AMERICAN CARS

AMERICAN CARS

THE AUTOMOBILES THAT MADE AMERICA

GENERAL EDITOR: CRAIG CHEETHAM

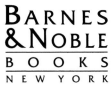

BARNES
&NOBLE
BOOKS
NEW YORK

This edition published by Barnes and Noble, Inc.,
by arrangement with Amber Books Ltd

2004 Barnes & Noble Books

M 10 9 8 7 6 5 4 3 2

ISBN: 0-7607-5448-9

Produced by
Amber Books Ltd
Bradley's Close
74–77 White Lion Street
London N1 9PF
www.amberbooks.co.uk

Printed in Singapore

CONTENTS

Introduction

America has a profound love of the automobile. Ever since the early pioneers of motoring took to the roads in their horseless carriages, the nation fell in love with the notion of personal mobility. This book celebrates the achievements of the engineers responsible for some of America's finest and most distinctive cars. Cars that, for over a century, have brought freedom and convenience to generations of people, not just in the United States, but all over the world. Although German visionary Karl Benz is credited with creating the very first car to be powered by the internal combustion engine, he wasn't the first man to create a vehicle that could run independently of horses. That honour fell to Nicolas Cugnot of France, with his steam car. A similar principle was applied to the first American "horseless carriage." Although crude in comparison to modern vehicles, the machine created by 24-year-old Oliver Evans in 1772 could propel itself by steam power. Steam power continued apace and in 1851 the American Steam Carriage Co. was established, with a fleet of vehicles capable of reaching up to 15 mph.

Inventors persisted with steam for over a century, but the machines were heavy, slow and expensive to build. The notion of personal transportation remained a distant dream. However, that dream would be realized before the end of the nineteenth century. In 1890, America's first successful internal combustion engine, designed by Charles Duryea of Springfield, Massachussetts, powered a vehicle independently. By 1896, 13 Duryea vehicles had been built and the American auto industry was in business.

The Early Years

From these humble roots, the motor industry grew rapidly. In 1903, a Winton four horsepower became the first car to travel across the United States coast-to-coast, proving the great potential that lay with the automobile concept.

That potential was realized almost exclusively by one man. Previously, the car had been solely the preserve of the wealthy. Cars were expensive, temperamental machines that required high maintenance. But Henry Ford had other ideas. The son of an Irish potato farmer whose family had migrated to Michigan, Ford believed there

Cadillac introduced its most expensive car to date with the Eldorado Brougham in 1957. Each car was hand-built and featured a huge range of extras.

was a way to create cars for the general populous. "I will build a car for the multitudes," he told a conference of local businessmen at a trade fair in 1906, while showing them the plans for his car. It won their financial backing, and the Model T was in production two years later, albeit at a slightly higher price than originally intended.

But that, too, would change. Thanks to humane working conditions and yet another visionary idea, Ford introduced the first continuously working production line in 1913. Production of Model T's increased to over a million units a year as it took just an hour and a half to build one, and the use of black paint only meant all parts could be prepared before assembly. Ford opened factories in England and Germany, and all of a sudden the car became a worldwide phenomenon.

Massive Growth
Ford's simple idea created massive industrial growth. Steel mills and engineering factories started to sprawl across his home city of Detroit, and America's economy boomed. But Ford was a modest man. His dream was to create cars for the masses, and he never patented his production line method. That meant other auto makers moved to the area to cash in on the skilled labor Ford had developed and the wide availability of the core products needed to build a car. Detroit became known as Motor City, or "Motown," and even today is the epicenter of the world's motor industry.

Car manufacturers sprouted up everywhere, and some of America's most prestigious brands were founded. Chevrolet, Pontiac, Buick, Chrysler, Dodge, Cadillac, Plymouth, Hudson, DeSoto, and Oldsmobile appeared, each with a varied range of models. Like all industries, however, only the

strongest would survive, and following the Great Depression of the 1930s, money in the car industry became hard to find, consumers were not buying new cars, and the smaller manufacturers started to struggle. By the end of the decade, America's motor industry consisted of just three major manufacturers: Ford, which incorporated Lincoln and Mercury; Chrysler, including Dodge and Plymouth; and General Motors, which incorporated Chevrolet, Pontiac, Oldsmobile, Cadillac, and Buick, among others. By 1937, GM became America's best-selling manufacturer, with Chevrolet cars outselling Fords for the first time in history. The 1930s also saw the introduction of some of America's most

The 1959 Pontiac Bonneville was the first model to include Pontiac's now famous split front grille, which has been used on virtually every model since.

extravagant cars. The growth of Hollywood and the multi-million dollar film industry was responsible for cars such as the Duesenberg SJ and Auburn Speedster—cars built purely for excess, with no thought to cost-cutting build practices. Today, they are revered by collectors and command high premiums at auction. America's car industry developed into the strongest in the world, and it grew even stronger when its rivals in Europe suffered badly due to the ravages of World War II (1939–45).

While the ravages of World War II knocked back the development of Europe's car industry, it allowed America's manufacturers to prosper. Extra money was gained from supplying vehicles to the Allied armies, including those from the United States, while valuable technical expertise was gleaned from creating military hardware such as aircraft and weaponry.

Post-war Boom

By the time war was over and the 1950s dawned, America was entering a new period of prosperity. The country's new-found wealth would affect its motor industry, as cars took on new forms and shapes. America's first true sports car appeared in 1953. Although other companies had built roadsters in the pre-war years, the Chevrolet Corvette was something completely new. With a lightweight body molded from glass-reinforced plastic—an entirely new build method—the Corvette had an overhead-valve V8 engine. Its performance, too, was impressive and it sold by the million, mostly to young American men who wanted to impress the girls. Determined not to be outdone, Ford unveiled the Thunderbird. Built to more traditional methods and much larger, the T-Bird was no less stylish, with hooded fenders and stylized rear fins. It was also a roaring success, becoming synonymous with the youth culture of the era.

But it was not just younger and sporty motorists that enjoyed the rapid advances in America's car industry. The decade also saw a number of family cars that would become icons of their era. Who could forget such classic shapes as the stunning 1957 Chevy Bel Air, or Chevrolet Nomad Station Wagon? Then, for the wealthy, there was the Cadillac Series 62 or Chrysler Imperial, each very different, but regarded as classics of their time. By the end of the decade, America's big three were launching a new model every year and more than one in two homes in the United States owned their own cars.

However, not all the new models were a success. In 1956, Ford launched a new brand known as Edsel, in a bid to create a market between its basic Ford and more upmarket Mercury models. Canadian designer Roy Brown was chosen to spearhead the project, but it was a disaster. The car's distinctive grille was out of keeping with the rest of its styling, and mechanical problems did not help, either. By 1960, the Edsel name had disappeared, and Ford's reputation suffered with it.

Swinging Sixties

It would not just be Ford that suffered embarrassment through poor design, however. In 1960, concerned by the growing popularity of foreign budget cars such as the VW Bug, Chevrolet unveiled the Corvair. The car was designed to be a rear-engined, air-cooled economy offering with cheap, swing-arm rear suspension. In hindsight, it became one of the most important automobiles in history, after it

The classic 1960s Ford Mustang was such a huge hit that Ford created a mass of aftermarket components to deal with the demand for modification.

was namechecked in Ralph Nader's book *Unsafe At Any Speed*, which highlighted the inbuilt dangers of certain American automobiles. The chapter about the Corvair's wayward handling forced the government to introduce over-zealous safety regulations that would see the flair and free spirit of 1950s designs disappear almost overnight. The early and mid 1960s were a wilderness for car designers, as safety rules meant any flair was immediately designed out by terrified committees. But there were some highlights, not least of which was the original and best "Pony Car"—the Ford Mustang.

Launched in 1964, the Mustang became the fastest-selling car in the world, a record that even today has not been beaten. Available in a variety of styles and sizes, from an economy six-cylinder sedan to a macho V8 fastback, there was a Mustang for everyone, and it was the country's best-selling car for almost a decade.

But aside from the Mustang and the evergreen Corvette, it was not until 1966 when American cars became great again. It was in that year that General Motors hit on the idea of combining an ordinary sedan shell with a high performance engine, the first incarnation of which was the legendary Pontiac GTO. The "muscle car" was born. Others soon followed, and by 1968 buyers could choose from a variety of uprated sedans with engines of up to 440 cubic inches. Today, the GTO—along with the Dodge Challenger, Plymouth Road Runner, Ford Torino Talladega, Oldsmobile 4-4-2, and Shelby GT350—are held in high esteem by enthusiasts.

Enforced Change
But the muscle car era did not last. By the 1970s, safety legislation was becoming ever more stringent and the post-Vietnam War oil crisis

meant economy engines were becoming much more important. Instead of speed, car manufacturers used safety and low running costs to market their vehicles, and although the cars of the era are not as emotive as those that went before, they are still highly significant. It was through the 1970s and early 1980s that safety items such as airbags, anti-lock braking and bodywork crumple zones were introduced, and without them the ultra-safe cars of today would never have been developed.

America's love of the SUV (sports utility vehicle) was also born, with vehicles such as the Ford Bronco, Chevy Suburban, and Chevy Blazer coming onto the market.

The GT40 was Ford's first foray into motor racing. In 1966 it spectacularly won the Le Mans 24-hour race, with three Mk IIs crossing the line in an historic first win.

Today, the American car industry is still the strongest in the world, and design flair is once again making a comeback—and some of the more interesting designs, such as the Dodge Viper, Cadillac Catera, and Ford F150 Lightning are covered here. These cars prove how far the American auto industry has come since those early days, and if Henry Ford, Oliver Evans, and Charles Duryea were alive to see how far their dreams had progressed, they would have plenty to be proud of…

AC **COBRA**

When Texan racing driver Carroll Shelby wanted a real performance sports car, he put a Ford V8 into AC's Ace chassis and produced a legend—the mighty Cobra. Engines grew, power outputs soared and the Cobra reached supercar status.

"...oozing raw power."

"Turn the key and the huge V8 rumbles into life, shaking the car and oozing raw power. The driving position and seats are comfortable, which is just as well because you'll be working hard. The Cobra is almost all engine and the chassis had to be strengthened to take the 7-liter V8. Despite the wider tires of the 427, there's still a huge surplus of power over grip. Power oversteer is available whenever you want it. When 100 mph can come up in 10 seconds it's hard to breathe."

Hang on tight! Hair raising performance is what the Cobra is all about. The interior is comfortable, but very windy at 150 mph.

Milestones

1962 Carroll Shelby installs a 260-cubic inch Ford V8 into an AC Ace chassis to create the first Cobra, shown at the New York Motor Show, and production begins.

The Cobra was based on the AC Ace.

1963 The original 260 V8 engine is replaced with 289 V8 that makes 271 bhp.

1964 Shelby builds the Daytona coupe and a prototype 427 Cobra. Having outgrown the Venice facility building Cobras, Shelby Mustangs and Sunbeam Tigers, Shelby American moves to the Los Angeles airport.

Massive performance made the Cobra a natural for racing.

1965 The Daytona Cobras win the World Sports Car Championship ahead of Ferrari. This is the first championship of its kind won by an American car. The 427 Cobra goes into production.

1966 Shelby American liquidates its Cobra inventory at its famous 'fire sale' and closes its doors in February.

UNDER THE SKIN

Beef it up

To take the bigger engine and its massive power output, the two main longitudinal chassis tubes were replaced by larger diameter, thicker section tube. Suspension pick-up points were strengthened. Original 260 and 289 Cobras retain the Ace's leaf-sprung rear end, but the MkII versions gained more sophisticated coil-sprung suspension which improved handling.

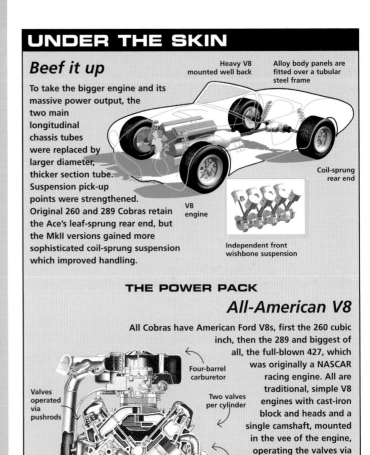

Heavy V8 mounted well back

Alloy body panels are fitted over a tubular steel frame

Coil-sprung rear end

V8 engine

Independent front wishbone suspension

THE POWER PACK

All-American V8

All Cobras have American Ford V8s, first the 260 cubic inch, then the 289 and biggest of all, the full-blown 427, which was originally a NASCAR racing engine. All are traditional, simple V8 engines with cast-iron block and heads and a single camshaft, mounted in the vee of the engine, operating the valves via pushrods and rockers. The impressive power and torque outputs are due more to the engine's sheer size rather than clever tuning.

Four-barrel carburetor

Valves operated via pushrods

Two valves per cylinder

Single camshaft

Pressed steel sump

Cast-iron block and heads

Baby Cobra

It's not as powerful as the 427 and it uses the leaf-spring chassis, but the early Cobra 289, built from 1963 is capable of 138 mph and 0-60 mph in 5.7 seconds. Because the body is so light, the little car had no problem getting the power to the ground.

Not as powerful as the 427, the 289 still has enough performance to thrill.

Brash and completely over the top, the 427 looks like a caricature of a sports car. Thanks to Shelby American and Ford's massive American V8 engines, the Ace finally has an edge to be competitive in road racing.

Flared wheel arches

To cover the much larger wheels and tires of the 427 model, the wheel arches are drastically flared rather than the whole body being redesigned.

Side exhausts

Side exhausts make the 427 look even more muscular. They are a feature of the 427 S/C (Street/Competition) models, which are basically racing models sold as road cars.

427-cubic inch big block V8

The 427 engine is 97 lbs. heavier than the 289 but much more powerful. Its this engine that gave the Cobra its legendary status.

Wide track

When the Ace first appeared it was a small and quite narrow car, but the track was widened for the Cobra conversion to fit its massive wheels and tires.

Halibrand alloy wheels

These wheels were very popular in the U.S. where the Ace was transformed into the Cobra. Although the original Cobras run on wire wheels, they cannot handle the power of Ford's potent 427 engine.

Tubular steel chassis

The Cobra's chassis features two main tubular steel chassis members connected by cross braces.

Coil spring suspension

The leaf-spring chassis of the original Cobra was updated for the 427 model and more modern coil-spring suspension is installed at the front and rear.

Quick-release fuel filler

Practical as well as stylish, the big alloy fuel filler cap can be opened in a split second for refueling during a race.

Roll-over hoop

This 427 has a roll-over hoop to protect the driver in the event of an accident, but standard Cobras do without it.

Alloy bodywork

To be as light as possible, all Cobra bodies are made of alloy, and were hand-built at AC's Thames Ditton factory.

Specifications

1965 AC Cobra 427

ENGINE

Type: V8

Construction: Cast-iron block and heads

Valve gear: Two valves per cylinder operated by single block-mounted camshafts via pushrods and rockers

Bore and stroke: 4.24 in. x 3.78 in.

Displacement: 427 c.i.

Compression ratio: 10.5:1

Induction system: Holley 750 CFM four-barrel carburetor

Maximum power: 425 bhp at 6,000 rpm

Maximum torque: 480 lb-ft at 3,700 rpm

Top speed: 165 mph

0-60 mph: 4.7 sec.

TRANSMISSION

Borg-Warner four-speed manual

BODY/CHASSIS

Tubular steel ladder frame with cross braces and alloy two-door, two-seat convertible

SPECIAL FEATURES

Large chrome side grill vents hot air from the 427's crowded engine compartment.

Quick-release fuel filler cap was a style as well as practical feature.

RUNNING GEAR

Steering: Rack-and-pinion

Front suspension: Double wishbones with coil springs and telescopic shocks

Rear suspension: Double wishbones with coil springs and telescopic shocks

Brakes: Discs, 11.6 in. dia. (front), 10.8 in. dia. (rear)

Wheels: Alloy 15 in. x 7.5 in.

Tires: 7.3 in. x 15 in. (front), 7.7 in. x 15 in. (rear)

DIMENSIONS

Length: 156 in.   **Width:** 68 in.

Height: 49 in.   **Wheelbase:** 90 in.

Track: 156 in. (front), 56 in. (rear)

Weight: 2,530 lbs.

AM GENERAL HUMMER

Built for the military, and one of the stars of the Gulf War, the massive go-anywhere, over-anything off-roader—originally known as a Humvee—has become a cult vehicle guaranteed to get you noticed anywhere.

"... Unstoppable off-roader."

"You're cocooned high above traffic in your Hummer feeling an enormous sense of security and take-on-anything confidence. The ride is softer than you imagine, but its sheer bulk makes it awkward on normal roads—as does its lethargic performance—and the noise at highway speeds batters you. None of this matters off-road, though, where the Hummer shrinks around you and really comes into its own. Poor flat-out performance becomes irrelevant because this unstoppable off-roader will ford rivers and climb mountains all day long."

Because of the huge transmission tunnel, the Hummer is not as spacious as you might expect.

12

Milestones

1980 AM General's version of the High Mobility Multi-purpose Wheeled Vehicle (HMMWV) starts tests in the Nevada desert, just 11 months after design work began.

1983 U.S. Army orders 55,000 HMMWVs, to be delivered in the following five years. The clumsy title is soon modified to Humvee just so it can be spoken. The Humvees would be produced in more than a dozen different versions. It could be bodied as an armored car, personnel carrier or ambulance.

Long suspension travel helps off-road traction.

1992 Sales to the public begin after a lot of publicity is generated by seeing the Humvees in the Gulf War.

1994 Original Chevy 350-cubic inch gasoline V8 is supplanted by the new 378-cubic inch GM diesel V8 engine with little change to the power output.

1996 Hummer buyers now have a choice of normally aspirated or turbo diesel engines and the range comprises seven variants, including a five-door, two- and four-door pickups and a four-door convertible, available from 40 dealers across the US.

UNDER THE SKIN

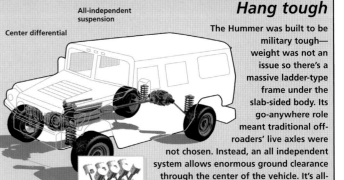

Hang tough

The Hummer was built to be military tough—weight was not an issue so there's a massive ladder-type frame under the slab-sided body. Its go-anywhere role meant traditional off-roaders' live axles were not chosen. Instead, an all independent system allows enormous ground clearance through the center of the vehicle. It's all-wheel drive, of course, with a four-speed auto transmitting to a two-speed transfer case and center differential.

All-independent suspension
Center differential
Ladder chassis
Gas or diesel V8

THE POWER PACK

Gasoline or diesel?

Hummers started with the 350-cubic inch Chevrolet small-block V8 (shown). In the Hummer, it was tuned for torque rather than outright power. In 1994, it switched to GM's bigger 395-cubic inch V8 diesel as standard. It's a development of the 387-cubic inch diesel produced for GM by its Detroit Diesel Division and it is designed with turbocharging very much in mind. The turbocharged version of the big diesel, launched in the late-1990s, gained another 10 bhp, and up to 430 lb-ft of stump-pulling torque.

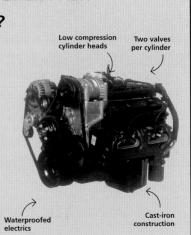

Low compression cylinder heads
Two valves per cylinder
Waterproofed electrics
Cast-iron construction

No stopping it

It's heavy and it's slow. Conventional pick-up trucks at half the price can carry more and go much faster. However, with 430 lb-ft of torque at 1,700 rpm there's no other off-roader that can get you over more rugged mountains or through deeper rapids than a Hummer.

There's nowhere you can't go in a Hummer.

Intimidated by Peterbilts and Kenworths? If you want to get on more equal terms without going the whole 18-wheeler route, get yourself a Hummer. Just don't get upset when the trucks still go faster.

Extra wide
As a military vehicle, the Hummer wasn't designed to fit on the road, so it could be made very wide, making it stable even with that high ground clearance. How wide is it? At 86.5 inches it's 13.8 inches wider than a full-size Chevrolet sedan.

Turbocharged option
One of the engine options is a turbocharged version of the 395-cubic inch diesel. It only produces an extra 10 bhp, but adds a great amount of torque which is what the heavyweight Hummer needs to move it along.

No overhangs
The wheelbase is almost as long as the vehicle itself. This wheel-at-each-corner design means there's nothing to get in the way when the Hummer climbs and descends. It has an excellent approach angle of 73 degrees.

Two-speed transfer case
With a two-speed transfer case to give low and high ratio gears, there are eight forward gears available and a gear for every situation. The Hummer also uses advanced Torsen differentials in the front and rear.

Separate chassis
Because it was intended to have many different bodies fitted to it, the basic Hummer structure had to be a traditional ladder-type chassis rather than a unitary monocoque structure.

Diesel V8
Although the Hummer started out with GM's small-block Chevy V8 gasoline engine the larger 395-cubic inch, GM diesel—used in the Chevrolet Tahoe and GMC Yukon—was added to the series as the standard powerplant in the mid-1990s.

Independent suspension
To allow high ground clearance and better individual wheel articulation, the Hummer has all-around independent suspension instead of the usual live rear axle arrangement employed by most off-roaders.

Enormous ground clearance
Hummers ride high, with an excellent 16-inch ground clearance, helped by the independent suspension design which allows 9.1 inches of suspension travel on each wheel.

Specifications
1997 AM General Hummer

ENGINE
Type: V8 diesel
Construction: Cast-iron block and heads
Valve gear: Two valves per cylinder operated by single block-mounted camshaft via pushrods, rockers and hydraulic lifters
Bore and stroke: 4.06 in. x 3.82 in.
Displacement: 395 c.i.
Compression ratio: 21.5:1
Induction system: Electronic fuel injection with turbocharger
Maximum power: 195 bhp at 3,400 rpm
Maximum torque: 430 lb-ft at 1,700 rpm
Top speed: 87 mph
0-60 mph: 17.3 sec

TRANSMISSION
Four-speed GM 4L80-E automatic with two-speed transfer case and center differential; four-wheel drive with Torsen differentials

BODY/CHASSIS
Steel ladder frame with choice of five bodies

SPECIAL FEATURES

The optional tire inflation/deflation system enables you to drop the tire pressure for extra traction in slippery off-road conditions, then reinflate them automatically to their standard pressures. Each tire costs $500, though.

Front and rear tow hooks come standard so Hummer drivers can easily pull humbler vehicles from mud or snow.

RUNNING GEAR
Steering: Power-assisted recirculating ball
Front suspension: Unequal length wishbones, coil springs, telescopic shocks and anti-roll bar
Rear suspension: Unequal length wishbones, coil springs and telescopic shocks
Brakes: Vented discs front and rear
Wheels: Steel discs 8.3 in. x 16.5 in.
Tires: 37 in. x 12.5 in. R16.5

DIMENSIONS
Length: 184.5 in.   **Width:** 86.5 in.
Height: 72 in.   **Wheelbase:** 130 in.
Track: 72 in. (front and rear)
Weight: 6,620 lbs.

AMC **AMX**

American Motors struggled to establish the sort of market identity that the other manufacturers had gained. Its 'character' car, possibly aimed at the Chevrolet Corvette, was the curious AMX two-seat coupe.

"...serious performance."

"Turn the V8's starter motor and your senses awaken—this really sounds like a muscle machine. The deep reserves of torque make driving very easy, and there is plenty of power for fast take offs. Add in the optional quick-rack power steering, front disc brakes and limited-slip differential and you have a serious performance machine that is just as capable of tackling twisty mountain roads as taking part in a traffic light drag race."

The dashboard is trimmed with wood grain trim which was very stylish in the late 1960s.

Milestones

1968 Mid-season, AMC launches its new compact sports coupe with a choice of three V8 engines.

Another of AMC's compact muscle cars of the period was the Hurst SC Rambler.

1969 This year the AMX remains very much as the previous year.

1970 A mild restyle includes moving the spotlights to the front grill and adding a prominent hump to the hood. The standard engine expands to 390 cubic inches and power outputs rise. This is the last year of AMX sales.

Due to its design, many thought the AMX was supposed to compete with the Corvette.

1971 The AMX name is reduced to an option package on a larger and curvier Javelin. After 1973 it is more show than go.

UNDER THE SKIN

A classic Detroiter

Basically a shortened Javelin, the AMX is surprisingly usable and has an independent wishbone front suspension, with coil springs, shocks and an anti-roll bar. At the rear are semi-elliptic leaf springs and a rigid axle, plus telescopic shocks. Quick-ratio power-assisted steering options aid driveability.

THE POWER PACK

Muscle car V8

The standard engine in the AMX is a 225-bhp, 290-cubic inch V8, although larger 343 and 390-V8s were optional. The 390 has a forged steel crankshaft and connecting rods, and a Carter AFB four-barrel carburetor. Its 315 bhp power output is more than adequate and the 425 lb-ft of torque gives it pulling power which modern cars can only dream of. Though very underrated, this two-seat machine is one of the most potent cars to ever have seen action on American pavement.

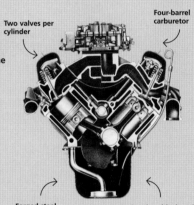

Super rare

Few changes occurred in 1969, but the 1970 AMX received a new grill with air vents, plus an improved interior, revised graphics and optional 15-inch wheels. Just 4,116 of the 1970 model were built, making it the rarest and most desirable of all AMXs.

The 1970 AMC AMX muscle cars are the most sought-after by collectors.

By shortening the Javelin, AMC produced a cheap all-American two-seater sports coupe. Just 19,134 AMXs were built, making it a highly desirable muscle car today.

Bulging hood
A popular and sporty option on the AMX was the performance hood complete with dual air scoops. In 1968 the hood bulge was only decorative, but in 1970 the 'Go' package included a fully functional ram air system.

Racing paintwork
The typical paint scheme for the AMX in its first two years was twin racing stripes running down the center. Late 1970 models lose the hood stripes but have side stripes instead.

Sporty rear styling
The rear end is styled to give the car a smooth side profile but a ridged-out appearance from behind.

Short wheelbase
Riding on a 97-inch wheelbase, the AMX is 12 inches shorter than the Javelin. This is even shorter than the Corvette, and qualified the AMX as one of the most compact American cars on the market at the time.

Chrome sills
With AMC's move toward flashier styling, the AMX featured chrome-plated sill covers. Later, these sills gained mock vents, mimicking a side-mounted exhaust.

Two-seat interior
Shortening the bodyshell of the 2+2 Javelin means the AMX has room for just two passengers sitting on bucket seats, although there is a large space behind the seats for extra luggage.

V8 power
Emphasizing its sporty role, the AMX was only ever sold with V8 engines. It was the only AMC at the time not to be offered with a straight-six engine as standard.

Specifications
1968 AMC AMX

ENGINE
Type: V8

Construction: Cast-iron block and cylinder heads

Valve gear: Two valves per cylinder operated by a single camshaft, pushrods and rockers

Bore and stroke: 4.16 in. x 3.57 in.

Displacement: 390 c.i.

Compression ratio: 10.2:1

Induction system: Single four-barrel carburetor

Maximum power: 315 bhp at 4,600 rpm

Maximum torque: 425 lb-ft at 3,200 rpm

Top speed: 125 mph

0-60 mph: 6.6 sec.

TRANSMISSION
Three-speed automatic or four-speed manual

BODY/CHASSIS
Integral with two-door steel coupe body

SPECIAL FEATURES

AMX meant something special after AMC showed a stunning mid-engined sports car with the AMX badge

The 390-cubic inch V8 was AMC's biggest engine in the late 1960s.

RUNNING GEAR
Steering: Recirculating ball

Front suspension: Wishbones with coil springs and shocks

Rear suspension: Rigid axle with leaf springs and shocks

Brakes: Drums (front and rear)

Wheels: Steel, 14-in. dia.

Tires: E70 x 14 in.

DIMENSIONS
Length: 177 in.   **Width:** 71.5 in.

Height: 51.7 in.   **Wheelbase:** 97 in.

Track: 58.8 in. (front), 57 in. (rear)

Weight: 3,400 lbs.

AMC REBEL MACHINE

After the overachieving little SC/Rambler of 1969, AMC returned to the muscle car market with the Rebel Machine. It still sported loud graphics, but thanks to a 390-cubic inch, 340-bhp V8, it was more than capable of outshining the competition and backing up its flashy appearance.

"...built to be a performer."

"It may have a horizontal-sweep speedometer, but a four-on-the-floor and bucket seats assure you that this car was built to be a performer. The 390-cubic inch V8 is a lot more tractable than some others in everyday driving, and although throttle control is required to really get the Machine moving, the end result is worth it. Through corners, the AMC feels quite nimble for its size, with much less understeer than you would expect."

A four-speed transmission with a cue-ball shifter is nestled between the front seats.

Milestones

1968 American Motors releases

photographs of a menacing mid-size Rebel. It has semi-gloss dark paint with matching bumpers and wheels. Called the Machine, it is intended for production in 1969, but none are actually sold.

The SC/Rambler was American Motors' first serious muscle car.

1969 With help from

Hurst Performance, AMC stuffs its biggest engine in the compact Rogue, resulting in the Hurst SC/Rambler. Packing 315 bhp and capable of 14.3-second quarter miles, 1,512 of these patriotic-looking cars are built.

The two-seater AMX could also get the big 390-c.i. V8.

1970 Replacing the

SC/Rambler is a new, larger Rebel Machine. Packing 340 bhp from a 390 V8, it is a potent performer too, but lasts for only one model year.

UNDER THE SKIN

Street racer

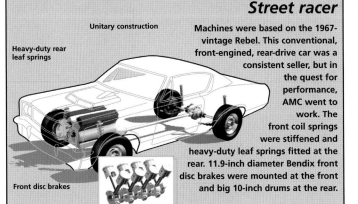

Unitary construction

Heavy-duty rear leaf springs

Front disc brakes

Big-block V8

Machines were based on the 1967-vintage Rebel. This conventional, front-engined, rear-drive car was a consistent seller, but in the quest for performance, AMC went to work. The front coil springs were stiffened and heavy-duty leaf springs fitted at the rear. 11.9-inch diameter Bendix front disc brakes were mounted at the front and big 10-inch drums at the rear.

THE POWER PACK

AMC's biggest

In order to compete with the big three, American Motors realized that the best way was to stuff its largest engine in a mid size car. The 390-cubic inch mill that powered all Machines is an enlarged version of the 343 unit. It followed customary practice with a cast-iron block and heads, plus two valves per cylinder. Where the 343 has cast-iron rods and crankshaft, the 390 has forged-steel items and larger bearings. The 390 is a moderate performer, producing its 340 bhp at 5,100 rpm.

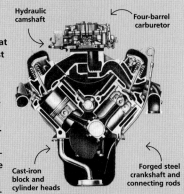

Hydraulic camshaft

Four-barrel carburetor

Cast-iron block and cylinder heads

Forged steel crankshaft and connecting rods

Patriotic

Rebel Machines were offered for only one year, and with a production total of 2,326 are not exactly common. The first 1,000 cars built had a special white, blue and red color scheme, making them particularly sought-after in AMC circles.

Later Machines could be ordered in any Rebel factory color.

Although AMC stated 'The Machine is not that fast,' the car could give many muscle cars from the big three a run for their money, particularly with an experienced driver behind the wheel.

King of the cubes

In 1970, the 390-cubic inch V8 was the biggest engine offered by American Motors. With a big four-barrel carburetor and functional hood scoop, it produces a credible 340 bhp and 430 lb-ft of torque, good enough for mid-14-second ¼-mile ETs.

Power steering

Manual steering was standard, but many buyers considered it too heavy and thus ordered the optional power setup. It was, however, boosted and contemporary road testers wrote that it was 'grossly over-assisted.'

Stiff suspension

Rebel Machines rode on some of the stiffest suspension from Detroit. Fitting the Rebel wagon's heavy-duty rear leaf springs gave a street racer stance, and although handling is good for a muscle car, the jacked-up rear results in severe wheel hop if the gas is floored from a standing start.

Strong transmission

Like the AMX and Javelin, the Machine was offered with a Borg-Warner T-10 four-speed manual transmission and a Hurst shifter. This enabled lightning-quick getaways from the lights.

Twin-Grip

Transmitting power to the rear tires is a Twin-Grip differential with standard 3.54:1 final drive. Steeper gearing was offered over the counter—up to an incredible 5.00:1 for hardcore drag-racer types.

Hood scoop

Besides having an interesting look, the vacuum-operated hood scoop is functional too, forcing cooler, denser air into the engine. The scoop assembly also contains an integrated 8,000-rpm tachometer, which can be difficult to read in harsh sunlight or rain.

AMC **JAVELIN AMX**

After the previous generation two-seater, the 1971 Javelin AMX seemed cumbersome and unwieldy. Even so, with a 360 or 401 under the hood, it is a real mover and something few people would expect from AMC.

"...smooth, satisfying torque."

"The instrument panel with the gauges angled toward the driver was unique to the AMX through the 1970s. Because of its long front end styling, the car feels much bigger than it actually is. With plenty of power under your right foot and loads of smooth, satisfying torque, the AMX shines when going in a straight line. Despite its size and light steering, the AMX is surprising around corners, demonstrating better agility than its appearance would suggest."

A curved dash gives the driver a clear view of all the gauges.

Milestones

1971 A bigger and heavier second generation Javelin goes on sale. For buyers wanting performance, the AMX option is available with a 360- or 401-cubic inch V8.

The 1970 Rebel Machine used a 390 V8, the forerunner of the 401 found in the 1971 AMX.

1972 With Detroit scaling down on performance, all hi-po engines are now required to run on unleaded fuel. New SAE power ratings result in a drop in output, the big 401 now producing just 255 bhp.

In its last year as a two-seater, 1970, 4,116 AMX's were built.

1974 The writing is on the wall for the Javelin and AMX due to a drop in demand for ponycars and the onset of the first fuel crisis. Despite this, second-generation Javelin sales reach an all-time high and 4,980 AMXs leave the factory. There is no AMC ponycar for 1975.

UNDER THE SKIN

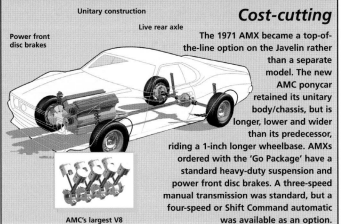

Unitary construction
Live rear axle
Power front disc brakes
AMC's largest V8

Cost-cutting

The 1971 AMX became a top-of-the-line option on the Javelin rather than a separate model. The new AMC ponycar retained its unitary body/chassis, but is longer, lower and wider than its predecessor, riding a 1-inch longer wheelbase. AMXs ordered with the 'Go Package' have a standard heavy-duty suspension and power front disc brakes. A three-speed manual transmission was standard, but a four-speed or Shift Command automatic was available as an option.

THE POWER PACK

AMC's finest

The standard performance Javelin, the SST, has a 304-cubic inch V8, but the AMX was fitted with the bigger 360 engine. An enlarged 343, the increased displacement was needed mainly to meet tightening emissions requirements without too much sacrifice in performance. With a two-barrel carburetor, it was rated at 245 bhp, and with a four-barrel, 285 bhp. A step up the ladder was AMC's largest engine, the 401. With a 9.5:1 compression ratio, it is able to run on low octane fuel but can still crank out 330 bhp and 430 lb-ft of torque. For 1972, net power is down in the 360 to 195 and 220 bhp, and the 401 to 255 bhp.

AMXcitement

After the original two-seat AMX of 1968-1970, the second-generation Javelin AMX is the most collectible AMC ponycar. Find one with the 'Go Package' and a 360-cubic inch four-barrel or 401-cubic inch V8 and you have a rare and unusual ponycar.

The AMX is one of the more fun-to-drive early 1970s Detroit cars.

Although less special than the original, the 1971–1974 AMX still differs from regular Javelins in having its own grill and standard front and rear spoilers. Equipped with a 401 V8, it is also a potent performer.

'Go Package'
This package included stiffer rate springs and shocks, 15-inch wheels shod in Goodyear Polyglas G60 F-15 tires, a cowl induction setup that draws in air from the base of the windshield and a T-stripe on the hood.

Dual exhausts
AMXs came with a standard single exhaust, but included with the four-barrel 360 was a set of full-length dual exhaust pipes with twin mufflers. These reduce back pressure and help the V8 to fully exploit its power.

V8 engine
The AMX, as a high-performance machine, came with the largest engines offered by the American Motors stable, the 360 and 401. Most buyers ordered the 360, which in four-barrel form propelled the AMX through the ¼-mile in 14.9 seconds.

Limited-slip differential
With 315 lb-ft of torque from the 360 four-barrel V8 and 430 lb-ft from the 401, a limited-slip differential was almost essential to help prevent the rear tires from going up in smoke.

Longer wheelbase
One of the major criticisms of the early ponycars (including the Javelin) had been the lack of interior room. So for the second-generation car, AMC stretched the wheelbase from 97 to 110 inches.

Optional transmissions
Javelins came with a standard three-speed manual transmission, though a four-speed was optional and recommended for the big engines. A Shift Command automatic was also available and buyers could choose between a floor- and column-mounted shifter.

Specifications
1971 AMC Javelin AMX

ENGINE
Type: V8

Construction: Cast-iron block and heads

Valve gear: Two valves per cylinder operated by a single V-mounted camshaft with pushrods and rockers

Bore and stroke: 4.08 in. x 3.44 in.

Displacement: 360 c.i.

Compression ratio: 8.5:1

Induction system: Four-barrel carburetor

Maximum power: 285 bhp at 5,000 rpm

Maximum torque: 315 lb-ft at 3,400 rpm

Top speed: 114 mph

0-60 mph: 6.9 sec.

TRANSMISSION
Four-speed manual

BODY/CHASSIS
Unitary steel construction

SPECIAL FEATURES

Bulging front fenders mimicked the contemporary Corvette.

The AMX models got their own unique grill.

RUNNING GEAR
Steering: Recirculating-ball

Front suspension: Unequal-length A-arms with coil springs, telescopic shock absorbers and anti-roll bar

Rear suspension: Live axle with semi-elliptic leaf springs and telescopic shock absorbers

Brakes: Discs (front), drums (rear)

Wheels: Stamped steel, 15 x 7 in.

Tires: Goodyear Polyglas, E60-15

DIMENSIONS
Length: 191.8 in. **Width:** 75.4 in.

Height: 51.5 in. **Wheelbase:** 110.0 in.

Track: 59.3 in. (front) 60.0 in. (rear)

Weight: 3,244 lbs.

Auburn SPEEDSTER

Auburn's 851 Speedster was the sleekest car on American roads in the 1930s. It followed the lead of the big Mercedes SSK of the 1920s with its supercharged engine, and its eight cylinders were enough to give a guaranteed top speed of more than 100 mph.

"The faster the better."

"That was the opinion of road testers in 1935. In America that year there was nothing to touch the Auburn Speedster for the price. The supercharged 280-cubic inch eight-cylinder engine gives lots of smooth power, and thanks to the two-speed axle and three-speed transmission, the driver has six gears to play with. The hydraulic brakes are man enough to haul the heavy car down, and the handling is impressive for its day. Because of its low-geared steering and excessive body roll, the car shows its age around tight corners."

The Auburn Speedster offered a high level of comfort as well as serious art-deco fittings.

Milestones

1928 First Auburn 'boat tail' Speedster is introduced. It has a similar tiny swept-back windshield, but an upright grill and open fenders. Most powerful is the eight-cylinder, 125-bhp 8-125, produced in 1930.

This 1929 Model 115 evolved into the 120 and the 125.

1932 By adding a 160-bhp Lycoming V12 to the speedster chassis, Auburn creates the similarly styled 12-160 Speedster. Top speed is 117 mph but it is not a success and is dropped for 1934.

1935 The Speedster 851 is introduced.
Restyled by new designer, Gordon Buehrig, it uses a 150-bhp supercharged version of the Lycoming straight-eight engine.

Auburn's dynamic president, Errett Lobban Cord, arrived at Auburn in 1924.

1936 Name changes to 852 from 851. Sales are slow and production ends. The total number of 851/852 Speedsters built is just over 500.

UNDER THE SKIN

Two in one

It looks spectacular, but the Speedster is quite conventional except for its rear axle. It has two sets of final-drive gears—low and high ratio—to give good acceleration with one set or relaxed high-speed cruising with the other. The driver could also play with the gear and axle controls to give the same effect as a six-speed transmission.

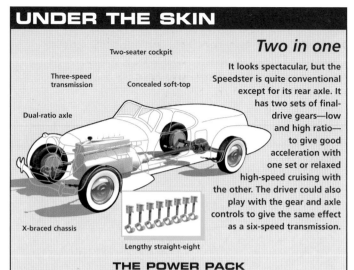

Two-seater cockpit
Three-speed transmission
Concealed soft-top
Dual-ratio axle
X-braced chassis
Lengthy straight-eight

THE POWER PACK

Eight supercharged cylinders

Built by Lycoming, better known for its aircraft engines, the Speedster's engine was not advanced—a simple side-valve design, it was a vintage layout for such a sporty engine. But with a mechanically driven supercharger running at four pounds of boost, the straight-eight engine gives a good deal of low-end torque. Although the centrifugal supercharger runs at six times crankshaft speed, the limited amount of boost means the engine is hardly over-stressed.

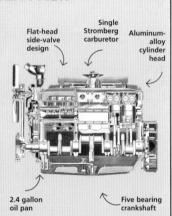

Flat-head side-valve design
Single Stromberg carburetor
Aluminum-alloy cylinder head
2.4 gallon oil pan
Five bearing crankshaft

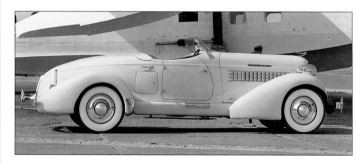

Auburn record

In 1935, the classy Auburn Speedster became the first American production car to exceed 100 mph for more than 12 hours, averaging 102.9 mph. It was driven by racing driver Ab Jenkins. He also set a new record in the flying mile with a top speed of 104.17 mph.

Using a centrifugal supercharger, the Speedster really lives up to its name.

Auburn's famous designer Gordon Buehrig wanted the Speedster to appear to be the fastest car on the road. He succeeded, using features like the low V windshield, sloping grill and flowing wing-line to give a streamlined look to the car.

Teardrop headlights
The Auburn's styling is supposed to suggest speed. The streamlined lights, with bulging convex lenses, help achieve this impression.

Supercharged engine
The Auburn's mechanically driven supercharger runs at six times engine-speed and helps the Lycoming engine generate 150 bhp—35 bhp more than without the supercharger.

Top cover
The Auburn's top folds away neatly under this rigid cover to maintain the car's sleek lines.

Drum brakes
All the cars in the 1930s had drum brakes, but the Auburn's hydraulically-operated drums were more modern than most.

Flexible exhaust headers
Each of the four flexible exhaust headers serve two cylinders. The conventional rigid pipes are hidden under the flexible tubes.

Dual-ratio rear axle
The driver could switch from a low- to a high- axle ratio, and with a three-speed transmission that gave six gears overall. In high-ratio top gear, the Speedster's engine rotated at only 2,250 rpm at 60 mph.

Winged mascots
Each of the side 'flying lady' mascots was made by slicing the radiator mascot in two.

Boat-tail design
From above, the description is obvious. The style was popular in the 1920s and '30s and here it is mirrored in in its rearend styling.

Luggage hatch
A carriage key opens this hatch. The compartment is just large enough to take a set of golf clubs, a feature much appreciated by the typical playboy Speedster owner.

Hydraulic lever-arm shocks
Before telescopic shocks were introduced, cars like the Auburn used hydraulic lever arms to replace the previous friction shocks.

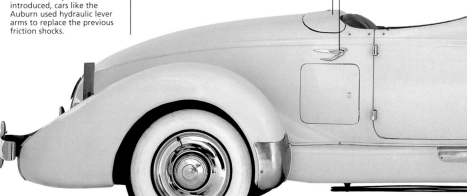

Specifications
1935 Auburn Speedster 851

ENGINE
Type: In-line eight
Construction: Cast-iron block and light alloy cylinder head
Valve gear: Side-valve with two valves per cylinder and single block-mounted camshaft
Bore and stroke: 3.06 in. x 4.75 in.
Displacement: 280 c.i.
Compression ratio: 6.5:1
Induction system: Single downdraft Stromberg carburetor with Schwitzer-Cummins supercharger
Maximum power: 150 bhp at 4,000 rpm
Top speed: 108 mph
0-50 mph: 10.0 sec

TRANSMISSION
Three-speed manual with dual-ratio rear axle

BODY/CHASSIS
Steel two-door, two-seat speedster body with steel box-section ladder-type chassis rails

SPECIAL FEATURES

Each Speedster has a signed plaque guaranteeing it has been tested to more than 100 mph.

Mechanically-driven supercharger is used to boost power.

RUNNING GEAR
Steering: Worm-and-peg
Front suspension: Solid axle with semi-elliptic leaf springs and Delco hydraulic shock absorbers
Rear suspension: Live axle with semi-elliptic leaf springs and Delco hydraulic shock absorbers
Brakes: Four-wheel Lockheed drums, hydraulically operated with Bendix vacuum booster
Wheels: Pressed steel or wire spoke, 6.5 in. x 15 in.
Tires: Crossply 6.5 in. x 16 in.

DIMENSIONS
Length: 194.4 in. **Width:** 71.5 in.
Height: 56.5 in.
Track: 59 in. (front), 62 in. (rear) **Wheelbase:** 127 in.
Weight: 3,753 lbs.

Buick ROADMASTER

The combination of just about the most comfortable ride in any large sedan and the total convenience of the pioneering two-speed Dynaflow transmission made the 1949 Roadmaster a huge success.

"...comfortable and relaxing."

"Its incredibly soft suspension may not give the Roadmaster the best hand-ling, but it does mean that it is blissfully comfortable and relaxing. This is enhanced by the quiet, refined, and strong straight-eight engine. The pioneering and impres-sively smooth Dynaflow transmission comes into its own as you accelerate to around 30 mph, when it performs really well. You just select 'Drive' and forget the rest—the Buick can easily soak up hundreds of miles in a day."

The view of the gauges through the large steering wheel is excellent.

Milestones

1945 Buick production gets underway again after WWII. Its cars changed from the 1942 models. Among the range is a Roadmaster.

By 1953, the Roadmaster had an OHV V8 engine.

1949 There is a fundamental restyle for the Roadmaster, with the top line of the front fender carried all the way through the doors to the top of the rear fender. The modern look complements the pioneering two-speed automatic transmission, with Dynaflow-drive.

1958 is the last year for the Buick Roadmaster.

1953 The straight-eight engine is replaced by a new, overhead-valve, pushrod 322-cubic inch V8 producing 188 bhp.

1958 The name Roadmaster is discontinued. It is resurrected in 1991.

UNDER THE SKIN

"Dynaflow Drive"

Even by 1949 the chassis design was little different from pre-war GM cars, so the Roadmaster has a strong separate chassis frame carrying a live rear axle, although mounted on leaf springs. Front suspension is by double A-arms and coil springs, but one feature is very advanced for the time: the Dynaflow transmission. Buick was the first to offer a torque converter transmission with advanced fluid couplings, making it a two-speed automatic transmission.

Dynaflow automatic transmission

Separate steel chassis

12-inch drum brakes

In-line eight

THE POWER PACK

Pre-war power

Buick's fine straight-eight engine, with its cast-iron block and cylinder head has its origins in the pre-war period. With the use of long crankshafts mounted on five bearings, by 1936 the capacity had increased to 320 cubic inches. A single block-mounted camshaft operates in-line overhead valves with pushrods and rockers. It is very unstressed and has a small 6.9:1 compression ratio. The engine is tuned for torque rather than outright power with its long stroke. The maximum power output of 150 bhp and 260 lb-ft of torque are produced, at 3,600 rpm and 2,400 rpm respectively.

Open-top joy

The two-door convertible is the most sought-after Roadmaster. At the time, it was more affordable than the two-door coupe. This helped account for its popularity, with over 8,200 sold in the model year—almost twice as many as the Riviera coupe.

The open-top Roadmaster is the ideal model for cruising.

For 1949, the Roadmaster's new flatter side styling and the first appearance of portholes in the front fenders were an instant hit. Buick sales increased by more than 100,000.

Foot starter

To start the Roadmaster, the ignition is switched on and then, with the transmission in 'Park' or 'Neutral,' the throttle is pressed right to the floor, activating the starter button.

Recirculating-ball steering

The Roadmaster is a big and very heavy car, so the recirculating-ball steering needed more than five turns to go from lock to lock. This was improved with the power steering introduced in 1952. By 1954, there were 4.5 turns lock to lock, but the steering was still vague.

Drum brakes

Large, cast-iron drums give the Roadmaster good stopping power and can halt the car from 60 mph in 240 feet. Brake fade soon sets in if the car is driven hard.

Straight-eight engine

The design of Buick's straight-eight engine dates back to 1931. Straight-eights were built for prestige and, although very smooth, had drawbacks, such as length and the very long crankshaft, which limited engine speeds.

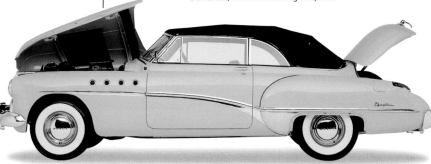

Dynaflow transmission

Buick was not the first to offer an automatic transmission but was the first to have a torque converter. It called its new transmission dynaflow. It is a much more sophisticated version of a fluid coupling, which magnifies the effect of the torque produced by the engine, so Drive is the only selection really needed.

Rear wheel covers

The 1949 Buicks, including the Roadmaster, were the last to have enclosed rear wheels. A removable panel allows the wheel to be changed.

A-arm front suspension

Coil-sprung double A-arm suspension and an anti-roll bar are used at the front to give the best possible ride.

Split windshield

The 1949 Roadmaster was one of the last Buicks to have a split windshield. Soon technology enabled curved, one-piece windshields to be produced.

Specification

1949 Buick Roadmaster

ENGINE

Type: In line eight-cylinder

Construction: Cast-iron block and head

Valve gear: Two valves per cylinder operated by a block-mounted camshaft.

Bore and stroke: 3.44 in. x 4.25 in.

Displacement: 320.2 c.i.

Compression ratio: 6.9:1

Induction system: One two-barrel Stromberg carburetor/ or carter carburetor

Maximum power: 150 bhp at 3,600 rpm

Maximum torque: 260 lb-ft at 2,400 rpm

Top speed: 100 mph

0-60 mph: 17.1 sec.

TRANSMISSION

Two-speed Dynaflow automatic with a torque converter

BODY/CHASSIS

Separate steel chassis with two-door convertible body

SPECIAL FEATURES

The Roadmaster has four portholes compared to the three of other Buicks.

The Dynaflow transmission was the first torque-converter automatic on a production car.

RUNNING GEAR

Steering: Recirculating-ball

Front suspension: Double A-arms with coil springs, telescopic shock absorbers and anti-roll bar

Rear suspension: Live axle with leaf springs, torque arm and telescopic shock absorbers

Brakes: Drums, 12-in. dia. (front and rear)

Wheels: Steel disc, 15-in. dia.

Tires: 8.20 x 15

DIMENSIONS

Length: 214.1 in. **Width:** 80.0 in.

Height: 63.2 in. **Wheelbase:** 126.0 in.

Track: 59.1 in. (front), 62.2 in. (rear)

Weight: 4,370 lbs.

Buick SKYLARK

One of Harley Earl's long-standing projects, the Skylark was an exclusive convertible that arrived in Buick's 50th anniversary year and sold for just two seasons. It was the ideal car for the wealthy.

"...a cut above the rest."

"Buicks of this period ooze refinement and civility, and the Skylark is one of the shining examples. The 200-bhp V8, coupled to the Dynaflow transmission means the car has more than enough power, but it is more of a fast cruiser than sportster. Fit and finish are top rate, with quality materials inside and out. As a top-of-the-line car, the Skylark is laden with luxury features and pampers its driver and passengers, making them feel a cut above the rest."

Skylarks came with a four-way power bench seat, power windows and a Selectronic radio.

Milestones

1953 In its 50th year, Buick gets its first overhead-valve V8 and a new top-level offering, the Skylark. Based on the Roadmaster™ chassis, it has a custom coachbuilt body and standard Dynaflow transmission. Priced at $5,000, only 1,690 are sold this year.

Five other convertibles were offered in 1954; this is a Super.

1954 The Skylark returns but as a regular production model, now based on the shorter Century™ chassis. The price is trimmed to $4,883, but sales are even less than in 1953, totaling 836. The 322-cubic inch Buick V8 now puts out 200 bhp.

The Skylark nameplate lasted up until 1998. Its final incarnation was the N-body compact.

1961 Skylark is revived, but as a top-level hardtop on the new 112-inch wheelbase Special™ compact.

UNDER THE SKIN

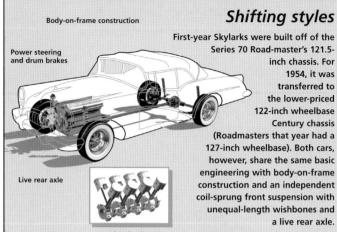

Body-on-frame construction

Power steering and drum brakes

Live rear axle

Overhead-valve V8

Shifting styles

First-year Skylarks were built off the Series 70 Road-master's 121.5-inch chassis. For 1954, it was transferred to the lower-priced 122-inch wheelbase Century chassis (Roadmasters that year had a 127-inch wheelbase). Both cars, however, share the same basic engineering with body-on-frame construction and an independent coil-sprung front suspension with unequal-length wishbones and a live rear axle.

THE POWER PACK

'Fireball' V8

Besides the Skylark, 1953 also saw the introduction of a new overhead-valve V8 at Buick. Known as the Fireball Eight, it followed the basic engineering pattern of the original Cadillac® and Olds™ engines of 1949, with cast-iron construction, two valves per cylinder and an oversquare design. With a 4.0-inch bore, 3.2-inch stroke and 8.5:1 compression ratio, it produces 164/170 bhp in Supers and 188 bhp in uplevel Roadmasters. At the time, it was the highest output of any Detroit-production V8.

Two valves per cylinder operated by pushrods and hydraulic lifters

Carter four-barrel carburetor

Cast-iron block and cylinder heads

Five main-bearing crankshaft

Sky's the limit

Of the 1950s Skylarks, the 1953 models are the most special, with their custom-built bodies. The 1954 models are lighter and more powerful, with 200 bhp versus 188. Despite being more ostentatious, the 1954 versions are much rarer.

Only 836 Skylarks were built in 1954, despite the drop in price.

Rare and exclusive, the Skylark was a short-lived image maker for General Motors' other premium division. It showed that the cars from Flint could compete with the best luxury automobiles that Lincoln had to offer.

Fireball power

A 200-bhp, 322-cubic inch version of Buick's famed 'Fireball' overhead-valve V8 powers the 1954 Skylark. This engine was stroked to 364 cubic inches in 1957 and remained as an option until 1967, in 401- and 425-cubic inch forms.

Changing chassis

When introduced in 1953, the Skylark rode a 121.5-inch Roadmaster chassis. For 1954, as a cost-saving measure, this was changed to the 122-inch Series 60 Century chassis.

Luxurious interior

Power steering, brakes, four-way front bench seat and a power convertible top are all standard equipment. A Selectronic radio, which automatically searches for stations at the touch of a button, and 'Easy-Eye' tinted glass are also included.

Dynaflow

While some critics called it the Dynaslush, Buick's fully automatic Dynaflow transmission was, for the most part, well received. In 1953, an improved twin-turbine unit was introduced and proved more responsive. It was standard on all Skylarks.

Drum brakes

The Skylark used four-wheel drum brakes. A power brake booster was standard, but repeated firm applications on the pedal could result in fading.

Special touches

Skylarks have a number of distinguishing features, including the absence of fender vents, unique wheel well styling (flared at the rear), special front fenders and big chrome fins grafted on the rear quarter panels.

Specifications
1954 Buick Skylark

ENGINE

Type: V8

Construction: Cast-iron block and heads

Valve gear: Two valves per cylinder operated by a single V-mounted camshaft via pushrods and rockers

Bore and stroke: 4.00 in. x 3.20 in.

Displacement: 322 c.i.

Compression ratio: 8.5:1

Induction system: Carter four-barrel carburetor

Maximum power: 200 bhp at 4,100 rpm

Maximum torque: Not quoted

Top speed: 105 mph

0-60 mph: 11.5 sec

TRANSMISSION

Dynaflow two-speed automatic

BODY/CHASSIS

Separate steel chassis with two-door convertible body

SPECIAL FEATURES

Skylarks even have their own special steering wheel boss.

The stylish Kelsey-Hayes 15-inch wire wheels have knock off spinners.

RUNNING GEAR

Steering: Recirculating ball

Front suspension: Unequal-length wishbones with coil springs and telescopic shock absorbers

Rear suspension: Live axle with semi-elliptic leaf springs and lever-arm shock absorbers

Brakes: Drums (front and rear)

Wheels: Kelsey-Hayes wire, 15-in. dia.

Tires: 6.70 x 15 in.

DIMENSIONS

Length: 206.3 in. **Width:** 69.8 in.

Height: 55.8 in. **Wheelbase:** 122.0 in.

Track: 59.0 in. (front and rear)

Weight: 4,260 lbs.

Buick LIMITED

For 1958, Buick decided bigger was better and added the lengthened Limited to the range. Along with it came advances such as air suspension and alloy brake drums. However, by 1959 Buick had discontinued it.

"...the softest of rides."

"You don't so much drive the air-suspended Limited as set sail. Be prepared for the softest of rides, as the springs cannot keep up with the motion of the very long body on its comparatively short wheelbase. Sharp corners have the Buick heeling hard over, although it sticks adequately. The good news is the more effective braking from the alloy drums, which helps make up for the lack of response from the Flight-Pitch Dynaflow three-speed automatic."

The large cabin of the Limited glistens thanks to copious amounts of chrome.

Milestones

1957 Buick introduces a new X-braced chassis with deep side rails available with either a 122- or 127.5-inch wheelbase.

The 1958 Roadmaster was priced below the Limited.

1958 The longer-wheelbase chassis is chosen as the basis for the new Limited model, which revives an old Buick nameplate. It comes with the new Flight-Pitch automatic transmission as standard and optional air springs. It is built in three body-styles: two- and four-door hardtop, or two-door convertible.

In later years, the Limited became a trim option on a wide variety of Buicks like this 1983 Century.

1959 The Limited does not prove a success (with just 7,436 sold) and is discontinued for the 1959 model year. The Limited name reappears as a trim option on up-market Buicks in the mid-1970s.

UNDER THE SKIN

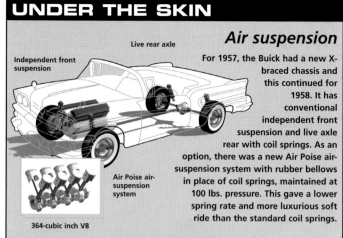

Live rear axle

Independent front suspension

Air Poise air-suspension system

364-cubic inch V8

Air suspension

For 1957, the Buick had a new X-braced chassis and this continued for 1958. It has conventional independent front suspension and live axle rear with coil springs. As an option, there was a new Air Poise air-suspension system with rubber bellows in place of coil springs, maintained at 100 lbs. pressure. This gave a lower spring rate and more luxurious soft ride than the standard coil springs.

THE POWER PACK

Modern design

Buick's 364-cubic inch V8 was a fine engine and quite compact, thanks to its oversquare dimensions (4.25 inch x 3.40 inch). The design follows the normal layout with cast-iron block and heads, single V-mounted camshafts and two valves per cylinder with hydraulic valve lifters. It was powerful, and in 1958 was still a recent design, created for the 1957 lineup. It produces some 300 bhp at 4,600 rpm in standard trim and 400 lb-ft of torque at 3,200 rpm.

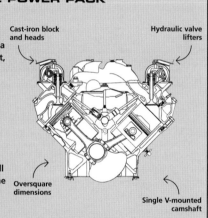

Cast-iron block and heads

Hydraulic valve lifters

Oversquare dimensions

Single V-mounted camshaft

Collectible

The Limited to choose is the convertible, with its power top and leather upholstery. It is very rare, with only 839 made. This accounts for its high price in the collector-car market where they can cost $40,000. The four-door hardtop will cost you about $20,000.

Rarest of all Limiteds is the two-door convertible.

The attraction of the Limited is its sheer scale, extravagant length and excessive chrome, but it was already as doomed as the dinosaurs when it came out, destined to be replaced by Buick's superbly styled 1959 range.

Alloy front brakes

One real advance for 1958 were the new front brakes. They are very large finned alloy castings, with a vented iron insert on which the larger-than-usual brake shoes rub. They performed exceptionally in brake-fade tests. The rear has conventional drums.

V8 engine

For the heavyweight Limited models, Buick used the 364-cubic inch V8 in its most advanced state of tune, which consists of a higher, 10.0:1 compression ratio (instead of 9.5:1) and a Carter or Rochester four-barrel carburetor. This increased power to 300 bhp at a slightly higher 4,600 rpm, with an excellent torque output of 400 lb-ft.

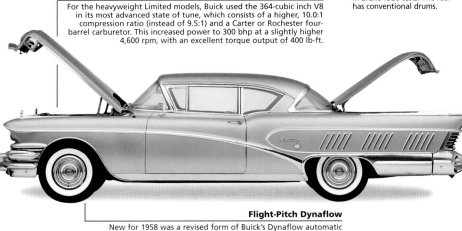

Variable ride height

One feature of the air suspension is that it can be used to raise the car's ride height by 5 inches. A manual override knob on the dash activates a compressor, which inflates the springs.

Flight-Pitch Dynaflow

New for 1958 was a revised form of Buick's Dynaflow automatic transmission. This has three rather than two turbines inside, with variable pitch, and was designed to give a smoother transition across the range of gears. It also features a 'G' (grade-retarding) gear for use when going down steep hills.

Huge rear overhang

The Limited is really an example of size just for the sake of it. The extra length, compared with even the standard big Buicks like the Roadmaster™, is all in the tail, with a rear overhang of more than 60 inches. Despite this great length, rear legroom is still very poor.

Bigger radiator

Because the V8 had to work hard hauling huge cars like the Limited around, in 1958 the radiator was made wider by 3 inches. There was another change to the cooling system: fan speed became independent of the engine's speed.

Specifications

1958 Buick Limited

ENGINE

Type: V8

Construction: Cast-iron block and heads

Valve gear: Two valves per cylinder operated by a single V-mounted camshaft with pushrods, rocker arms and hydraulic lifters

Bore and stroke: 4.25 in. x 3.40 in.

Displacement: 364 c.i.

Compression ratio: 10.0:1

Induction system: Single Carter or Rochester four-barrel carburetor

Maximum power: 300 bhp at 4,600 rpm

Maximum torque: 400 lb-ft at 3,200 rpm

Top speed: 110 mph

0-60 mph: 11.2 sec.

TRANSMISSION

Three-speed automatic Flight-Pitch Dynaflow

BODY/CHASSIS

Separate steel X-braced chassis frame with steel two-door hardtop body

SPECIAL FEATURES

The Limited's gas cap is tucked away under the rear bumper.

These angled rear taillights set the Limited apart from the other Buicks.

RUNNING GEAR

Steering: Recirculating-ball

Front suspension: Unequal length A-arms with coil springs, telescopic shock absorbers and anti-roll bar

Rear suspension: Live axle with coil springs, trailing arms, Panhard rod and telescopic shock absorbers

Brakes: Alloy-cased drums (front), drums (rear)

Wheels: Stamped steel disc, 15-in. dia.

Tires: 8.00 x 15

DIMENSIONS

Length: 227.1 in. **Width:** 79.8 in.

Height: 59.4 in. **Wheelbase:** 127.5 in.

Track: 60.0 in. (front), 61.0 in. (rear)

Weight: 4,691 lbs.

Buick **RIVIERA**

The name Riviera was first affixed to the Buick Roadmaster® during the 1950s. By 1963 Roadmasters were long gone and Riviera became its own model. With a 325-bhp 401 cubic inch engine the Riviera had the power to match its luxurious image.

"...a true 100 mph cruiser."

"As its looks suggest, the Riviera is a sporty yet powerful full-size car. Once behind the wheel of this plush mobile, its striking features become obvious. The power steering is light and the ride immensely soft. The Riviera is fast and is a true 100 mph cruiser. It also has quick acceleration, reaching 60 mph in just 8 seconds. By the mid-1960s disc brakes had still not appeared, and the Riviera's drums require a delicate touch to minimize fade."

1960s Buicks have always had well-trimmed interiors and the Riviera is no exception.

Milestones

1963 Buick produces a Riviera model. It has a large number of standard features, including sporty bucket seats, automatic transmission and power steering; sales top out at 40,000 units.

1964 Minor styling changes and a 340-bhp, 425-cubic inch engine are introduced.

The Wildcat® 445® was also offered in the Skylark®-based Gran Sport®.

1965 This is the last year for the original bodyshell. Headlights are now stacked behind electrically-operated 'clamshell' covers. The Gran Sport produces 360 bhp and the turbohydramatic transmission is now a three-speeder.

The Riviera was rebodied for 1966, and continued in this form until 1970.

1966 A revised Riviera goes on sale. It has smoother, but less distinctive, lines.

UNDER THE SKIN

Nothing new

Buick raided the corporate parts bin for the Riviera's underpinnings. It has a separate chassis for good noise isolation, with coil and wishbone suspension up front and a live axle with coil springs and radius arms at the rear. Like most Detroiters of the time, it has drum brakes front and rear.

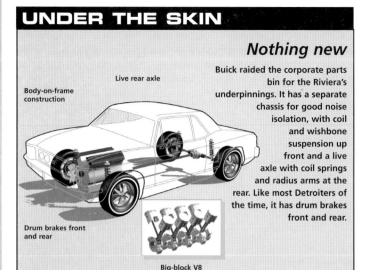

Body-on-frame construction

Live rear axle

Drum brakes front and rear

Big-block V8

THE POWER PACK

Nailhead V8

In 1963 the standard engine for the Riviera was the 401-cubic inch unit that was also used in other big Buicks like the Invicta®, Le Sabre® and Electra®. It has a cast-iron block and cylinder heads and a five main-bearing, cast-iron crankshaft. It is nicknamed the 'Nailhead' due to the small, vertical intake valves. With a 10.25:1 compression ratio and four-barrel carburetor, it produces 325 bhp. Rivieras could also be ordered with a larger 425-cubic inch mill which thumped out 340 bhp.

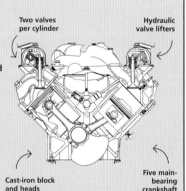

Two valves per cylinder

Hydraulic valve lifters

Cast-iron block and heads

Five main-bearing crankshaft

Luxury coupe

The 1963-1965 Rivieras reflect the influence of styling supremo Bill Mitchell who wanted a clean, European-looking luxury coupe. Enthusiasts also approved, and these classic early models are, without doubt, the most collectable Rivieras.

The 1963 Riviera was Buick's first true luxury coupe.

The Riviera demonstrated that Americans were capable of styling really beautiful cars rather than merely flashy ones. Fast, yet restrained, it was an alternative to expensive, temperamental European coupes.

Eggcrate grill
The classically simple grill was based on Ferrari 250 GT styling. This car has visible turn signals, but on 1965 models the lights are located in clamshell covers in the ends of the fenders.

Smooth V8
The 325-bhp engine is smooth and quiet and gives the Riviera enormous straight-line performance. Uprated Gran Sports, with the 360-bhp, 425-cubic inch V8 and dual carburetors, are even faster.

Discreetly trimmed
Apart from the simulated wire wheel covers and non-functional side scoops, the Riviera's appearance is quiet and discreet.

Conventional chassis engineering
Like most American cars of the period, the Riviera has a separate body and chassis and conventional suspension with coil springs and a live rear axle. The more enthusiast-orientated Gran Sport model has a Posi-Traction limited-slip differential.

Pillarless styling
The side windows are electrically operated to give a clean, pillarless look.

Less bulk
Although massive by European standards, the Riviera was a more modest size compared to the domestic Cadillac and Lincoln competition.

'Coke-bottle' profile
A kicked-up rear fender line over the wheel opening became a trend in American styling and continued until the mid 1970s.

Specifications
1963 Buick Riviera

ENGINE
Type: V8

Construction: Cast-iron block and heads

Valve gear: Two valves per cylinder operated by hydraulic valve lifters with pushrods

Bore and stroke: 4.19 in. x 3.64 in.

Displacement: 401 c.i.

Compression ratio: 10.25:1

Induction system: Single four-choke carburetor

Maximum power: 325 bhp at 4,400 rpm

Maximum torque: 445 lb-ft at 2,800 rpm

Top speed: 125 mph

0-60 mph: 8.0 sec.

TRANSMISSION
Two-speed automatic

BODY/CHASSIS
Steel body on separate X-frame chassis

SPECIAL FEATURES

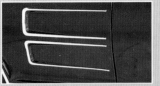

Rear fender scoops are purely cosmetic but accentuate the Riviera's lines.

Wildcat 445 refers to the torque figure rather than the engine displacement.

RUNNING GEAR
Steering: Recirculating ball

Front suspension: Wishbones with coil springs and telescopic shock absorbers

Rear suspension: Live axle with radius arms, coil springs and telescopic shock absorbers

Brakes: Drums, 12-in. dia. (front and rear)

Wheels: Steel discs, 15-in. dia.

Tires: 7.10 x 15

DIMENSIONS
Length: 208.0 in.   **Width:** 79.4 in.

Height: 69.7 in.   **Wheelbase:** 117.0 in.

Track: 62.0 in. (front), 61.0 in. (rear)

Weight: 4,367 lbs.

Buick **RIVIERA GRAN SPORT**

Bigger and heavier for 1971, Buick's personal luxury coupe also got dramatic new styling—especially at the rear, which gave rise to its 'boat-tail' nickname. Some saw it as the ultimate land yacht, but the GS™ model's 330 bhp made for fast, executive-style driving.

"...easy and effortless ."

"When viewed from the outside, the Riviera looks positively huge, but take your place behind the wheel and it feels much smaller. Easy and effortless to drive, this big Buick is at its best on long, straight roads, but with the GS package it will corner hard, ultimately only let down by its tires and sheer girth. The V8 is another matter; with the GS option it packs 330 bhp and 455 lb-ft of torque. This car will reach 60 mph quicker than many other personal luxury cars of its era."

A radiused gauge cluster and close-mounted console garnish the Riviera's lavish interior.

Milestones

1971 Replacing the 1966 vintage Riviera is a new, larger model, with a wheelbase three inches longer and swoopy styling. Weighing about 100 lbs. more, sales drop to 33,810 due in part to its controversial rear end.

The Riviera was reborn as a personal luxury coupe in 1963.

1972 Chrome side spears and a new grill mark the 1972 model. The Gran Sport package is still around, though power is down because of its low-lead, 8.5:1 compression ratio. The big 455-c.i. V8 makes 225 bhp—250 in GS tune.

1974 saw the heaviest Riviera yet, weighing in at 4,572 lbs.

1973 A bigger front bumper and toned down rear deck styling give the Buick's personal luxury car a less distinctive look. Sales creep up slightly to 34,080.

UNDER THE SKIN

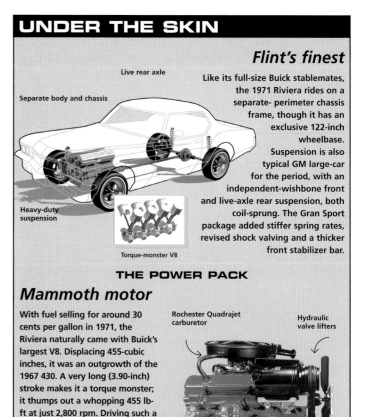

Flint's finest

Live rear axle

Separate body and chassis

Heavy-duty suspension

Torque-monster V8

Like its full-size Buick stablemates, the 1971 Riviera rides on a separate- perimeter chassis frame, though it has an exclusive 122-inch wheelbase. Suspension is also typical GM large-car for the period, with an independent-wishbone front and live-axle rear suspension, both coil-sprung. The Gran Sport package added stiffer spring rates, revised shock valving and a thicker front stabilizer bar.

THE POWER PACK

Mammoth motor

With fuel selling for around 30 cents per gallon in 1971, the Riviera naturally came with Buick's largest V8. Displacing 455-cubic inches, it was an outgrowth of the 1967 430. A very long (3.90-inch) stroke makes it a torque monster; it thumps out a whopping 455 lb-ft at just 2,800 rpm. Driving such a car as the Riviera Gran Sport, it is possible to entice drivers of smaller and lighter muscle cars to a traffic light duel. Though it has a lot of torque, the engine is still well behaved and will provide relaxed high-speed cruising.

Rochester Quadrajet carburetor

Hydraulic valve lifters

Cast-iron construction

Long stroke for maximum torque

Speed boat

Although large and unique, the boat-tail Riviera does have a following. The 1971-1972 models have the unusually styled rear end, which was toned down for 1973. The 1971 GS is also the most sporty version and luckily can still be bought at reasonable prices.

1971 is the pinnacle year for boat-tails in terms of styling and performance.

Penned by Jerry Hirschberg, the 1971 Riviera was a unique design because it broke away from the conservative luxury so often associated with Buick cars. This is what elevated this short-lived car to cult status in later years.

Giant V8

Powering one of the largest and heaviest Rivieras is Buick's largest passenger car engine. Displacing a monster 455-cubic inches, this giant packs 330 bhp in Gran Sport trim and 455 lb-ft of torque. The Riviera GS was the perfect street sleeper for those who were looking for something different.

Cornering lights

Costing just $36 in 1971, cornering lights are mounted in the front fenders. These come on with the turn signals. At night, the front and side signals flash alternately instead of in time.

Heavy-duty suspension

Ordering the Gran Sport package in 1971 brought with it stiffer coil springs and shock absorbers, plus a thicker stabilizer bar. It made for one of the most sporty luxury coupes then on sale.

Body-on-the-frame construction

Rivieras in 1971 had their own E-body chassis but shared their separated chassis structure with the other GM B- and C-body full-size cars.

Boat-tail deck styling

Riviera stylist Hirschberg gave the new Riviera a very dramatic rear deck style which extended right to the bumper. This necessitated an offset rear license plate bracket.

Dual exhaust

Initially, Rivieras had dual exhaust, each with individual mufflers. This system prevailed until 1975, when the adoption of a catalytic convertor necessitated the need for a single setup.

Counterbalanced hood

Like most U.S. cars of the period, the 1971 Riviera has a counterbalancing hood. When opened, heavy-duty hinges support it, eliminating the need for a prop rod. The hood latch is located in the front-grill assembly.

Specifications

1971 Buick Riviera Gran Sport

ENGINE

Type: V8

Construction: Cast-iron block and heads

Valve gear: Two valves per cylinder operated by pushrods and rockers

Bore and stroke: 4.31 in. x 3.90 in.

Displacement: 455 c.i.

Compression ratio: 8.5:1

Induction system: Rochester Quadrajet four-barrel carburetor

Maximum power: 330 bhp at 4,600 rpm

Maximum torque: 455 lb-ft at 2,800 rpm

Top speed: 120 mph

0-60 mph: 8.1 sec.

TRANSMISSION

GM TurboHydramatic 400 three-speed automatic

BODY/CHASSIS

Steel-perimeter chassis with separate two-door coupe body

SPECIAL FEATURES

Pillarless styling is a feature of Rivieras built up to 1974.

1971-72 models are the only true boat-tail-styled Rivieras.

RUNNING GEAR

Steering: Recirculating ball

Front suspension: Unequal-length A-arms with coil springs, telescopic shock absorbers and stabilizer bar

Rear suspension: Live axle with coil springs and telescopic shock absorbers

Brakes: Discs (front), drums (rear)

Wheels: Steel 7 x 15

Tires: G70-15 in.

DIMENSIONS

Length: 217.4 in. **Width:** 79.9 in.

Height: 56.4 in. **Wheelbase:** 122.0 in.

Track: 60.4 in.

Weight: 4,325 lbs.

Buick **GS 400**

While the competition offered bare-knuckled street fighters, Buick loaded its GS 400 with luxury features. It may have looked like an overstuffed luxury coupe, but with 400-cubic inches it was not to be taken lightly.

"...few can rival its power."

"It is hard to judge the GS 400 when you slide behind the wheel, but its character soon becomes clear. The big-block engine has enough torque to light the back tires up on even the driest pavement, yet unlike some other hi-po mills it's turbine smooth. The Buick is more at home on the straights than through corners—push it too hard and it begins to understeer. But for its intended purpose—a stop-light racer—few can rival its power."

A modest-looking sweep speedometer belies this car's searing performance.

Milestones

1965 Buick jumps into the muscle car fray by dropping its 'nailhead' V8 into the intermediate Skylark™, creating the Gran Sport™.

1967 The Gran Sport gets a new 400-cubic inch engine and is renamed GS 400.

The 400-cubic inch engine was first seen in the 1967 GS 400 sport coupe.

1968 All GM A-body intermediates get new two-door bodies and ride on a shorter, 112-inch wheelbase. The GS 400 returns with a standard 340-bhp, 400-cubic inch V8.

The successor to the GS 400 was the 1970 GS 455™ sport coupe.

1969 Functioning hood scoops are made standard and a new Stage 1 option boosts power to 345 bhp. A Stage 2 package is also offered with 360 bhp.

1970 The GS 400 is replaced by the GS 455.

UNDER THE SKIN

Power brakes

The GS 400 has front wishbones with coil springs and telescopic shock absorbers. For the rear, there is a live axle with coil springs and telescopic shocks. To match the stopping power to that of the 400 V8 engine, disc brakes are fitted at the front, though drums are retained at the rear. Modifications were made to both the four-speed manual and three-speed automatic transmissions so they would be more suited to handle the engine's massive surge of power.

Live rear axle

Wishbone front suspension

Front disc brakes

V8 engine

THE POWER PACK

Nasty nailhead

The 400-cubic inch 'nailhead' engine in the GS 400 is a bored and stroked version of the 340, the extra power supplied to match the car's sporty image. It has a special 'Cool Air' induction system fitted to increase the power output. The two scoops in the hood feed a system which features a twin-snorkel air cleaner with two foam muffs that seal the hood's air inlets. Buick claimed that the system increased horsepower by 8 percent. Two optional power packages were also available. Stage 1 used specially tuned carbs to reach 345 bhp, and the rare Stage 2 increased power to 360 bhp.

Rare treat

If there is a choice to be made between the 1968-1969 GS models, it is arguably the convertible. Just 1,776 were built, making them hard to track down. Find one with the hot Stage 1 setup and you have one of the finest muscle cars of the 1960s.

The 1969 convertible models are among the most desirable for collectors.

Although it wasn't the best selling muscle car, the GS 400 certainly did not take a back seat when it came to performance. With 440 lb-ft of torque on tap, the GS400 Stage 1 was the perfect weapon to shut down the competition with.

Large bore V8
The 400-cubic inch engine in Stage 1 trim received a higher lift cam, 11.0:1 compression pistons, a special Quadrajet carburetor, plus low-restriction exhaust pipes. The result was a 0-60 time in the high 5-second range.

Subtle changes
GM's Astro Ventilation system dispensed with the need for vent windows, and the grill and taillights were also mildly altered.

Functional hood scoops
Buick stole a lead, not only on rival manufacturers but on other GM divisions too, by offering a standard 'Cold Air' package. It uses a twin-snorkel air cleaner to increase power.

Power disc brakes
By 1969, engineers were beginning to pay more attention to making cars stop as well as they accelerated. Therefore, power front disc brakes were standard on the GS 400, though drums were still fitted at the rear.

Shorter wheelbase
For 1968, all GM A-body intermediates received revised styling and split wheel-bases—two-door models were three inches shorter than the 4-door versions.

Live rear axle
Like most muscle cars, the GS put power to the pavement through a live axle. With the Stage 1 package, a set of 3.64:1 gears and a Positraction limited-slip differential were standard—the latter helping the skinny, bias-ply tires to hook up under fierce acceleration.

Specifications

1969 Buick GS 400 (Stage 1)

ENGINE

Type: V8

Construction: Cast-iron block and heads

Valve gear: Two valves per cylinder operated by a single block-mounted camshaft with pushrods and rockers

Bore and stroke: 4.04 in. x 3.90 in.

Displacement: 400 c.i.

Compression ratio: 11.0:1

Induction system: Single Rochester Quadrajet four-barrel downdraft carburetor

Maximum power: 345 bhp at 4,800 rpm

Maximum torque: 440 lb-ft at 3,200 rpm

Top speed: 125 mph

0-60 mph: 5.8 sec.

TRANSMISSION

TurboHydramatic three-speed automatic

BODY/CHASSIS

Separate steel chassis with two-door convertible body

SPECIAL FEATURES

The 'Cold Air' induction system helps to boost engine power.

The Turbo-Hydramatic three-speed transmission was fortified to handle the engine's massive torque output.

RUNNING GEAR

Steering: Recirculating ball

Front suspension: Unequal length wishbones with coil springs, telescopic shock absorbers and anti-roll bar

Rear suspension: Live axle with coil springs and telescopic shock absorbers

Brakes: Discs (front), drums (rear)

Wheels: Magnum 500 steel, 6 x 14 in.

Tires: G-70 14

DIMENSIONS

Length: 200.7 in. **Width:** 81.0 in.

Height: 54.0 in. **Wheelbase:** 112.0 in.

Track: 59.0 in. (front and rear)

Weight: 3,594 lbs.

Buick **GSX**

If the 1970 mid-size GS™ 455 wasn't wild enough, Buick raised the muscle car ante with the fearsome GSX. It had all the power of the regular GS 455, but included a better suspension and wild appearance package. When ordered with the optional 455 Stage I engine the GSX became lethal.

"...the Velvet Hammer."

"Unlike most other muscle cars of the era, Buick's GSX offered creature comforts that were mostly associated with luxury cars. Included in the package was a brutal 455 V8. The GSX combined luxury with high performance, earning it the nickname the 'Velvet Hammer.' With more than 510 lb-ft of torque, its low-end power was nothing short of insanity. Thanks to its heavy duty suspension and 15-inch wheels, the GSX handled great for such a heavy car."

Although one of the quickest muscle cars built, the GSX is definitely not a stripped-out racer.

Milestones

1970 Buick unveils a restyled Skylark™. The Gran Sport (GS) model receives a 455-V8. The GSX option package also appears but the cars are only available painted in Apollo White or Saturn Yellow. Production for the model year is just 687 units.

Although overshadowed by the GSX, regular GS models continued into 1972.

1971 The GS and the GSX option continue. A wider assortment of colors is now available. GM drops the compression ratio in the 455 engines down to 8.5:1 to meet stricter emission standards. The regular 455 now makes 315 bhp while the Stage 1 engine makes 345 bhp.

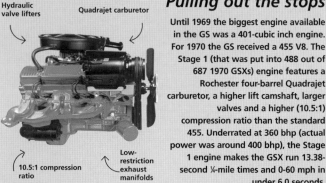

When Buick launched the GN™ in the 1980s, it made one of the fastest late model street cars.

1972 The GS reverts to an option package on the Skylark models. The GSX package is still available, but only 44 cars are ordered. The Stage 1 455 only makes 270 bhp.

UNDER THE SKIN

Beefed up

Like rival GM intermediates of the era, the GSX has independent wishbone front suspension and a live rear axle with coil springs. For improved handling the shocks and springs are stiffened and large front and rear anti-roll bars are installed. Stopping power is provided by big 11-inch discs up front and finned 9.5 inch drum brakes at the rear.

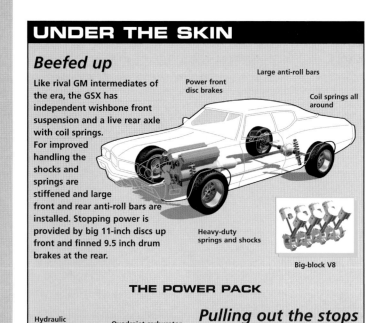

Large anti-roll bars

Power front disc brakes

Coil springs all around

Heavy-duty springs and shocks

Big-block V8

THE POWER PACK

Hydraulic valve lifters

Quadrajet carburetor

10.5:1 compression ratio

Low-restriction exhaust manifolds

Pulling out the stops

Until 1969 the biggest engine available in the GS was a 401-cubic inch engine. For 1970 the GS received a 455 V8. The Stage 1 (that was put into 488 out of 687 1970 GSXs) engine features a Rochester four-barrel Quadrajet carburetor, a higher lift camshaft, larger valves and a higher (10.5:1) compression ratio than the standard 455. Underrated at 360 bhp (actual power was around 400 bhp), the Stage 1 engine makes the GSX run 13.38-second ¼-mile times and 0-60 mph in under 6.0 seconds.

Still potent

Although the GSX was Buick's muscle flagship for 1970, regular GS models were just as powerful and could also be ordered with the 360-bhp, 455-cubic inch Stage 1 V8. Only 1,416 GS convertibles with this package were built for the 1970 model year.

Standard GS 455s may have a more subtle appearance, but they are still fast.

With its loud paintwork, spoilers, scoops and graphics, plus a monstrous 455 engine, the GSX is Buick's finest muscle car and comes complete with all the trimmings.

Front disc brakes

With so much performance just a stab of the throttle away, the GSX needs powerful brakes. It uses 11-inch diameter disc brakes at the front, but made do with finned drum brakes at the rear.

Awesome power

1970 marked the introduction of 455-cubic inch engines in GM intermediates. A standard Buick GS 455 churns out 350 bhp, but the optional Stage 1 produces 360 bhp due to a more aggressive cam and a higher compression ratio.

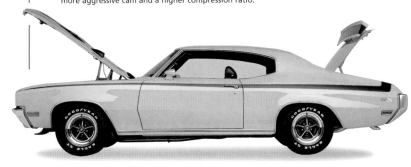

Transmissions

Three different transmissions were available: three- or four-speed manual, or a TurboHydramatic 400 automatic transmission with a Hurst gear shifter.

Suspension upgrades

The GSX has heavy-duty suspension and powered front disc brakes, plus uprated shock absorbers and stiffer springs for better handling.

Color availability

Introduced halfway through the model year, the 1970 GSX was available in only two colors: Apollo White or Saturn Yellow.

Chrome wheels

The GSX package included a handsome set of 7-in wide Magnum 500 chrome-plated steel wheels and Goodyear Polyglas GT series tires.

Restyled body

Some people criticized the 1968-1969 GS for looking out of proportion. For the 1970 model year, the Skylark received an attractive facelift and full rear wheel cut-outs.

1970 Buick GSX

ENGINE

Type: V8

Construction: Cast-iron block and heads

Valve gear: Two valves per cylinder operated by pushrods and rockers

Bore and stroke: 4.33 in. x 3.9 in.

Displacement: 455 c.i.

Compression ratio: 10.5:1

Induction system: Rochester four-barrel Quadrajet carburetor

Maximum power: 360 bhp at 4,600 rpm

Maximum torque: 510 lb-ft at 2,800 rpm

Top speed: 123 mph

0-60 mph: 5.5 sec.

TRANSMISSION

Four-speed close-ratio manual

BODY/CHASSIS

Steel coupe body on separate chassis

SPECIAL FEATURES

A hood-mounted tachometer came standard on all GSX models.

The rear spoiler and black accent stripes are some of the GSX's styling features.

RUNNING GEAR

Steering: Power-assisted recirculating ball

Front suspension: Independent wishbones with coil springs, telescopic shocks and heavy-duty roll bar

Rear suspension: Live axle fitted with 3.64:1 axle gears, heavy-duty coil springs, telescopic shocks and anti-roll bar

Brakes: Vented discs, 11-in. dia. (front), finned drums, 9.5-in. dia. (rear)

Wheels: Magnum 500, 7 x 15 in.

Tires: Goodyear Polyglas GT G60-15

DIMENSIONS

Length: 202 in.   **Width:** 75.9 in.

Height: 53 in.   **Wheelbase:** 112 in.

Track: 60.1 in. (front), 58.9 in. (rear)

Weight: 3,561 lbs.

Buick **GNX**

The basic idea of the GNX was to mimic what Buick did with the GSX™ project in 1970. Because 1987 marked the end of the rear-wheel drive Regal™, Buick wanted to build a killer limited edition performance car using its turbo V6 engine.

"...B-B-Bad to the Bone."

"The caption on 1987 Buick GNX promotional poster read: 'The Grand National™ to end all Grand Nationals.' When the simple V6 is fired up it sounds docile. With one foot on the brake and the other on the gas the boost needle rises to 1 psi. Release the brake and drop the accelerator and the 3.8 liter engine quickly makes 15 psi of boost rocketing the car down the ¼ mile in 13.43 seconds at 104 mph. Another Turbo Buick promotion labeled the car as 'B-B-Bad to the Bone'—and it lives up to this reputation."

The standard GN gauges were scraped in favor of analog instruments from Stewart-Warner.

Milestones

1978 A downsized Buick Regal is launched with a turbo 3.8 liter V6 engine that kicks out 150 bhp.

The turbo V6 was also offered in Regal T-Types.

1982 215 Grand Nationals and 2,022 T-Types are built.

1984 GNs return with an all-black exterior and a 200-bhp turbo V6 engine. Grand Nationals are nothing more than an appearance package on the Buick T-Type.

1986 The Grand National and T-Types get an air-to-air intercooler revised fuel management system and relocated turbocharger. The engine makes 235 bhp.

Buick sold 20,193 GNs in 1987.

1987 Stock turbo Buicks make 345 bhp. Buick and ASC/Mclaren build 547 GNX cars to commemorate the final year of the turbocharged cars.

UNDER THE SKIN

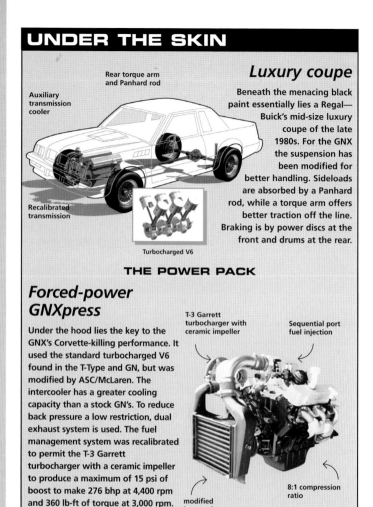

Luxury coupe

Beneath the menacing black paint essentially lies a Regal—Buick's mid-size luxury coupe of the late 1980s. For the GNX the suspension has been modified for better handling. Sideloads are absorbed by a Panhard rod, while a torque arm offers better traction off the line. Braking is by power discs at the front and drums at the rear.

Rear torque arm and Panhard rod

Auxiliary transmission cooler

Recalibrated transmission

Turbocharged V6

THE POWER PACK

Forced-power GNXpress

Under the hood lies the key to the GNX's Corvette-killing performance. It used the standard turbocharged V6 found in the T-Type and GN, but was modified by ASC/McLaren. The intercooler has a greater cooling capacity than a stock GN's. To reduce back pressure a low restriction, dual exhaust system is used. The fuel management system was recalibrated to permit the T-3 Garrett turbocharger with a ceramic impeller to produce a maximum of 15 psi of boost to make 276 bhp at 4,400 rpm and 360 lb-ft of torque at 3,000 rpm.

T-3 Garrett turbocharger with ceramic impeller

Sequential port fuel injection

8:1 compression ratio

modified intercooler

Modern Muscle

During the 1980s late-model muscle cars were beginning to resurface. It was the first time since the 1960s that American cars were running the S/S ¼ mile in under 14 seconds. The Buick GNX was the fastest production car in 1987 and is a landmark car for collectors.

Surprisingly, the 1987 GNX was faster than the new Corvette that year.

Buick had three objectives with the GNX; to drop its 0-60 by almost a second over a stock GN, to revise the body and interior in functional areas, and to build a limited number to create exclusivity and collectability. It met them all.

Flared wheel arches

Because of the larger and wider wheels and tires, the front and rear wheel well openings had to be modified and fitted with composite fender flares. They blend in nicely with the rest of the GNX's styling.

Upgraded turbocharged engine

The 3.8 liter SFI turbocharged engines are refitted with a better turbo, improved intercooler, recalibrated fuel management system and a low restriction exhaust system.

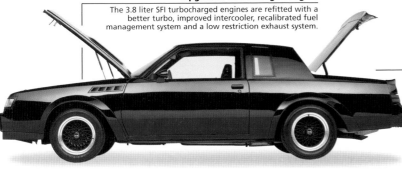

Live axle

The same 8.5-inch rear that is found in the GN and T-Type is retained in the GNX. It also uses the same 3.42:1 axle ratio. All GNX cars came equipped with aluminum rear brake drums to help save weight.

Powermaster brakes

A unique braking system was used on all turbocharged Buicks. Instead of a vacuum-assisted system it uses a hydraulic system that works off the power steering pump.

Modified transmission

A stock GN 200-4R transmission with a 2.74:1 first-gear ratio and an increased stall speed torque converter was used in the GNX. It was recalibrated for increased line pressure, resulting in firmer shifts.

16 x 8-inch alloy wheels

Larger 16 x 8-inch BBS style black mesh wheels were used on all GNXs. It's a very similar wheel used on the Trans Am GTA, but with a different offset.

Stiffer suspension

The GNX has a unique rear suspension. It uses a Panhard rod and torque arm. It also uses the same 19 mm anti-roll bar and Delco shocks found on GNs and T-Types.

Stewart-Warner gauges

A special Stewart-Warner analog instrument cluster replaces the stock gauges. It includes a 140 mph speedometer, 8,000 rpm tachometer, turbo boost gauge, amp meter, oil pressure and water temperature gauge.

Black out

Like all 1984-1987 Grand Nationals, the GNX was only available in black. Tinted glass, black wheel centers and a complete lack of exterior chrome further enhanced its menacing appearance. It did receive special 'GNX' badging on the front fenders, grill and rear trunk lid.

Fender vents

Vents were incorporated into the fenders to reduce engine bay heat.

Specifications

1987 Buick Regal GNX

ENGINE

Type: V6

Construction: Cast-iron block and heads

Valve gear: Two valves per cylinder operated by a camshaft with .389/.411 inch lift and 294/290 degrees of duration

Bore and stroke: 3.80 in. x 3.40 in.

Displacement: 231 c.i.

Compression ratio: 8.0:1

Induction system: SFI with modified intercooler and Garrett T-3 turbocharger

Maximum power: 276 bhp at 4,400 rpm

Maximum torque: 360 lb-ft at 3,000 rpm

Top speed: 124 mph

0-60 mph: 5.5 sec.

TRANSMISSION

Modified GM 200-4R four-speed automatic

BODY/CHASSIS

Steel two-door four-seater

SPECIAL FEATURES

GNXs have special fender vents which release hot air from the engine compartment.

Each GNX is numbered and has a plaque on the dashboard. Anyone who ordered one new received a GNX book and jacket.

RUNNING GEAR

Steering: Recirculating ball

Front suspension: Double wishbones with shocks and anti-roll bar

Rear suspension: Live axle with Panhard rod, torque arm, trailing links, coil springs, and anti-roll bar

Brakes: Discs, 10.5-in. dia. (front), drums, 9.5-in. dia. (rear)

Wheels: Alloy, 8 x 16 in.

Tires: Goodyear Gatorbacks, 245/50 VR16 (front), 255/50 VR16 (rear)

DIMENSIONS

Length: 200.6 in. **Width:** 71.6 in.

Height: 56.0 in. **Wheelbase:** 108.1 in.

Track: 59.4 in. (front), 59.3 in. (rear)

Weight: 3,545 lbs.

Cadillac ELDORADO BROUGHAM

The most expensive Cadillac of the 1950s, the Eldorado Brougham is a huge four-door hardtop derived from a show car. Each one was hand built and came with just about every conceivable option. However, its steep price resulted in it being dropped in 1960.

"...you can feel its quality."

"The most luxurious of all 1950s Cadillacs, the Eldorado Brougham is glitzy but not overtly so. You can almost feel the quality in the massive hand-stitched bench seat and door panels. The best part about this car is that it's whisper quiet at speed and the air suspension makes you feel like you're floating on a cloud. The automatic transmission is amazingly precise for a 1950s car. The steering is exceedingly light, while the brake pedal has almost no feel."

Buyers could choose from 44 trim and color combinations, including lamb's-skin seats.

Milestones

1956 In December, the Eldorado Brougham is announced for 1957. A total of 400 are built in its first year.

The Eldorado Seville was the next most expensive Cadillac after the Brougham.

1958 While regular Cadillacs receive an exterior facelift, the Brougham remains externally unchanged, although the interior door panels are now leather instead of metal.

1959-1960 Broughams were larger and sharper looking.

1959 All Cadillacs are new this year, and standard models have Detroit's tallest fins. The Brougham returns with more power and a new, four-door, hardtop body built by Pininfarina in Italy.

1960 As a result of high production costs and slow sales, the Brougham is dropped. Its styling previews 1961 Cadillacs.

UNDER THE SKIN

State of the art

When the Brougham arrived in 1957 it rode an exclusive 126-inch wheelbase;—other Cadillacs were larger. It adopted a new X-braced separate chassis, and shunned conventional coil springs in favor of air suspension. Separate piston-operated airbags were used at each corner and operated with a central air pump. Braking was less high tech, with power-assisted drums in the front and rear.

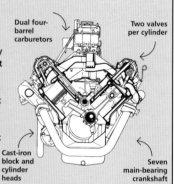

Body-on-frame construction

Air suspension front and rear

X-braced chassis

Milestone V8

THE POWER PACK

Ever more power

V8s powering Cadillacs during the 1950s were versions of the 331-cubic inch overhead-valve powerplant developed by engineers Ed Cole, Harry Barr and Jack Gordon in 1949. The unit was light, with a low reciprocating mass, and was reliable. By 1957 it had grown to 365 cubic inches and put out 325 bhp in Eldorados, increasing to 335 bhp the following year. In 1959 the engine was bored out to 390 cubic inches and, while standard Series 62s had 325 bhp, upmarket Eldorados produced 345 bhp.

Dual four-barrel carburetors

Two valves per cylinder

Cast-iron block and cylinder heads

Seven main-bearing crankshaft

U.S.-built

Broughams can be divided into two distinct series, the 1957-1958 cars, hand-built in Detroit, and the later 1959-1960 models. These Pininfarina-built cars are larger and have much sleeker styling that other Cadillacs. Collectors tend to prefer the earlier models.

Earlier Broughams have proved to be very popular with collectors.

Cadillac was the 'Standard of the World' back in the 1950s and the Brougham was the ultimate expression of luxury on wheels. At a staggering $13,075 in 1957, however, few could afford it.

Powerful V8

By 1957 the 1949 vintage Cadillac V8 had been stroked to 365 cubic inches and produced a muscular 325 bhp on Eldorados (300 bhp on other models). All Cadillacs got an extra 10 bhp for 1958.

Sumptuous interior

Eldorado Broughams were laden with luxury options inside, including power steering, brakes and windows, plus air-conditioning, electric memory seats and cruise control. Buyers also had the choice of 44 interior and exterior trim and color combinations.

Huge chrome grill

Broughams have a unique eggcrate mesh-pattern grill which is neater than those on other Cadillacs. Broughams were also the first to get quad headlights.

Air suspension

A state-of-the-art feature, air suspension, was introduced on the Brougham. It basically consisted of a rubber diaphragm and piston at each wheel controlled by a central compressor. The system was not very reliable and many owners chose to replace it with coil springs.

Suicide doors

Another feature unique to the 1957-1958 Eldorado Brougham are the suicide doors. Those at the front open in the normal manner, but the back doors are hinged at the rear. This allows easy access for passengers and also means that the Brougham was a pillarless four-door sedan that allowed the elimination of the rear quarter windows.

Modest fins

Cadillac pioneered fins among domestic manufacturers as far back as 1948. In 1955 Eldorados gained tall blade-like items, and these were adopted for the Brougham when it was launched in 1958. Interestingly, although regular Cadillacs had fins of gigantic proportions for 1959, Broughams had fairly small fins with dagger-shaped taillight lenses.

Smooth styling

Panoramic windshields were first seen on the limited production Eldorado convertible in 1953. By 1958 all Cadillacs had them. They offered good visibility, but were costly to replace and necessitated a front dog-leg A-pillar which could make entry into the car rather difficult.

Specifications

1957 Cadillac Eldorado Brougham

ENGINE
Type: V8

Construction: Cast-iron block and heads

Valve gear: Two valves per cylinder operated by a single camshaft via pushrods and rockers

Bore and stroke: 4.00 in. x 3.63 in.

Displacement: 365 c.i.

Compression ratio: 10.0:1

Induction system: Two four-barrel carburetors

Maximum power: 325 bhp at 4,800 rpm

Maximum torque: 435 lb-ft at 3,400 rpm

Top speed: 110 mph

0-60 mph: 11.4 sec

TRANSMISSION
Three-speed automatic

BODY/CHASSIS
Separate chassis with two-door steel convertible body

SPECIAL FEATURES

A full-length stainless-steel roof was standard on 1957-1958 Broughams —a feature lifted intact from the Eldorado show car of 1954.

A gold anodized air cleaner is mounted atop the 365-cubic inch V8.

RUNNING GEAR
Steering: Recirculating ball

Front suspension: Wishbones with airbags and shock absorbers

Rear suspension: Live axle with airbags and shock absorbers

Brakes: Drums (front and rear)

Wheels: Steel, 15-in. dia.

Tires: 8.0 x 15.0 in.

DIMENSIONS
Length: 216.3 in.   **Width:** 78.5 in.

Height: 55.5 in.   **Wheelbase:** 126.0 in.

Track: 61.0 in. (front and rear)

Weight: 5,315 lbs.

Cadillac **SERIES 62**

In response to Chrysler's tail-finned cruisers General Motors fielded all-new C-body cars in 1959—all with outrageous styling. The 1959 Cadillac was the most flamboyant of all and became etched in the public's imagination because of its classy styling and large tail fins.

"...the definitive Cadillac."

"For its size the 1959 Cadillac is quick in a straight line, with lots of low rpm torque to get it moving. It's easily capable of maintaining a smooth, silent 80 mph. Feather-light power steering makes for easy turning, but over-enthusiastic cornering reveals the Caddy's tendency to pitch and roll in an unsettling manner. But as we already know, this isn't designed to be a race car. Rather it's a sleek and sophisticated luxury cruiser. And to most people, it's the definitive Cadillac."

The emphasis is on luxury. This car has power everything, including cruise control.

Milestones

1955 Eldorados get a revised body with a new gold anodized grill and larger, more protruding fins than the Series 62s.

In 1953 the Series 62 was the entry-level Cadillac.

1957 The ultra-exclusive Eldorado Brougham, costing $13,074, is a new flagship built to challenge the Lincoln Continental. Among a huge list of luxuries this model previews the air suspension available on the 1959 cars. The fins are made larger too.

By 1964, fins on Cadillacs had become quite modest.

1959 Totally restyled on a massive 130-inch wheelbase, the 1959 has some of the wildest fins ever, plus a huge chrome grill. All Cadillacs are powered by a V8 stretched to 390 cubic inches. The 1960 models have cleaner styling.

UNDER THE SKIN

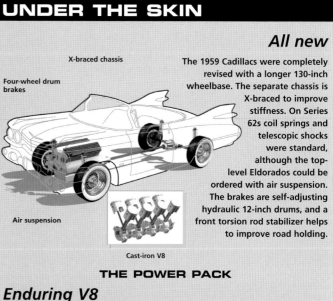

X-braced chassis

Four-wheel drum brakes

Air suspension

Cast-iron V8

All new

The 1959 Cadillacs were completely revised with a longer 130-inch wheelbase. The separate chassis is X-braced to improve stiffness. On Series 62s coil springs and telescopic shocks were standard, although the top-level Eldorados could be ordered with air suspension. The brakes are self-adjusting hydraulic 12-inch drums, and a front torsion rod stabilizer helps to improve road holding.

THE POWER PACK

Enduring V8

By 1959, the Cadillac V8 had been enlarged to 390 cubic inches and was offered in two states of tune. Series 62s, DeVilles, Sixty-Specials and 75s came with a 325-bhp unit and a Carter four-barrel carburetor. The Eldorado models were fitted with a 345-bhp version and three Rochester two-barrel carburetors. The V8 is a conventional unit, constructed from cast iron, with two valves per cylinder and hydraulic lifters. Each engine was run in before being fitted in the car.

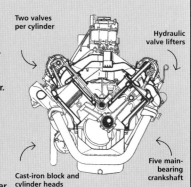

Two valves per cylinder

Hydraulic valve lifters

Cast-iron block and cylinder heads

Five main-bearing crankshaft

Biarritz special

Next up the scale from the series 62 is the DeVille, offered in hardtop coupe and sedan form. The four window sedan De Ville may not have quite the allure of a drop top but it is distinctive nonetheless and presently is cheaper to buy than a convertible.

in 1959 Sedan DeVilles came in either four- or six-window forms.

The 1959 Cadillacs were at their most glamorous in convertible form, either as Series 62 models or the flagship Eldorado Biarritz. As one of the world's premier luxury cars of the late 1950s, they were almost unchallenged.

Big-block V8
Displacing 390 cubic inches, the Cadillac V8 cranks out 325 bhp in the Series 62. A four-barrel carburetor is standard.

Power top
Power accessories were a major selling point of the Cadillac convertibles. With the flick of a switch, the top folds back neatly behind the rear seat.

Automatic headlights
Cadillac's 'Twilight Sentinel' headlights switch on automatically at dusk and also switch from high to low beams for oncoming traffic.

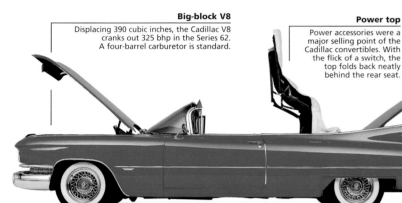

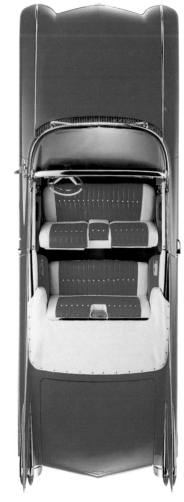

Drum brakes
Although it accelerates quickly, the Series 62 is not an all-out performer. Repeated heavy braking from high speed may cause the four-wheel drums to lock and quickly fade.

Separate chassis
A separate chassis provides greater ride comfort, which is essential for a luxury cruiser. The frame is X-braced for greater stiffness.

Mass-produced quality
For a mass-produced vehicle, the 1959 Cadillac was well put together. Only the finest quality materials were used during the manufacturing process.

Chromed bumper
In the 1950s, designers looked to the space program for inspiration. The 1959 Cadillac has a heavy, full-width chromed rear bumper with back-up lights built into the center of its fins.

Flamboyant styling
The 1959 Caddy was one of the last cars styled by the legendary Harley Earl and marked the end of an era.

Specifications
1959 Cadillac Series 62

ENGINE
Type: V8
Construction: Cast-iron block and heads
Valve gear: Two valves per cylinder operated by a single camshaft via pushrods and rockers
Bore and stroke: 4.00 in. x 3.88 in.
Displacement: 390 c.i.
Compression ratio: 10.5:1
Induction system: Carter four-barrel carburetor
Maximum power: 325 bhp at 4,800 rpm
Maximum torque: 435 lb-ft at 3,400 rpm
Top speed: 121 mph
0-60 mph 11.0 sec.

TRANSMISSION
GM TurboHydramatic automatic

BODY/CHASSIS
Steel body on steel X-frame chassis

SPECIAL FEATURES

By 1959, quad headlights were in fashion. For the ultimate in excess, all 1959 Cadillacs have dual parking lights in chrome housings which form the lower part of the bumper.

The most recognizable feature are the fins—the tallest ever on a production car. Huge chrome bumpers further accentuate its advanced styling.

RUNNING GEAR
Steering: Recirculating ball
Front suspension: Wishbones with coil springs and telescopic shock absorbers
Rear suspension: Live axle with coil springs and telescopic shock absorbers
Brakes: Drums, 12-in. dia. (front and rear)
Wheels: Steel discs, 15-in. dia.
Tires: 8.20-15

DIMENSIONS
Length: 224.8 in. **Width:** 79.9 in.
Height: 55.9 in. **Wheelbase:** 130.0 in.
Track: 61.0 in. (front), 60.2 in. (rear)
Weight: 4,885 lbs.

Cadilliac **ALLANTE**

In the late 1980s, Cadillac entered the ultra-luxury market with the Allanté. Sadly, it was not a success and was dropped in 1993, by which time it had become a world-class luxury touring machine.

"...no ordinary Cadillac."

"Everything tells you that this is no ordinary Cadillac—from the bite and efficiency of the vented disc brakes to the minimal body roll when cornering, the precise rack-and-pinion steering and remarkably stiff convertible body. The Northstar V8 has incredible low-down torque and a raspy exhaust note, but as this is a powerful front-drive car there is a hint of torque steer. Apart from that, the Allanté is a quiet, competent and comfortable cruiser."

By 1993 a driver's airbag was a standard fitting in the Allanté.

Milestones

1986 Cadillac launches the Allanté late in the year as an 1987 model. The company hopes that the Pininfarina styling will broaden Cadillac's appeal.

In the 1960s, Cadillac's only convertibles were four-seaters, like this Eldorado.

1989 Only 3,300 Allantés are sold during the first year and substantial changes are made for 1989. These include an enlarged 4.5-liter V8 with 200 bhp. Computer control suspension switches between three shock absorber settings, and larger wheels and tires are fitted.

The Allanté shares its inner structure with the Eldorado and Seville.

1993 The Allanté is given the brand-new Northstar V8, resulting in a 0-60 time of 7.0 seconds and a top speed of 145 mph. However, GM decides that the Allanté will not return for 1994.

UNDER THE SKIN

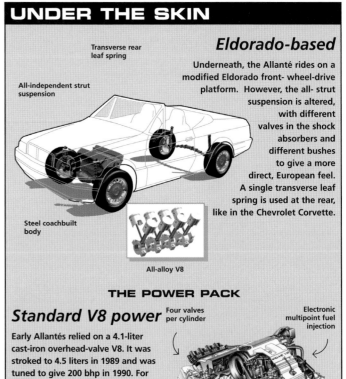

Transverse rear leaf spring

Eldorado-based

All-independent strut suspension

Underneath, the Allanté rides on a modified Eldorado front-wheel-drive platform. However, the all-strut suspension is altered, with different valves in the shock absorbers and different bushes to give a more direct, European feel. A single transverse leaf spring is used at the rear, like in the Chevrolet Corvette.

Steel coachbuilt body

All-alloy V8

THE POWER PACK

Standard V8 power

Four valves per cylinder

Electronic multipoint fuel injection

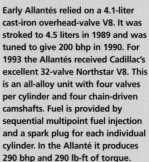
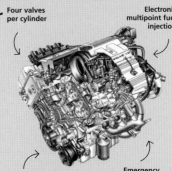

Early Allantés relied on a 4.1-liter cast-iron overhead-valve V8. It was stroked to 4.5 liters in 1989 and was tuned to give 200 bhp in 1990. For 1993 the Allantés received Cadillac's excellent 32-valve Northstar V8. This is an all-alloy unit with four valves per cylinder and four chain-driven camshafts. Fuel is provided by sequential multipoint fuel injection and a spark plug for each individual cylinder. In the Allanté it produces 290 bhp and 290 lb-ft of torque.

Alloy block and cylinder heads

Emergency limp-home mode

Last and best

For 1993 the Allanté finally became a world-class automobile, with traction controls, road-sensing suspension and a magnificent 290-bhp Northstar V8. Only a small number were built and were a stylish alternative to a Mercedes-Benz SL.

The 1993 Allanté is the most desirable model.

The production of the Allanté was one of the most complicated ever undertaken. The bodies and chassis were flown between Detroit and Pininfarina in Italy by Boeing 747s.

V8 engine
Early examples were powered by 4.1- and 4.5-liter pushrod V8s, but 1993 Allantés, like this one, rely on the exotic all-alloy overhead-cam 4.6-liter Northstar V8.

Manual soft top
Surprisingly for a Cadillac, the Allanté has a manually-operated convertible top. It was designed to be raised and lowered easily and quickly and was used to save the weight of the electric motors needed for a power top. A powered top did appear on the later, more powerful models.

Automatic transmission
Cadillac considered a five-speed manual version of the Allanté, but settled on a four-speed automatic. To smooth the gearchanges and preserve the transmission, the engine timing is retarded the merest fraction before each change, but not enough for the driver to notice.

Anti-lock brakes
Cadillac opted for Bosch's compact ABS III system because it leaves space for the long tuned engine intake runners under the hood.

Pininfarina styling
For an appealing and wind cheating style, the Allanté's coachwork was built by Pininfarina. The bodies were built in Turin and then flown to the U.S. Final assembly of the Allanté was carried out at GM's Hamtramck plant in Detroit.

Specifications
1993 Cadillac Allanté

ENGINE
Type: V8

Construction: Alloy block and heads

Valve gear: Four valves per cylinder operated by twin overhead camshafts per cylinder bank

Bore and stroke: 3.7 in. x 3.3 in.

Displacement: 279 c.i.

Compression ratio: 10.3:1

Induction system: Sequential multipoint fuel injection

Maximum power: 290 bhp at 5,600 rpm

Maximum torque: 290 lb-ft at 4,400 rpm

Top speed: 145 mph

0-60 mph: 7.0 sec

TRANSMISSION
THM-440 four-speed automatic

BODY/CHASSIS
Unitary construction with modified Eldorado/Seville platform and Pininfarina styling

SPECIAL FEATURES

Later Allantés have these distinctive taillight inserts.

The gas cap is located just behind the driver's door, which is unusual for a Cadillac.

RUNNING GEAR
Steering: Rack-and-pinion

Front suspension: Modified MacPherson struts with anti-roll bar

Rear suspension: Modified MacPherson struts with transverse composite leaf spring

Brakes: Vented discs, 10.3-in. dia. (front), 10.0-in. dia. (rear)

Wheels: Alloy, 16-in. dia.

Tires: Goodyear Eagle GA, P225/60 ZR16

DIMENSIONS
Length: 178.4 in.   **Width:** 73.5 in.

Height: 52.2 in.   **Wheelbase:** 99.4 in.

Track: 60.0 in. (front and rear)

Weight: 3,720 lbs.

Cadilliac **CATERA**

Cadillac decided that the best way to fight back against foreign imports was to have its own. The Catera is an Americanized version of the German Opel Omega, which has an advanced quad-cam V6 engine.

"...European style."

"With features such as leather seats and air conditioning, this Cadillac is no poor relation. Fire up the quad-cam V6 and the Catera offers the right combination of handling and performance. It might be small for a Cadillac, but it doesn't feel it inside. The ride is comfortably soft and yet there's roll-free handling through the corners. Switching to performance mode on the four-speed automatic utilizes all the power on offer to keep the driver happy."

The cabin of the Catera retains a European flavor, with leather used to add luxury.

Milestones

1994 Opel launches the Omega. It has a conventional front-engined, rear-wheel-drive layout and is designed with an eye to the North American market.

The Catera has its origins in the European Opel/Vauxhall Omega.

1996 Before the car goes on sale in the U.S., a traditional Cadillac grill is added and the rear is restyled; the car is now called the Catera. Engine power suffers slightly as a result of having to meet stiffer emissions and safety requirements.

Cadillac's largest current car is the DeVille.

1997 Catera equipment is improved with an optional power sunroof and the OnStar system, with theft detection and tracking. There is also improved traction control. A new optional radio comes with a one-slot CD player rather than the remote stack, and there are audio controls on the steering wheel.

UNDER THE SKIN

Omega-based

Large four-wheel disc brakes

Unitary-construction steel monocoque

MacPherson-strut front suspension

Quad-cam V6

Behind the Cadillac badges, there is an Opel Omega with subtle changes. The Cadillac retains the Opel's strut front and semi-trailing arm rear suspensions, with a toe-control link added to improve handling. Powerful braking is guaranteed, thanks to large vented front discs and solid rears, and there is automatic leveling at the rear to compensate for heavy loads. The power-assisted recirculating-ball steering is also from the Omega.

THE POWER PACK

Compact V6

It may not be a V8, but the German 3.0-liter V6 is a fine engine. Its cast-iron block is topped by two alloy cylinder heads at an unusual angle of 54 degrees. The heads have twin overhead belt-driven camshafts opening four valves per cylinder. Although there's no variable valve timing, the length of the intake manifold is altered through the rev range, with flaps opening to give three different intake lengths. This has a significant effect on torque production.

Alloy cylinder heads

Electronic fuel injection

Cast-iron block

Four valves per cylinder

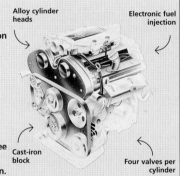

Attractive pricing

Although it is based on the Opel Omega MV6, the Catera brings European-style driving to American buyers. As the entry-level Cadillac in the current lineup, it boasts outstanding levels of equipment and an excellent chassis, plus a very attractive base price of around $30,000, undercutting several of its prime rivals.

The Catera offers European looks at an affordable price.

Cadillac produced a compact luxury car that competes directly with Lexus, Infiniti and BMW. The idea is to attract a younger market than what Cadillac currently had.

Front struts

Front MacPherson struts are commonly used on front-drive cars, as they are easy to package. However, Cadillac also uses struts on the rear-drive Catera.

V6 engine

The engine is a compact, 3.0-liter, quad-cam V6 with a narrower angle between the cylinder heads. This means it can fit into smaller models made by the European subsidiaries of GM, such as the Saab 9.5.

Full-width lights

The elegant front grill, complete with prominent Cadillac badge, and the full-width rear lights are the only visual differences between the Catera and its European cousin.

All-weather tires

Cadillac decided that it is better to equip the Catera with all-weather tires to avoid the inconvenience of changing them for the winter.

OnStar system

Current Cateras have the option of OnStar, which uses onboard diagnostics, global positioning system (GPS) satellite technology and the cellular network to link the driver and car with an OnStar advisor. Services include stolen vehicle tracking, route support, remote door unlock and emergency assistance.

Specifications

1998 Cadillac Catera

ENGINE

Type: V6

Construction: Cast-iron block and alloy cylinder heads

Valve gear: Four valves per cylinder with twin overhead camshafts per bank of cylinders

Bore and stroke: 3.39 in. x 3.35 in.

Displacement: 2,962 cc

Compression ratio: 10.0:1

Induction system: Electronic fuel injection

Maximum power: 200 bhp at 6,000 rpm

Maximum torque: 192 lb-ft at 3,600 rpm

Top speed: 125 mph

0-60 mph: 8.5 sec.

TRANSMISSION

Four-speed automatic

BODY/CHASSIS

Unitary monocoque construction with rear subframe and four-door steel sedan body

SPECIAL FEATURES

To comply with federal regulations, the Catera has revised lighting and a bigger front bumper.

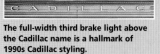

The full-width third brake light above the Cadillac name is a hallmark of 1990s Cadillac styling.

RUNNING GEAR

Steering: Recirculating-ball

Front suspension: MacPherson struts with lower control arms and anti-roll bar

Rear suspension: Semi-trailing arms with toe-control link, coil springs, telescopic shock absorbers and anti-roll bar

Brakes: Vented discs, 11.7-in. dia. (front), solid discs, 11.3-in. dia. (rear)

Wheels: Alloy, 6 x 16 in.

Tires: Goodyear Eagle, 225/55 HR16

DIMENSIONS

Length: 194.0 in.   **Width:** 70.3 in.

Height: 56.3 in   **Wheelbase:** 107.4 in

Track: 59.3 in. (front), 59.8 in. (rear)

Weight: 3,800 lbs.

Callaway CORVETTE SPEEDSTER

When turbocharging specialist Reeves Callaway built his mighty ZR-1-beating, twin-turbo Sledgehammer version of the Corvette it was difficult to see what else could match it. The answer was the incredible and amazing-looking Corvette Speedster.

"...astounding acceleration."

"The chopped roof is disconcerting and the wraparound rear window and headrests make it difficult to see out, but practicality is not the Speedster's forté. Acceleration is astounding—it can reach 100 mph in 12.1 seconds. Callaway has reworked the Corvette suspension to increase its handling characteristics. And when you take into account the powerful brakes, enormous grip from the tires and outrageous style, the sky-high price becomes understandable."

The blue-trimmed interior is outrageous—but then so is the performance.

Milestones

1985 Reeves Callaway fits twin turbos to an Alfa Romeo GTV6, boosting its power output to 230 bhp and taking top speed to 140 mph. Chevrolet is so impressed that it approaches Callaway to develop a twin-turbo version of the Corvette.

Callaway used the standard C4 Corvette as the basis for his turbocharged specials.

1988 Callaway produces the incredible 225-mph, 880-bhp Sledge-hammer version of the Corvette. French Canadian stylist Paul Deutschman is charged with improving the stock Corvette's aerodynamics.

Callaway also has a racing program and has entered Corvettes at Le Mans.

1991 The first Speedster appears at the Los Angeles Auto Show, and is the first car identified purely as a Callaway. The reception is amazing and Callaway prepares to make the Speedster a special edition; only 50 are built.

UNDER THE SKIN

Reworked

Callaway has comprehensively reworked the standard C4 Corvette. Composite transverse leaf springs are almost a Corvette trademark, but these have been replaced with coil-over-shock units for all four wheels which give greater chassis tuning possibilities. At the same time the brake system is uprated with a Callaway/Brembo set up with four-piston calipers and vented cross-drilled discs.

Fiberglass body panels

Four-wheel disc brakes

All-independent suspension

Twin-turbo V8

THE POWER PACK

Totally revised

Callaway completely stripped and rebuilt the Corvette 350-cubic inch L98 V8, fitting a stronger crankshaft which is made fromforged steel rather than cast iron. The compression ratio has been lowered to 7.5:1 using Cosworth or Mahle pistons to allow for turbocharging with twin RotoMaster turbos. The aluminum-alloy heads are milled and have stronger valve springs plus stainless-steel valves, and thestandard electronic fuel injection has been recalibrated to help boost the new power output.

Dual intercoolers

Steel crankshaft

Dual RotoMaster turbochargers

7.5:1 compression pistons

Dream Vette®

With its incredible acceleration, superior handling and braking,plus outrageous style and very limited production, the Callaway Corvette Speedster ranks among the most desirable performance car ever built, anywhere.

Only a select few are lucky enough to own a Callaway Speedster.

Callaway proved that there was no need to go down the ZR-1 route with a complex quad-cam, 32-valve V8. It showed that all you need for huge horsepower is twin intercooled turbochargers producing 420 bhp.

V8 engine

Callaway spent 75 hours on each stock Corvette iron-block engine, rebuilding it to exact tolerances and, with stainless-steel valves, turning it into the more powerful twin-turbo version. If the 'ordinary' 420-bhp twin-turbo unit wasn't enough, the even more powerful 450-bhp version could be bought for an extra $6,000.

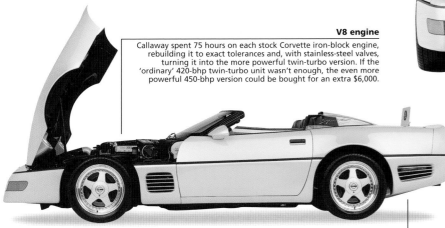

Intercooled turbochargers

Most of the increase in power is due to the twin turbochargers. The watercooled RotoMaster units produce power quickly with little lag. The air is fed through twin intercoolers to keep it dense and to help release more power.

Leather interior

Callaway would fit the very highest quality full-leather trim to the Speedster on request, but it cost an extra $12,000.

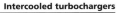

Extra vents

The Speedster features a variety of very large vents at both the front and rear to guarantee that the engine receives enough air and that the big brakes are properly cooled. Their exaggerated size is due to style as well as function.

Wraparound rear window

The side glass is continued onto the rear deck and complements the prominent twin headrest humps which are a big part of the Speedster theme.

Lowered windshield

Callaway chopped seven inches from the Corvette's A-pillars to lower the windshield. However, it is not a full seven inches lower because of exaggerated rake, but it does aid aerodynamics at high speed.

Exotic colors

Speedsters were available in 12 different colors, but some of the more exotic, including Old Lyme Green, Hot Pink or Nuclear Meltdown Orange, were an expensive option at $7,500.

Specifications

1991 Callaway Corvette Speedster

ENGINE

Type: V8

Construction: Cast-iron block and alloy heads

Valve gear: Two valves per cylinder operated by a single vee-mounted camshaft via pushrods and rockers

Bore and stroke: 4.0 in. x 3.48 in.

Displacement: 350 c.i.

Compression ratio: 7.5:1

Induction system: Electronic fuel injection with Callaway Micro Fueler controller and twin RotoMaster turbochargers

Maximum power: 420 bhp at 4,250 rpm

Maximum torque: 562 lb-ft at 2,500 rpm

Top speed: 185 mph

0-60 mph: 4.5 sec

TRANSMISSION

Six-speed manual

BODY/CHASSIS

Separate steel chassis frame with two-seater fiberglass open speedster body

SPECIAL FEATURES

A lowered windshield prevents air from buffeting inside the cabin.

The Speedster has a special plaque mounted on the console next to the boost gauge.

RUNNING GEAR

Steering: Rack-and-pinion

Front suspension: Double wishbones with coil springs, telescopic shock absorbers and anti-roll bar

Rear suspension: Multi-link with coil springs, telescopic shock absorbers and anti-roll bar

Brakes: Brembo vented discs with four-piston calipers (front and rear)

Wheels: Alloy, 9.5 x 18 in. (front), 11 x 18 in. (rear)

Tires: Bridgestone RE71 285/35 ZR18

DIMENSIONS

Length: 176.5 in.   **Width:** 71.0 in.

Height: 39.7 in.   **Wheelbase:** 92.2 in.

Track: 59.6 in. (front), 60.4 in. (rear)

Weight: 3,200 lbs.

USA 1963-1982

Checker A11

For more than 30 years, the Checker was an unmistakable sight on the streets of Manhattan. Its familiar bulbous shape has been etched, not only in the minds of New Yorkers, but in people all over the world.

"...built for the human race."

"Picture the scene. It's Saturday night in midtown Manhattan and you and your Checker are experiencing one of the busiest nights of the week. The high-set driving position gives you a commanding view of the pot-holed avenues, and the huge bumpers mean other drivers stay clear of your path. This car is built like a tank and with more than 30 years of severe duty, the Checker's sturdy design and tough suspension proved it was built for the human race."

Primitive but hard-wearing, the A11's interior has everything a cabbie needs.

Milestones

1956 Checker Motors launches its A8 taxicab. It has slab-sided yet fairly restrained styling and a coil-sprung front suspension.

From 1964, Checkers were called Marathons.

1958 This year, quad headlights and a 125-bhp engine are featured.

1959 The A10 series replaces the A8 and is offered in passenger trim as the Superba Special.

Chevrolet's Impala was the main rival to the Checker in terms of NYC taxicab sales.

1963 Checker's A11 makes its debut.

1969 A 350-cubic inch Chevrolet V8 is optional.

1974 Big aluminum bumpers are fitted to comply with federal legislation. Production ends in 1982.

UNDER THE SKIN

Live rear axle

Separate steel chassis

Power front disc brakes

Six or V8 power

Built to last

Checkers were built to withstand the harsh life of a taxi. The chassis is a massive X-braced steel item, offered in 120- or the longer 129-inch wheelbase form for taxi cabs. Suspension is classic 1950s Detroit style, with wishbones at the front and leaf springs at the rear. A11s have 15-inch wheels. Early cars had four-wheel drum brakes, but by the time production ceased, front disc brakes were standard.

THE POWER PACK

Myriad of options

Checker never built its own engines for the A11, but obtained them from outside sources. Initially, the A11 was powered by a 226-cubic inch Continental six, although from 1967 Chevy small-block V8s became available in 327-cubic inch form at first and in 350-cubic inch form from 1969. During the 1970s, the Checker's only full decade of production, engine choice centered around the Chevy 250-cubic inch six and 350 V8, although a debored 305 arrived for 1977. By 1980, a 229-cubic inch Chevy V6 was the base engine found in the majority of New York Cabs, but 327 and 350 V8s were offered for those who craved more torque.

New York taxi

Having led demanding and harsh lives, particularly in major U.S. cities, it is rare to find a decommissioned cab in great shape. Checkers do not command much money, but with fewer cabs out there, finding a genuine, running New York taxi that's not beat to death is rare.

This A11 is one of the last working Checkers in the Big Apple.

Although operated by cab companies in many different cities across the U.S., New York is considered the Checker's natural habitat. Big Apple cabs even had their own special NYC package.

New York certified
Manhattan cabs are operated under the control of the NYC Taxi and Limousine Commission. Official cabs have yellow paint and a medallion number, which is assigned to each driver and marked on the roof, rear doors and license plates. A driver is not allowed to pick up fares in the Big Apple without it.

V6 or V8
By 1980, when this cab left the factory, engine choices were 229-cubic inch V6s or V8s displacing 267 or 305 cubic inches. A diesel V8 was also listed on the order form.

Heavy-duty suspension
Traveling thousands of miles over cratered and broken pavement requires heavy-duty suspension. The Checker's proven setup of stiff coils and leaf springs is well up to the job.

Propane
Although most Checkers run on gas, some have been converted to use propane. These cars are identified by a fairing over the gas cap on the rear valance.

Spacious interior
Two different wheelbases were available (120 or 129 inches). The longer A11E version has rear-facing jump seats and can seat up to eight instead of six passengers.

Bumper guards
Due to heavy traffic in New York, many cabs were fitted with bumper guards to keep wayward motorists at bay.

Specifications

1980 Checker A11

ENGINE
Type: V8

Construction: Cast-iron block and heads

Valve gear: Two valves per cylinder operated by pushrods and rockers

Bore and stroke: 3.74 in. x 3.48 in.

Displacement: 305 c.i.

Compression ratio: 8.6:1

Induction system: Rochester four-barrel carburetor

Maximum power: 155 bhp at 3,800 rpm

Maximum torque: 250 lb-ft at 2,400 rpm

Top speed: 98 mph

0-60 mph: 15.5 sec.

TRANSMISSION
GM Turbohydramatic 350 three-speed automatic

BODY/CHASSIS
Steel-perimeter chassis with separate four-door sedan body

SPECIAL FEATURES

Cabs working 24 hour or night shifts were required to have a glass divider.

All official New York taxis have a medallion number on the roof sign.

RUNNING GEAR
Steering: Recirculating ball

Front suspension: Unequal-length wishbones with telescopic shock absorbers and anti-roll bar

Rear suspension: Live axle with semi-elliptic leaf springs and telescopic shock absorbers

Brakes: Discs (front), drums (rear)

Wheels: Pressed steel, 15-in. dia.

Tires: 155/70 R15

DIMENSIONS
Length: 201.0 in.

Width: 79.5 in.

Height: 71.6 in.   **Wheelbase:** 120.0 in.

Track: 64.6 in. (front and rear)

Weight: 3,830 lbs.

Chevrolet INDEPENDENCE

It is well known that early-1930s cars make great hot rods. But going several steps beyond the traditional format is this unique, awesome five-window coupe which, with its thunderous V8 engine and lightning acceleration, justifiably lives up to its name, 'Wild Thang.'

"...feel the ground shake."

"Looking like a refugee from a comic strip, this Chevy is like no other. The mighty motor explodes into life with a thunderous roar, and through open headers you can almost feel the ground shake. On the road, this car is a sight to behold. It turns heads everywhere it goes, but one thing will be etched in your memory—the acceleration. This rod will rocket to 60 mph in just under 5 seconds and is guaranteed to bring a smile."

Twin JAZ racing buckets and harnesses keep the occupants firmly in place.

Milestones

1931 Despite a model name change to Independence, the Chevrolet range is little changed from 1929, with almost Cadillac-like styling. Prices, however, are anything but, ranging from $475 to $650.

Chevrolets were popular in 1931 —this is a Police Sedan Delivery.

1932 In keeping with the yearly model change, the Confederate displaces the Independence. As before, all Chevrolets rely on the 127-cubic inches for power. Despite the onset of the Depression, 306,716 Chevrolets leave the assembly line.

The big 454 V8 gained prominence in the SS Chevelle.

1933 Chevrolet diversifies and introduces two new series—the Eagle on a 110-inch wheelbase chassis, and the Mercury with a 107.5-inch wheelbase.

UNDER THE SKIN

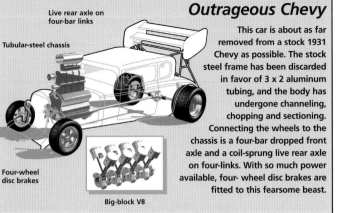

Live rear axle on four-bar links

Tubular-steel chassis

Four-wheel disc brakes

Big-block V8

Outrageous Chevy

This car is about as far removed from a stock 1931 Chevy as possible. The stock steel frame has been discarded in favor of 3 x 2 aluminum tubing, and the body has undergone channeling, chopping and sectioning. Connecting the wheels to the chassis is a four-bar dropped front axle and a coil-sprung live rear axle on four-links. With so much power available, four- wheel disc brakes are fitted to this fearsome beast.

THE POWER PACK

Overkill

In place of the 194-cubic inch six, with its 50 bhp, is a motor with a very different character. Above the firewall and radiator shell is a 454-cubic inch big-block overbored by 0.030 inch. Atop the block sit a Weiand intake manifold and a custom-built intercooler, mated to a 6-71 Weiand positive displacement supercharger. To enable this setup to run with reliability, the block carries eight 8.5:1-compression pistons, and fuel is fed through two massive Holley 750-cfm Double Pumper four-barrel carburetors. Spent gases are exhausted through eight individual pipes, directly from the engine exhaust ports.

Coupe to go

Not as popular with the street contingent as contemporary Fords, the early-1930s Chevrolets still have great potential for hot-rodding, and just about anything can be done with them. This radical 1931 five-window coupe is faster than many exotic supercars and will turn more heads on the sidewalk. Best of all, it is a unique and personal vehicle.

The term "extreme" is truly appropriate for this Chevy.

It is very difficult to know what to make of this car. Its appearance suggests that it was built strictly for show, but it is a fully functioning 200-mph-plus street rod that is also street-legal.

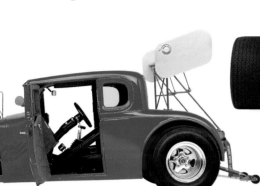

Straight pipes

Projecting from each cylinder head are individual exhaust pipes. They help the engine make an owner-estimated 900 bhp and contribute to the big V8's earth-shattering sound.

Widened body

A modification on this rod is the widening of the rear bodywork. It now measures an extra 3 inches across.

Killer V8 engine

The big 460-cubic inch V8, with its twin carburetors and massive intercooler/supercharger setup is enough to strike fear into the heart of any fellow hot-rodder.

Chopped top

The top has been chopped, which reduces its height. This also has the effect of exaggerating the height of the engine.

Parachute

Packed up behind the wheelie bars is a parachute that helps slow the car down after it reaches its maximum speed.

Aluminum rear wing

Because this car is capable of such incredible acceleration and speed, it needs to be kept firmly planted to the road in order to prevent rear-end liftoff. A huge aluminum rear wing, similar to those found on Outlaw sprint cars, ensures the rear end stays on the ground at high speeds.

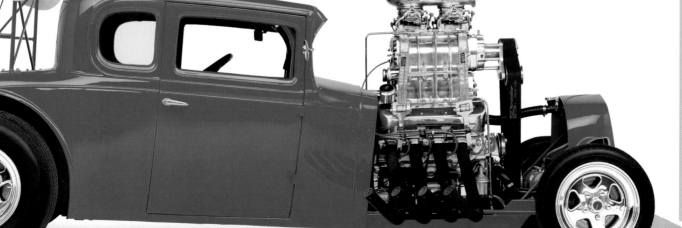

Specifications

1931 Chevrolet Independence

ENGINE

Type: V8

Construction: Cast-iron block and heads

Valve gear: Two valves per cylinder operated by a single V-mounted camshaft with pushrods and rockers

Bore and stroke: 4.28 in. x 4.00 in.

Displacement: 460 c.i.

Compression ratio: 8.5:1

Induction system: Dual Holley 750 DM four-barrel carburetors

Maximum power: 900 bhp at 6,400 rpm

Maximum torque: 710 lb-ft at 3,800 rpm

Top speed: 170 mph

0-60 mph: 4.5 sec

TRANSMISSION

TH400 three-speed automatic

BODY/CHASSIS

Steel tubular chassis with two-door coupe body

SPECIAL FEATURES

The whole engine assembly has been chrome-plated for maximum impact.

Wheelie bars help protect the rear pan when the throttle is mashed.

RUNNING GEAR

Steering: Recirculating-ball

Front suspension: Beam axle with transverse leaf spring, four-bar links and telescopic shock absorbers

Rear suspension: Live axle with four-bar links, coil springs and coil-over shock absorbers

Brakes: Discs (front and rear)

Wheels: Cragar Drag Star, 15 x 7 in. (front), 15 x 15 in. (rear)

Tires: BFGoodrich, 195/50 15 (front), Mickey Thompson, 29/18.5 15 (rear)

DIMENSIONS

Length: 152.6 in. **Width:** 74.7 in.

Height: 58.5 in. **Wheelbase:** 109.0 in.

Track: 51.3 in. (front), 57.1 in. (rear)

Weight: 2,850 lbs.

Chevrolet COUPE

If you were after a sporty Chevrolet in 1940, you bought a Coupe. Those old customers would have been shocked if they discovered it had the 125 mph performance like this one, with vast V8 power they could only have dreamt about.

"Fangio's winner."

"The Coupe was good enough for world champion driver Fangio to win an epic 6,000-mile marathon in 1940. Imagine how quick he'd have been in this one. The extra 215 bhp comes from a Corvette™ V8 and a new suspension all around, along with big sticky tires, makes it grip like Fangio could never imagine. Modern Corvette seats replace the high chairs of the original and hold you in place as the Coupe corners with g-forces Fangio never experienced. It'll rocket to 60 mph in under seven seconds and has a top speed of 125 mph."

Corvette leather seats, matching leather trim and a custom alloy-paneled dashboard complete the hot rod touch.

Milestones

1933 Chevy launches the new Master Eagle model line. It isn't Chevy's first six-cylinder, but its performance and style make it a huge seller.

1937 Redesign for the Master series makes it even more popular. From 1934 you can have independent front suspension on the Master Deluxe series.

The 1940 Chevy Coupe was quite a fast vehicle in its day.

1940 Longer wheelbase and restyling set the 1940 series apart. The year also marks the first use of some plastic parts and stainless-steel trim. Driving a Coupe version of the Chevrolet Master, Juan Manuel Fangio wins the 6,000-mile Gran Premio International del Norte race in South America by over an hour, averaging over 55 mph.

1941 214-cubic inch six gets another 5 bhp, taking it up to 90 bhp, to celebrate new longer, lower and wider bodies mounted on a longer wheelbase.

1942 All car production, Chevrolet included, comes to an end as factories turn to war production.

UNDER THE SKIN

Totally different

The only original components on this converted coupe are the deep separate perimeter chassis and the bodywork. Gone is Chevrolet's once advanced 'knee-action' independent front suspension in favor of modern double wishbones. The live rear axle and leaf springs are dropped in favor of an advanced Jaguar rear end to cope with the power that's generated by the Corvette V8.

Independent rear suspension

Standard, all-steel bodyshell

Wishbone front suspension

Chevy V8

THE POWER PACK

Three times the power

Where it once had an 85-bhp six, the Coupe now has a 327-cubic inch V8. The familiar small-block Chevy® had not even been thought of when the Coupe was being built, but the all-iron pushrod V8 is small enough to drop in the engine bay with ease. As an extra bonus, it's lighter than the engine it replaced. Here it's been dressed up with custom-made tubular headers to make a free-flow exhaust that liberates some extra power. The carbs changed to a trio of twin-choke Rochesters rather than the single four-barrel normally used.

Three two-barrel Rochester carburetors

Polished intake manifold

All-iron construction

Custom exhaust manifolds

Cute rear end

What made the Coupe stand out was the rear end design. From the front doors back, the standard clumsy upright (but more spacious) sedan lines were replaced with tiny rear windows and long flowing rear fenders on either side of a big curved trunk. It wasted passenger space but, as Chevrolet said, it certainly "had enhanced eye appeal" and gave room for plenty of luggage.

Long sloping rear end made the Coupe look better than the sedan.

If the small-block Chevy V8 had been around in 1940, Chevrolet would surely have installed it in the Coupe. But would they have been generous enough to give it 300 bhp and Jaguar independent rear suspension? No way—you have to do that yourself.

Vented disc brakes

The hydraulic drums of the original car were good in their day, but would be light years away from the stopping power of its current brakes. Vented discs at the front are gripped by the same four-piston calipers used on Triumph's old TR8 sports car.

Custom interior

A custom interior complements the late-model Corvette leather seats. In contrast, it has a classic steering wheel with sprung spokes.

Corvette V8

When this Business Coupe was built, it had Chevrolet's excellent 214-cubic inch straight-six engine with overhead valves, cast-iron block, heads and pistons, a low (6.5:1) compression ratio and a modest 85 bhp at 3,200 rpm. Now it's got a 327-cubic inch Corvette engine with as much as 300 bhp.

Rack-and-pinion steering

Recirculating ball steering was adequate for the Business Coupe, but with 300 bhp at its disposal, it needs a more precise steering system—the rack and pinion is from a European Ford.

Inboard rear brakes

Because it's now equipped with the complete Jaguar rear suspension unit, this Business Coupe has inboard rear disc brakes.

Jaguar rear suspension

The Coupe's live rear axle with its semi-elliptic leaf springs has been replaced by the advanced all-independent system from a Jaguar XJ6. Because the Jaguar is much wider than the old Chevy, the suspension had to be narrowed to fit.

Larger rear wheels and tires

To help give the Coupe its aggressive nose-down look, 15-inch wheels are used at the back and 14-inch rims up front. Its tires are also wildly different.

Specifications
1940 Modified Chevrolet Coupe

ENGINE

Type: Chevrolet Corvette V8
Construction: Cast-iron block and heads
Valve gear: Two valves per cylinder operated by single block-mounted camshaft via pushrods, rockers and hydraulic lifters
Bore and stroke: 4 in. x 3.24 in.
Displacement: 327 c.i.
Compression ratio: 10.5:1
Induction system: Three two-barrel Rochester carburetors
Maximum power: 300 bhp at 5,000 rpm
Maximum torque: 321 lb-ft at 3,200 rpm
Top speed: 125 mph
0-60 mph: 6.8 sec

TRANSMISSION
Four-speed automatic

BODY/CHASSIS
Box section perimeter chassis with steel two-door coupe body

SPECIAL FEATURES

Although the hood has been cleared of most ornamentation, the mascot has been left on.

A top quality paint job and super-shiny chromework are a must on a rod.

RUNNING GEAR

Steering: Rack-and-pinion
Front suspension: Double wishbones with coil springs and telescopic shocks
Rear suspension: Modified Jaguar XJ6 rear suspension with wishbones, four coil springs and telescopic shocks
Brakes: Ford vented discs with four-piston calipers front, Jaguar inboard discs rear
Wheels: Alloy Torq-Thrust, 14 in. dia. (front), 15 in. dia. (rear)
Tires: Bridgestone 185/70 14 (front), BF Goodrich 255/70 15 (rear)

DIMENSIONS

Length: 190.2 in. **Width:** 70 in.
Height: 68 in. **Wheelbase:** 112.2in.
Track: 57.5 in. (front), 59 in. (rear)
Weight: 2,900 lbs.

Chevrolet FLEETMASTER

Early postwar Chevrolets were solid, dependable cars, but comfort and finesse were overlooked. Their bulbous, slab-sided bodies and simple engineering, however, make these models very popular among street rodders.

"...smooth and satisfying."

"While postwar, fat-bodied Chevrolets aren't usually a customizer's first choice, they do make a striking street machine. An inviting interior and comfortable seats make this Chevy® an ideal summertime tourer. Plus, with 325 bhp from a mildly massaged 350 and an automatic transmission, satisfying performance is always on tap. With a better suspension, including a Mustang-II rack-and-pinion and a Ford 9-inch rear, this Chevy handles better than it did in stock guise."

A modern leather bench seat contrasts with the vintage instrument panel.

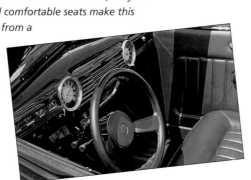

Milestones

1945 Like most Detroit manufacturers, Chevy resumes civilian production, fielding warmed-over 1942 cars as 1946 models. Although outpaced by rival Ford, the division still manages to churn out 398,026 cars.

A Chevy Fleetmaster was used to pace the 1948 Indy 500.

1947 Apart from a new grill and equipment changes, the Chevy lineup differs little from the previous year. Models are divided into Style-master®, Fleetmaster and Fleet-line®, the same since 1942. A 90 bhp, 216-cubic inch Stovebolt Six is standard across the board.

The hottest of the Stovebolt Six engines was the 'Blue Flame Special, found in the Corvette.

1948 Although its lineup changes very little, Chevrolet now outpaces Ford in the production stakes building a staggering 696,449 cars. An all-new Chevy debuts for 1949.

UNDER THE SKIN

Low to go

This 1948 custom is not a replica, but the real McCoy. Aside from the body mods, it retains a stock perimeter frame, but has a lowered Ford Mustang II independent front suspension and a hot-rodder's favorite Ford 9-inch rear differential mounted on reverse-eye rear leaf springs for an in-the-weeds stance. Monroe air shocks at the rear help improve the traction, ride and steering feel.

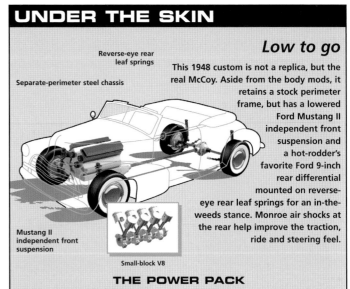

Reverse-eye rear leaf springs

Separate-perimeter steel chassis

Mustang II independent front suspension

Small-block V8

THE POWER PACK

Tri-carbed mouse

Chevrolets were exclusively powered by 216.5-cubic inch Stovebolt Sixes in 1948, making them not the most sporty automobiles. For much greater performance, a 350-cubic inch small-block V8 takes the original motor's place. The new mill has a Tri-Power intake manifold with three Rochester two-barrel carburetors, a progressive throttle linkage, Dart heads and low-restriction exhaust manifolds. All the engine accessories are vintage equipment to add nostalgia appeal.

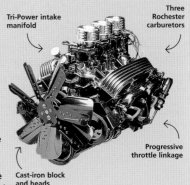

Tri-Power intake manifold

Three Rochester carburetors

Progressive throttle linkage

Cast-iron block and heads

Heavy Chevy

Big and chubby, the early postwar Chevys are not ideal for drag racing, but they do have great potential for lead sleds or customs. The convertibles especially, with chopped, channeled and smoothed bodies give new meaning to the term 'street machine.'

Smoothed and chopped, the 1948 Chevy takes on a whole new look.

Subtle but extremely well-detailed with a luxurious interior and sound yet simple mechanicals, this 1948 Chevy shows that old cars can be turned into immensely practical yet stylish drivers.

Tri-powered 350 V8

Multi-carb setups were one of the most straightforward routes to gaining more horsepower in the 1950s and 1960s. In keeping with its period image, this 1948 Chevy has a classic trio of two-barrel Rochesters.

Mustang II front suspension

Lurking under the front fenders is the street rodder's favorite front clip—a Mustang II independent front suspension. The spindles have been dropped 2½ inches. This serves to improve handling and accentuate the bulging front-end styling.

Bulletproof rear end

A Ford 9–inch rear end, packing streetwise 3.25:1 cogs replaces the stock rear. The axle is mounted on reverse-eye leaf springs to lower the ride height.

Chopped and channeled body

With their round fenders and bulbous stance, it seems only natural to exaggerate the contours of 1942-1948 Chevys. This stock OEM body has been chopped 3½ inches and smoothed, plus the fenders and hood have been reshaped to match the contours for a look appropriate to the car's name—48 Chubby.

Period piece

The whole shape of the car was done as a finished example of what original GM design sketches might have resulted in back in the 1940s, unencumbered by cost or manufacturing restrictions.

1948 Chevrolet Fleetmaster

ENGINE

Type: V8

Construction: Cast-iron block and heads

Valve gear: Two valves per cylinder operated by a single, V-mounted camshaft with pushrods and rockers

Bore and stroke: 4.00 in. x 3.48 in.

Displacement: 350 c.i.

Compression ratio: N/A

Induction system: Three Rochester two-barrel carburetors

Maximum power: 325 bhp at 5,500 rpm

Maximum torque: 340 lb-ft at 3,500 rpm

Top speed: 139 mph

0-60 mph: 6.8 sec

TRANSMISSION

GM TH400 three-speed automatic

BODY/CHASSIS

Perimeter steel chassis with separate two-door convertible body

SPECIAL FEATURES

A vacuum-controlled flap at the base of the windshield feeds cooler, denser air to the carburetors.

Both the front and rear bench seats have been neatly upholstered in soft, modern leather.

RUNNING GEAR

Steering: Rack-and-pinion

Front suspension: Short/long arms with coil springs, telescopic shock absorbers and anti-roll bar

Rear suspension: Live axle, semi-elliptic leaf springs and telescopic shock absorbers

Brakes: Discs (front), drums (rear)

Wheels: Stamped steel, 15-in. dia.

Tires: Kelley Springfield, 215 x 15 in. (front), 235 x 15 in. (rear)

DIMENSIONS

Length: 183.7 in. **Width:** 72.5 in.

Height: 58.1 in. **Wheelbase:** 116.0 in.

Track: 53.5 in. (front and rear)

Weight: 3,450 lbs.

Chevrolet **SEDAN DELIVERY**

If you wanted to deliver your goods efficiently and in style in the early 1950s, there was only one choice—Chevrolet's Sedan Delivery. This is a vehicle with all the practicality of a truck and the comfort and streetability of a contemporary passenger car.

"...relaxing yet capable."

"This mildly modified Chevy® still drives pretty much the way it always did. Inside, things are a little more comfortable, however, with custom trim and the added luxury of a passenger seat. The overhead-valve straight-six engine is a slow-spinning unit with plenty of bottom end torque, making for a relaxing yet capable drive. It'll never set the world on fire but it'll always get you where you want to go. Radial tires improve grip, but handling is still rather basic."

The Sedan Delivery's interior is just like that of the basic Chevy Styleline sedan up front.

Milestones

1928 Chevrolet introduces the Sedan Delivery model. It is based on the National AB Light Delivery chassis with a 107-inch wheelbase. More than 1,000 are built in its first year.

In 1931, Sedan Deliveries also had passenger car front ends.

1949 A new Sedan Delivery is launched, sharing the front-end styling of the new passenger car—the first true post-war Chevrolet. It is no longer listed as a commercial vehicle, but as a passenger car.

1955 A major facelift sees the Sedan Delivery now based on the 1955 passenger car range, the first of the 'Shoebox-Chevys.'

Sedan Deliveries are also popular customs. This is a 1933 model.

1960 Production of the Sedan Delivery finally comes to an end.

UNDER THE SKIN

Low axle ratio *Heavy-duty rear springs*

Passenger car chassis

Car chassis

The Sedan Delivery is based on the standard car chassis with a 116-inch wheelbase. It shares many parts with the contemporary passenger car range (in Styleline trim), although some body panels are unique to the model. A three-speed manual transmission drives through a low-ratio, 4.11:1 live rear axle to improve load-lugging ability. Heavy duty rear leaf springs allow a maximum 1,000-lb. payload in the back.

'Thriftmaster' six

THE POWER PACK

Ancient six

This Sedan Delivery still has its original overhead-valve straight-six engine. It is a simple power pack that can trace its origins back to 1929. The later 'Blue Flame' version even powered the early Corvette®. This version, the 'Thriftmaster,' displaces 217 cubic inches and gives 92 bhp in stock form. The owner of this car has fitted dual Rochester carburetors in place of the original single unit, as well as free-flowing Fenton exhaust headers and dual high-flow glass pack mufflers. It now produces 110 bhp.

Overhead valves *Low compression ratio*

Four main bearings *All cast-iron construction*

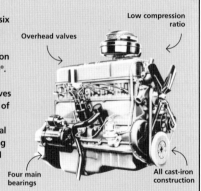

Classy cargo

The 1949-1954 Chevrolet passenger car range is certainly not lacking in style, but the Sedan Delivery is a more unusual sight today and is therefore more of a head-turner. Both make great promotional delivery vehicles too, and look great when the sides are lettered in vintage livery.

The Sedan Delivery combines style, comfort and practicality.

Chevrolet introduced its Sedan Delivery model in 1928. It proved a real success and helped Chevrolet reduce the sales gap between itself and the market leader Ford. Though modified this 1952 model retains much of its original styling cues.

Overhead-valve six
Chevrolet's stovebolt straight six was the company's main engine from the late 1920s until the mid-1950s.

Modern paint
Most Sedan Deliveries left the factory painted black. This car has been resprayed in 1998 Chevy Corvette Light Pewter Metallic, which really sets off the chrome.

Custom interior
This car has a custom vinyl headliner and vinyl and suede door panels. A passenger seat has also been added. It left the factory with only a driver's seat.

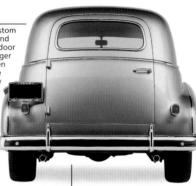

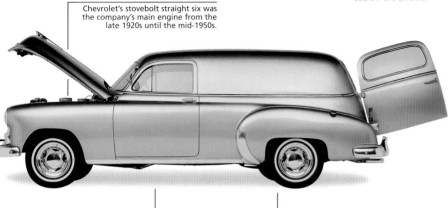

Independent front suspension
Like contemporary Chevrolet passenger cars, the Sedan Delivery has independent front suspension with unequal-length wishbones and coil springs.

Heavy-duty rear suspension
In order to deal with the heavy loads the Sedan Delivery was expected to carry, it has heavy-duty leaf springs and shock absorbers at the rear end.

Low axle ratio
A very low axle ratio (4.11:1) adds to the already excellent load-lugging capability of the torquey straight-six engine.

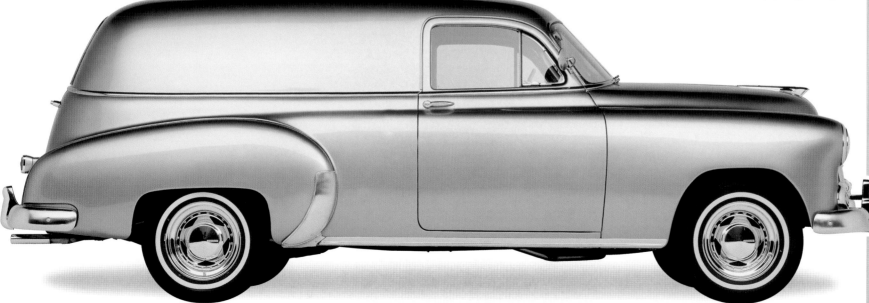

Specifications

1952 Chevrolet Sedan Delivery

ENGINE
Type: In-line six-cylinder
Construction: Cast-iron block and head
Valve gear: Two valves per cylinder operated by a single camshaft with pushrods and rockers
Bore and stroke: 3.50 in. x 3.75 in.
Displacement: 217 c.i.
Compression ratio: 6.6:1
Induction system: Twin Rochester carburetors
Maximum power: 110 bhp at 3,400 rpm
Maximum torque: 187 lb-ft at 1,700 rpm
Top speed: 92 mph
0-60 mph: 14.0 sec.

TRANSMISSION
Three-speed manual

BODY/CHASSIS
Separate chassis with steel two-door sedan delivery body

SPECIAL FEATURES

Swoopy rear fenders follow the style of those used on the 1952 passenger car lineup.

This interesting hood emblem was new for the 1952 model year.

RUNNING GEAR
Steering: Recirculating ball
Front suspension: Double wishbone with coil springs and telescopic shock absorbers
Rear suspension: Live axle with heavy-duty semi-elliptic leaf springs and telescopic shock absorbers
Brakes: Drums (front and rear)
Wheels: Pressed steel, 16-in. dia.
Tires: 6.25 x 16 in.

DIMENSIONS
Length: 197.9 in. **Width:** 70.2 in.
Height: 67.1 in. **Wheelbase:** 116.0 in.
Track: 57.6 in. (front), 60.0 in. (rear)
Weight: 3,100 lbs.

Chevrolet **CORVETTE**

Chevrolet was the first major car company in the world to dare to make a regular production car out of fiberglass. It was a crude affair at first but the sleek body and throaty engine captured the hearts of the American public, kick-starting the Corvette legend.

"...impressive in its day."

"You forget the modified sedan car origins of the Blue Flame Special six-cylinder engine when the throttle is floored and it roars to life. Despite the handicap of the two-speed Powerglide automatic, its 11 second 0-60 mph time is impressive for the day. Dynamically, the Corvette was closer to its traditional British sports car rivals than anything else made in the U.S. at the time, with stiff springs and a taut ride."

The interiors on early Corvettes were a bit confined and had a simple dashboard Layout.

Milestones

1952 The first full-size plaster model of the Corvette is presented to the GM president Harlow Curtice by Harley Earl. Curtice likes it and the Corvette is all set for production.

By 1957 the Corvette's V8 had gained optional fuel injection.

1953 The public sees the Corvette
for the first time at the GM Motorama Show. Production begins later in the year and all cars are painted Polo White. Changes are made for the 1954 model year with more colors and increased power.

A major facelift came for the Corvette in 1961.

1954 For the 1955 model
year Chevrolet's proposed facelift is shelved and the car's future is in doubt until the new V8 engine is used.

1955 It's the end of
of the line for the six-cylinder Corvette. The small block V8 is now the preferred power unit.

UNDER THE SKIN

Something old, something new

With the decision made to have a fiberglass body, the Corvette had a separate chassis. It is an X-braced perimeter steel section affair, given extra stiffness once the one-piece fiberglass floor molding is added. Having the semi-elliptic leaf springs for the rear axle mounted outside the chassis rails was a Corvette innovation.

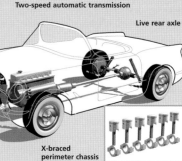

Two-speed automatic transmission

Live rear axle

X-braced perimeter chassis

Tuned six cylinder

THE POWER PACK

Transformation

Chevrolet transformed its existing low powered sedan engine into the Corvette's impressive 3.9-liter Blue Flame Special. A high-lift, long duration camshaft was used in the simple pushrod engine, the cylinder head was modified, compression ratio increased, and double valve springs, along with solid valve lifters, were fitted to deal with higher rpm. Induction was transformed by fitting three Carter sidedraft carburetors on a much improved alloy manifold.

High-lift camshaft

Two valves per cylinder

Cast-iron construction

Pushrod valve actuation

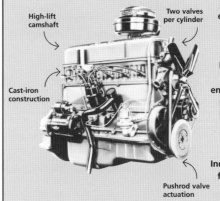

Rare original

Although the six-cylinder Chevrolet Corvettes aren't the best performing examples of the breed, they're now very valuable. Collectors value the 1953 and 1954 cars for their relative rarity, historical importance and purity of shape.

The early six-cylinder Corvettes are highly collectable today.

Because of poor sales, GM almost gave up on this little sports car. In 1955 it got a husky V8 engine and the car was making the power it lacked. Luckily, sales picked up and the Corvette has been in Chevrolet's line up ever since.

Six-cylinder engine
The first Corvettes used a modified Chevrolet sedan engine. Tuning made it an effective sports car powerplant with 150 bhp.

Wishbone front suspension
The Corvette's double wishbone and coil spring front suspension was a modified version of the contemporary Chevrolet sedans, with different spring rates to suit the sports car.

Whitewall tires
Whitewall tires were very fashionable in the 1950s. One advantage was that they broke up the high-sided look of the tall sidewalls.

Two-speed transmission
Incredibly, the only available GM transmission which would take the power and torque of the modified engine was the two-speed Powerglide automatic. A three-speed manual became available for the 1955 model year cars.

Live rear axle
Because it was a limited-production car, the first Corvettes had to use many off-the-shelf Chevrolet components and the engineering had to be as simple as possible.

Fiberglass body
Although there were a number of fiberglass-bodied specialty and kit cars around in the U.S. in the early 1950s General Motors was the first to make a regular production car out of the material. In production the fiberglass panels used were about half as thick as the prototype's.

Wrap-around windshield
The wrap-around style of windshield was popular in the early 1950s. Apart from looking great, it improved three-quarter vision compared with a conventional flat front glass with thick pillars.

Specifications
1954 Chevrolet Corvette

ENGINE
Type: Inline six cylinder

Construction: Cast iron block and head

Valve gear: Two valves per cylinder operated by single block-mounted camshaft via pushrods and solid valve lifters

Bore/stroke: 3.56 in. x 3.94 in.

Displacement: 235 c.i.

Compression ratio: 8.0:1

Induction system: Three Carter YH sidedraft carburetors

Maximum power: 150 bhp at 4,200 rpm

Maximum torque: 233 lb-ft at 2,400 rpm

Top speed: 107 mph

0-60 mph: 11.0 sec.

TRANSMISSION
Two-speed Powerglide automatic

BODY/CHASSIS
X-braced steel chassis with fiberglass two-seater convertible body

SPECIAL FEATURES

The first Corvettes have very curvaceous rear ends with subdued fins and prominent taillights.

Stone guards over the front headlights were purely a styling feature and unnecessary on ordinary roads.

RUNNING GEAR
Steering: Worm-and-sector

Front suspension: Double wishbones with coil springs, telescopic shocks and anti-roll bar

Rear suspension: Live axle with semi-elliptic leaf springs and telescopic shocks

Brakes: Drums (front and rear), 11-in. dia.

Wheels: Steel disc, 15-in. dia.

Tires: Crossply 5.5 x 15

DIMENSIONS
Length: 167 in. **Width:** 72.2 in.

Height: 51.3 in. **Wheelbase:** 102 in.

Track: 57 in. (front), 59 in. (rear)

Weight: 2,851 lbs.

Chevrolet CORVETTE

By the end of the 1950s, the Corvette had grown into one of the fastest sports cars in the world and one of the biggest performance bargains too. With so many power and handling options, the Vette™ could be just what you wanted it to—from civilized sportster to awesome mile-eater.

"...a unique experience."

"For the lucky few that will ever own or even drive a vintage Corvette, it's a unique experience. What's it like? Well, if you exploited the option list, your Corvette turned into a fearsome sports car, which by 1962, could have 360 bhp. Brakes were never its strong suit and even the optional linings are no solution. Despite the live axle, the handling is excellent for the time and the power steering is surprisingly precise. It has to be, because you need to be quick to catch the power-oversteer."

There are few car interiors that can rival the dramatic styling of an early Corvette.

Milestones

1956 Corvettes are introduced with a streamlined body style; powered by the 265-cubic inch small-block V8.

1958 Revised styling adds twin headlights, among other body modifications. The Vette is about 2 inches wider, 10 inches longer and 200 lbs. heavier. Cockpit is improved and the base engine power rises to 230 bhp.

Twin headlights were added for the 1958 restyle.

1961 Styling changes again, but like the 1958, the 1961 change is more major, with a new design for the rear of the car that gives a welcomed boost to the trunk space.

1962 Styling is toned down again and a larger engine is installed, the bored and stroked 327-cubic inch V8 with power ranging from 250 bhp to 360 bhp.

1963 A new generation of Corvette, the Sting Ray®, appears totally restyled and with independent rear suspension.

1961 Corvette has a restyled rear, a hint of what was to come with the 1963 Sting Ray.

UNDER THE SKIN

Cover-up

Simple ladder-frame chassis

Leaf-sprung live rear axle

Fiberglass bodywork

Double-wishbone front suspension

Traditional American V8

The Corvette's spectacular looks mask a very simple ladder-frame chassis with its two main rails joined and strengthened by a massive cruciform brace. The live rear axle is located and sprung by semi-elliptic leaf springs. At the front is a double-wishbone system with anti-roll bar. Although the big V8 is mounted up front with the transmission, it is set well back to give a very reasonable distribution of weight.

THE POWER PACK

Rumbling V8s

Corvettes of this generation are all V8-powered. All of these V8s are simple cast-iron, single camshaft, pushrod designs with two valves per cylinder. All have a short stroke and increasingly larger bore. Displacement rose from 265-cubic inches in 1956, through 283 and then, in the last year of this type, to 327. Outputs ranged from 210 bhp for a carbureted 265, right up to 360 bhp at 6,000 rpm, with the high, 11.25:1 compression ratio of the rare Rochester 'Ramjet' fuel-injected version, available as an option from 1957.

Single camshaft

Two valves per cylinder

Short-stroke crankshaft

Cast-iron construction

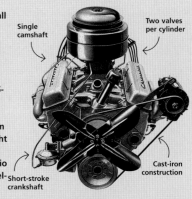

Best Vette

The best of the second generation of Corvettes was the 1957 model-year—after that they became bigger and more sleek. A 1957 equipped with Rochester Ramjet fuel injection produced 283 bhp and could reach 135 mph with 0-60 mph in 6.8 seconds.

The 1957 is the best vintage of second-generation Vette.

Style, power and performance. In the 1950s and early-1960s, the Corvette had it all. Despite its fiberglass body it was no lightweight but no one cared—it had power to burn.

Color schemes
In 1961, the Corvette was available in a choice of seven colors: Tuxedo Black, Ermine White, Roman Red, Sateen Silver, Jewel Blue, Fawn Beige and Honduras Maroon. For an extra $16, you could have the side cove highlighted in silver or white, an option deleted the next year.

Concealed hood
Unlike some of its European convertible rivals, the Corvette has a top which folds down completely to be hidden out of sight under a lockable cover.

Front vents
When the Corvette was widened for the 1958 model year, some of that extra width was taken up by vents behind the front bumper, there purely for styling.

Jaguar wheelbase
Chevrolet evaluated the Jaguar XK120 while developing the Corvette, but the only sign of any influence is that both cars have exactly the same wheelbase.

Limited slip differential
To stop the Corvette from spinning away its power on relatively narrow tires, the option of a Positraction limited slip differential was offered from 1957 on.

Power windows
From 1956 onward, Vettes were available with electrically-operated windows. In 1961, that option would have cost you just under $60.

'Duck tail' rear
The major styling change introduced for the 1961 model is this 'duck tail' rear, created by stylist Bill Mitchell and carried over into the '62 models.

Fiberglass body
Vettes have always been fiberglass and Chevrolet became better at producing it as the years passed. Early bodies were made from 46 different panels but that process had been streamlined by 1961.

Live rear axle
By 1961, the Corvette was only two years away from independent rear suspension. Until then it soldiered on with an old-fashioned live axle.

Specifications
1961 Chevrolet Corvette

ENGINE
Type: V8
Construction: Cast-iron block and heads
Valve gear: Two valves per cylinder operated by single block-mounted camshaft, pushrods and rockers
Bore and stroke: 3.87 in. x 2.99 in.
Displacement: 283 c.i.
Compression ratio: 11:1
Induction system: Rochester Ramjet mechanical fuel injection
Maximum power: 315 bhp at 6,200 rpm
Maximum torque: 295 lb-ft at 4,000 rpm
Top speed: 135 mph
0-60 mph: 6.1 sec.

TRANSMISSION
Four-speed manual

BODY/CHASSIS
X-braced ladder frame with fiberglass two-seat convertible body

SPECIAL FEATURES

All 1958-1962 Corvettes have a side cove, but the detail design and amount of chrome was changed every year.

From 1957 a Rochester Ramjet fuel injection option offered owners even more power to play with.

RUNNING GEAR
Steering: Worm-and-ball
Front suspension: Double wishbones with coil springs, telescopic shocks and anti-roll bar
Rear suspension: Live axle with semi-elliptic leaf springs and telescopic shocks
Brakes: Drums, 11 in. dia. (front and rear)
Wheels: Steel discs 6 in. x 17 in.
Tires: Crossply 6.70 in. x 16 in.

DIMENSIONS
Length: 177.5 in. **Width:** 72.8 in.
Height: 52.4 in. **Wheelbase:** 102 in.
Track: 57 in. (front), 59 in. (rear)
Weight: 2,905 lbs.

Chevrolet **CORVETTE**

As one of the U.S.'s few sports cars, the Corvette has been desirable since the day it first rolled of the assembly line in 1953. Although fast in stock trim, some people just cannot resist the urge to make these cars even more powerful.

"...A 409-powered Corvette?"

"A 409-powered Corvette? It is a fact that no such production car was built, but then, this is not your run-of-the-mill sports car. There are few creature comforts inside, but once on the move, this ceases to matter. The classic Chevy V8 gives plenty of power right through the rev range, and six speeds enable you to get the most from it. Turn-in is sharp thanks to the steering, and a low center of gravity results in race car-type handling."

Cream leather seats are the only concession to luxury in the functional interior.

Milestones

1958 The Corvette is heavily facelifted, with chrome accents on the coves and trunk, plus quad headlights, vents on the hood and revised wheel covers. In this recession year, production jumps from 6,339 to 9,168. The base 283 gets an extra 10 bhp while the fuelie version makes up to 290.

The Corvette entered production in 1953. They were all painted white and had red interiors.

1959 Minor changes, including the elimination of the trunk straps and hood vents conspire to give a cleaner appearance. Power ratings remain unchanged, but sales near the 10,000 mark.

The 1963 Sting Ray® marked a new direction for the Corvette.

1961 New rear styling, inspired by the 1957 Sting Ray racer, mates well with the front-end design. The grill is changed to a mesh pattern and the headlight bezels are painted instead of chrome. The fuelie V8 is up to 315 bhp.

UNDER THE SKIN

Radical racer

It would be fair to say that this Corvette is almost a totally new car underneath. A tubular-steel chassis has been fabricated with mounts grafted on for the tilting front end. A live rear axle with 3.23:1 gears is still fitted out back, but the old leaf springs have been discarded in favor of parallel links and coil over shocks for better traction.

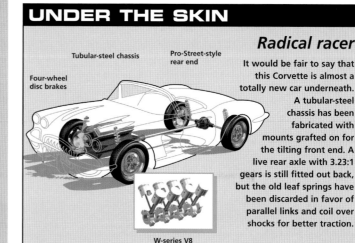

Tubular-steel chassis · Pro-Street-style rear end · Four-wheel disc brakes · W-series V8

THE POWER PACK

Not as it seems

Solid-axle Corvettes came from the factory with 283 and 327 small-block V8s, but this one was built with a little more performance in mind. One of the most legendary engines of the early 1960s now sits between the fenders: a 409-cubic inch W-series engine. Outside, the engine looks almost stock, but it has Venolia 10.3:1 compression pistons, ported and polished heads with 2.19 intake valves, Competition Cams valve springs and a Lunati camshaft. It is fully balanced and blue printed like a real race engine.

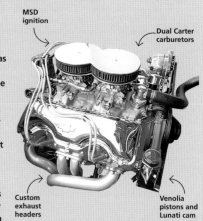

MSD ignition · Dual Carter carburetors · Custom exhaust headers · Venolia pistons and Lunati cam

Solid axle

Somewhat overshadowed by the Sting Ray, the 1958-1962 Corvettes still have strong collector interest and are among the most popular Corvettes with the custom fraternity. They are fairly rare and considerably expensive, but the end result is often worth it.

Pre-1963 Corvettes are nicknamed 'solid axles' because of their live rear axle.

Few cars can capture the spirit of the late 1950s as well as the Corvette. This tasteful though radically modified example does a lot more than capture spirits—it captures show trophies, too.

Performance engine
The Beach Boys sang its praise, justifiably, considering the 409 was one of the most potent hi-po V8s of the early 1960s. Although expensive to build and not easy to modify, experienced engine builders are able to coax tremendous power from it.

Fiberglass body
Since its introduction in 1953, the Corvette has always had fiberglass bodywork. This was decided late in the development stage, as it would prove more cost effective than steel and Kirksite—which was originally intended.

Tubular chassis
A completely custom-fabricated chassis lies beneath the bodywork, though thanks to considerable ingenuity, the stock front suspension has been mated to it.

Lowered suspension
By dropping the front and rear ends, the center of gravity is lowered, which, combined with the gas shocks and Goodyear GSC tires results in one of the sharpest-handling Corvettes around.

Cleaned-up body
The 1958 Vette has more glitz than its predecessors, but this was only in keeping with buyer tastes of the time. This one looks positively demure, with its monochromatic Rally Orange paint and absence of chrome accents on the door coves.

Spartan interior
Everything about this car screams performance and function. The interior may be draped in cream colored leather, but there is no convertible roof, air conditioning or stereo. However, a full set of Stewart-Warner gauges keeps the driver fully informed.

Small windshield
It may look cut down, but the windshield is actually the stock full-length piece, just lowered four inches into the cowl.

Stock hood
Even though the whole front end can be tilted forward, the hood can still open independently for routine maintenance and tuning so essential for hot rods.

Specifications

1959 Chevrolet Corvette (modified)

ENGINE

Type: V8

Construction: Cast-iron block and heads

Valve gear: Two valves per cylinder operated by pushrods and rockers

Bore and stroke: 4.31 x 3.50 in.

Displacement: 416 c.i.

Compression ratio: 10.3:1

Induction system: Dual Carter AFB four-barrel carburetors

Maximum power: 454 bhp at 5,500 rpm

Maximum torque: 460 lb-ft at 5,500 rpm

Top speed: 164 mph

0-60 mph: 4.6 sec

TRANSMISSION

Richmond six-speed manual

BODY/CHASSIS

Tubular-steel chassis with fiberglass convertible body

SPECIAL FEATURES

The whole front end tilts forward for access to the engine.

Auxiliary gauges are neatly housed in the center console, which is color-keyed with the rest of the interior.

RUNNING GEAR

Steering: Worm-and-ball

Front suspension: Unequal-length A-arms with coil springs, telescopic shock absorbers and sway bar

Rear suspension: Live axle with upper and lower parallel links, coil springs and telescopic shock absorbers

Brakes: Discs, (front and rear)

Wheels: Slotted Magnesium 15.0-in. dia.

Tires: Goodyear Eagle GS-C

DIMENSIONS

Length: 177.2 in.   **Width:** 70.5 in.

Height: 48.2 in.   **Wheelbase:** 102.0 in.

Track: 56.2 in. (front), 55.6 in. (rear)

Weight: 2,620 lbs.

Chevrolet **CORVETTE STING RAY**

The ground-breaking Corvette Sting Ray Coupe of 1963 is among the most collectable of all Corvettes. The car's distinctive split rear window wasn't liked very well by the press and owners at the time, but it is this feature that makes it one of the most desirable Sting Rays today.

"...outstanding racers."

"For its first year with a brand new body and suspension, the 1963 Vette® was virtually flawless. With its independent rear suspension, it handled better than it ever did before—it had truly evolved. Offering a near-perfect 49/51 percent weight ratio, this fiberglass fastback was finally able to compete with the Jaguar's XKE. Thanks to the race-inspired vision of Zora Arkus Duntov, cars equipped with the ZO6 competition package were outstanding racers right out of the showroom."

The cabin of the 1963 Corvette differs from that of later Sting Rays.

Milestones

1959 Using the chassis from the cancelled Corvette SS racing program, Bill Mitchell and Larry Shinoda style a body for a new racer called the Stingray (first raced in 1959) that anticipates the shape of the next-generation Vette.

The final iteration of the first-generation Corvette was in 1962.

1963 Chevrolet launches the second-generation Corvette. With styling influenced by the Stingray racer, the new Corvette Sting Ray is available in open or, for the first time, coupe forms. The Coupe has a distinctive central bar dividing the rear window.

The shark's basic body style lasted from 1968 until 1982.

1968 The Sting Ray is replaced by the third-generation, shark-styled, Corvette, known as the Stingray (one word).

UNDER THE SKIN

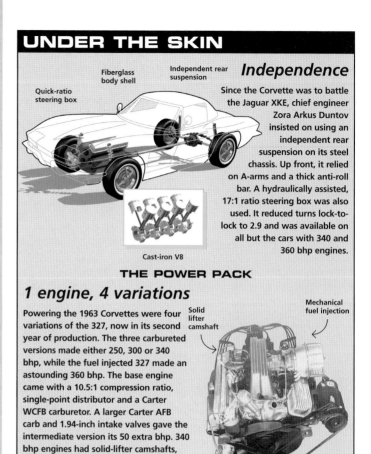

Fiberglass body shell

Quick-ratio steering box

Independent rear suspension

Independence

Since the Corvette was to battle the Jaguar XKE, chief engineer Zora Arkus Duntov insisted on using an independent rear suspension on its steel chassis. Up front, it relied on A-arms and a thick anti-roll bar. A hydraulically assisted, 17:1 ratio steering box was also used. It reduced turns lock-to-lock to 2.9 and was available on all but the cars with 340 and 360 bhp engines.

Cast-iron V8

THE POWER PACK

1 engine, 4 variations

Powering the 1963 Corvettes were four variations of the 327, now in its second year of production. The three carbureted versions made either 250, 300 or 340 bhp, while the fuel injected 327 made an astounding 360 bhp. The base engine came with a 10.5:1 compression ratio, single-point distributor and a Carter WCFB carburetor. A larger Carter AFB carb and 1.94-inch intake valves gave the intermediate version its 50 extra bhp. 340 bhp engines had solid-lifter camshafts, aluminum intake manifolds and 11.25:1 compression ratios. The FI engines were basically the same as the 340 bhp versions but used mechanical fuel injection systems.

Solid lifter camshaft

Mechanical fuel injection

11.25:1 compression ratio

Steel crankshaft

One year only

The split rear window was a favorite feature of GM Chief Stylist Bill Mitchell. He had to fight tooth and nail against other GM executives who wanted a solid rear window. Mitchell won the battle, but only for one year. In 1964 the Sting Ray had a one-piece rear window.

It's the split rear window that makes this Sting Ray Coupe so collectable.

Without Bill Mitchell, the Sting Ray would never have been. He built and campaigned the original Stingray racer with his own money. It certainly paid off—the Sting Ray is one of the most sought after of all Corvettes.

Thunderous 300

While the hot setup in 1963 was the 360 fuelie engine, most (8,033) buyers opted for the 300 bhp version. It was less temperamental but still offered plenty of power-on oversteer.

Split window

Although the automobile magazine test editors detested 'that bar in the middle of the rear window,' customers loved it. In fact, the Sting Ray Coupe was so popular that it set a new sales record, almost outselling the previous model 2 to 1.

Competition upgrade

Although GM was 'officially' adhering to the 1957 AMA racing ban, the ZO6 package was available so buyers who wanted to race had the best chance of winning. To get it, owners had to first specify the 360 bhp Coupe with a 4-speed and Posi rear then pay the extra $1,818.45 for the option. In exchange they would receive Al-fin power brakes with sintered metallic linings, a heavy duty front stabilizer bar, uprated shocks, stiffer springs, a dual master cylinder, and a 36-gallon fuel tank.

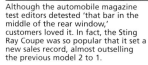

In-house 4-speed

In 1963, GM switched from using Borg Warner-manufactured 4-speeds to its own in-house manual transmissions. The division was in Muncie, Indiana and the wide-ratio, manual transmission simply became known as the Muncie 4-speed, or just M20.

Independent rear end

The 1963 Corvette was the first to have an independent rear suspension. It incorporated a frame-mounted differential and U-joint halfshafts held together by a transverse leaf spring.

Daytona Blue

There was a choice of seven exterior colors for 1963. This example is one of the 3,475 Sting Rays painted Daytona Blue.

Optional axle ratios

Corvettes with the Powerglide or 3-speed transmissions came standard with 3.36:1 rear axle ratios. 4-speed cars came with 3.70:1s but 3.08:1, 3.55:1, 4.11:1 and 4.56:1 gears were optional.

Pop-up headlights

The Corvettes headlights were mounted in a rotating section that, when closed, gave a flush fit to the contour of the nose. It was the first U.S. production car to use this system since 1942.

Specifications

1963 Chevrolet Corvette

ENGINE

Type: V8

Construction: Cast-iron block and heads

Valve gear: Two valves per cylinder operated by a single camshaft with pushrods and rockers

Bore and stroke: 4.00 in. x 3.25 in.

Displacement: 327 c.i.

Compression ratio: 10.5

Induction system: Single Carter four-barrel carburetor

Maximum power: 300 bhp at 5,000 rpm

Maximum torque: 360 lb-ft at 3,200 rpm

Top speed: 118 mph

0-60 mph: 6.1 sec.

TRANSMISSION

Four-speed manual

BODY/CHASSIS

Steel perimeter chassis with fiberglass two-door coupe body

SPECIAL FEATURES

Because of poor visibility, the split rear was eliminated in 1964.

The 1963 model was the first Corvette to use pop-up headlights. This feature has stuck with the Corvette ever since.

RUNNING GEAR

Steering: Recirculating ball

Front suspension: Double A-arms, coil springs, shock absorbers and anti-roll bar

Rear suspension: Independent by trailing arms and lower transverse rods with halfshafts acting as upper links, single transverse leaf spring and shock absorbers

Brakes: Drums (front and rear)

Wheels: Steel, 5.5 x 15 in.

Tires: 6.70 x 15

DIMENSIONS

Length: 175.3 in.   **Width:** 69.6 in.

Height: 49.8 in.   **Wheelbase:** 98.0 in.

Track: 56.3 in. (front), 57.0 in. (rear)

Weight: 3,160 lbs.

Corvette STING RAY

When Chevrolet® introduced the Corvette Sting Ray in 1963, it was the quickest roadster Detroit had ever made. Its 327-cubic inch V8 gave the new Corvette serious muscle, and for the first time, an American sports car could out-gun its European rivals.

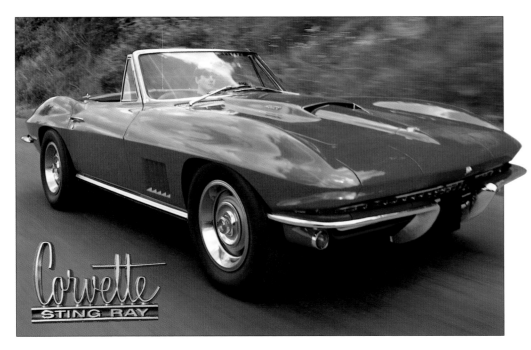

"America's favorite sports car."

"Off the line, this Vette™ has the kind of low-end grunt that will leave most modern sports cars in a cloud of dust and burning rubber. First you hear the throaty rumble of the big-shouldered 427 V8, then the three two-barrel carbs snarl to life and you can feel the power throb through the chrome shifter. Both the steering and clutch are heavy, while the handling and brakes are crude by today's standards. But that snap-your-head-back lunge of power still makes the Sting Ray America's favorite sports car."

The cockpit is Spartan and functional with a classic hot rod feel often imitated but never quite equaled.

Milestones

1953 The first Motorama Corvette show car enters production with a six-cylinder engine.

1955 Zora Arkus-Duntov, father of the Sting Ray, becomes head of the Corvette program, a position he held until retirement in 1982. Under him, manual transmission and the V8 engine are offered as options (1955) and fuel injection becomes available (1957).

1957 The Vette is the fastest real production car in the world, showing what can be done when conventional engineering is applied well.

The 1963 convertible. Soft top is stored under a panel behind the seats.

1963 The first Sting Ray production car is built, with all-independent suspension and the first coupe body. Its styling is based on a racing car design originally developed in 1958 by Bill Mitchell.

1965 Big-block engine and disc brakes are available. The 396-cubic inch V8 with a solid cam is introduced with 425 bhp.

1967 Pinnacle of performance is the L88 427-cubic inch V8. This also marks the last year of this body style.

UNDER THE SKIN

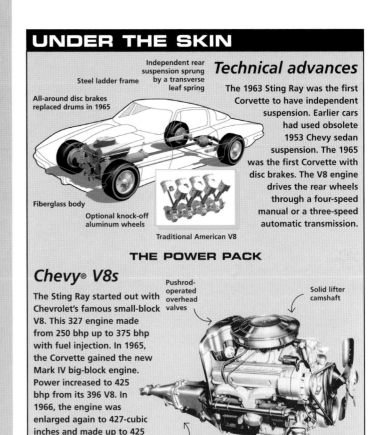

Technical advances

The 1963 Sting Ray was the first Corvette to have independent suspension. Earlier cars had used obsolete 1953 Chevy sedan suspension. The 1965 was the first Corvette with disc brakes. The V8 engine drives the rear wheels through a four-speed manual or a three-speed automatic transmission.

Independent rear suspension sprung by a transverse leaf spring

Steel ladder frame

All-around disc brakes replaced drums in 1965

Fiberglass body

Optional knock-off aluminum wheels

Traditional American V8

THE POWER PACK

Chevy® V8s

The Sting Ray started out with Chevrolet's famous small-block V8. This 327 engine made from 250 bhp up to 375 bhp with fuel injection. In 1965, the Corvette gained the new Mark IV big-block engine. Power increased to 425 bhp from its 396 V8. In 1966, the engine was enlarged again to 427-cubic inches and made up to 425 bhp. The 435 bhp 427 L88 was offered the very next year.

Pushrod-operated overhead valves

Solid lifter camshaft

M-22 manual transmission

Cast-iron block

Split rear window

The most sought-after Sting Ray is the 1963 split rear window coupe model. The designer, Bill Mitchell, intended it to form a visual connection with the central raised sections on the hood. The feature was dropped because it spoiled rear vision. Some later cars have been retro-fitted with the center pillar in an attempt to raise their values.

The split rear window coupe was only available in 1963.

The Sting Ray was introduced in 1963, 10 years after the Corvette's first appearance. The engine is set well back in the frame, giving nearly 50/50 weight distribution and excellent handling for the day.

V8 engine
Apart from the very early models, all Corvettes are powered by V8 engines. There is a wide variety of displacements and states of tune. The 327-cubic inch engine in 350-bhp tune is typical.

Disc brakes all around
Vented discs with dual-pot calipers on each wheel were fitted from 1965. While old stocks lasted, buyers could opt for the discontinued drums to save money.

Fiberglass body
Like all Corvettes, the Sting Ray has a body made from a number of fiberglass panels mounted on a traditional separate frame.

Alloy gearbox and clutch housing
To save weight, the Sting Ray was given an alloy clutch housing and an alloy-cased gearbox. This also improved weight distribution.

Optional side exhausts
The Sting Ray's enormous options list included the Side Mount Exhaust System. The side pipes are covered with a perforated shield to prevent the driver or passengers from burning themselves. Side exhausts were chosen mainly for visual effect.

Independent rear suspension
Another Corvette first, the Sting Ray has a crude but effective system with a transverse leaf spring mounted behind the differential.

Flip-up headlights
The headlights are rotated by two reversible vacuum operated motors—a postwar first for an American car.

No trunk lid
To preserve the contour of the car, there is no trunk lid and access to the luggage compartment is from behind the seats.

Foldaway top
The Corvette's convertible top folds away completely when not in use and is stored beneath a flush-fitting fiberglass panel behind the driver. Optional hard top cost $231.75 in 1966.

Triple side vents
Side vent arrangement, like many minor details, changed over the years. The 1965 and '66 models like this one have three vents.

Specifications
1966 Chevrolet Corvette Sting Ray

ENGINE
Type: V8, 90°
Construction: Cast-iron block and heads; Single cam, pushrods
Bore and stroke: 4.0 in. x 3.25 in.
Displacement: 327 c.i.
Compression ratio: 11:1
Induction system: Rochester fuel injection or one/two Carter four-barrel carbs
Maximum power: 375 bhp at 6,200 rpm
Maximum torque: 350 lb-ft at 4,000 rpm
Top speed: 135 mph
0-60 mph: 5.6 sec.

TRANSMISSION
Three-speed automatic (optional four-speed manual)

BODY/CHASSIS
Steel ladder frame with two-door convertible or coupe fiberglass body

SPECIAL FEATURES

Innovative retractable headlights.

Soft top folds away neatly into compartment behind seats, with luggage space below.

RUNNING GEAR
Front suspension: Double wishbone, coil springs, anti-roll bar
Rear suspension: Semi-trailing arms, half-shafts and transverse links with transverse leaf spring
Brakes: Vented discs with four-pot calipers (optional cast-iron drums)
Wheels: Five-bolt steel (knock off aluminum optional) 6 in. x 15 in.
Tires: 6.7 in. x 15 in. Firestone Super Sport 170

DIMENSIONS
Length: 175.3 in.   **Width:** 69.6 in.
Height: 49.8 in.   **Wheelbase:** 98 in.
Track: 56.3 in. (front), 57 in. (rear)
Weight: 3,150 lbs.

Chevrolet CORVETTE

In 1968 Chevrolet introduced the third generation Corvette. Not everyone liked it but with a 427-cubic inch engine under the hood, it was one of the quickest production vehicles made in the late 1960s.

"...strong and torquey."

"Compared to contemporary European sports cars, the 1969 Corvette is big and brash. The styling is controversial and the interior tight, but once you put your foot down all these criticisms are forgotten. The 427-cubic inch V8 is strong and torquey and will push the 'Vette to 60 mph in under six seconds. Though most of the Corvette's weight is over the front wheels, it can hold a line or corner with most any other sports car."

Early third generation Corvettes had easy-to-read gauges and comfortable bucket seats.

Milestones

1966 Mako Shark show car which is designed by GM stylist Larry Shinoda, is revealed.

Early third generation Corvettes use the optional 427 that first appeared in the 1967 model.

1968 The new Corvette, with both small-block and big-block V8s, debuts to mixed reviews. There are initial quality control problems, but testers comment on the excellent performance. The new model sets a production record, with 28,566 Corvettes built.

By 1977 the Corvette was more cruiser than bruiser.

1969 Chevrolet makes detail changes. The name Stingray is revived, but now as one word. The doors and rear taillights are slightly redesigned. The 350 replaces the 327 as the base small-block V8, and it also marks the final year the 427 V8 will be used. The following year will see the arrival of the 454 big block.

UNDER THE SKIN

Fiberglass body — Rear-wheel drive

All-independent suspension

Big-block V8

Low-tech

Although it has an all-new body, underneath the Corvette is little different from the midyear models. This means a separate perimeter frame chassis with an unequal length wishbone suspension at the front and an independent rear with a single transverse leaf spring and halfshafts, which also act as upper control arms. Braking is provided by discs all around.

THE POWER PACK

Codes of power

In 1969 Chevrolet offered five 427 big-block V8 engines. The lowest powered 427 was the L36 which 'only' made 390 bhp, while the L68 made 400 bhp. Those who wanted more performance ordered the L71 (435 bhp) which was available with optional aluminum heads. Both the L68 and L71 came with tri-power carbs. The over-the-edge engine was the L88 which was underrated from the factory at 430 bhp (the actual figure was closer to 530 bhp). There were also two all-alloy ZL-1 427s produced which made over 500 bhp.

Cast-iron construction — Rochester or Holley carbs

Forged-steel crankshaft and con rods — Aluminum heads available as an option

Special order

Some of the rarest and most desirable of all the muscle-era Corvettes are those powered by the L88 engine. Factory rated at 435 bhp, the true output is estimated at around 530 bhp. Only 116 were built in 1969, and today are worth around $90,000.

The L88 Corvettes were only available by special order.

Although overshadowed by the 1963-1967 Sting Ray, the later big-block Corvettes were equipped with some of Detroit's most powerful engines and are highly sought after because of their performance.

Optional hard top

For an extra $252, owners who bought convertibles could order an optional hardtop that attaches to twin locating slots on the rear decklid and two on the top of the windshield frame. It can be installed when the soft top is down.

Big-block engine

Known as the Mark IV, the big-block 427 was only available in full-size Chevrolets and the Corvette as a regular production option in 1969. With this engine, Corvettes are capable of 13-second 1/4-mile times at around 100 mph.

Limited-slip differential

A GM Positraction limited-slip differential was available for an extra $46.35 and most owners specified it. It helps to control wheel spin under hard acceleration.

Revised interior

The 1968 Corvette was criticized for it's small interior, and so for 1969 it was modified with a smaller-diameter steering wheel and thinner door panels. A map pocket was also included in the glove compartment door.

Windshield wiper panel

An unusual feature is a vacuum-operated panel which conceals the windshield wipers. When the wipers are turned on, it pops up and forward and can be left up to facilitate changing the wiper blades.

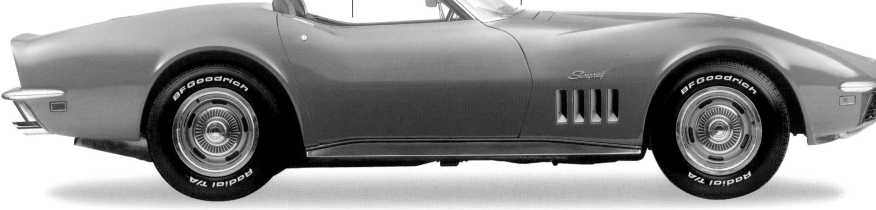

Specifications

1969 Chevrolet Corvette

ENGINE
Type: V8
Construction: Cast-iron block and heads
Valve gear: Two valves per cylinder operated by pushrods and rockers
Bore and stroke: 4.25 in. x 3.76 in.
Displacement: 427 c.i.
Compression ratio: 11.0:1
Induction system: Single Rochester Quadrajet four-barrel carburetor
Maximum power: 435 bhp at 5,600 rpm
Maximum torque: 460 lb-ft at 4,000 rpm
Top speed: 135 mph
0-60 mph: 5.5 sec.

TRANSMISSION
Muncie M22, close ratio, four-speed

BODY/CHASSIS
Perimeter chassis with fiberglass body

SPECIAL FEATURES

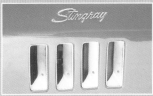

1968-1969 Corvettes contain these gill-like fender air extractors.

Quad headlights are hidden under pop-up panels.

RUNNING GEAR
Steering: Recirculating ball
Front suspension: Unequal length wishbones with coil springs and telescopic shock absorbers
Rear suspension: Independent with lower control arms, transverse leaf spring and telescopic shock absorbers
Brakes: Discs (front), drums (rear)
Wheels: Slotted Rally, 7 x 15 in.
Tires: F60 15

DIMENSIONS
Length: 171.0 in.   **Width:** 67.8 in.
Height: 48.9 in.   **Wheelbase:** 98.0 in.
Track: 57.9 in. (front), 59.6 in (rear)
Weight: 3,145 lbs.

Chevrolet **CORVETTE PACE CAR**

The Corvette was 25 years old in 1978, and a special Silver Anniversary addition was released to celebrate. Plus, America's only sports car was chosen to pace the 62nd Indianapolis 500, and more than 6,000 replicas were built and sold through select dealers.

"...incredibly civilized."

"After the late-1960s screamers, the 1978 Pace Car replica feels incredibly civilized. The seats are soft, but more supportive than those in earlier cars, and all the gadgets suggest relaxed cruising is more appropriate than straightline grunt. The L82 engine is keen enough, and when coupled with the automatic transmission, it delivers respectable performance. Handling and balance are good, and the Goodyear tires give excellent grip."

All Pace Car replicas have silver-lined interiors; most are automatics, too.

Milestones

1968 A third-generation Corvette, with sleek new lines inspired by the Mako Shark show car of 1965, is unveiled. Under the skin, it's mainly a carryover.

The last year for the 'Shark' Corvette was 1982.

1969 The name Stingray returns, this time as one word. The small-block 327 is bored to 350 cubic inches.

1974 This is the last year for big-blocks and for Corvettes that run on leaded gasoline.

The C5 Corvette was chosen to pace the Indy 500 in 1998.

1978 A new rear window arrives, as does the 25th-anniversary edition. In May, the Corvette paces the Indianapolis 500, and 6,502 replicas are available for sale to the public.

UNDER THE SKIN

New over old

Ladder-type chassis frame

Independent rear suspension

Front disc brakes

Although the styling was all new for 1978, the chassis was carried over. The ladder-type frame supports a coil-sprung independent front and transverse leaf-sprung rear end. Pace Car replicas are fitted with the FE7 Gymkhana Suspension package, which includes heavy-duty front and rear shock absorbers, a larger-diameter front anti-roll bar, a rear anti-roll bar and higher-rated springs. Front disc brakes were standard.

Emissions controlled V8

THE POWER PACK

Greater power

With a cast-iron block and head, the high-performance 350-cubic inch L82 V8, rated at 220 bhp, was standard in the Pace Car replica. This unit has greater power and torque than the L48 engine (standard in other Vettes), achieved through a higher-lift camshaft, special heads with bigger valves and specially forged pistons. The L82 also features four-bolt, main bearing caps and a slightly higher 8.9:1 compression ratio. Induction is by a four-barrel carburetor and a dual-snorkel cold-air induction system. For a finishing touch, there is a larger exhaust, larger tailpipes and finned aluminum rocker arm covers.

High demand

Typical of the 1970s genre of visual performance cars, the Corvette Pace Car replica was more for show. Nevertheless, it was instantly snapped up. Demand remained high in subsequent years, resulting in a spate of fakes.

Demand for Pace Cars resulted in a number of 'bogus' replicas.

Despite the onset of emissions regulations, federal fuel-economy mandates and high insurance premiums, the Corvette turned into a money making machine during the 1970s, selling 47,667 examples in 1978 alone.

Special V8

A special-order-code—(L82) V8—improved performance from the 350-cubic inch unit with a host of improvements designed to release more power. The L82 engine has a higher-lift camshaft, special cylinder heads and forged pistons and crankshaft.

Special Pace Car decals

To indicate that this Corvette was a special edition, it could be literally covered in Indianapolis 500 Pace Car decals. However, these were packaged separately in the car.

Luxurious cabin

The Pace Car replica came standard with just about every option available on a standard Corvette. It also had a special silver interior, including new lightweight high-back seats upholstered in either silver leather or leather with gray cloth inserts.

Front air dam

Corvette Pace Cars feature a front airdam and a rear decklid spoiler, which were both functional and sporty-looking.

Performance wheels

The Pace Car replica came with P225/60 R15 Goodyear GT white-letter radial tires on polished-aluminum spoke wheels.

Redesigned rear end

In 1978, the Corvette underwent major body restyling with a new fastback roofline and rear window. The new rear end not only gave a sleeker profile, but improved driver visibility and luggage space.

1978 Chevrolet Corvette Pace Car replica

ENGINE

Type: V8

Construction: Cast-iron block and head

Valve gear: Two valves per cylinder operated by a single camshaft with pushrods and rockers

Bore and stroke: 4.00 in. x 3.48 in.

Displacement: 350 c.i.

Compression ratio: 8.9:1

Induction system: Rochester Quadrajet four-barrel carburetor

Maximum power: 220 bhp at 5,200 rpm

Maximum torque: 260 lb-ft at 3,600 rpm

Top speed: 125 mph

0-60 mph: 8.2 sec.

TRANSMISSION

TH350 three-speed automatic

BODY/CHASSIS

Welded steel box section chassis with fiberglass body

SPECIAL FEATURES

Official Pace Car graphics came in the trunk and were dealer-installed items.

Pop-up headlights were very popular styling cues in the late 1970s.

RUNNING GEAR

Steering: Recirculating-ball

Front suspension: Unequal length control arms with coil springs, telescopic shock absorbers and anti-roll bar

Rear suspension: Independent with halfshafts, lower links, transverse semi-elliptic leaf spring, telescopic shock absorbers and anti-roll bar

Brakes: Discs (front and rear)

Wheels: Aluminum, 15-in. dia.

Tires: Goodyear Radial, P255/70 R15

DIMENSIONS

Length: 185.2 in.   **Width:** 69.0 in.

Height: 48.0 in.   **Wheelbase:** 98.0 in.

Track: 58.7 in. (front), 59.5 in. (rear)

Weight: 3,401 lbs.

Chevrolet **CORVETTE**

By 1982, the venerable third-generation Corvette was outclassed. With a replacement on the way, Chevrolet released a special 'Collector Edition.' Today, as its name suggests, this Corvette is indeed being collected.

"...all the essential ingredients."

"If you have ever driven a late 1960s Vette®, then you will feel at home in the Collector Edition. The 350 V8 offers adequate go for a car of this vintage, and although a four-speeder would be better, the automatic transmission still yearns for enthusiastic driving. Best of all, the handling and steering are truly in the sports car league, reminding you that, despite its luxury content, it is still a real Corvette with the essential ingredients of 'America's Sports Car'."

This Vette is truly civilized, with thick carpeting, good insulation and comfortable seats.

Milestones

1974 This marks the last year for the 454 V8.

1976 Despite only one body style, Corvette production reaches an all-time high, with 46,558 built.

Another special third generation Vette is the 1978 Pace Car.

1978 Celebrating its 25th anniversary, the car gets a facelift with a new aero-style back window. It also paces the Indianapolis 500. 6,200 Pace Car replicas are issued.

1980 The Corvette sheds 250 lbs. due to greater use of aluminum.

A special Collector Edition was released in the C4's final year.

1982 Fuel injection reappears, but only 25,407 Corvettes, 6,759 of which are Collector Editions, are made. It is the end of the third generation.

UNDER THE SKIN

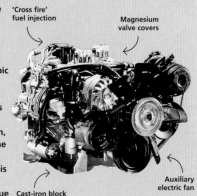

All-independent suspension

Four-wheel vented disc brakes

Box-section steel chassis

Small-block V8

Strength in depth

Although the Corvette got a new body for 1968 (which was used through 1982), beneath it the chassis was a carryover from the Sting Ray. The box-section steel chassis has five crossmembers and is very stiff. It has an independent suspension, with unequal-length A-arms and coil springs fitted at the front, while at the rear are lower lateral arms, trailing arms, a transverse leaf spring and tube-type shocks. Vented discs provide the braking.

THE POWER PACK

Improved formula

By the early 1980s, the Corvette had become more of a refined boulevard sports car than a straightline screamer. Only one engine is available on the 1982 Corvette, a 200-bhp L83 350-cubic inch small-block V8. It is a reworked version of the long-running L82 engine but features a number of improvements, including cross-fire fuel injection, an electric fan to supplement the engine-driven fan and GM's Command Control computer. This provides fuel metering and governs the transmission's torque convertor.

'Cross fire' fuel injection

Magnesium valve covers

Cast-iron block and heads

Auxiliary electric fan

Cool, collected

Since 1982 marked the end of the third generation Corvette body style, Chevrolet decided to make a special edition package to commemorate its 1968-1982 production run. This model has may options including silver-beige paint and seat covers and special wheels.

The Collector Edition was the first Vette to break the $20,000 price barrier.

Along with the Camaro® and Firebird®, the Corvette was one of the only American sports cars to survive the tumultuous events of the 1970s. The Collector Edition, produced in small numbers, signified the end of an era.

Lift-up rear window
Originally intended to be introduced in 1978, high costs kept the lift-up rear hatch from appearing on the Corvette until 1982. It provides improved rear access and is mounted on twin hydraulic rams.

Fuel-injected engine
In 1982, fuel injection reappeared on the Corvette in 1984. This throttle body system, called cross-fire injection, boosts power by 10 bhp to 200 bhp. With this engine, the 1982 Collector can sprint to 60 mph in 8.0 seconds.

Mild facelift
For the 1980 model year, the 12-year-old Corvette was revised to achieve more integrated front and rear ends. This minor facelift brought a slight decrease in aerodynamic drag and a reduction in overall weight.

All-independent suspension
Since 1963, all Corvettes have employed fully independent suspension. Anti-roll bars are fitted front and rear and give outstanding handling for a car of this period.

T-top roof panels
With the absence of convertible Corvettes in the late 1970s and early 1980s, T-tops, which offer a wind-in-the-hair feel plus the practicality of a solid roof, grew in popularity. On the Collector Edition, these are etched in bronze. The twin glass panels can be lifted off with a special key and stowed behind the seats.

Collector Edition package
Items unique to the Collector Edition Corvette include silver-beige metallic paint, silver cloth upholstery, silver leather door trim, graduated shadow graphics, a lift-up rear window, special emblems, bronze-colored T-top roof panels and finned aluminum wheels.

Specifications
1982 Chevrolet Corvette Collector Edition

ENGINE
Type: V8
Construction: Cast-iron block and heads
Valve gear: Two valves per cylinder operated by pushrods and rockers
Bore and stroke: 4.00 in. x 3.48 in.
Displacement: 350 c.i.
Compression ratio: 9.0:1
Induction system: GM throttle-body fuel injection (cross-fire injection)
Maximum power: 200 bhp at 4,200 rpm
Maximum torque: 285 lb-ft at 2,800 rpm
Top speed: 125 mph
0-60 mph: 8.0 sec.

TRANSMISSION
Four-speed automatic

BODY/CHASSIS
Steel ladder-frame chassis with glass-reinforced plastic two-door coupe body

SPECIAL FEATURES

cross-fire-injection

Chevrolet's special injection system was revolutionary when first introduced.

The finned aluminum wheels are among the Collector's most distinctive features.

RUNNING GEAR
Steering: Recirculating ball
Front suspension: Unequal-length A-arms with coil springs, telescopic shock absorbers and anti-roll bar
Rear suspension: Lower lateral arms, half shafts, trailing arms, transverse leaf spring, telescopic shock absorbers and anti-roll bar
Brakes: Vented discs, 11.75-in. dia. (front and rear)
Wheels: Cast-aluminum, 8 x 15 in.
Tires: Goodyear Eagle GT, P55/60 VR15

DIMENSIONS
Length: 185.3 in.   **Width:** 69.0 in.
Height: 48.4 in.   **Wheelbase:** 98.0 in.
Track: 58.7 in. (front) 59.5 in. (rear)
Weight: 3,425 lbs.

Chevrolet CORVETTE ZR-1

With its Lotus-designed quad-cam V8 engine, the ZR-1 has a more advanced powerplant and superior performance than the current C5 Corvette. It is the ultimate Corvette—a genuine world-class supercar.

"...the ultimate Corvette?"

"Above 3,500 rpm, when all 16 injectors are pumping fuel as fast as the engine can use it, the ZR-1's performance is astounding, even for early models. With the later 405 bhp engines there were few cars on the road to challenge the ZR-1's performance. The chassis easily copes with the huge power output. The ride may be harsh and the interior cramped, but this is a supercar with sensitive steering, powerful brakes, and fine rear-wheel drive road manners."

Lateral support in the ZR-1 is excellent, although the cockpit is difficult to enter.

Milestones

1984 A new Corvette is finally introduced in 1983 as a 1984 model. The fourth-generation Corvette is the best in years, but, although it retains the front-engine rear-drive format, it severely needs more power.

By 1956 the Corvette finally matured, and turned into a serious sports car.

1986 The Corvette roadster is revived, and goes on sale this year. It is selected as a pace car for the Indianapolis 500.

1990 After much hype, the ZR-1 finally enters production. It has unique rear end styling to distinguish it from the standard Corvette.

An all-new, fifth-generation Corvette debuted in 1997.

1993 Power is boosted to 405 bhp and a special 40th anniversary trim package is available on all Corvettes. The ZR-1 returns for two more seasons with new five-spoke alloy wheels.

UNDER THE SKIN

American technology

Beneath the fiberglass body lies the heart of the ZR-1, the high-tech LT5 V8 engine. Backing it up is a standard six-speed ZF transmission (automatic was not available), which transmits power to a fully independent rear end. The rear body panels had to be widened to fit the huge 315/35 Goodyear tires.

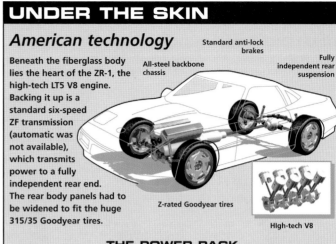

Standard anti-lock brakes

All-steel backbone chassis

Fully independent rear suspension

Z-rated Goodyear tires

High-tech V8

THE POWER PACK

Lotus-designed

It's a V8, but not as we know it. Although it is the classic small block 350 V8, the fuel-injected LT5 engine is all-alloy with two chain-driven camshafts per cylinder bank, which operate four valves per cylinder. The crankshaft is a very strong, cross-drilled, forged steel unit and the connecting rods are made from forged steel alloy. Chevrolet employed Lotus, in England, to design the engine and Mercury Marine, in the U.S., to build it. The sophisticated design meant that it could be tweaked to produce even more power.

Four camshafts and 32 valves

Nikasil-coated cylinder liners

All-alloy construction

Forged steel crankshaft

Brute force

In 1993 Chevrolet began to make use of the powerful Lotus-designed LT5 V8, pushing up its output to 405 bhp at 5,800 rpm and the torque to 385 lb-ft. The early ZR-1s may have been fast, but the extra power of the later model really makes them move.

This post-1993 model has an increased power output of 405 bhp.

With the ZR-1, Chevrolet proved that an exotic mid-mounted engine and $100,000 price tag are not required to offer true supercar performance.

Plastic springs
Like all Corvettes since the launch of the 1963 Coupe, the ZR-1 features transverse leaf springs. These are now made from plastic for reduced weight.

Quad-cam V8
A technological masterpiece, the LT5 was originally intended for boats. Although all-alloy, it weighs more than a cast-iron Chevy small block.

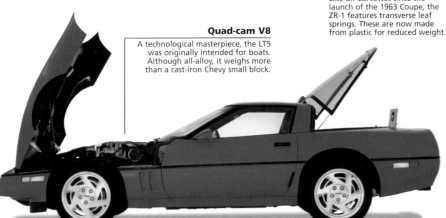

Valet key
To prevent certain individuals from experiencing the ZR-1's full performance, a special key can be used to restrict horsepower.

Fiberglass bodywork
The ZR-1, like all Corvettes, retains fiberglass bodywork. The back half of the car had to be widened to fit the ZR-1s large wheels.

Traction control
Corvettes were often tricky to control on slippery roads. The introduction of ASR (Anti-Slip Regulation) considerably reduced the tendency for the car to slide on wet roads.

Tire-pressure monitor
For 1989 all Corvettes received a tire-pressure monitoring device which warns the driver, by means of a flashing light, if tire pressures are low.

CAGS gear selection
Computer-Aided Gear Selection (CAGS) is a device which skips shifts in low gears at light throttle openings.

Selective ride control
At the touch of a switch the ZR-1 driver can select three different suspension settings: Touring, Sport, or Performance. As speed increases, the shocks are stiffened by a computer that is able to make 10 adjustments per second.

Variable fuel injection
During normal driving, the ZR-1's engine uses only eight primary ports and injectors. With the throttle floored and the engine turning above 3,500 rpm, the eight secondary injectors are brought into action, producing truly awesome performance.

Specifications
1991 Chevrolet Corvette ZR-1

ENGINE
Type: LT5 V8
Construction: Alloy block, heads and cylinder liners
Valve gear: Four valves per cylinder operated by four overhead camshafts
Bore and stroke: 3.90 in. x 3.66 in.
Displacement: 350 c.i.
Compression ratio: 11:1
Induction system: Multi-port fuel injection
Maximum power: 375 bhp at 5,800 rpm
Maximum torque: 371 lb-ft at 4,800 rpm
Top speed: 180 mph
0-60 mph: 5.0 sec.

TRANSMISSION
ZF six-speed manual

BODY/CHASSIS
Separate steel chassis with fiberglass two-door coupe body

SPECIAL FEATURES

A unique feature of the LT5 is the three-stage throttle control.

Prototype ZR-1s retained the original 1984 instrument panel layout.

RUNNING GEAR
Steering: Rack-and-pinion
Front suspension: Double wishbones, transverse plastic leaf springs, and telescopic adjustable shocks
Rear suspension: Upper and lower trailing links, transverse plastic leaf spring, telescopic adjustable shocks, and anti-roll bar
Brakes: Vented discs front and rear, 13 in. dia. (front), 12 in. dia. (rear)
Wheels: Alloy, 17 x 9.5-in. dia. (front), 17 x 11-in. dia. (rear)
Tires: Goodyear Eagle ZR40, 275/40 ZR17 (front), 315/35 ZR17 (rear)

DIMENSIONS
Length: 178.5 in.   **Width:** 73.2 in.
Height: 46.7 in.
Wheelbase: 96.2 in.
Track: 60 in. (front), 62 in. (rear)
Weight: 3,519 lbs.

Chevrolet CORVETTE

Some might say that the Corvette looks good enough and goes fast enough as standard. Others, though, will always crave individuality or more speed from their car and set out to create their version of the ideal Vette™.

"...always entertaining."

"A Corvette will always be entertaining to drive, whatever the year, whatever the power output. On these late cars, it's just a case of rechipping the engine management system to boost the power and give you the extra performance you need. Heads turn as you plant your foot and the deep-chested V8 rumble changes to a hard-edged howl from the aftermarket exhaust system and the car tears away. The standard Corvette steering is retained and handling is just as good, but the ride suffers on the lowered suspension, especially on poorly surfaced roads."

Corvette interior looks good as stock, especially with the optional leather bucket seats.

Milestones

1953 First Corvette introduced with a straight-six engine and fiberglass body.

1955 In response to the launch of the V8 Ford Thunderbird, Chevrolet added the new 265-cubic inch small-block V8 engine.

The third generation Corvettes lasted from 1968 through 1982.

1963 New restyled Sting Ray® is launched. The chassis is new and the car features all-around independent suspension. A larger big-block V8 engine is added in 1965.

1968 Corvette restyled again and is known as the Stingray from 1969.

There are many specialists who modify Corvettes. This car has been modified by Kaminari Design.

1984 Corvette receives a total redesign with new styling, chassis and new front and rear suspension. From 1985 to 1992, the standard engine is the L98 350 V8.

1990 Ultimate factory Corvette development arrives, the 379-bhp ZR-1.

UNDER THE SKIN

Plastic fantastic

As with the standard Corvette, modified cars use a fiberglass body on a separate chassis. Suspension is via plastic transverse leaf springs front and rear, with double wishbones at the front and trailing arms at the rear. On modified cars, Chevrolet's Z51 performance handling package and the FX3 selective ride control are frequently installed to sharpen up the handling.

Custom rear wing

Upgraded engine management microprocessor

Upgraded suspension

Polished alloy wheels

Small-block Chevy V8

THE POWER PACK

Ultimate power

The ultimate engine for a modified Corvette is the LT5 unit installed in the mighty ZR-1. With two cams per cylinder bank operating four valves per cylinder, the LT5 produces an incredible 379 bhp, while still offering similar levels of driveability as a standard, small-block engined Corvette. The capacity remains the same at 350 cubic inches. Other modified Corvettes use the single camshaft small-block V8 (shown here) with an array of tuning equipment. Later cars can have their power boosted by simply upgrading the microchip in the engine control management system.

Single camshaft

Cast-iron block

Upgraded engine management

Callaway

The ultimate in modified Corvettes is the Callaway Corvette. Early models used turbochargers to give a boost in power, but later versions relied on increased capacity. In 1994, Callaway launched the Corvette-based C7R racer with carbon fiber bodywork.

This C7R is the ultimate Corvette-based car with nearly 660 bhp.

The Corvette holds a place next to any American's heart. Some like their car standard, others feel the need for a little personalization. Modifications range from the subtle to the outrageous.

'Chipped' engine
The Corvette has a sophisticated computerized engine management system, making it difficult for the amateur mechanic to tune the engine. The easiest way to raise power is to replace the control module with an upgraded unit which controls ignition timing and the fuel metering.

Leather bucket seats
Although some modified Vettes feature custom upholstery, many opt for the leather bucket seats, which hold the driver firmly in place under the high cornering forces the Corvette is capable of generating. The driver's seat is electrically adjustable.

ASR system
A popular and useful performance option, especially on modified Vettes, is the Acceleration Slip Regulation (ASR) system which limits wheelspin under heavy acceleration.

ABS brakes
Despite the boost from the tweaked engine, the Corvette's standard brakes are sufficient. For extra stopping power, the larger 13-inch front discs from the ZR-1 can be used.

Transmission
This car has the standard four-speed plus overdrive gearbox, but the ultimate Corvette transmission package would use the optional six-speed manual gearbox and low ratio performance axle.

Suspension
Adding Chevrolet's own Performance Handling Package improves the car's handling further. There is also a Selective Ride Control system available which allows the driver to select one of three different shock settings.

Body modifications
Because it's fiberglass, the Corvette's bodyshell is relatively easy to modify. This subtle rear deck wing has been added by the owner.

Upgraded exhaust system
Extra horsepower and a whole lot of V8 rumble can be released by adding an aftermarket system. This car uses a B&B Tri-Flow stainless-steel exhaust system.

Polished alloy wheels
Although this is a 1994 car, the owner has installed the wheels from a 1996 Corvette. The 17-inch rims have been polished to a mirror finish.

Specifications
1994 Modified Chevrolet Corvette

ENGINE
Type: V8, LT1
Construction: Cast-iron block and aluminum cylinder heads
Valve gear: Two valves per cylinder actuated by a single block-mounted camshaft via pushrods, rocker arms and hydraulic lifters
Bore and stroke: 4 in. x 3.48 in.
Displacement: 350 c.i.
Compression ratio: 10.1:1
Induction system: Computer-controlled sequential fuel injection
Maximum power: 330 bhp at 5,500 rpm
Maximum torque: 340 lb-ft at 4,000 rpm
Top speed: 158 mph
0-60 mph: 5.0 sec.

TRANSMISSION
Four-speed plus overdrive automatic transmission

BODY/CHASSIS
Two-seater fiberglass convertible body on 'uniframe' chassis

SPECIAL FEATURES

The owner of this Corvette has subtly modified the body with a color-coded wing added to the rear deck.

An upgraded engine control module gives a significant increase in power.

RUNNING GEAR
Steering: Power-assisted rack and pinion
Front suspension: Double wishbones with semi-elliptic fiberglass transverse spring, telescopic shock absorbers
Rear suspension: Five link with trailing arms and semi-elliptic fiberglass transverse leaf spring, telescopic shock absorbers
Brakes: Discs, front and rear with anti-lock system
Wheels: 1996 model chromed alloy, 17 in. x 8.5 in. (front) 17 in. x 9.5 in. (rear)
Tires: Goodyear Eagle GS-C, 255/45ZR-17 (front), 285/40ZR-17 (rear)

DIMENSIONS
Length: 178.5 in.   **Width:** 70.7 in.
Height: 46.3 in.   **Wheelbase:** 96.2 in.
Track: 56.8 in. (front), 59.1 in. (rear)
Weight: 3,504 lbs.

Chevrolet CORVETTE GRAND SPORT

With the advent of the new C5 model on the horizon, Chevrolet wanted to send off the fourth generation version in typical Corvette style. So for its final year in production, Chevy® added a 330-bhp LT4 small-block V8 and some interesting graphics that hark back to the original sports racer of the 1960s and called it the Grand Sport.

"...a driving enthusiast's dream."

"Because this is a limited edition Corvette it needed more than radical graphics to give it collectible status. The engine reaches 330 bhp thanks to redesigned cylinder heads and intake manifold. Its stable road manners and flat-out handling leave the driver with a strong feeling of confidence and enthusiasm. The firm suspension, responsive steering and potent brakes mated with the one-year-only engine option are a hard-core driving enthusiast's dream come true."

'Grand Sport' embroidery on each seat back is just one exclusive touch to this special Vette®.

Milestones

1954 The first V8 Corvette is built. It uses the 195-bhp 'Turbo-Fire' 265-cubic-inch V8.

1967 Most coveted of all Corvettes is the L88 Sting Ray®. Only 20 are built.

1984 Late-model technology in the form of a rigid chassis and race-car style suspension is the focus on the fourth-generation model.

The original Grand Sport cars were built for SCCA racing.

1990 'King of the Hill' is the name given to the ZR-1®. It boasts a special Lotus-designed 32-valve all-alloy engine.

For the Corvette's 40th anniversary in 1993, a special appearance package was offered.

1996 The end of an era coincides with the one-year-only LT4 small-block V8. Grand Sport production is limited to 1,000 units.

UNDER THE SKIN

Good breeding

Blasting through sweeping turns, the race-bred suspension provides excellent driver feedback, as does the power steering. The ZF six-speed transmission shifts precisely, its ratios being well matched to the engine's powerband. Larger tires are installed on the rear wheels requiring inconspicuous bolt-on fender flares.

Traction differential

Fiberglass body on steel chassis

Four-wheel anti-lock brakes

LT4 V8

THE POWER PACK

LT4 upgrades

The 405 bhp LT-5 was dropped in 1995, but GM wanted an engine for the Corvette that would offer 10 percent more power than the base LT1. The LT4 was the answer. The foundation is a 350-cubic inch engine with modified pistons. They are required to clear the 2.00/1.55-inch hollow valves. This brings the compression ratio up to 10.8:1 from 10.5:1. Redesigned cylinder heads with modified ports are used along with 100 lb. valve springs, a hot cam and roller rocker arms. The LT4 makes 330 bhp and also has a higher 6,300 rpm redline.

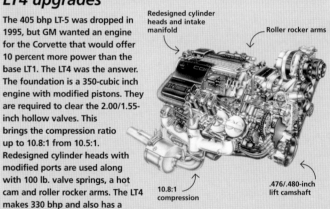

Redesigned cylinder heads and intake manifold

Roller rocker arms

10.8:1 compression

.476/.480-inch lift camshaft

Neat package

Models with the Z51 'Performance Handling Package' have a special attraction. The package increases the Grand Sport's cornering ability by means of thicker anti-roll bars, firmer shocks and stiffer springs. The ride is firm, but the trade-off is worth it.

In addition to its many dynamic qualities, the Grand Sport is very attractive.

All Grand Sports were finished in the identical color scheme. This makes the cars very distinctive, while the limited production run guarantees a desirable degree of exclusivity.

Six-speed shifting

GM didn't think that an automatic unit would be strong enough to handle the engine's 10 percent power gain. Because of this, all Grand Sports were only available with a strong ZF 6-speed manual transmission.

Small-block V8

To separate the 330-bhp LT4 small-block from the base LT1, the ignition wires, intake manifold and 'Corvette' lettering on the plastic manifold covers are all painted red.

High-flow heads

The LT4's heads are a completely different casting than the LT1's. The exhaust ports are widened, the intake ports are raised by .100-inch and the radius has been smoothed for better flow. They are assembled with larger 2.00-inch hollow-stem intake valves, and 1.55-inch sodium-filled exhaust valves and use stiffer valve springs.

Special identification

To celebrate the Grand Sport's limited production run of only 1,000 models, Chevrolet gave them a separate serial number sequence.

Distinctive color

All Grand Sports are painted Admiral Blue Metallic with a white stripe down the center of the body and red hash marks on the driver's side front fender.

Performance wheels and tires

High-performance Z-rated Goodyear GS-C tires are fitted to black, powder-coated 17-inch five-spoke wheels. Although they look like ZR-1 wheels, their offset is slightly different.

Aero shape

Although they have a large frontal area, fourth-generation Corvettes slice through the air quite effectively. Special fender flares in the rear have been added to house the wider 315/35 ZR17 tires.

ENGINE

Type: V8 (LT-4)

Construction: Cast-iron block and aluminum cylinder heads

Valve gear: Two valves per cylinder operated by a centrally-mounted camshaft with pushrods and roller rocker arms

Bore and stroke: 4.00 in. x 3.48 in.

Displacement: 350 c.i.

Compression ratio: 10.8:1

Induction system: Sequential fuel injection

Maximum power: 330 bhp at 5,800 rpm

Maximum torque: 340 lb-ft at 4,500 rpm

Top speed: 168 mph

0-60 mph: 4.7 sec.

TRANSMISSION

Six-speed manual

BODY/CHASSIS

Fiberglass body on steel chassis

SPECIAL FEATURES

The five-spoke wheel design resembles that of the ZR-1, but is in fact unique.

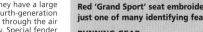

Red 'Grand Sport' seat embroidery is just one of many identifying features.

RUNNING GEAR

Steering: Rack-and-pinion

Front suspension: Independent with aluminum upper and lower control arms, transverse leaf spring, gas shock absorbers and anti-roll bar

Rear suspension: Independent with five-link, transverse leaf spring and anti-roll bar

Brakes: Discs, 12-in. dia. (front and rear)

Wheels: Aluminum, 9.5 x 17 in.

Tires: Goodyear, 275/40 ZR17 (front), P315/35 ZR17 (rear)

DIMENSIONS

Length: 178.5 in.   **Width:** 70.7 in.

Height: 46.3 in.   **Wheelbase:** 96.2 in.

Track: 57.7 in. (front), 59.1 in. (rear)

Weight: 3,298 lbs.

Chevrolet **CORVETTE**

Corvettes have been around for well over 40 years, but none has the sophistication of the latest model. It still has typical stunning performance, but without the compromise that made previous Corvettes hard to live with.

"...return to greatness."

"The C5 signals Corvette's return to greatness: it is truly a perfect blend of performance and comfort. The alloy LS1 V8 engine revs instantly in response to its new electronic throttle control and sends the car soaring to 60 mph in less than five seconds and past 150 mph with ease. But thanks to a redesigned body that is four times stiffer than that of its predecessor, the car doesn't creak, groan or shudder over bumps, and the longer wheelbase and roomier cabin combine to make it much more comfortable."

The completely redesigned cockpit makes the C5 Corvette more comfortable and user-friendly.

Milestones

1990 The ZR-1® gives the Corvette supercar status. Its quad-cam 32-valve V8 engine produces 375 bhp and can reach 60 mph in under five seconds.

The latest Corvette is the fifth generation car.

1995 ZR-1 production ends to make way for a more advanced Corvette, which will be launched the following year.

1997 A new generation of Corvette appears. It is slightly wider and taller, but the biggest difference is in the wheelbase, which is significantly longer and adds to the car's stability. The quad-cam V8 is not used because the all-alloy LS1 small block can produce 345 bhp without the complexity of multiple overhead valves and cams.

The Coupe was launched eight months before the Convertible.

1997 The Convertible appears eight months later. It is slightly heavier than the Coupe and has the same specification, but the Convertible's inferior aerodynamics reduces the top speed—but only by three mph.

UNDER THE SKIN

Super stiff

Because the Corvette has a fiberglass body, it has to have a separate steel frame. A new composite floor has been added, with a balsa wood layer sandwiched between two steel sheets, to stiffen the whole structure. The suspension features cast-alloy arms, a multi-link rear end for maximum control and monofilament leaf springs made of composite material which are lighter and more space efficient.

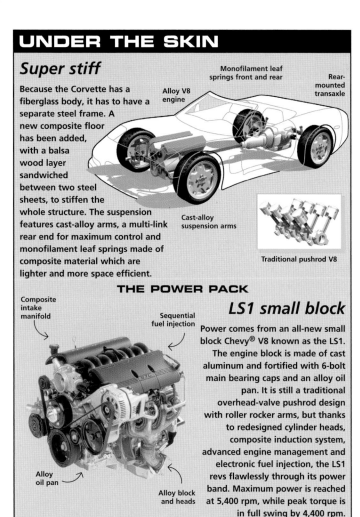

Monofilament leaf springs front and rear

Alloy V8 engine

Rear-mounted transaxle

Cast-alloy suspension arms

Traditional pushrod V8

THE POWER PACK

LS1 small block

Power comes from an all-new small block Chevy® V8 known as the LS1. The engine block is made of cast aluminum and fortified with 6-bolt main bearing caps and an alloy oil pan. It is still a traditional overhead-valve pushrod design with roller rocker arms, but thanks to redesigned cylinder heads, composite induction system, advanced engine management and electronic fuel injection, the LS1 revs flawlessly through its power band. Maximum power is reached at 5,400 rpm, while peak torque is in full swing by 4,400 rpm.

Composite intake manifold

Sequential fuel injection

Alloy oil pan

Alloy block and heads

Newcomer

The Convertible features a body-color tonneau cover which extends between the front seats, echoing the original Corvettes. But as in more modern cars, the easy-folding convertible top has a lightweight magnesium alloy frame.

The Corvette Convertible looks good with its top up or down.

It looks softer and less aggressive than the ZR-1, but don't be deceived. With its latest Corvette, Chevrolet has produced one of the best sports cars in the world.

Magnesium roof frame

The suspension is not the only area where Chevrolet has opted for alloy rather than steel. The convertible roof frame is made from light, yet very strong, magnesium.

Alloy V8

The 347-cubic inch engine is new to the Chevy V8 family. Some of its features include 6-bolt main bearing caps, a composite intake manifold and an electronic throttle.

Fiberglass body

A fiberglass body is as much a Corvette tradition as the front-mounted V8 engine and both are retained on the new Corvette.

Alloy suspension arms

The Corvette's suspension deserves to be exposed rather than hidden away, as the various control arms are made from forged alloy instead of heavier pressed steel.

Balsa wood floor

One of the many innovative features on the Corvette is the use of a balsa wood and steel sheet sandwich material for the floor. This is light, but extremely rigid, and makes the car feel more like a conventional steel monocoque design, despite the separate steel chassis.

Six-speed transmission

For the first time, the Corvette benefits from a rear transaxle. Standard equipment is a four-speed automatic, but buyers can order a six-speed manual with a very high overdrive ratio of 0.50:1.

Traction control

Working in tandem with the ABS, the Corvette has traction control. When wheelspin is detected, the system automatically reduces the power until traction is restored.

Rear transaxle

For even better packaging and weight distribution, the transmission is now mounted at the rear. This means that a slim torque tube is used, which makes the interior roomier.

Tire-pressure monitor

Like the previous Vette®, the C5 has a tire-pressure monitor which alerts the driver when the tire pressure is low. As a backup (and because there is no room for a spare) the tires can run flat for 200 miles.

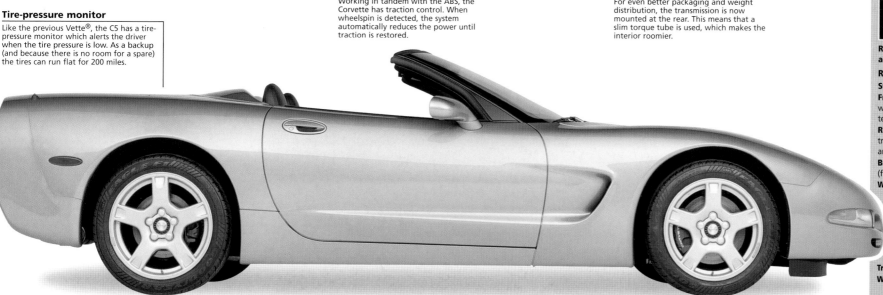

Specifications
1998 Chevrolet Corvette

ENGINE

Type: V8

Construction: Alloy block and heads

Valve gear: Two valves per cylinder operated by a single block-mounted camshaft

Bore and stroke: 3.9 in. x 3.62 in.

Displacement: 347 c.i.

Compression ratio: 10.1:1

Induction system: Electronic sequential fuel injection

Maximum power: 345 bhp at 5,400 rpm

Maximum torque: 350 lb-ft at 4,400 rpm

Top speed: 175 mph

0-60 mph: 4.7 sec.

TRANSMISSION

Four-speed automatic or optional six-speed manual, rear-mounted transaxle

BODY/CHASSIS

Separate steel chassis with fiberglass and composite two-door convertible body

SPECIAL FEATURES

The roof folds neatly under this stylish, body-colored cover.

Rear-mounted transaxle and lightweight alloy V8 give even weight distribution.

RUNNING GEAR

Steering: Rack-and-pinion

Front suspension: Double unequal length wishbones, transverse leaf spring, telescopic shocks and anti-roll bar

Rear suspension: Five-link system with transverse leaf spring, telescopic shocks and anti-roll bar

Brakes: Vented discs with ABS, 12.8 in. dia. (front), 12 in. dia. (rear)

Wheels: Magnesium, 17 in. x 8.5 in. (front), 18 in. x 9.5 in. (rear)

Tires: Goodyear F1 EMT 245/45 ZR17 (front), 275/40ZR18 (rear)

DIMENSIONS

Length: 179.7 in. **Width:** 73.6 in.

Height: 47.7 in. **Wheelbase:** 104.5 in.

Track: 62 in. (front), 62.0 in. (rear)

Weight: 3,220 lbs.

USA 1998-PRESENT

Chevrolet **CORVETTE**

In building the Hardtop, it was Chevrolet's intention to create a lightweight, budget Corvette designed for the hard-core driving enthusiast. Standard features in the new fixed-head model include a six-speed transmission, rigid Z51 suspension and a leaner, weight-reducing option list—all for $37,500.

"...less garb means more go."

"Jump inside. The interior may be stark but remember: less garb means more go. Now fire it up. If the Hardtop's engine sounds like the one in the Coupe, it's because it relies on the same blistering 345-bhp LS1 for power. Hope you like manual trans-missions, because a six speed is the only one the Hardtop comes with. Replacing the adjustable suspension system found on other C5s is the all-business, Z51 system. It, along with the Hardtop's rigid body, give a firm and reassuring ride."

Luxury items have been sacrificed in favor of performance, but the cabin is still attractive.

Milestones

1997 The fifth generation Corvette

is introduced. Known as the C5, it was designed to be the best Vette® yet. The designers started with a clean sheet of paper to create a state-of-the-art Corvette using cutting edge technology.

The long-running C4 Corvette finally bowed out in 1996. This is a 1990 coupe.

1997 Joining the C5 Corvette Coupe

later this year is the Convertible, complete with sophisticated features such as a magnesium roof frame. The latest Vette® was designed to be both a coupe and convertible from the beginning.

The C5 has state-of-the-art technology and a new sleek body.

1998 For the 1999 model year, the

Corvette range is extended with the introduction of the lighter and stiffer Hardtop model. It has a tauter suspension and its steering is improved with a revised Magna Steer II system.

UNDER THE SKIN

State of the art

The Hardtop's structure is the same as the other C5s in the Corvette family. It relies on a separate steel frame supporting the fiberglass body. The Corvette's suspension has been very advanced for some time now—alloy arms in the front and double-wishbones and multi-link rear, sprung by the Corvette's familiar composite transverse leaf springs. Improved rack-and-pinion steering and the rear-mounted, six-speed, manual transmission complete the picture.

Fixed hardtop
Rear-mounted transmission
Stiff Z51 suspension
Cutting edge LS1 V8

THE POWER PACK

Back to its roots

Relying on the same engine that powers the Coupe and Convertible models, the Hardtop has a 345 bhp LS1 under its sleek fiberglass hood. Though derived from Chevrolet's original small block V8, the new all-aluminum LS1 has no inter-changeable parts with its predecessor. Instead, it relies on 6-bolt main bearing caps, a sequential port fuel injection system and a composite intake manifold. Thanks to redesigned cylinder heads and an updated camshaft profile, the engine offers lots of torque all the way up to 4,400 rpm.

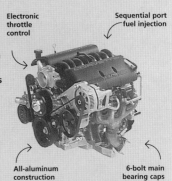

Electronic throttle control
Sequential port fuel injection
All-aluminum construction
6-bolt main bearing caps

Exclusive look

The Hardtop is bound to become a collector's item even if it is less expensive than the regular production Corvette. This is because it will be built in fewer numbers and will have exclusivity as well as superior performance and different looks on its side.

The stiffer structure of the hardtop produces improved feel and response.

You won't be seeing that many Hardtops on the road. Because of their aggressive nature and light option list, Chevrolet estimates that only 15 percent of Corvette buyers will select this high performance model.

High-tech LS1
The hardtop uses the same engine as the other C5 Corvettes—the all-alloy, 5.7-liter, small-block, LS1 V8. It has advanced features such as a composite intake manifold and electronic throttle control.

Stiff structure
Because of the new fixed-head design, the Hardtop is much more rigid than the Coupe or Convertible models. Squeaks, rattles and body flex are virtually eliminated—even on rural switchback roads. This stiff body really helps to get the most out of the taut but tolerable Z51 sport suspension.

Less interior embellishments
To save weight, the C5 Hardtop does without several amenities that are in the other C5 models. The dual-zone air conditioning and memory package for the powerseats, mirrors and radio are not available. Magna Steer II and power windows and locks are standard.

Brakes with bite
With massive 12.6 inch vented front discs and 11.8 vented rear discs, it's no wonder that the Hardtop comes to a halt from 60 mph in only 126 feet.

Standard six-speed
Because the Hardtop is designed for aggressive driving enthusiasts, you will not find 'automatic transmission' on the option list—this car is only available with a sure-shifting six speed. Like other C5s, it's mounted to the rear suspension which results in moderate understeer.

Roll control
Fitted with Goodyear Eagle F1 tires and the Z51 suspension package (which consists of stiffer springs, meatier anti-roll bars and revalved shocks), the Hardtop remains composed up to .90gs of lateral acceleration through the skidpad.

Specifications

1999 Chevrolet Corvette Hardtop

ENGINE

Type: V8

Construction: Alloy block and heads

Valve gear: Two valves per cylinder operated by a single camshaft

Bore and stroke: 3.90 in. x 3.62 in.

Displacement: 5.7 liter

Compression ratio: 10.1:1

Induction system: Electronic sequential fuel injection

Maximum power: 345 bhp at 5,600 rpm

Maximum torque: 350 lb-ft at 4,400 rpm

Top speed: 168 mph

0-60 mph: 5.3 sec.

TRANSMISSION

Six-speed manual

BODY/CHASSIS

Separate steel chassis frame with fiberglass two-door body

SPECIAL FEATURES

Most of the weight saving (around 70 lbs.) comes from the fiberglass hardtop.

All C5 Corvettes come standard with daytime running lights.

RUNNING GEAR

Steering: Power-assisted rack-and-pinion

Front suspension: Composite transverse monoleaf spring, shocks and anti-roll bar

Rear suspension: Toe-control link, transverse composite monoleaf spring, shocks and anti-roll bar

Brakes: 12.6-in. vented front discs, 11.8-in. vented rear discs

Wheels: Alloy, 17 x 8.5 in. (front), 18 x 9.5 in. (rear)

Tires: Goodyear Eagle F1 245/45 ZR17 (front), 275/40 ZR18 (rear)

DIMENSIONS

Length: 179.1 in. **Width:** 73.6 in.

Height: 47.9 in. **Wheelbase:** 104.5 in.

Track: 62.0 in. (front), 62.1 in. (rear)

Weight: 3,245 lbs.

Chevrolet **NOMAD**

One of the most stylish wagons of all time, the 1955-1957 Chevrolet Nomads are a favorite with both collectors and customizers. The owner of this car has taken a traditional approach when customizing his 1956 Nomad.

"...supercharged performance."

"With its bucket seats and thick-rimmed steering wheel, this 1956 Nomad has a sporty edge. Push down on the throttle and feel its supercharged performance that can only come from a 1970 Corvette® small-block V8 with a B&M blower. It rockets the car to 60 mph in less than six seconds. No expense has been spared underneath either, and the 1986 Corvette suspension enables this car to corner much better than it did stock.

The dashboard is original, but the Connolly leather bucket seats have been added and give the car a more upmarket feel.

Milestones

1955 Chevrolet announces its new models, totally restyled and with magnificent new V8 engines. Top of the range is the distinctive Nomad, combining hardtop styling with station wagon practicality.

Designed by Carl Renner, the Nomad first appeared in 1955.

1956 Performance is improved with up to 265 bhp available from the small-block V8. Nomads, like the rest of the line, adopt busier styling.

The Nomad was subtly restyled for the 1956 model year.

1957 The two-door Nomad is again listed and receives another, and arguably more attractive, facelift. A Ramjet mechanical fuel injection system is available with the 283 V8 giving up to 283 bhp. Due to its high cost, its two-door styling and several seal problems, sales are moderate. Chevrolet decides to drop the model for its 1958 model line-up.

UNDER THE SKIN

Body-on-the-frame construction

Lowered Corvette suspension

Custom small-block V8

Totally unique

Although it retains the X-braced chassis frame of the original 1956 Chevrolet, a Corvette front subframe and rear end have been grafted on. The suspension is all-independent with plastic transverse leaf springs front and rear, and four-wheel disc brakes to help improve stopping power.

THE POWER PACK

Old school mill

Many hot rodders use a small-block Chevy® to power their cars. The owner of this Nomad has installed a 1970-vintage Corvette LT-1®, (similar to the one shown here) and had it overbored to 358-cubic inches. The reciprocating assembly has been balanced, while the rest of the engine features ported heads, stainless-steel valves, roller-rocker arms, a forged steel crankshaft and a B&M supercharger.

Two valves per cylinder

Single camshaft

Cast-iron construction

Tuned for maximum torque

The Cormad

Although it looks like a mild custom, this Nomad has been drastically modified. Underneath is a 1986 Corvette front and rear suspension, complete with brakes and shocks. With a reworked LT-1 engine, this car will surprise many drivers on the road.

With their classic lines, Shoebox-Chevy Nomads are collector's favorites.

This Shoebox-Chevy Nomad combines style with performance. Using a Corvette powerplant and running gear, this 1956 Nomad can surprise many newer performance cars.

Corvette front end

The front suspension employs a 1986 Corvette subframe. Not only does it lower the car, giving it a ground-hugging stance, but it greatly improves the car's handling.

Modern paint

The body has been resprayed in two-tone Corvette dark red metallic and tan pearl.

Modified transmission

A 1976 Turbo 400 automatic transmission backs up the sinister LT1 engine. To extract maximum power from the engine, it has a high-stall torque converter.

Custom wheels

No street machine would be complete without aftermarket wheels. This Nomad is fitted with a set of custom chromed 16-inch wheels.

Clean lines

Even in 1956, the Nomad was a fairly clean-looking car. The two-tone paintwork and chrome spears accentuate the classic lines of this Chevrolet.

Small-block power

For massive performance, this ubiquitous 1970 LT-1 small-block V8 has been bored over .060-inch in and features a forged-steel crank, ported and polished cylinder heads, roller rocker arms plus a B&M supercharger and a Holley carburetor.

Specifications

1956 Chevrolet Nomad

ENGINE

Type: V8

Construction: Cast-iron block and heads

Valve gear: Two valves per cylinder operated by pushrods and rockers

Bore and stroke: 4.06 in. x 3.48 in.

Displacement: 358 c.i.

Compression ratio: 10.5:1

Induction system: B&M supercharger and Holley four-barrel carburetor

Maximum power: 400 bhp at 4,800 rpm

Maximum torque: 320 lb-ft at 3,000 rpm

Top speed: 131 mph

0-60 mph: 5.5 sec.

TRANSMISSION

1976 Turbo HydraMatic 400 with a high-stall torque converter

BODY/CHASSIS

Separate two-door station wagon steel body on X-braced steel frame and Corvette front subframe.

SPECIAL FEATURES

The fuel cap is neatly hidden behind the tail light.

With the rear seat folded down, luggage space is cavernous.

RUNNING GEAR

Steering: Recirculating ball

Front suspension: Double wishbones with plastic transverse leaf spring and shocks

Rear suspension: Trailing arms with plastic transverse leaf spring and shocks

Brakes: Discs (front and rear)

Wheels: Custom Boyds, 15-in. dia.

Tires: Goodyear P22560VR15

DIMENSIONS

Length: 196.7 in.   **Width:** 77.2 in.

Height: 53 in.   **Wheelbase:** 115 in.

Track: 59.5 in. (front), 55.8 in. (rear)

Weight: 3,352 lbs.

Chevrolet **BEL AIR**

Think of America in the 1950s and an image of a 1957 Chevy® will appear, parked outside a period diner. This, the most popular of the so-called classic 'Shoebox-Chevys,' is also a favorite basis for a hot rod.

"...apple pie dynamite."

"This is what American hot-rodding is all about: a classic '57 Chevy® with some serious get-up-and-go. Think of it as apple pie with a stick of dynamite baked right in. Tap the throttle and the whole car rocks with the engine's inertia. Off the line, this car could beat almost any modern production car. Once the huge Mickey Thompson racing rear tires have stopped spinning, the violent acceleration shoves you back into your seat as you hang, white-knuckled, onto the tiny steering wheel."

Flame theme is apparent inside the car, with the graphic appearing on the steering wheel, interior trim and upholstery.

Milestones

1955 Chevrolet releases its new modern line of cars, the 150, 210 and Bel Air series. It is the first sedan to use the new 265-cubic inch V8 small-block engine. Harley Earl's design team matches the engine to well-balanced and modern styling. Its box-styling and clean looks give it the name 'shoebox Chevy.'

The 1957 Bel Air convertible was the top of the line.

1956 The car receives a $40 million restyle for the new model year. Power is boosted on both six- and eight-cylinder models. The top spec V8 with Power-Pak produces 225 bhp.

The 150-series models are identifiable by the 1955-styled side trim.

1957 Another restyle produces the classic 1950s American sedan. The 1957 model uses a larger 283-cubic inch version of the small-block engine with fuel injection for 283 bhp.

1990s By this time, the 1955-57 'shoebox-Chevys' have become true classics in standard and hot-rod forms.

UNDER THE SKIN

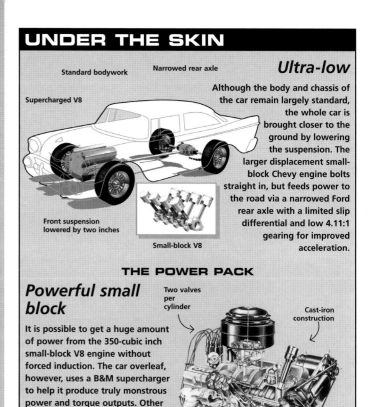

Ultra-low

Although the body and chassis of the car remain largely standard, the whole car is brought closer to the ground by lowering the suspension. The larger displacement small-block Chevy engine bolts straight in, but feeds power to the road via a narrowed Ford rear axle with a limited slip differential and low 4.11:1 gearing for improved acceleration.

Standard bodywork

Narrowed rear axle

Supercharged V8

Front suspension lowered by two inches

Small-block V8

THE POWER PACK

Powerful small block

It is possible to get a huge amount of power from the 350-cubic inch small-block V8 engine without forced induction. The car overleaf, however, uses a B&M supercharger to help it produce truly monstrous power and torque outputs. Other modifications include custom-fabricated tubular exhaust headers and electronic exhaust cut-outs. The rest of the exhaust system uses 2.5-inch diameter tubing and Mac mufflers to create a very free-flowing system.

Two valves per cylinder

Cast-iron construction

Single block-mounted camshaft

Custom exhaust

Boyd's best

Master hot-rod builder Boyd Coddington created the Boydair as a showcase for his hot-rod building company. It has a custom-made chassis clothed in modified 1957 Chevy panels. It's centered around the cowl and windshield of a 1959 Chevrolet Impala®. The engine and running gear are from a 1997 Corvette®.

Ultra-low 'Boydair' uses modern Corvette mechanicals.

Huge tires, an immaculate custom paint job, a wild interior, low aggressive stance and a powerful blown V8 engine installed in a classic American car—all the ingredients of a great hot rod.

Chromework
Although this car has been built as a high-performance vehicle, little has been done to reduce its weight. Even the heavy chrome bumpers are retained.

Blown engine
A B&M supercharger gives a huge boost to the power and torque outputs of this car's 350-cubic inch small-block Chevy V8 engine.

Custom interior
It looks just as good inside. The flame motif is carried through to the interior and even appears on the headlining and steering wheel.

Alloy wheels
The popular American Racing Torq-Thrust five-spoke wheels are used. They are similar in style to racing wheels often used in the 1960s.

Lowered suspension
To lower the lines of the car and give it that road-hugging stance, the suspension has been lowered. Two-inch drop spindles and chopped coil springs lower the front, while custom semi-elliptic leaf springs, relocated on the chassis, ease down the rear end.

Huge rear tires
The Mickey Thompson tires added to the rear of the car are designed to give maximum traction off the line.

Standard bodywork
Apart from the removal of some badges, the bodywork remains largely as standard. The custom look is achieved with a fantastic paint job, wide wheels and lowered suspension.

Narrowed rear axle
To transmit the power to the road, a narrowed Ford axle is used with a Positraction limited slip differential. The axle is narrowed to keep the huge rear tires within the standard bodywork.

Smoothed hood and trunk
Both the hood and rear deck have been smoothed off and stripped of badges to give the car a much cleaner look.

Specifications
1957 Modified Chevrolet Bel Air

ENGINE

Type: V8

Construction: Cast-iron block and heads

Valve gear: Single block-mounted camshaft operating two valves per cylinder via pushrods

Bore and stroke: 4 in. x 3.5 in.

Displacement: 350 c.i.

Compression ratio: 8.5:1

Induction system: B&M 4-71 mechanical supercharger with Holley four-barrel carb

Maximum power: 420 bhp at 5,400 rpm

Maximum torque: 435 lb-ft at 2,500 rpm

Top speed: 147 mph

0-60 mph: 3.9 sec.

TRANSMISSION

350 Turbo automatic

BODY/CHASSIS

Standard 1957 Bel Air steel body with smoothed hood and rear deck on steel perimeter chassis

SPECIAL FEATURES

Above: To achieve its enormous power output, the hot 350-cubic inch V8 uses a B&M supercharger. *Left:* This car features outstanding chromework. The hidden gas filler cap is a typical feature for a car of the '50s.

RUNNING GEAR

Steering: Power-assisted recirculating ball

Front suspension: Fabricated tubular wishbones, 2-in. drop spindles, chopped coil springs, telescopic shock absorbers

Rear suspension: Custom semi-elliptic leaf springs, lowering blocks, traction bars and air shock absorbers

Brakes: Discs (front and rear)

Wheels: American Racing Torq-Thrust D, 7.5 in. x 15 in. (front), 11 in. x 15 in. (rear)

Tires: BF Goodrich 205/60-15 (front), Mickey Thompson Sportsman I N50/15 (rear)

DIMENSIONS

Length: 200 in.   **Width:** 73.9 in.

Height: 46.9 in.   **Wheelbase:** 115 in.

Track: 58 in. (front), 58.8 in. (rear)

Weight: 3,197 lbs.

Chevrolet **BEL AIR 409**

As the horsepower wars began to heat up in the early 1960s, Chevrolet unleashed its hot 409-cubic inch engine, primarily aimed at drag racers. With it, the lightweight Bel Airs cleaned up, both on the track and on the street.

"...legendary racing status."

"This is the quintessential early-1960s factory hot rod in its purest form. Take your place behind the wheel—everything about the car is plain and boring, but once the key is turned, your attitude changes. Grab the shifter and release the clutch. With 420 lb-ft of torque, the rear tires will chirp in every gear. Although strong at low speed, give the 409 a little gas and it really pulls hard. It is at this point you realize why the 409 has achieved such legendary racing status."

A column-mounted tach and cue-ball shifter are the only clues to performance inside.

Milestones

1961 Midway through the year, Chevrolet unleashes its 409-cubic inch V8, as a larger, more powerful version of the 348. There is also a Super Sport™ option on the Impala™ series, but by the end of the year, only 142 cars are fitted with the 409.

The 409 debuted in 1961 along with the Impala Super Sport.

1962 In competition, Chevy 409s do exceedingly well. In the NHRA's Stock Eliminator class, Hayden Proffitt sets a class record at the Nationals at Indy with a 12.83-second ET at 113.92 mph. He also took the Super Stock championship this year.

Only 2,828 Chevy 409s were built in its last year, 1965.

1963 Chevrolet offers the Z-11. It's a bored and stroked version of the 409. This elusive race engine displaces 427 cubic inches and is rated at 430 bhp.

UNDER THE SKIN

Steel and alloy

Separate-perimeter steel chassis

Standard 3.68:1 rear axle ratio

Sintered metallic brake linings

Big-block V8

For 1961, full-size Chevrolets had shorter and narrower bodies. The chassis was still a separate steel structure, and suspension was by unequal-length wishbones with coil springs at the front and a live axle with coils at the rear. Cars ordered with the 409 required a mandatory manual transmission—either a three or four speed. Late in 1962, a small number of lightweight cars with aluminum front sheet metal were built.

THE POWER PACK

Top flight 409

Having its parentage in the 348 W-series V8, the 409 has few interchangeable parts with the former. It does, however, share the same block, W-shaped cylinder heads and wedge-shaped combustion chambers. The 409's wedge originated from the top of the block, cut at a 74-degree angle to the cylinder walls. This also required high-compression heads and pistons (11.25:1), making the 409 a handful for the average driver on the street and very difficult to tune. For 1962, a revised cam and 11.0:1 compression heads boosted power from 360 to 380 bhp, and a dual-quad intake resulted in 409 bhp.

Bold and bubbly

With just 15,019 built, the 409-equipped Chevy is rare today. Aesthetically, the lightweight 1962 Bel Air bubble-top models are perhaps better looking than the Impalas. In fact, they were the best choice for drag racing and won that year's NHRA S/S championship.

Bel Air 409s were strong performers on the street and unbeatable at the strip.

When the Beach Boys sang about it, the 1962 Chevy 409 gained a reputation few other engines or cars possessed. But as the competition found out, this reputation was entirely justified.

W-series V8
It may have been derived from a 348 truck engine, but the solid-lifter 409 is a true high-performance motor. In 1962, it was rated at 380 bhp with a four-barrel carburetor, or 409 bhp with two four barrels—achieving the magical one horsepower per cubic inch.

Separate chassis
Like most full-size cars of the time, 1962 Chevrolets ride on a separate chassis. Suspension is fairly standard for the day—wishbones at the front and a live axle at the rear. Big GM cars differed from rivals by having rear coil springs for a smoother ride.

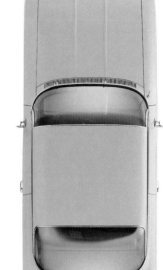

Lightweight panels
Late in 1962, Chevrolet built 12 Chevy 409s with lightweight aluminum front sheet metal aimed purely at drag racers. These parts could also be ordered over the counter and were fitted to some steel-bodied cars.

Hardtop bodystyle
Full-size Chevrolets were fitted with shorter and narrower bodies for 1961 but retained the 119-inch wheelbase separate chassis. In 1962, the Impala hardtop coupe adopted a more formal roofline, leaving the Bel Air as the sole bubble-top coupe. The 409 could be ordered in any bodystyle, but the majority were fitted in coupes.

Optional rear gearing
A manual transmission was mandatory with the 409, and the standard rear axle ratio was 3.68:1. Dealers could install 4.10:1 or 4.56:1 cogs for better low-end launches.

Spartan interior
Most buyers who ordered 409s were interested only in speed, and thus many Bel Airs had spartan interiors. This one has a meager front bench seat, manual windows and no heater or radio. A column-mounted tachometer was standard, however.

Specifications

1962 Chevrolet Bel Air 409

ENGINE

Type: V8

Construction: Cast-iron block and heads

Valve gear: Two valves per cylinder operated by a single block-mounted camshaft with pushrods and rockers

Bore and stroke: 4.31 in. x 3.50 in.

Displacement: 409 c.i.

Compression ratio: 11.25:1

Induction system: Carter AFB four-barrel downdraft carburetor

Maximum power: 380 bhp at 6,000 rpm

Maximum torque: 420 lb-ft at 3,200 rpm

Top speed: 115 mph

0-60 mph: 7.3 sec.

TRANSMISSION

Four-speed manual

BODY/CHASSIS

Separate steel chassis with two-door hardtop body

SPECIAL FEATURES

The 409 features a 7,000-rpm, column-mounted tachometer.

1962 was the second and last year for the bubble-top roof.

RUNNING GEAR

Steering: Recirculating ball

Front suspension: Unequal-length A-arms with coil springs, telescopic shock absorbers and anti-roll bar

Rear suspension: Live rear axle with coil springs and telescopic shock absorbers

Brakes: Drums (front and rear)

Wheels: Pressed steel, 15-in. dia.

Tires: 8.00 x 14

DIMENSIONS

Length: 209.6 in. **Width:** 84.2 in.

Height: 69.4 in. **Wheelbase:** 119.0 in.

Track: 60.3 in. (front), 59.3 in. (rear)

Weight: 3,480 lbs.

Chevrolet **3100 STEPSIDE**

Since the day they were introduced, the 1955-1957 Chevy® 3100 series trucks have always been hugely popular. They make great custom haulers, too, as witnessed by the thousands of them on the roads.

"...stylish and dependable."

"The door swings on vault-like hinges and closes with reassuring firmness. It may look stylish, but this truck is still dependable to the core. The big bench seat takes you back to the 1950s, but the digital instruments are right up to date. A torquey small-block under the hood moves you along with a constant flow of power from its tri-power carburetors. The ride is fairly good for an old truck and modern tires keep it in line even on the most slippery roads."

By 1957, Chevy pickups were becoming more and more carlike, inside and out.

Milestones

1955 In March, Chevrolet unveils a new line of light-duty trucks. These are offered with a ½- to 1-ton carrying capacity. Big news is a new overhead-valve V8 engine and the 3100 Cameo™, a deluxe ½-ton pickup with a long box, slab-sided bed and deluxe trim. Only 5,219 of these are built.

The previous Bullnose 3100 lasted from 1948 until 1954.

1956 Styling is virtually unchanged this year save for a new hood ornament, but engine tweaks result in an extra 17 bhp on the standard six, and power is up to 205 bhp from the four-barrel V8.

Most expensive of the 3100 series in 1957 was the Cameo.

1957 A flatter hood with twin bullets and a new grill with a center loop mark the major changes. Four-wheel drive Chevrolet pickups are offered for the first time.

UNDER THE SKIN

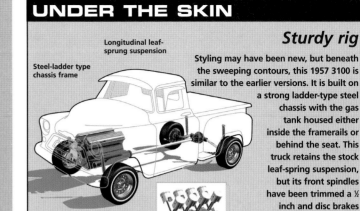

Longitudinal leaf-sprung suspension

Steel-ladder type chassis frame

Power front disc brakes

Small-block V8

Sturdy rig

Styling may have been new, but beneath the sweeping contours, this 1957 3100 is similar to the earlier versions. It is built on a strong ladder-type steel chassis with the gas tank housed either inside the framerails or behind the seat. This truck retains the stock leaf-spring suspension, but its front spindles have been trimmed a ½ inch and disc brakes pirated from a Chevy II™ Nova™. At the rear is a 10-bolt rear axle with 3.27:1 gearing.

THE POWER PACK

Sports car power

In 1955, Chevrolet released its infamous 265-cubic inch, small-block V8. This small block would vary from size to size, but the basic block has been used for more than five decades now. This 1957 3100 came from the factory with V8 power, but where the original 165-bhp mill once sat, there is now a 1970 Corvette® 350. It has been mildly tweaked with a free-flowing aluminum intake and three Rochester two-barrel carburetors, a late-model MSD ignition system and a heavy-duty alternator. It currently produces a streetwise 330 bhp at 5,200 rpm and a strong 360 lb-ft of torque. This makes the truck easy to drive, but also incredibly quick off the line.

Choice Chevy

Some of the most stylish pickups built during the mid-1950s are the the 3100 series. They are collectors' and enthusiasts' favorites today. Many have been turned into modified drivers that are high on looks, performance and practicality, too.

A 1957 hot-rodded Stepside is a popular choice for those who modify trucks.

Classic styling combined with detailed yet subtle touches makes this 3100 Series a real head-turner on the street. With some serious power under the hood, this truck is a performer as well as a first-rate looker.

Class designation
In 1957, Chevrolet light-duty trucks were offered in a variety of forms depending on their carrying capacity. The smallest (3100) was certified for 5,000 lbs. GVW while bigger 3442/3542 and 3742 series trucks could haul up to 7000 lbs. With its varnished wood bed, this truck is more for showing than hauling.

Mighty Mouse engine
Nicknamed the Mouse, the small-block Chevy V8's abundance and simplicity made it the first choice of power for hot-rodders. This 1957 truck has a 350-cubic inch version from 1970.

Old and new interior
Inside this Chevy is a mixture of both old and new. A traditional-style bench seat is retained, as are the stock door panels and dash. A leather-wrapped, thick-rimmed steering wheel and digital gauges are modern touches.

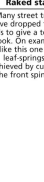

Raked stance
Many street trucks have dropped front ends to give a tough look. On examples like this one with leaf-springs, it is achieved by cutting the front spindles.

Turbo 350 automatic
As one of the best automatic transmissions ever built, the TH350 was a mainstay of GM cars and trucks during the 1970s and is one of the most reliable units ever made.

Stepside bed
While the classy Cameo got a slab-sided bed with unique taillights and trim, other 3100s stuck with the traditional, for the time, stepside bed. Custom truck builders today tend to prefer the look of the nostalgic stepside bed.

Car-derived styling
With trucks beginning to move into the personal transportation sector during the 1950s, the 1955-1957 3100 trucks took many cues from regular passenger cars, including the swept-forward fenders and wraparound windshield.

Chrome trim
Back in the 1980s, body color and blackout trim were all the rage, though today, chrome has made a comeback on the custom scene. Chromed C-pillars, floor bed brackets, and side steps add to this truck's appeal.

1957 Chevrolet 3100 Stepside

ENGINE
Type: V8
Construction: Cast-iron block and heads
Valve gear: Two valves per cylinder operated by a single centrally-mounted camshaft via pushrods and rockers
Bore and stroke: 4.00 in. x 3.48 in.
Displacement: 350 c.i.
Compression ratio: 10.25:1
Induction system: Three Rochester two-barrel carburetors
Maximum power: 330 bhp at 5,200 rpm
Maximum torque: 360 lb-ft at 3,400 rpm
Top speed: 115 mph
0-60 mph: 7.2 sec.

TRANSMISSION
GM TH350 three-speed automatic

BODY/CHASSIS
Steel ladder-type chassis with steel cab and pickup bed

SPECIAL FEATURES

1957 Chevy trucks have a unique one-year-only, loop-style grill.

Chromed Chevrolet lettering on the tailgate adds a touch of class.

RUNNING GEAR
Steering: Recirculating ball
Front suspension: Beam axle, with semi-elliptic leaf springs and telescopic shock absorbers
Rear suspension: Live axle, with semi-elliptic leaf springs and telescopic shock absorbers
Brakes: Discs (front), drums (rear)
Wheels: Centerline 7 x 14 in.
Tires: BF Goodrich radial 205/75/R14

DIMENSIONS
Length: 185.7 in.	**Width:** 69.6 in.
Height: 75.5 in.	**Wheelbase:** 114.0 in.
Track: 57.3 in. (front), 56.4 in. (rear)	
Weight: 3,230 lbs.	

Chevrolet **IMPALA**

One of the most popular cars to turn into a low rider is the Chevrolet Impala. It's not built for all-out power, nor does it handle like a fine Italian sports car. Lowriders were simply made to cruise with class.

"...built to turn heads"

"Despite its long and low appearance, this beautiful Impala drives pretty much as it did when it left the factory in 1959. The 315-bhp engine really makes the heavy car move at indecent speeds when you put your foot down. But it has been built to turn heads, not to break the land speed record. Its ground-hugging stance means that it can bottom-out on really rough surfaces, and so it's best to sit back, take it easy and cruise."

Wide bench seats allow the Impala to carry up to six people in total comfort.

Milestones

1958 Chevrolet introduces the Impala name, as the top model in the Bel Air line. The 348-cubic inch big-block V8 is launched.

The earlier 1955-1957 shoebox-Chevys had much more rounded styling. This is a 1957 Nomad.

1959 The Impala becomes a model in its own right. Despite somewhat wild styling, it is well received by the motoring press. There are three body styles: a four-door sedan, a two-door coupe, and a convertible coupe.

The new-for-1959 El Camino™ pick-up had a great deal in common with the Impala.

1960 A subtle restyle is undertaken for the 1960 model range. The new car has a more conventional front end without the previous year's headlight 'eyebrows'. The distinctive 'cat's eye' tail lights are replaced by a trio of more conventional round lights. The top-spec 348-cubic inch engine now produce 315 bhp.

UNDER THE SKIN

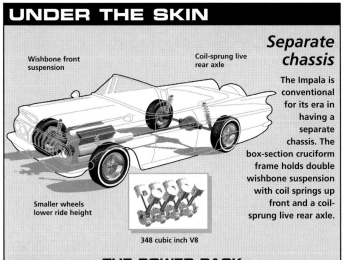

Wishbone front suspension

Coil-sprung live rear axle

Separate chassis

The Impala is conventional for its era in having a separate chassis. The box-section cruciform frame holds double wishbone suspension with coil springs up front and a coil-sprung live rear axle.

Smaller wheels lower ride height

348 cubic inch V8

THE POWER PACK

Stock big block

The 1959 Impala was offered with a choice of engines, from a 236 cubic inch straight-six producing 135 bhp, right up to a 315-bhp, 348 cubic inch V8. The V8 was typical for the time, being a simple design with a single central camshaft operating two valves per cylinder via pushrods and rockers. Top-spec V8s had three two-barrel Rochester carburetors, while the less powerful engines made do with a single four-barrel unit. This car has a stock V8 with three two-barrel carburetors.

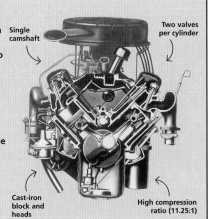

Single camshaft

Two valves per cylinder

Cast-iron block and heads

High compression ratio (11.25:1)

Long and low

The 1959 Impala was designed to look as long and low as possible. Today, this makes it a popular choice for those who want to build a lowrider. By bringing the car closer to the ground, the Impala's low lines are accentuated even further.

The sleek and elegant Impala was a big car even by 1959 standards.

Top of the 1959 Chevrolet range, the Impala had it all—wild styling, luxury fittings, and a huge amount of horsepower. It makes an ideal choice for a stylish custom lowrider.

Big-block engine
Introduced in 1958, the 348-cubic inch V8 is capable of producing astounding power outputs. The top 1959 engine produces 315 bhp.

Huge trunk
The 1959 Impala has one of the biggest trunks ever made by Chevrolet. The wheelbase was increased 3.9 inchbetween 1956 and 1959.

Wild style
The 1959 Impala must rate as the wildest-looking Chevrolet ever even rivaling the overtly-stylized 1959 Cadillac. Chevrolet tamed the car's appearance for 1960 with revised front and rear styling.

Ground-hugging stance
This Impala's low-slung appearance has been achieved without modifying the suspension. The owner has simply fitted 13-inch wheels instead of the stock 14-inch rims. The factory spring length remains unaltered.

Factory custom
Although this car looks highly customized, all the modifications (except for the wheels) were factory options. A buyer could have ordered an Impala like this in 1959, but few customers specified this many options. It has side skirts, spot lights, a continental kit, bumper guards, remote trunk release, cruise control, air-conditioning, and power-assisted everything.

Coil-sprung rear axle
The Impala has a simple rear suspension set-up. The live rear axle is coil-sprung with telescopic shocks. In order to prevent wheel hop, Chevrolet engineers added trailing arms, a Panhard rod, and a central torque reaction arm to locate the rear axle.

Continental kit
The continental kit was a highly desirable option on late-1950s cars. Although it was fitted mainly for aesthetic appeal, it does have a practical use. By mounting the spare wheel behind the rear bumper, more trunk space is available for luggage.

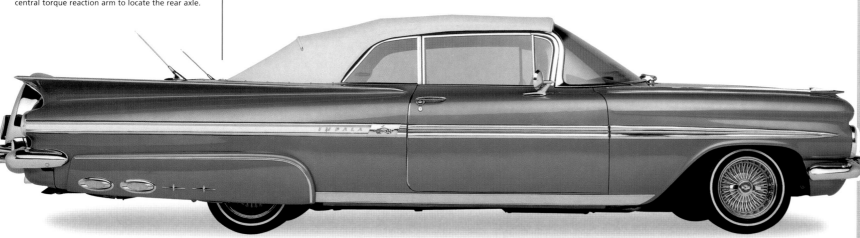

Specifications

1959 Chevrolet Impala

ENGINE

Type: V8

Construction: Cast-iron block and heads

Valve gear: Two valves per cylinder operated by a single central camshaft

Bore and stroke: 4.133 in. x 3.26 in.

Displacement: 348 c.i.

Compression ratio: 11.25:1

Induction system: Three two-barrel Rochester carburetors

Maximum power: 315 bhp at 5,600 rpm

Maximum torque: 357 lb-ft at 3,600 rpm

Top speed: 134 mph

0-60 mph: 9.0 sec.

TRANSMISSION

Optional three- or four-speed manual or two-speed automatic

BODY/CHASSIS

Steel box-section cruciform chassis with two-door convertible body

SPECIAL FEATURES

These wide, low-profile chrome wire wheels are particularly eye-catching.

The continental kit looks smart, but it adds more than 11 inches to the car's overall length.

RUNNING GEAR

Steering: Recirculating ball

Front suspension: Double wishbones with coil springs and telescopic shocks

Rear suspension: Live axle with coil springs and telescopic shocks

Brakes: Four-wheel drums

Wheels: Wire wheels, 13-in. dia.

Tires: 155/80 R14

DIMENSIONS

Length: 223.4 in.   **Width:** 80 in.

Height: 57 in.   **Wheelbase:** 119 in.

Track: 60.2 in. (front), 59.5 in. (rear)

Weight: 3,649 lbs.

Chevrolet **IMPALA SS427**

When Chevrolet put the engine used in the Corvette® in very nearly the same tune into the big Impala SS™, the car's sheer size meant the result wasn't quite as dramatic. It did, however, produce a high-speed cruiser with plenty of power to spare.

"...full-size muscle monster."

"For some, bigger is better, and this is certainly true of the SS 427. The front bucket seats are huge. The monster 427-cubic inch V8 has enough torque to move mountains and motivates the tremendous bulk of the Impala down the road at maximum velocity. It would be natural to think that the SS 427 would plow through corners, but a wide track and well-located rear end ensure this is one of the better behaved full-size muscle monsters of the late 1960s.

The Impala SS has full instrumentation and tremendous interior space.

Milestones

1965 Impalas are redesigned with smoother, more modern contours and a new perimeter chassis, plus revised suspension. The Impala SS returns with available bucket seats and a new optional Mark IV 396-cubic inch V8 engine. The 409 will be dropped at the end of the year.

The last year for the boxy, square Impala SS was 1964.

1966 Externally, few changes mark this year's full-size Chevys®. The big news is under the hood. The 396 engine is joined by a larger 427-cubic inch unit available in 390-bhp and 425-bhp versions.

1965 Impala SS models came standard with an in-line six.

1967 A new fastback roof is grafted to the Impala Sport Coupe.

1969 Having reverted to an option package in 1968, the Impala SS is retired this year.

UNDER THE SKIN

Strong frame

Body-on-frame construction

Power front disc brakes

Live rear axle

For the 1965 model year, Chevrolet introduced a new perimeter chassis frame for the Impala, plus revised the suspension with a wider front and rear track which made the car more stable during high-speed cornering. The frame had to be strong so that the pillarless two-door coupe bodies of the SS versions could be fitted without flexing. The faster SS versions had superior rear axle location with four, rather than three, links.

Big-block V8

THE POWER PACK

The fat rat

In 1966, Chevrolet launched its 427, an enlarged version of the 396-cubic inch V8 which was more common to find in a Corvette than a full-size car. The following year, it was available in full-size cars. The standard 427 engine returned for 1968 with a power output of 385 bhp and a four-barrel carburetor in full-size cars (GM outlawed multi-carb setups in 1967 on all models but the Corvette). The engine continued until 1969, by which time it thumped out 390 bhp.

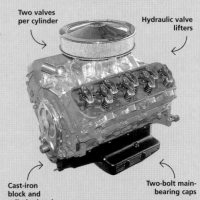

Two valves per cylinder

Hydraulic valve lifters

Cast-iron block and cylinder heads

Two-bolt main-bearing caps

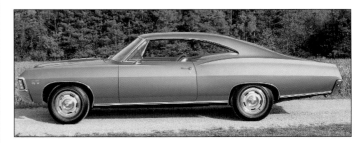

Milestone SS

1967 was a milestone for the SS Impala. The Impala was reskinned with larger, swoopier sheet metal. It was also the first and last year that the SS 427 was a model in its own right. Today, these cars make an interesting alternative to Chevelles and Camaros.

The 1967 Impala SS with fastback styling and the 427 is the one to go for.

'For the man who'd buy a sports car if it had this much room' was how Chevrolet marketed the Impala SS 427. It was a fine machine, with a huge torquey V8, seating for five and a well-engineered suspension.

V8 engine

The fastest of all the Impalas, the SS 427 is powered by the same short-stroke cast-iron 427-cubic inch engine found in the Corvette. Despite its size, it is happy to rev and produces its maximum power at 5,200 rpm with maximum torque coming in at 3,400 rpm. In its highest state of tune, Chevrolet claimed 385 bhp for the Impala engine.

Front parking lights

The ends of the front fenders contain what look like turn signals. In fact, they are just parking lights, with the turn signals located in the lower grill assembly.

Four transmissions

The big V8s could be matched to a variety of transmissions: a three- or four-speed heavy-duty manual; Powerglide; or strong TurboHydramatic 400 three-speed automatic.

Front disc brakes

Front disc brakes are a necessity for the faster SS models with their high performance and weight. For the SS, Chevrolet made front discs an option, which came with different wheels for $121.15.

Heavy-duty suspension

The best-handling SS Impalas use the optional heavy-duty F41 suspension with its stiffer springs and shocks. At just $31.60, it was a very small price to pay for the extra handling security.

Fastback style

The fastback style was very fashionable in the 1960s and helped give a sporty look to very large cars. The size of cars like the Impala and the Ford Galaxie meant they could have a long sloping rear roof line and still have room for rear passengers.

Pillarless construction

Chevrolet gave the Impala its sleek look by the use of two styling features. As well as the long, sloping rear fastback, the car has pillarless construction. This accentuates the side window glass area and makes it appear bigger than it really is.

Specifications

1968 Chevrolet Impala SS 427

ENGINE

Type: V8

Construction: Cast-iron block and heads

Valve gear: Two valves per cylinder operated by a single camshaft with pushrods and rockers

Bore and stroke: 4.25 in. x 3.76 in.

Displacement: 427 c.i.

Compression ratio: 10.3:1

Induction system: Single four-barrel carburetor

Maximum power: 385 bhp at 5,200 rpm

Maximum torque: 460 lb-ft at 3,400 rpm

Top speed: 125 mph

0-60 mph: 8.4 sec.

TRANSMISSION

M21 four-speed manual

BODY/CHASSIS

Box-section perimeter chassis with two-door fastback hardtop body

SPECIAL FEATURES

In 1968, the 427-cubic-inch V8 was offered in 390- or 425-bhp form.

For 1968, all cars sold in the U.S. had to have side marker lights. In addition to the lights the SS also had proper engine identification.

RUNNING GEAR

Steering: Recirculating ball

Front suspension: Double wishbones with coil springs, telescopic shock absorbers and anti-roll bar

Rear suspension: Live axle with four links, Panhard rod, coil springs and telescopic shock absorbers

Brakes: Discs, 11-in. dia. (front), drums, 11-in. dia. (rear)

Wheels: Steel discs, 6 x 15 in.

Tires: 8.25 x 15 in.

DIMENSIONS

Length: 213.2 in. **Width:** 79.9 in.

Height: 55.4 in. **Wheelbase:** 119.0 in.

Track: 62.5 in. (front), 62.4 in. (rear)

Weight: 3,835 lbs.

Chevrolet **IMPALA SS**

When launched as a 1994 model, the Impala SS struck a chord with enthusiasts and hot rodders. It was a big, powerful sedan that could seat six, yet still had enormous tuning potential.

"...breathtaking acceleration."

"Once settled behind the wheel of this hot rod Impala SS, take in the amount of attention to its detail. This car gives new meaning to the term 'fully loaded.' The heavily modified LT1 engine, combined with a 100-mph nitrous oxide system, results in breathtaking acceleration, yet the V8 is still docile enough for commuting. The air suspension not only gives a very smooth ride, but also outstanding cornering ability."

A billet steering wheel, carbon-fiber inserts and a TV screen add a futuristic touch.

Milestones

1993 At the Detroit auto show, Chevrolet reveals the Impala SS concept car. It is powered by a 300-bhp LT1 and wears 17-inch rubber.

The first car to carry the Impala SS name was in 1961.

1994 Following favorable public response, the Impala SS goes into production. Initially only available in black, it has a cop-spec suspension and a 260-bhp LT1.

It may look plain compared to the Impala, but the Caprice™ is basically the same car under the skin.

1995 With the Impala SS having proved to be a success, production is increased at the Arlington, Texas plant, which builds B-body cars. Changes include a slightly revised interior with a center console, bigger mirrors and a new color palette. Production of all B-body GM cars ends the following year, however.

UNDER THE SKIN

Separate body and chassis · Four-wheel disc brakes · Full air suspension · 5.7 Liter LT1 V8

1970s vintage

Just like the original 1961 Impala SS, the 1996 model is a family car that has been turned into a true performance machine. Impala SS models are fortified with police specification spindles, springs, de Carbon shocks and variable-rate steering. This car differs somewhat in having air springs at all four corners and Bilstein shocks. The brakes are Billet four-wheel disc items.

THE POWER PACK

Firebreathing LT1

Although the show car packed a mighty 300 bhp, stock Impala SS models got a 260-bhp mill, mainly due to more restrictive cast-iron exhaust manifolds and cast-iron cylinder heads. It may still have the original LT1 V8, but this particular car puts both stock Impala and the show car on the bench by adding much more power. The addition of Edelbrock exhaust headers, Flowmaster mufflers, a Hypertech performance chip, K&N air filter and a cold-air induction kit help the engine kick out all of 360 bhp. A 100-bhp nitrous oxide system adds more power on demand.

SS scope

It may be the favorite of New York City cabbies in Caprice guise, but the Impala SS has a loyal band of followers. Because of its relatively simple enginer-ing, it has considerable potential for hot-rodding, but prices for used examples remain high due to demand.

The Impala SS makes for a great late-model street machine.

One of the biggest late-model cars on the road and also one of the quickest, the Impala SS has already become a part of the popular cruising scene in both stock and modified forms.

Tweaked V8

Thanks to less restrictive exhaust system, an aftermarket computer chip and other changes, the LT1 in this Impala now puts out 360 bhp and 410 lb-ft of torque—more than enough to haul a 4,000-plus-lbs. cruiser to 60 mph in less than 4.5 seconds.

Four-wheel disc brakes

Stock SS Impalas came with standard disc brakes. This modified Impala had its factory system replaced with billet rotors and calipers.

Futuristic wheels

In keeping with the cutting-edge theme, the Impala rides on a set of 20-inch Boyd billet chrome rims. These are shod with huge Michelin Z tires, 245s at the front and 275s out back.

Subtle body alterations

Custom Caprice front and rear rollpans blend well with the body contours, but perhaps the neatest body mod is the substitution of original 1961 Impala SS cross-flag emblems in place of the stock 1996 appliqués and not-so-subtle purple flames.

Air suspension

Replacing the stock coil springs are air bags at all four corners. The ride height can be raised or lowered with an onboard compressor. Performance anti-roll bars are fitted front and rear to deliver razor-sharp handling.

Chrome details

Under the hood, no hot rod looks right without a smattering of chrome. Thus, the coolant cap, throttle body, relay box, radiator supports and hood latch have all been given the chrome treatment.

Specifications

1996 Chevrolet Impala SS

ENGINE

Type: V8

Construction: Cast-iron block and heads

Valve gear: Two valves per cylinder operated by a single V-mounted camshaft with pushrods and rockers

Bore and stroke: 4.00 in. x 3.48 in.

Displacement: 350 c.i.

Compression ratio: 10.5:1

Induction system: Electronic fuel injection

Maximum power: 360 bhp at 5,400 rpm

Maximum torque: 410 lb-ft at 3,400 rpm

Top speed: 165 mph

0-60 mph: 4.2 sec.

TRANSMISSION

GM 4L60E four-speed automatic

BODY/CHASSIS

Separate steel chassis with four-door sedan body

SPECIAL FEATURES

White taillight lenses with sequential bulbs are very interesting.

A nitrous oxide system in the trunk adds 100 extra bhp.

RUNNING GEAR

Steering: Recirculating-ball

Front suspension: Unequal length A-arms with air springs, telescopic shock absorber trailing arms and anti-roll bar

Rear suspension: Live axle with air springs, telescopic shock absorbers and anti-roll bar

Brakes: Discs (front and rear)

Wheels: Boyd Vertigo, 20-in. dia.

Tires: Michelin XGTZ4, 245/40 ZR20 (front), 275/35 ZR20 (rear)

DIMENSIONS

Length: 213.6 in. **Width:** 77.0 in.

Height: 55.7 in. **Wheelbase:** 115.9 in.

Track: 61.2 in. (front), 61.7 in. (rear)

Weight: 4,350 lbs.

Chevrolet **CORVAIR**

It was supposed to be a new, small Chevrolet in response to foreign imports, but the Corvair turned into a giant controversy regarding its safety. Later models were remedied of the handling problem and some were even fitted with turbochargers.

"...unbelievable power."

"The Corvair is a simple car to enter and all the instruments are very easy to read. While suspension problems plagued the first generation Corvairs, by 1965 this was all in the past. The handling from the four-wheel independent suspension is outstanding. It doesn't roll and there is just a slight hint of understeer. The Corsa®, optioned with a 180 bhp, turbocharged flat-six engine, was the most desirable Corvair and offered unbelievable power."

Corsas were available with a deluxe interior complete with a full set of instruments.

Milestones

1960 Chevrolet announces its Corvair, with a 140-cubic inch rear engine and three levels of specification (500, 700 and 900 Monza®) to compete with imported compacts.

Corvair (here a 700) was the most revolutionary of the big three compacts for 1960.

1962 Suspension improvements attempt to answer handling criticisms, and a convertible is added to the range. The most exciting debutante, however, is the turbocharged Monza Spyder®.

1965 A radically overhauled second-generation Corvair is launched. A new Corsa coupe and convertible displaces the Monza as the top of the range.

Second generation Corvairs included a hardtop sedan.

1969 Production finally comes to an end.

UNDER THE SKIN

Radical Chevy

Beneath its new swoopy styling, the second-generation Corvair embodied many improvements. The swing axle rear suspension is replaced by a fully independent set up with coils on both sides and double control arms, the uppers being the axle half-shafts. The front suspension is also tuned to match the rear with stiffer springs. Drum brakes are standard all around.

Unitary construction · All-independent suspension · Rear-mounted engine

Turbocharged flat-six

THE POWER PACK

Sophisticated flat-six

Although inspired by the Volkswagen Beetle, the Corvair's power unit is more sophisticated, perhaps echoing engineer Ed Cole's background in aviation. It has six separate cylinder barrels with cast-iron walls mounted in an aluminum block with a divided crankshaft. Outputs initially varied from 80 to 95 bhp, but the addition of a Thompson turbocharger in 1962 resulted in 150 bhp. This rose to 180 bhp for the revised 1965 models, making this one of the most powerful sixes in production.

Thompson turbocharger · Progressively linked carburetors · Individual cylinder barrels · Aluminum block with divided crankshaft

Choice Corsa

With the 1965-1966 Corsa, Chevrolet thought it had a winner on its hands. Alas, it proved to be short-lived; the Corsa and turbocharged engine were dropped after 1966. Today, not surprisingly, the Corsa is the most collectible of all Corvairs.

The Corsa only lasted for two model years and offered the most power.

The Corvair was a true cutting edge car, but Ralph Nader's book *Unsafe at Any Speed* tarnished its image. In fact, the Corvair was later vindicated by Congress, and today it has a reputation as an enthusiast's car.

Coke-bottle styling
1965-1969 Corvairs look very different from early models, with smooth Coke-bottle contours and a raised rear fender top line.

Revised suspension
For 1965, the Corvair received a revised rear suspension employing upper and lower control arms to better monitor wheel movement. Rods connect the lower arms to the main rear cross-member to absorb longitudinal forces.

Unibody construction
The Corvair is a rare example of a 1960s American car with integral body/chassis construction. This makes the whole structure very rigid, especially in convertible form.

Wire wheel covers
Corsas came with standard steel wheels and full wheel covers, although wire covers with knock-off spinners were factory options.

Grill-less nose
Like the Beetle, the Corvair does not have a front grill. The headlights are set back in chrome bezels, which results in a striking and attractive appearance.

Rear-mounted air-cooled engine
The rear weight bias of the rear-mounted engine arrangement led to handling problems on early cars. Besides the turbocharged engine, the Corsa could also be specified with the 140-bhp atmospheric unit.

Choice of transmissions
As launched, the Corvair had a three-speed floor shift manual or Powerglide automatic. A four-speed transmission was introduced as an option in 1961, boosting the model's appeal as an enthusiast's car.

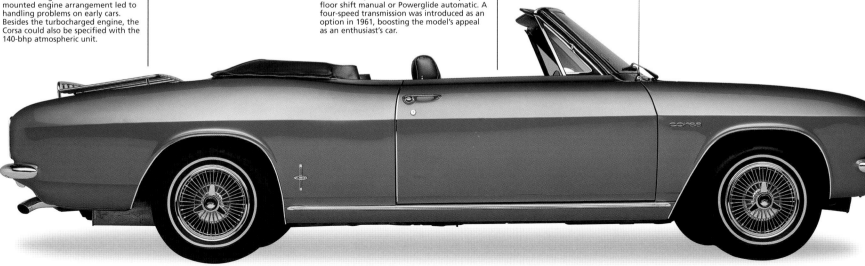

Chevrolet **CHEVELLE 300**

By the mid-1960s, NASCAR was heating up. It was also at this time that a new breed of drivers, who would dominate the sport in the 1970s and 1980s, began appearing on the scene. One was Florida's Bobby Allison.

"...a test of endurance."

"Lined up on the grid, you savor the experience. The small-block engine makes a raucous sound due to the straight exhaust and lack of sound deadening. The whole car shakes when the throttle is tapped. The big slicks give incredible grip on the banked NASCAR ovals, but the Chevelle jolts over even the slightest bump, and both the steering and pedals need a firm touch. Driving around the track for four hours at speeds of 130 mph soon becomes a true test of driver endurance."

This NASCAR racer shares precious few appointments with a standard Chevelle.

Milestones

1961 Native Floridian Bobby Allison enters NASCAR racing following a spate of successes in Jalopy and Modified classes.

Bobby Allison soon made a name for himself as one of the most successful drivers of the 1970s.

1966 Having taken to NASCAR racing full time, Bobby Allison's perseverance pays off; he wins three races this year.

Modern stock-car racers bear little resemblance to their road-going counterparts.

1972 In NASCAR's first 'modern season,' Allison wins 10 races, the most victories that season.

1983 After two decades, Allison finally wins the Winston Cup, ahead of Darrell Waltrip. He retires in 1988 with 84 victories.

UNDER THE SKIN

Modest update

It may look like a regular Chevelle from the outside and, indeed, it does have stock steel panels and a separate steel chassis, but it also has a 12-point roll-cage fitted to improve stiffness. The stock front A-arms are retained, but Koni shocks and Eaton springs replace the stock pieces. At the rear is a 10-bolt rear end with a set of 3.00:1 rear gears. It has four-wheel drum brakes with sintered metallic linings.

Box-section separate steel chassis

Twelve-point roll-cage

Four-wheel drum brakes

Small-block V8

THE POWER PACK

Not so stock

By 1965, the term "stock" was more tightly applied, but, even so, most NASCAR racers still ran with production-size engines. This Chevelle 300, thus, has a 283-cubic inch V8. It was the base V8 offered that year. Apart from its stock block and heads, the engine has been altered since it was raced by Allison in 1965. Today it has a Milodon oil pan capable of holding eight quarts, Mr. Gasket exhaust headers, a high-volume oil pump, a Griffin radiator cooler to keep temperatures down and reliability up, Ross aluminum pistons, stainless-steel valves, a high-lift cam and an Edelbrock Torker intake manifold. This helps the engine kick out an honest 300 bhp.

Street stock

Fully restored to its original race-ready appearance, this Chevelle is amazingly street-legal. Most historic NASCAR racers have been destroyed or are on display in museums, which demonstrates their rarity and value. A driveable racer with history is worth more than $100,000.

This particular Chevelle was Allison's back-up car during the 1965 season.

With 84 victories, Bobby Allison ranks as one of the most popular and successful NASCAR drivers. Today, he is the third most winning NASCAR racer of all time.

Small-block V8
It may be a 283-cubic incher like one found in a regular Chevelle, but this mill differs quite radically, thanks to its deeper-capacity oil pan, racing-style fuel pump, Edelbrock intake and Carter four-barrel carburetor.

Roll cage
Even in the 1960s, a roll cage was deemed essential to compete in NASCAR. This Chevelle has a 12-point full roll cage welded to the frame.

Production based suspension
In the mid-1960s, NASCAR race cars still had stock suspensions and running gear. This Chevelle has been further improved with the addition of Koni shocks, modern coil springs, and a Global West rear anti-roll bar.

Straight side exhausts
Helping to achieve the legendary NASCAR V8 sound is a set of Mr. Gasket exhaust headers, bolted to straight pipes which exit ahead of the rear wheels.

Rugged rear end
With sustainable speed and endurance being prime factors in NASCAR, the cars need rugged drivetrains and fairly tall gearing. Housed in the strong 10-bolt live axle is a set of 3.00:1 gears—ideal for track use.

Stock steel body panels
Unlike modern NASCAR racers, this car retains stock steel body panels. Because they were in poor condition before the restoration began, they have been acid-dipped prior to their refinishing.

Specifications

1965 Chevrolet Chevelle 300

ENGINE
Type: V8

Construction: Cast-iron block and heads

Valve gear: Two valves per cylinder operated by a single camshaft with pushrods and rockers

Bore and stroke: 3.875 in. x 3.00 in.

Displacement: 283 c.i.

Compression ratio: Not quoted

Induction system: Holley 750-cfm four-barrel carburetor

Maximum power: 300 bhp at 6,400 rpm

Maximum torque: 360-lb-ft at 4,200 rpm

Top speed: 148 mph

0-60 mph: 5.2 sec.

TRANSMISSION
Four-speed manual

BODY/CHASSIS
Separate steel chassis with two-door sedan body

SPECIAL FEATURES

Durable Koni shock absorbers help improve the Chevelle's handling.

A passenger-side bucket seat has been added for street use.

RUNNING GEAR
Steering: Recirculating-ball

Front suspension: Unequal-length A-arms with coil springs, telescopic shock absorbers and anti-roll bar

Rear suspension: Live axle with coil springs and telescopic shock absorbers

Brakes: Drums (front and rear)

Wheels: Steel, 12 x 15 in.

Tires: BF Goodrich, P245/50 R15H-11

DIMENSIONS
Length: 192.3 in. **Width:** 80.9 in.

Height: 56.4 in. **Wheelbase:** 115.0 in.

Track: 58.0 in. (front and rear)

Weight: 2,750 lbs.

Chevrolet **CHEVELLE SS 454**

In 1970, Chevrolet introduced the ultimate powerhouse for its midsize muscle car. It was also the year GM lifted its displacement ban on all of its midsize cars. For the Chevelle, it meant 450 bhp from a stout LS-6 454 V8 for the Super Sport model. Today, it is regarded as one of the most fearsome muscle cars of all time.

"...all-out performance."

"This is not a toy—it's an LS-6 Chevelle SS. It's one of those cars GM built just to show up Ford and Mopar. For years, the SS used semi-powerful 396 V8s, but when Chevy® released the LS-6 454, the competition shuddered. The all-out performance engine has a factory rating of 450 bhp—no other muscle car production engine had a higher rating. The LS-6 Chevelle's only limitation was its tires. But even with the stock tread, the SS could be power shifted to 13.7 seconds in the ¼ mile."

While most Chevelle Super Sports were ordered with custom buckets, this one has a bench seat.

Milestones

1969 SS is an option package. Top-of-the-line engine continues to be the L78 396 with 375 bhp. However, Vince Piggins, GM's performance products manager, had 323 COPO (Central Office Production Order) Chevelles built with L72 427 V8s. They produce 425 bhp, and run the ¼ mile in 13.3 seconds at 108 mph.

Earlier Chevelles had much boxier styling.

1970 General Motors unleashes its wildest muscle cars yet, with revised styling. The LS-5 (360 bhp) and LS-6 (454 bhp) 454 V8s join the 396 in the Chevelle SS line up as a regular production order.

In 1970, the smaller-engined SS 396 was still available.

1971 The SS 454 returns, though the LS-6 option is dropped. The less powerful LS-5 actually gains 5 bhp, to 365. Only 9,402 SS 454s are built. A new Chevelle arrives for 1973.

UNDER THE SKIN

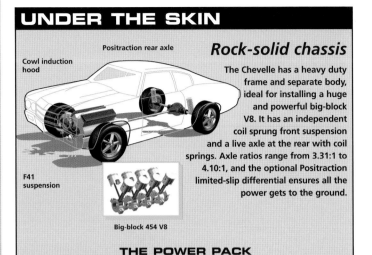

Cowl induction hood

Positraction rear axle

F41 suspension

Big-block 454 V8

Rock-solid chassis

The Chevelle has a heavy duty frame and separate body, ideal for installing a huge and powerful big-block V8. It has an independent coil sprung front suspension and a live axle at the rear with coil springs. Axle ratios range from 3.31:1 to 4.10:1, and the optional Positraction limited-slip differential ensures all the power gets to the ground.

THE POWER PACK

Hard-core power

The lightning and thunder raging under the hood of the highest performance Chevelle SS—the infamous LS-6—produces 450 bhp and 500 lb-ft of torque. The block shares the same 4.25-inch bore as the 427 V8, but the stroke was increased to 4.00 inches. The longer stroke helps produce gobs of low end power. The powerful LS-6 uses high (11.25:1) compression forged pistons, steel crankshaft, high-lift camshaft with mechanical lifters and closed-chamber, rectangle-port cylinder heads. It uses an aluminum intake manifold and a Holley 800 cfm carburetor. This engine means business.

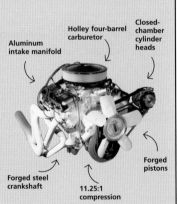

Aluminum intake manifold

Holley four-barrel carburetor

Closed-chamber cylinder heads

Forged pistons

Forged steel crankshaft

11.25:1 compression

Collector's cars

The 1970 Chevelle Super Sport was restyled from the 1969 model and again in 1971. A 1970 SS with the LS-6 is as rare as it is powerful. Only 4,475 of these venomous vehicles were produced, making them popular and valuable among auto collectors.

Not many muscle cars come close to the tire-shredding power of the LS-6 SS.

The LS-6 Chevelle was one of the most powerful muscle cars ever produced. It combined Chevrolet's largest engine with its sporty midsize car to give outrageous results.

Body stripes

By 1970 style was every bit as important as performance, and SS Chevelles were available with twin stripes running over the hood and rear decklid.

LS-6 454-cubic inch V8

The biggest performance option in 1970 was the LS-6 engine. It produces 450 bhp at 5,600 rpm and 500 lb-ft of torque at 3,600 rpm. It has high compression pistons, rectangle port cylinder heads, and solid valve lifters. Few other muscle machines could rival the power of the LS-6.

M-22 'Rock crusher' transmission

With 500 lb-ft of torque, only two transmissions were strong enough to cope with the LS-6 engine. This one has a Muncie M22 'Rock crusher' four-speed. This stout unit has a 2.20:1 straight-cut first gear.

Magnum 500 wheels

Magnum 500 steel wheels were used on all 1970 Chevelle Super Sports. The Polyglas F70x14 could barely handle the engine's torque.

Hardtop body

While all LS-6 engines were supposed to be installed in hardtops only, it's rumored that a few found their way into convertibles.

Upgraded suspension

The SS package included the F41 suspension which has stiffer front springs to compensate for the weight of the big-block engine.

Dual exhaust

A full-length 2.5-inch dual exhaust system enables the LS-6 to optimize the engine's performance.

Cowl induction hood

A vacuum-controlled flap at the top of the hood draws air in from the high-pressure area at the base of the windshield to help the engine exploit its power. This is known as cowl induction.

Specifications

1970 Chevrolet Chevelle SS 454

ENGINE

Type: V8

Construction: Cast-iron block and heads

Valve gear: Two valves per cylinder operated by pushrods and rockers

Bore and stroke: 4.25 in. x 4.00 in.

Displacement: 454 c.i.

Compression ratio: 11.25:1

Induction system: Holley four-barrel carburetor and aluminum intake manifold

Maximum power: 450 bhp at 5,600 rpm

Maximum torque: 500 lb-ft at 3,600 rpm

Top speed: 125 mph

0-60 mph: 6.1 sec

TRANSMISSION

Manual four-speed, close-ratio M-22

BODY/CHASSIS

Steel body on separate steel chassis

SPECIAL FEATURES

All Chevelle Super Sports came with Magnum 500 steel wheels and Polyglas F70x14 tires in 1970.

These NASCAR-style tie down hood pins were a popular item and helped keep the hood from lifting at high speed.

RUNNING GEAR

Steering: Recirculating ball

Front suspension: Independent with wishbones, anti-roll bar, coil springs and telescopic shock absorbers

Rear suspension: Live axle with coil springs and telescopic shock absorbers

Brakes: Disc, 11-in. dia. (front), drum 9-in. dia. (rear)

Wheels: Magnum 500, 14-in. dia.

Tires: Polyglas F70x14

DIMENSIONS

Length: 189 in.	**Width:** 70.2 in.
Height: 52.7 in.	**Wheelbase:** 112 in.
Track: 56.8 in. (front), 56.9 in. (rear)	
Weight: 4,000 lbs.	

Chevrolet SUBURBAN 1966

Launched in 1935, the Suburban is one of Chevy's best-loved and longest-lasting nameplates. With examples like this outstanding high-riding 1966 model, it is easy to see why.

"...a perfect match."

"If there was ever a near-perfect match between classic looks and modern levels of comfort and dependability, this is it. The seats are supportive and the cabin is light-years away from a stock 1966 Suburban. Performance is better, especially with a 300-bhp small-block under the hood. This rig can hold its own on the highway and gobbles up the miles with ease, but with its big, grippy tires and strong 4-WD driveline, it makes light work of rock crawling, too."

Digital gauges and modern seats are a tasteful and practical addition.

Milestones

1935 The Model EB Suburban, a steel-bodied station wagon built off the Master Series Truck, arrives on the scene. It can seat eight people and is offered with a number of different door configurations.

The shorter C/K-5 Blazer supplemented the Suburban from 1969.

1960 Like the rest of Chevy's C10 series, the Suburban gets new angular sheetmetal, yet is still available with rear doors or a tailgate, plus six cylinder or V8 power.

Suburbans are still built off the full-size pickup platform.

1962 The full-size trucks revert to single headlamps and front-end styling, and model designations are simplified.

1966 A revamped C10 arrives.

UNDER THE SKIN

Complete Jimmy driveline

Power front disc brakes

Separate steel chassis

Worked small-block V8

Four by far

In 1966, the Suburban was built off the short-wheelbase C-14 pickup, which meant a separate, ladder-type chassis and a choice of two-wheel or four-wheel drive configurations. With four-wheeling in mind, the owner of this rig decided to upgrade his vehicle. It now rides on front and rear axles and wheels from a 1980 Jimmy, which also donated its power front disc brakes. Airlift shocks mean the ride height can be raised or lowered depending on changes in terrain.

THE POWER PACK

Better than stock

The base powerplant for the 1966 Suburban was the ancient Thriftmaster six, which, with its 140 bhp and single one-barrel Rochester carburetor, was not very sporty. Bigger 250 and 292 sixes, plus 283- and 327-cubic inch small-block V8s, were available for those who wanted more grunt; but for the owner of this truck, even these were not enough. Sitting between the light blue fenderwells is a 1970-vintage 350-cubic inch motor. With an 8.5:1 compression ratio, Edelbrock Performer intake manifold, and four-barrel carburetor, it packs a whopping 300 bhp and 380 lb-ft of torque.

Sixties simplicity

Back in the 1960s, the Suburban was far from the luxury wagon it is today. Most were still purchased for commercial duties, which explains why only 12,051 were built for 1966. Nevertheless, these old trucks possess plenty of character and simple, robust mechanicals, making them ideal candidates for resto-mod duty.

With only a few modifications, this 1966 Suburban really turns heads.

Amazingly, the turquoise paintwork of this 1966 Suburban is the original factory color. Subtle graphics and stock 8 x 15-inch color-coded wheels lend it a thoroughly modern look, however.

Original and modern

One of the most appealing aspects of this truck is the interior. The stock dash is kept, but the instruments have been replaced. The old seats have been replaced by late-model buckets, which offer more support for the driver and passengers.

Jimmy suspension

With greater ground clearance than a stock K-14 Suburban, this vehicle owes its increased ride height to a 1980-vintage GMC Jimmy. The modern sport utility also donated its front and rear axles, plus the center differential. With less weight than a stock 1980 Jimmy, this Suburban can tackle all but the roughest terrain with considerable ease.

Rear tailgate

In 1966, as today, the Suburban could be ordered with either twin rear hinging doors or a drop-down tailgate. This one has the latter and it opens in two sections making the truck easier to load and unload.

Final year styling

The 1966 full-size trucks were the final iteration of the 1960 design. Over the seasons, the appearance of these rigs was cleaned up to satisfy buyer tastes. The grill and hood brightwork were simplified for 1962, and single headlamps returned for the first time. The 1967 line was even cleaner.

Hi-po small-block

A torquey 350-cubic inch V8 is just the ticket for towing and off-road excursions. With 380 lb-ft, it can power the Suburban to 60 mph in 10.4 seconds.

Specifications

1966 Chevrolet Suburban

ENGINE

Type: V8

Construction: Cast-iron block and heads

Valve gear: Two valves per cylinder operated by a single V-mounted camshaft with pushrods and rockers

Bore and stroke: 4.00 in. x 3.48 in.

Displacement: 350 c.i.

Compression ratio: 8.5:1

Induction system: Edelbrock Performer four-barrel carburetor

Maximum power: 300 bhp at 4,800 rpm

Maximum torque: 380 lb-ft at 3,200 rpm

Top speed: 114 mph

0-60 mph: 10.4 sec.

TRANSMISSION

700RS four-speed automatic

BODY/CHASSIS

Separate steel chassis with two-door station wagon body

SPECIAL FEATURES

The embroidered bowtie logo on the headrest is just one of several subtle touches.

These wheels are stock items on 1980 Blazers and Jimmys.

RUNNING GEAR

Steering: Recirculating-ball

Front suspension: Live axle with semi-elliptic leaf springs and telescopic shock absorbers

Rear suspension: Live axle with semi-elliptic leaf springs and telescopic shock absorbers

Brakes: Discs (front), drums (rear)

Wheels: Pressed steel, 8 x 15 in.

Tires: BF Goodrich All Terrain

DIMENSIONS

Length: 193.19 in. **Width:** 86.8 in.

Height: 81.6 in. **Wheelbase:** 115.0 in.

Track: 74.9 in. (front), 66.7 in. (rear)

Weight: 3,850 lbs.

Chevrolet SUBURBAN

When Chevrolet introduced the new Suburban model in 1992, it redefined the large sports utility vehicle. Massive in every sense of the word, it is able to carry up to nine people in comfort, has 149 cubic feet of load space and can tow up to 10,000 lbs.

"...a living room on wheels."

"It is impossible not to notice the Suburban's immense size. When driving around town the bulk is quite noticeable, but on the open road it cruises along in perfect comfort. Over the years, the Suburban has become a popular vehicle to customize. In addition to the body graphics, this example has been modified on the inside to living room comfort. It has an alarming stereo, VCR and video game player for the rear occupants. It's nothing short of a living room on wheels"

The upgrades to the interior are designed for maximum comfort and enjoyment.

Milestones

1992 Chevrolet introduces the restyled C-series pickup and Suburban. The pickup comes in C1500™ and C2500™ variants which are available with a 262-cubic inch V6 and V8s in the form of 305, 350 small blocks, a 398-cubic inch turbo-diesel and a massive 454-cubic incher.

The smaller Chevrolet Tahoe™ uses the same 350-cubic inch engine.

1995 Changes are made to the interior. Twin airbags are fitted, a more modern-looking dash is added and the front grill is changed.

The four-wheel drive Suburban also comes in GMC® guise.

1999 Chevy® pickups are redesigned but Suburbans carry on unchanged.

2000 A new Suburban model is slated for release, using the LS1-derived power plant.

UNDER THE SKIN

Rear-wheel drive, though four-wheel drive is available

Standard front anti-lock disc brakes

Lowered rear leaf spring suspension

Revised V8

Off-roader

The Suburban was not designed as a performance vehicle. Thus the rear leaf-sprung suspension does not inspire aggressive driving. However, in four-wheel drive form, it is a very capable off-road vehicle. This is further aided by the optional Autotrac computer-activated transmission which automatically distributes torque between the front and rear wheels according to the demands of the terrain.

THE POWER PACK

Power boosted

The Suburban was initially offered only with 350- and 454-cubic inch gasoline engines. Latera 398-cubic inch turbo diesel was offered. The model shown here has the popular 350-cubic inch engine but with a few modifications. To complete the custom look, the coolant tank, battery cover and air cleaner are made of Billet aluminum. Doug Thorley headers with 3-inch Flow Master dual exhaust are used along with a high performance computer chip to extract more power. In standard form this unit produces 210 bhp at 4,000 rpm and 325 lbs. of torque at 2,400 rpm, which is sufficient to enable it to pull a massive 10,000 lbs. load.

Luxury cruiser

Suburbans naturally lend themselves to modifications because there is so much to work on. In this model, power leather seats, a rosewood dash and built in phone system have enlivened the cabin. In the rear there is a TV, VCR and video game player.

This modified Suburban has a complete entertainment system in the rear.

Big, bold and brash, the Chevrolet Suburban lends itself to being customized. By fitting a complete entertainment system this vehicle has been turned into a living room on wheels.

Luxury cabin

To increase its comfort and to add some class, the cabin has been fitted with power leather seats and a 56-piece Bahia rosewood overlay on the center console.

Engine changes

The venerable 350-cubic inch Chevrolet engine has been modified using billet aluminum, chrome and polished brass. Also all of the pulleys and the underside of the hood have been painted.

Entertainment system

The electrical system has been altered to handle the entertainment system. Two Optima batteries have been fitted and the wiring has been reworked and covered in a blue and black loom casing.

Lowering

This truck has been lowered 3½ inches in the front and 5½ in the rear. This is done with custom front coils and rear leaf spring lowering blocks.

Bodywork changes

The 1998 chrome grill has been upgraded with a polished aluminum phantom grill insert. The front bumper has chrome plated teardrop inserts and the rear bumper is painted white.

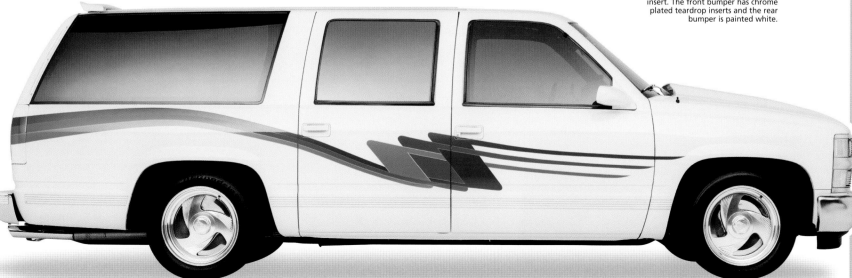

Specifications

1993 Chevrolet Suburban

ENGINE

Type: V8

Construction: Cast-iron block and heads

Valve gear: Two valves per cylinder operated by a single overhead camshaft

Bore and stroke: 4.00 in. x 3.48 in.

Displacement: 350 c.i.

Compression ratio: 10.5:1

Induction system: Single four-barrel throttle body

Maximum power: 210 bhp at 4,000 rpm

Maximum torque: 300 lb-ft at 2,800 rpm

Top speed: 98 mph

0-60 mph: 11.2 sec

TRANSMISSION

Four-speed automatic

BODY/CHASSIS

Steel four-door sport utility body

SPECIAL FEATURES

The two rows of rear seats fold down to provide 149.5-cubic feet of space.

The unique and lively graphics were designed by the owner.

RUNNING GEAR

Steering: Recirculating ball

Front suspension: Independent with unequal length control arms, coil springs, KYB shocks and anti-roll bar

Rear suspension: Live axle with leaf springs and KYB shocks

Brakes: Discs (front), drums (rear)

Wheels: Aluminum, 8 x 17 in. (front), 9.5 x 17 in. (rear)

Tires: BF Goodrich, 255/50 ZR17

DIMENSIONS

Length: 219.5 in. **Width:** 76.8 in.

Height: 71.3 in. **Wheelbase:** 131.5 in.

Track: 61.1 in. (front), 61.7 in. (rear)

Weight: 4,675 lbs.

Chevrolet CAMARO Z28

General Motors' answer to the Ford Mustang needed plenty of power to compete with the original pony car. The Z28 performance option on the Chevrolet Camaro was the answer. It dramatically improving handling and power.

" ...factory built race car."

"Designed to compete in Trans Am racing, the high-revving Z28 is a factory built race car. Underrated at 290 bhp, the over-square 302 V8 engine is peaky and nothing much happens until the engine revs past 4,000 rpm. Suddenly the tachometer needle is pointing to 7,000 rpm and the car really comes to life. It's upper end power like this where the Z28 gives you easy 120 mph performance. Complementing the overabundance of high end power, the Z28 is garnished with a four-speed transmission, seven-inch rims and competition suspension."

The interior of this race-modified Z28 uses bucket seat, roll cage and a fire extinguisher.

Milestones

1966 First Camaro appears based on the Chevy II frame. The standard powertrain is only a 230-cubic inch six cylinder.

Only 602 Camaro Z28s were built in its first year, 1967.

1967 Regular production option Z28 is introduced with a 302-cubic inch engine, just inside the 305-cubic inch limit set for Trans Am racing. Z28s finish third and fourth at the Sebring 12 Hours, winning the Trans Am category.

1968 Z28 dominates Trans Am, easily winning the championship with the Roger Penske-prepared cars. Driver Mark Donohue wins 10 out of the 13 rounds.

The Camaro's styling was radically altered for 1970.

1969 Crossram induction is made available, but is put in only 205 cars.

1970 Model restyled to be longer and heavier with egg-crate type grill, but the Z28 option lives on and is still found on today's hottest Camaros.

UNDER THE SKIN

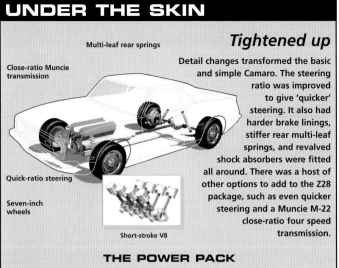

Tightened up

Detail changes transformed the basic and simple Camaro. The steering ratio was improved to give 'quicker' steering. It also had harder brake linings, stiffer rear multi-leaf springs, and revalved shock absorbers were fitted all around. There was a host of other options to add to the Z28 package, such as even quicker steering and a Muncie M-22 close-ratio four speed transmission.

Multi-leaf rear springs

Close-ratio Muncie transmission

Quick-ratio steering

Seven-inch wheels

Short-stroke V8

THE POWER PACK

Hybrid V8

For the Z28, GM used the 327 cast iron block to give a four-inch bore and added a forged crankshaft (similar to the 283) with a three-inch stroke to make a rev-happy, over-square 302-cubic inch V8. It operated a high (11.0:1) compression ratio, had 'Camelback' cylinder heads fitted with large 2.02-inch intake and 1.60-inch exhaust valves and had very radical valve timing. The engine is designed to give loads of top end performance with its maximum power not coming in until 6,000 rpm.

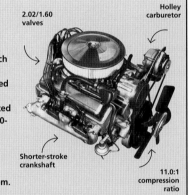

2.02/1.60 valves

Holley carburetor

Shorter-stroke crankshaft

11.0:1 compression ratio

Longer, sleeker

The distinctive egg-crate grill is a definitive feature on the second-generation Camaro and was included on the Z28. It may not be the original, the rarest, or the most collectable Camaro variant, but it has a more obvious, overtly-sporting image. This shape remained in production, largely unchanged, until 1974.

The 1970 Camaros are more streamlined than first generation cars.

To compete in the prestigious Trans Am championship, the rules required that Chevrolet had to build 1,000 suitable cars ready for sale to the public to homologate the car for racing. The result was the Z28, a racing car for the road.

Performance V8

Chevrolet originally rated the Z28's short-stroke V8 at 290 bhp. Some critics thought its potential was being deliberately underrated, and it could really produce something nearer to 350 bhp at well over 6,000 rpm.

Coupe-only body style

You could not order the Z28 package with the convertible body because Chevrolet only needed to homologate the coupe for Trans Am racing.

Vented disc brakes

Z28s are heavy cars, so with the performance available they have to have vented front disc brakes. Even with the harder pads though, the Z28's braking isn't its strongest feature.

Close-ratio transmission

Standard Z28 transmission was an automatic but for $184 a Muncie four-speed manual was available that could also be ordered with close-ratio gears.

Harder brake linings

Although the Z28 carries rear drum brakes, just like stock Camaros, the linings are a harder compound to improve performance under sustained high-speed braking.

Wide tires

The Z28 used Goodyear WideTread tires on relatively wide (for the time) seven-inch rims.

Stiffer rear springs

The one major suspension change was the switch to multi-leaf instead of the stock single-leaf rear springs which were 25 percent stiffer than standard. Despite this change, the front spring rates did not need to be altered at all.

Rear spoiler

The rear spoiler is as much about adding just a touch of style to the rear of the Camaro as managing the airflow over the car to improve rear downforce.

Specifications
1967 Chevrolet Camaro Z28

ENGINE.

Type: V8

Construction: Cast-iron block and heads

Valve gear: Two valves per cylinder operated by single block-mounted camshaft via pushrods and hydraulic lifters

Bore and stroke: 4.0 in. x 3.0 in.

Displacement: 302 c.i.

Compression ratio: 11.0:1

Induction system: Single four-barrel 800-cfm Holley carburetor

Maximum power: 290 bhp at 5,800 rpm

Maximum torque: 290 lb-ft at 4,200 rpm

Top speed: 123 mph

0-60 mph: 6.5 sec.

TRANSMISSION

Three-speed automatic or four-speed manual

BODY/CHASSIS

Unitary steel construction with two-door coupe body

SPECIAL FEATURES

The 302-cubic inch engine was new for the Z28. It combined 327 block with a 283 crank to achieve a capacity of less than 305 cubic inches for SCCA racing.

This car has been fitted with a roll cage to comply with SCCA racing regulations.

RUNNING GEAR

Steering: Recirculating ball

Front suspension: Double wishbones with coil springs, telescopic shocks and anti-roll bar

Rear suspension: Live axle with multi-leaf semi-elliptic springs and telescopic shocks

Brakes: Front vented discs, 11 in. dia., and rear drums, 9 in. dia.

Wheels: Steel disc, 7 in. x 15 in.

Tires: Goodyear WideTread E70-15

DIMENSIONS

Length: 184.7 in. **Width:** 72.5 in.

Height: 51.4 in. **Wheelbase:** 108 in.

Track: 59.6 in. (front), 59.5 in. (rear)

Weight: 3525 lbs.

Chevrolet **CAMARO RS/SS**

SS was the Camaro's high performance range. RS was its luxury package. For the best of both worlds, Chevrolet offered the RS/SS. This one happens to have a big-block V8.

"...outlandish performance."

"Super Sport (SS) Camaros have become classics, and after driving one it is easy to see why. Small bucket seats and a skinny steering wheel take you back to the 1960s, as does the outlandish performance. Fire up the big-block V8 and head out—the sound is fantastic. Stab the gas pedal and the SS shows you who is in charge. Despite heavy-duty suspension, understeer is the dominant handling characteristic through corners, but this is of little significance in such a machine."

Automatic-equipped SS Camaros have a stirrup-type shift lever.

Milestones

1966 In September, Chevrolet releases its new ponycar, the Camaro. It is available as a two-door coupe or a convertible. The main performance model has a Super Sport tag and a standard 285-bhp, 350-cubic inch V8; the big 396 is optional. Over 34,000 SS Camaros are sold during the debut season.

An SS package was still part of the redesigned 1970½ Camaro.

1967 Fine-tuning is the order of the day for the 1968 model. Staggered rear shocks help reduce wheel hop on big-block SS Camaros and GM's new Astro ventilation system dispenses with the need for vent windows. Mechanically, the SS version remains unchanged.

The Camaro SS was reborn in 1995; this is a 1998 model.

1969 Squared-up sheetmetal marks the last of the first-generation Camaros.

UNDER THE SKIN

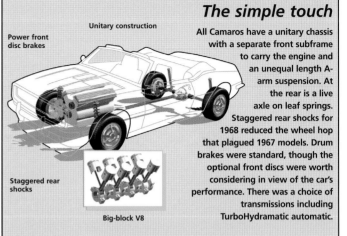

The simple touch

All Camaros have a unitary chassis with a separate front subframe to carry the engine and an unequal length A-arm suspension. At the rear is a live axle on leaf springs. Staggered rear shocks for 1968 reduced the wheel hop that plagued 1967 models. Drum brakes were standard, though the optional front discs were worth considering in view of the car's performance. There was a choice of transmissions including TurboHydramatic automatic.

THE POWER PACK

Classic big-block

Making its debut during 1965 in the Corvette and full-size Chevrolet, the 396-cubic inch, big-block V8 was the first of the so-called MK IV engines. Like the 409 it supplanted, it had a cast-iron block and heads, with canted valves for improved flow, which gave rise to the nickname Porcupine. When the Camaro arrived, the 396 was available as an option. The base version was rated at 325 bhp, although there was also a 350-bhp version. Top of the range was the infamous L78, with a higher-lift cam and solid lifters. With 375 bhp and 415 lb-ft, it was enough to make the Camaro a serious street racer.

8 is great

Possibly the best all-around first-generation Camaro is the 1968 model in SS form. It is more refined than the 1967 version but still retains the original clean lines. An RS/SS convertible with the L78 engine is one of the most desirable Camaros of all.

A perfectly restored RS/SS 396 will set you back around $35,000.

Externally, only detail changes mark the 1968 Camaro, but beneath the skin it features a number of improvements making it a more pleasing package overall.

Live rear axle

Like most Detroit cars of the time, the Camaro has a live rear axle. It also has semi-elliptic single leaf springs. Problems with wheel hop were reduced by fitting multileaf springs and staggered shock absorbers.

V8 engine

In standard form, the big 396 V8 puts out 325 bhp and 410 lb-ft of torque, but the solid-lifter, 375-bhp L78 was optional. Although this engine is more powerful, it produces only 5 extra lb-ft. of torque.

Heavy-duty transmission

Base Camaros had a three-speed manual, or Powerglide listed as an option, but for the 396-engined cars, a stronger M21 four-speed or TurboHydramatic transmission was necessary to harness the engine's extra torque.

Convertible top

A convertible top was available for 1968 Camaros. In standard form the top was manually operated, but for an extra $52.70 you could order a power-operated top, which was available in black, blue, or white. Despite the reasonable strength of the F-body's shell, convertible Camaros still needed some additional strengthening along the unibody rails.

Recirculating-ball steering

In theory, power steering for the recirculating-ball system was not necessary, but few buyers would have ordered a car that way. Only 2.8 turns were needed to wind the steering wheel from lock to lock.

Larger wheels

The SS Camaro would normally ride on 14-inch diameter steel wheels with 6-inch wide rims, but it made sense with the 396 engine to have the optional 7-inch rims along with the wide-tread Goodyear F70 x 14 tires.

Super Sport package

For an additional $210 the Super Sport (SS) package included a heavy-duty suspension, a 285-bhp 350 V8, a nose stripe and SS emblems. For 1968, this package also included a set of non-functional hood scoops. To avoid confusion, the 396 V8 engine was an additional option.

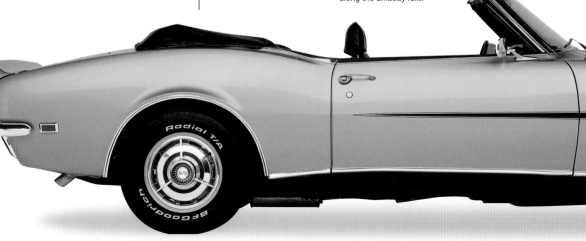

Specifications

1968 Chevrolet Camaro RS/SS

ENGINE

Type: V8

Construction: Cast-iron block and heads

Valve gear: Two valves per cylinder operated by a single V-mounted camshaft with hydraulic lifters, pushrods and rockers

Bore and stroke: 4.09 in. x 3.76 in.

Displacement: 396 c.i.

Compression ratio: 10.25:1

Induction system: Single Rochester four-barrel Quadrajet carburetor

Maximum power: 325 bhp at 4,800 rpm

Maximum torque: 410 lb-ft at 3,200 rpm

Top speed: 130 mph

0-60 mph: 6.6 sec

TRANSMISSION

Three-speed automatic

BODY/CHASSIS

Semi-unitary construction with steel two-door convertible body

SPECIAL FEATURES

Rally Sport-equipped Camaros have full-width taillights with the back up lights below the bumper.

Twin non-functional hood scoop clusters were a new SS item for 1968.

RUNNING GEAR

Steering: Recirculating-ball

Front suspension: Unequal length A-arms with coil springs, telescopic shock absorbers and anti-roll bar

Rear suspension: Live axle with semi-elliptic leaf springs and telescopic shock absorbers

Brakes: Discs, 11.0-in. dia. (front), drums, 9.5-in. dia. (rear)

Wheels: Stamped-steel disc, 14 x 7 in.

Tires: F70 x 14

DIMENSIONS

Length: 184.7 in.   **Width:** 72.3 in.

Height: 51.6 in.   **Wheelbase:** 108.0 in.

Track: 59.6 in. (front), 58.0 in. (rear)

Weight: 3,860 lbs.

Chevrolet CAMARO Z28 RS

Perhaps the most famous Chevrolet Regular Production Order (RPO) ever, the Z/28 package turned the base Camaro into a rip-roaring road racer. The crisply styled 1969 car was perhaps the best of all and is certainly the most collected today.

"...barely tamed for the street."

"The Z/28 is, without a doubt, the trickiest Camaro to drive. It's a real racer, barely tamed for the street. The highly tuned 302 is a pesky engine and makes the car hard to launch and pretty fussy under 3,000 rpm. Once the engine's spinning, though, it pulls hard well into triple digit speeds. The handling is sharp, with the F41 suspension package and wider wheels and tires. The rare optional four-wheel disc brakes are easily up to the job, too."

A complete set of gauges is mounted in the console just above the shifter.

Milestones

1967 Chevy introduces its Camaro special version, the Z28. It includes a 302-cubic inch engine, handling package and quick-ratio steering. Only 602 are ordered in its first year.

The Camaro's mainstream performance offering was the SS, here a 1968 model.

1968 The cars gain Z/28 badges as well as multileaf rear springs, staggered rear shocks and optional transmissions. The car wins the Trans-Am Championship, and 7,198 cars are built this model year.

Meanest and most expensive of all 1969 Camaro is the ZL-1.

1969 A crisp facelift arrives, together with four-bolt mains, rear-facing hood scoop and optional four-wheel disc brakes. An incredible 19,014 are built before the redesigned 1970 car arrives.

UNDER THE SKIN

Upgraded package

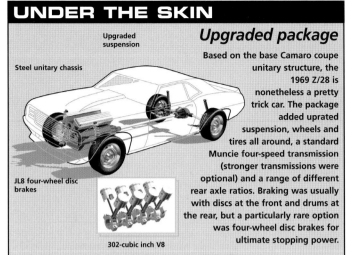

Upgraded suspension

Steel unitary chassis

JL8 four-wheel disc brakes

302-cubic inch V8

Based on the base Camaro coupe unitary structure, the 1969 Z/28 is nonetheless a pretty trick car. The package added uprated suspension, wheels and tires all around, a standard Muncie four-speed transmission (stronger transmissions were optional) and a range of different rear axle ratios. Braking was usually with discs at the front and drums at the rear, but a particularly rare option was four-wheel disc brakes for ultimate stopping power.

THE POWER PACK

Trans Am power

Because the Z/28 was going to be Chevrolet's Trans-Am contender, it needed an engine that was less than 305 cubic inches. The smallest existing V8 was the 327, so Chevrolet engineers had to do a little mixing and matching. By combining the old 283's crankshaft and the 327's block, they achieved a displacement of 302 cubic inches. Other changes included heads from the L69 engine, solid lifters, a hot cam, a baffled oil pan and a high-pressure oil pump. There were a number of carburetor setups; this car has two 600-cfm Holleys on a cross-ram manifold. Chevrolet quoted a power output of 290 bhp, but the true figure is probably about 350 bhp.

Fine '69

Despite the relative rarity of the earlier 1967 and 1968 Camaro Z/28s, the 1969 model, with 19,014 built, is considered the most collectible of the bunch. Options can add further desirability. For example, this car is fitted with the extremely rare four-wheel disc brake package.

The sharp lines of the 1969 Camaro make it one of the most desirable.

Developed to compete against Ford's market-leading Mustang in the popular Trans-Am racing series, the Camaro Z/28 stole two championships from the Mustang in the late 1960s and also became a legendary road car.

302-cubic inch engine
In order to comply with Trans-Am regulations, which restricted the maximum engine size to 305 cubic inches, Chevrolet engineers combined the crankshaft from one engine with the block from another to give an ideal displacement of 302 cubic inches.

Improved axle location
The severe wheel hop of 1967 Z/28s led to the fitment of multileaf rear springs and staggered shock absorbers in 1968.

Rally Sport package
Chevrolet's RPO packages could be combined. This car has option RPO-Z22—the RS (Rally Sport) package—which includes hidden headlights.

Wide wheels and tires
The wider wheels and tires are part of the Z/28 option package. The wheels are Corvette 6-inch Rally steel rims, and the tires are E70-15 Firestone SC-200s.

Coupe bodystyle
In 1969, the Z/28 package was only available on the Camaro's new facelifted coupe bodystyle.

(JL8) Four-wheel disc brakes
Corvette four-wheel disc brakes became an option for 1969. Most of the 503 cars ordered with this option were for race use. This is one of a handful of road cars with this very rare option.

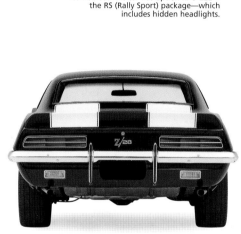

USA 1969

Chevrolet **CAMARO ZL1**

GM supported the Automotive Manufacturers Association (AMA) ban in the 1960s by only using its 400 cubic-inch and larger engines in full size cars and Corvettes. Through the Central Office Production Order system Vince Piggins, one of Chevrolet's officers, found a loop hole with the ban and created the ultimate Camaro—the ZL-1.

"...the apex of Chevy muscle."

"This is the apex of Chevy's muscle cars. In the driver's seat the car resembles a typical six-cylinder Camaro. When you start it up and listen to the aggressive engine you soon realize you've slid behind the wheel of a true factory-built racer. With the addition of tubular headers, drag slicks and a super tune, one of these nasty Camaros could run the ¼ mile in 11.68 seconds at more than 120 mph. Few cars come close to offering the level of thrill that a ZL-1 can."

Most ZL-1s had stripped cabins, but this one has a deluxe interior with woodgrain trim.

Milestones

1967 In response to the Mustang, Chevrolet launches the Camaro. The most powerful engine available is the 375 bhp, 396 V8. Because of the AMA ban, GM's intermediates weren't available with engines larger than 400 cubic inches. Meanwhile, a handful of Chevy dealers were installing 427 V8s into these cars, especially Camaros.

In 1967 car dealers were installing 427 V8s into new Camaros.

1968 Don Yenko of Yenko Sports Cars becomes the largest dealer converting these Camaros. GM's Vince Piggins takes notice. Later that year, Piggins and Yenko get together to offer the conversion package from GM's COPO (Central Office Production Order) department for 1969.

Don Yenko's YSC Camaros got the ball rolling for the ZL-1.

1969 A few hundred COPO Camaros are built. While most come with cast iron 427s, 69 versions known as ZL-1s are built with aluminum big-block engines. Tuned ZL-1s made 500+ bhp and could cover the ¼ mile in just under 12 seconds.

UNDER THE SKIN

Stock Camaro

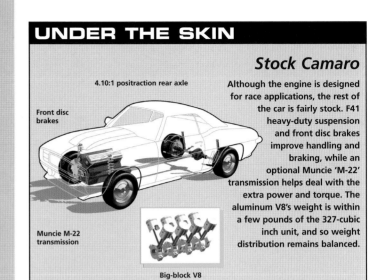

Although the engine is designed for race applications, the rest of the car is fairly stock. F41 heavy-duty suspension and front disc brakes improve handling and braking, while an optional Muncie 'M-22' transmission helps deal with the extra power and torque. The aluminum V8's weight is within a few pounds of the 327-cubic inch unit, and so weight distribution remains balanced.

THE POWER PACK

Exotic big-block

The ZL-1 was unlike any other engine that GM made at that time. The engine is roughly equivalent to the L88 Corvette racing V8 but has an aluminum instead of cast-iron block. The reciprocating assembly consisted of a forged steel crankshaft, forged pistons that slide in steel cylinder liners and four-bolt main bearing caps. The aluminum cylinder heads have closed chambers and rectangle intake ports. A Holley 850-cfm four-barrel carburetor fed the massive engine the fuel it required.

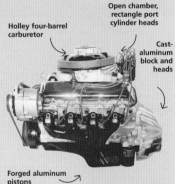

Pure racer

ZL-1s are ranked with the Hemi Cuda convertible and Ram Air IV™ GTO® as one of the most desirable muscle cars ever produced. With only 69 built with the all-aluminum engine, they attract a premium price and often trade hands for $150,000 or more.

To this day, Chevrolet hasn't built a more powerful production car than the ZL-1.

Most ZL-1s had plain bodies with skinny steel wheels—they didn't even have any badging to designate their model or engine size. This unique ZL-1 has the RS appearance package, vinyl top and 427 badging.

ZL2 cowl hood

All ZL-1s came with cowl induction hoods. It forced cool air into the engine from the high pressure area just below the windshield.

Expensive engine

You had to have a healthy bank account to be able to afford a ZL-1 Camaro. The engine's all-aluminum construction saved 160 lbs. over the cast-iron 427. Because it is virtually hand built, the engine alone cost $4,160—more than most cars of the period.

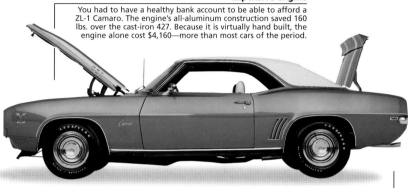

Better balance

Although it is a big-block unit, the ZL-1 engine weighs about 500 lbs. which is roughly the same as a 327, and so these special Camaros actually handle better than the stock SS 396™. However, these cars were designed for use in NHRA Super Stock drag racing events.

Standard exhaust system

ZL-1s left the factory with lots of mismatched parts because the owners were expected to do a lot of race development themselves. The stock exhaust manifolds restrict the flow of exhaust gases and were usually among the first items to be replaced.

The ZL-1 option package

All ZL-1s began life as SS 396s, but the engine and Super Sport™ option were deleted. Instead, the special cars received the ZL-1 option package which included the aluminum engine, F41 suspension, front discs and a cowl induction hood.

Heavy duty suspension components

All ZL-1s were equipped with the heavy duty F41 suspension and front disc brakes. To better handle the 450 lb-ft of torque from the powerful engines, ZL-1s were equipped with 12-bolt rear ends with 4.10 gears.

Performance transmission

Only two transmissions were strong enough to cope with the ZL-1 V8: the Muncie M-22 'Rock Crusher' four-speed or the equally stout TurboHydramatic 400 automatic.

Specifications

1969 Chevrolet Camaro ZL-1

ENGINE

Type: V8

Construction: Aluminum block and cylinder heads

Valve gear: Two valves per cylinder operated by a single camshaft

Bore and stroke: 4.25 in. x 3.76 in.

Displacement: 427 c.i.

Compression ratio: 12.0:1

Induction system: Holley four-barrel carburetor

Maximum power: 430 bhp at 5,200 rpm

Maximum torque: 450 lb-ft at 4,400 rpm

Top speed: 125 mph

0-60 mph: 5.3 sec

TRANSMISSION

Muncie M-22 four-speed manual

BODY/CHASSIS

Unitary steel chassis with two-door hardtop coupe body

SPECIAL FEATURES

Each ZL-1 engine has a special sticker on the valve cover.

Most ZL-1s have exposed headlights, but this car has the RS package.

RUNNING GEAR

Steering: Recirculating ball

Front suspension: Double wishbones with coil springs, telescopic shock absorbers and anti-roll bar

Rear suspension: Live axle with semi-elliptic leaf springs and telescopic shock absorbers

Brakes: Discs (front), drums (rear)

Wheels: Steel, 6 x 15 in.

Tires: Goodyear Wide Tread GT, E70-15

DIMENSIONS

Length: 186.0 in.　**Width:** 74.0 in.

Height: 51.0 in.　**Wheelbase:** 108.0 in.

Track: 59.6 in. (front), 59.5 in. (rear)

Weight: 3,300 lbs.

Chevrolet **CAMARO SS 396**

Unveiled in February 1970, the all-new second-generation Camaro was an instant design classic. Benefitting from a smoother ride and better handling, it could still be optioned with a pile-driving 375 bhp 396. Because of the immediate popularity of the then-new 350 bhp, 350 LT-1™, few buyers specified the big engine.

"...no ordinary Camaro."

"If you want a good handler, try the Z28® but if it's outright power that makes your mouth water, slide in and start 'er up. Inside the SS396, you're quickly greeted with a rough-idling engine and a loudly roaring exhaust. That's just one sign that lets you know this is no ordinary Camaro. Coax the shifter into first, bring up the rpm and drop the clutch—the tires spin with ease from the SS396's massive 415 lb-ft of torque. Then, powershift into second and hang on—it'll reach 60 mph in 6.2 seconds."

Supportive front bucket seats and a well laid-out instrument panel are Camaro traits.

Milestones

1970 An all-new, second-generation

Camaro makes its debut in February. Offered only as a coupe, it comes in base, SS™ and Z28 versions. A United Auto Workers strike causes production to dip to 124,889 units. The SS gets a new 402 big block during the year but is still badged as a 396.

The Camaro was introduced in September 1966 in both coupe and convertible bodystyles.

1971 Few changes occur this year, although emissions begin to bite. The 402-cubic inch V8 has a lower 8.5:1 compression ratio and power drops from 350 to 300 bhp.

Second-generation Camaros got their final facelift for 1978.

1972 Power ratings are switched to SAE net ratings, with all engine ancillaries attached. The SS is still offered with 350-cubic inch, four-barrel and 402-cubic inch engines, but power is down to 200 and 240 bhp, respectively. The SS is replaced by the LT for 1973.

UNDER THE SKIN

SS packaging

Ten-bolt live axle on leaf springs

Two-door coupe body only

Power front disc brakes

Big-block V8

All SS396 Camaros came with the heavy-duty F41 performance suspension (stiffer springs and 1-inch front and ⁵⁄₁₆-inch rear sway bars), 12-bolt positraction rear with a choice of ratios, power brakes, and 14x7 wheels. Cars ordered with close-ratio, Muncie 4-speeds came with Hurst shifters. Though the massive 402-cubic inch engine made plenty of torque, one unfortunate side effect was that it made the SS396 Camaros nose-heavy.

THE POWER PACK

Is it a 396 or a 402?

Though the popular combination for the Camaro in 1970 was the Z-28 with 360-bhp, LT-1 power, customers were still offered the 396 big block. Although its bore was increased to 4.125 inches making its actual displacement 402-cubic inches, GM still badged the engine as a 396. If ordered in Camaro SS trim, the massive motor was available in two states of tune—350 (L-34) or 375 bhp (L-78). 350 bhp versions had 10.25:1 compression, a cast-iron intake manifold and a Rochester Quadrajet carburetor. 375-bhp versions came with higher compression, an aluminum intake manifold and a Holley four-barrel carburetor.

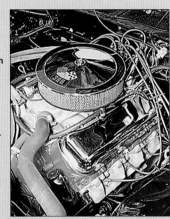

Rare find

Although the SS was in its prime in 1969, one year later it was eclipsed by the LT-1-powered Z28. The rarest of the 1970 SS396 Camaros have the elusive 375-bhp, L78 engines. Only 600 were built. Today, these powerful Camaros are hard to find and have kept their value well.

The original SS leaves the lineup in 1972 due to a changing market.

Overshadowed by the better balanced Z28, the 1970 SS396 was the weapon of choice for drag racers. As the muscle car dynasty of the 1960s began to unfold during the early 1970s, Chevrolet still offered a truly brutal performer.

Standard front
The standard front-end treatment consists of a full-length chrome bumper with turn signals mounted below it. RS-equipped Camaros have an Endura nose and twin bumperettes.

Big-block V8
With more than 400-cubic inches and 415 lb-ft of torque, the SS396 could run with the best cars the competition had to offer. Improved suspension also gave the factory SS ¼-mile times in the low 14-second range.

Unitary chassis
Camaros retained a unitary body/chassis for 1970, but greater attention was paid to refinement, including greater use of sound-deadening in the body.

Small rear window
GM stylists originally intended to give the 1970 Camaro a wraparound rear window, but problems with the installation delayed this until 1975. Thus, all early cars got small back windows, which led to criticism of rearward visibility.

Hardtop styling
Two bodystyles were initially planned, although with a growing buyer preference for closed bodystyles, it was decided to drop the convertible early in the development stage.

SS equipment group
The SS package included a stiffer suspension and a refreshing appearance package with twin sport mirrors, blacked-out grill and a sporty interior.

External spoilers
Front and rear spoilers were optional on any Camaro. The rear spoilers increased in size later in the 1970 model year.

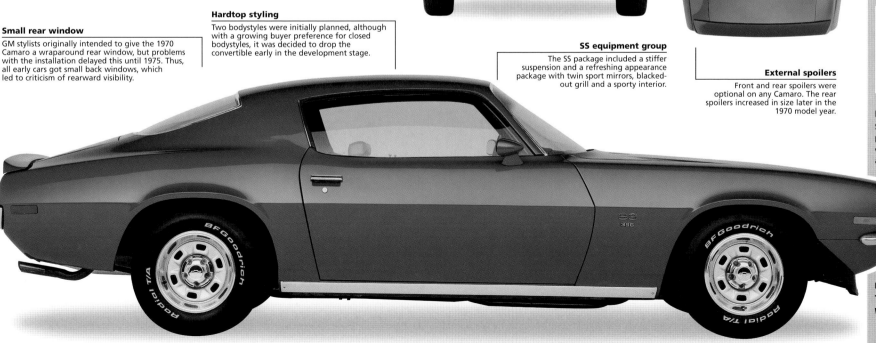

Specifications

1970 Chevrolet Camaro SS396

ENGINE
Type: V8

Construction: Cast-iron block and heads

Valve gear: Two valves per cylinder operated by pushrods and rocker arms

Bore and stroke: 4.125 in. x 3.76 in.

Displacement: 402 c.i. (396 c.i.)

Compression ratio: 10.25:1

Induction system: Rochester Quadrajet carburetor

Maximum power: 375 bhp at 5,600 rpm

Maximum torque: 415 lb-ft at 3,200 rpm

Top speed: 128 mph

0-60 mph: 6.2 sec.

TRANSMISSION
Muncie M21 four-speed manual

BODY/CHASSIS
Steel unitary chassis with two-door body

SPECIAL FEATURES

Quad taillights mimic its big brother, the Corvette.

The SS396's transmission, the Muncie M21 four-speed, was named after the town they were made in—Muncie, Indiana.

RUNNING GEAR
Steering: Recirculating ball

Front suspension: Unequal-length A-arms with coil springs, telescopic shock absorbers and anti-roll bar

Rear suspension: Live axle with semi-elliptic leaf springs and telescopic shock absorbers

Brakes: Discs (front), drums (rear)

Wheels: Super Sport, 7 x 14 in.

Tires: Firestone Wide Oval, F70-14

DIMENSIONS
Length: 188.0 in. **Width:** 74.4 in.

Height: 50.1 in. **Wheelbase:** 108.0 in.

Track: 61.3 in. (front), 60.0 in. (rear)

Weight: 3,550 lbs.

Chevrolet CAMARO RS/SS

In February 1970, Chevrolet introduced a radical new Camaro. Almost since the beginning these cars have begged to be turned into street machines. Unlike most, however, which are built for the drag strip, this hot rod has been modified for street duty.

"...classic and modern blend"

"This Camaro has a nice blend of classic styling and modern mechanicals. It handles like a late-model car, its big tires stick to the road and the steering is razor sharp, with instant response. The tuned small-block V8 produces power all the way up to the 7,000-rpm redline. Stopping is no problem either, simply depress the brake pedal and the huge Baer discs slow the car immediately without any hint of fading. Everything about this Camaro is first class."

Two-tone upholstery and a wood rimmed steering wheel add a modern touch.

Milestones

1967 Chevrolet's Mustang Fighter, the Camaro, is finally launched in coupe and convertible body styles. The SS model is the mainstream performance variant. A 396-cubic inch V8 turns the Camaro into a major league muscle car.

An SS package debuted for 1967. This Camaro is a 1968 model.

1970 Delayed by an autoworkers strike, a new second generation Camaro is introduced. It is longer, lower and wider, with a smoother ride and improved handling. The SS is still listed and the 396 is bored out to 402 cubic inches

Camaro's other performance offering in the early 1970s was the Z28.

1971 The Camaro SS 396 returns, but power is down, from 375 to 300 bhp. The model enters a decline and after 1973, the performance SS is replaced by a Luxury Touring (LT) model.

UNDER THE SKIN

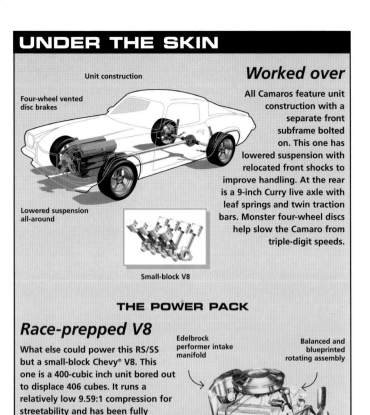

Unit construction

Four-wheel vented disc brakes

Lowered suspension all-around

Small-block V8

Worked over

All Camaros feature unit construction with a separate front subframe bolted on. This one has lowered suspension with relocated front shocks to improve handling. At the rear is a 9-inch Curry live axle with leaf springs and twin traction bars. Monster four-wheel discs help slow the Camaro from triple-digit speeds.

THE POWER PACK

Race-prepped V8

What else could power this RS/SS but a small-block Chevy® V8. This one is a 400-cubic inch unit bored out to displace 406 cubes. It runs a relatively low 9.59:1 compression for streetability and has been fully balanced and blueprinted. It has a custom baffled oil pan, to prevent oil surge during hard cornering, hyperutectic pistons, custom exhaust headers and an Edelbrock Performer intake topped by a 750-cfm Quadrajet carb, resulting in an honest 425 bhp.

Edelbrock performer intake manifold

Balanced and blueprinted rotating assembly

Cast-iron block and cylinder heads

Custom lubrication system and baffled oil pan

1971 RS/SS

As indicated by the front badge this Camaro is an SS (super sport), but since it has a split bumper, it's also a RS (rallye sport). The SS option is a performance package while the RS is an appearance option. So this Camaro RS/SS has the best of both worlds.

Although an SS, this street Camaro behaves more like a modern day racer.

The second generation Camaro has long been considered a design classic. This example was built to prove that muscle cars from the early 1970s can be made to handle and stop, too.

Modified small-block V8
Taken from a full-size Chevrolet, the 400-cubic inch V8 has been fully balanced and blueprinted and now has an output of 425 bhp. Other modifications include an aggressive camshaft and an Edelbrock induction system.

Stylish interior
Inside, major changes include Flo Fit sport bucket seats, a wood rimmed steering wheel, plus air conditioning and a premium Clarion sound system with remote CD player.

Nose treatment
If ordered with the RS (Rally Sport) package, 1970-73 Camaros received an endura-covered nose cap, with twin parking lights inboard of the headlights and small bumperettes.

Unique wheels
Large wheels are required in order to fit the monster 13-inch Baer Claw brakes. However, rather than source an existing set, renowned custom car builder Boyd Coddington was commissioned to build a unique set of five-spoke wheels which measure 17 inches in diameter. The large slots considerably help cool the brakes.

Stiffened chassis
To reduce body flex, this Camaro benefits from sub frame connectors and a custom welded roll bar.

Late model transmission
Many hot rodders rely on GM's 700R4 four-speed automatic transmission, because of its ability to handle so much extra power and torque. For this application, it has been fitted with a Transgo shift kit for shifting at higher rpm and a competition-style B&M ratchet shifter.

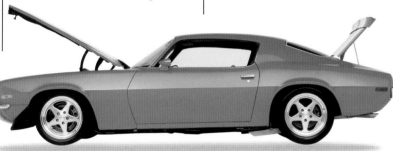
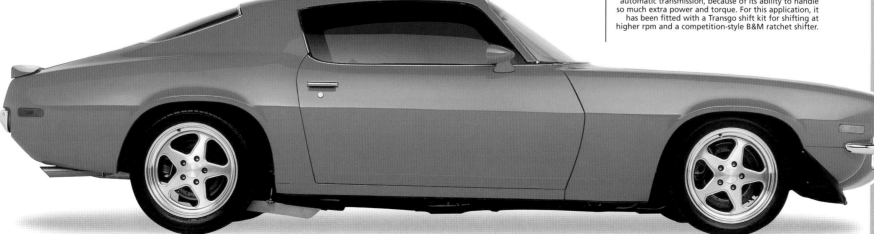

Specifications

1971 Chevrolet Camaro RS/SS

ENGINE
Type: V8

Construction: Cast-iron block and heads

Valve gear: Two valves per cylinder operated by pushrods and rockers

Bore and stroke: 4.12 in x 3.75 in

Displacement: 400 c.i.

Compression ratio: 9.59:1

Induction system: Rochester Quadrajet 750-cfm four-barrel carburetor

Maximum power: 425 bhp at 4,800 rpm

Maximum torque: 330 lb-ft at 3,000 rpm

Top speed: 143 mph

0-60 mph: 5.4 sec

TRANSMISSION
GM 700R4 four-speed automatic

BODY/CHASSIS
Unitary monocoque with steel two-door coupe body

SPECIAL FEATURES

Housed in the trunk are twin Orion amplifiers for the ultra-loud custom sound system.

RS Camaros feature an impact-absorbing front nose cone.

RUNNING GEAR
Steering: Recirculating ball

Front suspension: Unequal length wishbones with coil springs, telescopic shock absorbers and an anti-sway bar

Rear suspension: Live rear axle with semi-elliptical leaf springs, telescopic shock absorbers, traction bars and an anti-sway bar

Brakes: Baer Claw 13-in. dia.

Wheels: Boyd's alloy five-spoke 17-in. dia.

Tires: Bridgestone 27540ZR 17

DIMENSIONS
Length: 188.0 in **Width:** 74.4 in

Height: 49.5 in **Wheelbase:** 108.1 in

Track: 61.3 in (front) 60.0 in (rear)

Weight: 3,320 lbs.

Chevrolet **CAMARO Z28**

The legendary Z28 moniker has stuck with the Camaro well into its fourth generation. Since that magic three-figure code first appeared in 1967, it has always meant the same thing to buyers—added performance.

"...strong performance bias."

"Once you've settled yourself into the plush leather interior of the Z28, you realize that you're in a car with a strong performance bias. Start the car up and the V8 engine signals its intentions through its robust exhaust note. The deep-chested 305 cubic inch engine hauls you rapidly towards the horizon. Its suspension is tight through turns thanks to imprvments over the base Camaro model. With the 1LE package, handling is upgraded even further."

Red was one of three interior colors for the 1992 Heritage edition featured on the inset.

Milestones

1982 Chevrolet launches the third-generation Camaro to replace the previous 12-year-old model. It is available with a four-, six- or an eight-cylinder engine.

Second-generation Z28s continued until 1981, and still offer decent performance. The fastest is the 1970 LT-1 Z28.

1985 IROC-Z is added to the Camaro line. The new model features a special fascia, body skirts, and distinctive 16-inch cast-alloy wheels.

1987 The convertible returns to the range and is available in all Camaro trim levels.

The fourth generation Z28 appeared in 1993 and was the best balanced Camaro yet.

1988 The Z28 is dropped, only to be revived for 1991.

1992 Production of the third-generation Camaro ends to make way for the sleek, new fourth-generation model.

UNDER THE SKIN

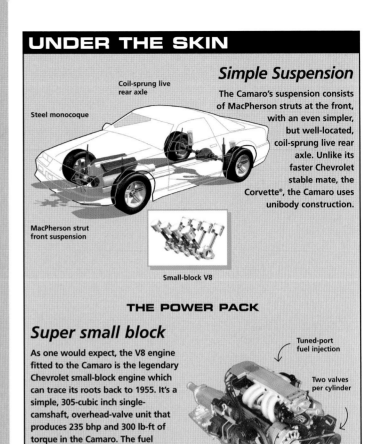

Simple Suspension

The Camaro's suspension consists of MacPherson struts at the front, with an even simpler, but well-located, coil-sprung live rear axle. Unlike its faster Chevrolet stable mate, the Corvette®, the Camaro uses unibody construction.

Coil-sprung live rear axle

Steel monocoque

MacPherson strut front suspension

Small-block V8

THE POWER PACK

Super small block

As one would expect, the V8 engine fitted to the Camaro is the legendary Chevrolet small-block engine which can trace its roots back to 1955. It's a simple, 305-cubic inch single-camshaft, overhead-valve unit that produces 235 bhp and 300 lb-ft of torque in the Camaro. The fuel injection system helps to lower emissions, boosts power and reduces fuel consumption. Although an LT1™-engined Camaro was proposed for 1992, it finally entered into production the following year.

Tuned-port fuel injection

Two valves per cylinder

Cast-iron block

Integral water pump

Final fling

The last year for the third-generation Camaro was 1992. The two main models available were the RS® that had a 189-cubic inch V6 as standard or with an optional V8, and the high-performance Z28. Both coupe and convertible body styles were available.

By 1992 the Camaro was a two-model range: the RS™ (shown) and the Z28.

Always a top seller, the Camaro has all the right ingredients to satisfy the enthusiastic driver—power, performance, fine rear-drive handling and head-turning looks.

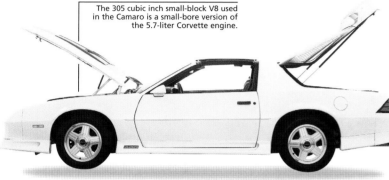

305 cubic inch V8

The 305 cubic inch small-block V8 used in the Camaro is a small-bore version of the 5.7-liter Corvette engine.

Body kit

To keep the third-generation Camaro looking as fresh as possible during its 10-year run, Chevrolet designers used a bolt-on body kit of extra spoilers and side skirts.

Live rear axle

The live rear axle is coil sprung and well located by longitudinal links to help prevent wheel hop during hard acceleration. A Panhard rod is used for lateral location.

Large hatchback

The luggage area of the Camaro is easily accessed through the lift-up hatch. More luggage space is available when the rear seat is folded forward.

Limited-slip differential

To help prevent wheelspin, a limited-slip differential is standard on the 1992 Camaro Z28 and has a 3.42:1 rear axle ratio.

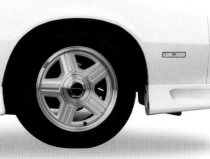

Heritage appearance package

To celebrate the Camaro's 25th birthday, in 1992 all models were finished with the Heritage appearance package, available in red, white or black.

Specifications

1992 Chevrolet Camaro Z28

ENGINE

Type: V8

Construction: Cast-iron block and heads

Valve gear: Single camshaft operating two valves per cylinder

Bore and stroke: 3.74 in. x 3.48 in.

Displacement: 305 c.i.

Compression ratio: 9.5:1

Induction system: Electronic fuel injection

Maximum power: 235 bhp at 4,400 rpm

Maximum torque: 300 lb-ft at 3,200 rpm

Top speed: 137 mph

0-60 mph: 6.5 sec.

TRANSMISSION

Five-speed manual

BODY/CHASSIS

Two-door coupe monocoque

SPECIAL FEATURES

Hood stripes are part of the Heritage appearance package to celebrate the Camaro's 25th birthday.

The rear spoiler is as much for looks as for its aerodynamic effect.

RUNNING GEAR

Steering: Recirculating ball

Front suspension: Independent with MacPherson struts, separate coil springs, telescopic shocks and anti-roll bar

Rear suspension: Live axle on longitudinal links with Panhard rod, coil springs and telescopic shocks

Brakes: Discs (front), drums or optional discs (rear)

Wheels: Alloy, 14-in. dia.

Tires: 205/70 R14

DIMENSIONS

Length: 192.6 in. **Width:** 72.4 in.

Height: 51.5 in. **Wheelbase:** 101 in.

Track: 60 in. (front), 60.9 in. (rear)

Weight: 3,105 lbs.

USA 1993-1997

Chevrolet CAMARO Z28

Since its introduction in 1967, the Camaro Z28 has been an all-American tire-frying, V8-powered coupe. In 1993, a fourth-generation version was introduced, which soon proved untouchable in the bang-for-the-buck performance stakes against the Ford Mustang.

"...a stunningly fast car."

"There is no sound like the rumble of a V8 engine, especially in a sports machine. And the Z28 has that sound in spades. It encourages you to turn up the revs. This is a stunningly fast car. Burnouts are not just possible, they are almost inevitable if you really start to use the power. The ride is good and the tires grippy, but if they come unstuck through sharp corners the nicely weighted power steering makes corrections easy.

A completely new interior arrangement and six-speed transmission arrived for 1993.

122

Milestones

1993 For the 1993 model year, Chevrolet announces an all-new Camaro range, initially available in coupe form only.

1994 Camaros are now also available in convertible form.

For the 1991 model year, the Z28 returned to the Camaro lineup.

1996 A 3.8-liter V6 engine is added to the range, supplementing the 3.4-liter V6 and 5.7-liter V8 units.

Mechanical twin to the Z28 is the Pontiac® Firebird™ Formula™.

1997 The 3.4-liter engine is dropped.

1998 Camaros are facelifted and the Z28 gets a new 305-bhp, 5.7-liter LS1 small-block V8.

UNDER THE SKIN

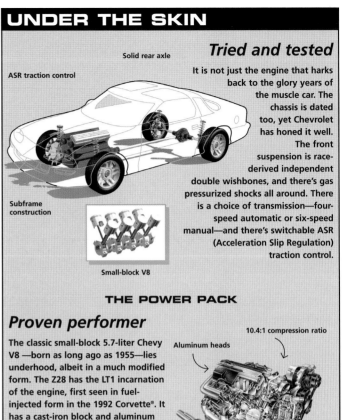

Solid rear axle

ASR traction control

Subframe construction

Small-block V8

Tried and tested

It is not just the engine that harks back to the glory years of the muscle car. The chassis is dated too, yet Chevrolet has honed it well. The front suspension is race-derived independent double wishbones, and there's gas pressurized shocks all around. There is a choice of transmission—four-speed automatic or six-speed manual—and there's switchable ASR (Acceleration Slip Regulation) traction control.

THE POWER PACK

Proven performer

The classic small-block 5.7-liter Chevy V8 —born as long ago as 1955—lies underhood, albeit in a much modified form. The Z28 has the LT1 incarnation of the engine, first seen in fuel-injected form in the 1992 Corvette®. It has a cast-iron block and aluminum heads and just two valves per cylinder, but cranks out anywhere from 275 to 300 bhp depending on year and application. Modifications include multiport electronic fuel injection and an Optispark ignition system.

10.4:1 compression ratio

Aluminum heads

Roller cam with .447/ .459-inch lift

Electronic multiport fuel injection

Top value

Fourth-generation Z28s offer one of the most invigorating driving experiences for under $20,000. If you crave all-American-style, acceleration combined with exceptional handling and braking, all for a reasonable price, the Z28 is a must.

Few cars can match the Z28's combination of performance and value.

The Camaro is ingrained into the minds of many auto enthusiasts as a truly affordable performance coupe, and the Z28 nametag adds a sharp edge of extra grunt to the equation.

High-performance brakes

Very few cars have vented disc brakes front and rear, certainly not at this price level. The Camaro also boasts a state-of-the-art Bosch ABS system that operates all four wheels.

Classic small-block V8

Unlike the lesser Camaros with their V6 engines, the Z28 packs a Corvette-derived LT1 small-block V8 with aluminum heads. Kicking out at least 275 bhp, the Z28 is good enough for 14-second ¼-mile times in factory stock form.

Composite body panels

When designing the fourth-generation car, plastics were chosen for the body due to their greater shape flexibility. The only steel items are the hood, roof and rear fenders.

Aluminum wheels

1993-1997 Z28s came with standard 16-inch aluminum wheels (optional on base models). Z-rated Goodyear Eagles enable speeds of over 150 mph. Wheel design was altered for the 1997 model year.

Simple rear suspension

Unlike the Corvette, the Camaro retains a live Salisbury rear axle. It is coil sprung, but the addition of a torque arm and Panhard rod keep it well located. DeCarbon gas shocks are fitted front and rear.

T-56 manual transmission

In 1993, the Camaro Z28 received a Borg-Warner T-56 six-speed transmission. The following year, CAGS (Computer Aided Gear Selection) became standard. This shifts the transmission from 1st to 4th under light throttle, improving gas mileage.

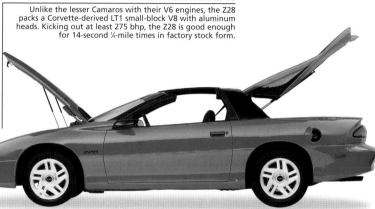

Specifications

1995 Chevrolet Camaro Z28

ENGINE

Type: V8

Construction: Cast iron block with aluminum cylinder heads

Valve gear: Two valves per cylinder operated by a single chain-driven camshaft with pushrods and rocker arms

Bore and stroke: 4.00 in. x 3.48 in.

Displacement: 350 c.i.

Compression ratio: 10.4:1

Induction system: Multiport electronic fuel injection

Maximum power: 275 bhp at 5,000 rpm

Maximum torque: 325 lb-ft at 2,400 rpm

Top speed: 155 mph

0-60 mph: 6.1 sec.

TRANSMISSION

Borg-Warner T-56 six-speed manual

BODY/CHASSIS

Subframe construction with composite two-door coupe or convertible body

SPECIAL FEATURES

The heart of the Z28 is the formidable 275-bhp LT1 small-block V8.

The Camaro's rear turn signals blend in nicely with the car's rear styling.

RUNNING GEAR

Steering: Rack-and-pinion

Front suspension: Wishbones with coil springs and telescopic shock absorbers

Rear suspension: Live axle with coil springs, torque arm, Panhard rod and telescopic shock absorbers

Brakes: Vented discs (front and rear)

Wheels: Alloy, 8 x 16 in.

Tires: 245/50 ZR16

DIMENSIONS

Length: 193.2 in. **Width:** 74.1 in.

Height: 52.0 in.

Wheelbase: 101.0 in.

Track: 60.7 in. (front), 60.6 in. (rear)

Weight: 3,475 lbs.

Chevrolet **CAMARO SS**

In 1998 the SS tag was applied to a Camaro for the third year straight. Early versions of this modified Z28® was developed by tuning company SLP (Street Legal Performance) but Chevrolet began building them in 1998.

"...balanced and brutally fast"

"Extremely well balanced and brutally fast, tight handling and braking that exceeds almost anything are some of the characteristics of the newest version of the Camaro SS. Thanks to the new LS1 347 V8, it can reach 0-60 mph in only 5.2 seconds. The Camaro SS will impress even the most dedicated enthusiasts. Even at speeds as high as 160 mph, the Camaro's 12 inch ABS enhanced brakes will slow the car down in record distance."

The SS interior screams performance thanks to its large analog gauges, supportive seats and perfect placement of pedals and shifter.

Milestones

1987 Ed Hamburger forms SLP Engineering, which is dedicated to making Camaros and Firebirds® go faster and look better.

The SS was the original Camaro performance package from 1967 until 1969. This is a 1968 model.

1996 This year SLP offers a package on the Chevrolet Camaro Z28. It includes ram-air induction and upgraded suspension. Harking back to the muscle car era, this package is named SS. In this first year 2,263 cars are built.

1998 Camaro SS models are based on the Z28.

1998 The Camaro is facelifted with a new front end and receives the all-alloy LS1 V8. Due to growing demand, SS models are now built in house by General Motors instead of being farmed out to Street Legal Performance.

UNDER THE SKIN

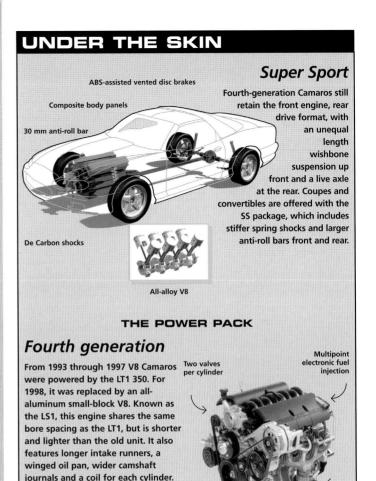

ABS-assisted vented disc brakes

Composite body panels

30 mm anti-roll bar

De Carbon shocks

All-alloy V8

Super Sport

Fourth-generation Camaros still retain the front engine, rear drive format, with an unequal length wishbone suspension up front and a live axle at the rear. Coupes and convertibles are offered with the SS package, which includes stiffer spring shocks and larger anti-roll bars front and rear.

THE POWER PACK

Fourth generation

From 1993 through 1997 V8 Camaros were powered by the LT1 350. For 1998, it was replaced by an all-aluminum small-block V8. Known as the LS1, this engine shares the same bore spacing as the LT1, but is shorter and lighter than the old unit. It also features longer intake runners, a winged oil pan, wider camshaft journals and a coil for each cylinder. In the Camaro Z28 it is rated at 305 bhp, but with ram-air induction installed, as on the SS, power is boosted to an impressive 320 bhp.

Two valves per cylinder

Multipoint electronic fuel injection

Alloy block and cylinder heads

Hydraulic roller camshaft

Future classic

Only a few thousand Camaro SS models are built in 1998. They all offer a 320-bhp 347 cubic inch LS1 V8 and a limited slip rear axle. With a 0-60 time of 5.2 seconds and a top speed of 161 mph, the SS is one of the fastest Camaros ever built.

Without doubt, the current SS Camaro will become a collector's car.

During its 10 years of modifying Pontiac Firebirds and Chevrolet Camaros, SLP Engineering has produced a performance package with outstanding acceleration, braking and handling.

V8 engine

For 1998 the Camaro Z28 and SS get an all-new engine, in the shape of the all-alloy small-block V8. Displacing 347 cubic inches, it includes a 10:0 compression ratio and a .500-inch lift hydraulic roller camshaft and thumps out 320 bhp in more powerful SS trim.

Front-heavy weight distribution

Even though the SS has a front-heavy weight distribution, with almost 57 percent of its bulk on the front wheels, it still accomplishes .90 gs of lateral acceleration on the skid pad and can slalom at 66 mph.

Big wheels and tires

SS Camaros have larger wheels and tires than standard Z28s, with meaty P275/40 ZR17 Goodyear Eagle F1s and 9 x 17-inch cast-alloy five-spoke wheels. Huge ABS-assisted vented discs and anti-roll bars front and rear ensure that handling and stopping are also not a problem.

Tuned exhaust

Fitting a freer-flowing exhaust is an established route for releasing more horsepower from an engine. SLP uses it to extract an additional 5 bhp from the LS1, bringing the total to 325 bhp.

Oil cooler

To ensure that the SS can meet the demands of ultra-high performance driving, SLP provides an engine oil cooler as an option. It can be ordered in conjunction with Castrol Syntec oil for driveline components, which are warranted for up to 500,000 miles.

Specifications

1998 Chevrolet Camaro SS

ENGINE

Type: V8

Construction: Cast-iron block and alloy head

Valve gear: Two valves per cylinder operated by pushrods and rockers

Bore and stroke: 4.0 in. x 3.48 in.

Displacement: 347 c.i.

Compression ratio: 10.1:1

Induction system: Sequential multipoint electronic fuel injection

Maximum power: 320 bhp at 5,200 rpm

Maximum torque: 345 lb-ft at 4,400 rpm

Top speed: 161 mph

0-60 mph: 5.2 sec

TRANSMISSION

Borg-Warner T56 six-speed manual

BODY/CHASSIS

Unitized stamped steel with composite two-door coupe body.

SPECIAL FEATURES

SS models are fitted with a single tailpipe, although dual pipes are offered as an option.

These smart five-spoke alloy wheels were first seen on the Corvette ZR-1.

RUNNING GEAR

Steering: Rack-and-pinion

Front suspension: Short and long arms with coil springs, telescopic shock absorbers and anti-roll bar

Rear suspension: Live axle with trailing arms, Panhard rod, torque arm, coil springs, telescopic shock absorbers and anti-roll bar

Brakes: Vented discs, 12-in. dia. (front), 11.9-in. dia. (rear)

Wheels: Alloy, 9 x 17 in.

Tires: Goodyear Eagle F1, P275/40 ZR17

DIMENSIONS

Length: 193.2 in.   **Width:** 74.1 in.

Height: 51.4 in.   **Wheelbase:** 101.1 in.

Track: 60.6 in. (front and rear)

Weight: 3,593 lbs.

Chevrolet **BLAZER K10**

The K10 Blazer is big, tough and rugged, and the immortal Chevy® V8 gives it the power to go anywhere. Since its revision in the 1990s, the Blazer is more civilized than the traditional Jeep.

"...four-wheel traction."

"On open roads, the full-size Blazer cruises effortlessly at around 70 mph, but its total lack of aerodynamics blunts performance above that speed. It has a harsh, choppy ride on poor surfaces due to its stiff leaf springs, but on a smooth road the big Blazer can hustle around corners. Off-road, and with low range selected, it will charge its way up, over or through just about anything. Even now, the Blazer is a great off-roader."

The utilitarian interior of the Blazer suits the requirements of the off-road driver.

Milestones

1969 Chevrolet introduces the Blazer as a roomy two- or four-wheel drive utility vehicle for use both on and off road. The base engine is a 120-bhp, 250-cubic inch straight-six, but Chevrolet's small-block 307 and 350 V8s are also available.

The first generation Blazers were crude, but tough.

1973 To bring it up to date. the Blazer receives a major facelift, including a larger, less boxy body. This style remains, albeit with minor detail changes, until well into the 1980s.

The 1998 Blazer is in fact an S10 and uses a V6 engine.

1992 A revised Blazer, with independent wishbone front suspension, a five-speed transmission and anti-lock brakes is introduced. This version is bigger than the first Blazer and has a longer wheelbase.

UNDER THE SKIN

Rough and tough

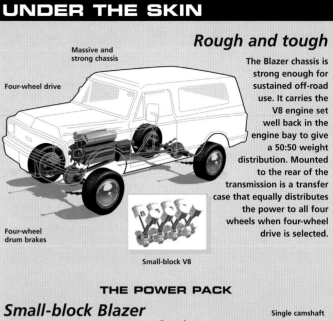

Massive and strong chassis

Four-wheel drive

Four-wheel drum brakes

Small-block V8

The Blazer chassis is strong enough for sustained off-road use. It carries the V8 engine set well back in the engine bay to give a 50:50 weight distribution. Mounted to the rear of the transmission is a transfer case that equally distributes the power to all four wheels when four-wheel drive is selected.

THE POWER PACK

Small-block Blazer

The biggest engine found in the Blazer is the very popular 350-cubic inch V8. Not only is it used in the Blazer but it is also used in a variety of other Chevrolets. It is a classic design and, despite being all iron, is compact and light. Although it is a simple overhead-valve, pushrod engine, it is also very tunable. In the Blazer, the V8 is in a moderate state of tune because torque is much more important than outright power.

Two valves per cylinder

Single camshaft

Cast-iron construction

Tuned for maximum torque

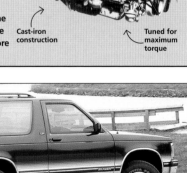

Still going

The full-size Blazer has survived into the 1990s even though it has been supplemented by the popular, but smaller, S10. It has become more advanced, with the introduction of independent front suspension and a five-speed manual transmission. The S10 is now known as the Blazer and the full-size truck is called the Tahoe®.

The smaller S10® Blazer arrived in 1983. This is a 1993 model.

The early model Blazer is not glamorous, but that's the last thing on your mind when you're miles from civilization. In these conditions you appreciate the truck's good qualities—simplicity, strength and reliability.

V8 engine
The 350-cubic inch small-block V8 which powers many other popular Chevrolets is equally capable in the off-road K5; but here it's tuned for torque, not power.

Permanent four-wheel drive
Drive to all four wheels is permanently engaged, with the torque split equally front and rear.

Limited slip differential
For even more traction, limited slip differentials can be added to the axles, but they are not standard equipment.

Front disc brakes
Most of the braking is undertaken by the front wheels, and so the Blazer has optional front discs. Drum brakes are retained at the rear.

High and low ratio
For road driving, the normal high range of gears is used, but for difficult off-road conditions and climbing, the Blazer has a lower ratio to take better advantage of its torque.

Rear tailgate
The rear tailgate folds flat, level with the floor, to allow loads to be slid inside. To carry large items, however, the spare wheel has to be removed.

High ground clearance
The body sits 8.5 inches off the ground to avoid damage from tree stumps and small rocks when four-wheeling. The clearance between the wheel and the body gives room for extreme suspension travel.

Live axles
Blazers are traditional off-road vehicles, with live axles at both the front and rear supported by semi-elliptic leaf springs. This system is extremely strong and allows excellent axle articulation in off-road conditions.

Specifications
1969 Chevrolet Blazer K5

ENGINE

Type: V8

Construction: Cast-iron block and cylinder heads

Valve gear: Two valves per cylinder operated by a single block-mounted camshaft, pushrods, rockers and hydraulic lifters

Bore and stroke: 4 in. x 3.48 in.

Displacement: 350 c.i.

Compression ratio: 8.5:1

Induction system: Single four-barrel Rochester carburetor

Maximum power: 165 bhp at 3,800 rpm

Maximum torque: 255 lb-ft at 2,800 rpm

Top speed: 98 mph

0-60 mph: 15.0 sec.

TRANSMISSION

Three-speed Turbo HydraMatic automatic, with two-speed transfer case and high and low ratios

BODY/CHASSIS

Separate chassis with steel five-door utility body

SPECIAL FEATURES

Large door mirrors are optional and allow a larger rear view when towing.

Front disc brakes are a worthwhile option for improved braking.

RUNNING GEAR

Steering: Recirculating ball

Front suspension: Live axle with semi-elliptic leaf springs and telescopic shock absorbers

Rear suspension: Live axle with semi-elliptic leaf springs and telescopic shock absorbers

Brakes: Discs, 11.6 in. dia. (front), drums, 11.1 in. dia. (rear)

Wheels: Pressed steel, 6 in. x 15 in.

Tires: LT10.15 H78 x 15

DIMENSIONS

Length: 184.4 in. **Width:** 79.6 in.

Height: 73.1 in. **Wheelbase:** 106.5 in.

Track: 66.7 in. (front), 63.7 in. (rear)

Weight: 5,157 lbs.

Chevrolet NOVA SS396

Redesigned and larger for 1968, Chevy's compact now had room for big-block engines. The 396-cubic inch rat motor was officially offered in 350-bhp tune, but those who lived by the phrase 'excess is best' selected the L78 engine option and got the 375-bhp 396 turning the plain-looking Nova into a street terror.

"...Dr. Jeckyll and Mr. Hyde aura."

"Traditionally, the Nova has been stereotyped as a timid base-model with zero performance potential. This 396 V8 version proves this to be a blatant misconception. True, inside and out, it is plain and unadorned, but upon start up, you soon realize that this so-called 'grocery-getter' has a real Dr. Jeckyll and Mr. Hyde aura. Grab the four-speed shifter, hit the gas and listen to the tires spin effortlessly. Its quick-ratio steering and stiff suspension give a fun-to-drive feel that is missing from other muscle cars.

Nova SSs are ideal racers because they're kept light with a minimum of interior embellishments.

Milestones

1968 The Chevy II is redesigned and now rides on a 111-inch wheelbase. Hardtop coupes are dropped, leaving just two-door, pillared coupes and four-door sedans. The SS option returns, and for the first time a 396-cubic inch, big-block V8 is available.

The Nova Super Sport finally got a 327-cubic inch V8 in 1965.

1969 Thanks to a strong advertising campaign, sales are high. Of the 106,200 Novas built, only 7,209 are ordered as SS™ models.

The most powerful engine available in 1971 was a four-barrel 270-bhp, 350-cubic inch V8.

1970 Nova is now the official name, ousting the original Chevy II title. Despite an auto workers' strike early in the year, production is up. The number of SS models that are sold are doubled from the previous year. This is the final season for the 396-cubic inch V8 in Novas.

UNDER THE SKIN

Sharing parts

Live rear axle

Double wishbone front suspension

Unitary construction

Big-block V8

Built on a bigger X-body platform from 1968, the Nova has unitary construction. Front end components, notably the subframe, suspension pieces, engine mounts and radiator, are shared with the Camaro®. All Novas from this period have front coil springs with a live rear axle suspended on leaf springs. SS models have stiffer shocks and springs and a standard front anti-roll bar. Quick-ratio power steering and front disc brakes were available as options.

THE POWER PACK

Mark IV monster

Introduced in 1965 as a replacement for the 409, the 396 was the smallest of the Mark IV series of big-block Chevrolet V8s. First made available in big Chevrolets and the Corvette®, the 396 became a Nova option partway through 1968. In L78 trim, it has a cast-iron block but features an aluminum dual-plane intake manifold and heads borrowed from the 427 with larger valves. Other high performance features include solid lifters and an 800-cfm Holley four-barrel carburetor. Horsepower is rated at 375 bhp at 5,600 rpm, while torque is a substantial 415 lb-ft. With this engine, the 3,400-lb. Nova could run the ¼-mile in 14.5 seconds bone stock.

Speed king

With a very favorable weight distribution, the Nova SS396 was one of the most surprising and quickest muscle cars of the late 1960s. Those equipped with the 375-bhp, solid-lifter, L78 engine are especially sought after by collectors today.

Those who wanted lots of power in a light car were drawn to the Nova SS396.

Serious racers saw the Nova as the perfect street brawler. For just $280 they could transform their bare-bones coupe into a machine that could nearly outrun just about every GTO, Mustang and Road Runner in town.

Pillared coupe styling

When the Chevy II was enlarged in 1968, the hardtop bodystyle was dropped, leaving the pillared coupe and sedan as the only choices. Even with SS badging, the 1969 Chevy II Nova is still demure in appearance.

Rat motor

The key to the Nova's surprising performance is the 396-cubic inch, big-block V8. Although not highlighted in factory brochures, the L78 version of this engine with its solid cam could be ordered by those who wanted a serious performance machine.

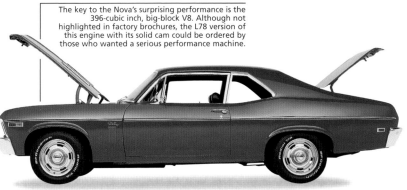

Rally wheels

When new, the SS396 came from the factory with 14-inch steel wheels and poverty hubcaps. Chevy Rally wheels were available as an option and were without a doubt more attractive. Unusually, not many Novas were ordered with them.

Four-speed transmission

Back in the late 1960s, most racers still wanted a manual transmission. The Muncie M21, close-ratio four-speed was an ideal companion to the torquey 396 engine.

Side marker lights

From 1969, all cars sold in the U.S. required side marker lights (amber) front and (red) rear.

Short gearing

With its greater size and weight, plus multileaf springs at the rear, the SS396 is better at launching off the line than its predecessor. To further lower 0-60 mph acceleration, this Nova is equipped with a set of 3.55:1 rear gears and a Positraction limited-slip differential.

Specifications

1969 Chevrolet Nova SS396

ENGINE

Type: V8

Construction: Cast-iron block and heads

Valve gear: Two valves per cylinder operated by a single centrally-mounted camshaft with pushrods and rockers

Bore and stroke: 4.09 in. x 3.76 in.

Displacement: 396 c.i.

Compression ratio: 10.0:1

Induction system: Holley 800-cfm four-barrel downdraft carburetor

Maximum power: 375 bhp at 5,600 rpm

Maximum torque: 415 lb-ft at 3,600 rpm

Top speed: 120 mph

0-60 mph: 5.9 sec

TRANSMISSION

Muncie M21 four-speed manual

BODY/CHASSIS

Unitary steel chassis with two-door coupe body

SPECIAL FEATURES

These non-functional hood vents are part of the SS package.

'SS396' front fender badges give a clue to what lies under the hood.

RUNNING GEAR

Steering: Recirculating ball

Front suspension: Unequal length A-arms with coil springs, telescopic shock absorbers and anti-roll bar

Rear suspension: Live axle with semi-elliptic leaf springs and telescopic shock absorbers

Brakes: Discs (front), drums (rear)

Wheels: Rally, 7 x 14 in.

Tires: E70 14

DIMENSIONS

Length: 189.4 in. **Width:** 70.4 in.

Height: 52.4 in. **Wheelbase:** 111.0 in.

Track: 59.0 in. (front), 58.9 in. (rear)

Weight: 3,400 lbs.

Chevrolet YENKO CHEVELLE

Best known for his hopped-up Camaros®, Don Yenko also offered a small number of hot Chevelles during 1969—made possible due to a GM corporate loophole—powered by 427-cubic inch engines. Properly tuned these cars could run the ¼ mile in around 12 seconds.

"...highly tuned street car."

"If the bold stripes don't tell you that this Chevelle is a highly tuned street car then upon start up, the loud engine note will. Replacing the nasty 375 bhp 396 is an even more belligerent Corvette-spec 427 that cranks out a whopping 450 bhp. During part throttle acceleration, the Yenko Chevelle is notchy and disobedient. But if it's all-out racing excitement you crave, step on the accelerator all the way and listen to the throaty 427 bellow its true intention."

The interior looks stock with the exception of the column-mounted Stewart Warner tach.

Milestones

1967 After building a small number of hot Corvairs, Cannonsburg speed shop owner Don Yenko strikes a deal with Vince Piggins at Chevrolet to build 427 c.i. Camaros. Stock SS 396 models are sent to the Yenko dealership where their engines are swapped out for 427s. A total of 118 are built up to 1968.

The factory Chevelle for 1969 was the SS 396—mainstream muscle.

1969 Using a loophole known as the Central Office Production Order, Yenko convinces Chevrolet to build 427 powered Camaros on the production line. These are then sent to Cannonsburg for installation of decals and trim

Filling the Yenko's shoes in 1970 was the mighty Chevelle SS 454.

1969 Following on from the Camaros are a small number of 427 Chevelles. Yenko orders 99 with SS hoods, 4.10 gears and front disc brakes.

UNDER THE SKIN

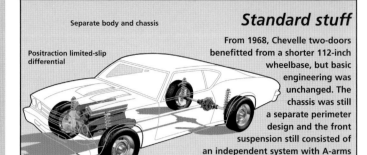

Separate body and chassis

Positraction limited-slip differential

Highly tuned engine

Big-block V8

Standard stuff

From 1968, Chevelle two-doors benefitted from a shorter 112-inch wheelbase, but basic engineering was unchanged. The chassis was still a separate perimeter design and the front suspension still consisted of an independent system with A-arms and coil shocks. At the rear is a live axle, also coil sprung. Like COPO, the Yenko Chevelle came with a standard heavy duty suspension, front disc brakes and a 12-bolt differ-ential with 4.10:1 final drive gearing.

THE POWER PACK

Tyrannical L-72

Due to a corporate edict, the largest engine officially available in the Chevelle in 1969 was a 396. By ordering his cars as COPO specials tuning specialist Don Yenko was able to have 427s factory installed in Chevelles. All these cars have L-72 engines which feature a cast-iron block with four-bolt main bearing caps, rectangular exhaust ports with closed combustion chambers, low restriction exhaust manifolds, an aluminum intake, a solid lifter camshaft and a 800 cfm Holley four-barrel carburetor. GM quoted output at a conservative 425 bhp, however Yenko and the National Hot Rod Association rated them as a more truthful 450 bhp.

Super Car

Only 99 1969 Yenko Chevelles were built. All models had L-72 engines and Positraction 12-bolt rear ends. As some of the quickest GM intermedi-ates of the 1960s, these cars command high prices today and perfectly restored examples sell for $80,000 or more.

Rarest of all Yenko Chevelles are the automatic cars—only 28 were built.

Going a step beyond what the factory had to offer, the Yenko Chevelles, adorned with Yenko SC (Super Car) logos, were part of a select band of street warriors and among the finest Detroit muscle cars ever built.

Heavy-duty transmission

The only transmissions deemed strong enough to cope with the raucous 427 were a Muncie M21 and M22 'Rock-crusher' four-speed manual or, as in this car, a strengthened TH400 three-speed automatic.

Big-block engine

All Chevelles built as part of the COPO order received L-72 427-cubic inch V8s with four-barrel carburetors and solid lifters. For an additional charge, Yenko could fit a pair of Mickey Thompson Super Scavenger headers making the Chevelle a genuine 12-second street car.

Heavy-duty rear axle

Intended as straight-line screamers, the 427 COPO Chevelles and Yenkos were fortified with strengthened GM 12-bolt rear ends with 4.10:1 gearing for maximum acceleration. A Posi-traction limited-slip differential was standard.

Gaudy graphics

Yenko liked to dress up his cars, so the Chevelles got side and hood stripes with SC (Super Car) emblems. Like the factory 396SS Chevelles, Yenkos came with a blacked-out Super Sport grill and rear valance along with the intimidating SS hood.

Base interior

As all the 427 Chevelles were part of a COPO order, they received base Malibu interiors, but many had front bench seats and a center console. Some of the Yenko cars also came with three-spoke, wood-rimmed steering wheels and Hurst shifters.

Power front disc brakes

Because it could scream to 60 mph in less than six seconds, the Chevelle needed considerable power to brig it to a halt. Front disc brakes were thus mandatory.

Specifications

1969 Chevrolet Yenko Chevelle

ENGINE

Type: V8

Construction: Cast-iron block and heads

Valve gear: Two valves per cylinder operated by a single camshaft with pushrods and rockers

Bore and stroke: 4.25 in. x 3.76 in.

Displacement: 427 c.i.

Compression ratio: 11.0:1

Induction system: Holley cfm 800 four-barrel carburetor

Maximum power: 450 bhp at 5,000 rpm

Maximum torque: 460 lb-ft at 4,000

Top speed: 110 mph

0-60 mph: 5.7 sec.

TRANSMISSION

TH400 three-speed automatic

BODY/CHASSIS

Separate steel chassis with two-door coupe body

SPECIAL FEATURES

All 427-cubic inch V8s were built at GM's Tonawanda plant in NY.

A vinyl roof was a popular option in the late 1960s.

RUNNING GEAR

Steering: Recirculating ball

Front suspension: Unequal length A-arms, coil springs, telescopic shock absorbers and anti-roll bar

Rear suspension: Live axle, coil springs, lower links and telescopic shock absorbers

Brakes: Discs (front), drums (rear)

Wheels: Steel Rally 7 x 15 in.

Tires: Goodyear Polyglas GT F70-15

DIMENSIONS

Length: 186.4 in.   **Width:** 77.2 in.

Height: 55.6 in.   **Wheelbase:** 112.0 in.

Track: 61.9 (front), 61.0 (rear)

Weight: 3,800 lbs.

131

Chevrolet **EL CAMINO SS454**

Part car, part truck—the El Camino was always an exclusive vehicle. In the late 1960s, however, the horsepower race could not be ignored, and in 1970 Chevrolet released the meanest El Camino of them all—the SS454.

"...Super Sport hauler."

"From behind the wheel you would think you were sitting in a Chevelle™ SS™: the dashboard, front bucket seats and console are identical. It feels the same too, with a throaty growl from the big V8 and instant acceleration. However, with an unloaded bed, great care is needed when cornering and braking because it's easy to bring out the rear end. At the drag strip this particular El Camino is unique—few pick ups are capable of 14-second ¼-mile times."

Sportiness abounds inside, with front bucket seats and full instrumentation.

Milestones

1964 After a four-year absence the El Camino is relaunched, although it is now based on the midsize Chevelle. A Super Sport package is available, and a big-block 396-cubic inch V8 is optional from 1966.

In 1959, the El Camino was revealed as a stylish pick up.

1968 This year the El Camino receives a major facelift with softer, more flowing styling. Engines range from a straight-six to the 396-cubic inch V8.

1970 Like the Chevelle SS, the El Camino is now available with a 454-cubic inch V8 in either 360-bhp or 450-bhp tune.

In 1970, the Chevelle SS rode the same chassis as the El Camino.

1971 The El Camino SS454 returns, but the 450-bhp LS6 engine is dropped and all V8s have lowered compression; performance and horsepower are also down. A restyled El Camino is still available with the 454-cubic inch V8.

UNDER THE SKIN

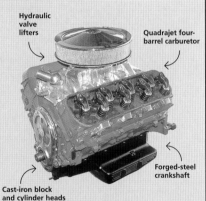

Chevelle-based

From 1964 the El Camino was based on GM's midsize 'A'-body also used by the Chevelle. A body-on-frame design, it has an independent front suspension and a live rear axle. Telescopic shock absorbers at all corners smooth out the ride even further. Unlike the Chevelle SS, it is based on the longer 116-inch wheelbase to improve carrying capacity.

Body-on-the-frame construction

Limited-slip differential

Independent front suspension

Big-block V8

THE POWER PACK

Killer rat motor

SS454s could be ordered with two versions of the 454-cubic inch rat-motor: the LS5 or LS6. Both versions are all-iron, pushrod, short-stroke V8s, although the LS5 has a 10.25:1 compression ratio, hydraulic valve lifters and is rated at 360 bhp. The LS6 features forged-aluminum pistons and forged-steel crankshaft and connection rods. Topped by a huge Holley 850-cfm four-barrel carburetor, it puts out an incredible 450 bhp and 500 lb-ft of torque.

Hydraulic valve lifters

Quadrajet four-barrel carburetor

Cast-iron block and cylinder heads

Forged-steel crankshaft

Power lust

The most desirable of all El Caminos is the 1970 SS454 equipped with the LS6 engine. This monster thumps out 450 bhp and is the quickest of all El Caminos. Only a handful were built and they are now highly sought-after for their performance.

The 1970 LS6-engined El Camino SS454 was only built for one year.

The SS454 was the pinnacle of the El Camino's career. It has the perfect combination of style and practicality, together with the sheer power and performance of the big-block V8.

Big-block V8
The Turbo Jet 454 engine was available in two states of tune. The hydraulic lifter LS5 (as fitted to this car) was rated at 360 bhp and the killer LS-6 at 450 bhp.

Bench or buckets
Like the Chevelle, the El Camino could be specified with either a front bench or twin bucket seats. This example has bucket seats with a center-mounted console. The dashboard layout on both models is identical.

Close-ratio four-speed
To handle all the torque from the Turbojet LS5 engine, this El Camino uses a Muncie M21 close-ratio four-speed transmission. It is named after GM's transmission plant in Muncie, Indiana.

Disc brakes
Early El Camino SS models could definitely go, but stopping was more of a problem. By 1970 the Super Sport package offered power front disc brakes, which helped make the monster pickup slightly safer.

Positraction differential
The combination of an empty load bed and 500 lb-ft of torque can result in the rear wheels spinning under hard acceleration. An optional Positraction limited-slip differential helps to reduce this.

Large load area
The El Camino was extremely practical with a load area of 32.14 sq ft.

Dealer-installed tarp
To help protect both the bed and loads, a dealer-installed tarp was available.

Specifications

1970 Chevrolet El Camino SS454

ENGINE
Type: V8

Construction: Cast-iron block and heads

Valve gear: Two valves per cylinder operated by a single camshaft via pushrods, rockers and hydraulic lifters

Bore and stroke: 4.25 in. x 4.00 in.

Displacement: 454 c.i.

Compression ratio: 10.25:1

Induction system: Single Rochester Quadrajet four-barrel carburetor

Maximum power: 360 bhp at 4,400 rpm

Maximum torque: 500 lb-ft at 3,200 rpm

Top speed: 130 mph

0-60 mph: 7.0 sec.

TRANSMISSION
Muncie M21 (close ratio) four-speed

BODY/CHASSIS
Separate steel perimeter frame with two-door cabin and exposed cargo area

SPECIAL FEATURES

For 1970 only, El Camino SS models were fitted with these Magnum 500 Super Sport wheels.

A special cowl induction hood draws air into the engine at the base of the windshield.

RUNNING GEAR
Steering: Recirculating ball

Front suspension: Double wishbones with coil springs, telescopic shock absorbers and anti-roll bar

Rear suspension: Live axle with control arms, coil springs and telescopic shock absorbers

Brakes: Discs, 11.0-in. dia (front), drums, 9.5-in. dia (rear)

Wheels: Magnum 500, 7 x 15 in.

Tires: HR70-15

DIMENSIONS
Length: 206.8 in. **Width:** 75.4 in.

Height: 54.4 in. **Wheelbase:** 116.0 in.

Track: 60.2 in. (front), 59.2 in. (rear)

Weight: 4,270 lbs.

Chevrolet **C10**

Chevrolet trucks have always been popular workhorses, but with the advent of a new C/K series in the 1970s, they began to take on a different role as family hauler or tricked out street machine.

"...a serious muscle truck."

"This generation of C/K series has a much improved cabin, with a better dash layout and more space. The bench seat may be utilitarian, but starting the big-block rat motor soon erases any feelings of a work truck. The V8 is a torque monster at low rpm and enables you to out perform many late model performance cars. With dual exhaust, the sound is truly awesome and lets any challenger know that this is a serious muscle truck."

The interior has been upgraded with many machined aluminum trim pieces.

Milestones

1973 General Motors launches a new generation of full-size trucks, which are larger and more spacious than their predecessors. Also joining them are a redesigned Blazer® sport utility and Suburban®. Both the engines and chassis are carried over from the previous models.

The featured truck uses a 454-V8 from a Corvette®.

1978 There are minor improvements to the interior of the big trucks.

1979 All full-size trucks are fitted with a catalytic convertor and require unleaded fuel. The hood and grill treatment are also altered.

An all-new Chevy® half-ton pickup made its debut for 1988.

1981 Both the Chevrolet C/K and GMC® Sierra® get a new front grill with square, stacked headlights. Electronic spark control is added to the small-block V8.

UNDER THE SKIN

Made to order

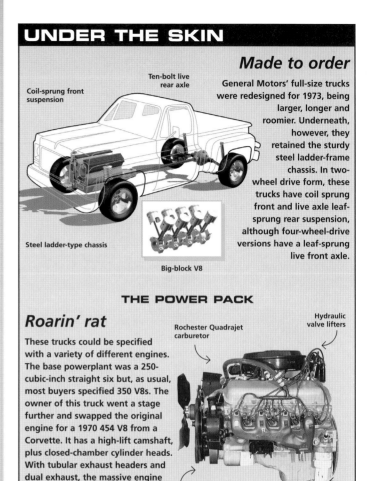

General Motors' full-size trucks were redesigned for 1973, being larger, longer and roomier. Underneath, however, they retained the sturdy steel ladder-frame chassis. In two-wheel drive form, these trucks have coil sprung front and live axle leaf-sprung rear suspension, although four-wheel-drive versions have a leaf-sprung live front axle.

Ten-bolt live rear axle

Coil-sprung front suspension

Steel ladder-type chassis

Big-block V8

THE POWER PACK

Roarin' rat

These trucks could be specified with a variety of different engines. The base powerplant was a 250-cubic-inch straight six but, as usual, most buyers specified 350 V8s. The owner of this truck went a stage further and swapped the original engine for a 1970 454 V8 from a Corvette. It has a high-lift camshaft, plus closed-chamber cylinder heads. With tubular exhaust headers and dual exhaust, the massive engine thumps out a mighty 425 bhp and 500 lb-ft of torque.

Rochester Quadrajet carburetor

Hydraulic valve lifters

Reinforced crank journals and main caps

Large-capacity oil pan

Stepside

Because of its small bed, it wasn't very utilitarian when new. Today, the half- ton Stepside has become a popular truck to modify. Rugged construction and huge engine bays make it an ideal street machine They are also easy to build and modify.

The Stepside version is the preferred C10 for street duty.

Its chunky styling still looks almost contemporary, and the tasteful and subtle modifications give little indication that underneath its meek exterior, this is a killer street pickup.

Stepside bed
Although the Fleetside style was the most popular, hot rodders seem to prefer the narrow bed and large rear fenders of the Stepside models.

Billet grill
Another popular modification on these trucks is to replace the stock grill assembly with billet-style mesh.

Big-block V8
Although C10s use 350 cubic-inch small-block engines, this one has a 1970 Corvette 454-cubic inch mill. With high-flowing heads and an aggressive cam, this pickup can cover the ¼-mile in 15.8 seconds.

Lowered suspension
A popular modification on street pickups is to lower the suspension. On this two-wheel drive C10, the coil-sprung front has been dropped four inches, while the rear has been lowered by 3½ inches.

TurboHydramatic transmission
Due to the incredible torque from the 454 V8, an equally stout transmission is required. This Chevy is fitted with a tough TurboHydramatic 400 three-speed automatic with a 1,800-rpm stall speed torque convertor and shift kit.

Aftermarket wheels
No custom pickup is complete without a set of aftermarket wheels. In keeping with the period look, this Chevy rides on slotted Western cast-aluminum wheels, shod in modern Goodyear Eagle GT performance tires.

Dual exhaust
A full-length dual exhaust system is usually the first modification done to a street machine. This truck uses a dual 2½ inch diameter system to quickly release the engine's exhaust. It lets out a great bellow in the process.

Square styling
The 1973 Chevy and GMC trucks differed considerably from the 1967-1972 models. The later versions have bulkier squared off styling. In fact, this redesign proved so successful and popular that it lasted in various guises until 1992.

Specifications

1974 Chevrolet C10

ENGINE

Type: V8

Construction: Cast-iron block and heads

Valve gear: Two valves per cylinder operated by pushrods and rockers

Bore and stroke: 4.25 in. x 4.0 in.

Displacement: 454 c.i.

Compression ratio: 10.25:1

Induction system: Rochester Quadrajet four-barrel carburetor

Maximum power: 425 bhp at 6,200 rpm

Maximum torque: 500 lb-ft at 3,400 rpm

Top speed: 122 mph

0-60 mph: 7.8 sec.

TRANSMISSION

GM TurboHydramatic three-speed automatic

BODY/CHASSIS

Steel cab and bed on separate steel ladder-type chassis

SPECIAL FEATURES

The engine bay has been dressed up with chrome valve covers, air cleaner and radiator support.

The original wood floor has been replaced with finished oak boards.

RUNNING GEAR

Steering: Recirculating ball

Front suspension: Unequal-length wishbones with coil springs

Rear suspension: Live axle with semi-elliptic leaf springs and telescopic shock absorbers

Brakes: Discs (front), drums (rear)

Wheels: Western cast-aluminum, 8 x 15 in. (front), 10 x 15 in. (rear)

Tires: Goodyear Eagle, P225/60 R15 (front), P275/60 R15 (rear)

DIMENSIONS

Length: 182.6 in. **Width:** 80.4 in.

Height: 61.7 in. **Wheelbase:** 117.5 in

Track: 67.5 in. (front), 68.2 in. (rear)

Weight: 4,045 lbs.

Chevrolet MONTE CARLO

A big seller in the 1970s, the third-generation Monte Carlo has become especially popular in recent years with the lowrider community. Some of these cars are turned into works of automotive art.

"...reserved for special occasions."

"You can tell just by looking that this car is reserved for special occasions. There is no dash—instead the firewall panel is covered in buttoned velour upholstery. Then there's the absence of side glass and B-pillars. Performance is average, but this car is all about looks. Watch passersby crane their necks as you glide along the street. Flick the switches and feel the car dance. Lowrider is an automotive culture unlike any other."

The whole interior is color coordinated in four-tone velour upholstery.

Milestones

1973 A second-generation Monte Carlo on a new G-body platform arrives. With its curvy sheet metal it is a big hit and finds 290,693 buyers.

The Monte Carlo has the longest hood ever fitted to a Chevy®.

1976 Having proved a success, the Monte Carlo is mildly facelifted with stacked headlights and a new grill, plus slight alterations to the interior. The big-block 454 engine option is dropped.

1978 Following in the footsteps of the full-size cars, GM intermediates are downsized, including the Malibu™ and related Monte Carlo.

A second-generation Monte Carlo arrived for 1973.

1980 The Monte Carlo is facelifted at the front with quad headlights. A crisp restyle marks the 1981 Monte Carlo.

UNDER THE SKIN

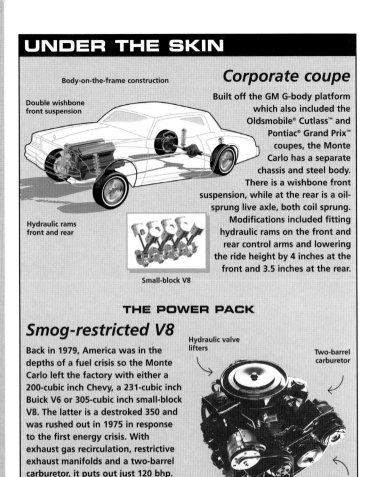

Body-on-the-frame construction

Double wishbone front suspension

Hydraulic rams front and rear

Small-block V8

Corporate coupe

Built off the GM G-body platform which also included the Oldsmobile® Cutlass™ and Pontiac® Grand Prix™ coupes, the Monte Carlo has a separate chassis and steel body. There is a wishbone front suspension, while at the rear is a oil-sprung live axle, both coil sprung. Modifications included fitting hydraulic rams on the front and rear control arms and lowering the ride height by 4 inches at the front and 3.5 inches at the rear.

THE POWER PACK

Smog-restricted V8

Back in 1979, America was in the depths of a fuel crisis so the Monte Carlo left the factory with either a 200-cubic inch Chevy, a 231-cubic inch Buick V6 or 305-cubic inch small-block V8. The latter is a destroked 350 and was rushed out in 1975 in response to the first energy crisis. With exhaust gas recirculation, restrictive exhaust manifolds and a two-barrel carburetor, it puts out just 120 bhp. However, with 240 lb-ft of torque it makes the Monte a fine long-distance cruiser. This engine remains stock.

Hydraulic valve lifters

Two-barrel carburetor

Five main-bearing nodular cast-iron crankshaft

Cast-iron block and cylinder heads

Plentiful

These cars were tremendously popular when new, and simple, rugged engineering with a plentiful and inexpensive parts supply means that they make a practical buy today. These cars make excellent starting points for one-of-a-kind customs.

1978-1980 Monte Carlos are a favorite choice for lowrider enthusiasts.

East Los Angeles is the center for the lowrider movement and boasts some of the finest cars anywhere. This 1979 Monte Carlo is no exception and can be regarded as a benchmark for lowrider aficionados.

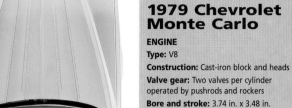

V8 engine
Back in the late 1970s, V6s and economically tuned small-block V8s were the norm in most American cars. This Monte Carlo is no exception, being fitted with a 305-cubic inch (5.0-liter) V8 with a two-barrel carburetor.

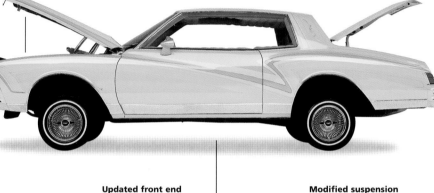

Separate chassis
Although it may seem antiquated, having a separate chassis saved on tooling costs and enabled a soft ride and reduced vibration on the road—an important selling point for what was, after all, a personal luxury coupe.

Body modifications
The unmistakable baroque styling of the late-1970s Monte Carlo is still there, but has been considerably altered. The side glass and B-pillars have been completely removed, turning this Monte into a true hardtop.

Updated front end
Appearances can be deceptive, for although this Monte Carlo has a 1980 nose piece, it is a 1979 model. The owner choose to fit this nose in order to stand out from the crowd. The major changes for 1980 were quad headlights and repositioned turn signal/running lights.

Modified suspension
All true lowriders have customized suspensions that are able to raise and lower the car by using an 8-inch hydraulic pump. This system replaces the stock suspension and is activated by three car batteries.

Wild paint
Perhaps the greatest attention was applied to the paint finish. A rough texture base coat was applied, followed by 'School Bus' yellow pearl and accentuated by five shades of yellow/orange pearl and gold pinstriping. The result is striking, to say the least.

Lounge-style interior
The interior has also been totally reworked, including the removal of the dashboard and all the gauges. A custom center console with a built-in TV has been fabricated and the interior cockpit trimmed with crushed velour.

Specifications
1979 Chevrolet Monte Carlo

ENGINE

Type: V8

Construction: Cast-iron block and heads

Valve gear: Two valves per cylinder operated by pushrods and rockers

Bore and stroke: 3.74 in. x 3.48 in.

Displacement: 305 c.i.

Compression ratio: 8.6:1

Induction system: Rochester two-barrel carburetor

Maximum power: 120 bhp at 3,800 rpm

Maximum torque: 240 lb-ft at 2,400 rpm

Top speed: 118 mph

0-60 mph: 9.4 sec.

TRANSMISSION

GM 2004-R three-speed automatic

BODY/CHASSIS

Separate steel chassis with two-door body

SPECIAL FEATURES

Dayton chrome 13-inch wire wheels are a must for any lowrider.

Swivel front seats hark back to the larger 1973-1977 Monte Carlos.

RUNNING GEAR

Steering: Recirculating ball

Front suspension: Unequal length wishbones with coil springs, telescopic shock absorbers and anti-roll bar

Rear suspension: Live axle with coil springs and telescopic shock absorbers

Brakes: Discs (front), drums (rear)

Wheels: Dayton wires, 7 x 13 in. (front and rear)

Tires: Premium Sportway, 5 x 13 in.

DIMENSIONS

Length: 189.5 in. **Width:** 79.8 in.

Height: 51.4 in. **Wheelbase:** 108.1 in.

Track: 64.6 in. (front), 65.7 in. (rear)

Weight: 3,169 lbs.

Chevrolet 454 SS

As performance made a comeback in the late 1980s, a new automotive phenomenon began to take hold in the U.S.—muscle trucks. One of the first to arrive on the scene was the potent Chevrolet 454 SS.

"...massive amount of torque."

"When you take your place behind the wheel, the 454 feels almost like any other C/K-series pickup. The coil-sprung front suspension gives the SS a smoother ride than most trucks of the era, but the lightly loaded back end can get upset over rough surfaces. What really sets this truck apart, however, is its massive amount of torque. With a large engine, acceleration from lights is tremendous and it pulls the full-size pickup all the way to 120 mph."

Dual bucket seats are comfortable and give the big truck a dash of sportiness.

Milestones

1988 Chevrolet releases a radically reworked version of its popular full-size pickup. It boasts up-to-the-minute styling, an improved interior, a stiffer frame and better handling and ride.

The huge Suburban™ shares its sheet metal with the C1500.

1989 Realizing that there is a potential market for performance pickups, Chevrolet decides to drop its monster 454 engine into the standard-cab, short-bed C1500 truck. The resulting 454 SS goes on sale as a 1990 model. It is initially available only in black.

Chevy 2500 pickups could be offered with a 454-cubic inch V8 but in lower tune than the SS.

1992 There are few changes for the 454 SS, but the color choice is expanded to include red and white.

1993 Having spawned a number of competitors, production of the 454 SS comes to an end.

UNDER THE SKIN

Rough and ready

Beneath the smooth exterior lies a tough ladder-type chassis frame. The front suspension on C/K pickups is very carlike, with unequal length A-arms and coil springs, although a traditional leaf spring setup is fitted at the rear. For the 454 SS, engineers chose to upgrade the suspension for better handling. This was achieved by fitting higher-rate springs, replacing the stock shocks with Bilsteins and regearing the steering for a quicker response.

Live rear axle

Separate ladder-type chassis

Coil-sprung independent front suspension

Big-block V8

THE POWER PACK

Gen V big block

Chevrolet was first on the scene with a muscle truck, and for maximum impact it decided to fit the largest engine it could. The huge 454-cubic-inch engine, used in the standard C/K 3/4- and 1-ton pickups, was chosen. With a fairly long stroke, it is designed for power and torque delivery at low rpm, making it extremely tractable under normal driving conditions. Updates to the 454 unit in the SS truck included Delco electronic ignition, low restriction cast-iron exhaust manifolds and a new intake.

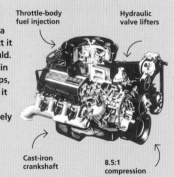

Throttle-body fuel injection

Hydraulic valve lifters

Cast-iron crankshaft

8.5:1 compression

Collector C/K

Among the 1988-1998 generation of C/K-series trucks, the 454 SS is the most sought after. It boasts more power than the others and has truly phenomenal acceleration, improved handling and unique paint and graphics. Good ones can sell for $12,000.

Among all C/K-series trucks, the 1991 454 SS is the best performer.

With this high performance truck, Chevrolet uncovered a new market for factory hot rodded pickups. When the 454 SS first appeared, the division could claim that it was the most powerful production pickup truck on sale at the time.

Stiffened frame

When the new big pickups arrived for 1988, Chevrolet engineers paid considerable attention to the chassis, strengthening the crossmembers and adding thicker rubber bushings to increase stiffness.

Monster powerplant

Chevrolet's catch phrase in the early 1990s was 'The Heartbeat of America.' The heartbeat of this truck is one of the largest engines ever shoehorned into a production pickup. With 405 lb-ft of torque under the hood, it was a serious street brawler.

Smooth styling

Smoother, more rounded styling marked a dramatic departure from the rough-and-ready look of previous Chevy trucks. Until 1992, these aero-styled trucks were available only in standard cab form.

Front disc brakes

By the 1990s, many full-size trucks had front disc brakes. The SS is no exception, although 9.5-inch drums are still fitted at the rear. Anti-lock braking (ABS) is standard.

Less restrictive exhaust system

In 1991, GM replaced the truck's single exhaust with a true dual system. The change brought power up to 255 bhp and 405 lb-ft of torque. This figure is up from 230 bhp and 385 lb-ft of torque in 1990.

Rugged rear end

In 1990, a TH400 three-speed was coupled to a 10-bolt differential with 3.73:1 gears. In 1991, an all new 4L80-E four-speed automatic was introduced. It was basically an electronically shifted TH400, but with overdrive. In addition to the new transmission, the truck also came with steeper 4.10:1 gears.

Handling suspension

Because buyers wanted muscle trucks to go around corners as well as they could accelerate in a straight line, the 454 SS was treated to suspension upgrades. The ZQ6 setup, with stiffer front coil and rear leaf springs, was specified, as were Bilstein shocks and a beefy front anti-roll bar. This results in the truck having a street-rod-like raked stance.

Specifications

1991 Chevrolet 454 SS

ENGINE

Type: V8

Construction: Cast-iron block and heads

Valve gear: Two valves per cylinder operated by a single camshaft with pushrods and rockers

Bore and stroke: 4.25 in. x 4.00 in.

Displacement: 454 c.i.

Compression ratio: 8.5: 1

Induction system: Throttle-body fuel injection

Maximum power: 255 bhp at 4,000 rpm

Maximum torque: 405 lb-ft at 2,400 rpm

Top speed: 120 mph

0-60 mph: 7.2 sec.

TRANSMISSION

GM 700R4 three-speed automatic

BODY/CHASSIS

Steel ladder frame with steel cab and bed

SPECIAL FEATURES

In the SS, the 7.4-liter big-block engine was known as the Tonawanda V8.

These slotted aluminum wheels are unique to Chevrolet 454 SS pickups.

RUNNING GEAR

Steering: Recirculating ball

Front suspension: Unequal-length A-arms with coil springs, telescopic shock absorbers and anti-roll bar

Rear suspension: Live axle with semi-elliptic leaf springs, coil springs and telescopic shock absorbers

Brakes: Discs (front), drums (rear)

Wheels: Cast-aluminum, 15-in. dia.

Tires: Goodyear GT+4, P225/60 VR15

DIMENSIONS

Length: 185.1 in.   **Width:** 75.4 in.

Height: 77.9 in.   **Wheelbase:** 115.0 in.

Track: 62.8 in. (front), 61.9 in. (rear)

Weight: 4,535 lbs.

Chevrolet **LUMINA STOCK CAR**

In 1992, 1993 and 1994, NASCAR's legendary Dale Earnhardt drove a Chevrolet Lumina, but the only connection between that machine and the stock production car was the shape. It was hugely successful and won the championship in 1993 and 1994.

"...here comes the Intimidator."

"Move over Jeff Gordon, here comes the Intimidator—Dale Earnhardt. The sound of the small-block V8 tells you there's over 650 bhp straining to get out. The clutch and gearshift are surprisingly light and easy to use, while the steering has plenty of feel and the car seems massively strong and stable. It has an offset suspension for the endless left-hand turns. This helps fight against the understeer that throws the car to the edge of the oval."

Dale Earnhardt sits nestled among the tubes, with the bare minimum of creature comforts.

Milestones

1993 After a dismal 1992 season, the Chevrolet team doubles its efforts for 1993. By the middle of the season Dale Earnhardt leads the championship. A 10th place at the Hooter's 500 in Atlanta gives him his sixth Winston Cup championship.

Earnhardt moved to racing the Chevrolet Monte Carlo in 1995.

1994 The great Earnhardt, known as 'The Intimidator,' sets off to win his seventh championship. He does so even though he only wins four races, with the Daytona 500 eluding him once again. He finishes the year ahead of Thunderbird driver Mark Martin.

Dale Earnhardt drove the Lumina for three seasons.

1995 The Lumina's career at the top comes to an end as Chevrolet uses the new Monte Carlo® body to promote excitement for the streetgoing versions.

UNDER THE SKIN

Much modified

Tubular-steel chassis   Standard Lumina profile

All NASCAR stock cars are built on a massive separate tubular-steel chassis. Where the production Lumina has independent rear suspension, the NASCAR version has a live axle (like all other NASCAR stockers), together with long trailing arms and a Panhard rod. Front suspension is a double-wishbone system, which is different from the production car.

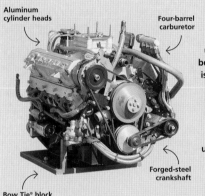

Live rear axle

Race V8

THE POWER PACK

Aluminum cylinder heads

Four-barrel carburetor

Race-spec 358

A reworked version of the small-block Chevrolet V8 is used, but tuned to take power beyond 650 bhp. The crankshaft is forged steel, the con rods are stronger and the raised compression ratio requires 108 octane fuel. The reciprocating assembly is balanced and aluminum cylinder heads are used in place of cast-iron ones. For safety reasons, these engines are limited by using restrictor plates between the high performance four-barrel carburetor and intake manifold.

Forged-steel crankshaft

Bow Tie® block

Chevy® choice

The choice of which car to use in NASCAR is based to an enormous degree on the aerodynamic possibilities because everything else but the shape can be changed. That was why Ford raced the sleek Thunderbird rather than the Crown Victoria.

The Lumina was Chevrolet's most suitable car for NASCAR.

Years ago the term 'stock' car meant that the vehicle being raced is to be right off of the showroom floor with minor modifications. Today, the only part of a stock car that is 'stock' is the roof.

Lexan windshield
Even the strongest laminated glass would be dangerous in crashes, and is therefore replaced by a very strong material known as Lexan.

Kevlar nose
The front body panels are made from Kevlar. It is essential in keeping weight to the specified 3,500 lbs.

V8 engine
A tuned version of the 680-bhp small-block Chevrolet V8 is used. On tracks where speeds can easily exceed 200 mph a restrictor plate is placed between the carburetor and the intake manifold. This restricts fuel flow and power to keep the cars competitive and their speeds safe.

Different tires
The two front tires are different. The tire on the right is slightly heavier and also runs at a higher pressure than the left tire, typically 55 psi rather than 35 psi.

Shapes checked
Before each race a template with the exact dimensions of the particular model is passed over the car by the technical inspectors to make sure that it is within the correct specifications.

Four-speed transmission
As all the racing is flat out in fourth, the only time the driver needs to change gear is to the pits. Cars are still equipped with a four-speed manual transmission, however.

Tubular-steel chassis
Because NASCAR stockers have to weigh at least 3,500 lbs. the chassis can consist of massive constructions of mostly round seamless tubular- steel with some rectangular steel tubes.

Rear wing
The only spoiler allowed on NASCAR stockers of this era was a fairly crude affair riveted to the back of the car. Its 35-degree angle could only be altered by bending it—they didn't have different settings.

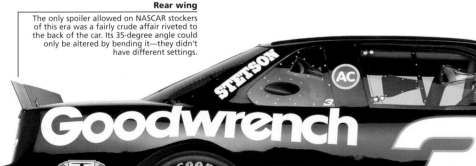

Specifications

1993 Chevrolet Lumina Stock Car

ENGINE
Type: V8

Construction: Cast-iron block and alloy cylinder heads

Valve gear: Two valves per cylinder operated by a single camshaft, pushrods and roller rockers

Bore and stroke: Not quoted

Displacement: 358 c.i.

Compression ratio: 13.0:1

Induction system: Single four-barrel carburetor and restrictor plate

Maximum power: 680 bhp approx.

Maximum torque: Not quoted

Top speed: 200 mph

0-60 mph: 3.5 sec. approx.

TRANSMISSION
Borg-Warner T-10 four-speed manual

BODY/CHASSIS
Tubular-steel chassis with welded-on steel roof and steel and Kevlar panels

SPECIAL FEATURES

Netting over the window keeps the driver's arms inside the car in the event of an accident.

The racing-type gas-filler cap allows quick refuelling during pit stops.

RUNNING GEAR
Steering: Recirculating ball

Front suspension: Adjustable double wishbones with coil springs, adjustable shock absorbers and anti-roll bar

Rear suspension: Live axle with trailing arms, coil springs, adjustable shock absorbers and Panhard rod

Brakes: Vented discs (front and rear)

Wheels: Bassett steel discs, 9 x 15 in.

Tires: Goodyear Eagles, 15-in. dia

DIMENSIONS
Length: 198.4 in.   **Width:** 71.1 in.

Height: 53.5 in.

Wheelbase: 110.0 in.

Track: 59.4 in. (front), 57.9 in. (rear)

Weight: 3,500 lbs.

Chrysler AIRFLOW

The Airflow was one of the most revolutionary and adventurous American cars of the 1930s, an extraordinary study of aerodynamic lines and novel packaging. It was a brilliant car, but too revolutionary for the masses of mainstream buyers.

"...inspires confidence."

"Press the gas pedal and the straight-eight rumbles willingly ahead of you. There is power to take it above 80 mph if you want, but it's better to enjoy the unbelievable amount of torque at your disposal and sit back at a gentle cruise of around 72 mph. In traffic it is tractable, and the view from the high driving position inspires confidence. The hydraulic brakes are surprisingly good and the worm-and-roller steering is remarkably accurate."

The Airflow has comfortable bench seats and an unusual instrument panel.

Milestones

1934 The wind tunnel-tested Airflow range receives straight-eight power, a choice of four wheelbases and various bodystyles. There are three lines—Standard, Imperial and Imperial Custom. It sets speed records and wins the Monte Carlo Concours d'Elegance for design.

Chrysler Airflows are all powered by straight-eight engines.

1935 The 298-cubic inch engine is dropped. The famous waterfall grill is replaced by a curious 'skyscraper' design.

Chrysler also offered a more conventional Airstream model.

1936 The flowing rear end is toned down with the addition of a built-in trunk. Only one engine (a 323-cubic inch) is now offered.

1937 In the final year of production the range is reduced to just two models, and sales dwindle to 4,600 cars.

UNDER THE SKIN

Ahead of its time

Rear-wheel drive
Tubular-steel frame

Hydraulically-operated drum brakes all around

Cast-iron straight-eight

It is not only its striking bodywork—the Airflow is advanced under the skin too. The structural concept of a steel cage and network of girders and trusses onto which the body panels fitted followed aircraft principles for strength and light weight and resembles a modern-day 'safety cell,' All models are fitted with a ride stabilizer bar and the front end has longer and softer front springs. The Airflow's brakes are hydraulically operated, whereas most cars of the era still used rod or cable systems.

THE POWER PACK

Straight-eight power

Chrysler used its range of straight-eight engines in the Airflow series. Carburetion was by Ball & Ball or dual Stromberg downdrafts with automatic choke and an integral air cleaner. During its first year of production there were three engine sizes—298-, 323- and 384-cubic inches—but the 298 was dropped after the first year and the 384 was not available after 1935. Airflows sold under the De Soto badge are fitted with straight-six engines instead of eights.

Integral air cleaner
Twin carburetors

Cast-iron block and cylinder head
Cast-iron crankshaft

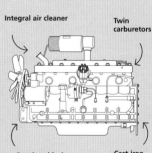

1934 Imperial

The most stylish Airflow is the imposing long-wheelbase Imperial Custom —the 145-inch wheelbase best suits the car's aerodynamic lines. The most desirable model is the first year 1934, with its classic waterfall grill and sloping tail.

Airflow Custom Imperials from 1934 are highly sought after today.

The Airflow was supposed to represent the future, but like so many advanced ideas the public was skeptical of this strange-looking new car, even though it offered new levels of comfort, space and driveability.

Straight-eight power

The straight-eight engine has a healthy power output and masses of torque. In addition, the unit is positioned directly over the front axle, making the hood quite short for a car of this period and allowing more room for passengers.

Advanced transmission

The three-speed manual transmission is renowned for its silent operation. It is fitted with helical gears and later examples gained a hypoid rear axle. Above 45 mph, when you lift your foot off the accelerator, overdrive is automatically engaged.

Wind-tunnel-honed body

The Airflow was one of the first cars to be tested in a wind tunnel. The aerodynamic lines helped a 1934 Imperial coupe to complete the flying mile at the Bonneville Salt Flats at 95.6 mph.

Bold nose

The front end of the1934 model features an amazing 'waterfall' grill, 'shaped by the wind' badging and triple bumper strips. The faired in headlights look curiously like bug eyes, especially on later cars.

A glazing world first

Although most Airflows, like this one, have split windshields, some later-model Imperials boasted a new curved glass design.

Aircraft-type construction

The method of construction was inspired by aviation principles. The body is mounted on steel beams and trusses, in a similar way to contemporary aircraft's.

Puncture-proof tires

By 1936 all Airflows were fitted with new Lifeguard tires with special heavy-duty tubes and a second 'floating' tube inside.

Specifications
1934 Chrysler Airflow Sedan

ENGINE
Type: In-line eight-cylinder
Construction: Cast-iron block and head
Valve gear: Two sidevalves per cylinder
Bore and stroke: 3.25 in. x 4.50 in.
Displacement: 298 c.i.
Compression ratio: Not quoted
Induction system: Two carburetors
Maximum power: 122 bhp at 3,400 rpm
Maximum torque: Not quoted
Top speed: 88 mph
0-60 mph: 19.5 sec.

TRANSMISSION
Three-speed manual

BODY/CHASSIS
Steel girder chassis with four-door steel sedan body

SPECIAL FEATURES

The rear wheel skirts are evocative of the 1930s art deco era.

The rigorously curved surfaces of the Airflow, shaped by Oliver Clark, were unique for 1930s design.

RUNNING GEAR
Steering: worm-and-roller
Front suspension: Beam axle with leaf springs and shock absorbers
Rear suspension: Rigid axle with leaf springs and shock absorbers
Brakes: Drums (front and rear)
Wheels: Steel, 16-in. dia.
Tires: Crossply, 16-in. dia.

DIMENSIONS
Length: 235.0 in.   **Width:** 77.9 in.
Height: 68.9 in.   **Wheelbase:** 146.5 in.
Track: 63.0 in. (front), 61.1 in. (rear)
Weight: 4,166 lbs.

Chrysler TOWN & COUNTRY

Introduced as Chrysler's first woody station wagon in 1941, the Town & Country returned after World War II as a top-level series of sedans, convertibles and coupes built on the New Yorker chassis. The most elegant variant in the post-war years was the convertible.

"...unique driving experience."

"You can tell that a lot of effort went into building this car. The doors shut with vault-like firmness and everything feels rock solid. The huge steering wheel adds an air of authority. Once on the move, it's fun to watch others gaze as you glide by. While the Town & Country with its thick padded bench seat was designed for cruising, it has more than ample power, a satisfyingly smooth ride and comfortable seating—it's a unique driving experience."

Town & Countrys could be well equipped— this one has a cigarette lighter and clock.

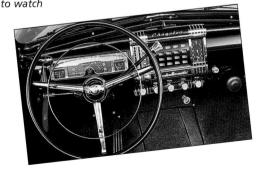

Milestones

1941 Created under the direction of Dave Wallace, the Town & Country is Chrysler's first station wagon. It has clamshell doors and can seat six or nine. Based on the Windsor chassis, 997 are built.

Ford and Mercury were Chrysler's only rivals in 1946-1948. This is a Mercury Sportsman.

1942 The Town & Country becomes a Windsor, but production of all models ceases in February due to World War II.

1950 was the last year of sale for the T&C convertible.

1946 Automobile production resumes. The Town & Country is now an entire series instead of just a wagon. A Brougham, sedan, convertible and coupe are offered.

1947 Only the Town & Country sedan and convertible are offered this year.

UNDER THE SKIN

Playing it safe

Chrysler fielded restyled cars for 1942, but although sheet metal was new, mechanicals were essentially carried over. Town & Countrys rode two different wheelbases for 1947. The chassis is a separate steel affair with independent front suspension and solid axle attached to the rear. Springs are coils at the front, with semi-elliptics at the rear. Braking is courtesy of four-wheel drums.

Separate steel chassis

Independent front suspension

Four-wheel drum brakes

Dependable eight

THE POWER PACK

Proven eight

When relaunched for the 1946 model year, the Town & Country was available with either straight-six or straight-eight engines. Eights were first introduced for 1931, spanning 240 to 385 cubic inches and producing from 82 to 125 bhp. By 1947, only a single straight eight was still available—a 324-cubic inch unit. By then, the basic design was slightly dated, but the cast-iron unit, with a low 6.7:1 compression ratio and a five-main-bearing crankshaft, was very reliable and was used until 1951.

Rare woody

Town & Countrys, convertibles in particular, have long been coveted collectibles. They were little short of handmade cars and production was always low—only 8,368 convertibles were built. This makes them exceedingly rare today.

All T&C convertibles were powered by straight-eight engines.

The name Town & Country came from Mr. Boyertown—the man who built the bodies for these special cars. He said the front of the car 'looked town, while the rear looked country,' and the name stuck.

Semi-automatic transmission

Chrysler's fluid-drive transmission was standard on the Town & Country. This semi-automatic unit has two high and two low gears. The fluid drive means acceleration is slightly on the leisurely side.

Exclusively straight eight

Production 1946-1948 Town & Countrys are powered by Chrysler's venerable straight-eight engine sized at 324-cubic inches. With two Ball and Ball carburetors, it produces 135 bhp.

Structural wood

Besides looking great, the wood is structural on the Town & Country. The door, quarter panel and trunk-lid framing are made from white ash, and the inserts are real Honduras mahogany, changed to DI-NOC decals in late 1947.

Fender skirts

Available as a dealer-installed accessory, rear fender wheel well skirts gave the car a more streamlined appearance.

Long wheelbase

In 1947, the Town & Country was available either as a sedan or convertible. The six-cylinder powered sedans had a 121.5-inch wheelbase, while the eight-cylinder convertibles had 127.5 inches between the wheel centers.

Specifications

1947 Chrysler Town & Country

ENGINE

Type: Inline eight-cylinder

Construction: Cast-iron block and head

Valve gear: Two side valves per cylinder operated by a single block-mounted cam

Bore and stroke: 3.25 in. x 4.88 in.

Displacement: 324 c.i.

Compression ratio: 6.7:1

Induction system: Twin Ball and Ball E7A1 carburetors

Maximum power: 135 bhp at 3,400 rpm

Maximum torque: Not quoted

Top speed: 105 mph

0-60 mph: 20.0 sec

TRANSMISSION

Fluid-drive four-speed semi-automatic

BODY/CHASSIS

Steel chassis with steel and wood two-door convertible body

SPECIAL FEATURES

Chrysler's fluid-drive semi-automatic transmission is fitted on this car.

Its body and door frames were made from ash with mahogany inserts.

RUNNING GEAR

Steering: Recirculating ball

Front suspension: Unequal-length wishbones with coil springs and telescopic shock absorbers

Rear suspension: Live axle with semi-elliptic leaf springs and telescopic shock absorbers

Brakes: Drums (front and rear)

Wheels: Pressed steel, 15-in. dia.

Tires: 8.20 x 15

DIMENSIONS

Length: 202.9 in. **Width:** 84.2 in.

Height: 66.8 in. **Wheelbase:** 127.5 in.

Track: 64.7 in. (front), 65.7 in. (rear)

Weight: 4,332 lbs.

Chrysler **C-300**

The Chrysler 300 is widely recognized as one of America's first muscle cars. However, the 300 wasn't about brute power; it also was a refined, full-size sportster with an abundance of luxury features.

"...immensely powerful."

"The immensely powerful 331-cubic inch Hemi engine produces superb performance by 1950s standards. It pushes the 4,005-lbs. Chrysler to 60 mph in less than 9 seconds, and cruising at over 120 mph is easily possible. Despite its considerable size, the big C-300 remains rock-steady at speed, and although it leans through corners, it manages to hold the line better than any of its contemporaries. It truly deserves its legendary status."

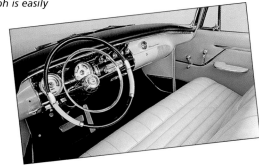

Power windows and a 150-mph speedometer are standard in the C-300.

Milestones

1951 Chrysler introduces its first mass-produced, widely available overhead-valve V8—the 331-cubic inch firepower Hemi. Although a late entry in the OHV V8 race, Chrysler's engine gains a fine reputation for its rugged, powerful and technically well-engineered design.

1958 was the last year for the original Hemi in Chrysler cars, here a DeSoto Adventurer.

1955 Chrysler installs a tuned 300-bhp Hemi into a two-door Windsor coupe and adds heavy-duty suspension and an Imperial grill. The result is the potent C-300.

The last of the tailfinned 300s was the 1961 300G.

1956 More power (340 bhp) and integrated fins mark the second-season 300B, which also starts the letter legacy, culminating in the square-rigged 300L of 1965.

UNDER THE SKIN

Separate steel perimeter chassis

Heavy-duty springs and shock absorbers

Four-wheel power drum brakes

Hemi-head V8

Windsor factor

Based on the Windsor two-door hardtop coupe, the C-300 shares many components with the New Yorker and Imperial, including its dual-cylinder braking system. The standard Windsor suspension setup of an independent front with coil springs and a live rear axle on semi-elliptics was upgraded with stiffer springs and shock rates. This made the C-300 one of the most responsive big cars on the road at the time.

THE POWER PACK

Hemi Legacy

Chrysler gained a lead on its competition when it launched its new overhead-valve V8 in 1951. This 331-cubic inch cast-iron engine featured hemispherical combustion chambers, which enabled it to produce more power than rival V8s at a lower compression ratio. In initial form, it was rated at 180 bhp, but more power was easily possible. For 1955, engineers fitted a tuned version into a two-door Windsor hardtop and christened it the 300. This engine featured bigger valves, a higher-lift camshaft, and a slightly higher compression. The result was nearly 1 bhp per cubic inch and staggering performance.

Bargain Blaze

Competing in the great American horsepower race, the C-300 packed a fearsome punch. It was faster than nearly every other car on sale in the U.S. in 1955, and although it cost a towering $4,110, this early muscle car was a bargain.

Back-up lights and external mirrors were not available on the C-300.

America's first mass-produced car to break the 300-bhp ceiling, the C-300 was also incredibly stylish and dominated NASCAR, winning 37 races in the hands of drivers like Buck Baker and Tim Flock.

Stiffened suspension

While the front coil springs of the New Yorker are rated at 480 lbs./in., those on the C-300 are rated at 800 lbs./in. Likewise, the New Yorker's rear leaf springs are rated at 100 lbs./in., whereas the C-300's are 160 lbs./in.

Solid lifters

Chrysler engineers replaced the hydraulic lifters with solid lifters for the 300. Revving up to 5,200 rpm, the heat generated by the engine could 'pump up' hydraulic lifters as they expand and hold the valves open.

Automatics only

All C-300s came with two-speed PowerFlite automatic transmissions. However, experts agree that there was one car (number 1206) that was built with a three-speed manual transmission.

Axle ratios

The standard rear axle ratio for the C-300 is a 3.54:1 ring-and-pinion, but steeper cogs were available.

Unique wheels

Chrysler C-300 buyers had a choice of two wheel styles. The standard ones are steel with Imperial wheel covers and unique 300 center caps; or, for an extra $617, buyers could opt for a set of chrome, 48-spoke wheels by Motor Wheel.

Specifications

1955 Chrysler C-300

ENGINE

Type: V8

Construction: Cast-iron block and heads

Valve gear: Two valves per cylinder operated by a single camshaft with pushrods and rockers

Bore and stroke: 3.81 in. x 3.63 in.

Displacement: 331.1 c.i.

Compression ratio: 8.5:1

Induction system: Two Carter four-barrel carburetors

Maximum power: 300 bhp at 5,200 rpm

Maximum torque: 345 lb-ft at 3,200 rpm

Top speed: 130 mph

0-60 mph: 8.9 sec.

TRANSMISSION

PowerFlite two-speed automatic

BODY/CHASSIS

Separate chassis with steel two-door body

SPECIAL FEATURES

The protruding stalk shifter was only found on 1955 300s.

Fins on the C-300 were little more than extra chrome pieces grafted on.

RUNNING GEAR

Steering: Recirculating-ball

Front suspension: A-arms with coil springs and telescopic shock absorbers

Rear suspension: Live axle with semi-elliptic multileaf springs and telescopic shock absorbers

Brakes: Drums (front and rear)

Wheels: Wire, 15 x 5 in.

Tires: Goodyear Super Cushion Nylon Special tubeless white sidewalls 6-ply, 8.00 x 15

DIMENSIONS

Length: 218.8 in.   **Width:** 79.1 in.

Height: 60.1 in.   **Wheelbase:** 126.0 in.

Track: 60.2 in. (front) 59.6 in. (rear)

Weight: 4,005 lbs.

Chrysler 300C

Chrysler's letter cars went from the 300B to the 300L. One of the greatest was the stylish 300C, which was capable of an incredible 149 mph thanks to its tuned 392-cubic inch hemi V8 engine.

"...it's all about class."

"The 300C has so much power on tap that Chrysler stepped the throttle action, requiring quite deliberate pressure to get all eight carburetor barrels to pour in fuel. Floor the pedal and the vast bulk of the 300C leaps forward, flinging the car to 60 mph in a mere 8.3 seconds. Direct power steering and stiff springs mean that the handling gives you a fighting chance of keeping the 300C on the road. But this car isn't about handling—it's all about class."

The 300C is a 1950s style-fest both inside the cabin as well as out.

Milestones

1955 The first of the 300 series—the C300— appears. A modified Chrysler New Yorker with a 300-bhp V8, it becomes an all-conquering stock car champion in NASCAR racing.

The first Chrysler 300s appeared in 1955.

1956 Next in the Chrysler letter car series is the 300B with tail fins and a TorqueFlite transmission. Power output rises to 340 bhp.

The 300F model of 1960 was the first 300 with unit construction.

1957 Better looking than the 300B, the 300C arrives. It has a further increase in power, up to 375 bhp, with an optional 390-bhp V8.

1959 This year marks a turning point in the letter cars' history as the hemi engine is dropped for the 300E. The series continues until 1965, ending with the 300L.

UNDER THE SKIN

Torsion bars

Like all Chrysler cars in 1957, the 300C has torsion bars in place of the earlier front coil spring suspension. They are stiffer than those used in the Chrysler New Yorker to give good handling. Similarly, the rear semi-elliptic leaf springs are stiffer than lesser Chryslers. The company's own Oriflow shocks are used all around. With power steering only 3.3 turns of the wheel are needed lock-to-lock. Braking is by four-wheel drums.

Torsion bar front suspension

Body-on-frame construction

Four-wheel drum brakes

Hemi-head V8

THE POWER PACK

Original hemi

For 1957 Chrysler increased the power of the hemi-headed, all-iron V8 by boring and stroking the engine to increase the displacement to 392 cubic inches. Coupled with two four-barrel carburetors, a 9.25:1 compression ratio, mechanical valve lifters and a higher-lift camshaft than in the standard Firepower engine, power rose to 375 bhp. And it didn't end there. As an option you could have a higher-lift camshaft and a 10:1 compression ratio to take the power output to 390 bhp.

Two four-barrel carburetors

Mechanical lifters

Cast-iron block and heads

Cast-iron crankshaft

Open top

With the 300C came the first convertible in the letter car range. Although significantly more expensive than the hardtop model, it had a hydraulically powered top that folded away automatically; it was rather slow to operate, however.

The 300C was the first of the 300s to be offered in convertible form.

Some styling experts claim that no other cars on sale in the U.S. in 1957 could match the dramatic style and sheer overwhelming presence of the Virgil Exner-designed 300C—one of the greatest of all post-war Chryslers.

Hemi V8 engine

Chrysler's first hemi-headed V8 engine appeared as early as 1951 in the shape of the 331-cubic inch Firepower with 180 bhp. By 1957 this engine, with the help of many tweaks, produced a massive 375 bhp.

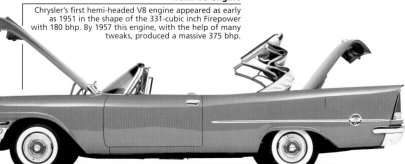

TorqueFlite transmission

The earliest letter cars are fitted with Chrysler's two-speed PowerFlite automatic, but the 300C has the advantage of the superior three-speed TorqueFlite auto. It features push-button gear selection via buttons on the left-hand side of the dash.

Torsion bar suspension

The 300C saw Chrysler switch from coil springs at the front to torsion bars. The bars run lengthwise, operating off the lower wishbones. It is a system that Chrysler retained for many years and used on its later, more powerful cars like the Dodge Charger and Plymouth Superbird.

Drum brakes

In 1957 disc brakes were still not fitted on American production cars and, consequently, the 300C is fitted with drums all around. They are as big as the 14-inch wheel diameter allows to maximize braking power.

Brake cooling scoops

Due to the immense weight of the 300C and its capability of very high speeds, Chrysler fitted scoops below the headlights to direct cooling air to the overworked front brakes.

Tail fins

Although Cadillac is credited with starting the craze for tail fins, by 1957 Chrysler was well in on the act. Chrysler's famous head of styling, Virgil Exner, gave the 300C some of the most pronounced fins seen in the U.S. up until that time.

Specifications

1957 Chrysler 300C

ENGINE

Type: V8

Construction: Cast-iron block and heads

Valve gear: Two inclined valves per cylinder operated by a single V-mounted camshaft via pushrods, rockers and solid valve lifters

Bore and stroke: 4.0 in. x 3.9 in.

Displacement: 392 c.i.

Compression ratio: 9.25:1

Induction system: Two four-barrel Carter carburetors

Maximum power: 375 bhp at 5,200 rpm

Maximum torque: 435 lb-ft at 3,600 rpm

Top speed: 149 mph

0-60 mph: 8.3 sec.

TRANSMISSION

Three-speed TorqueFlite automatic

BODY/CHASSIS

Separate steel chassis frame with two-door hardtop or convertible body

SPECIAL FEATURES

Even the side-view mirrors on the Exner-designed 300C received a considerable amount of attention.

The 300C was one of the most powerful cars on the road in 1957, thanks to the amazing hemi engine.

RUNNING GEAR

Steering: Recirculating ball

Front suspension: Double wishbones with longitudinal torsion bars and telescopic shock absorbers

Rear suspension: Live axle with semi-elliptic leaf springs and telescopic shock absorbers

Brakes: Drums (front and rear)

Wheels: Steel disc, 6.5 x 14 in.

Tires: Goodyear Blue Streak nylon-belted

DIMENSIONS

Length: 219.2 in. **Width:** 66.75 in.

Height: 54.7 in. **Wheelbase:** 126.0 in.

Track: 61.25 in. (front), 60.0 in. (rear)

Weight: 4,389 lbs.

Chrysler **300G**

As a major player of Chrysler's infamous 'letter' dynasty, the 1961 300 G was one of the finest performance/luxury packages on the road during its day, something that endears it to car enthusiasts all over the world.

"...Subtly deceptive."

"With swivelling front bucket seats, access to the cabin is almost effortless. From behind the wheel it becomes all too obvious why few cars can match the 300 G's charisma. Start the engine and just listen to the subtly deceptive sound of the cross-ram 413 V8. The unique pushbutton-operated TorqueFlite transmission is perfectly mated to the engine's torque curve. Despite its size, the 300 feels quite nimble through corners, helped by a finely tuned suspension."

A well-appointed interior and wide bucket seats make the G inviting.

Milestones

1959 Replacing the costly 392-cubic inch Hemi in this year's 300 E is a more conventional 413-cubic inch wedge head. Packing 375 bhp, it is one of the fastest U.S.-built cars on the road.

The first incarnation of the 'letter' cars was the 1955 C300.

1960 Unitary construction and substantially revised styling appear on the heavily revised 300F. It comes with a French-built Pont-a-Mousson four-speed or TorqueFlite automatic. A 400-bhp, 413 V8 is a performance enthusiast's dream option.

In 1957, Chrysler introduced its 300 convertible.

1961 Canted headlights and mild styling revisions are seen on the 300 G. Taller wheels and tires fill its wheelwells. The four-speed option is dropped, but prices are unchanged from 1960.

1962 The 300 sheds its fins on the new H model.

UNDER THE SKIN

Trademark traits

Unitary construction

Dana rear axle with 3.23:1 gears

Torsion-bar front suspension

413 max-wedge V8

For 1960, all Chryslers adopted a unitary body/chassis foundation, and this was carried over for the 1961 model year. The 300 G also has another Chrysler characteristic—a torsion-bar front suspension supplemented by a leaf-sprung live rear axle. The 300 G features stiffer spring rates and has a tough Dana rear end with 3.23:1 gears. Four-wheel drum brakes are standard.

THE POWER PACK

Cross-ram credence

All 300 Gs were powered by the incredible 413-cubic inch max-wedge V8. An outgrowth of the 383 unit that arrived for 1959, the 413 was procured as a less expensive and more practical alternative to the original, first-generation Hemi. This heavy engine offers an incredible 495-lb-ft of torque at a low rpm, making the 300 G very quick from 0-60 mph. Atop the malicious max wedge is a highly unusual, though very effective, cross-ram intake manifold with a Carter four-barrel carb on each side of its seemingly endless ports. The long runners force the air/fuel mixture at a high velocity into the heads and combustion chambers, further maximizing its power.

Hard or soft

Without question one of the most powerful and polished cars of its time, the 300 G is highly regarded today. Two body-styles were offered, and although the hardtop was more popular when new, it is the convertible that captures hearts today.

Extremely stylish though sadly elusive, only 337 drop-top 300 Gs were built.

Unleashing an overabundance of output from its dual-quad, cross-ram, max-wedge engine, the Chrysler 300 G became a legend on the street. However, its first-class styling and massive size kept its brutality well concealed.

Big-block V8

Created under the guidance of chief engineer Robert M. Rodger, the cross-ram induction system made Chryslers some of the hottest cars in their day. Although a 375-bhp V8 was standard in the 300 G, buyers could step up to an even more potent 400-bhp 413 motor. It had even longer runners on its unusual looking intake manifold.

Larger wheels and tires

For the first time since 1956, the 300 featured 15-inch wheels giving the car a taller stance. They also resulted in improved road holding and ride qualities.

TorqueFlite transmission

Chrysler's proven TorqueFlite automatic transmission is operated by pushbutton controls mounted on the dashboard. A three-speed manual was listed on the options list, but few 300 Gs were ordered with it.

Stiffer suspension

The 300 G has a stiffer suspension than other Chryslers, making this 4,315-lb. cruiser one of the most nimble big cars of its time.

Crisp styling

The 300 G was the last of the 'letter' cars to really bear the hallmarks of what is perhaps Virgil Exner's finest work. Canted fins were dramatic and futuristic but times were changing, and for the 1962 300 H they were discarded completely, marking the end of the tail-fin era.

Generous list

As befitting its flagship status, the 300 G came loaded with equipment, including power steering, brakes and windows, a safety cushion dashboard, waterproof ignition, tachometer and front and rear center armrests.

Popular options

Besides the extensive standard equipment that garnished the 300, popular options included air conditioning, electric mirrors and a Music Master radio.

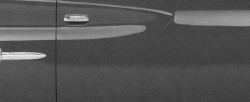

Specifications

1961 Chrysler 300 G

ENGINE

Type: V8

Construction: Cast-iron block and heads

Valve gear: Two valves per cylinder operated by pushrods and rockers

Bore and stroke: 4.18 in. x 3.75 in.

Displacement: 413 c.i.

Compression ratio: 10.0:1

Induction system: Twin Carter four-barrel carburetors, cross-ram intake manifold

Maximum power: 375 bhp at 5,000 rpm

Maximum torque: 495 lb-ft at 2,800 rpm

Top speed: 130 mph

0-60 mph: 8.4 sec

TRANSMISSION

TorqueFlite 727 three-speed automatic

BODY/CHASSIS

Steel unitary chassis with two-door convertible body

SPECIAL FEATURES

The 300 G's swivelling seats were a popular feature on lavish Chryslers.

The year 1961 was significant because it was the final appearance of large, pointed fins on 300s.

RUNNING GEAR

Steering: Recirculating ball

Front suspension: Unequal-length A-arms with longitudinal torsion bars and telescopic shock absorbers

Rear suspension: Live axle with semi-elliptic leaf springs and telescopic shock absorbers

Brakes: Drums (front and rear)

Wheels: Steel disc, 15-in. dia.

Tires: Blue Streak, 8.00 x 15

DIMENSIONS

Length: 219.8 in.   **Width:** 79.4 in.

Height: 55.6 in.   **Wheelbase:** 126.0 in.

Track: 61.2 in. (front and rear)

Weight: 4,315 lbs.

Chrysler **TURBINE**

The 1963 Turbine was an experimental vehicle supplied to 45 families across the U.S., with each having a three-month trial. Although it had potential, there were too many problems for it to gain any commercial application.

"...makes a heat haze."

"When you start up the engine, there is an extraordinary whining sound. Look down at the tachometer and you will see that the engine idles at an incredible 20,000 rpm. The hot air from the tail pipes makes a heat haze behind the car. Despite its bulk, acceleration is good, although you need to get used to the curious sensation of the delay between pressing the throttle and feeling the power. In most other respects you could be driving any 1960s Detroit sedan."

The attractive interior is color-keyed to match the paintwork.

Milestones

1955 Chrysler fits a gas turbine to a stock Plymouth Belvedere as an experiment.

The more conventional 1963 Lincoln Continental had the same designer as the Turbine.

1963 As an exercise in evaluation and publicity, Chrysler releases 45 gas-turbine cars to members of the public for testing.

1964 One turbine car is sent around the world to test public reaction.

The GM EV-1 is the latest attempt at mass-marketing an alternative-fuel car.

1977 Chrysler pursues its turbine experiments throughout the 1960s and 1970s, culminating in a seventh-generation turbine in a 1977 Dodge Aspen.

UNDER THE SKIN

Conventional

Live rear axle

Power-assisted steering

The Chrysler Turbine was engineered just like any other Detroit product of the time. That means coil-spring independent front suspension and a leaf-sprung live rear axle. Despite the car's considerable weight, drum brakes are fitted front and rear, although there is power assistance. Likewise, power steering was standard. The three-speed automatic transmission is conventional, too, though the lever gate has 'Idle' instead of 'Neutral.'

Drum brakes front and rear

Coil-sprung front suspension

THE POWER PACK

Gas Turbine

Chrysler may not have been the first to produce a gas-turbine engine, but it was the world's greatest turbine exponent. The pistonless gas turbine engine has some very strong advantages: it can run on all sorts of fuel (from diesel and kerosene to aircraft fuel), it can rev to very high speeds (as much as 44,600 rpm) very quietly, it warms up instantaneously and boasts a huge amount of torque. However, the disadvantages outweigh the benefits. In pure horsepower terms the engine is quite feeble (only 130 bhp). It's heavy, and worst of all, it has appalling gas mileage figures, at around 12 mpg.

Museum piece

When Chrysler canned its Turbine experiment, 46 of the 55 examples were destroyed simply to avoid paying import duty on the Italian-built cars. The remaining 9 machines were dispatched to car museums and private collections across America.

The Chrysler's styling is particularly outlandish from the rear.

The sight and sound of a car powered by a high-revving gas-turbine engine sounded very space-age in 1963. Chrysler's bold experimental Turbine car worked surprisingly well in many areas and looked futuristic to boot.

Turbine engine
Central to the Chrysler is its gas-turbine powerplant, a neat installation under the hood. Able to spin up to 44,600 rpm, its power is available right across the rev band, as is its torque. But it is too thirsty, even though it can run on a wide variety of fuels.

Turbine gauges
There is a turbine inlet temperature gauge to indicate the temperature at the first-stage turbine wheel.

Turbine styling theme
This Chrysler was the only one of Detroit's multitude of jet-age design concepts to actually reach the public. It lays on the turbine styling theme pretty thick, with deeply indented rear light clusters, rear turbines, turbine-style hubcaps and a bumperless front end with headlamps surrounded by turbine cowls.

Orange paintwork
All 55 cars were built to basically the same specifications, including orange metallic paint and orange leather upholstery. Most, but not all, also had a black vinyl roof.

Designed by Mr. Thunderbird
The cigar-shaped Turbine body was designed by Elwood Engle, the father of the 1961 Ford Thunderbird. Many similarities exist in the profile of the two designs.

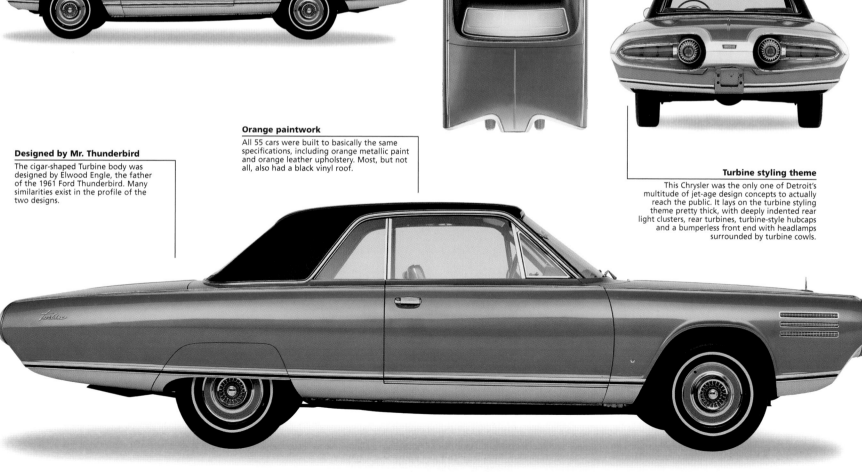

Specifications

1963 Chrysler Turbine

ENGINE
Type: Gas turbine
Construction: Centrifugal air compressor with vaned power turbine
Valve gear: Compressor turbine operating power turbine
Bore and stroke: N/A
Displacement: N/A
Compression ratio: N/A
Induction system: Pressurized air in flame tube
Maximum power: 130 bhp at 44,600 rpm
Maximum torque: 425 lb-ft at zero rpm output shift speed
Top speed: 115 mph
0-60 mph: 10.0 sec.

TRANSMISSION
Three-speed automatic

BODY/CHASSIS
Separate chassis with steel two-door sedan body

SPECIAL FEATURES

The rear-end styling drew inspiration from Flash Gordon.

Spent gases exit from under the car, as in a conventional engine.

RUNNING GEAR
Steering: Recirculating-ball
Front suspension: Upper and lower wishbones, coil springs and shock absorbers
Rear suspension: Live axle with leaf springs and shock absorbers
Brakes: Drums (front and rear)
Wheels: Steel, 14-in. dia.
Tires: 7.50 x 14

DIMENSIONS
Length: 201.6 in. **Width:** 72.9 in.
Height: 53.5 in. **Wheelbase:** 110.0 in.
Track: 59.0 in. (front), 56.7 in. (rear)
Weight: 3,900 lbs.

Chrysler **JEEP GRAND CHEROKEE**

Capitalizing on the past success of the Jeep name and heritage, Chrysler launched the Grand Cherokee for 1993. It's a large, luxurious, all-purpose machine and is capable of the sort of high performance normally reserved for sports cars.

"...an off-road sports car."

"Equipped with a V8 engine, the Grand Cherokee can take on all comers with the acceleration to rival sports cars. Furthermore, it does not roll through corners like most off-roaders. Ride quality is also good, even in rough conditions, and the sophisticated 4x4 system makes light work of difficult terrain. Inside, the Grand Cherokee Limited is fully equipped, better than many luxury cars on the market."

The Grand Cherokee has full instrumentation and features such luxuries as power seats and climate control.

Milestones

1992 Chrysler boss Bob Lutz reveals the Grand Cherokee by driving the first one from the factory, along the streets of Detroit and through a plate-glass window at the Detroit Auto Show.

The Wrangler is currently the entry-level vehicle and the most traditional in the Jeep range.

1994 European production begins at Chrysler's plant in Graz, Austria.

1996 The 1,000,000 Grand Cherokee rolls off the assembly line.

Since 1984 the Cherokee has remained a consistent winner in terms of sales.

1997 The new Grand Cherokee 5.9 Limited, equipped with a larger, 360-cubic inch V8, makes its debut to American buyers.

UNDER THE SKIN

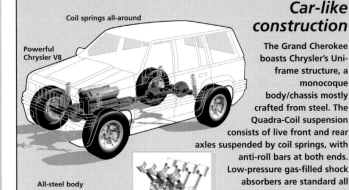

Coil springs all-around

Powerful Chrysler V8

All-steel body

5.9-liter V8

Car-like construction

The Grand Cherokee boasts Chrysler's Uni-frame structure, a monocoque body/chassis mostly crafted from steel. The Quadra-Coil suspension consists of live front and rear axles suspended by coil springs, with anti-roll bars at both ends. Low-pressure gas-filled shock absorbers are standard all around.

THE POWER PACK

Awesome pulling power

While the Grand Cherokee is available with a six-cylinder engine and smaller V8, the Limited LX has the throaty growl of a 360-cubic inch V8, which dates from the 1960s. This engine also powers the mid-size Dodge Dakota, Durango sport-utility vehicle, and the full-size Ram pick-up. In the Limited, it produces 237 bhp and a huge 345 lb-ft of torque. This large engine enables the Grand Cherokee Limited LX to pull a trailer of up to 5,000 lbs.

Overhead valves

Single camshaft

Heavy cast-iron block and heads

Oversquare design

Limited LX

Launched in September 1997, the 5.9 Limited is the current flagship. The fastest Jeep ever marketed, it is also exceedingly capable off road and has one of the most luxurious and well-equipped interiors of any sport-utility vehicle. It may not be for everyone, but the 5.9 Limited is one of the best 4x4s in the world.

Enduring style is part of the Grand Cherokee's popularity.

Taking up its position at the top of the Chrysler Jeep tree, the 5.9 Limited provides the performance of a sports car, the luxury of a limousine, and the off-road ability of a Jeep.

Big V8 engine
The 360-cubic inch V8 runs smooth and provides ample torque. Sophisticated fuel injection and tough cast-iron construction, make for a reliable and robust powerplant.

Quadra-Trac four-wheel drive
An on-demand 4x4 system uses a viscous coupling center differential to split the torque between front and rear axles depending on ground surface conditions.

Aerodynamic design
Compared to contemporary cars, a drag coefficient figure of 0.45 seems quite high. The Grand Cherokee, however, is one of the most aerodynamic sports-utility vehicles ever built thanks to its raked front windshield and relatively low roof line.

Built-in roof rack
The sleek, contoured built-in roof rack increases the already-large luggage capacity.

Steep approach angle
With its small front overhang, the Grand Cherokee has an approach angle up hills of 37 degrees and a departure angle of 30 degrees.

Specifications
1998 Jeep Grand Cherokee Limited LX

ENGINE
Type: V8
Construction: Cast-iron block and heads
Valve gear: Two overhead valves per cylinder with hydraulic lifters
Bore and stroke: 4.02 in. x 3.58 in.
Displacement: 360 c.i.
Compression ratio: 8.7:1
Induction system: Fuel injection
Maximum power: 245 bhp at 4,050 rpm
Maximum torque: 345 lb-ft at 3,050 rpm
Top speed: 124 mph
0-60 mph: 8.2 sec.

TRANSMISSION
Four-speed automatic

BODY/CHASSIS
Steel monocoque five-door sport-utility

SPECIAL FEATURES

It's a tight squeeze under the hood, but the 360-cubic inch V8 engine gives outstanding performance.

Hood vents distinguish the 5.9 Limited from lesser models.

RUNNING GEAR
Steering: Power-assisted recirculating ball
Front suspension: Live axle suspended by coil springs with leading arms, shocks, and anti-roll bar
Rear suspension: Live axle suspended by coil springs with trailing arms, shocks, and anti-roll bar
Brakes: Vented discs front and rear, anti-lock brake system
Wheels: Alloy, 16-in. dia.
Tires: 225/70 R16

DIMENSIONS
Length: 177.2 in. **Width:** 70.7 in.
Height: 64.9 in. **Wheelbase:** 105.9 in.
Track: 58.5 in. (front), 58.8 in. (rear)
Weight: 4,218 lbs.

USA 1998

Chrysler **SEBRING**

Replacing the popular Le Baron, Chrysler's Sebring convertible is based on the coupe that shares its name, but it has a unique personality and elegance that makes it a consistent sales champion.

"...well designed and equipped."

"This is the best-selling U.S.-built convertible and it is easy to see why. Well designed and well equipped, it has plenty of room, even for back seat passengers. It could do with more power, however. An all-coil suspension makes the Sebring a fine handler, plus its big tires and front drive give good traction and grip, even in adverse conditions. With the top up or down, wind noise and cowl shake are less than you would expect for such an affordable car."

Top-of-the-line JXi models come with a V6 engine and leather upholstery.

Milestones

1995 Chrysler's new JA family sedans arrive as the Cirrus and Stratus. These replace the veteran A-body cars and come with either four-cylinder or V6 engines mated to five-speed manual or four-speed automatic transaxles.

Sebring coupes are built at the Diamond Star factory in Illinois.

1996 Replacing the top-selling Le Baron drop-top is a new Sebring convertible. It shares its name with the Mitsubishi-built coupe but uses Cirrus/Stratus running gear and has all-new sheet metal. Two trim levels and powertrains are offered.

Sebring convertibles share floorpans with the Cirrus.

1997 Autostick transmission control becomes available on JXi models along with a Limited package.

1999 Changes are limited to new exterior colors and depowered airbags.

UNDER THE SKIN

Four-wheel disc brakes with ABS

Unitary construction

All-independent suspension

Smooth V6

Not as it seems

Chrysler's convertible shares little under the skin with the Sebring coupe apart from engines. Core parts, namely floorpan, suspension and steering, all come from the JA series sedans, which means unitary construction. There are unequal-length wishbones with coils at the front and a complex dual wisbone and trailing arm arrangement at the rear.

THE POWER PACK

Civilized motoring

Sebring convertibles are offered with two different engines. The base unit, as fitted to JX models, is a 2.4-liter in-line four with 150 bhp. With a base curbweight of 3,331 lbs, the Sebring is no lightweight and not surprisingly, many buyers opt for six-cylinder power. The 2.5-liter, alloy-head, overhead-camshaft V6 is built by Mitsubishi and has a maximum power output of 168 bhp at 5,800 rpm and 170 lb-ft of torque at 4,350 rpm. Equipped with the V6, Sebring ragtops can reach 60 mph from a standing start in 10.2 seconds and can cover the ¼-mile in around 17.4 seconds—hardly drag strip material but good for a cruiser.

Sky's the limit

Attractive looks, a roomy interior and sound engineering mean the Sebring is the best of both worlds: a convertible you can live with year round. The Limited package is perhaps the best choice, offering a V6, leather seats and fancier trim.

Limited models can be distinguished by different pattern wheels.

One of the most attractive convertibles on the market, the Sebring is also one of the easiest to live with, thanks to its superbly engineered top mechanism, good handling and smooth powertrain.

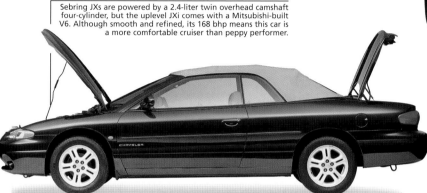

V6 engine
Sebring JXs are powered by a 2.4-liter twin overhead camshaft four-cylinder, but the uplevel JXi comes with a Mitsubishi-built V6. Although smooth and refined, its 168 bhp means this car is a more comfortable cruiser than peppy performer.

Handling suspension
Making an already fine-handling car even better are firmer springs and shock rates, plus 16-inch cast-aluminum wheels and P215/55 R16 touring tires.

Automatic transmission
A four-speed overdrive automatic transmission transmits power to the front wheels. This car has an Autostick, first introduced in 1997, which lets you shift gears manually by moving the shifter from side to side.

Integral seatbelt reels
Lap/shoulder seatbelts are built into the front seats. This has two advantages: first, it eliminates the need for B-pillars or a roll-over hoop; second, it does not hinder passenger access to the roomy rear seat.

Slick styling
Part of the Sebring's sales success is due to the styling. The convertible has a distinctive body, which gives it a long, low appearance. Sheet metal on the convertible is entirely unique, not being shared with other models.

Specifications

1998 Chrysler Sebring

ENGINE

Type: V6

Construction: Cast-iron block and alloy heads

Valve gear: Four valves per cylinder operated by a single camshaft per bank

Bore and stroke: 3.29 in. x 2.99 in.

Displacement: 152 c.i.

Compression ratio: 9.4:1

Induction system: Sequential multipoint fuel injection

Maximum power: 168 bhp at 5,800 rpm

Maximum torque: 170 lb-ft at 4,350 rpm

Top speed: 122 mph

0-60 mph: 10.2 sec.

TRANSMISSION

Four-speed automatic

BODY/CHASSIS

Unitary monocoque construction with steel two-door convertible body

SPECIAL FEATURES

It takes just 10 seconds to lower the Sebring's power top.

The mandatory third brake light is housed in the rear deck trim.

RUNNING GEAR

Steering: Rack-and-pinion

Front suspension: Unequal-length wishbones with coil springs, telescopic shock absorbers and anti-roll bar

Rear suspension: Unequal-length wishbones with trailing arms, coil springs telescopic shock absorbers and anti-roll bar

Brakes: Vented discs (front), Drums (rear)

Wheels: Cast-aluminum, 6.5 x 16 in.

Tires: Michelin XGT4, P215/55 R16

DIMENSIONS

Length: 192.6 in. **Width:** 70.1 in.

Height: 54.8 in. **Wheelbase:** 106.0 in.

Track: 60.2 in. (front and rear)

Weight: 3,382 lbs.

Cord **L-29**

In the late 1920s, America's rich required novelty as well as luxury. Auburn's solution was to produce the long and low L-29 with front-wheel drive and a straight-eight engine. Alas, it arrived on the eve of the stock market crash.

"...tight turning circle."

"Get past the L-29's tendency to go through universal joints and its slightly sluggish performance, and you will discover that in many respects it is a great car. The steering is light and direct and despite its size, the L-29 feels very maneuverable, boasting an incredibly tight turning circle. Near perfect weight distribution and a low center of gravity help give impressive roadholding. Also, befitting its luxury status, the ride is truly excellent."

A distinctive feature of the cockpit is the gearshift, which projects from the dash.

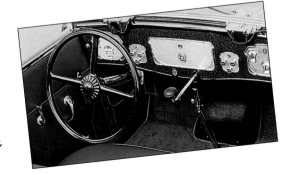

Milestones

1928 Auburn Automobile Company president E.L. Cord decides the time is right for a different luxury car and sets his engineers an extremely tight deadline to produce a front-wheel-drive machine.

E.L. Cord took control of Auburn, and later Duesenberg, before building his own cars.

1929 Named after the company owner, a new car appears as the Cord L-29, powered by 298.6-c.i. Lycoming straight eight. However, it is introduced at the time of the Wall Street crash and sales are disappointing.

Last and most coveted of all Cords is the 812.

1930 Cord L-29s prove an enormous hit on the Concours d'Elegance circuit in Europe.

1931 Prices are slashed to help boost sales, but the L-29's days are numbered and it bows out in December.

UNDER THE SKIN

Clever design

Simple separate chassis
Central X-brace
Front-mounted transmission

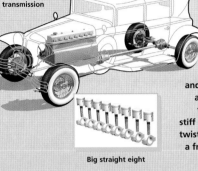

Big straight eight

These front-drive Cords have some of the simplest-looking frames ever made. The twin chassis rails are almost flat, as there was no need to accommodate a live rear axle. The engine is mounted behind the transmission to give almost perfect weight distribution, and it also acts as a chassis brace at the front. There are another five crossmembers including a stiff 'X' brace to stop the structure twisting. Inboard front brakes and a front De Dion axle set the Cord apart from anything else.

THE POWER PACK

Extensively modified

As Lycoming was part of the Auburn-Cord-Duesenberg group, it seemed a logical choice to use one of its straight eights for the L-29. This has a cast-iron block topped by a flat alloy cylinder head, the two inline valves per cylinder are mounted in the block operating upward into the combustion chambers in an L-head design. However, because the L-29 is front-wheel drive, the engine had to be modified considerably and has some 70 unique parts, including the cylinder heads (which got a front-mounted water outlet). During 1932, the bore was increased to give a cubic capacity of 322-cubic inches and 125-bhp.

Fab Phaeton

Although it took a long time for the L-29 to garner collector interest, the car has now been certified a classic. Most sought after of all the factory-bodied L-29s is one of the four-door convertible Phaetons, very closely followed by the two-door cabriolet.

Low and sleek, the L-29 was styled by John Oswald and Al Leamy.

The configuration of the Cord enabled chief body engineer John Oswald to create long, swooping front fenders and a profile that was one of the most striking of its era.

Dashboard-mounted shifter
Because the gear linkage had to go all the way from the cockpit to the transmission in front of the engine, it was easier to take the linkage over the engine and have the shift lever project from the dashboard.

Inboard front brakes
Saving weight is vital at the front on a front-wheel-drive car, so the front brake drums were mounted inboard next to the differential rather than being outboard.

Eight-cylinder engine
Changes to the Lycoming straight eight were necessary for use in the L-29. The engine is mounted back-to-front in the Cord. The crankshaft, camshaft, cylinder head and its oil pan were modified; the camshaft drive was moved aft.

Low ride height
The Cord is lower than any other comparable luxury car because it dispensed with a central driveshaft and thus did not need the usual kick-up at the rear to clear a live axle.

Central chassis lubrication
The L-29 has the Bijur chassis lubrication system in which a pedal pressed by the driver's left foot sends oil from a central reservoir to the water pump, fan, brake pedal linkage, clutch release bearing and rear springs.

Beam-axle rear
Because there was no drive to incorporate in it, the rear axle could be a light A-section beam between the hubs. This is held in place by two semi-elliptic leaf springs, with shackles at the rear to allow for changes in spring length as the axle moves up and down.

Specifications
1930 Cord L-29

ENGINE
Type: Inline eight

Construction: Cast-iron block and alloy head

Valve gear: Two side valves per cylinder operated upwards by single block-mounted camshaft

Bore and stroke: 3.25 in. x 4.50 in.

Displacement: 299.0 c.i.

Compression ratio: 5.25:1

Induction system: Single updraft Schleber carburetor

Maximum power: 115 bhp at 3,300 rpm

Maximum torque: N/A

Top speed: 78 mph

0-60 mph: 24.0 sec.

TRANSMISSION
Three-speed manual

BODY/CHASSIS
Separate-perimeter chassis frame with four-door convertible sedan body

SPECIAL FEATURES

Twin spare wheels can be mounted on the front fenders. Leather straps help keep them on their mountings.

The front-mounted differential helps achieve perfect weight distribution.

RUNNING GEAR
Steering: Gemmer center point

Front suspension: De Dion axle with four reversed quarter-elliptic leaf springs and Houdaille Hershey shock absorbers

Rear suspension: Beam axle with semi-elliptic leaf springs and Houdaille Hershey shock absorbers

Brakes: Drums, inboard at front, hydraulically operated

Wheels: Wire spoke, 5.5 in. x 18 in.

Tires: 7.00 x 18

DIMENSIONS
Length: 205.5 in.   **Width:** 71.5 in.

Height: 66.5 in.   **Wheelbase:** 137.5 in.

Track: 58.0 in. (front), 60.0 in. (rear)

Weight: 4,710 lbs.

Cord 810/812

Produced by a company that was on the verge of bankruptcy, the Cord 810 made its debut as the most advanced front-wheel drive car in the world offering amazing performance and handling.

"...a motoring revelation."

In the mid-1930s the Cord 810 was a motoring revelation. With the addition of a supercharger, performance is excellent and the engine is quiet and refined at speeds above 80 mph. The ride is equally civilized, while handling and roadholding are unbelievable for this type of car. Despite the power being fed to the front wheels, the steering, even without power assistance, is light and precise. The gearshift too is light and delicate."

The interior design is as much a visual delight as the exterior styling.

Milestones

1934 Renowned designer Gordon Buehrig creates a prototype for a new baby Duesenberg.

Due to the unusual styling, the 810 and 812 are often referred to as the 'coffin-nosed' Cords.

1935 A new Cord, the 810 styled by Buehrig along the lines of his stillborn Duesenberg, is rushed into production, but manufacturing difficulties result in orders being delayed.

A Lycoming engine also powers the Duesenberg Model J.

1936 The Cord 810 goes on sale in sedan and Phaeton styles, in addition to a two-seater Sportsman convertible.

1937 Cord introduces the 812. This is a mildly modified 810 and the company's final model before the Cord empire collapses.

UNDER THE SKIN

Body-on-the-frame construction

Front-wheel drive

Front-mounted gearbox

Side-valve in-line eight

New ground

Apart from the chassis, the 810 is a high-tech wonder. The front suspension uses trailing arms, together with a transverse semi-elliptic spring, to keep the wheels vertical—other systems would allow too much camber change and poor handling. The transmission is even more advanced, with a four-speed unit in front of the engine. The change is activated by an electro-vacuum mechanism and a miniature gearshift lever in the cabin.

THE POWER PACK

Aircraft-inspired

Lycoming, an aircraft engine manufacturer, built the Cord engine. It is a 289-cubic inch V8, with the valves on the side of the cylinder heads toward the center of the 'V' between the heads. Unlike modern engines, these are operated by a cam-and-roller mechanism. In normally-aspirated form it produced a reasonable 125 bhp, but the addition of a Schwitzer-Cummins supercharger increased the power initially to 170 bhp and later to a more useful 190 bhp.

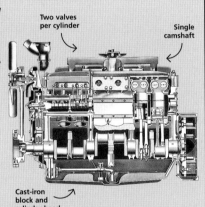

Two valves per cylinder

Single camshaft

Cast-iron block and cylinder head

812 Sportsman

The most desirable of all the 810/812 range is the 812 Sportsman convertible. The supercharged engine gives great performance and the styling is timeless. The car has long been recognized as one of the ultimate American automobiles.

The 812 Sportsman became a legend in its time.

Although more than 50 years old, the Cord still looks advanced. Designed to almost impossible deadlines, the Gordon Buehrig-styled V8-engined Cord 810 was a sensation at the New York Auto Show in 1935.

Pop-up lights
The 810 and 812 pioneered the use of pop-up lights. They were produced by another Auburn-Cord-Duesenberg subsidiary, Stinson, and were actually adapted aircraft landing lights.

Symmetrical window frames
Cord made the front and rear window frames in the doors symmetrical for a very streamlined look. In addition, the front door is rear-hinged and the rear door opens the opposite way to promote its cutting edge styling.

Louvered radiator grill
Although the front of the Cord looks like it contains a stylized version of the old exposed radiators, it is actually a styling feature which hides a conventional radiator.

Lycoming V8
Errett Cord's Auburn-Cord-Duesenberg company also owned the Lycoming engine manufacturers which produced the cast-iron side-valve L-head V8. It produced 125 bhp from 289 cubic inches before the supercharger was installed.

Beam rear axle
In front-wheel drive cars, the rear suspension is lightly loaded and has a simpler design than the front suspension. The Cord has a beam suspended on semi-elliptic leaf springs.

Specifications
1936 Cord 810

ENGINE

Type: V8

Construction: Cast-iron block and heads

Valve gear: Two valves per cylinder operated by a single camshaft and rollers

Bore and stroke: 3.50 in. x 3.75 in.

Displacement: 289 c.i.

Compression ratio: 6.5:1

Induction system: Single carburetor

Maximum power: 125 bhp at 3,500 rpm

Maximum torque: Not quoted

Top speed: 90 mph

0-60 mph: 20.0 sec.

TRANSMISSION

Four-speed pre-selector

BODY/CHASSIS

Separate steel box-section chassis with four-door sedan body

SPECIAL FEATURES

This handle is used to crank the headlights up and down.

The Cotal gearshift is operated by a miniature gearshift lever attached to the steering column.

RUNNING GEAR

Steering: Gemmer centerpoint

Front suspension: Independent with trailing arms and transverse semi-elliptic leaf spring

Rear suspension: Beam axle with longitudinal semi-elliptic leaf springs

Brakes: Drums, 12-in. dia. (front and rear)

Wheels: Steel disc, 16-in. dia.

Tires: Crossply, 6.5 x 16 in.

DIMENSIONS

Length: 195 in. **Width:** 70.9 in.

Height: 57 in. **Wheelbase:** 125 in.

Track: 55.9 in. (front), 60.9 in. (rear)

Weight: 3,650 lbs.

Cosworth **VEGA**

A limited production of Vegas received an engine transplant and turned it into a performance machine. It looks good, handles well and has an advanced twin-cam engine designed by British Formula One racing experts Cosworth.

"...exotic twin-cam engine."

"For its time the standard Vega was an advanced car, offering more power than its rivals, and the Cosworth version was even better. Unfortunately, because the U.S. was new at building emission-controlled performance cars, the exotic 2.0-liter, twin-cam engine lacks sufficient torque. The four-speed Muncie transmission offers precise shifts and the steering is responsive. The handling is exceptional and the Cosworth Vega can corner with the best of its rivals."

The interior is very European in character—stark but very functional.

Milestones

1970 Chevrolet introduces the Vega

as a 1971 model in sedan and coupe forms. Chevy's® import fighter was available with a 2.3 liter engine with up to 110 bhp, but the engine is criticized for its roughness

Although Cosworth was known for its race engines, the Vega was never raced seriously.

1973 Further improvements make

the Vega quicker, but the appearance of the Cosworth, with a twin-cam engine, sees the fastest Vega yet. Chevrolet plans to build 5,000 for the 1975 model year.

Cosworth later helped Ford with rally cars like the Sierra and Escort Cosworth.

1976 Sales never reach projected figures and

having sold just 1,447 units in the 1976 model year, the Cosworth Vega is discontinued.

UNDER THE SKIN

Euro technology

Wishbone front suspension

Live rear axle

Chin spoiler

Twin-cam four

Launched as a 1971 model, the Vega adopted monocoque construction for reduced weight, just like the European imports. Running gear consists of a double wishbone front suspension and a live rear axle, located by control arms and an anti-roll bar. Cosworth Vegas have a quicker steering ratio, and larger radial tires on wide alloy wheels give improved grip.

THE POWER PACK

Hi-tech engine

The standard 140 cubic inch (2.3-liter) alloy block/iron head Vega engine was a disaster, but the Cosworth engine is quite different, with a shorter stroke and smaller, 2-liter displacement. It was an advanced unit, featuring dual overhead cams, four valves per cylinder and electronic fuel injection. The pistons, designed and machined by Cosworth, run in the alloy etched block without the iron plating used in the Chevrolet engine. In stock tune, the small engine produces 110 bhp.

four valves per cylinder

Electronic fuel injection

Electronic engine management system

8.5:1 compression ratio

Tubular header

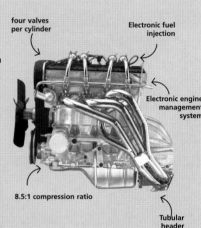

A hotter Vega

With just 3,508 built over a two-year production run, the Cosworth Vega is a real collector's item. It is also a historically important car, because it was built as an economical performance car when gasoline prices were driven up by the fuel crisis of the time.

The Cosworth is by far the most desirable Vega.

Using electronic fuel injection and four valves per cylinder in a 2-liter engine might have been normal in Europe during the 1970s, but not in the U.S. It's too bad this high-tech hot rod wasn't more successful.

Wide radials

Due to its better performance, the Cosworth deserves bigger tires so it uses with fatter BR70-13 radials as standard equipment.

High-tech horsepower

Small displacement, overhead cams and electronic fuel injection are common on U.S. cars today. But these features made the Cosworth an exotic high-tech hot rod with 110 bhp from its very small 122 cubic inch engine in 1975.

Low rear axle ratio

All 1975 Cosworth Vegas used 3.73:1 rear axle ratios, while in 1976 they used 4.10:1s. The Cosworth's rear suspension is upgraded to handle the engine's power.

Twin-cam engine

Chevrolet followed the exotic import route and fitted the Vega with a Cosworth-designed twin-cam cylinder head, the first in a U.S. car for many years. When the engine first appeared the power output was an excellent 130 bhp and 115 lb-ft of torque, but in production the figures were much lower.

Four-speed transmission

In attempt to attract buyers of would-be imported small cars, the Cosworth Vega came with a Muncie four-speed transmission.

European styling

Vegas bore styling cues from the larger Camaro®, which was unmistakably European, although this was later marred by big bumpers.

Alloy wheels

The standard Vega wheels have been replaced by wider 6-inch alloy wheels.

Specifications

1975 Cosworth Vega

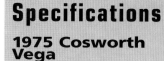

ENGINE

Type: In-line four-cylinder twin-cam

Construction: Light alloy block and head

Valve gear: Four valves per cylinder operated by twin belt-driven overhead camshafts

Bore and stroke: 3.50 in. x 3.14 in.

Displacement: 122 c.i.

Compression ratio: 8.5:1

Induction system: Bendix electronic injection

Maximum power: 110 bhp at 5,600 rpm

Maximum torque: 107 lb-ft at 4,800 rpm

Top speed: 112 mph

0-60 mph: 12.3 sec.

TRANSMISSION

Four-speed Muncie

BODY/CHASSIS

Unitary monocoque construction with two-door coupe body

SPECIAL FEATURES

Each Cosworth Vega has a dash-mounted plaque making it exclusive.

The twin-cam alloy engine is highly exotic for a 1970s American compact.

RUNNING GEAR

Steering: Recirculating ball, 16:1 ratio

Front suspension: Double wishbones with coil springs, telescopic shocks and anti-roll bar

Rear suspension: Live axle with upper and lower control arms, coil springs, telescopic shocks and anti-roll bar

Brakes: Discs, 9.9-in. dia. (front), drums, 9-in. dia. (rear)

Wheels: Alloy, 6 in. x 13 in.

Tires: Radial BR70-13 in. x 6 in.

DIMENSIONS

Length: 170.2 in. **Width:** 65.4 in.

Height: 47.9 in. **Wheelbase:** 97 in.

Track: 55.2 in. (front), 54.1 in. (rear)

Weight: 2,639 lbs.

DeSoto FIREFLITE

The name may have long passed into the annals of history, but that still does not stop a small but ardent band of followers from restoring and maintaining these great cars. The Fireflite is a one-of-a-kind street machine.

"...exceedingly quick."

"Every now and then it's nice to try something different, and this Fireflite is it. The capacious interior has been tastefully altered, and although it is stock, the Hemi V8 is powerful and the Fireflite is exceedingly quick in a straight line. The automatic transmission is excellent for a car of this era, effortlessly shifting between gears. By modern standards, the steering is very light and the ride soft, but when cruising, these factors pale into insignificance."

There's no shortage of flair in the way the cabin has been finished on this 'special.'

Milestones

1949 The all-new DeSotos arrive in March. The power of the straight-six engine is 112 bhp. A total of 94,371 new models are built.

1952 DeSoto's first-ever V8, of 276 cubic inches with 160 bhp, arrives. V8 models are more popular than the six-cylinder Custom/Deluxe variants.

By 1939, DeSoto offered only closed bodystyles.

1955 New, more aggressive styling spruces up the line.

1956 The standard Hemi is bored out to 330 cubic inches with 230 bhp in Firedomes and 255 bhp in Fireflites. The 'Adventurer' hardtop is given a 320-bhp engine.

The 1955 DeSoto Adventurer II was an exotic Ghia-styled four-seater show car.

1957 An all-new range of heavily redesigned DeSotos is launched.

UNDER THE SKIN

Hidden heritage

All-new styling sets the 1955 DeSotos apart from their predecessors, but many items are carryovers. The separate steel perimeter chassis is retained, as is the suspension: double wishbones and coils at the front, plus a live axle with leaf springs at the rear. In common with Detroit practice at the time, braking is by drums. Apart from a later engine and an aftermarket exhaust system, the underside of this 1955 Fireflite remains stock.

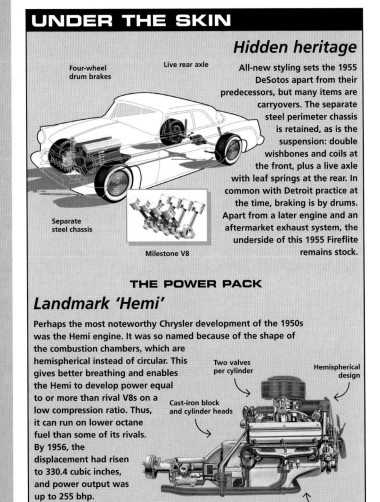

Four-wheel drum brakes

Live rear axle

Separate steel chassis

Milestone V8

THE POWER PACK

Landmark 'Hemi'

Perhaps the most noteworthy Chrysler development of the 1950s was the Hemi engine. It was so named because of the shape of the combustion chambers, which are hemispherical instead of circular. This gives better breathing and enables the Hemi to develop power equal to or more than rival V8s on a low compression ratio. Thus, it can run on lower octane fuel than some of its rivals. By 1956, the displacement had risen to 330.4 cubic inches, and power output was up to 255 bhp.

Two valves per cylinder

Hemispherical design

Cast-iron block and cylinder heads

255 bhp

Adventurer

If there is a favorite among the 1955-1956 DeSotos, it is the high-performance Adventurer, but with only 996 built, it is rare. Besides this, the Fireflite Sportsman hardtop is an ideal choice, with its handsome lines and 200-/255-bhp V8.

Fireflite Sportsmans have sharp styling and offer plenty of V8 power.

Even in their day, these cars were considered flamboyant, to say the least, but this period-modified example takes the idea a step further with its stunning paint finish and classic custom touches.

Hemi V8
Although this car originally came with a Hemi V8, the original engine is long gone. In its place is a 1956 330 Hemi. Unlike many other street machines, which have radically modified engines, the owner chose to leave the V8 stock. With 255 bhp, however, performance is still far from sedate.

Toothy grill
The distinctive grill treatment is a trademark of DeSotos from 1953 to 1955. This car's owner has retained it but has modified the front bumper.

Custom paint
This Fireflite has been painted using DuPont Sonic Purple as the main color, with the roof and lower rear fenders covered in contrasting Eggshell White. This two-tone combination is well suited to the sweeping lines.

Swoopy styling
DeSotos were fairly stodgy-looking cars until 1955. Although all Chryslers were restyled that year, the DeSotos benefited most of all. Some even claimed these cars were among the most beautiful automobiles ever to come out of Detroit.

Aftermarket exhaust
In the 1950s and 1960s, it was common for many speed freaks to fit aftermarket exhausts to help the engine produce more power. This DeSoto has a classic stainless-steel system with true dual pipes and glass pack mufflers. This results in an extra 7 bhp and makes for a terrific-sounding engine.

Shaved and smoothed body
A popular modification on many cars of the 1940s and 1950s is to smooth the body, accentuating the sheet metal contours. On this Fireflite, the body has been nosed and decked, and all emblems and the door handles have been removed.

Two-tone interior
Many 1950s cars had factory interiors that matched the two-tone exterior. Although the paint finish on this car is not stock, the owner has chosen a matching interior. The seats and doors are Eggshell White, with purple inserts in the headlining.

Specifications

1955 DeSoto Fireflite Sportsman

ENGINE
Type: V8

Construction: Cast-iron block and heads

Valve gear: Two valves per cylinder operated by a singe camshaft via pushrods and rockers

Bore and stroke: 3.72 in. x 3.80 in.

Displacement: 330.4 c.i.

Compression ratio: 10.0:1

Induction system: Dual four-barrel carburetors

Maximum power: 255 bhp at 5,200 rpm

Maximum torque: 340 lb-ft at 2,800 rpm

Top speed: 118 mph

0-60 mph: 8.2 sec.

TRANSMISSION
TorqueFlite three-speed automatic

BODY/CHASSIS
Separate steel chassis with two-door hardtop body

SPECIAL FEATURES

Half-moon headlight covers are a typical custom feature for this kind of car.

In DeSotos, the Hemi V8 was known as the Firedome Eight.

RUNNING GEAR
Steering: Recirculating ball

Front suspension: Unequal-length wishbones with coil springs and telescopic shock absorbers

Rear suspension: Live axle with semi-elliptic multi-leaf springs and telescopic shock absorbers

Brakes: Drums (front and rear)

Wheels: Steel discs, 5 x 14 in.

Tires: F70-14

DIMENSIONS
Length: 204.0 in. **Width:** 85.4 in.

Height: 58.9 in. **Wheelbase:** 126.0 in

Track: 65.7 in. (front), 63.2 in. (rear)

Weight: 3,930 lbs.

DeSoto PACESETTER

Arriving midway through 1956 was a new top-of-the line DeSoto—the Adventurer. Packing a bigger 341-cubic inch version of the Hemi engine, it was distinguished by gold anodized trim. A convertible version, which was the Indianapolis 500 pace car that year, was aptly named the Pacesetter.

"...majestic interior design."

"The majestic interior design in the Pacesetter really strikes a chord. Sitting on sofa-like seats, you grasp a huge, narrow-rimmed steering wheel with push button shift controls to the left of the wheel. The wonderful-sounding Hemi V8 sings enthusiastically, combining seamlessly with the PowerFlite transmission. Despite its bulk, the DeSoto was quick for its day and will keep pulling past 100 mph long after its competition has reached its terminal top speed."

Anodized gold on the dash and door panels was an Adventurer/Pacesetter exclusive.

Milestones

1956 DeSoto launches a limited-production hardtop, the Adventurer. A convertible version, the Pacesetter, is also built in very small numbers.

1957 As part of an all-new Chrysler range, a new DeSoto lineup debuts, with the Adventurer coupe and convertible (replacing the Pacesetter) at the top of the range. The Hemi is bored out to 345 cubic inches and has 345 bhp.

1951 saw the arrival of the Hemi V8 in DeSotos.

1958 With a larger bore, the engine size grows to 361 cubic inches. There are minor changes to the grill and trim.

For 1958, the Pacesetter and Adventurer gained a 361-cubic inch engine.

1959 The size of the V8 increases again, to 383 cubic inches.

UNDER THE SKIN

Special touches

In 1956, DeSotos followed the customary Detroit practice in engineering with a separate perimeter chassis and independent coil-sprung wishbone suspension. At the rear was a live axle supported by semi-elliptic leaf springs. Adventurers came with standard power-assisted hydraulic drum brakes and steering and heavy-duty front suspension.

THE POWER PACK

Highland Park power

Regular Firedomes and Fireflites came with 330-cubic inch versions of Chrysler's superb hemi-head V8, rated at 230 and 255 bhp, respectively. In 1956, the Adventurer name first appeared and was the perfect limited-edition showcase for a larger, more powerful 341-cubic inch Hemi. With 320 bhp coupled to a PowerFlite automatic transmission, the new DeSoto flagship was a star performer with 0-60 mph acceleration in the 10- to 12-second range. This engine formed part of the so-called 'Highland Park' performance stable of that year, which included the legendary Chrysler 300B and Dodge D-500.

Trendsetter

Although the 1956 Adventurer is an undisputed collectible, offering fine performance and style, its lesser known derivative, the Pacesetter, is worth a look. For 1956, its only year, just 100 were built compared to 996 hardtops.

Pacesetters are extremely rare these days.

DeSotos were always clean, stylish and classic. The Adventurer and Pacesetter, with their 320-bhp Hemi V8s and luxury trim, were flagships, and still look fresh and stylish today.

Tailfins

1956 was a pivotal year for Chrysler products, which began sprouting true fins. Those on the Pacesetter were tasteful and mated well with the rest of the body. As the decade wore on, Desotos gained increasingly taller and more outlandish fins.

DeSoto Fireflite Eight

Chrysler's Hemi V8 was an engineering milestone of the 1950s. In the DeSoto Pacesetter it was known as the Fireflite Eight. It had smoother porting and manifold passages and better spark plug and valve location than rival V8s, which helped produce more power.

One-year wonder

Chosen as the pace car for the 1956 Indianapolis 500, the Pacesetter paid homage to the famous race with a checkered-flag motif carried on the rear fenders. For 1957, the Pacesetter was replaced by a regular Adventurer convertible.

Coil-sprung suspension

Like rivals of the time, the Pacesetter has independent front suspension with upper and lower wishbones and telescopic shocks. Adventurers and Pacesetters have standard heavy-duty suspension, which slightly improves roadholding.

126-inch wheelbase

The Pacesetter is a full-size car riding a 126-inch wheelbase. In 1957, when Virgil Exner's 'Forward look' cars arrived, the entry-level Firesweep got a shorter 122-inch wheelbase; other DeSotos had a 126-inch wheelbase.

Single color scheme

In its debut year, the Adventurer and the Pacesetter were available only in two-tone white and gold. Special gold badging, interior paneling, grill and wheel covers completed the package. The result was one of the most striking Detroit cars in 1956.

Convenience options

Pacesetters came with standard power steering, chrome exhaust tips and whitewall tires, which were optional on the Firedome and Fireflite. Air Temp air conditioning, power antenna and Solex safety glass were also available to Pacesetter buyers in 1956.

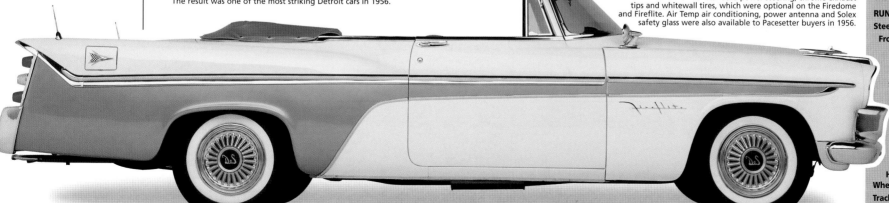

1956 DeSoto Pacesetter

ENGINE

Type: V8

Construction: Cast-iron block and heads

Valve gear: Two valves per cylinder operated by a single camshaft via pushrods and rockers

Bore and stroke: 3.78 in. x 3.80 in.

Displacement: 341 c.i.

Compression ratio: 9.5:1

Induction system: Two Carter four-barrel carburetors

Maximum power: 320 bhp at 5,200 rpm

Maximum torque: 365 lb-ft at 2,800 rpm

Top speed: 115 mph

0-60 mph: 10.2 sec.

TRANSMISSION

PowerFlite two-speed automatic

BODY/CHASSIS

Separate steel chassis with two-door convertible body

SPECIAL FEATURES

Fins were fashionable in 1956 and twin antennas were a popular option.

A dealer installed record player was just one of the DeSoto's unusual options.

RUNNING GEAR

Steering: Recirculating ball

Front suspension: Double wishbones with coil springs and telescopic shock absorbers

Rear suspension: Live axle with semi-elliptic leaf springs and telescopic shock absorbers

Brakes: Drums (front and rear)

Wheels: Pressed steel, 15-in. dia.

Tires: 7.60 x 15

DIMENSIONS

Length: 220.9 in.   **Width:** 76.5 in.

Height: 58.12 in.

Wheelbase: 126.0 in.

Track: 60.4 in. (front), 59.6 in. (rear)

Weight: 3,870 lbs.

Dodge **CHARGER**

Based on the intermediate Coronet, the Charger created a sensation when it arrived for 1966. The dramatic fastback shape also lends it to custom modifications, as demonstrated by this example.

"...modernized muscle car."

"This modified Charger is a uniquely modernized classic muscle car. The interior still looks cool, even today, and with a small-block, 360-cubic inch V8, performance is better than average. 0-60 mph takes just eight seconds and, thanks to its relatively tall gearing, this Charger can cruise happily at 100 mph. With a lowered suspension and modern tires, it holds the road too, and front disc brakes mean it stops far better than with the original drums."

A Le Carrera steering wheel and Auto Meter gauges give it a roadracing flair.

Milestones

1966 The Charger is launched as a stylish two-door fastback based on the intermediate Coronet 117-inch wheelbase chassis. Flashy touches include a hidden headlight grill and a four-bucket-seat interior. Engines range from a 318-cubic inch unit to the monster 425-bhp, 426 Hemi.

A second-generation Charger arrived for 1968. This is the limited-production 1969 500.

1967 After selling 37,344 units in its debut year, the Charger returns with few changes. A new performance-oriented R/T package arrives with a standard 440-cubic inch V8 and heavy-duty suspension. Sales drop to 15,788 in its sophomore year.

A Ram pickup donated its 360 V8 for this particular Charger.

1968 An all-new, Coke-bottle styled, second-generation Charger arrives.

UNDER THE SKIN

Front disc brakes

Unitary construction

Lowered suspension

Small-block V8

Making it handle

Derived from the intermediate Coronet, the new-for-1966 Charger shares its unitary construction, torsion-bar front suspension and leaf-sprung live rear axle. The torsion bars have been cranked lower to drop the front, and lowering springs have been fitted at the back—resulting in a 1.5-inch lower ride height. Front disc brakes and stainless-steel brake lines replace the stock items.

THE POWER PACK

Mid-1970s muscle

Back in 1966, this Charger had a 318-cubic inch V8 nestling between the fenders. Now long gone, the original V8 has been replaced with something a little more potent: a 1978 360-cubic inch engine taken from a Dodge Ram pickup. This 360, which is an excellent high-performance V8 in its own right, has been further improved with the aid of Sealed Power pistons, a high-lift Mopar Performance camshaft, Edelbrock performer intake manifold and four-barrel carburetor. Retaining the stock manifolds, the V8 delivers 365 bhp at 4,700 rpm and 400 lb-ft of torque, making an excellent, head-turning driver.

Base model

Most common of the first-generation Chargers are the 1966 models. The big-block cars are the most sought after, but regular examples are cheaper to buy and are more readily available. They easily accept more power and can be modified to handle well, too.

Eclipsed in popularity by later Chargers, the early cars are still a good buy.

First generation Chargers almost beg for custom treatment, and even with subtle modifications they are guaranteed head-turners on the street. This one has won numerous awards at shows and cruises.

Updated interior
Besides late-model seats, the transmission shift indicator on the console has been modified to read Skully (the car's name), instead of the normal P-R-N-D-2-1 pattern.

More modern
For reasons of practicality, the owner has fitted a small-block, 360-cubic inch V8 of late-1970s vintage. It has been mildly reworked with an aftermarket intake and carb, a hotter camshaft and late-model ignition.

Fastback roof
Although essentially a Coronet with a fastback roof, the 1966 Charger evidently proved to be a hit, with 37,344 sold that year.

Lowered suspension
Although this car retains the stock suspension, it has been lowered. The front torsion bars have been cranked down and lowering blocks fitted on the rear leaf springs, reducing its ride height. This means cornering limits are far greater than Chrysler could have imagined in the 1960s.

Low-profile tires
Besides the lowered suspension, modern BF Goodrich radial tires improve handling even further. Those at the rear are slightly larger than those at the front (255/45x17 versus 215/45x17), which gives excellent traction during standing-start acceleration.

Unitary construction
Like all intermediate Mopars built in the mid- and late-1960s, the Charger has a unitary body/chassis resulting in a stiffer structure than that of some of its rivals.

Specifications

1966 Dodge Charger

ENGINE
Type: V8

Construction: Cast-iron block and heads

Valve gear: Two valves per cylinder operated by a single camshaft with pushrods and rocker arms

Bore and stroke: 4.00 in. x 3.58 in.

Displacement: 360 c.i.

Compression ratio: 9.1:1

Induction system: Edelbrock Performer four-barrel downdraft carburetor

Maximum power: 365 bhp at 4,700 rpm

Maximum torque: 400 lb-ft at 2,800 rpm

Top speed: 135 mph

0-60 mph: 8.0 sec.

TRANSMISSION
TorqueFlite three-speed automatic

BODY/CHASSIS
Unitary steel chassis with two-door fastback body

SPECIAL FEATURES

Given the nickname 'Skully,' this car has subtle custom body graphics.

Full-length dual exhaust pipes help the 360 V8 produce its 365 bhp.

RUNNING GEAR
Steering: Recirculating ball

Front suspension: Unequal-length A-arms with torsion bars, telescopic shock absorbers and anti-roll bar

Rear suspension: Live axle with semi-elliptic leaf springs and telescopic shock absorbers

Brakes: Discs (front), drums (rear)

Wheels: Centerline Scorpion, 7 x 17 in. (front), 8 x 17 in. (rear)

Tires: BF Goodrich Comp ZR, 215/45x17 (front), 255/45x17 (rear)

DIMENSIONS
Length: 204.2 in.   **Width:** 75.0 in.

Height: 55.2 in.   **Wheelbase:** 117.0 in.

Track: 59.5 in. (front), 58.5 in. (rear)

Weight: 3,900 lbs.

Dodge CHARGER

One of the biggest two-door coupes built, the awesome Charger had the extrovert style and extreme performance to go with its massive size, making it the ideal street machine.

"...obeys every command."

"Don't be fooled by the Charger's size. It has enough power under the hood to tame the wildest performance cars in its class. While the 400-bhp 440-cubic inch V8 engine and TorqueFlite automatic transmission is the common driveline, a 425-bhp, 426 Hemi V8 with dual four-barrel carburetors and heavy duty four-speed transmission unleashes the Charger's true potential. Hemi-powered Chargers, if equipped with a Traction Loc differential and 4.10:1 gears, will run the standing 1/4 mile in 13.7 seconds."

Black plastic fascia dominates the Charger's interior. The tachometer carries a clock in its center.

Milestones

1966 The first Chargers are genuine high performers, especially with the 425-bhp Hemi-engined version.

More than 400 Chargers were destroyed during the filming of the TV series 'The Dukes of Hazzard.'

1968 Second-generation Chargers get a restyle. Seven different power outputs are available from a range of V8 engines. The 1969 model year Charger 500 is a limited edition NASCAR special.

The 1970 Charger is more refined than the 1968 model.

1969 Dodge dominates NASCAR with the Charger Daytona, a racing car with aerodynamic nose, tall rear wing and a top speed beyond 200 mph.

1970 Last year of the classic Charger, in which styling is changed from the previous year. Its dimensions are almost the same but the car loses its appeal as the 1970s unfold.

UNDER THE SKIN

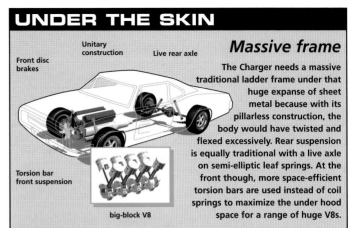

Front disc brakes

Unitary construction

Live rear axle

Torsion bar front suspension

big-block V8

Massive frame

The Charger needs a massive traditional ladder frame under that huge expanse of sheet metal because with its pillarless construction, the body would have twisted and flexed excessively. Rear suspension is equally traditional with a live axle on semi-elliptic leaf springs. At the front though, more space-efficient torsion bars are used instead of coil springs to maximize the under hood space for a range of huge V8s.

THE POWER PACK

Classic V8

There were seven different power outputs available from a range of V8s in this style of Charger from 1968 to 1970, culminating in the mighty Hemi with 426-cubic inches and 425 bhp. The name 'Hemi' derives from the engine's hemispherical combustion chamber design. This design has the same efficient combustion chamber as overhead-cam engines while using pushrods and a single cam. This enables the engine to produce more power at higher rpm. Since they were made to run in the upper rpm range, street Hemis came equipped with dual carburetors. The larger 440 V8 would give 375 bhp as standard, which nearly equaled the Hemi.

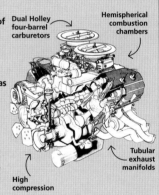

Dual Holley four-barrel carburetors

Hemispherical combustion chambers

Tubular exhaust manifolds

High compression

Charger Daytona

Pride of the 1969 Charger fleet was the Daytona, built for long-distance NASCAR races like the Daytona 500. It was distinguished from the rest of the range by an aerodynamic nose with chin spoiler and concealed headlamps, a flush-window fastback roof and a huge rear adjustable wing. Dodge built only 503 examples in order to homologate the car for competition.

The Charger Daytona was conceived for long-distance NASCAR races.

With style and performance to burn why modify a good thing? When the changes are subtle, unseen and increase performance and handling, why not make a good thing even better?

Tuned V8

The 440-cubic inch Chrysler V8 relies on neat design and its sheer size to give 375-bhp standard output without stressing the engine at all. This modified car has been fitted with two large four-barrel carburetors and a free-flowing exhaust to liberate further power without sacrificing reliability.

Concealed headlamps

One of the Charger's consistent features is its concealed headlamps, seen on all the models from 1966 to 1970. When the four lights were not needed all you could see was the full-width grill.

Radial tires

In the late-1960s, R/T Chargers rode on F70 x 14 tires like most of the powerful opposition. Tire technology has moved on and this modified Charger has far more grip and control thanks to its modern radials.

Torsion bar front suspension

It would have been hard to place the right sized front coil springs between the Charger's double wishbones so the bottom wish-bone is connected to a long torsion bar on each side.

TorqueFlite transmission

A manual four-speed was a no-cost option on the Charger, but most buyers opted for the superb Chrysler TorqueFlite three-speed auto without really losing anything in performance.

Leaf spring rear suspension

Although the Charger only has a leaf spring rear suspension the faster versions were given stiffer springs thanks to six rather than four leafs.

Optional disc brakes

Even on the most powerful of the 1968 to 1970 generation Charger front discs were listed as an option, costing $41.75 extra.

Standard bodywork

Given the rising value of the 1968-1970 Charger as a classic car it pays to make modifications reversible so as not to affect the car's value. This car has immaculate standard bodywork.

Specifications
1968 Modified Dodge Charger 440

ENGINE

Type: V8

Construction: Cast-iron block and heads

Valve gear: Two valves per cylinder operated by single block-mounted camshaft via pushrods, rockers and hydraulic lifters

Bore and stroke: 4.32 in. x 3.75 in.

Displacement: 440 c.i.

Compression ratio: 10.0:1

Induction system: Two four-barrel carburetors

Maximum power: 400 bhp at 4,800 rpm

Maximum torque: 410 ft-lb at 3,600 rpm

Top speed: 140 mph

0-60 mph: 7.5 sec.

TRANSMISSION

Three-speed TorqueFlite automatic

BODY/CHASSIS

Unitary construction with additional ladder frame and two-door pillarless coupe body

SPECIAL FEATURES

The 'vents' pressed into the door panels are non-functional but help give the Charger a distinguishing look.

R/T stands for Road/Track and denotes the installation of Dodge's popular performance package.

RUNNING GEAR

Steering: Recirculating ball

Front suspension: Double wishbones with longitudinal torsion bars and telescopic shocks

Rear suspension: Live axle with semi-elliptic leaf springs and telescopic shocks

Brakes: Drums, 11 in. dia. (front), drums 10 in. dia. (rear)

Wheels: Alloy, 14 in. x 5.5 in.

Tires: F70 x 14

DIMENSIONS

Length: 208 in.   **Width:** 76.6 in.

Height: 53.2 in.   **Wheelbase:** 117 in.

Track: 59.5 in. (front), 59.2 in. (rear)

Weight: 3,574 lbs.

Dodge CHARGER 500

'Win on Sunday, sell on Monday' was a Detroit mantra in the late 1960s. With Chrysler being trounced by Ford on the super speedways, it needed a worthy contender. The result was the high-performance, limited-production Dodge Charger 500.

"...breathtaking acceleration."

"Turn the key and hear the distinctive starter crank the mighty Hemi. Although it requires premium fuel, the 426-cubic inch V8 powers the Charger around town without stumbling in low revs like some engines, although fast street racing is its call. Planting your foot to the floor brings a howl of delight from under the hood and, combined with the four-speed transmission, the acceleration is breathtaking—the Hemi pulls all the way up to the redline."

Charger 500s came with a stock R/T (Road and Track) interior, and woodgrain trim.

Milestones

1967 A second-generation Charger, with coke bottle fender line, is released for 1968. The R/T model comes with either a 375-bhp, 440-cubic inch or 425-bhp, 426-cubic inch Hemi V8.

The Charger debuted for 1966 with fastback styling.

1968 With Chrysler losing the battle in NASCAR to Ford, Mopar produce the Charger 500. It has a plugged grill with exposed headlights and a flush back window. It is sold as a 1969 model.

Regular Charger R/Ts got a split hidden headlight grill for 1969.

1969 The slippery Charger 500s manage to capture 18 NASCAR victories this year. Unfortunately, Ford's more aerodynamic Talladega's won 30.

1969 A more streamlined Daytona replaces the 500 later this year. It has a pointed nose cone and tall rear wing.

UNDER THE SKIN

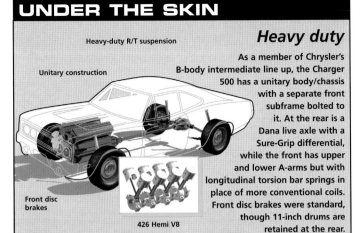

Heavy-duty R/T suspension

Unitary construction

Front disc brakes

426 Hemi V8

THE POWER PACK

Heavy duty

As a member of Chrysler's B-body intermediate line up, the Charger 500 has a unitary body/chassis with a separate front subframe bolted to it. At the rear is a Dana live axle with a Sure-Grip differential, while the front has upper and lower A-arms but with longitudinal torsion bar springs in place of more conventional coils. Front disc brakes were standard, though 11-inch drums are retained at the rear.

Ultimate Hemi

Like the standard Charger R/T, the 500 was offered with just two engines—the 375-bhp, 440-cubic inch Magnum or 426-cubic inch Hemi V8. The Hemi, installed in a mere 32 Charger 500s, was perhaps the ultimate muscle car engine. With 425 bhp, 490 lb-ft of torque and an aluminum intake manifold with twin Carter AFB four-barrel carburetors, it is a fearsome powerplant. Equipped with this engine and 4.10:1 rear gearing, a Charger 500 can zip through the ¼-mile in just 13.7 seconds.

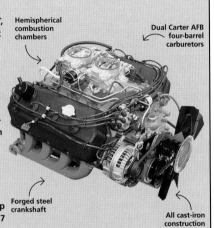

Hemispherical combustion chambers

Dual Carter AFB four-barrel carburetors

Forged steel crankshaft

All cast-iron construction

Rare Hemis

Built as a homologation exercise, the Charger 500 is exceedingly rare. The Hemi V8-engined cars are even more exclusive, with just 32 built. As with all muscle Mopars, these machines are highly sought after today and mint examples can cost $50,000.

Exposed headlights, flush-fit grill and smooth rear window distinguish the 500.

Although marginally faster than the standard Charger on the speedways, the 500 really came into its own on the street. One magazine even went as far as to call it a showroom racer—surprisingly docile on the street circuit.

Body modifications

To combat problems of turbulence on the second-generation Charger, the 500 was fitted with a flush-mounted grill and smooth rear window. The latter necessitated a shorter trunk lid and an extended rear backlight shelf.

Hemi V8

Only two engines were available in the limited edition 500. The first was the big 440-cubic inch Magnum, installed in the majority (340) of the cars. The second was the mighty Hemi, which produced an incredible 425 bhp and 490 lb-ft of torque.

Front disc brakes

Base model Chargers came with four-wheel drum brakes, although R/T models have 11-inch units front and rear. Charger 500s, however, have front discs as standard equipment.

Heavy-duty suspension

All Charger 500s were fitted with the same suspension. This included heavy-duty shocks, stiffer front torsion bars and an extra leaf in the right rear spring, plus a thicker and tighter front anti-roll bar.

Out-of-house conversion

The Charger 500 started life as a 1968 Charger but, besides the nose and window alterations, it got 1969 style taillights and was marketed as a 1969 model. The conversion was undertaken by Creative Industries—an aftermarket car crafter based in Michigan.

Dual exhaust

Like the vast majority of muscle cars, the Charger 500 needed a large exhaust system. It is fitted with twin full-length 2¼-inch diameter pipes.

Specifications

1969 Dodge Charger 500

ENGINE
Type: V8

Construction: Cast-iron block and heads

Valve gear: Two valves per cylinder operated by a single camshaft with pushrods and rockers

Bore and stroke: 4.25 in. x 3.75 in.

Displacement: 426 c.i.

Compression ratio: 10.25:1

Induction system: Twin Carter AFB four-barrel carburetors

Maximum power: 425 bhp at 5,000 rpm

Maximum torque: 490 lb-ft at 4,000 rpm

Top speed: 138 mph

0-60 mph: 6.1 sec.

TRANSMISSION
Four-speed manual

BODY/CHASSIS
Steel unitary chassis with two-door fastback body

SPECIAL FEATURES

All Chargers from 1968 to 1970 have this racing style fuel filler cap on the left rear quarter panel.

The Charger 500s flush-fit grill was modeled after the 1968 Coronet R/T.

RUNNING GEAR
Steering: Recirculating ball

Front suspension: Unequal length A-arms with longitudinally-mounted torsion bars, telescopic shock absorbers and anti-roll bar

Rear suspension: Live axle with semi-elliptic leaf springs and telescopic shock absorbers

Brakes: Discs, 11-in. dia. (front), drums, 11-in. dia. (rear)

Wheels: Steel discs, 5 x 14 in.

Tires: F70-14

DIMENSIONS
Length: 208.0 in.   **Width:** 76.5 in.

Height: 53.1 in.   **Wheelbase:** 116.0 in.

Track: 59.5 in. (front), 29.2 in. (rear)

Weight: 4,100 lbs.

Dodge **CHARGER DAYTONA**

There was a street version of the Charger Daytona because Dodge had to build a certain number to qualify for NASCAR racing. With its Hemi-engined 200-mph missile, Dodge went on to win 22 races in 1969.

"...shattering performance."

"You do not notice the aerodynamic aids until you are well past 120 mph, but they really come into play on superspeedways, helping to keep the cars stable as they passed each other at around 200 mph. It is unlikely you will not reach that in street-spec Hemi V8 since it only has 425 bhp; but that is still enough for earth shattering performance and acceleration. Low gearing and light steering do not give an immediate sense of confidence, but it is fairly accurate."

The interior of the street Charger is much more civilized than its NASCAR sibling.

Milestones

1969 Race goers at Alabama's Talledega track get the first sight of the racing Charger Daytona. Charlie Glotzbach laps the track at just under 200 mph. Charger driver Richard Brickhouse wins the race, and the Charger Daytona goes on to take another 22 checkers this season.

Plymouth's version of the Charger was the Superbird.

1970 Plymouth builds a sister to the Charger Daytona in the shape of the almost-identical Superbird.

Chargers and Superbirds often went head to head on the track.

1971 Both the Charger Daytona and the Plymouth Superbird are effectively outlawed from racing when NASCAR insists on a reduction in engine size by 25 percent. To prove a point, Dodge organizes a run at Bonneville on the Salt Flats, where Daytona 500 winner Bobby Isaacs reaches over 217 mph.

UNDER THE SKIN

Standard layout

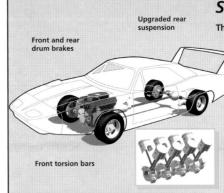

Upgraded rear suspension

Front and rear drum brakes

Front torsion bars

Famous V8 engine

The layout from the roadgoing Charger was kept for the Daytona, with suspension of A-arms, longitudinal torsion bars, recirculating-ball steering at the front and a live axle at the rear. The running gear was fortified, having far stiffer springs and shocks, with extra leaves in the rear springs and bigger front torsion bars; the Charger's unibody structure was made far stronger for the racers.

THE POWER PACK

MOPAR Muscle

The immortal Hemi engine first appeared in 1964, when Chrysler seriously decided to take on Ford in NASCAR. It is an all-cast-iron unit with a single camshaft in the V operating canted valves in highly efficient hemispherical combustion chambers through a combination of pushrods, solid lifters and rockers. It is oversquare with a large bore to allow room for the large valves. With its shorter stroke, it is designed to rev high, up to 7,200 rpm. The 426-c.i. alloy-headed, high-compression race engines gave over 650 bhp when fitted into the front of the Charger Daytona.

Special

The distinctive looks of the Charger Daytona have ensured its status as a cult classic. All cars are supremely powerful, but Keith Black (builder of MOPAR performance engines) prepared a promotional version with hair-raising performance.

The Daytona has one of the most outrageous wings ever seen on a stock car.

The Charger Daytona's outrageous look was no styling gimmick; the sharp extended nose and huge rear wing really did make the car more aerodynamic and quicker around the track.

426-c.i. Hemi

The street version of the Hemi gave less power than the higher tuned race engines, with their outputs between 575 and 700 bhp. Also, they ran with iron heads, lower compression ratios, and later hydraulic rather than solid tappets which kept the potential engine speeds lower.

Four-speed transmission

Street versions of the Charger Daytona came with a standard three-speed manual, but the racers were equipped with a close-ratio, four-speed with a Hurst shifter. Customers could specify a four-speed as a no-cost option or opt for the TorqueFlite three-speed auto.

Extended nose

The new nose was made of Fiberglass and was some 17 inches long. It made the car more aerodynamically efficient. The poor fit, that is a feature of all Charger Daytonas and Plymouth Superbirds, clearly had no effect on the aerodynamics of this 200-mph car.

Unitary construction

Although it looks like a classic example of a traditional body-on-frame piece of American design, the Charger Daytona is a unitary vehicle, with the bodywork acting as the chassis.

Two four-barrel carburetors

For the street Hemi engine there were two Carter four-barrel carburetors, arranged to open progressively. Just two barrels of the rear carb open at low throttle.

Pop-up lights

With the addition of the sharp extended nose, the standard headlights were covered and had to be replaced by a new arrangement of pop-up light pods, with each having two headlights.

Rear wing

That distinctive rear wing is mounted more than two feet above the trunk lid, so there is room for the trunk to open. But its real benefit is to allow it to operate in clean air.

1969 Dodge Charger Daytona

ENGINE

Type: V8

Construction: Cast-iron block and heads

Valve gear: Two valves per cylinder operating in hemispherical combustion chambers opened by a single V-mounted camshaft with pushrods, rockers and solid lifters

Bore and stroke: 4.25 in. x 3.75 in.

Displacement: 426 c.i.

Compression ratio: 10.25:1

Induction system: Two Carter AFB 3084S carburetors

Maximum power: 425 bhp at 5,600 rpm

Maximum torque: 490 lb-ft at 4,000 rpm

Top speed: 135 mph

0-60 mph: 5.0 sec.

TRANSMISSION

Four-speed manual

BODY/CHASSIS

Unitary monocoque construction with steel body panels and fiberglass nose section

SPECIAL FEATURES

The aerodynamic fiberglass nose houses the unique pop-up headlights.

The black rear wing distinguishes the Charger from the Plymouth Superbird.

RUNNING GEAR

Steering: Recirculating-ball

Front suspension: A-arms with longitudinal torsion bars, telescopic shock absorbers and anti-roll bar

Rear suspension: Live axle with asymmetrical leaf springs and telescopic shock absorbers

Brakes: Drums, 11.0-in. dia. (front), 11.0-in. dia. (rear)

Wheels: Stamped steel, 14 in. x 6 in.

Tires: F70 x 14

DIMENSIONS

Length: 208.5 in.   **Width:** 76.6 in.

Height: 53.0 in.   **Wheelbase:** 117.0 in.

Track: 59.7 in. (front), 59.2 in. (rear)

Weight: 3,671 lbs.

Dodge HURST HEMI DART

In the 1960s, drag racing was a great way for the auto industry to advertise its high-performance cars. The 1968 Hemi Darts became legendary as soon as they started racing in NHRA's Super Stock class. In fact, no other cars racing in this category could even come close. Their instant racing successes helped sell many Chrysler products.

"...Super Stock race rocket."

"NHRA Super Stock race rockets don't come any meaner than a Hurst-modified Hemi Dart. The engine was a high-strung, 500-plus-bhp race Hemi that was mated to a four-speed tranny and 4.88:1 gears. This deadly drivetrain was put into a stripped out 1968 Dart body shell (it didn't even come painted). The combo made for unwieldy 10-second ¼ mile sprints. While many other S/S cars loosely resembled stripped-out showroom cars with big engines, the Hemi Dart couldn't have been built as a more blatant factory racer."

To reduce weight, the heater, radio, window cranks and sound deadeners were deleted.

Milestones

1964 Chrysler introduces 426 Hemi V8s. They prove to be an instant success and nearly dominate NHRA Super Stock racing throughout the 1960s.

Run-of-the-mill Darts come with standard slant-six engines.

1967 In an attempt to dominate NHRA's Super Stock class, Chrysler plans to unleash its deadliest weapons—Hemi-powered Darts and Barracudas for 1968.

Another Mopar conceived for drag racing was the 440 'Cuda.

1968 Chrysler and Hurst Performance build the all-out Hemi race cars. 72 stripped-out primered Darts are sent from the Chrysler plant to Hurst where they receive their lightweight body panels, drivetrain and special suspension.

1968 The Hemi Darts and Barracudas become the fastest accelerating factory built production cars of all time.

UNDER THE SKIN

Option L023

Every part put in the L023-optioned Hemi Dart is designed for ¼-mile drag racing. It uses a custom front K-member and the shock towers have been modified to fit the wide Hemi engine. Revalved shocks, B-body front disc brakes and six-cylinder A-body torsion bars are fitted to the front. Cars that were built with automatics use an 8¾-inch rear axle with 4.86:1 gears. Those cars equipped with four-speeds use Dana 60 assemblies with 4.88:1 gearing.

THE POWER PACK

Mighty elephant

Super Stock domination was the objective of the Hemi-powered Dart. Under the hood is a full-tilt, race-prepped engine fortified with the strongest parts available in 1968. It has a cross-drilled, forged-steel crankshaft, 12.5:1 compression, a solid lifter 'Stage II' camshaft, and a light magnesium crossram intake manifold. Other race components include a high-capacity oil pump, transistorized ignition, dual Holley four barrel carbs, and headers. Rated at 425 bhp, NHRA quickly refactored the power to a closer-to-the-truth 500 bhp.

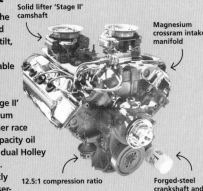

Paint not included

When buyers marked the L023 box on their new Dart's option list, they got a stripped out car that didn't come with much—no heater, radio, rear seat, sound deadening or window cranks. It didn't even come painted. What they did get was a full-tilt, Hemi-powered race car. This 'new' car wasn't even street legal.

Owners who indicated the L023 option on their new Dart got quite a ride.

Putting a huge engine in a small, light car was the idea for nearly every muscle car, but few took this formula to such extremes as the 1968 Hurst Hemi Dart. These cars have been consistent front-runners in NHRA events.

Monster hood scoop

A distinctive feature of the Hemi Dart is the monster hood scoop. It is needed to clear the twin Holley carburetors but also enables them to ingest large quantities of air. Hood pins keep the lift-off fiberglass hood in place

Bare-bones interior

Unnecessary weight was shed by deleting such non-essentials such as the radio, heater, window cranks, sound deadeners, body sealer, rear seat and even the passenger's side seat belt. The stock seats were also replaced with lighter Dodge van seats.

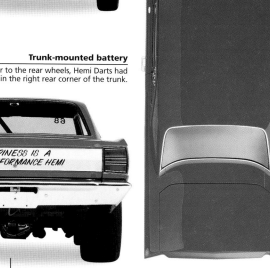

Trunk-mounted battery

For better weight transfer to the rear wheels, Hemi Darts had their batteries located in the right rear corner of the trunk.

Lightweight body

Further dietary supplements include fiberglass front fenders and hoods, while the doors and bumpers were acid-dipped. In addition, all of the side windows were replaced by light Corning Chemcor glass.

A-833 four-speed transmission

All cars with manual transmissions had specially modified 'Slick Shift' four speeds (every other synchro tooth was removed). They also came with scattershields, B&M high stall torque converters, Hurst shifters and 10.5-inch clutches.

Modified quarter panels

The standard Dart's rear wheel arches were never meant to accommodate large wheels and racing slicks. Because the Hemi versions were S/S race cars they needed more rear wheel clearance so the wheel arches were made larger.

Factory-flat finish

Because Chrysler knew that these future S/S race cars would be immediately receiving custom paint and lettering, none of the Hemi Darts were sold painted. The bodies were finished in an ugly flat-gray primer while the fiberglass fenders and hoods retained their black gelcoats.

B-body rear end

Because the narrow Hemi Dart uses a Dana 60 9¾-inch rear end, which is normally used in wider B-body cars, rear wheels with special offsets were required. The Dana 60 rear end came from the factory with a 4.88:1 rear axle ratio.

Specifications

1968 Dodge Hurst Hemi Dart

ENGINE

Type: V8

Construction: Cast-iron block and heads

Valve gear: Two valves per cylinder operated by pushrods and rockers

Bore and stroke: 4.25 in. x 3.75 in.

Displacement: 426 c.i.

Compression ratio: 12.5:1

Induction system: Two Holley four-barrel carburetors

Maximum power: 425 bhp at 6,000 rpm

Maximum torque: 480 lb-ft at 4,600 rpm

Top speed: 140 mph

0-60 mph: 3.6 sec.

TRANSMISSION

Hurst-shifted four-speed

BODY/CHASSIS

Steel unitary chassis with fiberglass and steel two-door body

SPECIAL FEATURES

This monster hood scoop was found on Hemi- and 440-powered A-body Mopars.

A special plaque was fitted to each car to remind drivers that the Hemi Dart was not really suitable for street use.

RUNNING GEAR

Steering: Recirculating ball

Front suspension: Unequal length A-arms with longitudinally-mounted torsion bars and telescopic shock absorbers

Rear suspension: Live axle with semi-elliptic multi-leaf springs and telescopic shock absorbers

Brakes: Drums (front and rear)

Wheels: Cragar S/S, 6 x 15 in. (front), 9 x 15 in. (rear)

Tires: Goodyear Eagle radials (front), Mickey Thompson slicks (rear)

DIMENSIONS

Length: 195.4 in.   **Width:** 69.6 in.

Height: 53.9 in.   **Wheelbase:** 110.0 in.

Track: 57.4 in. (front), 55.6 in. (rear)

Weight: 3,000 lbs.

Dodge **DART GTS**

In 1968, the humble Dart finally entered the muscle car fraternity when it was fitted with the 383 V8. An even larger 440 V8 was fitted in 1969. This turned the Dart into a very accomplished performer and a serious threat on the streets.

"...pulls hard to 120 mph."

"A horizontal sweep speedometer and a plain interior give away the budget-based origins of the GTS, but its 383 V8 performance puts the car in an entirely different league. At idle, the massive 330-bhp engine vigorously and uncontrollably shakes the car. With the sure-shifting TorqueFlite at the command of your right hand, the Dart will rocket off the line with the slightest touch of the throttle, but its real strength lies when the throttle is nailed from about 20 mph; then it pulls hard to 120 mph."

The narrow steering wheel and pedestrian-looking dash show the Dart's humble character.

Milestones

1967 Chrysler offers new A-body

compacts with unitary construction. Both the Dodge Dart and Plymouth Valiant get more important and curvier styling. At Dodge, performance is endowed in the Dart GT, which can get a 230-bhp, 270-cubic inch V8.

The Dart GTS was only offered for 1968 and 1969.

1968 A hotter GTS

version is launched with a standard 340-cubic inch small-block engine. With an excellent power-to-weight ratio, it can run 14-second ¼-mile times. A larger 383-cubic inch unit is optional.

Based on the Dart, the Dodge Demon 340 debuted for 1971.

1969 In an attempt to improve

performance, the 383 engine undergoes some tweaks, resulting in 330 bhp. This is the final year for the GTS. The Swinger is the sole performance Dart for 1970.

UNDER THE SKIN

Unitized lightweight

Early Darts had body-on--frame construction, but when the little A-body was redesigned for 1967 it adopted unitary construc-tion but retained a 111-inch wheelbase. Chrysler's customary torsion bar front suspension is fitted up front, with semi-elliptic leafs at the rear. GTS models got bigger torsion bars, a front anti-roll bar and six-leaf rear springs. The Dana rear axle has standard 3.23:1 gearing.

THE POWER PACK

Magnum force

The GTS was powered by a standard 340-cubic inch engine, but in 1968 Dodge finally gave the Dart some serious muscle under the hood when the little compact was fitted with a big block. The 383-cubic inch V8, the staple of run-of-the-mill big Dodge sedans, underwent some modifications for 1969 using experience from the 1968 Super Bee. These included free-breathing cylinder heads, a stronger crankshaft, stiffer valve springs, a higher lift camshaft and low-restriction exhaust manifolds. Fuel is fed through a single Carter AFB four-barrel carburetor. With 330 bhp and 410 lb-ft of torque, 14.4-second ¼-miles are a regular occurrence.

GT Sport

One of the most unassuming performers of the late 1960s, the Dart is still underrated when compared with its larger stablemates. Good 383-equipped cars can sell in the $20,000 range and have equal if not better acceleration than B-bodies.

GTS Darts could be bought with 340- and 383-cubic inch engines.

Although adding the 383 engine upset the Dart's balance somewhat, the problem was addressed in 1969 by modifying the front suspension. The resulting car runs excellent ETs, provided care is taken with the throttle.

Small- or big-block V8

The standard engine in the GTS is the free-revving, small-block 340 which offers outstanding performance. The big 383, despite its extra 55 bhp, offers only marginally better acceleration but in the right hands it makes for a lethal junior muscle car. Power for the Darts didn't stop there. Some GTSs received 375-bhp 440 V8s.

TorqueFlite transmission

In 1969, either a four-speed manual or a TorqueFlite automatic transmission could be ordered. Typically, the smooth, quick-shifting TorqueFlite was tough to beat.

Torsion-bar front suspension

Because the 383 engine puts more weight over the front wheels than the 340, the front torsion bars were increased and a thicker front anti-roll bar fitted. This gives a stiffer ride and better handling than the base model Darts.

Bias-ply tires

The E70 x 14 tires are not really capable of harnessing 410 lb-ft of torque and careless acceleration can result in uncontrollable wheelspin. Deflating the tires a few psi greatly improves its traction under hard acceleration.

Unitary chassis

From 1967, Darts adopted unitary construction, which gives a stiffer structure. The front suspension is attached to a subframe.

Rugged rear end

A Dana 9¾ rear axle with a Sure-Grip limited-slip differential and standard 3.23:1 gears transfer the power to the pavement. Shorter 3.55:1 or 3.90:1 ratios were available for those who craved quicker acceleration.

Plain interior

Most Darts have spartan interiors—the GTS included—but optional front bucket seats, a center console and deluxe steering wheel add a little luxury.

Dodge SUPER BEE

In the late 1960s, Chrysler went all out to better the competition when it came to muscle cars. One of the fastest of all was the Super Bee, created by stuffing the monster 440 into the lightest intermediate bodyshell.

"...throws you back in the seat."

"Take a good, long look at the Super Bee before you slide behind the wheel. The matte-black, fiberglass hood with its massive scoop and bare-bone steel wheels tell you that this Dodge means business. A full set of instruments greets you inside, but otherwise the interior is fairly plain. Punch the gas pedal and this car turns into a real animal. It throws you back in the bucket seat, and there is little you can do but stare at the rising speedometer and listen to the screaming engine."

Super Bees came with full instrumentation, but a center console was optional.

Milestones

1966 The Chrysler Corporation issues a paper about a new high-performance engine designed for regular street driving.

1968 Dodge releases the no-frills Super Bee in response to the Plymouth Road Runner. It is initially offered as a two-door coupe with a 383- or a 426-cubic inch Hemi V8.

The classic 1969 Charger R/T came with standard 440 power.

1969 Realizing that there is still a market for outlandishly fast, yet low-buck, street racers, Dodge unveils the Super Bee 440 Six Pack. It comes with a fiberglass lift-off hood. 1,907 are built this year.

Super Bees are the performance variant of base Coronets.

1970 The Coronet is facelifted with a twin horsecollar front grill. The Super Bee 440 Six Pack returns for its second and final season.

UNDER THE SKIN

Dodge derivative

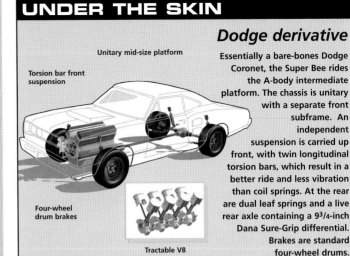

Unitary mid-size platform

Torsion bar front suspension

Four-wheel drum brakes

Tractable V8

Essentially a bare-bones Dodge Coronet, the Super Bee rides the A-body intermediate platform. The chassis is unitary with a separate front subframe. An independent suspension is carried up front, with twin longitudinal torsion bars, which result in a better ride and less vibration than coil springs. At the rear are dual leaf springs and a live rear axle containing a 9³/4-inch Dana Sure-Grip differential. Brakes are standard four-wheel drums.

THE POWER PACK

Best of both worlds

For the Six Pack, the 440 cubic inch engine was used as a starting point. Items such as the forged steel crank-shaft, connecting rods and aluminum pistons were retained. To boost performance, a higher lift camshaft, stronger valve springs and free-flowing heads were specified. Sitting atop the engine is a special Edelbrock aluminum manifold and three Holley two-barrel carburetors. Although it has less power than the 426 Hemi, the 440 is more tractable and easier to keep in tune.

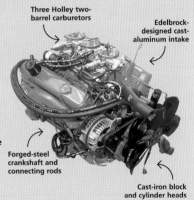

Three Holley two-barrel carburetors

Edelbrock-designed cast-aluminum intake

Forged-steel crankshaft and connecting rods

Cast-iron block and cylinder heads

First year

Six Pack Super Bees were only built for two years and only in small numbers. Collectors tend to prefer the 1969 models with their cleaner styling, plus the fiberglass scoop which is unique to this year and the aluminum intake. Good Six Packs can cost $35,000.

Super Bee 'Six Packs' left the factory with 14-inch steel wheels.

With its enormous cop-baiting hood and loud paint, the Super Bee Six Pack is certainly no street sleeper. It is, however, a true high performance machine, able to take on any challenger on the street or at the strip.

Fiberglass hood
The feature that probably brings more attention than any other element of the car is the hood. It is a one-piece fiberglass affair with a massive functional scoop.

Six Pack 440 engine
In normal driving, the engine only requires the fuel from the center carburetor. However, when the accelerator pedal meets the floorboard, the front and rear carburetors feed the engine more fuel. With this engine, the Super Bee can run the ¼-mile in a shade under 14 seconds.

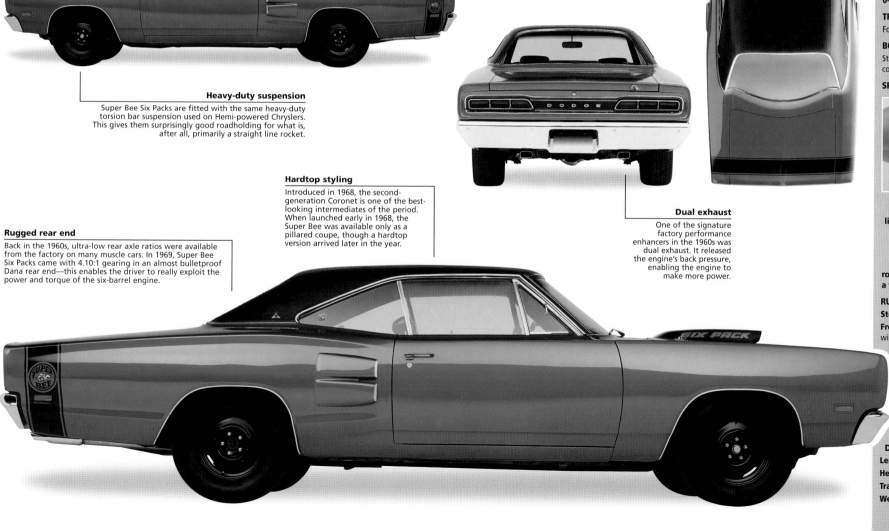

Heavy-duty suspension
Super Bee Six Packs are fitted with the same heavy-duty torsion bar suspension used on Hemi-powered Chryslers. This gives them surprisingly good roadholding for what is, after all, primarily a straight line rocket.

Hardtop styling
Introduced in 1968, the second-generation Coronet is one of the best-looking intermediates of the period. When launched early in 1968, the Super Bee was available only as a pillared coupe, though a hardtop version arrived later in the year.

Rugged rear end
Back in the 1960s, ultra-low rear axle ratios were available from the factory on many muscle cars. In 1969, Super Bee Six Packs came with 4.10:1 gearing in an almost bulletproof Dana rear end—this enables the driver to really exploit the power and torque of the six-barrel engine.

Dual exhaust
One of the signature factory performance enhancers in the 1960s was dual exhaust. It released the engine's back pressure, enabling the engine to make more power.

Specifications
1969 Dodge Super Bee 440

ENGINE
Type: V8

Construction: Cast-iron block and heads

Valve gear: Two valves per cylinder operated by a single camshaft via pushrods and rockers

Bore and stroke: 4.32 in. x 3.75 in.

Displacement: 440 c.i.

Compression ratio: 10.5:1

Induction system: Three Holley two-barrel carburetors (Six Pack)

Maximum power: 390 bhp at 4,700 rpm

Maximum torque: 490 lb-ft at 3,200 rpm

Top speed: 130 mph

0-60 mph: 6.0 sec.

TRANSMISSION
Four-speed manual

BODY/CHASSIS
Steel unitary chassis with two-door hardtop coupe body

SPECIAL FEATURES

Because of its bare-bone image, the only wheels that the Super Bees came with were these low-budget black steel wheels with chrome lug nuts.

The one-piece, lift-off fiberglass hood is held in place by four tie-down pins and made routine oil checks a two-person job.

RUNNING GEAR
Steering: Recirculating ball

Front suspension: Unequal length wishbones with longitudinally-mounted torsion bars, telescopic shock absorbers and anti-roll bar

Rear suspension: Dana 60 rear axle with semi-elliptic leaf springs and telescopic shock absorbers

Brakes: Drums (front and rear)

Wheels: Steel discs, 7 x 14 in.

Tires: F70-14

DIMENSIONS
Length: 206.6 in.   **Width:** 76.7 in.

Height: 54.8 in.   **Wheelbase:** 117.0 in.

Track: 59.5 in. (front), 58.5 in. (rear)

Weight: 4,100 lbs.

Dodge CHALLENGER T/A

With the SCCA's Trans Am wars in full swing, Dodge jumped in to the foray with its aptly-named Challenger T/A. Built for only one year and powered by a 340 cubic inch V8, it was conceived as a road racer but became a factory street rod.

"...mindwarping acceleration."

"Unlike its big-block counterparts, the T/A is a better-balanced package with less weight over the front wheels. It therefore offers more nimble handling. The rev-happy 340 V8 engine, with its triple carburetors and the bulletproof TorqueFlite transmission give mind-warping acceleration. For its time, the power-assisted steering is smooth and the brakes firm, but the sound of the V8 blowing through the side pipes is enough to stir anyone's soul."

Full instrumentation and black upholstery give the interior a real sporty feel.

Milestones

1970 Dodge finally launches its own ponycar—the Challenger. An R/T performance model is offered with standard big-block power. With the popularity of Trans Am racing Dodge develops a homologation special: the Challenger T/A. Street versions are fitted with a 340-cubic inch V8, a fiberglass lift-off hood, side pipes and large rear tires. Only 2,142 are built this year.

In 1969, the top performing Dodge small block muscle car was the Dart GTS 383.

1971 With factory support in Trans Am racing on the decline, the T/A does not return, although the big-block R/T makes it second and last appearance. Only 4,630 R/Ts are built and Challenger sales in general are less than half those of 1970.

The 1971 Demon is also powered by a 340-cubic inch V8.

1972 Big-block engines are no longer available and the performance model is a new Challenger 360 Rallye. The Challenger itself lasts until 1974.

UNDER THE SKIN

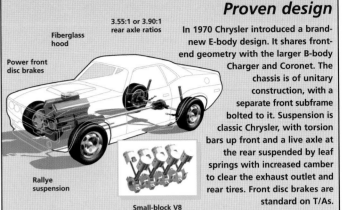

Proven design

In 1970 Chrysler introduced a brand-new E-body design. It shares front-end geometry with the larger B-body Charger and Coronet. The chassis is of unitary construction, with a separate front subframe bolted to it. Suspension is classic Chrysler, with torsion bars up front and a live axle at the rear suspended by leaf springs with increased camber to clear the exhaust outlet and rear tires. Front disc brakes are standard on T/As.

THE POWER PACK

Rev-happy magnum

The T/A proved that the hemi or the 440 Magnum are not necessary to produce real power. The 340-cubic inch unit used in the Dart Swinger is fitted with a special Edelbrock intake manifold, on which sits three two-barrel Holley carburetors. The advertised output was 290 bhp at 5,000 rpm, although this was purely for insurance reasons. With this engine the Challenger T/A and its AAR 'Cuda twin are a serious threat on the street and hydraulic lifters ensured that they were always ready for action.

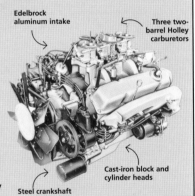

Loud T/A

In 1970 Dodge finally got serious about SCCA racing and launched its T/A. On the race circuit all cars ran a 305-cubic inch V8 which was nothing more than a destroked 340. To make the street versions more fun, an Edelbrock intake and trio of Holley carbs were added.

The Challenger T/A has handling to match its massive power output.

With its matte black hood and wide stripes, the Challenger T/A might just be one of the most stylish cars Dodge built during the heyday of muscle cars. It was equally at home taking high speed turns or accelerating in a straight line.

V8 engine
When all six barrels of the carburetors are wide open, the 340 has rocket-like acceleration. Though it's a smaller engine than what most Mopar enthusiasts consider to be powerful, the 340 really holds its own against larger-engined cars.

Panther Pink paint
Believe it or not, this color was offered by Dodge. It's called Panther Pink and it's one of the optional High Impact colors.

Big rear wheels
The Challenger T/A was one of the first Detroit production cars to feature different size front and rear tires. At the back are massive G60 x 15 Goodyear Polyglas GTs, which give the T/A excellent straight-line traction.

Limited-slip differential
Despite the larger rear tires, many T/A buyers specified a Positraction limited-slip differential to reduce wheel spin and increase bite.

'Six-pack' carburetors
In order to extract maximum performance out of the 340-cubic inch small-block, Dodge installed three Holley two-barrel carburetors atop the engine. During normal driving only the center carburetor is used, but punching the throttle opens the outboard units and produces astonishing acceleration.

Torsion bar suspension
Unlike its rivals, Chrysler used torsion bar front suspension on its cars in the early 1970s. These are more robust than coil springs and result in a smoother ride over rough surfaces.

Four-speed transmission
The standard transmission on the T/A is a Hurst-shifted four-speed with a direct-drive top ratio. The only option was a TorqueFlite three-speed automatic.

Hardtop body
The Challenger was available in coupe and convertible forms, but all T/A models were hardtop coupes. However, a vinyl roof was available.

Specifications

1970 Dodge Challenger T/A

ENGINE

Type: V8

Construction: Cast-iron block and heads

Valve gear: Two valves per cylinder operated by pushrods and rockers

Bore and stroke: 4.03 in. x 3.31 in.

Displacement: 340 c.i.

Compression ratio: 10.5:1

Induction system: Three Holley two-barrel carburetors

Maximum power: 290 bhp at 5,000 rpm

Maximum torque: 345 lb-ft at 3,200 rpm

Top speed: 125 mph

0-60 mph: 5.8 sec

TRANSMISSION

TorqueFlite three-speed automatic

BODY/CHASSIS

Unitary steel construction with two-door four-seater coupe body

SPECIAL FEATURES

All Challengers are fitted with this racing-style chromed fuel filler cap.

At the rear, Challengers have a single, large back up light behind the Dodge lettering.

RUNNING GEAR

Steering: Recirculating ball

Front suspension: Double wishbones with longitudinal torsion bars, telescopic shock absorbers and anti-roll bar

Rear suspension: Live axle with semi-elliptic leaf springs, telescopic shock absorbers and anti-roll bar

Brakes: Discs (front), drums (rear)

Wheels: Steel discs, 7 x 15 in.

Tires: E60 x 15 (front), G60 x 15 (rear)

DIMENSIONS

Length: 191.3 in.   **Width:** 76.1 in.

Height: 51.7 in.   **Wheelbase:** 110.0 in.

Track: 60.7 in. (front), 61.2 in. (rear)

Weight: 3,650 lbs.

Dodge **CORONET R/T**

The Coronet R/T was the first mid-size Dodge muscle machine to feature all the performance and luxury features in a single package. With a powerful 440-cubic inch V8, it didn't disappoint.

"...it just keeps on going."

"Unlike previous mid-size Chrysler muscle cars, the Coronet R/T has a more sporty feel. With a distinctive start-up sound, the giant Magnum V8 roars into life. Smooth and refined, the big V8 has plenty of torque. Dropping the pedal launches the car forward and it just keeps on going, daring you to go faster. Watch out for the corners though; the nose-heavy R/T doesn't handle very well and its 480 lb-ft of torque will surely result in oversteer."

The Coronet R/T has standard bucket seats, a center console and full instrumentation.

Milestones

1967 Dodge introduces its Coronet R/T (Road and Track). It is a complete high-performance package and is fitted with a standard 440-cubic inch V8, although the Hemi engine is also available. This year sales figures total 10,181.

The Coronet R/T debuted in both hardtop and convertible forms.

1968 The R/T returns with handsome new sheet-metal on an unchanged wheelbase.

1969 After a major facelift in 1968, changes this year are minor, with a new grill and rear tail panel. Engine choices remain the same.

The race-ready Super Bee was the Coronet's high performance stablemate.

1970 Greater competition in a heavily crowded market takes its toll on the Coronet R/T and sales fall to just 2,615. Only 13 of these cars are fitted with the Hemi V8.

UNDER THE SKIN

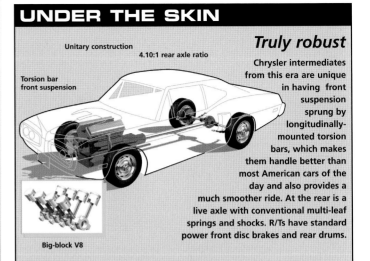

Unitary construction
4.10:1 rear axle ratio
Torsion bar front suspension
Big-block V8

Truly robust

Chrysler intermediates from this era are unique in having front suspension sprung by longitudinally-mounted torsion bars, which makes them handle better than most American cars of the day and also provides a much smoother ride. At the rear is a live axle with conventional multi-leaf springs and shocks. R/Ts have standard power front disc brakes and rear drums.

THE POWER PACK

More reliable

Only two engines were available with the R/T package: the more common 440-cubic inch Magnum and the street-lethal 426-cubic inch Hemi. The Magnum was lifted from the full-size Chrysler line, but in the R/T it has a longer duration camshaft profile, bigger exhaust valves, a dual snorkel intake, a four-barrel Carter carburetor, and free-flowing exhaust manifolds. It produces 375 bhp and 480 lb-ft of torque. By including the 'Six Pack,' the 440 received 3x2 carburetors for 490 bhp.

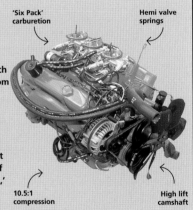

'Six Pack' carburetion
Hemi valve springs
10.5:1 compression
High lift camshaft

Short life

When the Coronet was launched in 1967, its styling was boxy and upright. A new, smoother body was introduced the following year, which was carried over to 1969 with few changes. 1970 models feature an aggressive twin 'horse collar'-type grill.

1970 was the last year for the convertible Coronet.

This peppermint green 1970 Coronet 440 is one of just 2,615 R/Ts built that year. With so much competition in the muscle car arena, sales plummeted in 1970, making this a desirable muscle car today.

Torsion bar suspension

Chrysler was unique in employing torsion bars for the front suspension. Mounted lengthways, they are extremely simple and robust.

Street racer's powerplant

Easier to maintain, more flexible and less temperamental than the Hemi, the 440 delivers plenty of torque and is perfect for drag racing. It is nicknamed the 'Wedge' because of the shape of its combustion chambers.

Bulletproof TorqueFlite

The V8 in this R/T is backed up by the optional 727 TorqueFlite three-speed automatic. This transmission is extremely reliable and has been used in countless Mopars over the years.

Bigger wheels

For 1970 handsome 15-inch Rallye wheels became available on the Coronet R/T. They feature chrome beauty rings and center caps.

Aggressive front

Twin 'horse collar'-type grills are unique to 1970 Coronets and give the car an aggressive appearance. The hood scoops are an R/T-only feature and are non-functional.

Bumble bee stripe

A tail end stripe, usually in black, white or red, was available at no extra cost.

Specifications

1970 Dodge Coronet R/T

ENGINE

Type: V8

Construction: Cast-iron block and heads

Valve gear: Two valves per cylinder operated by pushrods and rockers

Bore and stroke: 4.32 in. x 3.75 in.

Displacement: 440 c.i.

Compression ratio: 10.5:1

Induction system: Single Carter AFB downdraft four-barrel carburetor

Maximum power: 375 bhp at 4,600 rpm

Maximum torque: 480 lb-ft at 3,200 rpm**Top speed:** 123 mph

0-60 mph: 6.6 sec

TRANSMISSION

TorqueFlite 727 three-speed automatic

BODY/CHASSIS

Steel monocoque with two-door body

SPECIAL FEATURES

Side-mounted scoops are only fitted to 1970 Coronet R/Ts and are purely decorative features.

Though the engine in this Coronet R/T makes 375 bhp, it is the base engine. Also available was a 390 bhp version with three two-barrel carbs, and a 426 Hemi that made 425 bhp.

RUNNING GEAR

Steering: Recirculating ball

Front suspension: Longitudinally-mounted torsion bars with wishbones and telescopic shocks

Rear suspension: Live rear axle with semi-elliptic leaf springs and telescopic shocks

Brakes: Discs (front), drums (rear)

Wheels: Steel disc, 15-in. dia.

Tires: Goodyear Polyglas GT F60 15

DIMENSIONS

Length: 207.7 in. **Width:** 80.6 in.

Height: 52.5 in.

Wheelbase: 117 in.

Track: 58.9 in. (front and rear)

Weight: 3,546 lbs.

Dodge **LI'L RED EXPRESS TRUCK**

Offered as a performance variant to Dodge's common full-size pickup truck, the Li'l Red Express with a 360 cubic-inch V8 as the standard engine was actually the fastest U.S. production vehicle in 1978. It is a true hot hauler in every sense of the term.

"...sense of authority."

"Sitting in the bucket seat behind the Tuff sport steering wheel and with a 225-bhp, 360-cubic inch V8 under foot, you have a commanding sense of authority on the road. The big, twin, chromed exhaust stacks behind the cab, the wide chrome wheels and the bold red and gold color represent a very 1970s image, but this truck's performance is definitely not 1970s. It rockets to 60 mph in just 6.6 seconds—faster than most contemporary cars."

For a pickup, the Li'l Red Express Truck is well equipped and quite civilized.

Milestones

1976 The Warlock is Chrysler's first attempt at attracting young buyers of the fast growing light-duty truck market. This customized D-100 pickup is built from 1976 to 1979 in black, dark green or red with gold stripes.

The big Dodge Ram marched into the 1980s with few changes.

1978 The Li'l Red Express attracts 2,188 buyers in its first year of production.

A new 'Big Rig'-styled Ram pickup arrived for 1994 and sales exploded.

1979 Production of the final Express comes to an end after 5,118 have been built, bringing the total to 7,306. Quad rectangular headlights set it apart from the 1978 version. The basic Ram pickup on which it is based soldiers on until 1993.

UNDER THE SKIN

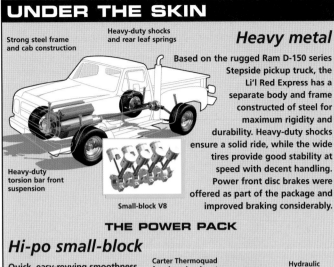

Strong steel frame and cab construction

Heavy-duty shocks and rear leaf springs

Heavy-duty torsion bar front suspension

Small-block V8

Heavy metal

Based on the rugged Ram D-150 series Stepside pickup truck, the Li'l Red Express has a separate body and frame constructed of steel for maximum rigidity and durability. Heavy-duty shocks ensure a solid ride, while the wide tires provide good stability at speed with decent handling. Power front disc brakes were offered as part of the package and improved braking considerably.

THE POWER PACK

Hi-po small-block

Quick, easy-revving smoothness backed by adequate torque makes the 360-cubic inch small-block V8 very entertaining to drive. This 5.9-liter cast-iron powerhouse has a high-lift camshaft from the 1968 340 V8, a large 850-cfm Carter Thermoquad four-barrel carburetor in a dual-snorkel air cleaner and a windage tray to reduce parasitic oil drag on the cast crankshaft. These modifications also made the engine a favorite with police departments, which operated 360-powered big sedans.

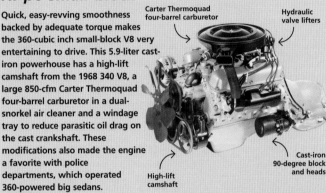

Carter Thermoquad four-barrel carburetor

Hydraulic valve lifters

Cast-iron 90-degree block and heads

High-lift camshaft

Pre-emissions

The Li'l Red Express Truck was not the first Dodge 'factory custom' pickup, but it remains the best known. As far as collectability is concerned, the 1978 edition is slightly more desirable as fewer were built, plus 1978 was also the last year that light trucks were exempt from EPA emissions regulations and thus performance is marginally better than the 1979 version.

The heavy-duty bed is trimmed with wood.

Ram pickups ordered with the Li'l Red Express Truck package are coded YH6. This includes the special engine, transmission and exhaust system, plus a wood-trimmed bed, chrome engine accessories and Canyon Red paint.

Smog equipment
This 1979 model is equipped with pollution control equipment, including a smog pump, EGR (Exhaust Gas Recirculating) system and catalytic converters. These power robbing devices aren't required on the 1978 models.

Heavy-duty suspension
In keeping with its performance image, heavy-duty shocks and rear leaf springs are fitted all around. Torsion bars control the front wheels.

Rectangular headlights
Identifying the year of manufacture is easy, since the 1978 model has a pair of round headlights as opposed to the more modern-looking quad rectangular headlight set up on the 1979 model.

Step side bed
Varnished solid oak side boards line the rugged step side steel bed and tailgate for added appeal.

Exhaust stacks
The eye-catching exhaust system is quite unique with its twin 2.5-inch chrome stacks exiting vertically behind the cab in a similar fashion to a giant 18-wheeler.

Cab interior
A bench seat is standard, although front bucket seats were optional. Durable red or black vinyl were the only two interior trim colors available.

Police power
The 360-cubic inch V8 is a police spec engine with a high-lift camshaft and Thermoquad carburetor.

Specifications

1979 Dodge Li'l Red Express Truck

ENGINE

Type: V8

Construction: Cast-iron block and heads

Valve gear: Two valves per cylinder operated by a single camshaft, pushrods, rockers and hydraulic lifters

Bore and stroke: 4.00 in. x 3.58 in.

Displacement: 360 c.i.

Compression ratio: 8.4:1

Induction system: Carter Thermoquad four-barrel carburetor

Maximum power: 225 bhp at 3,800 rpm

Maximum torque: 295 lb-ft at 3,200 rpm

Top speed: 118 mph

0-60 mph: 6.6 sec.

TRANSMISSION

Three-speed LoadFlite automatic

BODY/CHASSIS

Separate steel body and frame

SPECIAL FEATURES

The package even included an engine dress-up kit with a chrome air cleaner.

Li'l Red Express trucks were based on the Adventurer 150 series Ram.

RUNNING GEAR

Steering: Recirculating ball

Front suspension: Torsion bars with shock absorbers and anti-roll bar

Rear suspension: Live solid axle with leaf springs and shock absorbers

Brakes: Discs (front), drums (rear)

Wheels: 7 x 15 in.

Tires: GR60-15 (front), LR60-15 (rear)

DIMENSIONS

Length: 186.0 in.   **Width:** 76.0 in.

Height: 74.0 in.   **Wheelbase:** 115.0 in.

Track: 70.4 in. (front and rear)

Weight: 3,855 lbs.

USA 1991-1992

Dodge SPIRIT R/T

Surprising just about everyone, Dodge dropped its potent 224-bhp turbo engine into the almost invisible Spirit sedan. The resulting Spirit R/T could outperform nearly every sports car on sale in the early 1990s.

"...rapid acceleration."

"Like the exterior, there is very little inside to distinguish the R/T from the basic Spirit commuter sedan—until you drive it. The 2.2-liter four-cylinder is an absolute jewel. Smooth and vibration-free for its size and coupled to a five-speed trans-mission, it produces extremely rapid acceleration: 60 mph comes up in less than 7 seconds. But with 224 bhp going through the front wheels, torque steer can take the inexperienced driver completely by surprise."

All Spirit R/Ts have front bucket seats and a Getrag five-speed manual transmission.

188

Milestones

1988 As a replacement for the aging Aries compact, Dodge introduces the Spirit as a slightly larger, more upscale model. Both cars are assembled side by side for awhile. Unlike the Aries, the Spirit is available only as a four-door sedan. A 2.5-liter four cylinder is standard, but a 150-bhp turbo version is fitted to the top-of-the-line ES model. A 3.0-liter V6 is optional.

The earlier Omni GLH was also powered by a 2.2-liter turbo four.

1990 Late in the year, Dodge fits a 224-bhp, 2.2-liter turbo four in the Spirit. The result is the rapid Spirit R/T, which goes on sale as a 1991 model.

The Spirit was superseded by the Stratus in 1995.

1991 Revised alloy wheels are the major change for the R/T's last season—the 1992 model year.

UNDER THE SKIN

K-car ancestry

The Spirit owes much to its K-car predecessor, the Aries, which means a unitary chassis, MacPherson-strut front suspension and a beam axle on semi-trailing arms at the rear. For the R/T, Dodge engineers stiffened up the standard Spirit springs, and added bigger anti-roll bars and 15-inch wheels and tires. All R/Ts have standard four-wheel disc brakes and ABS was offered as an option. Even so, handling is one of the car's less redeeming features.

THE POWER PACK

Let your spirit fly

What really makes the Spirit R/T is its engine. It was based on the proven 2.2-liter four-cylinder that had been around in various forms since 1982 and was fitted to the overtly sporty Omni and Charger GLH-S. The Spirit motor features a cast-iron block and alloy head, which has twin belt-driven, overhead camshafts and four valves for each cylinder. Twin rotating balancer shafts in the motor reduce vibration (a trademark problem of Mopar small displacement four cylinders) and a Garrett T3 turbocharger, with an intercooler, helps to produce as much power as possible—in this case, a respectable 224 bhp at 6,000 rpm.

Fast commuter

In standard form, the Spirit is a fairly accomplished but ordinary midsize sedan. In R/T form, it is an absolute scorcher and can run the ¼-mile as quickly as some hallowed 1960s muscle cars. Best of all, production was kept low, guaranteeing collectibility.

1990 and 1991 Spirit R/Ts have unusual snowflake-style wheels.

Externally almost indistinguishable from the lesser ES model, the Spirit R/T also represented a terrific buy at under $20,000 in 1991. Like the Omni GLH before it, the R/T is a true wolf in sheep's clothing.

Five-speed transmission

While buyers of ordinary Spirits most often ordered automatic transaxles, the R/T model was available with a Getrag five-speed manual transmission.

Powerful turbocharged four

With four valves per cylinder, twin overhead camshafts, a single turbocharger and an intercooler, the 135-cubic inch four is an absolute screamer. Maximum power (224 bhp) comes in at 6,000 rpm, while the torque (217 lb-ft) peaks at a low 2,800 rpm.

Big wheels and tires

Helping the car make the most of its 224 bhp are a set of beefy Michelin XGT V4 tires and 15-inch cast-aluminum wheels (also shared with the ES and Daytona). For 1992, the Spirit R/T was fitted with revised wheels.

Bucket seats

Whereas regular Spirits could be specified with a split front bench seat, the R/T model came standard with front buckets and a center console. Even so, the dash and door panels are nearly identical to other Spirits.

Uprated suspension

With so much power, the stock Spirit running gear was deemed insufficient. Therefore, stiffer springs and shocks and thicker anti-roll bars are fitted. The rear also features a Panhard rod in the interest of controlling lateral movement.

Dodge VIPER

The Viper was designed as a modern incarnation of the legendary Shelby Cobra of the 1960s—no nonsense, no frills, just big bags of brute power. The massive V10 is the biggest engine currently shoehorned into a production car.

"...a street brawler."

"Some owners describe it as 'a great motor looking for a car.' Cruising at 75 mph, the wind batters you, the exhaust drones, engine and exhaust heat cook your feet. But when you put your foot down, all of the faults disappear. The engine has so much torque it's possible to drive away in 3rd, then shift to 6th at 35 mph. With its eight liters, the V10 actually pulls at 500 rpm. This is a no-holds-barred street brawler that will rattle your fillings and your neighbors' windows."

A functional cockpit with stark white instruments. A very high 6th gear (53 mph per 1,000 rpm) is required to pass California emission laws.

Milestone

1989 The Viper was originally a 'concept car'—a car taken to the motor shows to gauge public reaction. It is shown at the Detroit International Auto Show in January 1989. Public reaction is overwhelming.

Early racers had a huge rear spoiler.

1991 Carroll Shelby drives a prototype Viper as the pace car in the Indianapolis 500.

1992 The car goes on sale and proves a massive success. Chrysler has taken a huge risk building a car that costs nearly $60,000 and doesn't even have windows or air conditioning. It is a long-odds gamble that soon proves to be a winner for Chrysler.

1996 The GTS Coupe, first seen as a 'concept car' in 1993, finally goes on sale in Europe. Its chassis is stiffer and the engine and car are lighter, while the V10's power is increased to 450 bhp. The superior aerodynamics of the fixed hard top also help make it faster.

Sleek and fast: Viper GTS Coupe.

UNDER THE SKIN

...the bonded beast

All independently sprung

Six-speed transmission

Composite fiberglass roadster body

Built-in roll bar

Rear-wheel drive

Tubular steel frame

Four-wheel disc brakes

Front engine V10

The mechanical arrangement of the Viper is conventional—front engine, rear drive, disc brakes and independent double-wishbone suspension all around. These are mounted on a rock-solid tubular steel chassis to which the composite body panels are bonded or bolted.

THE POWER PACK

...Outstanding V10 performance

The Viper is an outrageous sports car, so it makes sense that its power plant be equally impressive. During this time, Dodge was in ownership of Lamborghini, so it employed the Italian supercar company to develop an all-aluminum V10 mechanical masterpiece. Its sheer size of 488-cubic inches helps make 400 bhp and 488 lb-ft of torque for those made in 1992. By 1998, power was increase to 450 bhp.

Alloy block and heads

Two valves per cylinder with hydraulic tappets

Dry sump

Five-into-one exhaust manifold

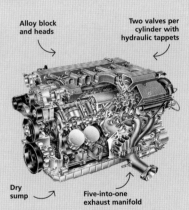

Viper Venom

As if the normal car wasn't powerful enough, John Hennessey has produced the Venom version with a staggering 550 bhp—150-bhp more than the original. It's enough to send a brave Viper driver to 100 mph in under 10 seconds and on to a top speed of 174 mph.

With 150-bhp extra bite, the Viper Venom is a car for the brave.

The Viper's dramatic look of controlled aggression expresses the elemental power of its awesome V10 8-liter engine. It was styled by an in-house Chrysler design team led by Tom Gale.

Options

Air conditioning and color choice were the only options in 1994.

Ellipsoidal headlights

Dodge describes the headlights on the Viper as Aero-Polyellipsoid. Behind those teardrop-shaped lenses are powerful halogen bulbs.

V10 engine

The world's only production passenger car V10, at 8 liters (488 cubic inches) it is also the largest production engine in the world. Power in this all-aluminum dynamo has increased from 400 bhp in 1992 to 450 bhp in 1998.

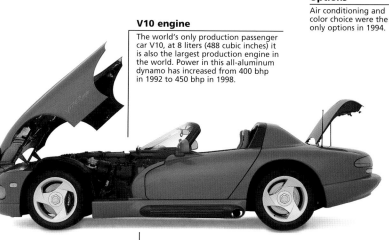

Tubular steel chassis

Steel tube chassis with steel cowl and sill structures; some composite body panels are bolted or bonded to the frame.

Unequal-sized tires

Different size tires and wheels front and rear help balance handling.

Six-speed transmission

Borg-Warner six-speed transmission has an electronic shift lockout that automatically changes from 1st to 4th at light throttle.

Functional roll bar

Built-in roll bar stiffens body structure as well as adding protection. Removable rear window snaps into roll bar.

Limited slip differential

Limited slip differential helps to put the Viper's huge power down onto the road by reducing wheel spin.

Exhaust air vents

The exaggerated cutaway sections in front of the doors form functional vents through which the hot engine compartment air is exhausted.

Plastic composite body

With a separate chassis, you would expect a fiberglass body, but the Viper uses more advanced plastic composite material with far greater damage resistance properties.

Specifications

1992 Dodge Viper RT/10

ENGINE

Type: V10, 90°

Construction: Aluminum heads and block with cast iron sleeves

Valve gear: Two valves per cylinders pushrods, roller hydraulic lifters

Bore and stroke: 4.0 in. x 3.9 in.

Displacement: 7,998 cc

Compression ratio: 9:1

Induction system: Multi-port electronic injection with ram tuning

Maximum power: 400 bhp at 4,600 rpm

Maximum torque: 488 lb-ft at 3,600 rpm

Top speed: 162 mph

0-60 mph: 5.4 sec

TRANSMISSION

Borg-Warner T-56 six-speed manual with electronic shift lock out

BODY/CHASSIS

Tubular steel chassis with two-seat fiberglass reinforced plastic convertible body

SPECIAL FEATURES

The six-speed transmission was specially designed to handle the immense torque.

The Viper is the only production car with a V10 engine.

RUNNING GEAR

Steering: Power-assisted rack-and-pinion

Front suspension: Unequal A-arms, anti-roll bar, coil springs, adjustable gas shocks

Rear suspension: Unequal A-arms, anti-roll bar, coil springs, toe-control links, adjustable gas shocks

Brakes: Brembo 13 in. vented disc with four-piston caliper (front); Brembo 13 in. vented disc with sliding caliper (rear)

Wheels: Alloy 10 in. x 17 in. (front), 13 in. x 17 in. (rear)

Tires: 275/40 ZR17 (front), 335/35 ZR17 (rear)

DIMENSIONS

Length: 175 in.   **Width:** 75.6 in.

Height: 44 in.   **Wheelbase:** 96.2 in.

Track: 59.5 in. (front), 60.6 in. (rear)

Weight: 3,477 lbs.

Dodge VIPER GTS

Its has a quicker ¼ mile time than a Ferrari F355, has better lateral acceleration than a Porsche 911 Carrera and can out-slalom a C5 Corvette. The Dodge Viper GTS might just be the best all around performance car built that doesn't cost more than $100,000.

"...fantastic all around."

"After just a few minutes at the wheel, you have no doubt that the Viper GTS is a fantastic all-around sports car. It takes effort to depress the clutch pedal, the gear shift is notchy and the brakes require a big stamp to get the most out of them. However, the sheer torque of the V10 engine allows a ¼ mile time of 12.6 seconds at 117 mph, its handling is tuned to give a lateral acceleration of .98 g and it can reach over 60 mph in a 700 ft. slalom. Enough said."

The GTS features power windows, a CD player and even has adjustable pedals.

Milestones

1989 The Viper legend is born when a revitalized Chrysler Corporation displays it as a concept car at the Detroit Motor Show.

Race-prepared Vipers have been successful in GT endurance racing since they were introduced.

1991 A Viper RT/10 paces the prestigious Indianapolis 500 race with Carrol Shelby behind the wheel.

1992 The production Viper RT/10 roadster finally goes on sale and buyers line up.

By popular demand the Viper RT/10 roadster was put into production in 1991.

1993 A GTS coupe version is put on display as a future production proposition.

1996 The GTS finally goes on sale after tremendous media acclaim. Current Viper roadster owners are allowed to put their orders in first for the new car.

UNDER THE SKIN

Improved snake

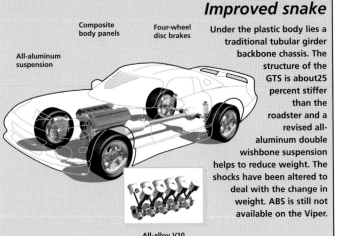

Composite body panels

Four-wheel disc brakes

All-aluminum suspension

All-alloy V10

Under the plastic body lies a traditional tubular girder backbone chassis. The structure of the GTS is about 25 percent stiffer than the roadster and a revised all-aluminum double wishbone suspension helps to reduce weight. The shocks have been altered to deal with the change in weight. ABS is still not available on the Viper.

THE POWER PACK

King of the cubes

The Viper's visceral heart is its amazing engine. There is no substitute for cubic inches, and the Viper has 488 of them. The Lamborghini-designed V10 engine features two valves per cylinder, pushrods and hydraulic valve lifters. The block is all-aluminum and uses cross-bolted main bearing caps. It is basically the same engine found in the Viper R/T. In the GTS coupe version power has been bumped up to 450 bhp, although torque still stands at an incredible 490 lb-ft.

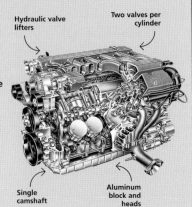

Hydraulic valve lifters

Two valves per cylinder

Single camshaft

Aluminum block and heads

Hard nut

By adding a solid roof, Dodge took the Viper to a new level with the GTS model. Thanks to its 490 lb-ft of torque the GTS gets up to its maximum speed of 179 mph in no time. With this much torque it's no wonder why it's designed to have mild understeer.

The GTS takes the original Viper concept a stage further.

In a world where the premiere performance cars are thought to come from Maranello, Italy and Stuttgart, Germany, it is great to know that, with the Viper GTS, the U.S. has a supercar that can crush both Ferrari and Porsche.

V10 engine
The V10 puts out 450 bhp and an incredible 490 lb-ft of torque. The Viper is the only current production car powered by a V10 engine.

Large trunk
The GTS satisfies that seemingly overridingly important criterion, namely that the trunk should be able to accommodate more luggage than you would expect.

Sleeker shape
Compared to the RT/10 roadster, the GTS has smoother, more aerodynamic lines and a drag figure of 0.39. Body panels are not interchangeable with the roadster.

Six-speed transmission
The Viper was one of the first road cars to use a six-speed transmission. However, in reality, the six-speed unit was specified to obtain an improved fuel economy rating to satisfy tough fuel consumption standards. Both fifth and sixth are overdrive gears.

Huge brakes
Vented disc brakes at all four corners are among the largest used on any production car. They measure 13 inches across and can stop the GTS from very high speeds.

Polished alloy wheels
The alloy wheels have a beautifully polished finish and are huge—17-inch diameter and 10 inches wide at the front and 13 inches at the rear.

Plastic bodywork
The body of the GTS is made almost entirely of composite materials, with some steel strengthening in the doors. This suits the low-volume production of the Viper. The GTS weighs 42.2 lbs. less than the RT/10 roadster.

Specifications
1998 Dodge Viper GTS

ENGINE

Type: V10

Construction: Aluminum cylinder block and heads

Valve gear: Two valves per cylinder operated by a single chain-driven camshaft

Bore and stroke: 4 in. x 3.88 in.

Displacement: 488 c.i.

Compression ratio: 9.6:1

Induction system: Sequential fuel injection

Maximum power: 450 bhp at 5,200 rpm

Maximum torque: 490 lb-ft at 3,700 rpm

Top speed: 179 mph

0-60 mph: 4.7 sec

TRANSMISSION

Six-speed manual

BODY/CHASSIS

Monocoque tubular backbone chassis with composite two-door coupe body

SPECIAL FEATURES

Massive 17-inch five-spoke wheels were first seen on Viper roadsters in 1995.

The push-button door handles are electrically operated.

RUNNING GEAR

Steering: Rack-and-pinion

Front suspension: Unequal length wishbones with coil springs, shocks and anti-roll bar

Rear suspension: Unequal length wishbones with coil springs, shocks and anti-roll bar

Brakes: Vented discs, 13-in. dia. (front and rear)

Wheels: Alloy, 17-in. dia.

Tires: 275/40 ZR17 (front), 335/35 ZR17 (rear)

DIMENSIONS

Length: 175.1 in. **Width:** 75.7 in.

Height: 44 in. **Wheelbase:** 96.2 in.

Track: 59.6 in. (front), 60.6 in. (rear)

Weight: 3,384 lbs.

Dodge RAM

Since its introduction, the latest Ram, with its bold, extroverted styling, spacious interior, and unprecedented refinement, has proven immensely popular. It currently holds 12 percent of the full-size truck market.

"...rugged and spacious."

"From any angle the Ram is huge. Inside, it boasts one of the most spacious cabs in its class, with ample room even in standard form. Turning the key brings the huge V10 to life. The largest engine available in a production pick-up, it offers an incredible amount of power and torque. The column shifted four-speed automatic is effortless. Rugged and spacious, the Dodge Ram is perfect for a night on the town or working on the ranch."

Inside, the Ram is car-like and boasts considerable refinement for a full-size pick-up.

Milestones

1994 After years of fielding a boxy and outmoded design, Dodge jumps back into the truck market with a huge splash. The new Ram has bold styling and the best interior in its class.

Introduced in late 1997, the Quadcab has twin rear doors.

1995 In order to compete with rival Ford, a Ram Sport model, with a body-colored grill and bumpers, is launched. It is only available in standard cab, short wheel-base configuration and a V8 is the only engine choice.

Big Ram styling cues have also been extended to the mid-size Dakota pick up, and the Durango sport utility (above).

1997 Turning the industry on its ear yet again, Dodge introduces its unique Quadcab model, with suicide doors on both sides.

UNDER THE SKIN

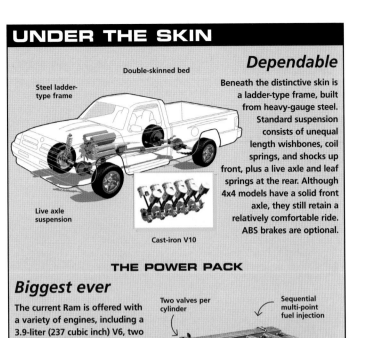

Double-skinned bed

Steel ladder-type frame

Live axle suspension

Cast-iron V10

Dependable

Beneath the distinctive skin is a ladder-type frame, built from heavy-gauge steel. Standard suspension consists of unequal length wishbones, coil springs, and shocks up front, plus a live axle and leaf springs at the rear. Although 4x4 models have a solid front axle, they still retain a relatively comfortable ride. ABS brakes are optional.

THE POWER PACK

Biggest ever

The current Ram is offered with a variety of engines, including a 3.9-liter (237 cubic inch) V6, two V8s and a diesel. Top of the range, available in ¾- and 1-ton models, is an 8.0-liter (488 cubic inch) V10, which is also used in the Dodge Viper. It retains two valves per cylinder and pushrods, but also incorporates a highly sophisticated sequential electronic fuel injection system. In the Ram, the V10 produces 300 bhp and a huge 440 lb-ft of torque at only 2,800 rpm. Despite this power, compression is relatively low at 8.6:1.

Two valves per cylinder

Sequential multi-point fuel injection

Forged steel crankshaft

Cast-iron block and cylinder heads

Macho style

Part of the Ram's tremendous sales appeal is its big grill and 18-wheeler appearance. This gives it a traditional all-American look combined with modern styling cues. Love it or hate it, you certainly cannot ignore the current Dodge Ram pickup.

With 440 lb-ft of torque the Ram is a great tow vehicle.

With the current Ram, Dodge is on to a winner. Buyers love the brawny exterior styling and the spacious and luxurious interior. A variety of body styles, lengths and powertrains is available.

Monster V10

The Ram is unique in being the only current American pickup to be fitted with a V10. Based on the Viper's engine, the truck unit is cast-iron instead of alloy but still produces an impressive 300 bhp.

Roll bar

Many 4x4 pick-ups are fitted with roll bars. Although they are installed for safety reasons, they also give the truck a rugged and durable look.

Big rig style

From the front, the Ram looks like a scaled-down Peterbilt or Freightliner conventional. This contrasts with the car-like appearance of other pickups.

Plush ride

With gas-filled shock absorbers, even 4x4 models, such as this 2500, offer a supple ride and make them ideal for regular open road use.

Car-like interior

Trevor Creed styled the interior and placed considerable emphasis on ergonomics with all controls logically placed. King-size cup holders are also fitted.

Different bed lengths.

Like its main rivals, the Ram is available with two different bed lengths—6.5 and 8 feet. This example has the longer bed and is able to carry ¾-ton loads, as specified by its 2500 designation.

Optional ABS

With safety in mind, anti-lock brakes (ABS) are available and help stop rear-wheel lock-up with an empty load bed.

195

Specifications
1995 Dodge Ram 2500 V10

ENGINE

Type: V10

Construction: Cast-iron block and heads

Valve gear: Two valves per cylinder operated by pushrods and hydraulic lifters

Bore and stroke: 4 in. x 3.88 in.

Displacement: 488 c.i.

Compression ratio: 8.6:1

Induction system: Sequential multi-point fuel injection

Maximum power: 300 bhp at 4,000 rpm

Maximum torque: 440 lb-ft at 2,800 rpm

Top speed: 113 mph

0-60 mph: 7.5 sec.

TRANSMISSION

Four-speed automatic

BODY/CHASSIS

Steel frame with separate steel body

SPECIAL FEATURES

Roll bar-mounted spotlights are a favorite accessory for many buyers.

Big Goodyear Wrangler off-road tires ensure maximum grip.

RUNNING GEAR

Steering: Recirculating ball

Front suspension: Live front axle with coil springs and telescopic shocks

Rear suspension: Live rear axle with multi-leaf springs and telescopic shocks

Brakes: Vented discs, 12.5-in. dia. (front), drums, 13-in. dia. (rear), optional ABS

Wheels: Styled steel, 16-in. dia.

Tires: Goodyear Wrangler RT/S P245/75R16

DIMENSIONS

Length: 224.3 in. **Width:** 79.4 in.

Height: 72.1 in. **Wheelbase:** 134.7 in.

Track: 68.6 in. (front), 68 in. (rear)

Weight: 5,383 lbs.

Dodge DURANGO

Unashamedly based on the Dakota truck, the new Dodge Durango SUV combines the best of both worlds: trucklike strength and size, and carlike comfort, ride and handling.

"...balanced and comfortable."

"For all its Dakota truck underpinnings the Durango does everything many more purpose-built SUVs do, and it does a few things even better. There's feel and accuracy in the steering, plus balanced handling and a comfortable ride. Add to this the fierce acceleration from the big V8, which sees you hitting 60 mph in 8.7 seconds, and the ground clearance which makes it very practical off road, and the appeal of the Durango is obvious."

The Durango has the biggest interior in its class with seating for up to eight people.

Milestones

1986 Dodge introduces the Dakota. Its
first new mid-size truck, it fits in between the full-size D150 and the compact Ram. Two wheelbase lengths are available and engines start with the 2.2-liter four and include the 125-bhp 3.9-liter V6.

The Ramcharger was Dodge's only SUV for many years.

1996 A new Dakota is launched. With an
imposing style clearly inspired by the successful Ram, it is bigger and heavier than the 1980s version. Engines include a larger 2.5-liter four-cylinder, a 3.9-liter V6 and Magnum 5.2-liter V8.

The Durango gets its styling cues from the bigger Ram pickup.

1997 The Dakota forms the basis of the
new Durango. Engines start with the 3.9-liter V6, and the next step up is a 5.2-liter V8. The top of the range SLT Plus is powered by the 250-bhp, 5.9-liter V8.

UNDER THE SKIN

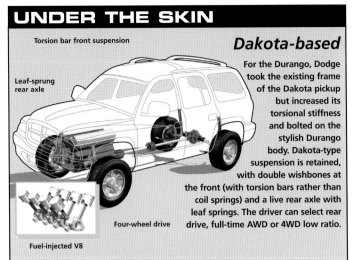

Torsion bar front suspension

Leaf-sprung rear axle

Fuel-injected V8

Four-wheel drive

Dakota-based

For the Durango, Dodge took the existing frame of the Dakota pickup but increased its torsional stiffness and bolted on the stylish Durango body. Dakota-type suspension is retained, with double wishbones at the front (with torsion bars rather than coil springs) and a live rear axle with leaf springs. The driver can select rear drive, full-time AWD or 4WD low ratio.

THE POWER PACK

Conventional V8

The top of the range Durango uses the big 5.9-liter fuel-injected V8 Magnum engine used by the Ramcharger. It has the traditional cast-iron block and heads, plus the usual two valves per cylinder operated by single V-mounted camshafts and hydraulic valve lifters. Over the years it has been given a little more power to bring it up to its current 250 bhp, but it is tuned for low rpm power (peaking at only 4,000 rpm) and torque, with all 335 lb-ft being on tap by 3,200 rpm.

Fuel injection

Two valves per cylinder

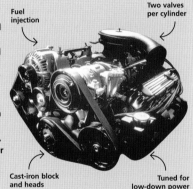

Cast-iron block and heads

Tuned for low-down power

Smaller V8

The Durango is good even without the mighty 5.9-liter V8 in the SLT Plus. The SLT, with a 5.2-liter version of the Magnum V8, has just 20 bhp and 35 lb-ft of torque less than the Plus model. It is a better bet than the 175-bhp, 3.9-liter V6 base model.

The Durango is one of the most striking SUVs in its class.

Add a generous eight-seater body and a 250-bhp V8 engine to a truck chassis and you have the Durango SLT Plus—a carry-all SUV with the type of acceleration sports car owners used to brag about not all that long ago.

V8 engine
The fuel-injected 5.9-liter Magnum V8 is a short-stroke pushrod design with plenty of power and torque, but the all-iron construction helps to contribute to the Durango's front-heavy (56:44 front/rear) weight distribution.

Four-speed automatic
There is no need to have a manual transmission with the 5.9-liter engine. The top of the range SLT Plus is fitted with a four-speed automatic with a high and relaxing overdrive.

Torsion bar front suspension
Dodge's long allegiance with torsion bar front suspension is continued in the Durango, in which the lower wishbones operate a torsion bar.

Separate chassis
Like all rugged trucks, the Durango is built on a separate chassis. The Durango's body is fixed to the frame with bolts and rubber bushings to help reduce noise and vibration.

High and low ratios
The driver only needs to select 'low' ratio in four-wheel drive in extreme circumstances. Creeping along at 3.4 mph per 1,000 revs, even a driver who is not skilled with the throttle is unlikely to spin the wheels on ice.

Specifications

1998 Dodge Durango SLT Plus

ENGINE
Type: V8

Construction: Cast-iron block and heads

Valve gear: Two valves per cylinder operated by a single V-mounted camshaft via pushrods, rockers and hydraulic tappets

Bore and stroke: 4.0 in.x 3.58 in.

Displacement: 5,898 cc

Compression ratio: 8.9:1

Induction system: Electronic port fuel injection

Maximum power: 250 bhp at 4,000 rpm

Maximum torque: 335 lb-ft at 3,200 rpm

Top speed: 115 mph

0-60 mph: 8.7 sec.

TRANSMISSION
Four-speed overdrive automatic transmission with selectable four-wheel drive in low and high ratio with lockable center differential

BODY/CHASSIS
Separate steel chassis frame with bolted-on steel four-door SUV body

SPECIAL FEATURES

The 5.9-liter V8 gives the Durango excellent performance.

The Durango is available in both two- and four-wheel drive versions.

RUNNING GEAR
Steering: Recirculating ball

Front suspension: Double wishbones with torsion bars, telescopic shock absorbers and anti-roll bar

Rear suspension: Live axle with leaf springs, telescopic shock absorbers and anti-roll bar

Brakes: Vented discs, 11.3-in. dia (front), drums, 11.0-in. dia (rear)

Wheels: Cast-aluminum alloy, 8 x 15 in.

Tires: 235/75 R15

DIMENSIONS
Length: 193.2 in.   **Width:** 71.5 in.

Height: 72.9 in.   **Wheelbase:** 115.9 in.

Track: 63.0 in. (front), 62.5 in. (rear)

Weight: 5,050 lbs.

USA • ITALY 1956-1958

Dual GHIA

Virgil Exner was a great styling talent for Chrysler for several decades. One of his show cars even made it to the road, thanks to the intervention of Eugene Casaroll, a longtime Chrysler consultant.

"...a cruising machine."

"Considering its extraordinarily high price, the Dual Ghia had to compete with some very fine imported machinery, though the driving experience is very definitely American, not European. When you start the V8 engine and engage the PowerFlite floorshift transmission, the feel is distinctly 1950s and distinctly Dodge. The short wheelbase and low center of gravity make it stable, but this is still a cruising machine, not a sports car."

Only the finest leather and trim were used on the ultra-exclusive Dual Ghia.

Milestones

1952 Virgil Exner's Dodge Firearrow show car breaks new ground.

The Dual Ghia uses a Dodge D-500 chassis and running gear.

1953 A more practical, restyled show car called the Firebomb impresses a certain Mr. Eugene Casaroll.

1956 Production of the Dual Ghia gets underway. For the greatest prestige possible, only select people may purchase them.

Among Virgil Exner's later lavish creations was the Stutz.

1958 Warranty claims force the Dual Ghia out of production after only 117 have been built. Eugene Casaroll returns in 1960 with another design based on Chrysler parts. Named the Ghia L-610, it boasts unitary construction and a 335-bhp, 383-cubic inch V8. It is unsuccessful and production ends after 26 cars are built.

UNDER THE SKIN

Step-down floor

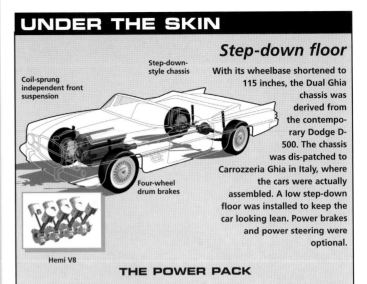

Coil-sprung independent front suspension

Step-down-style chassis

Four-wheel drum brakes

Hemi V8

With its wheelbase shortened to 115 inches, the Dual Ghia chassis was derived from the contemporary Dodge D-500. The chassis was dis-patched to Carrozzeria Ghia in Italy, where the cars were actually assembled. A low step-down floor was installed to keep the car looking lean. Power brakes and power steering were optional.

THE POWER PACK

Mighty Red Ram

Dual Motors took one of the most powerful engines from Chrysler's lineup, the Dodge Red Ram V8. This featured hemispherical combustion chambers, enabling it to produce more power on a lower compression engine than its V8 rivals. This massive engine was offered in three power levels starting with a 315-cubic inch Dodge V8 out of the D-500. It had an 8.0:1 compression ratio and 230 bhp on tap. Next up was the larger 325-cubic inch D-500-1 motor. This $100 offer had an 8.5:1 compression ratio and 260 bhp. The top of the line was a 285-bhp version of the engine that was not far off Chrysler's '1-bhp-per-cubic-inch' dream.

Status symbol

In its day, the Dual Ghia was a Hollywood special. It may not have the same mystique today, but its status as a high-quality Italian-American hybrid will always ensure it has a high collector value. Especially if its former owner has celebrity status.

Opinions on it may be divided, but the Dual Ghia is a definite collector's piece.

Virgil Exner's 1953 Firebomb styling prototype for Dodge impressed Eugene Casaroll so much that he ambitiously launched a modified version of the show car for an independent production run.

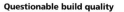

Hardtop or convertible

Almost all Dual Ghias were convertibles, but a hardtop was available. This was made from fiberglass rather than steel. However, only two hardtops are known to have been built.

Ghia-built bodywork

Chassis were shipped from the U.S. for the new bodywork to be fitted and trimmed by Ghia in Turin, Italy. They were then shipped back for final assembly and sale.

Questionable build quality

Because it was handbuilt by Italian craftsmen who used a lot of body filler to get the smooth lines right, the Dual Ghia was not the most durable. This resulted in an over-whelming number of warranty claims, which led to the company's demise.

Hollywood style

The Dual Ghia was brashly advertised with the line: 'Rolls-Royce is the car of those who cannot afford a Dual Ghia.' Casaroll himself decided who would be permitted to buy one of his cars. Frank Sinatra was one such owner.

Modified Dodge chassis

The Dual Ghia body sat on what was essentially a Dodge D-500 chassis. It was shipped to Ghia in Italy, and its wheelbase was shortened seven inches for a total length of 115 inches. Ghia's Giovanni Savonuzzi designed the new step-down floor for the car.

Luxury interior

At over $7,500, the Dual Ghia ranked as one of the most expensive cars on sale in 1956. Some justification was provided by the luxury specification, including hand-finished English leather upholstery for the four seats, a radio and a heater.

Exner styling

Chrysler's chief of styling, Virgil Exner, created the Firebomb's shape. It was translated into the pro-duction Dual Ghia with very few changes. The front and rear bumpers were, however, stock Dodge pieces.

Specifications

1956 Dual Ghia

ENGINE

Type: V8

Construction: Cast-iron block and heads

Valve gear: Two valves per cylinder operated by a single camshaft with pushrods and rocker arms

Bore and stroke: 3.63 in. x 3.80 in.

Displacement: 315 c.i.

Compression ratio: 8.0:1

Induction system: Single Carter four-barrel carburetor

Maximum power: 230 bhp at 4,300 rpm

Maximum torque: Not quoted

Top speed: 125 mph

0-60 mph: 8.5 sec.

TRANSMISSION

Two-speed automatic

BODY/CHASSIS

Separate chassis with steel two-door convertible body

SPECIAL FEATURES

Sharp, blade-like fins were typical styling features in the 1950s.

Spinner wheel covers represent the Dual Ghia's exotic image.

RUNNING GEAR

Steering: Recirculating ball

Front suspension: Double wishbone with coil springs and telescopic shock absorbers

Rear suspension: Live axle with semi-elliptic leaf springs and telescopic shock absorbers

Brakes: Drums (front and rear)

Wheels: Steel, 15-in. dia.

Tires: 6.70 x 15

DIMENSIONS

Length: 203.5 in.

Width: 79.0 in.

Height: 51.0 in.

Wheelbase: 115.0 in.

Track: 58.9 in. (front), 59.2 in. (rear)

Weight: Not quoted

Duesenburg MODEL J

One of the greatest of all prewar luxury cars was built not in Europe, but in the U.S. The mighty Duesenberg Model J has a straight-eight engine with twin overhead camshafts, four valves per cylinder, and 265 bhp.

"...as though on rails."

"Unlike a Rolls-Royce, the Duesenberg was a sporty luxury car intended for keen drivers. The twin-overhead-cam, 32-valve straight-eight was basically a racing car engine that would easily rocket the Model J past 100 mph. The handling and roadholding are superior for a 1930s car, and live up to the Duesenberg catch phrase that the car takes curves 'as though on rails.' It's a big heavy car that needs a strong person behind the wheel to get the best from it."

The seat of the stars. *The Duesenberg Model J was a favorite of 1930s film stars like Clark Gable and Gary Cooper.*

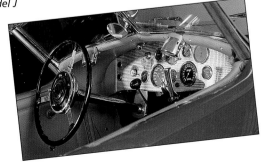

Milestones

1921 The Duesenberg company, run by brothers Fred and August, build their first production car, the Model A. It is the first straight-eight-engined car built in the U.S.

Duesenbergs often carried stunning bodywork.

1926 Duesenberg is taken over by Errett Lobban Cord, who eventually owns the Auburn, Cord and Duesenberg companies.

1928 Duesenberg's masterpiece, the Model J, is launched in December.

1932 Despite the Wall Street Crash, Duesenberg introduces the Model SJ.

Duesenberg brothers, Fred and August, founded the company.

1937 The Auburn/ Cord/Duesenberg group goes out of business. Duesenberg is later bought up and its new owners stop car production after 436 Model Js and 36 SJs have been made.

UNDER THE SKIN

Huge chassis

The Model J was built to deal with power. It had six cross members on its huge chassis. It is quite conventional, with a three-speed transmission, solid axles and leaf springs. Duesenberg was ahead of the rest in two areas. It pioneered hydraulic brakes in the 1920s (the Model J's are very efficient) and the car also has the first mechanical onboard computer.

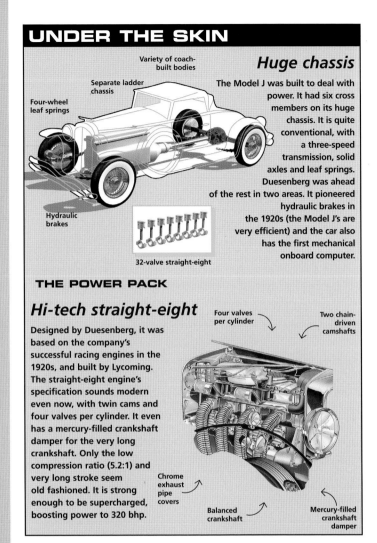

Variety of coach-built bodies
Separate ladder chassis
Four-wheel leaf springs
Hydraulic brakes
32-valve straight-eight

THE POWER PACK

Hi-tech straight-eight

Designed by Duesenberg, it was based on the company's successful racing engines in the 1920s, and built by Lycoming. The straight-eight engine's specification sounds modern even now, with twin cams and four valves per cylinder. It even has a mercury-filled crankshaft damper for the very long crankshaft. Only the low compression ratio (5.2:1) and very long stroke seem old fashioned. It is strong enough to be supercharged, boosting power to 320 bhp.

Four valves per cylinder
Two chain-driven camshafts
Chrome exhaust pipe covers
Balanced crankshaft
Mercury-filled crankshaft damper

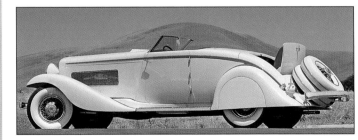

Supercharged

If a Model J was not enough you could, like Clark Gable, have the supercharged SJ. It had a centrifugal supercharger running at six times engine speed that boosted power by 55 bhp more than the standard car. Just 36 SJs were built.

Film stars Clark Gable and Gary Cooper had supercharged Duesenberg SJs.

Duesenberg was the only American automaker to win a Grand Prix and put that experience to good use in building racing-inspired engines to power cars like the Model J.

Solid front axle
Though the Duesenberg brothers were fantastic engineers, they still had no problems about using a solid front axle.

Bodies made to order
Customers could choose to have any body they liked fitted to the Model J. Coachbuilders like Le Baron, Rollston, and Weymann built bodies to complement Duesenberg's own offerings. This model is a LeGrande convertible.

Swivelling spotlights
An intriguing feature on the Model J are the spotlights that turn along with the steering wheel so the lights follow the direction of the car.

Single stop light
In the late-1920s, it was not compulsory to have two brake lights, but this Duesenberg's single huge white stop light is still very unusual.

Straight-eight engine
It's an impressive technical feat to make a twin-cam straight-eight. The camshafts and crankshaft are very long and need to be well supported.

Hydraulic brakes
Duesenberg pioneered hydraulic brakes in motor racing, so it's no surprise that the Model J has huge 15-inch hydraulic drum brakes.

Luggage trunk
The rear luggage compartment was nothing more than a trunk strapped to the rear of the car.

Duesenberg SJ

The Duesenberg J was one of the world's finest motor cars, but the SJ was even more powerful and opulent. The addition of a supercharger turned it into a phenomenal performer.

"...sense of superiority."

"When you enter the SJ, a sense of superiority pervades in terms of both design function and quality. It is not an obtrusive, heavy beast like so many of its contemporaries: indeed, the steering is light, accurate and full of feel. Open the throttle up and the gutsy noise from the engine and supercharger is almost overwhelming, as is the sheer speed—it is possible to top 100 mph in second gear! However, the antiquated chassis is not the equal of the engine."

The Duesenberg has an aura of quality that was only equaled by few of its peers.

Milestones

1926 Duesenberg brothers sell their car-manufacturing business to Cord.

Duesenberg was taken over by Cord when faced with the prospect of bankruptcy.

1928 An all-new Model J was announced, complete with the presupposed title of 'the world's finest car.'

The SJ uses the same engine as the J but has a supercharger.

1932 With a supercharger, the mighty SJ becomes one of the fastest road cars available. Fred Duesenburg is tragically killed behind the wheel of a SJ.

1935 A.B. Jenkins averages 135 mph on a 24-hour Bonneville run and clocks a 160-mph lap.

1937 Along with Cord and Auburn, Duesenberg is dragged down amid severe economic hardship.

UNDER THE SKIN

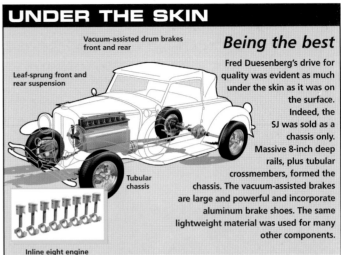

Vacuum-assisted drum brakes front and rear

Leaf-sprung front and rear suspension

Tubular chassis

Inline eight engine

Being the best

Fred Duesenberg's drive for quality was evident as much under the skin as it was on the surface. Indeed, the SJ was sold as a chassis only. Massive 8-inch deep rails, plus tubular crossmembers, formed the chassis. The vacuum-assisted brakes are large and powerful and incorporate aluminum brake shoes. The same lightweight material was used for many other components.

THE POWER PACK

Supercharged superlative

A centrifugal supercharger gives the straight-eight Duesenberg engine awesome power. Even in the naturally aspirated J model, the 420-cubic inch twin-overhead camshaft engine delivers an advertised 265 bhp. The addition of a blower, with 5 psi of boost at 4,000 rpm, rockets that to an incredible 320 bhp at 4,200 rpm in stock form, with an equally impressive 425 lb-ft of torque at 2,400 rpm. Modifications required for this power output included tubular-steel con rods. With different exhaust manifolds, one engine was dyno-tested at an incredible 400 bhp, way above other engines of the 1930s.

SSJ

Duesenbergs guarantee exclusivity, none more so than the two SSJ's that were specially made for Gary Cooper and Clark Gable. The 125-inch short-wheelbase cars had shattering performance. Both cars still exist as museum pieces.

Bigger and stronger than other cars, the SJ has real road presence.

With a stiffened-up engine and a blower fitted, Duesenberg's supremely accomplished Model J was transformed into the exclusive and powerful SJ. Only the extraordinarily wealthy could afford one.

Power brakes

The brakes were as advanced as the rest of the car's specification. With oversized shoes, braking power was impressive and was made easier by standard vacuum assistance.

Much use of aluminum

As many production SJs measured more than 20 feet long, there was naturally some concern to keep weight down. Therefore, many parts were made from aluminum, including some of the engine, dash, crankcase, water pump, intake manifold, brake shoes and gas tank.

Snaking pipes

One of the hallmarks of the SJ is its dramatic and beautifully plated exhaust headers emerging from the side of the engine. However, elaborate pipework like this does not necessarily mean the car is an SJ—the ordinary Model J was often fitted with such plumbing, even if there wasn't a supercharger.

Aircraft-quality engine

The undoubted centerpiece of any Duesenberg is its engine. The fabulous straight eight was extremely advanced, boasting twin overhead camshafts and four valves per cylinder. The basic engine was built by Lycoming to Fred Duesenberg's specifications.

Custom bodywork

In the best coachbuilt traditions, Duesenberg supplied only the chassis. Customers were expected to patronize independent coachbuilders to create whatever body-work struck their fancy. With its sporty bias, the SJ's performance suited a roadster or convertible body.

Supercharger

A centrifugal blower was added to the straight eight to deliver crushing performance on a mildly higher compression ratio. Power shot up to 320 bhp, making it easily the most powerful auto production engine in the world.

Specifications

Duesenberg SJ

ENGINE

Type: Inline eight

Construction: Cast-iron cylinder block and head

Valve gear: Four valves per cylinder operated by double chain-driven camshafts

Bore and stroke: 3.70 in. x 4.50 in.

Displacement: 420 c.i.

Compression ratio: 5.7:1

Induction system: Single Schebler carburetor plus supercharger

Maximum power: 320 bhp at 4,200 rpm

Maximum torque: 425 lb-ft at 2,400 rpm

Top speed: 130 mph

0-60 mph: 8.5 sec.

TRANSMISSION

Three-speed manual

BODY/CHASSIS

Separate chassis with convertible bodywork

SPECIAL FEATURES

A fold out rumble is available to fit two additional passengers.

As part of the effort to reduce weight, even the dashboard is aluminum.

RUNNING GEAR

Steering: Cam-and-lever

Front suspension: Beam axle with leaf springs and shock absorbers

Rear suspension: Live axle with leaf springs and shock absorbers

Brakes: Drums (front and rear)

Wheels: Wire, 19-in. dia.

Tires: Crossply, 9 in. x 16 in.

DIMENSIONS

Length: 222.5 in.

Width: 72.0 in.

Height: 70.0 in.

Wheelbase: 142.5 in.

Track: 37.5 in. (front), 58.0 (rear)

Weight: 5,000 lbs.

Edsel BERMUDA

Named after Henry Ford's only son, the Edsel has long been regarded as a flop. Today, however, these cars are prized by collectors, particularly the elusive and unusually styled Bermuda wagon.

"...glides along in comfort."

"Essentially, the Edsel drives like any other 1958 Detroit car, with ample power and an abundance of mid-range torque. Tele Touch drive—with its transmission's gear selectors mounted in the steering wheel hub—takes some getting used to, but shifts are seamless and the car glides along in total comfort. Braking and handling are on par with most Detroiters, with low-speed cornering and gentle stops being almost essential."

Tele Touch drive and a Cyclops-eye rotating drum speedometer were standard in 1958.

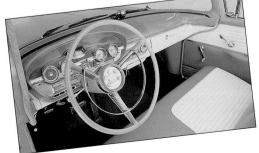

Milestones

1954 A new E-car program is set in motion, led by Ford chairman of the board Ernest R. Breech.

1958 was the only year for Edsels on split wheelbases.

1958 Edsel arrives in a recession year. Offered in four different series with two different V8s, it sells respectably, with 62,110 cars leaving the production line. However, this is not deemed sufficient by Ford's own estimates.

The most desirable Edsel is the 410-powered Citation convertible.

1959 The range is reduced to just two versions on a single wheelbase, the Corsair and Ranger. The 410-cubic inch V8 is dropped and a 292-cubic inch unit arrives as a base V8. Styling is toned down, but production still plummets.

1959 The 1960 model is axed in November.

UNDER THE SKIN

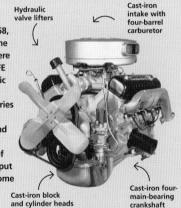

Ford parentage

From its launch, four models were offered on three different wheelbases. Wagons had the shortest, a 116-inch wheelbase chassis. Mechanically, the package was taken directly from other Ford models. Self-adjusting drum brakes were standard, as was a synchromesh transmission. Suspension is typical of the period with front coil and rear leaf springs.

Heavy-duty rear leaf springs
Body-on-frame construction
Four-wheel drum brakes
Powerful V8

THE POWER PACK

Big bang V8

When the Edsel was launched in 1958, its choice of engines fitted in with the rush for horsepower of that era. There were two engine options from the FE big-block family. One was a 361-cubic inch V8 with 303 bhp and came standard in the Ranger and Pacer series (these included the two Bermuda station wagons). Uplevel Corsairs and Citations used the monster 410-V8 engine with 345 bhp and 475 lb-ft of torque. Their substantial power output gave Edsels a reputation as being some of the quickest accelerating U.S. production cars in 1958.

Hydraulic valve lifters
Cast-iron intake with four-barrel carburetor
Cast-iron block and cylinder heads
Cast-iron four-main-bearing crankshaft

Rare hauler

1958 Edsels are the most recognized and consequently the most collected. From its debut year, the Bermuda station wagons ranked among the rarest of all Edsels with just 779 of the nine-seater version being built. Although ridiculed when new, Edsels have gained a cult following in recent years.

Bermudas were offered only for 1958.

Rushed into production and plagued with quality control problems, the Edsel was doomed from the start. Ultimately, Ford lost an estimated $250 million on the whole marketing fiasco.

Panoramic windshield
Still in vogue in 1958, panoramic windshields offered a clear line of vision, but the dog-leg A-pillars caused many a bruised knee upon entering the car.

Full equipment
In addition to the Tele Touch automatic transmission, Edsels came with air conditioning, power windows, steering and brakes and even power lubrication, which greased the steering points and front suspension.

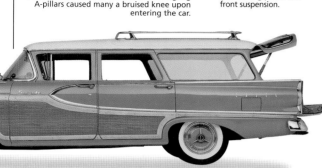

Horse collar grill
A distinctive styling feature is the horse collar vertical grill, which led to the remark that the Edsel looked like an Oldsmobile sucking a lemon.

Six- or nine-seater
Bermuda wagons formed part of the Pacer line, which, with 21,292 built, was the second most popular Edsel after the entry-level Ranger. Bermudas came in either six- or nine-seater configuration, the latter costing just $57 more.

Wood side moldings
By 1958, Ford Wagons had all-steel bodies, but woodgrain trim was still popular. The original Di Noc wood decals had a black pinstripe outline and are extremely valuable today.

Optional backup lights
Mounted outboard of the boomerang-type rear taillights are housings for the optional reverse lights. For a mere $8.50, it was a wise accessory.

1958 Edsel Bermuda

ENGINE
Type: V8
Construction: Cast-iron block and heads
Valve gear: Two valves per cylinder operated by a single camshaft with pushrods and rockers
Bore and stroke: 4.05 in. x 3.50 in.
Displacement: 361 c.i.
Compression ratio: 10.5:1
Induction system: Single Holley four-barrel carburetor
Maximum power: 303 bhp at 4,600 rpm
Maximum torque: 400 lb-ft at 2,600 rpm
Top speed: 108 mph
0-60 mph: 11.8 sec.

TRANSMISSION
Three-speed Tele Touch automatic

BODY/CHASSIS
Separate chassis with steel four-door station wagon body

SPECIAL FEATURES

This car even has an autograph by Roy Brown on the dashboard. Brown designed the Edsel.

Most Bermudas were ordered with the Tele Touch transmission.

RUNNING GEAR
Steering: Recirculating ball
Front suspension: Independent by unequal-length wishbones, coil springs and telescopic shock absorbers
Rear suspension: Live axle with semi-elliptic leaf springs and telescopic shock absorbers
Brakes: Drums (front and rear)
Wheels: Steel, 14-in. dia.
Tires: 8.50 x 14

DIMENSIONS
Length: 205.4 in.   **Width:** 78.8 in.
Height: 56.4 in.   **Wheelbase:** 116.0 in.
Track: 59.0 in. (front), 56.4 in. (rear)
Weight: 3,853 lbs.

Edsel CITATION

Recognized as one of the biggest flops of all time, the Edsel, in all honesty, was not really a bad car. The 1958 Citation convertible, in particular, was fast and well equipped, and had fairly restrained looks for its time.

"...cruises happily."

"Sitting on the big, padded bench seat, the Citation feels similar to most 1958 Detroit cars. Give her a little gas, however, and the picture begins to change. It has noticeably more urge off the line than many of its contemporaries, and on the highway, it cruises happily at speeds around 70 mph. Throw the Edsel into a sharp corner and it leans alarmingly, but then again, so does any other car built during the 1950s."

Citation was the top-of-the-line Edsel in 1958 and was loaded to the gills.

Milestones

1954 With Ford returning to prosperity after near collapse, chairman Ernest R. Breech lays plans to match GM with a five-make hierarchy.

Rarest of all the 1958 Edsels is the 9-seater Bermuda wagon—just 779 were built.

1958 After various delays, Ford launches its new medium-priced car—the Edsel—into a depressed market. Four series are offered (Ranger, Pacer, Corsair and Citation).

Citations and Corsairs shared their chassis with Mercurys.

1959 As a result of sluggish sales, the Edsel lineup is pared back to just Corsair, Ranger and station wagons, on a single 118-in. wheelbase. Less than 45,000 cars are built for the 1959 model year.

1960 Edsel production ends.

UNDER THE SKIN

Mercury chassis

Separate steel chassis with X-bracing

Four-wheel drum brakes

Live rear axle

Big-block V8

Citations used the 124-inch wheelbase Mercury chassis. It was a substantial affair with long side members kicking up at the rear to go over the live axle. On the convertible, a center cruciform X-bracing helped to increase overall stiffness. Suspension was straightforward, with double wishbones and coils at the front and a live axle on semi-elliptic leaf springs at the rear. Like the vast majority of U.S. cars in the late 1950s, the Citation had four-wheel drum brakes.

THE POWER PACK

Continental power

For the larger Edsels, Ford used basically the same engine as in the Lincoln Continental, but with a smaller (4.20 inch) bore, resulting in a displacement of 410 cubic inches instead of 430. Construction was typical for its time with a cast-iron block and cylinder heads, single cam, pushrods, rockers and hydraulic lifters. One different feature was having flat cylinder heads, with the wedge-shaped combustion chambers set in the block. With 345 bhp and 475 lb-ft of torque, the engine made the Edsel quite a performance-oriented car for its time.

Collectible

Considered a disaster when new, the Edsel—especially convertible models—has gained strong collector interest in recent years. The big 401-powered Citation, of which only 25 are believed to exist today, is sought after, and often sells for over $30,000.

With only 930 built, the 1958 Citation was rare.

There are many reasons the Edsel failed in the marketplace, but perhaps the greatest was poor quality control. This factor alone sent buyers scurrying almost immediately to other makes.

V8 engine
The Citation V8 was tuned for torque, as the output of 475 lb-ft at only 2,900 rpm indicates. Even the smaller 361 engine used in the Ranger and Pacer put out an impressive 303 bhp and 400 lb-ft of torque. That engine had its combustion chambers in the head, unlike the bigger 401 unit.

Convertible top
There was a choice of four colors available for the vinyl-covered convertible top on the Citation: black (seen here), white, turquoise and copper. The top folded down flush with the rear deck and was power-operated like most convertibles of the era. It had a flexible plastic rear window.

Power seats
An Edsel Citation convertible was a luxury vehicle and there was the $76 option of four-way power adjustable front seats which were formed by a 30/70 divided front bench seat.

Mercury chassis
There were three different wheelbase lengths for 1958 Edsels: 116 inches for wagons; 118 inches for Pacer and Ranger coupes, sedans and convertibles; and 124 inches for Corsairs and Citations. The latter two actually rode on a Mercury chassis and were built on the same assembly line as the slightly plusher Mercurys.

Recirculating-ball steering
The recirculating-ball steering could be ordered with or without power assistance (an $85 option). If you went without, the steering ratio was altered accordingly to make the wheel easier to turn. There were 5.25 turns lock to lock, compared with 4.25 when power was added.

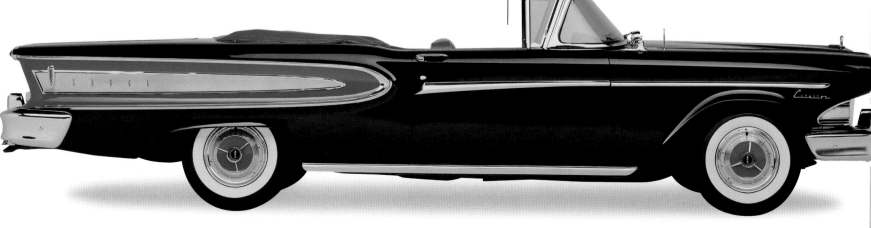

Specifications
1958 Edsel Citation

ENGINE

Type: V8

Construction: Cast-iron block and heads

Valve gear: Two valves per cylinder operated by single V-mounted camshaft

Bore and stroke: 4.20 in. x 3.70 in.

Displacement: 410 c.i.

Compression ratio: 10.5:1

Induction system: Single four-barrel carburetor

Maximum power: 345 bhp at 4,600 rpm

Maximum torque: 475 lb-ft at 2,900 rpm

Top speed: 105 mph

0-60 mph: 9.7 sec.

TRANSMISSION

Three-speed automatic

BODY/CHASSIS

Separate curbed-perimeter chassis frame with center X-brace and convertible body

SPECIAL FEATURES

A station seeking radio with an electric antenna was an expensive ($143.90) option.

One interesting gimmick on 1958 Edsels was the Cyclops Eye rotating-drum speedometer.

RUNNING GEAR

Steering: Recirculating-ball

Front suspension: Double wishbones with coil springs, telescopic dampers and anti-roll bar

Rear suspension: Live axle with semi-elliptic leaf springs and telescopic shock absorbers

Brakes: Drums, 11.0-in. dia. front, 11.0-in. dia. rear

Wheels: Pressed steel disc, 14 in. dia.

Tires: 8.50 -14

DIMENSIONS

Length: 218.8 in.   **Width:** 79.8 in.

Height: 57.0 in.   **Wheelbase:** 124.0 in.

Track: 59.4 in front, 59.0 in rear

Weight: 4,311 lbs.

Excalibur **SSK**

In the early 1960s industrial designer Brooks Stevens saw a market for a modern car with classic 1930s styling. The result was the Excalibur, a retro-styled roadster with modern General Motors mechanicals.

"...the best of both worlds."

"Because it doesn't have any doors, entry isn't that easy—but then the Excalibur isn't about practicality. With Corvette V8 power and a four-speed transmission you have the best of both worlds, a car that copes easily with traffic in town yet is super fast on the open road. Nail the throttle and the car almost takes off, due to its immense power and light weight. With wide tires, grip is good for a car of the 1960s, but the ride is very old fashioned."

The Excalibur has a simple, flat dash like the Mercedes-Benz after which it was styled.

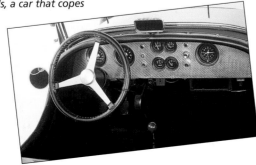

Milestones

1964 While working at Studebaker, Brooks Stevens starts to develop his own retro-style sports roadster.

1965 The first SSK roadsters with Corvette V8 power go into production. Performance and build quality are outstanding.

Styling of the Excalibur is based on the 1928 Mercedes-Benz SSK.

1966 A deluxe roadster with longer front and rear fenders and smart exterior running boards joins the line up.

Later Excaliburs were more luxurious and less sporty.

1967 An optional supercharged 327-cubic inch V8 with 400 bhp becomes available. Performance is now in the terrifying bracket. The SSK Series 1 continues in production until 1969 virtually unchanged.

UNDER THE SKIN

Off-the-shelf

Stevens chose the Studebaker Lark convertible chassis for the SSK. It is narrow enough to fit the slim 1930s-style body, plus it is cross braced for extra structural rigidity. Excaliburs have lower spring settings for safer handling. Suspension components are essentially Studebaker, with independent wishbones up front and a live rear axle. Braking is provided by four-wheel discs.

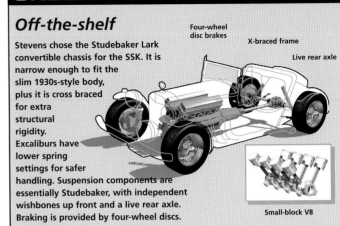

Four-wheel disc brakes

X-braced frame

Live rear axle

Small-block V8

THE POWER PACK

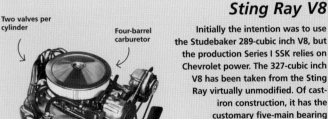

Two valves per cylinder

Four-barrel carburetor

Hydraulic valve lifters

Cast-iron block and heads

Sting Ray V8

Initially the intention was to use the Studebaker 289-cubic inch V8, but the production Series I SSK relies on Chevrolet power. The 327-cubic inch V8 has been taken from the Sting Ray virtually unmodified. Of cast-iron construction, it has the customary five-main bearing crankshaft and relies on a dual-plane intake manifold and a single Carter four-barrel carburetor. Available in only one state of tune, it churns out 300 bhp and 360 lb-ft of torque, and made the SSK one of the fastest cars on the road in 1965.

Exclusive

Excalibur builds some of the purest retro-styled cars in the world and the Series I SSK is undoubtedly the most sought-after model. Just 265 of these SSKs were built and, today, they command premium prices on the collector market.

The Series 1 Excalibur's clean lines and rarity make it highly collectable.

Brooks Stevens realized his dream of a 'modern classic' with the Excalibur, being able to offer a relatively inexpensive hand-built car with outstanding performance.

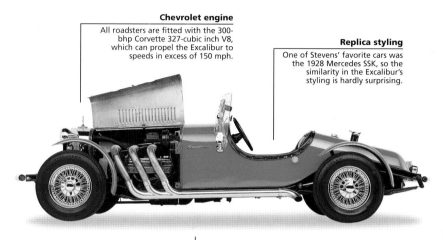

Chevrolet engine
All roadsters are fitted with the 300-bhp Corvette 327-cubic inch V8, which can propel the Excalibur to speeds in excess of 150 mph.

Replica styling
One of Stevens' favorite cars was the 1928 Mercedes SSK, so the similarity in the Excalibur's styling is hardly surprising.

Exhaust headers
The headers on either side of the hood are functional and look great even today. They were fabricated by the same German company used by Mercedes-Benz.

Spare tire
A full-size spare tire can be mounted on top of the trunk, in true 1930s sports car style.

Simple interior
The cockpit is spartan. The dashboard is covered in aluminum and features large and legible dials, plus a typically large German-style steering wheel.

Studebaker chassis
The convertible Studebaker Lark allowed the narrow body to be fitted without serious problems and results in little chassis flex and excellent roadholding.

Disc brakes
In 1965 most American cars had four-wheel drum brakes. The Excalibur has standard front disc brakes. Discs could also be installed on the rear wheels. With them, stopping power is outstanding for a car of this era.

Specifications

1965 Excalibur SSK Roadster Series I

ENGINE
Type: V8

Construction: Cast-iron block and heads

Valve gear: Two valves per cylinder operated by a single camshaft via pushrods and rockers

Bore and stroke: 4 in. x 3.25 in.

Displacement: 327 c.i.

Compression ratio: 10.0:1

Induction system: Single Carter four-barrel carburetor

Maximum power: 300 bhp at 5,000 rpm

Maximum torque: 360 lb-ft at 3,200 rpm

Top speed: 160 mph

0-60 mph: 4.8 sec.

TRANSMISSION
GM four-speed manual

BODY/CHASSIS
Steel X-braced frame with hand-built aluminum roadster body

SPECIAL FEATURES

External stainless steel headers add to the overall feel of a 1930s-vintage roadster.

Like the original Mercedes, the Excalibur has free-standing headlights.

RUNNING GEAR
Steering: Recirculating ball

Front suspension: Unequal length wishbones, coil springs, and telescopic shocks

Rear suspension: Live rear axle supported by semi-elliptic leaf springs, and telescopic shocks

Brakes: Discs (front and rear)

Wheels: Steel wire (chromed), 15-in. dia.

Tires: Firestone P21575 R15

DIMENSIONS
Length: 162.3 in.   **Width:** 73.9 in.

Height: 50.2 in.   **Wheelbase:** 109 in.

Track: 62.8 in. (front), 59.3 in. (rear)

Weight: 2,099 lbs.

Ford MODEL T

If ever a car helped the world get motoring it was the Ford Model T. Built in one piece, robust and reliable, Henry Ford's dream became a global reality. The Model T is rightly recognized by many as the world's most important car.

"...Living in the past."

"The Model T is a vastly confusing place to be for anyone who drives a modern car. The pedal layout is baffling, you have to think constantly about which lever or pedal controls what, and even then you sometimes get it wrong. Even when you've mastered the controls, the Model T isn't a pleasant car to drive. The ride is atrocious, the steering heavy and vague and the brakes practically useless. But to decry the driving experience is missing the point. The Model T was never intended to be a good drive—it was intended to be a reliable and efficient means for as many people as possible to get from A to B. It fitted the brief perfectly, and brought new -found freedom to over 15 million owners."

Today it might look basic, but the simple appearance disguises a very complicated layout.

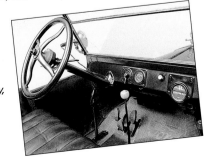

Milestones

1908 Ford's Model T goes on sale on 1 October. By the end of the year, 305 examples have been built.

1914 The Model T is famously offered by Henry Ford in "any colour as long as it's black," due to the low cost of lead-based black paint.

1915 Production levels exceed one million. Electric windscreen wipers are fitted.

One of the prettiest body styles: a Doctor's Coupé.

1919 A wish is answered: Model Ts get an electric starter. The original brass radiator is dropped and replaced by a black-painted nickel one.

Ford's first overseas factory was in Manchester, England.

1924 The different bodywork styles on offer are standardized and finished in the factory. The same year, Ford builds its 10 millionth Model T —a four-seat roadster.

1927 With 15 million cars built, production of the Model T ceases and the all-new Model A goes on sale to replace it.

UNDER THE SKIN

Unbreakable

The running gear is of very simple construction, with a direct gear linkage and a single propshaft to the rear axle. The axles are attached to two subframes, which are bolted to the chassis. The engine is mounted in the middle of the front subframe and sits low in the body, with a side-hinged bonnet for easy access should it need repairs or maintenance. The front bulkhead is fixed in place, meaning that owners had to build the bodywork from the rear in whatever style they chose.

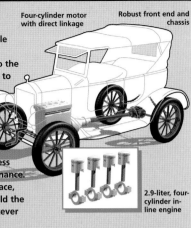

Four-cylinder motor with direct linkage

Robust front end and chassis

2.9-liter, four-cylinder in-line engine

THE POWER PACK

Built for longevity

With 2.9 liters displacement, the Model T's engine is quite big considering it is only a four-cylinder. On paper, the 20bhp sounds like a poor output for such a large capacity unit, but the engine was designed to operate at low speeds and provide effortless torque. Because the unit spins so lazily, it will go on for years without wearing out, but the inbuilt low compression means it can be very difficult to start up.

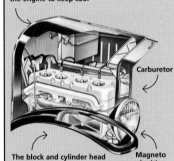

Slats in the bonnet allowed the engine to keep cool

Carburetor

The block and cylinder head were made from cast iron

Magneto ignition

Sporty Speedster

In 1910, a sporty version of the Model T appeared called the Speedster. With stripped-down bodywork and seating for just one occupant, it was designed primarily with racing in mind. it wasn't fast by today's standards, but the lighter weight meant performance, handling and braking were much better than a car with a standard body.

More show than go: The Speedster was an early attempt at a sports car.

Probably the single most important technical advance in motoring history, the Model T brought car ownership to the masses. Henry Ford's vision of an integrated production line is still used in automobile factories today.

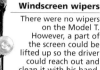

Gearbox

The Model T had two forward gears, which were selected by pulling an outside lever and then pressing a foot pedal, in order to change gear. Reverse gear was selected using the middle pedal.

Hand throttle

The three foot pedals were for changing gear, engaging reverse and braking, with the brake where the gas pedal can be found on a modern car. To accelerate, drivers had to use a lever on the steering wheel to increase the amount of fuel entering the engine.

Windscreen wipers

There were no wipers on the Model T. However, a part of the screen could be lifted up so the driver could reach out and clean it with his hand.

Quarter-elliptical leaf springs

Most contemporary cars came with semi-elliptic leaf springs as standard, but the Model T had smaller quarter-elliptic ones instead. This kept production costs to a minimum, but the trade-off was a harsh and bumpy ride.

Rear brakes

The right-hand foot pedal operated the cable brake, which applied itself to the front wheels only. It slowed the car down, but emergency stops were out of the question as it would heat up and fail completely. The rear brakes were more efficient and were operated with a hand lever.

Starting handle

Until an electric starter was introduced in 1919, Model T owners had to turn the engine by hand in order to get it to fire. The handle slotted in beneath the radiator grille and you had to turn on a tap to get fuel to the engine first.

Mudguards

This model features streamlined rear mudguards as it is a two-seater coupe. Saloon models had the guards integrated into the rear body, while van bodies sat over the axle to create a wheelarch. Basic and racing models had exposed wheels, but these were vulnerable to damage from road debris.

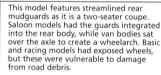

Under the hood

The Model T engine was typical of its time. The 2.9-litre four-cylinder unit ran at low compression and had a relatively small output of just 20bhp, but it had enormous reserves of torque and could pull from very low speeds.

Central fuel

The fuel tank of a Model T is a simple round barrel. It was mounted under the driving seat as it was most protected from damage here, which explains the car's rather high driving position.

Specifications

1908 Ford Model T

ENGINE

Engine: Four cylinder in-line
Construction: Cast iron block and cylinder head
Valve gear: Two valves per cylinder, mounted in block
Bore and stroke: 3.74 in. x 3.97 in.
Capacity: 2,895cc
Compression ratio: 4.5:1
Carburettor: One Holley direct unit
Power: 20bhp @ 1,800rpm
Top speed: 42mph
0–60mph: Not applicable

TRANSMISSION

Two-speed manual

BODY/CHASSIS

Chassis available in two lengths, wide range of bodies on offer.

SPECIAL FEATURES

Totally confusing: The left-hand pedal operates the forward gearbox, the middle pedal is used to select reverse and the right-hand pedal applies the brakes.

The Model T was equipped with quarter-elliptic leaf springs in order to cut production costs.

RUNNING GEAR

Steering: Direct linkage
Front suspension: Subframe, diagonal crosstubes, quarter-elliptic leaf springs
Rear suspension: Subframe, diagonal crosstubes, quarter-elliptic leaf springs
Brakes: Foot pedal operating cable to front, hand-operated cable linkage to rear
Wheels: Wooden, 30-spoke
Tires: 3.5 x 30 solid tyres

DIMENSIONS

Length: 140.0 in. **Width:** 66.0 in.
Height: Dependent on selected bodywork
Wheelbase: 100.5 in.
Track: 57.0 in. (front), 57.5 in. (rear)
Weight: 1475 lb.

Ford MODEL A

After 19 years and more than 15 million sales, the venerable 'Tin Lizzie' gave way to a new Ford, the Model A. It was more complex and boasted twice as much power and proved hugely succcessful with the public.

"...huge improvement from the T."

"Even today, the Model A is recognized as a huge improvement over its predecessor, the Model T; the big L-head four is much more torquey and smooth. Given a good road, it is possible to wind the car all the way up to 65 mph, though it takes time to get there. Greatly improved springing, bigger tires and four-wheel mechanical brakes also make the A feel much more stable and secure than the Tin Lizzie. Moreover, refinement is not far shy of contemporary luxury cars."

The basic interior design of the Model A lasted through the 1930s.

Milestones

1927 After a remarkable 19-year production run, the Ford Model T is phased out. Production stands at 15,007,033, a record which will remain unbroken until after World War II.

The Model A continued the legacy established by the versatile and popular 'Tin Lizzie.'

1927 Ford's Model A is introduced to much fanfare. Powered by a new 201 c.i. L-head four, 10 million people view the car during its first 36 hours on the market.

Replacing the A was the four-cylinder Model B.

1929 The two millionth Model A is built in July.

1931 Competition from Chevrolet and the Depression eat into sales. Production plumets amid rumors of a V8 Ford for 1932.

UNDER THE SKIN

Beam axles front and rear

Four-wheel mechanically operated drum brakes

Ladder-type chassis

Big in-line four

Moving forward

Like the T, the Model A has a ladder-type steel chassis frame on to which the separate body was added. The suspension is heavily based on that of the T, with a beam axle at the front and a live rear axle with longitudinally mounted leaf springs at the rear. A new feature was four-wheel brakes. Major changes occured for 1930, including higher effort steering, and fitting 19-inch wheels in place of 21-inchers.

THE POWER PACK

All-new motor

An all-new car needs an all-new engine and that was exactly what Ford did with the Model A. A new 201-cubic inch four-cylinder L-head design, it had a cast-iron block and cylinder head. With two valves per cylinder and fuel drawn in through a single Holley carburetor, it produced 40 bhp with a 4.22:1 compression ratio—20 more than the previous Model T engine—and was far more torquey, due to a much longer 4.25 inch stroke. It was the first Ford engine to have a battery-fed ignition.

Single Holley carburetor

L-head design

Cast-iron block and cylinder head

Water pump and battery fed ignition

Open-top

During its four-year life, the Model A was an undisputed best seller, so there are still a sizeable number around. Although not the most popular when new, Roadsters and Cabriolets are the most collected of these due to their sportier looks.

Back in 1930, a Cabriolet would set you back the princely sum of $645.

A huge gamble for the company, the Ford Model A nevertheless proved to be a hit, and its basic engineering was so sound that its legacy lived on in Ford cars built through 1948.

Big four-cylinder engine

Big displacement four-cylinder engines were common in the 1920s, offering good low end power. The Model A's 201-cubic inch 40 bhp enabled 0-60 mph times of just over 30 seconds.

Improved interior

1930 brought a number of noticeable changes, both inside and out. Highlighting a roomier interior was an improved dash with centrally placed instruments, including a 'cyclops eye' speedometer.

Four-wheel brakes

More complex than the T, the Model A introduced a few features worthy of merit. One such was four-wheel brakes, still mechanically operated, while 19-inch wheels were used instead of 21-inch wheels from 1930, resulting in greater safety and an improved ride.

Adjustable windshield

Like Roadsters, Phaetons had a windshield that could be lowered by hinging it forward to rest on the hood. This feature lasted until 1937, when fixed pillars were standardized.

Ladder-type frame

In keeping with Henry Ford's ideas of standardization in manufacturing, all Model As rode the same 103.5-inch, fully boxed steel chassis. This also saved production time and enabled competitive pricing in an increasingly crowded automobile market.

Phaeton body

Model As were offered with a variety of different bodies. The cheapest in 1930 was the two-seat roadster priced at $435 and followed by the four-door convertible phaeton at $440. The most popular Model A body style, however, was the Tudor sedan, of which 425,124 were built.

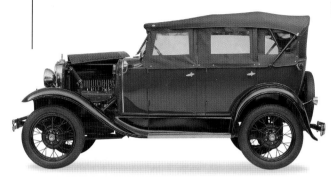

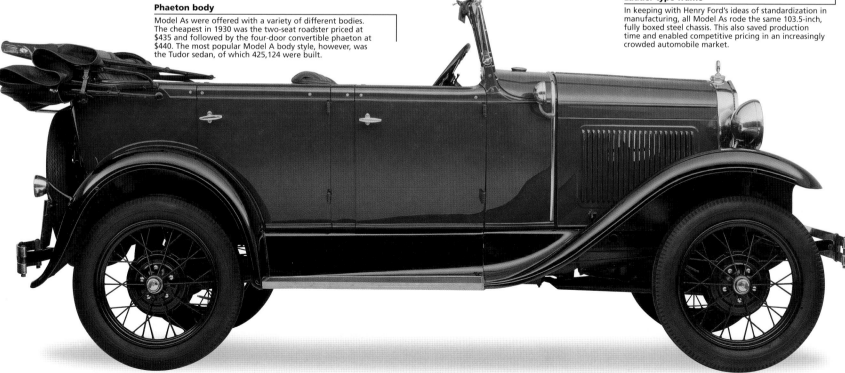

Specifications

1930 Model A Phaeton

ENGINE

Type: In-line four

Construction: Cast-iron block and head

Valve gear: Two valves per cylinder operated by a single camshaft via pushrods

Bore and stroke: 3.88 in. x 4.25 in.

Displacement: 201 c.i.

Compression ratio: 4.22:1

Induction system: Single Holley carburetor

Maximum power: 40 bhp at 2,200 rpm

Maximum torque: 128 lb-ft at 1,000 rpm

Top speed: 65 mph

0-60 mph: 32.0 sec.

TRANSMISSION

Three-speed manual

BODY/CHASSIS

Steel ladder chassis with steel Phaeton body

SPECIAL FEATURES

Turn signals are a later addition to this otherwise stock Phaeton.

The engine could still be started by turning a handle off the crankshaft.

RUNNING GEAR

Steering: Worm-and-roller

Front suspension: Beam axle with transverse leaf spring and lever arm type shock absorbers

Rear suspension: Live axle with longitudinal leaf springs and lever arm-type shock absorbers

Brakes: Drums, front and rear

Wheels: Steel, 19-in. dia.

Tires: 4.5 x 19 in.

DIMENSIONS

Length: 146.8 in. **Width:** 63.5 in.

Height: 71.6 in. **Wheelbase:** 103.5 in.

Track: 56.0 in. (front and rear)

Weight: 2,212 lbs.

Ford HI-BOY ROADSTER

If any car typifies the classic hot rod, it has to be the 1932 Ford Hi-boy Roadster. In the late 1940s and early 1950s, young men back from World War II wanted fast cars for low dollars. Stripping a Ford Roadster down to its bare bones and fitting a hot V8 was one of the most popular methods.

"...a nostalgic road rocket."

"If you're shy, then this car isn't for you. This Hi-boy, nostalgic, road rocket is a style icon today and can't help turning heads. The short stub exhaust pipes don't help either—the loud V8 rumble is deafening at higher engine speeds. It's only when the road clears that you realize that this car goes as as great as it looks. It doesn't weigh much and the engine puts out an unstressed 250 bhp, so acceleration is incredible. It takes a brave man to drive it at over 100 mph, though."

Stewart Warner, white-faced gauges give this hot rod a classic look.

Milestones

1931 With sales dropping due to the Depression, Chevrolet edges ahead of Ford in model-year sales figures.

Replacing the Model A for 1932 was the new four-cylinder Model B and V8 Model 18.

1932 In response, Ford improves its cars. The old, squared-off exposed radiator is replaced by a new smoother radiator cowl. This year also sees the launch of the famous Flathead V8. The four-cylinder Model B range is sold alongside the V8 Model 18s.

1932 Fords are still popular today, but fashions have indeed changed.

1933 The Ford lineup gets new graceful, low-slung styling.

UNDER THE SKIN

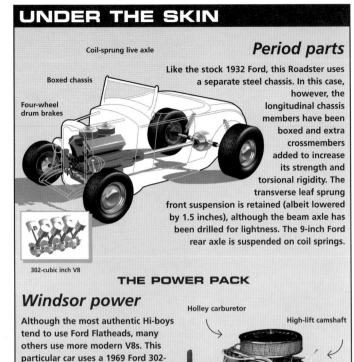

Period parts

Coil-sprung live axle

Boxed chassis

Four-wheel drum brakes

302-cubic inch V8

Like the stock 1932 Ford, this Roadster uses a separate steel chassis. In this case, however, the longitudinal chassis members have been boxed and extra crossmembers added to increase its strength and torsional rigidity. The transverse leaf sprung front suspension is retained (albeit lowered by 1.5 inches), although the beam axle has been drilled for lightness. The 9-inch Ford rear axle is suspended on coil springs.

THE POWER PACK

Windsor power

Although the most authentic Hi-boys tend to use Ford Flatheads, many others use more modern V8s. This particular car uses a 1969 Ford 302-cubic inch Windsor V8. It has been mildly tuned with a high-lift Crower camshaft, free-flowing tubular-steel headers, a high-rise Offenhauser intake manifold and a 600-cfm Holley four-barrel carburetor. All this takes the maximum power to a reliable 250 bhp at 4,500 rpm and 275 lb-ft of torque at 3,000 rpm.

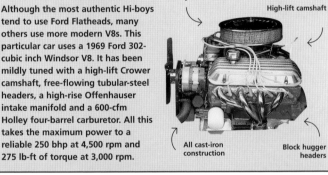

Holley carburetor

High-lift camshaft

All cast-iron construction

Block hugger headers

Top rods

Although there are many different styles of hot rod based on the 1932 Ford, these original-style Hi-boys are real classicsand even considered so by many enthusiasts of stock classic and vintage cars. They are part of America's post-war heritage, along with drive-in movies and rock and roll music.

Black paint and red steel wheels are classic 1950s hot rod touches.

To many, the first image that comes to mind when you say 'hot rod' would probably be something like this classic 1950s-style Hi-boy based on a 1932 Ford Roadster. Its simplicity of concept—less weight, more power—makes it a great and stylish custom.

Ford V8
The 1932 Ford Model 18 came with the then-new Flathead V8 engine. This car has a Ford 302-cubic inch Windsor V8. Mild tuning ensures reliability while still producing 250 bhp.

Fenderless styling
The first thing an early hot-rodder would do with his Ford would be to remove the floor boards and fenders. This cut weight and gave easier access to the mechanicals. The lack of fenders is the most important part of the classic Hi-boy look but can cause problems on wet roads—not only do you get wet with the spray from the front tires, but any cars following behind will be blinded by the huge fountains of spray from the massive rear tires.

Beam axle
The 1932 Ford used a beam axle and transverse leaf spring for the front suspension. This car has had the front end lowered by 1.5 inches for the classic nose-down stance and the axle has been drilled to reduce weight.

Drum brakes
Like the original car, this Hi-boy has four-wheel drum brakes. The front drums have been taken from a 1949 Buick and are finned to improve cooling and reduce brake fade.

Rumble seat
There were two styles of the 1932 Roadster. Externally they looked identical, but one version, such as this model, had a rumble seat in the trunk to carry extra passengers.

Steel wheels
With alloy wheels not yet available, the only options were pressed-steel or wire-spoked wheels. These were often painted in bright contrasting colors to liven them up.

Specifications

1932 Ford Hi-Boy Roadster

ENGINE
Type: V8

Construction: Cast-iron block and heads

Valve gear: Two valves per cylinder operated by a single camshaft with pushrods and rockers

Bore and stroke: 4.00 in. x 3.00 in.

Displacement: 302 c.i.

Compression ratio: 9.0:1

Induction system: Holley 600-cfm four-barrel carburetor

Maximum power: 250 bhp at 4,500 rpm

Maximum torque: 275 lb-ft at 3,000 rpm

Top speed: 120 mph

0-60 mph: 6.0 sec.

TRANSMISSION
Three-speed manual

BODY/CHASSIS
Steel chassis and steel and fiberglass body

SPECIAL FEATURES

The Roadster body style comes complete with a folding windshield.

Big-finned 1949 Buick front drums gives much improved braking.

RUNNING GEAR
Steering: Recirculating ball

Front suspension: Beam axle with transverse leaf springs, parallel control arms and telescopic shock absorbers

Rear suspension: Live axle with coil springs and telescopic shock absorbers

Brakes: Drums (front and rear)

Wheels: Steel, 15-in. dia. (front and rear)

Tires: 145 SR15 (front), 33 x 12.50 R15 (rear)

DIMENSIONS
Length: 132.5 in. **Width:** 63.9 in.

Height: 52.0 in. **Wheelbase:** 106.5 in.

Track: 56.2 in. (front), 56.2 in. (rear)

Weight: 2,250 lbs.

Ford COUPE

When Henry Ford launched America's first affordable V8 car, he could never have imagined that thousands of hot rodders would later choose it to modify into their dream machines.

"...it really takes off."

"This car's performance shouldn't be judged by its ancient appearance. Under the classic 1930s American coupe body, there is a 330-bhp small-block Chevy V8. It's not too highly stressed and idles quietly. With lots of low-down power, it can easily cope with modern traffic. If the road clears, though, and you floor the throttle, it really takes off. Its handling is is a little antiquated, but this car's Corvette rear end helps to keep things in line."

The tiny cockpit retains its 1930s look but has an extra touch of luxury.

Milestones

1932 Ford introduces America's first low-priced V8-engined car, ahead of arch-rival Chevrolet. Unfortunately, it is something of a rush job and early engine problems let Chevrolet take the production lead in1933.

Henry Ford's "any color as long as it's black" quote doesn't apply to this Ford hot rod.

1934 The Ford range becomes totally V8-powered after all the four-cylinder models were dropped. They are speedy, simple and affordable cars, offered with a wide range of body styles.

The first V8 Ford hot rods were stripped down and mildly tuned.

1940s and 1950s As a cheap way of getting a performance car, young men start to modify 1930s V8 Fords starting the hot-rodding craze.

UNDER THE SKIN

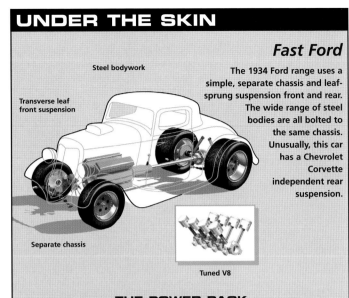

Fast Ford

The 1934 Ford range uses a simple, separate chassis and leaf-sprung suspension front and rear. The wide range of steel bodies are all bolted to the same chassis. Unusually, this car has a Chevrolet Corvette independent rear suspension.

Steel bodywork

Transverse leaf front suspension

Separate chassis

Tuned V8

THE POWER PACK

Flathead fun

The 1934, Ford was often chosen by hot rodders because it came with a highly-tunable flathead V8 (shown) as standard. In stock form, the 221-cubic inch V8 produced about 90 bhp, but tuners could get a whole lot more from it. Today, sources of original engines are drying up, so many hot rodders have turned to the immortal Chevrolet small block. It is a common engine and there is a wealth of tuning parts available from specialist suppliers. This car has a 350-cubic inch Chevy motor that has been overbored.

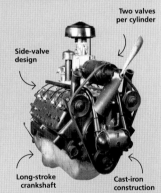

Two valves per cylinder

Side-valve design

Long-stroke crankshaft

Cast-iron construction

Classic custom

The 1934 Ford has always been a popular choice with hot rodders. At the start, it was just a case of stripping off all unnecessary components to reduce the weight and tuning up the flat-head V8. Nowadays, rodders are a little more sophisticated.

This customized full-fendered 1934 Ford retains its factory body panels.

Most stylish of the 1934 Ford model range, the V8 three-window Coupe turns even more heads today, especially when it looks as good as this hot rod.

Widened rear fenders
In order to cover the wider-than-stock rear tires, the fenders have been made larger by welding in a strip of steel.

Standard roof line
Many hot-rod Ford Coupes have a roof chop, in which the car's windshield pillars have been cut down by several inches to give the car a lower stance. This car has a standard roof line for a more classic look.

Filled roof
The original 1934 Fords had a fabric center roof section. This car has been modified with a custom welded sheet metal roof.

Nose-down, tail-up stance
The nose-down, tail-up stance clearly shows the Corvette-sourced rear suspension. It has been completely chromed to really show it off.

Simple front suspension
Like the Model T Ford, the 1934 car uses a transverse leaf-sprung solid front axle. Modern telescopic shocks help to keep it under control.

Corvette rear end
The original and simple leaf-sprung live rear axle has been replaced by a Corvette independent rear suspension with a single transverse leaf spring.

Chrome luggage rack
The chromed luggage rack is for show and is extremely unlikely to be used to carry any extra luggage.

Skinny front tires
In traditional hot-rod style, the front tires are a lot narrower (6.5 inches) than those at the rear (8 inches).

Sprung bumpers
The 1930s equivalent of modern impact-absorbing bumpers are these stylish sprung-steel ones.

Specifications
1934 Ford Coupe

ENGINE
Type: Chevrolet V8
Construction: Cast-iron block and heads
Valve gear: Two valves per cylinder operated by a single camshaft via pushrods and rockers
Bore and stroke: 4.06 in. x 3.48 in.
Displacement: 358 c.i.
Compression ratio: 9.5:1
Induction system: Single four-barrel carburetor
Maximum power: 330 bhp at 5,500 rpm
Maximum torque: 339 lb-ft at 3,400 rpm
Top speed: 127 mph
0-60 mph: 8.7 sec.

TRANSMISSION
Four-speed manual

BODY/CHASSIS
Two-door coupe body on a separate steel chassis

SPECIAL FEATURES

To retain the classic hot-rod look, this car has standard-looking steel wheels rather than modern alloys.

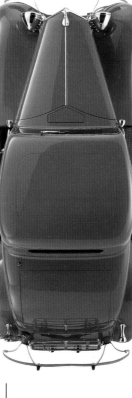

The Chevrolet small-block V8 engine gives great performance. It has been overbored from 350 to 358 cubic inches.

RUNNING GEAR
Steering: Chevrolet Vega recirculating ball
Front suspension: Transverse leaf spring with telescopic shocks
Rear suspension: Corvette-sourced independent suspension with transverse leaf spring and telescopic shocks
Brakes: Discs (front), drums (rear)
Wheels: Pressed steel, 6.5 in. x 15 in. (front), 8 in. x 15 in. (rear)
Tires: 165/70 R15 (front), 205/60 R15 (rear)

DIMENSIONS
Length: 153 in.   **Width:** 65.9 in.
Height: 55.5 in.   **Wheelbase:** 102.5 in.
Track: 58.7 in. (front), 59.1 in. (rear)
Weight: 2,403 lbs.

Ford DELUXE V8

The 1939-1940 Ford V8 is regarded by many collectors as the best of the famous pre-war V8 Ford line. With up-to-the-minute styling and plenty of power, it was immensely popular with buyers, too.

"...ride in total comfort."

"Open up the door and climb in. After you take your position behind the Deluxe's wide steering wheel and start up its flat-head V8, some of the embellishments that make this a Deluxe model become evident—namely the wood-grain dash and large-faced clock. Like all upgraded models, this Deluxe has the optional 85 bhp engine. Its firm body construction and advanced (for its time) suspension give a better than average ride in total comfort."

The stylish sprung steering wheel and beautiful dash make for a classic interior.

Milestones

1932 America's first bargain-priced V8 appears as Henry Ford boldly launches a range of eight-cylinder cars.

Fords gained fender-mounted headlights for 1938.

1933 New and widely admired airflow designs are now on a longer 112-inch wheelbase.

1935 More engine changes and a fuller body style enhance the V8's attractiveness.

A new grill and minor refinements distinguish the 1939 from the 1940 model.

1939 Distinctive styling changes are made, notably to the front grill.

1942 As Ford turns over its factories exclusively to war-time production, the V8 line is shut down.

UNDER THE SKIN

Stretched frame

Solid axles front and rear

Hydraulic drum brakes

Separate chassis frame

In 1933, the frame of the V8 was completely redesigned with a double drop and cross bracing, gaining an extra six inches in the wheelbase at the same time. As for the rest of the specification, that looks back to Model T days, with solid axles on transverse leaf springs front and rear. New for the 1939 cars were four-wheel hydraulic drum brakes. Henry Ford always believed that simpler is better.

Flathead V8

THE POWER PACK

Ford's first V8

Henry Ford had originally considered building a radical 'X8' engine but settled on a more conventional V8 for production. This was a classic piece of engineering, a simple yet effective flat-head cast-iron unit. In its original 221-cubic inch guise, it put out 65 bhp, rising to 85 bhp in 1934 thanks to a new carburetor and intake manifold. Initial reliability problems were soon cured, and the V8 gained a reputation as one of the most durable engines around, particularly with hot rodders. After the war, the V8 would return with a larger 239-cubic inch displacement.

V8 Deluxe

The V8 has a strong and enduring reputation and will always be regarded as one of the all-time greats. The 1940 Deluxes are among the most coveted pre-war Fords, due in part to their neat Bob Gregorie styling, rugged engineering and unabashed charm. Hydraulic brakes make stopping easier, too.

1940 Deluxes have long been collectors' favorites.

Durability and affordability were the hallmarks that established Ford, and though the V-8 boasted both of those qualities, its performance was the most impressive feature.

V8 engine

Crucial to Ford's success in the 1930s was its V8 powerplant. When other car makers had only fours and sixes, Ford could justly claim superiority with not one but two different V8 engines.

Deluxe interiors

All Deluxe models came with a woodgrain dashboard and a centrally mounted clock.

Faired-in headlights

The popular airflow look arrived for the Ford range in 1937. Apart from the chiseled front end styling, this took the form of fully faired-in, ellipsoid headlights.

V-grill

The distinctive V-shaped grill arrived in 1935 and developed into the streamlined profile seen on this 1939 Deluxe four-door sedan. The 1939 has vertical grill bars in place of the horizontal bars of the 1940 Deluxe.

Steel roof

Early V8 models had a fabric roof insert, but in 1937 Ford began using a full steel roof panel.

Optional taillight

Only the Deluxe models came with two taillights as standard. The base models only came with one taillight. However, certain states at this time required cars to have two taillights. So some standard models had the extra taillight installed at the dealership.

Specifications

1939 Ford Deluxe V8

ENGINE

Type: V8

Construction: Cast-iron cylinder block and heads

Valve gear: Two side-mounted valves per cylinder operated by a single camshaft

Bore and stroke: 3.06 in. x 3.75 in.

Displacement: 221 c.i.

Compression ratio: 6.2:1

Induction system: Single carburetor

Maximum power: 85 bhp at 3,800 rpm

Maximum torque: 155 lb-ft at 2,200 rpm

Top speed: 87 mph

0-60 mph: 17.4 sec

TRANSMISSION

Three-speed manual

BODY/CHASSIS

Separate chassis with steel two-door or four-door sedan, coupe or convertible body

SPECIAL FEATURES

Suicide-type rear doors were offered on four-door sedans in 1939.

Ellipsoid headlights were faired into the front fenders.

RUNNING GEAR

Steering: Worm-and-roller

Front suspension: Beam axle with transverse leaf spring and shocks

Rear suspension: Live axle with transverse leaf spring and shocks

Brakes: Drums (front and rear)

Wheels: Steel, 17-in dia.

Tires: 6 x 16 in.

DIMENSIONS

Length: 179.5 in. **Width:** 67.0 in.

Height: 68.6 in. **Wheelbase:** 112.0 in.

Track: 55.5 in. (front), 58.3 in. (rear)

Weight: 2,898 lbs.

Ford **CUSTOM TUDOR**

Long known as one of the toughest motorsport events, the Carrera Panamericana (Mexican Road Race) was the focal point for Ford competition in the early 1950s. Tough, simple cars like this Ford Custom did surprisingly well against faster and more exotic machinery.

"...true vintage performance."

"Fifty years of progress give this Ford the performance that 1950s Panamericana drivers could only have dreamed of. Despite the aftermarket gauges and six-point roll cage, the venerable flathead V8, which is quite content to push the car to 80 mph, remains under the hood. It is the suspension and brakes, though, which really set this car apart. The Custom Tudor grips like a sports car and goes where you want it to, and offers true vintage performance."

The interior is dominated by the aftermarket gauges, harness and roll cage.

Milestones

1948 An all-new car is required to save Ford from financial ruin, and it duly arrives for 1949. It has an improved suspension and a new chassis and styling. The model is an outstanding success, with Ford building 1,118,759.

The top model in the 1949 range was the Country Squire wagon.

1950 With such a winning formula, few changes are made this year. A new limited edition two-door sedan, the Crestliner, is launched in response to GM hardtops. Competition is tough and Ford falls behind its arch-rival Chevrolet in terms of sales.

The 1952-1954 Lincolns were also competitive in the Carrera.

1951 Ford finally produces a hardtop in the shape of the Victoria. This is also the last year for the true 'Woody' wagon and the 1949 vintage design. Sales are affected by government production quotas due to the Korean War.

UNDER THE SKIN

All-new Ford

The 1949 Ford was all-new, with a separate chassis, steel body and fully-independent coil-sprung front suspension. Cars built to compete in the Carrera Panamericana have uprated springs and thicker anti-roll bars. This replica also has a rear anti-roll bar and Watt linkage for better location, plus a rollcage for added safety.

Live axle with Watt linkage

Ladder-type chassis

Front disc brakes

Original V8

THE POWER PACK

Old faithful

By 1950, the venerable flathead V8 was putting out 100 bhp, and it also gained a number of improvements this year, including revised pistons which reduced the tendency to 'slap' when the motor was cold, plus a new camshaft with revised lobes to reduce lifter noise (a characteristic of the flathead). On this Carrera-prepared car, the engine has been reworked even further, with a longer stroke and twin electric fuel pumps, plus heavy-duty hoses and two extra radiators.

Single two barrel carburetor

Two valves per cylinder

Longer stroke crankshaft

Cast-iron block and cylinder heads

Ultra-tough

1949-1951 Fords are very rugged machines and easy to modify, making them ideal for competition use. The best model to go for is the no-frills Tudor sedan—it is the lightest and there are plenty available. These cars are still run in the gruelling Panamericana.

Tough, simple and plentiful, these Fords are ideal for historic road racing.

Today, nostalgic automobiles are popular and still run in the Carrera Panamericana. This Custom Tudor, which competed in the historic event in 1995, went on to achieve a class win and is a replica of a car which actually won the Sedan class in the 1950 race.

Flathead engine
Ford's venerable flathead V8 remained in production for 20 years and powered millions of Fords. Virtually unbreakable, it pushed out 100 bhp. Although it appears stock, this engine has been stroked from 239 to 290 cubic inches and tuned to produced a respectable 226 bhp.

Four-speed transmission
Automatics have been used on some Panamericana-prepared cars, although this Ford has a four-speed Borg-Warner T-10 transmission. It is a strong, durable unit and, due to its simplicity, repairs can be conducted at the side of the road.

Heavy-duty cooling system
Due to the extreme temperatures and steep elevations encountered during the event, engine reliability is a top priority. The cooling system has heavy-duty hoses and twin auxiliary radiators mounted under the rear floor. An external oil slave pump feeds the separate oil cooler and filter.

Roll-cage
Many hazards are encountered during the Carrera and some cars do get rolled. As a precaution, this Ford has a full six-point roll cage to protect the driver in the event of an accident. It also adds torsional stiffness to the body and chassis.

Sun visor
To reduce glare from sunlight, many cars of the late 1940s and early 1950s were fitted with large sun visors attached to the upper A-pillars.

Specifications

1950 Ford Custom Tudor

ENGINE
Type: V8

Construction: Cast-iron block and heads

Valve gear: Two valves per cylinder operated by pushrods and rockers

Bore and stroke: 3.30 in. x 4.40 in.

Displacement: 290 c.i.

Compression ratio: 7.5:1

Induction system: Single two-barrel carburetor

Maximum power: 226 bhp at 4,000 rpm

Maximum torque: 240 lb-ft at 2,600 rpm

Top speed: 110 mph

0-60 mph: 13.1 sec.

TRANSMISSION
Borg-Warner T-10 four-speed manual

BODY/CHASSIS
Steel ladder-type frame with two-door sedan body

SPECIAL FEATURES

A 22-gallon fuel cell with an isolated battery box is mounted in the trunk.

Leather straps are used to keep the hood closed at speed.

RUNNING GEAR
Steering: Recirculating ball

Front suspension: Double wishbones with coil springs, telescopic shock absorbers and anti-roll bar

Rear suspension: Live 9-in. axle with leaf springs, Watt linkage, telescopic shock absorbers and anti-roll bar

Brakes: Discs, 10-in. dia. (front), drums, 9.5-in. dia. (rear)

Wheels: Steel, 15-in. dia.

Tires: BF Goodrich Comp T/A 175/50 R15

DIMENSIONS
Length: 189.0 in.   **Width:** 71.8 in.

Height: 63.8 in.   **Wheelbase:** 114.0 in.

Track: 60.8 in. (front and rear)

Weight: 3,112 lbs.

Ford WOODY

A custom station wagon with real wood paneling was part of Ford's 1950 model line. Today these wagons, often called Woodies, are a favorite with car customizers young and old.

"...Built for straight-line speed."

"Equipped with a supercharged small-block Chevy V8, this Woody is quick off the line and hauls itself up to 60 mph in less than six seconds. Big rear tires provide excellent grip and enable rapid dragster-style launches from the lights. Although built for straight-line speed, the car retains relatively large front tires to provide some concession toward cornering grip and large disc brakes to make deceleration safer and quicker than the original drums."

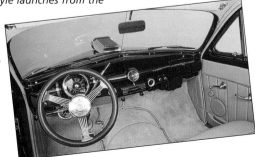

This pro-street car has a custom interior with an electrically-adjustable front bench seat.

Milestones

1949 An all new
Ford with independent front suspension makes its debut. Topping the line is the $2,000 Custom Wagon with real wood inserts. Two engines are available, a straight-six and the venerable 'Flathead V8.'

The 1950 Mercury was similar to the Ford, but more luxurious.

1950 The Custom
wagon is renamed Country Squire and all models receive a mild facelift with a revised grill. Handling and build quality are vastly improved over the 1949 car.

Henry Ford's original V8 engine was still powering Fords in 1950.

1951 Returning for
its final season, the wood-framed station wagon is now available with a three-speed Ford-O-Matic transmission. Ford debuts its all steel bodied station wagons for 1952.

UNDER THE SKIN

Exclusively Ford

The original Ford chassis has been retained, but modified with a Mustang front suspension consisting of unequal length wishbones, coil springs and telescopic shocks. At the rear is a narrowed Ford rear axle with 4.11 gears. Ladder bars prevent wheel hop under hard acceleration and four-wheel disc brakes taken from a Lincoln enable safe stopping.

Four-wheel disc brakes

Independent front suspension

Narrowed rear axle

Supercharged V8

THE POWER PACK

Racing camshaft

Stainless steel valves

Better durability

Originally powered by the venerable Flathead, this Woody now sports a 1974 Chevrolet 400-cubic inch V8 (similar in design to the engine shown here). It has been bored and benefits from forged steel connecting rods and crankshaft. Air is forced into the engine with a B&M supercharger. These modifications raise power output to an impressive 410 bhp, making this Woody a serious threat on the street.

Forged steel crankshaft

Forged steel connecting rods

1950 Woody

A Country Squire wagon was the most expensive Ford you could buy in 1950 and was only available in two-door form. Today, along with the Chevrolet Nomad, they rank as one of the most popular American station wagons of all time.

Even today the 1950 Woodys have popular, yet unusual, appeal.

The 1950s Fords were very popular custom cars in the 1960s. This 1950 Woody has been updated with modern running gear while retaining a classic yet custom look.

Chevrolet V8 engine
In its day, the Ford Flathead V8 was the powerplant of choice for hot rodding. Today its place has been taken by the ubiquitous small-block Chevy V8. This one features dual four-barrel carburetors and a supercharger to help it achieve its 410 bhp at 5,100 rpm.

Modified hood
In order to accommodate the large supercharger mounted on top of the engine the hood has been modified so the enormous air scoop can protrude through it.

Air conditioning
Although the back seat has been removed, the owner still wants some comfort, so a custom air conditioning system is fitted.

Predominantly steel
Most of the body is built from steel, only the doors, tailgate and quarter panels are fabricated from real wood.

Tinted windows
Woodys are a fashion statement in California and this one has tinted windows to enhance its street credibility.

Subtle modification
Although the body remains fairly standard, the tailgate features taillights taken from a 1946 Ford.

Specifications
1950 Ford Woody

ENGINE
Type: V8

Construction: Cast-iron block and heads

Valve gear: Two valves per cylinder operated by pushrods and rockers

Bore/stroke: 4.18 in. x 3.75 in.

Displacement: 406 c.i.

Compression ratio: 8.0:1

Induction system: Two four-barrel Holley 600 cfm carburetors

Maximum power: 410 bhp at 5,100 rpm

Maximum torque: 450 lb-ft at 3,100 rpm

Top speed: 147 mph

0-60 mph: 4.7 sec.

TRANSMISSION
GM 700R4 four-speed automatic with 2,500 stall torque converter and overdrive lockout

BODY/CHASSIS
Separate chassis with steel and wood two-door body

SPECIAL FEATURES

Supercharger assembly requires a cutout in the hood for clearance and for feeding air to the Chevy V8.

The center grill spinner bears an uncanny resemblance to that used on the contemporary Studebaker Champion.

RUNNING GEAR
Steering: Recirculating ball

Front suspension: Unequal length wishbones, coil springs and telescopic shocks

Rear suspension: Narrowed live axle with ladder bars and coil springs and telescopic shocks

Brakes: Four-wheel discs

Wheels: American Racing Torque Thrust D 7 x 15 (front) 10 x 15 (rear)

Tires: BF Goodrich radials (front) Mickey Thompson Prostreets (rear)

DIMENSIONS
Length: 174 in. **Width:** 73.3 in.

Height: 56.7 in. **Wheelbase:** 114 in.

Track: 56.5 in. (front) 50.2 in. (rear)

Weight: 3,402 lbs.

FORD CRESTLINE SUNLINER

Although 1949-1951 Fords are often considered the classic post-war street machine, the later, more refined 1952-1954 Fords are also great for customizing. This period-looking 1952 Sunliner convertible complete with flames and a roof chop is a fine example.

"...glide by in style."

"Fuzzy dice and tuck 'n' roll upholstery were almost essential for a cruisin' custom back in the late 1950s. With a carbureted 302 small-block under the flamed hood, this classy custom can drive happily in modern traffic yet still offers plenty of old-fashioned torque. Power steering and brakes and a column-shifted automatic transmission make this Sunliner really easy to drive, giving you time to take in the stares of others as you glide by them in style."

Functional as well as tasteful, the white and black interior is almost timeless.

Milestones

1952 Squared-up styling and a longer 115-inch wheelbase marks the new Ford line. Offered in Mainline, Customline and Crestline series, the latter includes a Sunliner convertible, Victoria hardtop and Country Squire wagon. The new cars prove to be a hit despite the ongoing Korean War; 671,733 Fords are built.

The basic design lasted through 1956—here is a Victoria glasstop.

1953 Ford celebrates its golden anniversary and all models get special steering wheel medallions. A special 'Production Blitz' is intended to help steal sales from rival Chevrolet.

Fords were all-new in 1957 and were fitted with engines up to 312-cubic inches.

1954 A new Y-block, overhead-valve V8 replaces the venerable flathead. A new ball-joint front suspension also arrives.

UNDER THE SKIN

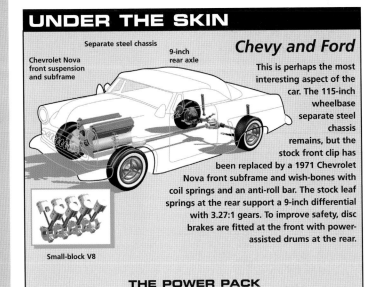

Separate steel chassis
Chevrolet Nova front suspension and subframe
9-inch rear axle

Chevy and Ford

This is perhaps the most interesting aspect of the car. The 115-inch wheelbase separate steel chassis remains, but the stock front clip has been replaced by a 1971 Chevrolet Nova front subframe and wish-bones with coil springs and an anti-roll bar. The stock leaf springs at the rear support a 9-inch differential with 3.27:1 gears. To improve safety, disc brakes are fitted at the front with power-assisted drums at the rear.

Small-block V8

THE POWER PACK

The mighty 302

Originally, this Sunliner had a Y-block 239 V8 under the hood packing 110 bhp. In the interest of better reliability, it has been replaced by a 302-cubic inch engine sourced from a 1972 Ford F-100 pickup. Introduced in 1968, the 302 is one of the most versatile Ford V8s. It has a reputation for being a torquey, tractable engine that easily responds to simple modifications. Retaining the stock, cast-iron intake and two-barrel Autolite carburetor, this engine puts out 150 bhp and 240 lb-ft of torque. This may not seem much on paper, but it is more than enough to make this custom a real mover.

Still cool

It may be the earlier post-war Fords that are raved about by customizers, but the 1952-1954 models can be converted into rides that are just as cool. Some of the modifications on this car include a chopped carson top, flames and removed door handles.

Clever touches make this Sunliner really stand out.

Flamed paint jobs are often depicted in contrasting hot/cold colors, but this Ford is ice-cool to the core, both inside and out. It puts a new face on the typical 1950s-style custom car.

Chopped windshield

The windshield has been dropped by three inches. The top is actually a Carson removable type rather than the normal folding power item.

Toothy grill

One car that is notorious for its chromed tooth grill is the 1955 DeSoto. In keeping with its 1950s custom style, this Sunliner has a DeSoto grill mounted in place of the stock item.

Small-block V8

Replacing the less-than-satisfactory Y-block is a 1972 302-cubic inch V8. The small-block Windsor is often considered a latter-day flathead and a tuner's friend. In this application, it produces 150 bhp and 240 lb-ft of torque.

C4 transmission

As it was conceived for cruising rather than all-out performance, this ride has a C4 three-speed automatic behind the engine. Despite its age, this unit boasts smoothness that some modern transmissions are hard pressed to match.

Radial tires

The tires on this car combine the safety of modern radials with the appearance of classic, wide, white bias-plys.

Handmade taillights

The 1952 Fords marked the beginning of trademark circular taillights, but this one has custom, handformed lights.

Tuck 'n' roll interior

Most customized cars of the late 1950s had tuck 'n' roll upholstery. Both the front and rear seats of this Sunliner are upholstered in this way, and the addition of fuzzy dice completes the period picture. An A/C system adds a touch of comfort for those hot summer nights.

Cool flames

The use of radiant 1990s colors like Jewel Green and black painted in the traditional 1950s-style flame pattern gives this Ford a classic, yet contemporary appearance.

Specifications

1952 Ford Crestline Sunliner

ENGINE

Type: V8

Construction: Cast-iron block and heads

Valve gear: Two valves per cylinder operated by a single camshaft with pushrods and rockers

Bore and stroke: 4.0 in. x 3.0 in.

Displacement: 302 c.i.

Compression ratio: 8.5:1

Induction system: Autolite two-barrel carburetor

Maximum power: 150 bhp at 4,200 rpm

Maximum torque: 240 lb-ft at 3,100 rpm

Top speed: 112 mph

0-60 mph: 10.5 sec.

TRANSMISSION

C4 three-speed automatic

BODY/CHASSIS

Separate steel chassis with two-door convertible body

SPECIAL FEATURES

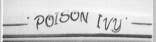

With its sharp green and black paint job, 'Poison Ivy' is an appropriate name.

Twin chrome spotlights were popular stock and custom accessories in the 1950s.

RUNNING GEAR

Steering: Recirculating ball

Front suspension: Unequal-length wishbones with coil springs, telescopic shock absorbers and anti-roll bar

Rear suspension: Live axle with leaf springs and telescopic shock absorbers

Brakes: Discs (front), drums (rear)

Wheels: Pressed steel, 14-in. dia.

Tires: Radial, 205/70 R14

DIMENSIONS

Length: 197.8 in. **Width:** 73.2 in.

Height: 56.8 in. **Wheelbase:** 115.0 in.

Track: 61.3 in. (front), 59.5 in. (rear)

Weight: 3,415 lbs.

Ford **THUNDERBIRD**

The 1955 Thunderbird was the first of a legendary line of Fords and was designed to compete with Chevrolet's Corvette. The Thunderbird was always more of a 'personal' car than an outright sports car. This example has been personalized much further with a 630-bhp supercharged V8.

"...seamless wall of torque."

"It's easy to feel at home once you are settled behind the wheel of this Thunderbird. The interior is a fantastic mix of classic 1950s feel with a slight techno edge. The monster V8 gives effortless performance, while the supercharger lends the engine a seamless wall of torque. The computer-designed suspension gives the T-bird handling that the original could never have dreamed of, and the four-wheel disc brake system stops the car with ease."

This Thunderbird has a subtle modern edge to its classic 1950s interior.

Milestones

1955 Two years after Chevrolet

launched the Corvette, Ford releases the V8-engined Thunderbird to rival it. More than 16,000 are sold in its first year, massively outselling the Corvette.

A 1971 Boss 351 Mustang gave up its Cleveland V8 for this modified 1955 T-bird.

1956 The T-bird gets an optional 312-

cubic inch engine, an exterior-mount spare, softer suspension and an optional 'Porthole' hardtop.

The T-bird debuted as a 1955 model with an optional 292-cubic inch V8.

1957 Ford launches the last two-seater T-bird.

A facelift added a more prominent grill and a longer deck. There is also more power and even a limited run of supercharged cars. The T-bird becomes a less sporty four-seater the following year.

UNDER THE SKIN

Computer designed

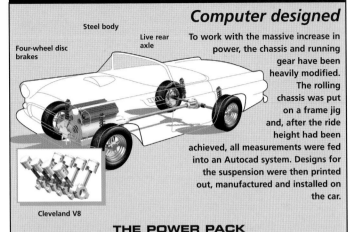

Steel body

Live rear axle

Four-wheel disc brakes

Cleveland V8

To work with the massive increase in power, the chassis and running gear have been heavily modified. The rolling chassis was put on a frame jig and, after the ride height had been achieved, all measurements were fed into an Autocad system. Designs for the suspension were then printed out, manufactured and installed on the car.

THE POWER PACK

Blown Boss

Gone is the original 292-cubic inch Mercury V8, replaced by a seriously-modified 351 Cleveland V8. It has been overbored to give a new displacement of 361 cubic inches and has a billet crankshaft and connecting rods. Forged pistons and early-style Yates NASCAR aluminum heads give an 8.2:1 compression ratio. There is also a NASCAR aluminum radiator to keep the engine operating at a reasonable temperature. The Custom-designed fuel injection system and Vortech supercharger, running 6 lbs. of boost, help this radical motor to pump out 630 bhp at 6,800 rpm and 550 lb-ft of torque at 4,900 rpm.

Blown 'Bird

Ford designers got the shape of the original Thunderbird just right, so there was no need to change it. This car retains its original styling but has the added bonus of earth-shattering performance and modern standards of handling and braking.

The owner of this model has left the bodywork largely untouched.

Two of Ford's most legendary cars of all time are the Mustang and the Thunderbird. This may be a 1955 two-seat T-bird, but under the hood beats the heart of a Mustang, in this case a blown Boss 351 Cleveland.

Custom interior
The interior retains the factory styling but is brought up to date with digital instruments. The front seat has been specially fitted for the driver to give a perfect and comfortable driving position.

Supercharged V8
Under the hood, there is a 351 Cleveland unit instead of the original 292-cubic inch mill. A Vortech supercharger, aluminum NASCAR heads and a custom fuel injection system help take the power output to a heady 630 bhp.

Bulletproof rear end
The ubiquitous 9-inch Ford rear axle sits under this car, with 4.56:1 gears and a limited-slip differ-ential for maximum traction off the line.

Powerful brakes
The Thunderbird's original drum brake setup would be nearly useless on this road rocket. This car is fitted with a twin master cylinder brake system with 11-inch Camaro front discs and Lincoln rear discs.

Rack-and-pinion steering
The old recirculating ball steering has been replaced with Mustang II spindles and a power-assisted rack-and-pinion steering system.

Near-stock body
This car retains its original steel body. The only modifications are the shaved trunk and doors. It is finished in striking Black Plum paint.

Specifications

1955 Ford Thunderbird

ENGINE
Type: V8

Construction: Cast-iron block and aluminum heads

Valve gear: Two valves per cylinder operated by a single camshaft with pushrods and hydraulic lifters

Bore and stroke: 4.06 in. x 3.50 in.

Displacement: 361 c.i.

Compression ratio: 8.2:1

Induction system: Custom fuel injection and Vortech supercharger

Maximum power: 630 bhp at 6,800 rpm

Maximum torque: 550 lb-ft at 4,900 rpm

Top Speed: 165 mph

0-60 mph: 3.6 sec

TRANSMISSION
Ford A40D automatic transmission

BODY/CHASSIS
Steel chassis and steel two-seater body

SPECIAL FEATURES

Digital gauges in the original housings are a neat touch.

A custom-built fuel injection system helps to produce 630 bhp.

RUNNING GEAR
Steering: Rack-and-pinion

Front suspension: Tubular A-arms with coil springs and telescopic shock absorbers

Rear suspension: Tubular A-arms with coil springs and telescopic shock absorbers

Brakes: Discs (front and rear)

Wheels: Weld Racing alloy, 15-in. dia.

Tires: Winston Radials

DIMENSIONS
Length: 175.3 in. **Width:** 70.3 in.

Height: 49.2 in. **Wheelbase:** 102.0 in.

Track: 57.8 in. (front), 55.86 in. (rear)

Weight: 2,980 lbs.

Ford THUNDERBIRD

Although there's been a Thunderbird in the Ford lineup since 1955, the sporty two-seater convertible version only lasted until 1957. In those first three years, it had all the style—and almost the performance—to match the Chevrolet Corvette.

"...the real T-Bird."

"They're very rare now, so just seeing one of the original two-seat Thunderbirds is a treat. For true car enthusiasts, this is the only real T-Bird. Driving this 1956 model, one of the last off the line, instantly puts a smile on your face. Yes, it's a little loose and a little soft, but none of its faults matter: its looks and style make up for everything. With the V8 working hard, the T-Bird has the performance to match its style, easily exceeding 100 mph."

The Thunderbird's interior is typical of a 1950s American car—loud, brash and very stylized, a little like a jukebox of the period.

Milestones

1954 The T-Bird first appears at the Detroit Auto Show in February and goes on sale in October as a 1955 model. It's powered by a 292-cubic inch V8 with three-speed manual or three-speed automatic transmission.

After 1958 the Thunderbird became a four-seater.

1955 Changes for the 1956 model year are minor. Cooling flaps are added to the front fenders. To make more room in the trunk, the spare wheel is mounted vertically outside behind the body, making the whole car longer. A larger, 312-cubic inch V8 is also available with 215 or 225 bhp. Round 'porthole' windows are installed in the sides of the hardtop.

1956 Much more obvious changes are made for the 1957 model year with fins added at the rear. The car is also lengthened enough to allow the spare wheel back inside the trunk. The front grill and bumpers are also changed and smaller wheels added. Power increases to 270 bhp, but with a supercharger, the engine makes much more.

1957 The last 1957 model T-Birds are produced on December 13, replaced by a larger, four-seater car for 1958.

UNDER THE SKIN

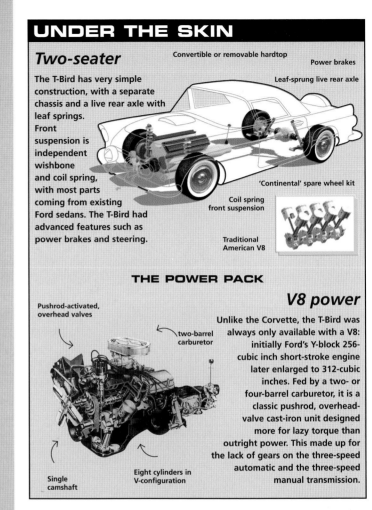

Two-seater

The T-Bird has very simple construction, with a separate chassis and a live rear axle with leaf springs. Front suspension is independent wishbone and coil spring, with most parts coming from existing Ford sedans. The T-Bird had advanced features such as power brakes and steering.

Convertible or removable hardtop

Power brakes

Leaf-sprung live rear axle

'Continental' spare wheel kit

Coil spring front suspension

Traditional American V8

THE POWER PACK

V8 power

Unlike the Corvette, the T-Bird was always only available with a V8: initially Ford's Y-block 256-cubic inch short-stroke engine later enlarged to 312-cubic inches. Fed by a two- or four-barrel carburetor, it is a classic pushrod, overhead-valve cast-iron unit designed more for lazy torque than outright power. This made up for the lack of gears on the three-speed automatic and the three-speed manual transmission.

Pushrod-activated, overhead valves

two-barrel carburetor

Single camshaft

Eight cylinders in V-configuration

Blown bird

The F-Bird, the Supercharged T-Bird, is the rarest, and now the most desirable, of all the early T-Birds. These are the supercharged 1957 models, with a Paxton-McCulloch supercharger added to a larger version (312 cubic inches) of the original V8 to give 300 bhp, or 340 bhp in race trim. Only 211 were sold.

The rare F-bird used a 340-bhp, supercharged engine.

The T-Bird was one of the smallest and most striking cars Ford built in the U.S. in many years. Ford called it a 'personal luxury' car rather than a sports car. It was never intended to be a serious rival to Jaguars or Ferraris.

Cooling flaps

The 1955 models had poor ventilation, so Ford added a flap in the front fenders which could be opened to let cold air into the footwells.

Wrap-around windshield

Like the Chevy Corvette, which came out two years before it, the T-Bird has a wrap-around-type front windshield, a design which avoided the blind spot caused by conventional front windshield pillars.

Choice of transmissions

There was a choice of three different transmissions: a three-speed Fordomatic automatic or the three-speed manual; and perhaps the best option—a manual transmission with high overdrive ratios.

V8 engine

From the beginning, the Thunderbird had a V8 engine. The prototype had only a 256-cubic inch engine with 160 bhp, but that was enlarged for production and became steadily more powerful year by year. By 1957, the most powerful engine—apart from the rare supercharged V8—was the 285-bhp, 312-cubic inch V8.

Open hardtop or convertible

As standard, the Thunderbird came with a bolt-on fiberglass hardtop. The car could also be ordered with a folding rayon convertible top instead of the hardtop, or in addition to it, for an extra $290.

Stretched rear

The original 1955 Thunderbird is very short, so the spare wheel had to be carried above the bumper. For 1957, Ford redesigned the back of the car to make the trunk longer so the spare wheel could be carried inside.

14/15-inch wheels

For its first two years, the Thunderbird ran on tall, 15-inch wheels. For the 1957 model year, they changed to 14-inch wheels which made the cars look sleeker.

Rear fenders

Setting the 1957 T-Bird apart from the 1955 and 1956 cars was the introduction of tail fins. This was the start of the fin era in the U.S., but those on the Thunderbirds are a little more restrained than those on some other models of the period.

Specifications
1957 Ford Thunderbird

ENGINE

Type: V8
Construction: Cast-iron block and heads
Valve gear: Two valves per cylinder operated via pushrods and rockers from a single block-mounted camshaft
Bore and stroke: 3.74 in. x 3.31 in.
Displacement: 292 c.i.
Compression ratio: 8.1:1
Induction system: two- or four-barrel carburetor
Maximum power: 212 bhp at 4,400 rpm
Maximum torque: 297 lb-ft at 2,700 rpm
Top speed: 122 mph
0-60 mph: 9.5 sec.

TRANSMISSION

Three-speed manual with optional overdrive or three-speed Fordomatic automatic

BODY/CHASSIS

Separate cruciform steel chassis with steel two-door body: choice of removable hardtop or convertible roof

SPECIAL FEATURES

Exhausts exiting through holes in the bumper are a typical 1950s American styling feature.

From 1956, the hardtop was available with 'porthole' windows to improve rear three-quarter vision

RUNNING GEAR

Steering: Power-assisted recirculating ball
Front suspension: Double wishbones, coil springs and telescopic shocks
Rear suspension: Live axle with semi-elliptic leaf springs and telescopic shocks
Brakes: Drums front and rear with optional power assistance
Wheels: Steel 14 in. dia.
Tires: Crossply, 7.5 in. x 14 in.

DIMENSIONS

Length: 181.4 in.   **Width:** 70.3 in.
Height: 51.6 in.   **Wheelbase:** 102 in.
Track: 56 in. (front and rear)
Weight: 3,050 lbs.

USA 1983-1988

Ford THUNDERBIRD TURBO COUPE

Ford's Thunderbird fell on hard times during the early 1980s, but new, aerodynamic styling and the arrival of a powerful turbocharged four-cylinder engine soon turned it into one of the most exciting and best-looking Detroit coupes of the late 1980s.

"...a plush yet fast cruiser."

"By taking a large, comfortable Thunderbird and adding a small turbocharged four cylinder engine, Ford created a plush yet fast cruiser. The engine has a raspy exhaust note and thrives on revs. On the back roads you can drive the T-bird exceedingly quick, provided you keep the revs up. On full boost the car becomes a road rocket, pushing you into its plush sports seat. Because of its low stance and wide tires, the Turbo Coupe handles fantastically."

The T-bird's leather-trimmed sports front seats give excellent support.

Milestones

1982 Replacing the boxy, slow-selling
1980-1982 Thunderbird is a rather different car with smooth 'aero' styling. A turbo version arrives halfway through the 1983 model year.

The original Thunderbird was designed to compete with the Chevrolet Corvette.

1985 Larger tail lights, a counterbalanced hood and restyled dash are new, plus the Turbo Coupe also gets a body-colored grill.

The Mustang SVO was the first Ford to use a turbo four cylinder.

1987 After a carryover for 1986,
the Thunderbird receives another facelift. It gets a new nose, flush headlights and larger taillights.

1988 Few changes are in the works for the 'Fox' T-bird, although the mid-range V6 engine gets tuned port injection and a balancer shaft. An all-new Thunderbird arrives for 1989.

UNDER THE SKIN

'Fox' platform

In the early 1980s, many Fords were built on the 'Fox' platform. The Thunderbird was no exception, riding a 104.2-inch wheelbase version. Front and rear anti-roll bars are standard on Turbo Coupes, as are four-wheel disc brakes and ABS from 1987. A five-speed transmission is standard, although an automatic was offered in later Turbo Coupes.

Live rear axle
MacPherson strut front suspension
Four-wheel disc brakes
In-line four

THE POWER PACK

Turbo four

For the Turbo Coupe, Ford adapted the 2.3-liter in-line four engine found in the Fairmont and Granada. This single overhead-cam iron-block engine was upgraded for use in the Turbo. Modifications include forged-aluminum pistons, alloy valves, lighter flywheel and an oil cooler. The turbocharger is mounted upstream of the induction system for reduced lag. Initially rated at 140 bhp, power jumped to 190 bhp in 1987 on the five-speed model thanks to the adoption of an intercooler from the Mustang SVO, although torque remained at 180 lb-ft.

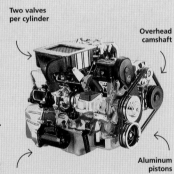

Two valves per cylinder
Overhead camshaft
Aluminum pistons
Cast-iron block and cylinder head

Intercooled

Out of all the Turbo Coupes, the later 1987-1988 cars are the ones to go for. Besides their smoother styling, they also have the more powerful intercooled four-cylinder turbo, plus larger 16-inch wheels and anti-lock disc brakes in the front and rear.

The later 1987-1988 Turbo Coupes have cleaner styling.

With its slick styling, turbocharged engine and proven rugged mechanicals, the Turbo Coupe offers all the performance of European GT cars but at much lower cost and with greater reliability.

Turbocharged engine

Known as the 'Lima' engine, the 2.3-liter single overhead-cam turbo four cylinder is rated at 190 bhp in this Turbo Coupe. An intercooler permits higher boost pressure from the Garret T3 turbocharger.

Fat tires

A big improvement on later cars are the meaty Goodyear Eagle GT tires with unidirectional tread. These are mounted on handsome 16-inch cast-aluminum wheels, which are unique to the Turbo Coupe.

Handling suspension

Turbo Coupes came as standard with a handling package with an uprated front anti-roll bar, plus higher rate coil springs and shocks. A variable rate damping system known as Automatic Ride Control was new for 1987.

Live rear axle

Although it embodies many high-tech features, the Thunderbird retains a live rear axle. It is coil sprung to improve the ride and features an extra pair of rear shocks, mounted horizontally to reduce axle tramp under hard acceleration.

Aero styling

The 1983 Thunderbird marked a radical change of direction for Ford. Minimal use of chrome trim resulted in one of the cleanest cars of the time. It was also exceptionally aerodynamic, having a drag co-efficient of just 0.35. The body was made even slicker for 1987 with smoother side glass and flush mounted headlights.

Five-speed transmission

Initially, the Turbo Coupe was only offered with a Borg-Warner T-5 manual transmission, but an automatic was later made available to increase sales.

Specifications

1987 Ford Thunderbird Turbo Coupe

ENGINE

Type: In-line four
Construction: Cast-iron bock and heads
Valve gear: Two valves per cylinder operated by a single overhead camshaft
Bore and stroke: 3.78 in. x 3.13 in.
Displacement: 2.3 liter
Compression ratio: 8.0:1
Induction system: Bosch electronic fuel injection
Maximum power: 190 bhp at 4,600 rpm
Maximum torque: 180 lb-ft at 3,600 rpm
Top speed: 137 mph
0-60 mph: 7.1 sec.

TRANSMISSION

Borg-Warner T-5 five-speed manual

BODY/CHASSIS

Unitary steel chassis with steel two-door coupe body

SPECIAL FEATURES

Later Turbo Coupes have this new smoother front-end styling.

 Smart 16-inch alloy wheels are another desirable feature of the later cars.

RUNNING GEAR

Steering: Recirculating ball
Front suspension: MacPherson struts with coil springs, telescopic shock absorbers, lower control arms and anti-roll bar
Rear suspension: Live axle with MacPherson struts, coil springs, telescopic shock absorbers and trailing arms
Brakes: Discs (front and rear)
Wheels: Cast aluminum, 16-in. dia.
Tires: Firestone, 8.00 x 16

DIMENSIONS

Length: 189.1 in. **Width:** 73.9 in.
Height: 50.6 in. **Wheelbase:** 104.2 in.
Track: 62.3. in. (front), 62.3 in. (rear)
Weight: 3,380 lbs.

Ford **F100**

When it comes to classic trucks, the 1956 Ford F-100 stands out. It was one of the most powerful and fastest trucks in its day and was also one of the first to achieve cult status.

"...straight back to the 1950s."

"Driving this truck is an experience in itself. The interior takes you straight back to the 1950s, as does the rumpity sound of the vintage Y-block that is nourished by three Stromberg two-barrel carburetors. The ride may still be a bit bumpy with the bed unloaded, but the F-100 is quick off the line and feels faster still, thanks to the manual transmission. The original suspension has been retained, but a custom lowering kit brings its belly closer to the ground."

Sliding behind the wheel is like stepping through a time warp.

Milestones

1953 Introduced in March, the new F-100 replaces the 1948-vintage F-1. It has all-new styling and a set-back front axle. A larger cab and improved suspension set new standards in pickup comfort and refinement. Powered by inline six or flathead V8 engines, a total of 116,437 are built.

The 1948-vintage F-1 got a new grill for the 1951 model year.

1954 A new Y-block overhead-valve V8 replaces the flathead. Known as the Power King, it is rated at 130 bhp and 214 lb-ft of torque.

Today, the F-series truck is the world's best-selling vehicle.

1956 The cab is restyled with a wraparound windshield, which alters its appearance. A 12-volt electrical system and a 273-cubic inch 'Power King' V8 debut. A 10.5-inch clutch is standard on all V8 F-100s. A new F-series truck arrives for the 1957 model year.

UNDER THE SKIN

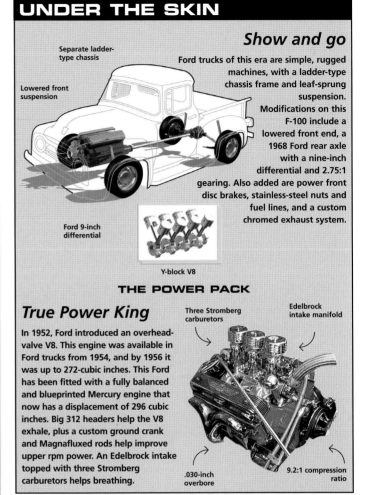

Show and go

Ford trucks of this era are simple, rugged machines, with a ladder-type chassis frame and leaf-sprung suspension. Modifications on this F-100 include a lowered front end, a 1968 Ford rear axle with a nine-inch differential and 2.75:1 gearing. Also added are power front disc brakes, stainless-steel nuts and fuel lines, and a custom chromed exhaust system.

Separate ladder-type chassis

Lowered front suspension

Ford 9-inch differential

Y-block V8

THE POWER PACK

True Power King

In 1952, Ford introduced an overhead-valve V8. This engine was available in Ford trucks from 1954, and by 1956 it was up to 272-cubic inches. This Ford has been fitted with a fully balanced and blueprinted Mercury engine that now has a displacement of 296 cubic inches. Big 312 headers help the V8 exhale, plus a custom ground crank and Magnafluxed rods help improve upper rpm power. An Edelbrock intake topped with three Stromberg carburetors helps breathing.

Three Stromberg carburetors

Edelbrock intake manifold

.030-inch overbore

9.2:1 compression ratio

Red hot roller

Collector interest in the 1956 F-100 has been very strong for a long time, and a ready supply of parts are available for these trucks. The classic styling and V8 power both respond well to custom modifications, and prices are reasonable compared to cars.

Although made in substantial numbers, the 1956 F-100 is coveted today.

Packing considerable power even in stock trim, and with timeless looks and simple yet sturdy mechanicals, the 1956 F-100 truly deserves the title of all-time classic pickup truck.

Stepside bed
One of the reasons these trucks are so popular today is the Stepside bed and full running boards. (1957 saw the introduction of the full bed—sheet metal flush with the cab.) Stepside trucks are not as practical, but in modified form they look much better than the full-bed versions.

Worked Y-block
A larger Mercury unit replaces the stock 272-cubic inch V8. It has been overbored by .030-inch and has an Iskendarian high-lift camshaft, Magnafluxed connecting rods, Edelbrock intake and triple Stromberg carburetors. It puts out an impressive 300 bhp at only 4,500 rpm.

Classic-style exhaust
Spent gases from the engine are exhaled through a custom exhaust system. The system gives an unmistakable, throaty, nostalgic sound.

Lowered nose
A set-back front axle gives these trucks a nose-in-the-weeds stance. Customizers often accentuate this look even further. This F-100 has been lowered by two inches, which improves handling, too.

Attention to detail
It may not appear radical on the outside, but this F-100 has many clever touches. The brake and fuel lines are steel braided, and every nut and bolt on the entire vehicle has been replaced with stainless steel hardware. The taillight wires are covered in chromed flexible tubing.

Quality interior
The leather used on the bench seat was sent to England to be dye-matched to the interior colors of red and orange on the door panels. Real wool was used for the interior carpet.

Wraparound rear window
A flat back window was standard on F-100s in 1956, but a wraparound piece was available as an option. If ordered, the buyer also got chrome windshield moldings. Few were fitted, making F-100s with this item very rare today.

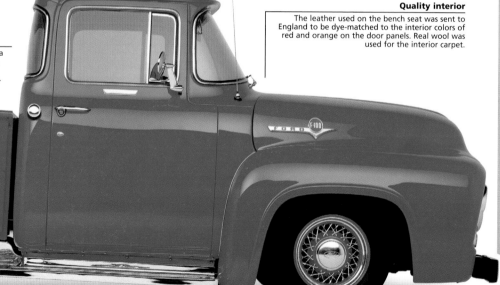

Specifications
1956 Ford F-100

ENGINE
Type: V8

Construction: Cast-iron block and heads

Valve gear: Two valves per cylinder operated by a single camshaft via pushrods and rockers

Bore and stroke: 3.78 in. x 3.30 in.

Displacement: 296 c.i.

Compression ratio: 9.2:1

Induction system: Three Stromberg two-barrel carburetors

Maximum power: 300 bhp at 4,500 rpm

Maximum torque: 270 lb-ft at 2,300 rpm

Top speed: 110 mph

0-60 mph: 8.1 sec.

TRANSMISSION
Three-speed manual

BODY/CHASSIS
Separate ladder-type steel chassis with steel cab and bed

SPECIAL FEATURES

V8-powered F-100s are identified by big grill badges. Sixes did without.

Chrome is used extensively underneath, including the shocks and differential.

RUNNING GEAR
Steering: Recirculating ball

Front suspension: Beam axle with semi-elliptic leaf springs and telescopic shock absorbers

Rear suspension: Live axle with semi-elliptic leaf springs and telescopic shock absorbers

Brakes: Discs (front), drums (rear)

Wheels: Sharp Spoke wire, 15-in. dia.

Tires: BF Goodrich, 15-in. dia.

DIMENSIONS
Length: 212.0 in. **Width:** 59.3 in.

Height: 80.9 in. **Wheelbase:** 114.0 in.

Track: 49.0 in. (front), 48.2 in. (rear)

Weight: 3,175 lbs.

Ford FAIRLANE CROWN VICTORIA

Dearborn first pioneered the use of a transparent roof on its 1954 Skyliner. When Fords were extensively restyled for 1955, the Plexiglas roof was retained for the new Crown Victoria. This novel idea is considered to be the forerunner of the modern 'moon' roof.

"...feather-light steering."

"Driving the Crown Victoria is like piloting any other mainstream Detroiter of the time. It has feather-light steering with a huge steering wheel as well as four-wheel, power-assisted, drum brakes. Although riding on big 15-inch wheels, the Ford is no handling champ, but it does ride smoothly. With Thunderbird power under the hood and lots of lowdown torque, acceleration is swift and instant once you step on the gas pedal."

Smart black and white, two-tone upholstery marks out the fairly restrained interior.

Milestones

1954 A longtime show car feature, a transparent Plexiglas roof finally makes production. It is offered on the Skyliner, a Crestliner hardtop coupe. Although a 223-cubic inch six is standard, the new 239-cubic inch, Y-block V8 is optional. Only 13,344 Skyliners are built this year.

The 312 V8 was also offered in the 1957 retractable top Skyliner.

1955 Restyled Fords are longer and lower with a more streamlined profile. Replacing the Skyliner is the glass-roof Crown Victoria. It does not prove popular, however, with fewer than 2,000 built compared to 33,165 steel-roof coupes.

Thunderbirds shared drivetrain choices with standard Fords.

1956 The Crown Victoria glass top returns, although very poor sales make it too costly to sustain and the model is banished for 1957.

UNDER THE SKIN

Proven simplicity

Body-on-frame construction

Four-wheel drum brakes

Live rear axle

Utterly conventional under the skin, the Crown Victoria has its origins in the new-for-1952 Fords. It has a separate steel-perimeter chassis and conventional suspension—double wishbones at the front suspended by coil springs and tube shocks, plus a live rear axle with semi-elliptic leaf springs. Transmissions are a three-speed manual or Ford-O-Matic automatic.

Y-block V8

THE POWER PACK

T-bird '12

Although the standard engine in all 1956 Fords—except the T-Bird—was a straight six, most buyers ordered one of the three optional V8s. The biggest and most powerful was the 312-cubic inch 'Thunderbird Special.' This Y-block engine (so named because of its cross-sectional shape) is an outgrowth of the original 239 unit but has a bigger 3.8-inch bore and a longer 3.44-inch stroke. It is a torquey engine, and its peak power of 225 bhp gives the Crown Victoria considerable grunt.

Fully loaded

Not popular when new, the 1955-1956 Fairlane Crown Victoria is a collectible automobile today. Many owners loaded these cars with dealer-installed options, which cost a lot of money. One of these cars with period extras is a real find.

Only 603 glass-topped Crown Victorias were built during the car's final season.

Dramatic-looking in its day, the Crown Victoria was not a great commercial success, and this, coupled with the new maximum-volume policy instigated by Ford, sounded the death knell for the bubbletop.

Lifeguard luxuries

Ford began touting safety in the mid-1950s, and the Crown Victoria boasted such features as a padded dashboard and sun visors, a deep-dish steering wheel, a breakaway rearview mirror and factory-installed seatbelts. All these items were grouped under the Lifeguard package.

Y-block power

Three versions, displacing 272, 292 and 312 cubic inches, of the new-for-1952 Y-block were available in the Crown Victoria. The top 312 unit, shared with the Thunderbird, put out 225 bhp with a four-barrel carburetor if teamed with the Ford-O-Matic automatic transmission.

Automatic transmission

The three-speed, Ford-O-Matic unit was a popular option and was smoother and more refined than arch rival Chevrolet's two-speed Powerglide.

Roof band

The Crown Victoria has a wraparound chromed roof band, which gives a tiara effect. The band adds no structural strength to the body, but gives the car a very 1950s, luxurious look.

Bubbletop roof

Costing an extra $70, the optional glass roof panel was heavily tinted, but on hot days it acted like a greenhouse, making the inside of the cabin unbearably hot. A zip-out headliner helped to reduce the problem.

Dual exhaust

Back in 1956, emissions regulations were still years away. Thus, a full-length dual exhaust system helps the engine make the most of its 225 bhp.

Specifications

1956 Ford Fairlane Crown Victoria

ENGINE

Type: V8

Construction: Cast-iron block and heads

Valve gear: Two valves per cylinder operated by a single camshaft with pushrods and rockers

Bore and stroke: 3.8 in. x 3.44 in.

Displacement: 312 c.i.

Compression ratio: 8.4:1

Induction system: Holley four-barrel carburetor

Maximum power: 225 bhp at 4,600 rpm

Maximum torque: 317 lb-ft at 2,600 rpm

Top speed: 107 mph

0-60 mph: 12.2 sec.

TRANSMISSION

Ford-O-Matic three-speed automatic

BODY/CHASSIS

Separate steel chassis with two-door hardtop body

SPECIAL FEATURES

The Continental kit hinges to the left to gain access to the trunk.

A rear-mounted antenna was a dealer-installed option.

RUNNING GEAR

Steering: Recirculating ball

Front suspension: Double wishbones with coil springs and telescopic shock absorbers

Rear suspension: Live axle with semi-elliptic leaf springs and telescopic shock absorbers

Brakes: Drums (front and rear)

Wheels: Pressed steel, 15-in. dia.

Tires: 7.10 x 15

DIMENSIONS

Length: 198.5 in. **Width:** 75.9 in.

Height: 52.5 in. **Wheelbase:** 155.0 in.

Track: 58.0 in. (front), 56.0 in. (rear)

Weight: 3,299 lbs.

Ford FAIRLANE 500

Ford's 1957 line-up was widely regarded as one of Detroit's most stylish. The Fairlane 500 sat at the top of the regular Ford tree, helping the company to achieve one of its best sales years.

"...effortless pulling power."

"This car was produced before the great horsepower race in which Detroit later indulged. Still, for a 1957 car, this Fairlane goes pretty well thanks to its Thunderbird engine. The V8 is tuned for low-down torque rather than absolute power, which means lazy cruising and effortless pulling power. But when you want to move a little faster, the big 312-cubic inch V8 pulls its weight. It's no slowcoach, and can easily deal with modern traffic conditions."

Getting behind the wheel of this Fairlane is like stepping back in time.

Milestones

1957 Ford presents
its new line up including the 118-inch wheelbase Fairlane and the range-topping Fairlane 500. In mid-1957 a new Skyliner version is added with a retractable hardtop roof.

One of the most desirable body styles is the Fairlane convertible.

1958 A facelift
includes the addition of a Thunderbird-style bumper and grill, quad headlights and tail lights and a choice of two new FE-series V8 engines (332-cubic inch and 352-cubic inch). There is also the option of the new Cruise-O-Matic transmission.

The 1956 Fairlane had more rounded rear styling but a similar front end.

1959 A major reskin
revives a more simple style, with a sculpted V-shape back panel and low-level grill with star-like ornaments. A choice of new Galaxie models is also available.

UNDER THE SKIN

Dependable

Excitement was mostly cosmetic on 1950s cars. Under the skin, simplicity was the order of the day. It comes as no surprise to find a separate chassis, a leaf-spring suspension at the rear, an independent coil-spring front end and four-wheel drum brakes.

Independent front suspension

Separate chassis frame

Hydraulically-assisted drum brakes

312-cubic inch Ford V8

THE POWER PACK

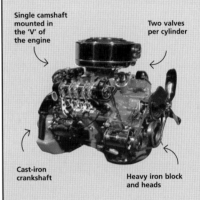

Single camshaft mounted in the 'V' of the engine

Two valves per cylinder

Cast-iron crankshaft

Heavy iron block and heads

Thunderbird V8

The 1957 Fords were offered with a large range of engines, starting with a 223-cubic inch six-cylinder and extending up through V8s of 272-, 292- and 312-cubic inch capacity. This particular car has the same 312-cubic inch engine found in the immortal Thunderbird. It develops a healthy 245 bhp in stock form, but the mildly uprated exhaust system liberates a further 10 bhp— enough to power the car to 120 mph. This performance is not far from the sporty Thunderbird.

Range topper

The 1957 Ford range began with the entry-level, sub-$2,000 Custom and spanned up to the Fairlane 500 Club Victoria and Skyliner with a retractable hardtop at the top end. Ford offered the cars with a 144 bhp six cylinder to a 240 bhp supercharged V8.

The Fairlane hardtop coupe is one of the best-looking of the 1957 range.

The 1957 Fairlane boasts tasteful styling for the period—a factor in its favor nowadays. Fords from this era are rarer than their popularity at the time might suggest.

Thunderbird engine
The base engine for the 1957 Fairlane was a modest six-cylinder. This car has received a useful increase in power by fitting a 255-bhp Thunderbird V8.

Modern paint
The body of this restored and customized car has been resprayed in yellow and white acrylic paint.

Automatic transmission
The Ford-O-Matic three-speed automatic transmission was optional on 1957 models and provides easy gear shifts.

Custom trim
The upholstery is black and charcoal velour, with yellow piping on the seats and rear package tray. Other additions include Auto Meter gauges, air-conditioning, and a powerful stereo.

Safety interior
Ford began its safety drive in 1956. This car is fitted with a dished steering wheel, padded dash, break-away rear-view mirror, and crash-proof door locks.

Partial dechroming
In order to give this car clean and uncluttered lines, much of the chrome trim has been removed.

Classic styling
Unlike the gaudy and contrived excesses of some late-1950s cars, the Fairlane was quite simple and understated.

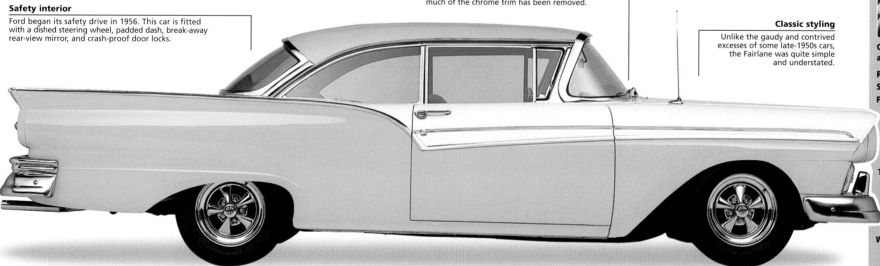

Specifications

1957 Ford Fairlane 500

ENGINE

Type: V8

Construction: Cast-iron cylinder block and cylinder heads

Valve gear: Two valves per cylinder operated by a single camshaft

Bore and stroke: 3.90 in. x 3.44 in.

Displacement: 312 c.i.

Compression ratio: 9.7:1

Induction system: Single Holley carburetor

Maximum power: 255 bhp at 4,600 rpm

Maximum torque: 354 lb-ft at 2,800 rpm

Top speed: 120 mph

0-60 mph: 10.2 sec.

TRANSMISSION

Ford-O-Matic three-speed automatic

BODY/CHASSIS

Separate chassis with steel two-door coupe bodywork

SPECIAL FEATURES

In 1957, the Fairlane had single rear lights; twin lights were fitted in 1958.

Chrome valve covers and air cleaner, and headers liven up the T-bird V8.

RUNNING GEAR

Steering: Recirculating ball

Front suspension: Independent with coil springs and telescopic shocks

Rear suspension: Rigid axle with leaf springs and telescopic shocks

Brakes: Four-wheel drums

Wheels: Cragar, 15-in. dia.

Tires: 235/60 x 15 in.

DIMENSIONS

Length: 207.5 in.   **Width:** 77 in.

Height: 56.5 in.   **Wheelbase:** 118 in.

Track: 59 in. (front), 56.4 in. (rear)

Weight: 3,400 lbs.

Ford FAIRLANE 427

To fight its opposition on the street Ford built the Fairlane 427 which had widened shock towers and larger front coil springs to fit a detuned 427 V8. Unfortunately, the Fairlane 427 was costly to build so only 70 units were made in 1966 and 200 in 1967. Most went to pro racers for NHRA Super Stock competition.

"...uses a detuned race engine"

"Only a Borg-Warner 'Top-Loader' four-speed transmission was able to handle the 480 lb-ft of torque that the massive engine was capable of making. Though it uses a detuned version of its race engine, the brutal 427, if equipped with dual four-barrel carbs, it 'only' makes 425 bhp. On the street, the Fairlane 427 was very competitive. Only a handful were made and at $5,100 were very pricey, thus giving a slight edge to the competition.

The only indication of power from the vinyl-clad interior was a 9,000 rpm tachometer.

Milestones

1964 After minimal success on the drag strips with the larger Galaxies, Ford creates the Thunderbolt—a specially prepared 427-powered lightweight Fairlane sedan. These factory-built race cars helped Ford secure the NHRA manufacturers' championship.

The first Fairlanes to be equipped with the 427 were the competition-only Thunderbolts.

1966 A new, bigger Fairlane is released, which has plenty of room for 427 FE V8 engines. Only 70 white hardtops and coupes are built to qualify for Super Stock drag racing.

The 1966 Fairlane has similar styling to the 1966-67 Galaxie.

1967 The 427 returns as a regular production option for its second and final season. Only 200 Fairlanes are equipped with the side-oiler 427 and are available in a variety of colors and optional trim packages.

UNDER THE SKIN

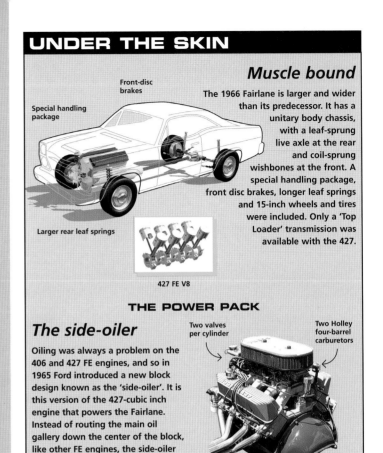

Muscle bound

The 1966 Fairlane is larger and wider than its predecessor. It has a unitary body chassis, with a leaf-sprung live axle at the rear and coil-sprung wishbones at the front. A special handling package, front disc brakes, longer leaf springs and 15-inch wheels and tires were included. Only a 'Top Loader' transmission was available with the 427.

Front-disc brakes

Special handling package

Larger rear leaf springs

427 FE V8

THE POWER PACK

The side-oiler

Oiling was always a problem on the 406 and 427 FE engines, and so in 1965 Ford introduced a new block design known as the 'side-oiler'. It is this version of the 427-cubic inch engine that powers the Fairlane. Instead of routing the main oil gallery down the center of the block, like other FE engines, the side-oiler has the main oil gallery positioned low on the left side near the pump outlet. It is rated at 410 bhp with a single four-barrel carburetor and 425 bhp with a dual carburetor set up.

Two valves per cylinder

Two Holley four-barrel carburetors

Side-mounted oil gallery

11.1:1 compression

Rare beast

Although the 1966 models are very rare, this no frills homologation special isn't very refined. For 1967, Ford offered the Fairlane 427 in a variety of colors and exterior trim. The cars still had the potent 427 V8 and also carried the equally potent price tag.

The 1967 Fairlane 427s were a serious threat on the streets and at the track.

Although it was one of the quickest muscle cars around in 1966, the rarity of the Fairlane 427 prevented it from having the same impact among street racers as a Chevelle SS396 or a tri-power GTO.

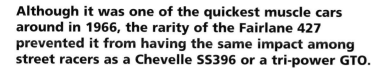

Heavy-duty suspension

To cope with the weight and power of the 427 engine, the standard Fairlane suspension was reworked with stiffer spring rates and larger front coil springs. This unit also took up considerable space, which necessitated relocating the front shock towers.

Race-derived engine

The 427-cubic inch engine was only available with the base model trim and was never used in the plusher GT/GTA model. After all, it was a thinly-disguised race car and potential purchasers were carefully screened by dealers.

Four-speed transmission

Unlike the Fairlane GT/GTA, the 427 was only available with one transmission: a Borg-Warner 'Top Loader' T-10 four-speed.

Handling package

A special handling package, consisting of manual front disc brakes, longer rear leaf springs and larger blackwall tires, was available. This particular car is one of the very few to be fitted with these items.

Smooth styling

For 1966, the Fairlane hardtop received similar styling to the Pontiac GTO, with stacked headlights and smooth-flowing contours.

Fiberglass hood

In 1966 all 427 Fairlanes were built with a fiberglass lift-off hood with four tie-down pins. For 1967 a steel hood was available alongside the fiberglass unit.

Specifications

1967 Ford Fairlane 427

ENGINE

Type: V8

Construction: Cast-iron block and heads

Valve gear: Two valves per cylinder actuated by a single camshaft via pushrods, rockers and solid lifters

Bore and stroke: 4.23 in. x 3.78 in.

Displacement: 427 c.i.

Compression ratio: 11.1:1

Induction system: Two Holley four-barrel downdraft carburetors with aluminum intake manifold

Maximum power: 425 bhp at 6,000 rpm

Maximum torque: 480 lb-ft at 3,700 rpm

Top speed: 121 mph

0-60 mph: 6.0 sec

TRANSMISSION

Borg-Warner 'Top Loader' T-10 four-speed

BODY/CHASSIS

Steel unitary chassis with two-door body

SPECIAL FEATURES

Stacked headlights are a feature of 1966-1967 Fairlanes. The lower units are the high beams.

Dual 652 cfm Holley four barrel carburetors are housed beneath an open element aircleaner

RUNNING GEAR

Steering: Recirculating ball

Front suspension: Double wishbones with heavy duty coil springs, telescopic shock absorbers, anti-sway bar

Rear suspension: Live axle with long semi-elliptic leaf springs and telescopic shock absorbers

Brakes: Discs front, drums rear

Wheels: 14 x 5.5-in.

Tires: 7.75 x 14

DIMENSIONS

Length: 197.0 in.	**Width:** 74.7 in.
Height: 54.3 in.	**Wheelbase:** 116.0 in.
Track: 58.0 in.	**Weight:** 4,100 lbs.

Ford **SKYLINER**

For the 1950s, the Skyliner was a technological miracle. At the touch of a button the car, which looks like a standard two-door hardtop coupe, lifts up its steel roof and tucks it neatly into the trunk. The idea has been revived by Mercedes-Benz for the SLK sports car.

"...retractable hardtop"

"The most dynamic feature of the Skyliner is its retractable roof. Just press the button under the dash and enjoy the show. The trunk opens to about 80 degrees and the roof emerges with the forward flap hanging down. It then moves forward and lowers and locks in place. As for performance, the Skyliner is quick and powerful, but rolls a bit through turns. It is an unstressed and comfortable car with a retractable hardtop."

By late-1950s standards, the interior is tastefully restrained.

Milestones

1957 Fords are totally restyled and the new Fairlane range is far lower and much longer than the 1956 models. The Skyliner, with its amazing electrically-powered, fully-retractable metal roof is launched; 20,766 are sold.

The Skyliner retractable appeared halfway through 1957.

1958 Minor styling changes are made, including four headlights and a fake hood scoop, and more power is available with the Interceptor Special V8 option. Ford V8 engines have an improved cylinder head, valve design, bearings and crankshafts. The roof is also strengthened.

The Skyliner proved unprofitable and was duly axed in 1959.

1959 Despite a complete restyle, sales fall to 12,915. A totally restyled range is scheduled for 1960 and production of the Skyliner comes to an end.

UNDER THE SKIN

Steel drop-top

Coil-sprung independent front suspension

Four-wheel drum brakes

Heavy duty X-braced chassis

Y-block V8

Apart from its incredible roof, the Skyliner is the same as the stock convertible but uses a stronger version of the already massive separate X-frame chassis with its five stronger cross braces. It has the usual live rear axle with semi-elliptic leaf springs, and wishbones and coil springs at the front. The large trunk allows room for the folding steel roof and associated electrics.

THE POWER PACK

Traditional V8 power

Fairlane engine options ranged from the base 200-bhp, 292-cubic inch V8 up to the 352-cubic inch Police Interceptor Special with 300 bhp. All are standard Ford cast-iron pushrod overhead-valve V8 designs. The Interceptor Special is a short-stroke (4.0 in. x 3.5 in.) engine with a high compression ratio and fuel is fed through a single four-barrel Holley carburetor. Like most V8 engines of the period, it is tuned to produce maximum power and torque at low rpm.

Dual plane intake manifold

Holley four-barrel carburetor

Cast-iron block and cylinder heads

Thin-wall block construction

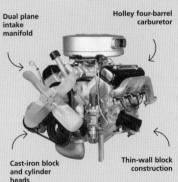

Vintage year

1959 Fords were regarded as the most attractive full-size cars the company had built up to that time. As far as Skyliners are concerned, the 1959 models are also the rarest—only 12,915 were produced. This makes them the most sought-after of all 1959 Fords.

The 1959 models are far more collectable than earlier Skyliners.

For three years Ford was the only car company brave enough to make a true mass-production car with a foldaway steel roof. It cost millions to develop, and is a real treat to see today.

Powerful V8
In 1959 the Skyliner came with a standard 292-cubic inch Mercury V8. With gas selling for around 20 cents a gallon at the time, big-blocks were popular. This car is fitted with a 352-cubic inch unit producing 300 bhp.

Folding rear deck
When the roof is folded away in the trunk, the deck is fully extended. When the roof is up, however, the end of the deck lid folds away. The end section of the deck is moved by an electric motor.

Automatic transmission
The standard transmission was a three-speed manual, but by 1958 the three-speed Cruise-O-Matic automatic could be ordered. There was also a manual transmission with automatic overdrive, but this was not popular.

Optional power brakes
To get the best from the four-wheel drum brakes, they are power-assisted. Brake fade is common after repeated hard use.

Round tail lights
One of the best styling changes made to 1959 Fords was to replace the four protruding taillights in the rectangular housings by single, large round lights. These became a trademark on early-1960s Fords.

Seven electric motors
To operate the roof, seven electric motors are required. The biggest is in the trunk and operates the two very long screw jacks that raise and lower the roof. Thirteen switches, 10 solenoids, eight circuit breakers and over 600 feet of wiring serve the electric motors.

Two-tone paintwork
The side trim of the 1957 model lent itself to a two-tone finish, and the 1958 model, with a long chrome-edged side panel, was ideal for a three-tone treatment. This panel became almost a stripe on the 1959 model.

Specifications
1959 Ford Skyliner

ENGINE

Type: V8

Construction: Cast-iron block and heads

Valve gear: Two valves per cylinder operated by a single V-mounted camshaft via pushrods and rockers

Bore and stroke: 4.00 in. x 3.50 in.

Displacement: 352 c.i.

Compression ratio: 9.6:1

Induction system: Four-barrel Holley carburetor

Maximum power: 300 bhp at 4,600 rpm

Maximum torque: 381 lb-ft at 2,800 rpm

Top speed: 112 mph

0-60 mph: 10.5 sec.

TRANSMISSION

Three-speed Cruise-O-Matic automatic

BODY/CHASSIS

Steel X-frame chassis with steel two-door convertible body

SPECIAL FEATURES

When the roof is up, the trunk is quite spacious.

With the top up the Skyliner looks like a normal hardtop car.

RUNNING GEAR

Steering: Recirculating ball

Front suspension: Double wishbones with coil springs and telescopic shock absorbers

Rear suspension: Live axle with semi-elliptic leaf springs and telescopic shock absorbers

Brakes: Drums (front and rear)

Wheels: Steel discs, 14-in. dia

Tires: 6.00 x 14

DIMENSIONS

Length: 208.1 in. **Width:** 76.6 in.

Height: 56.5 in. **Wheelbase:** 118.0 in.

Track: 59.0 in. (front), 56.5 in. (rear)

Weight: 4,064 lbs.

Ford **GALAXIE**

Ford Galaxie Starliners are powerful even in stock form. This particular model has been fitted with a variety of vintage Ford high performance running gear such as the infamous, ultra-rare, marginally street legal 427 SOHC.

"...prowess of performance."

"No matter what car you put the outlawed-by-NASCAR 427 SOHC engine in, it is guaranteed to give it an extraordinary prowess of performance. The only factor that keeps this Starliner from dropping its 0-60 mph elapsed time is the tires. Complimenting the hand-built 625-bhp engine is perhaps Ford's finest driveline. It includes a 'Top-Loader' 4-speed and a 9-inch rear that houses 4.30:1 gears. Though it's far from original, this street machine was sure done right."

Drop the pedal and hang on! Soon everything outside the windshield becomes a blur.

Milestones

1960 Ford introduces a new full-size hardtop line, and a new Starliner fastback hardtop joins the Galaxie series. It is conceived to reduce aerodynamic drag on NASCAR tracks and helps Ford to win the championship this year.

For 1960 the full-size Fords were completely revised.

1961 The Starliner returns, although full-size Fords are reduced by four inches in length and two in width. The FE series 352-cubic inch engine is stroked to 390 and the most powerful version produces 375 bhp at 6,000 rpm. Only 29,669 Starliners are built this year and poor sales ensure that it does not return for 1962.

Like their GM rivals, Ford 'biggies' had shorter and narrower bodies in 1961.

1965 A restyled full-size Ford, with all-coil suspension, goes on sale. A single overhead-cam version of the 427 is made available to racers.

UNDER THE SKIN

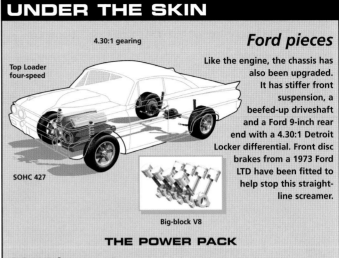

Ford pieces

Like the engine, the chassis has also been upgraded. It has stiffer front suspension, a beefed-up driveshaft and a Ford 9-inch rear end with a 4.30:1 Detroit Locker differential. Front disc brakes from a 1973 Ford LTD have been fitted to help stop this straight-line screamer.

THE POWER PACK

SOHC it to ya!

In 1965, Ford built the 427 SOHC in retaliation to Chrysler's 427 Hemi engines that were tearing up the NASCAR and NHRA circuits. The engine had single overhead cams and hemispherical combustion chambers. On Ford's dynamometer it made 675 bhp. The monster 427 mill proved to be so wicked that NASCAR disapproved the use of the engine. Seven factory sponsored A/FX cars that ran in NHRA in 1965 used the mighty engine and won the championship that year. The rest were never available in production models, but detuned versions could be bought over the counter form Ford. Though rare, some were used in street machines like this 1961 Starliner.

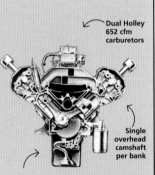

Fastback style

The Galaxie Starliner arrived in 1960—its main purpose was to keep Ford competitive in NASCAR. In its day the Starliner was one of the best looking Fords. Today its fastback design and low stance makes it a natural to be transformed into a street machine.

The Starliner debuted in 1960 but only lasted until the following year.

The 427 SOHC engines were never installed in any production cars. Although the handful that were offered were scoffed up by racers and hot rodders alike nearly as soon as they were available in 1965, their status is still legendary today.

Ultra-rare engine
Originally fitted with a 390, the owner of this car has installed a 427-cubic inch single overhead cam engine. This very rare power unit was developed by Ford to compete with the hemi Chryslers in NASCAR and NHRA sanctioned racing.

Manual transmission
Most Starliners are equipped with C6 automatics, but this one has a Borg-Warner T-10. To cope with the torque of the big V8, it has a heavy-duty clutch linkage.

Fastback styling
The fastback roof not only looks good, but it had a purpose. In 1961 Ford designed this car to be as aerodynamic as possible for specially prepared cars that raced in NASCAR. This was done to help reduce high speed aerodynamic drag.

Custom exhaust headers
For less restricted exhaust flow, the stock manifolds have been replaced by custom-fabricated tubular units. Doug Thorley was one of the largest suppliers of headers to drag racers in the 1960s.

Teardrop hood
Because the engine's induction system used a high rise intake manifold and dual carburetors, extra clearance was necessary. This stylish 'teardrop' shaped scoop was molded to a fiberglass hood to give the engine the space it required. Another added benefit was the two openings at the cowl that allowed hot air from the engine to escape. This hood style was immortalized in the 1964 lightweight Galaxie and Thunderbolt factory race cars. It quickly became a popular add-on for many other Ford models.

Full interior
As it is a street machine rather than a factory drag racer, this Galaxie still has a full stock interior and two-tone upholstery.

Specifications
1961 Ford Galaxie Starliner

ENGINE

Type: V8

Construction: Cast-iron block and heads

Valve gear: Two valves per cylinder operated by a single overhead camshaft per bank via rockers

Bore and stroke: 4.23 in. x 3.78 in.

Displacement: 427 c.i.

Compression ratio: 12.5:1

Induction system: Twin Holley four-barrel carburetors

Maximum power: 625 bhp at 7,000 rpm

Maximum torque: 515 lb-ft at 3,800 rpm

Top speed: 130 mph

0-60 mph: 5.4 sec.

TRANSMISSION

Borg-Warner 'Top-Loader' T-10 four-speed

BODY/CHASSIS

Perimeter steel chassis with two-door steel hardtop body

SPECIAL FEATURES

Starliner emblems garnish the rear quarter panels.

Round tail lights and a simulated grill treatment on the rear valance are hallmarks of early 1960s Fords.

RUNNING GEAR

Steering: Recirculating ball

Front suspension: Unequal length wishbones with coil springs and telescopic shock absorbers

Rear suspension: Live rear axle with semi-elliptic leaf springs and telescopic shock absorbers

Brakes: Drums (front and rear)

Wheels: Torque Thrust magnesium, 15-in. dia.

Tires: BFG radials

DIMENSIONS

Length: 463.0 in.   **Width:** 190.0 in.

Height: 124.0 in.   **Wheelbase:** 119.0 in.

Track: 145.0 in. (front), 136.0 in. (rear)

Weight: 3,660 lbs.

Ford **GALAXIE SUNLINER**

Not only was the Galaxie Ford's most popular car in the early 1960s, but the 1960-1961 models were the widest cars Ford ever built. The range-topping Sunliner improved the look of what was already arguably the cleanest styled sedan of its time.

"...designed for cruising."

"Ford's full-size cars of the 1960s are renowned for their power above all else. The fastest Galaxie can break seven seconds from 0-60 mph. It shifts smooth and trouble free. The heavy duty chassis is designed for cruising, and the car is too soft for hard cornering; also the tires are skinny for a car of its size. But drop the soft-top and turn up the radio, because the Sunliner is motoring that doesn't exist any more."

The plain and basic, color-coordinated interior of the Sunliner has class and style. The bench seat is also very comfortable.

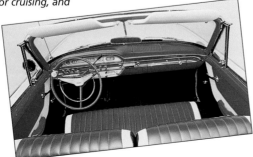

Milestones

1959 In October, Ford launches a bold, new lineup across three different ranges. The top of its full-size range is the Galaxie.

1959 model Fords were boxier and shorter.

1961 A minor facelift introduces a full-width concave grill and round taillights. A large, 390-cubic inch V8 is launched.

In 1963 a high-rise 427 V8 became an option in high performance Galaxies.

1962 A chunky new restyle and bigger engine options elevate the big Ford range, and a midseason Galaxie 500 Victoria/Sunliner is launched.

1964 This is the last year for the Galaxie in this body shape.

UNDER THE SKIN

Tried and tested

Leaf-sprung rear suspension

Optional power steering

Separate chassis

Big-block V8

Although its 1960 models were new, Ford did not undertake radical re-engineering. This meant a separate 119-inch wheelbase chassis with coil springs up front and leaf springs at the rear. In 1962, Ford adopted NASCAR-inspired suspension that transformed the behavior of the so-called 500 models. Drum brakes were fitted all around, and there were optional power steering and Cruise-O-Matic, Ford-O-Matic, and overdrive transmission options.

THE POWER PACK

FE-series power

The excellent FE-series V8 engines and drivelines were the only elements carried over from 1959 Fords. While a 223-cubic inch, six-cylinder engine remained in the lineup, the V8 was a better choice. In 1960, the regular engine had a 292-cubic inch displacement and developed 185 bhp, but the 352-cubic inch Interceptor engine had between 235 and 360 bhp. In 1961, the displacement grew to 390-cubic inches and power started at 300 bhp going up as high as 401 bhp in high-compression tune. That wasn't as big as it got, though: a 406-cubic inch V8 arrived in 1962 and the legendary 427-cubic inch V8 in 1963.

Sun seeker

The 1960 two-door Galaxie is regarded as one of the most handsome cars of the period. The pick of the range is the Sunliner convertible, especially with a Starlift detachable hard-top. The hot Interceptor V8 is the engine favored by most collectors.

The clean lines of the Sunliner have made it a favorite among collectors.

Elegant styling, powerful engine options and solid engineering were the Galaxie's strengths. And in Ford's best-selling range the sleek open-top Sunliner was a popular body style.

V8 power
Although a straight six was available, Ford's V8 engines were preferable. In 1960, a 292-cubic-inch unit was available, plus a 352-cubic-inch big-block with 235-350 bhp. In 1961, a 390-cubic-inch Thunderbird with 300-401 bhp was offered.

Ellipsoid arches
More than ever the shape of the front and rear wheel arches was a Ford trademark for 1960. The ellipsoid shape gives the impression of sleekness and speed.

Lush chrome trim
As the top model line for 1960, the Galaxie boasted chrome A-pillars, window moldings and side strips with ribbed aluminum stoneshields behind the rear wheels.

Special tires
Convertibles have wider tires than other models in Ford's full-size range (8.0 inches compared to 7.5 inches). A variety of tire options was also offered, including whitewalls and oversized tread.

Bat fins
Ford finally relented in the GM-led tailfin craze with an interesting fin detail of its own.

Single body crease
A single chrome strip, stretching from the front bumper right back to the tip of the rear fin emphasizes a very strong side body crease as part of the styling. The strip curves around the edge of the horizontal tailfin for extra emphasis.

Widest body
At 79.9 inches, the 1961 Galaxie ranks as one of the widest-bodied Detroit cars ever produced. Even this does not beat Chrysler's biggest model, the 1961 Imperial at 81.7 inches.

Specifications

1961 Ford Galaxie Sunliner

ENGINE

Type: V8

Construction: Cast-iron block and heads

Valve gear: Two valves per cylinder operated by a single camshaft with pushrods and rockers

Bore and stroke: 4.05 in. x 3.78 in.

Displacement: 390 c.i.

Compression ratio: 9.6:1

Induction system: Single carburetor

Maximum power: 300 bhp at 4,600 rpm

Maximum torque: 427 lb-ft at 2,800 rpm

Top speed: 122 mph

0-60 mph: 9.5 sec.

TRANSMISSION

Three-speed automatic

BODY/CHASSIS

Separate chassis with steel two-door convertible body

SPECIAL FEATURES

Optional fender skirts on the rear wheels add to the Galaxie's appearance.

With the huge sloping hood, guides are needed to assist with parking.

RUNNING GEAR

Steering: Recirculating-ball

Front suspension: A-arms with coil springs and shock absorbers

Rear suspension: Live axle with leaf springs and shock absorbers

Brakes: Drums (front and rear)

Wheels: Steel, 14-in. dia.

Tires: 8.00 x 14

DIMENSIONS

Length: 209.9 in. **Width:** 79.9 in.

Height: 55.0 in. **Wheelbase:** 119.0 in.

Track: 61.0 in. (front), 60.0 in. (rear)

Weight: 3,792 lbs.

Ford **GALAXIE 500 7 LITRE**

The Galaxie 500 7 Litre formula was a simple one. Tried-and-true mechanical components, luxury fittings, and a huge 428-cubic inch V8 came together in a single package that made for a powerful driving experience.

"...solidly built."

"Ford sought refinement with the Galaxie 500. It is solidly built, quiet, and very comfortable. Its soft suspension insulates passengers from severe road bumps. Because this is the sporty member of the Galaxie family, the steering is reasonably responsive and turn-in is good for such a large car. With 428-cubic inches under the hood, it is also a star performer; hit the gas pedal and this leviathan leaps forward. With front disc brakes, it stops well, too.

As it is a top-line model, the Galaxie 500 boasts leather-trimmed upholstery.

Milestones

1965 Like arch rival Chevy, Ford fields new big cars. They have more linear styling, stacked headlights, and all-new suspensions. Models are divided into Custom and Galaxie ranges, the latter including a top-line XL coupe, convertible, and plush LTD coupe and sedan. Engines range from a 240-cubic inch six up to the 427 V8.

Halfway through 1963, Galaxies could be fitted with the 427 V8 as an option.

1966 Joining the LTDs as big, upmarket Fords are the Galaxie 500 7 Litre coupes and convertibles, powered by 345-bhp 428 V8s. Only 11,073 7 Litres to 101,096 LTDs are built.

Big Fords were all restyled for 1965; this is a 427 Galaxie 500XL.

1967 More exaggerated Coke-bottle contours mark the Galaxies this year. Due to poor sales, the 7 Litre models do not return.

UNDER THE SKIN

Vast and fast

Unitary construction

Live rear axle

Independent front suspension

Massive FE V8

New from the ground up, the big Fords for 1965 received a stronger, unitary structure and an unequal length A-arm front suspension that proved to be so effective that it was used in NASCAR racing well into the 1970s. At the rear a live axle was retained, but coil springs and control arms replaced the leaf springs. The 1966 models differ only in detail. A front anti-roll bar was standard, as were four-wheel drum brakes, though front discs were available as an option.

THE POWER PACK

Torque monster

In 1965, the biggest engine offered in the Galaxie was the fearsome 427 unit. It had four-bolt main bearings, a forged-steel crank, and either a single four-barrel carburetor or two fours. For 1966, a new 428-cubic inch engine joined the option list. Still a member of the FE-series family of big-blocks, the cast-iron 428 was tuned more for torque than power and had two-bolt main bearings, a cast-iron crankshaft, and cast-alloy pistons. It was more streetable than the 427 and with 345 bhp on tap it still had more than enough power to satisfy the vast majority of drivers.

Extra luxury

The Mid-1960 Galaxie has a large following. The most popular model is the rare 1965 427 car with a dual-quad intake. The 1966 7 Litre model is also worth considering. It is quite rare (11,073 built) and in convertible form makes the ideal summer cruiser.

Galaxie 7 Litres were offered only for 1966.

As if to signify their departure from competition and the performance market, the 1965-1966 Fords were more formal-looking than their predecessors. The 7 Litres were among the most refined cars of their day.

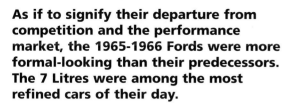

V8 engines
Because it was the flagship of the Ford line, the 7 Litre had to have the largest Ford powerplant available: in this case the 345-bhp, 428-cubic inch V8 also found in that year's Thunderbird. This engine makes the Galaxie a 16.5-second ¼-mile runner—impressive considering its 4,000-lbs. curbweight.

Front discs
Standard brakes on the Galaxie were 11-inch diameter drums. The front pair were wider than the one in the rear. However, by this stage, front discs were available and were standard equipment on the Galaxie 500 7-liter.

Independent front suspension
Through the 1960s, Ford played around with its unequal length A-arm front suspension in an effort to get the greatest ride comfort. This was achieved by improving the bushings in the lower A-arms.

Bucket seat interior
Galaxies could be ordered with a wide range of interior equipment including front power bucket seats with a power center console and power windows and door locks.

Coil-sprung rear
Although still retaining a live rear axle, from 1965 the big Fords got coil springs and semi-trailing arms. This was to improve the ride, which was said by some to be in the same league as a Rolls-Royce.

Three-speed automatic
The standard transmission with the V8 Galaxie 7 Litre is the C6 Cruise-O-Matic three-speed automatic transmission. This unit can also be shifted between first and second manually for improved acceleration off the line.

Power top
Unlike small sports cars, large convertibles had the space for proper power operation of the convertible top. In the Galaxie's case it folds down almost flush with the top of the car to give a smooth, uncluttered line.

Specifications
1966 Ford Galaxie 500 7 Litre

ENGINE
Type: V8

Construction: Cast-iron block and heads

Valve gear: Two valves per cylinder operated by a single V-mounted camshaft via pushrods, rockers and hydraulic valve lifters

Bore and stroke: 4.13 in. x 3.98 in.

Displacement: 428 c.i.

Compression ratio: 10.5:1

Induction system: Autolite four barrel carburetor

Maximum power: 345 bhp at 4,600 rpm

Maximum torque: 462 lb-ft at 2,800 rpm

Top speed: 105 mph

0-60 mph: 8.2 sec.

TRANSMISSION
C6 Cruise-O-Matic three-speed automatic

BODY/CHASSIS
Unitary steel construction, steel body panels and convertible top

SPECIAL FEATURES

One of the more noticeable changes for 1966 was using exposed turn signal lenses.

The "Galaxie 500" tag signifies Ford's involvement in NASCAR racing which it dominated in the mid 1960s.

RUNNING GEAR
Steering: Recirculating-ball

Front suspension: Unequal length A-arms with coil springs, telescopic shock absorbers and anti-roll bar

Rear suspension: Live axle with coil springs, control arms and telescopic shock absorbers

Brakes: Drums, 11 x 3 in. (front), 11 x 2.5 in. (rear)

Wheels: Stamped steel, 15-in. dia.

Tires: 8.45 x 15

DIMENSIONS
Length: 210.0 in.   **Width:** 78.0 in.

Height: 53.9 in.   **Wheelbase:** 119.0 in.

Track: 62.0 in. (front and rear)

Weight: 4,059 lbs.

Ford **GALAXIE 500XL**

Although it became progressively more formal during the 1960s, the Galaxie still remained a hot seller. However, few people then would have considered it to be a great basis for a street rod.

"...eye-popping paint."

"You may not remember much about driving a stock a 1968 Galaxie, but you won't forget this one. The custom interior is a world away from Ford's, with special seats, steering wheel and high-quality trim. A very low stance really helps this huge car corner, and stiff springs reduce body lean under high g loads. Handling, however, is incidental—this car's primary role is to turn heads, which it does with flames from the tailpipes and its eye-popping paint."

The billet aluminum wheel and painted metal dash are far removed from the stock interior.

Milestones

1965 With the intermediate Fairlane assuming the performance mantle, the new, redesigned big Fords adopt more formal lines and have stacked quad headlights. Engines range from a humble straight six to the big 427 V8. The top-of-the-line Galaxie range includes a new luxury model, the LTD.

The 1966 7-Litre marked a more formal role for the Galaxie.

1966 The Thunderbird's 345-bhp, 428-cubic inch V8 becomes an option and is standard on the new 7-Litre models. Styling is only slightly changed from 1965.

In 1968, the Mustang could also be ordered with a 390-cubic inch V8 engine.

1967 More fluid styling marks the big Fords this year.

1968 A new grill with hidden headlights is the major change.

UNDER THE SKIN

Low and large

Steel unitary chassis
Lowered front spindles
Live rear axle
Big-block V8

By 1968, the Galaxie had adopted unitary construction but retained independent front suspension and a live rear axle on leaf springs. In an effort to improve handling, which wasn't outstanding on these giants, the owner of this car has fitted 3-inch dropped spindles at the front and lowering blocks on the rear springs. Front disc brakes have been fitted, but stock drums remain at the rear.

THE POWER PACK

Fiery FE

The 345-bhp 428 engine could have been ordered in a Galaxie, but the buyer of this car chose the smaller 390-cubic inch V8. Like the 428, it is a member of the FE family of Ford big-blocks. Its basic construction consists of a cast-iron block, a crankshaft running on five main bearings, and a single central camshaft working the overhead valves with pushrods and hydraulic lifters. This motor has been fitted with a set of Hooker Super Comp exhaust headers, and an Edelbrock intake manifold and carburetors. Power is boosted from 315 bhp to an estimated 365 bhp.

Bargain buy

When it comes to street machines, most hot rodders choose intermediate- size cars, although really big cars, like the Galaxie, should not be forgotten. A 1968 hardtop or convertible is the best bodystyle. There are plenty around and they're very affordable.

1968 Galaxies in good condition can be bought for less than $2,000.

The stock 1968 Galaxie was a clean and rather understated design. That look has been totally transformed on this car by a combination of paint, perfect detailing, massive alloy wheels and flames—both painted and real.

Custom interior

Totally unique to this car are the combination of tweed and vinyl covering on the custom-made seats and the painted dashboard with Auto Meter phantom gauges. Not only has the steering wheel been changed to a Billet Specialities design, but it is now on a GM rather than Ford tilt steering column.

Modified V8

The 1968 Galaxie could be fitted with the 390-cubic inch V8 in various states of tune, from 265 bhp up to 315 bhp. This car has the base 390, but with a more efficient Edelbrock intake and four-barrel carburetor, plus a set of Hooker Super Comp headers.

Live rear axle

Live axles were still the industry standard in 1968. This one is a simple arrangement with angled telescopic shocks and long semi-elliptic leaf springs doing the dual task of suspending and locating the axle.

Independent suspension

Throughout the 1960s, Ford altered its A-arm and coil-spring front suspension design, trying to achieve the right degree of wheel control as well as the greatest comfort by minimizing the road shocks fed through the system. This was partly achieved by working on the bushings in the lower A-arm to give compliance in one direction only. In this case spring and shock rates have been increased to cope with the reduced suspension travel of a lowered car.

Seam-welded body

This Galaxie's body is much stiffer and stronger than any that left the production line in 1968. Instead of rows of individual spot-welds joining the body panels, there's a continuous run of weld along each seam.

Low ride height

Wide and flat, the original 1968 Galaxie was fairly low, but this one has been fitted with 3-inch drop spindles to lower the whole car, front and rear, to under 49 inches—about the height of a Porsche 928.

Ford **FALCON**

Super Gas is one of the toughest categories in NHRA drag racing, and most competitors run Chevy-powered vehicles. It is not so with this Falcon, which screams down the ¼-mile with Ford's finest under the hood.

"...breathtaking experience."

"Power and speed are everything at this level of NHRA racing, and one drive in this Falcon will show you that this little car delivers a lot of both. Strap yourself securely into the lightweight bucket seat, switch on the fuel pump and flip the starter switch. With around 700 bhp, the driving experience is breathtaking. Once you hit the gas, all you can do is just sit there and hold on as the car starts up and then rockets down the strip covering the ¼-mile in less than 10 seconds."

A custom-built interior houses a pair of lightweight buckets and a B&M shifter.

Milestones

1960 Ford launches its compact Falcon, an utterly conventional car offered in two- and four-door sedan forms or as a station wagon. A 144-c.i. inline six is the only engine available. In its debut year an incredible 435,676 are built.

Sprints finally got a V8 in 1963, in keeping with their sporty nature.

1961 A bigger, 170-c.i. six becomes available and a Futura coupe (with bucket seats) is added to the range, in an attempt to add sportiness. Falcon output this year numbers 474,191 units.

1965 was the last year for sprints and convertibles.

1963 The Futura becomes a separate series and a convertible is added to the range. A 260-c.i. V8 is also made available in the Futura this year. A redesigned Falcon arrives for the 1964 model year.

UNDER THE SKIN

Narrowed live axle on upper and lower links

Four-wheel disc brakes

Tubular steel chassis

Monster big-block V8

Little stock

It may look like a 1963 Falcon from the outside, but underneath it bears little resemblance. The chassis is a custom-built tubular-steel affair, with a four-link rear suspension and a narrowed 9-inch axle on Koni coil-over shocks. At the front, the radical Falcon employs Morrison struts and a power rack-and-pinion steering rack. A Panhard rod helps control sideways movement at the rear and disc brakes help the car stop.

THE POWER PACK

Simply overkill

With 164 bhp from its 260 V8, the 1963 Falcon Futura Sprint was quite a peppy little mover in its day, but this one gets its motivation from something bigger. Sitting in the custom-built chassis is a huge 460 V8 (Ford's largest production passenger car engine). It has been bored and stroked and has steel Manley Chevy rods pinned to Probe 13.5:1-compression pistons. It has a solid-lifter Crane camshaft that opens and closes the valves in a pair of ported and polished J. Bittle heads. Up top there's a Ford Performance aluminum intake manifold and a monster 1050-cfm Holley Dominator carburetor.

Sprinter

If you ask any Falcon aficionado which would be the best pick, a 289-poweredSprint convertible from 1964-1965 would be it. The earlier cars are great machines; simple, plentiful and relatively easy to build into a killer street or strip warrior.

Falcons are quite rare in Southern California Super Gas events.

It may resemble a 1963 Falcon, but this car is almost totally custom fabricated. Perhaps the most interesting thing about it is that the shell is actually from a convertible, with a hardtop from another Falcon grafted on.

Lightweight bumpers

Shaving as many pounds as possible was of primary concern when building this car. That approach extends to the bumpers, which are fiberglass items and have been sectioned to make them fit as close to the body as possible.

Killer V8

With a genuine 500 cubic inches and a huge 1050-cfm carburetor, this engine makes a tremendous amount of horsepower, more than 700, in fact. This enables the bantam weight Falcon to scream down the quarter-mile in just 9.2 seconds.

Custom interior

A whole new interior has been fabricated from aluminum sheeting, including the dash and the transmission tunnel (on which sits a B&M shifter for the Powerglide transmission). Safety is courtesy of a roll cage and Simpson twin harnesses.

Strut front suspension

Stock Falcons came with a short-long-arm front suspension and coil-over shocks, but both the stock chassis and IFS have been replaced by a pair of Morrison struts. In the interest of weight transfer, the anti-roll bar has been omitted and lightweight wheels, with skinnies, have been fitted.

Free-flowing exhaust

To expel the spent gases as quickly as possible, the big motor has a pair of Hooker 2½-inch diameter headers bolted to it. Besides getting rid of the spent gases, they help the engine make a truly thunderous trip down the strip.

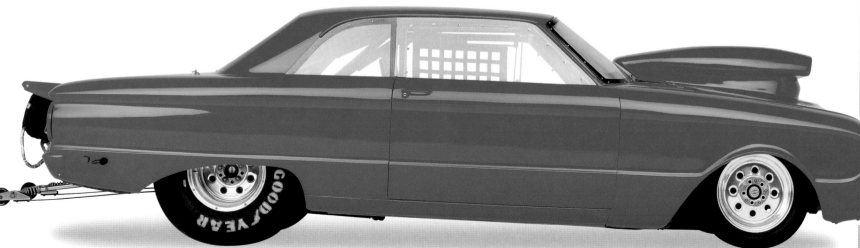

Specifications

1963 Ford Falcon Sprint

ENGINE

Type: V8

Construction: Cast-iron block with alloy heads

Valve gear: Two valves per cylinder operated by a single V-mounted camshaft with pushrods and rockers

Bore and stroke: 4.39 in. x 4.125 in.

Displacement: 500 c.i.

Compression ratio: 13.5:1

Induction system: Holley Dominator 1050-cfm four-barrel carburetor

Maximum power: 710 bhp at 7,000 rpm

Maximum torque: 685 lb-ft at 5,200 rpm

Top speed: 230 mph

0-60 mph: 2.8 sec.

TRANSMISSION

Powerglide two-speed automatic

BODY/CHASSIS

Tubular-steel chassis with two-door hardtop body

SPECIAL FEATURES

Lexan glass is used for all windows to save as much weight as possible.

Wheelie bars help keep the car straight off the tree.

RUNNING GEAR

Steering: Rack-and-pinion

Front suspension: Morrison struts, lower control arms and telescopic shock absorbers

Rear suspension: Live axle, four-bar links, coil springs, telescopic shock absorbers and Panhard rod

Brakes: Discs (front and rear)

Wheels: Centerline lightweight

Tires: BFGoodrich radial T/A (front), Goodyear Drag Slicks (rear)

DIMENSIONS

Length: 183.7 in. **Width:** 70.8 in.

Height: 51.5 in.

Wheelbase: 109.5 in.

Track: 56.9 in. (front), 48.5 in. (rear)

Weight: 2,015 lbs.

Ford **FALCON**

In the early 1960s, Ford embarked on its 'Total Performance' sales campaign. It also brought a number of Ford Falcons to Europe for use in racing and rallying, where they performed incredibly well.

"...means business."

"With its full roll cage and gutted interior, you can tell that this Falcon means business. Turn the key and the 289-cubic inch V8 rumbles to life. Thanks to its side mounted exhaust, the sound is impressive. Being fairly compact and light, the Falcon makes the most of its power and pulls hard in all gears. With stiffer springs than stock, a front anti-roll bar, and large tires it tackles sharp corners with enthusiasm, understeering mildly.

Only the bare essentials are retained, with just a single bucket seat for the driver.

Milestones

1960 Ford introduces its new compact car, the Falcon. It proves a tremendous success with 410,876 examples built.

1961 Midway through the year a sporty Falcon Sprint model is revealed with bucket seats and V8 power.

1964 Falcons gained boxier styling than the 1963 car.

1962 Ford begins its total performance campaign and sends race-prepared Falcons to Europe for use in rallying events.

1963 Driving a Falcon, Bo Ljungfeldt achieves a class win in the Monte Carlo Rally.

The Falcon Sprint was also available as a convertible.

1964 Restyled Falcons continue to do battle but are soon replaced in rallying by the sportier Mustang. The survivors continue in use as road racers through the 1960s.

UNDER THE SKIN

Mild alterations

Live rear axle

Independent front suspension

Unitary construction

Small-block V8

Underneath, the car basically remains stock, with unequal-length wishbones up front and a live rear axle. The front coil and rear leaf springs have been stiffened and a front anti-roll bar helps handling. Brakes are typical for the era with front discs and rear drums.

THE POWER PACK

High Performance

European competition Falcons used the High Performance 289-cubic inch V8. Typical of the times, it was a cast iron unit with two valves per cylinder. It developed 271 bhp, 46 more than the standard unit thanks to a slightly higher compression ratio, increased carburetor velocity, a higher-lift camshaft, and free-flowing exhaust headers. Although potent in this trim, the small-block V8 could be easily tweaked for more power and was the same engine used in the Shelby Mustangs.

High-lift camshaft

Free-flowing exhaust headers

Solid valve lifters

Cast-iron block and cylinder heads

Falcon Futura

For rallying, Ford campaigned Futura Sprint two-door hardtops with fiberglass body panels and standard 289 V8s. After their rallying career was over, a handful were raced in the British Saloon Car Championship until the early 1970s.

After rallying, a few Falcons raced in the British Saloon Car Championship.

While high performance Falcons were generally used for drag racing in the U.S., the European-spec cars had a more powerful engine and were successfully campaigned as road racers in the 1960s.

V8 engine

This Falcon has considerable go thanks to the 289 cubic inch V8 engine. This was the powerplant that made the cars highly competitive in rallying and circuit racing during the 1960s and continues to do so in historic events today.

Crisper styling

Falcons were restyled for 1964, with squarer, neater lines and a concave grille. This restyle carried over into 1965 with few changes. V8 engines transformed the Falcon's performance image.

Stiffened suspension

For more responsive handling, the springs have been stiffened. Today, Falcons demonstrate excellent poise in FIA historic racing events across Europe.

Original-style brakes

Under FIA rules, even the original braking set up of front discs and rear drums must be retained. Braking ability contrasts sharply with modern machinery.

Fiberglass body panels

In order to reduce weight and increase performance the front fenders, hood and trunk are made from fiberglass.

Four-speed transmission

Manual transmissions are essential for track racing so this Falcon features an original equipment Borg Warner T-10 four-speed transmission.

Specifications
1964 Ford Falcon

ENGINE

Type: V8

Construction: Cast-iron block and heads

Valve gear: Two valves per cylinder operated by pushrods and rockers

Bore/stroke: 4 in. x 2.87 in.

Displacement: 289 c.i.

Compression ratio: 10.5:1

Induction system: Twin four-barrel Holley cfm 600 carburetors

Maximum power: 271 bhp at 6,000 rpm

Maximum torque: 312 lb-ft at 3,400 rpm

Top speed: 135 mph

0-60 mph: 6.4 sec.

TRANSMISSION

Borg Warner T-10 four-speed

BODY/CHASSIS

Steel monocoque with two-door body

SPECIAL FEATURES

Circular taillights are a trademark of early 1960s Fords.

The elastic retaining strap on the hood looks crude but was actually homologated by Ford for racing.

RUNNING GEAR

Steering: Recirculating ball

Front suspension: Unequal length wishbones, coil springs, telescopic shocks and 1-in. dia. anti-roll bar

Rear suspension: Live rear axle with semi-elliptic leaf springs and telescopic shocks

Brakes: Discs to front, drums to rear

Wheels: 7 x 15 Minilite spoked alloy wheels

Tires: 205 60R 15

DIMENSIONS

Length: 180.2 in. **Width:** 76.6 in.

Height: 52.4 in. **Wheelbase:** 109.5 in.

Track: 47.5 in. (front), 43.1 in. (rear)

Weight: 2,811 lbs.

USA 1965

Ford FALCON RANCHERO

Adopting the compact Falcon platform in 1960, the Ranchero continued to tempt those who were looking for a recreational pickup truck. The V8 powerplant, light weight and unitary chassis all helped to make these vehicles excellent alternatives for those into modified cars.

"...no ordinary Ranchero."

"Rancheros were always among the most spartan Falcon derivatives, and this one maintains that theme. It has a front bench seat and a horizontal sweep speedometer, but the Grant steering wheel and aftermarket tach indicate that this is no ordinary Ranchero. Modern small-block power means this truck is a great daily driver, with ample power to spare. It will sprint to 60 mph in less than eight seconds, but the fun does not stop there —it can stop and take corners, too."

Grant GT steering wheel and tach give an almost competition feel to the cabin.

Milestones

1960 Ranchero transfers to the new compact Falcon chassis and is advertised as 'America's lowest price pickup' retailing for just $1,882. Powered by a 144-cubic inch, 90-bhp six, 21,027 are built.

Falcon got its first major restyling and V8 power for the 1964 model year.

1964 The Falcon gets a facelift, as does the Ranchero. A 200-cubic inch six and a 260-cubic inch V8 are options.

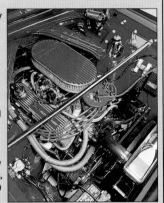

1965 would mark the last year for the Falcon Ranchero.

1965 A new grill with a center divider and revised trim marks this year's Ranchero. Performance gets a boost in the shape of two 289-cubic inch V8s, the latter boasting an Autolite four-barrel carb and 225 bhp. Production of Falcon-based Rancheros reaches 10,539 this year.

1966 Ranchero adopts the mid-size chassis.

UNDER THE SKIN

Car derived

Rancheros were essentially Falcon wagons under the skin, sharing their stiffer rear springs—essential for carrying heavy loads. The Falcon was a conventional car with a unitary body/chassis, independent-wishbone front suspension with coil springs, and a live axle at the rear. The suspension under this Ranchero remains mostly stock but has 1969 Mustang front disc brakes and traction bars.

Unitary construction

Front disc brakes

Leaf-sprung live rear axle

Fortified small-block V8

THE POWER PACK

Modern update

Early Falcons were powered exclusively by six-cylinder engines, though beginning in 1964, V8s began finding their way under the hood. This particular car originally came with a 200-bhp, 289, two-barrel V8, but this is long gone. A 1980 302-cubic inch small block has taken the original power plant's place. This engine, an outgrowth of the 289, originally produced just 130 bhp and 222 lb-ft of torque, but thanks to an Edelbrock Performer camshaft, intake manifold and carburetor, a recurved distributor, Heddman free-flow exhaust headers and Flowmaster mufflers, it puts out considerably more power—200 bhp and 285 lb-ft of torque.

Most athletic

Trimmest, and offering perhaps the greatest performance potential of all Rancheros, the Falcon-based pickup can be had for a very reasonable price today, and with the right modifications it can make for an excellent yet distinctive daily driver.

Based on its styling, the 1965 model is perhaps the nicest Ranchero of all.

The original car-based pickup, the Ranchero uncovered a new market during the late 1950s and early 1960s. Although it has been long out of production, it is still a well-respected cruising vehicle.

In view of performance
To improve torsional stiffness, this Ranchero has a shock-tower brace and stiffener between the fenders. This helps it handle much better than a similar stock example.

Later engine
Replacing the original 289 is a version of its successor, the 302. This one has been fitted with a classic 1960s-style chrome dress-up kit, but modern enhancements such as an Edelbrock intake and carburetor ensure that it is less temperamental and produces more power than a comparable 1960s engine.

Free-flowing exhaust
This Ranchero has been fitted with tubular Heddman headers and full-length dual Flowmaster pipes, resulting in a wonderful sound and quick 0-60 mph acceleration.

Stiffer suspension
Compared to standard Falcon sedans, Rancheros have stiffer rear springs in order to cope with the heavier loads. This means that hot-rodded versions suffer from poor weight transfer and traction with the bed unloaded. This problem has been cured somewhat on this car by using traction bars on the rear leaf springs.

Stock body
Virtually stock, the only modifications made to the body have been a respray in PPG Burgundy Pearl paint and the addition of a pair of 1969 Fairlane exterior door mirrors.

Late-model rubber
Tire technology has improved handling and grip beyond all other modifications since the 1960s. BF Goodrich radials feature a meaty 8 x 15 inches at the front and 10 x 15 inches at the back.

Specifications
1965 Ford Falcon Ranchero

ENGINE

Type: V8

Construction: Cast-iron block and heads

Valve gear: Two valves per cylinder operated by pushrods and rockers

Bore and stroke: 4.00 in. x 3.00 in.

Displacement: 302 c.i.

Compression ratio: 9.5:1

Induction system: Edelbrock Performer four-barrel carburetor

Maximum power: 200 bhp at 4,400 rpm

Maximum torque: 285 lb-ft at 3,200 rpm

Top speed: 120 mph

0-60 mph: 7.4 sec.

TRANSMISSION

Borg Warner T-10 four-speed manual

BODY/CHASSIS

Steel unitary chassis with two-door pickup body

SPECIAL FEATURES

Fender badges signify this Ranchero originally came with a 289-c.i. V8.

Centerline billet wheels add a 1990s theme to this custom pickup.

RUNNING GEAR

Steering: Recirculating ball

Front suspension: Unequal-length A-arms with coil springs, telescopic shock absorbers and stabilizer bar

Rear suspension: Live axle with semi-elliptic leaf springs, traction bars and telescopic shock absorbers

Brakes: 9.5-in. discs (front), 9.0-in. drums (rear)

Wheels: Centerline billet, 8 x 15 in. (front), 10 x 15 in. (rear)

Tires: BF Goodrich, 15-in. dia.

DIMENSIONS

Length: 190.0 in.   **Width:** 71.6 in.

Height: 54.2 in.   **Wheelbase:** 109.5 in.

Track: 55.9 in. (front), 53.3 in. (rear)

Weight: 2,820 lbs.

Ford MUSTANG

Following its 1964 launch, the Mustang was a massive hit. Creating a place in the pony car market, its sales continued to increase. A modification of a 1966 car was the next step for this almost perfect package.

"...no ordinary Mustang."

"Do not be fooled by its looks; this is no ordinary Mustang. Underneath there have been a multitude of changes. The supercharged engine delivers considerable power, and the modified chassis gives more stability and poise than the original. Great attention has been paid to the interior, which blends well with the orange exterior. You would be hard-pressed to find a better example of a 1966 Mustang."

The carpet of this car is taken from Mercedes and it certainly looks elegant.

Milestones

1961 Inspirational Ford President Lee Iacocca decides that the company should produce a sporty-looking car. Prototypes are built using a German four-cylinder engine.

1966 Mustangs came as convertibles as well as hardtops.

1964 Six months ahead of the 1965 calendar year, Ford releases the Mustang. It is an instant hit, sparking a host of imitators from other manufacturers as the pony car war heats up.

The Mustang's first major design changes were introduced on the 1967 model, a bigger car.

1974 After a series of styling changes, the original Mustang is replaced by the Mustang II. Initially a strong seller, it falls victim to the impending oil crisis and becomes a bloated, underpowered version of its previous self. Sales suffer as a result.

UNDER THE SKIN

Omni steering rack

DOHC 4.6L modular engine shock absorbers

Four wheel disc brakes

All-alloy V8

Uprated chassis

The original 1966 Mustang has a simple chassis layout that was adequate for the times, but feels its age now. Many changes have been made in the suspension. Up front, Mustang II parts have been incorporated and a chrome Ford 9-inch axle is in the rear. Disc brakes have been installed all around. Transmission is a Ford AOD-E automatic with a Lokar shifter. The rack-and-pinion steering is taken from a Dodge Omni.

THE POWER PACK

4.6 Liter "modular" V8

In 1966, the Mustang was available with a 200-c.i. inline six or a 289-c.i V8, in either 200 bhp or 225/271 bhp state of tune. The venerable cast-iron motor was considered too heavy for this Mustang and has been replaced by a 32-valve, 4.6 liter modular Ford V8 unit with all-alloy construction. From its relatively small displacement, 281 c.i., it produces 392 bhp with the aid of a Kenne Bell twin-screw whipplecharger running at 6 pounds of boost. This is in combination with a multipoint electronic fuel-injection system and a modern engine layout of four valves per cylinder operated by four chain-driven overhead camshafts.

Dynamite

For some people, the pre-1967 Mustangs are the best of the breed. The lines are uncluttered and classic. When mated with a stiff chassis and powerful engine, excellence is created—exactly what this 1966 example is.

Tasteful modifications have not betrayed the Mustang's good looks.

If you like the looks but not the performance, what can you do? Build your ideal car, of course. With nearly 400 bhp and a chassis that can handle the power, this Mustang would be your dream car.

Supercharged engine

To get phenomenal performance from the Mustang, a 32-valve, all-alloy 4.6 liter "modular" Ford V8 engine, from a late-model Mustang Cobra, has been fitted. The power has been upped to 392 bhp by the addition of a Kenne Bell supercharger running at 6 pounds of boost.

Tangerine dream

Completing the modified look is the tangerine pearl custom paint scheme. The side scallops are finished in a blend of gold pearl and candy root beer.

Billet grill

A lot of attention has been paid to the look of this car. This is illustrated by the six-bar chrome front grill and the five-bar rear fascia, which incorporates 900 LEDs.

Four-wheel disc brakes

To balance the enhanced performance, disc brakes have been installed. At the front these are 11 inches in diameter with 9-inch ones at the rear.

Custom interior

As much work has gone into customizing the interior as modifying the mechanicals of this car. There are two shades of leather upholstery, cream and biscuit. There is also a wool carpet from a Mercedes, as well as modified 1965 T-Bird front seats.

Upgraded suspension

As with many modified first-generation Mustangs, this car uses the coil-sprung front suspension from the Mustang II. A chrome 9-inch rear axle combines with a Global West stage III suspension system out back.

ENGINE

Type: V8

Construction: Alloy block and heads

Valve gear: Four valves per cylinder operated by four chain-driven overhead cams.

Bore and stroke: 3.61 in. x 3.60 in.

Displacement: 281 c.i.

Compression ratio: 9.8:1

Induction system: Multipoint fuel injection with Kenne Bell twin-screw whipple supercharger

Maximum power: 392 bhp at 5,800 rpm

Maximum torque: 405 lb-ft at 4,500 rpm

Top speed: 141 mph

0-60 mph: 4.3 sec.

TRANSMISSION

Three-speed automatic

BODY/CHASSIS

Steel chassis with steel body

SPECIAL FEATURES

Even the trunk has been upholstered in matching fabrics.

Budnick alloy wheels are a fine addition to the car.

RUNNING GEAR

Steering: Rack-and-pinion

Front suspension: A-arms with coil springs and telescopic shock absorbers

Rear suspension: Live rear axle with leaf springs and telescopic shock absorbers

Brakes: Discs, 11-in. dia. (front), 9-in. dia. (rear)

Wheels: Alloy, 17 x 7 in. (front); 17 x 8 in. (rear)

Tires: Toyo 215/45ZR17 (front), 245/45ZR17 (rear)

DIMENSIONS

Length: 176.0 in. **Width:** 71.0 in.

Height: 50.3 in. **Wheelbase:** 108.0 in.

Track: 58.6 in. (front and rear)

Weight: 2,358 lbs.

Ford MUSTANG BOSS 429

The Boss 429 Mustang was built to satisfy Ford's need to qualify at least 500 production vehicles with its new engine for NASCAR racing. Rather than putting the engine in the mid-size Torinos it ran in stock car racing, Ford put the engine in the sleek and exciting Mustang fastback instead.

"...a rippling mass of power."

"Those who expected the Mustang Boss 429 to be a Corvette® killer were disappointed by its true intent. With a semi-hemi engine that offered high-revving performance, the Boss 429 was a rippling mass of power, but was somewhat disappointing behind the wheel. It's at 6000 rpm and above where the 429 NASCAR engine makes its power, so its not much of a street dominator. It's hard to imagine why Ford made such a car. But the Boss 429 was actually a successful homologation exercise."

All Boss 429s were treated with plush interiors and an 8,000 rpm tachometer.

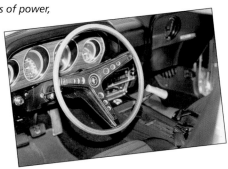

Milestones

1969 The Mustang

is redesigned with a sleeker body. Performance models include 857 Boss 429s, built to sanction Ford's new NASCAR 429 V8 engine. Once the Boss 429s were homologated for NASCAR, race-prepared Torinos known as Talladegas used the massive V8s. Ford took the title away from Dodge's Hemi Daytonas with more than 30 wins in the 1969 season thanks to the brawny 429 engines.

The early Shelby GT350 was the forerunner of the Boss Mustang.

1970 Mild restyling

for the second, and last, year of the Boss 429 includes a new nose, a revised tail light panel, plus a black hood scoop. Minor engine modifications include solid lifters. Again, Ford uses the same combination for NASCAR. Unfortunately, Plymouth's aerodynamic Hemi Superbird proves to be more successful.

The fearsome 428 Cobrajets were more fun on the street than the Boss 429s.

UNDER THE SKIN

Not quite stock

The Boss 429 features an altered front suspension, with relocated shock absorbers, which results in a wider track. All Boss 429s were equipped with a 4-speed Top Loader transmission, Traction Lok differential, relocated battery, front and rear stabilizers, quicker power steering and power front disc brakes.

Traction Lok differential with 3.91:1 gears

Massive '429' hood scoop

Chin spoiler

Wider front track

Big-block V8

THE POWER PACK

Bred for racing

This 429 engine was a homologation exercise—at least 500 had to be built to allow it to race in NASCAR, so it was no ordinary engine. It has four-bolt mains, forged steel crankshaft, high (10.5:1) compression, semi-hemi combustion chambers (similar to Chrysler's Hemi), Holley 735 cfm four-barrel carb, and headers. It could easily rev past 6,000 rpm. The big 429 engine was put in the restyled Mustang and not the mid-size Torinos it was used in for NASCAR racing.

Holley 735 cfm carburetor

Semi-hemi combustion chambers

Forged-steel crankshaft

10.5:1 compression

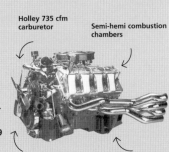

Race-bred?

In 1969, muscle car fans thought Ford had built a car to run with the big-block Corvettes. They were saddened to learn that the car was made to homologate the engine for use in NASCAR racing. Despite being a rev-happy engine, the Boss 429 could run the ¼ mile in 14 seconds. It was the most expensive non-Shelby Mustang.

Solid lifters, which allow for higher rpm, were used in 1970 Boss 429s.

Built for just two model years, the Boss 429 is one of the rarest and most valuable of all Mustangs. The homologated high-performance Boss 429 engine, however, earned Ford 30 wins in the 1969 NASCAR season.

Deluxe interior

All 429s have a deluxe interior with full instrumentation, including an 8,000 rpm tachometer deeply inset into the dashboard and improved seats, but air conditioning was not an option.

Front spoiler

A functional front airdam was optional. At highway speeds, it offers little aerodynamic advantage, however.

Close-ratio transmission

A close-ratio, four-speed manual is the only transmission available on the Boss 429. Automatics weren't strong enough and couldn't handle the 429's torque.

Trunk-mounted battery

The huge and heavy V8 leaves little room for anything else in the tightly-packed engine bay, including the battery. Ford engineers were forced to relocate it to the trunk.

Modified front suspension

As well as having the stiffest springs fitted to any Mustang up to that time, the Boss 429 has a thick, 1⁹⁄₁₆-inch diameter, front anti-roll bar and revalved shocks.

429-cubic inch engine

The 429s cylinder heads were so wide that not only did the battery have to be mounted in the trunk, but the shock towers had to be spread apart just to get the engine to fit.

Specifications

1969 Ford Mustang Boss 429

ENGINE

Type: V8

Construction: Cast-iron block and aluminum cylinder heads

Valve gear: Two valves per cylinder operated by a block-mounted camshaft

Bore and stroke: 4.36 in. x 3.59 in.

Displacement: 429 c.i.

Compression ratio: 10.5:1

Induction system: Four-barrel carburetor

Maximum power: 375 bhp at 5,200 rpm

Maximum torque: 450 lb-ft at 3,400 rpm

Top speed: 118 mph

0-60 mph: 6.8 sec.

TRANSMISSION

Top Loader close-ratio manual transmission

BODY/CHASSIS

Steel-frame chassis with steel two-door fastback body

SPECIAL FEATURES

These distinctive side scoops are unique to the 1969 model Boss 429.

The engine left no room for a battery or an air conditioning compressor.

RUNNING GEAR

Steering: Recirculating ball

Front suspension: Upper and lower wishbones, coil springs, telescopic shocks and anti-roll bar

Rear suspension: Live axle with semi-elliptical leaf springs, staggered telescopic shocks and anti-roll bar

Brakes: Discs front, drums rear

Wheels: Magnum 500, 7 in. x 15 in.

Tires: Goodyear Polyglas GT F60 x 15 in.

DIMENSIONS

Length: 187 in.   **Width:** 72 in.

Height: 49 in.   **Wheelbase:** 108 in.

Track: 59.3 in. (front), 58.8 in. (rear)

Weight: 3,870 lbs.

Ford MUSTANG BOSS 302

With its Mustangs getting trounced both on the street and on the race track by the ferocious Camaro Z28s, the Blue Oval brigade needed a solution. They found it in the small-block powered Boss 302, which was offered for 1969 and 1970.

"...really handles."

"High-back bucket seats and deeply set instruments take you back to the early 1970s. Start the small-block V8 and listen to the noisy solid lifters. Put the T-handle shifter into first gear and hit the gas. The big Polyglas tires have excellent bite and soon the car is in motion. To really get the most out of the V8, it needs to be revved above 4,000 rpm. Once there, it really makes maximum power. Thanks to its wide track, the Boss 302 handles well."

This Boss has the deluxe three-spoke wheel, but not the optional center console.

Milestones

1968 'Bunkie' Knudsen and stylist Larry Shinoda arrive at Ford from GM. One of their ideas is to position the Mustang as the sporty image-leader, with a 429-powered car and a small-block spinoff. Larry Shinoda designs the stripe package for the small-block car, and also coins the name Boss 302.

Bigger brother to the Boss 302 is the Boss 429.

1969 Boss 302 production begins in April. All the cars are built at the Dearborn assembly plant initially; some 1970 models are built in Metuchen, New Jersey.

The 1969 Boss 302 had distinctive C-type side stripes.

1970 Revised decals and single headlights mark this year's Boss 302. A Shaker hood option is offered and the 302 engines are fitted with aluminum instead of chrome valve covers.

UNDER THE SKIN

Heavy-duty

Still riding a 108-inch wheelbase in 1969, the Mustang was bigger and heavier than the 1965 original. It retains unitary construction and an independent double-wishbone front suspension, while at the rear there is a live axle on semi-elliptic leaf springs. Boss 302s have heavy-duty springs, shocks and spindles.

THE POWER PACK

A happy marriage

Originally, it had been intended to fit Ford's new Trans Am homologation Mustang with a special Le Mans 302 V8 with tunnel port heads. Knudsen, realizing that the bigger 351 Cleveland would be the division's staple small-block for the early 1970s, decided that the best solution would be to mate the 302 block with 351 Cleveland heads. With canted valves, the new heads helped the little 302 make 290 bhp (the same as the tunnel port version), but at a reduced cost. All Boss 302 engines have forged-steel cranks and rods, four-bolt main caps, a four-barrel Holley carburetor and dual-point ignition.

Double bill

One of the most legendary Mustangs of all, the Boss 302 is, not surprisingly, one of the most collectible. Only 8,252 were built in total (the majority were 1970 models), making them rare today. The 1970 models boast a number of improvements.

Many Boss 302s were ordered with Magnum 500 wheels.

Ironically, the Boss 302 was conceived partly by those who had been involved with its major rival, the Camaro Z28. Nevertheless, the little Boss made its mark by capturing the 1970 Trans-Am manufacturers' title.

Four-speed transmission

Both 1969 and 1970 Boss 302s came with the proven Borg-Warner T-10 four-speed manual transmission. A Hurst shifter with a T-handle was standard equipment.

Small-block V8 engine

Mating the Cleveland heads to the 302 Windsor resulted in a high-winding screamer of an engine. Fitted with a Holley 780-cfm four-barrel, it was pegged at 290 bhp, but real-world figures were closer to 350 bhp.

Rear window slats

Stylist Larry Shinoda conceived a set of rear window slats. These look terrific and help keep the cabin cool. They hinge upward to permit cleaning the rear windows.

Aerodynamics

Larry Shinoda was experienced in the field of aerodynamics, thus the Boss has a functional front spoiler. An optional rear spoiler helps further increase downforce at speeds above 70 mph.

Rev limiter

One major problem found on the 1969 Boss 302 was the durability of the engine, particularly as it required such high revs to get the most from it. Life expectancy of the V8 was improved for 1970, thanks to smaller valves and a 6,000-rpm rev limiter.

Specifications

1970 Ford Mustang Boss 302

ENGINE

Type: V8

Construction: Cast-iron block and heads

Valve gear: Two valves per cylinder operated by a single V-mounted camshaft with pushrods and rockers

Bore and stroke: 4.00 in. x 3.00 in.

Displacement: 302 c.i.

Compression ratio: 10.6:1

Induction system: Holley four-barrel downdraft carburetor

Maximum power: 290 bhp at 5,800 rpm

Maximum torque: 290 lb-ft at 4,300 rpm

Top speed: 128 mph

0-60 mph: 6.5 sec.

TRANSMISSION

Borg-Warner T-10 four-speed manual

BODY/CHASSIS

Unitary steel chassis with two-door fastback body

SPECIAL FEATURES

Flip-out rear quarter windows were a standard feature on Fastback Mustangs in 1970.

All Boss 302s came with a Hurst T-handle shifter.

RUNNING GEAR

Steering: Recirculating-ball

Front suspension: Unequal-length A-arms with coil springs and telescopic shock absorbers

Rear suspension: Live axle with semi-elliptic leaf springs and telescopic shock absorbers

Brakes: Discs (front), drums (rear)

Wheels: Magnum 500, 15 x 7 in.

Tires: Goodyear Polyglas, F70-15

DIMENSIONS

Length: 187.4 in.   **Width:** 71.9 in.

Height: 53.5 in.   **Wheelbase:** 108.0 in.

Track: 60.9 in. (front and rear)

Weight: 3,227 lbs.

Ford MUSTANG BOSS 351

Based on the newly redesigned SportsRoof, the Boss 351 superseded the previous Boss 302 and 429 versions. It was larger and less distinctive in appearance, but was quicker, less temperamental and still offered fine handling for a large muscle car of the period.

"...great all around performer."

"Compared to its predecessor, the Boss 351 is a great all-around performer. It offers quicker off-the-line acceleration and enjoys high speed cornering, although it still remains susceptible to oversteer. The massive size of the Boss 351 means it feels a little unwieldy in traffic, plus the harsh ride and low-set driving position can be tiring, but muscle-era Mustang performance does not come much more user friendly than this."

The 1971 model was the first Mustang not to use a dual cowl dashboard layout.

Milestones

1969 With its 'Total Performance' campaign in full swing, Ford releases two limited-production special Mustangs, the Boss 302 and 429. The 302 is built to satisfy Trans Am rules and has a high-revving 302-cubic inch Windsor V8. A big-block version, the 429, uses a 'semi-Hemi' V8 and is designed as a homologation special so the race-prepared Talladegas can run these engines in NASCAR.

A total of 8,641 Boss 302s were built between 1969 and 1970.

1970 The Boss 302 continues in production, but the 351 Cleveland V8 engine is developed with canted valve heads. A new larger Mustang on an inch-longer wheelbase arrives for 1971, and a new Boss 351 replaces both previous Bosses.

In 1971, the biggest-engined Mustang was the Mach 1 429 CJ.

1971 With Ford having pulled out of racing, the Boss 351 is dropped halfway through the model year.

UNDER THE SKIN

Biggest ever

Unitary construction

Power front disc brakes

For 1971, the Mustang grew eight inches in length and had a 1-inch longer wheelbase. It still had a unitary body/chassis and double wishbone front suspension, with a leaf-sprung rear axle. But the Boss 351 features a stiffer competition suspension with staggered rear shocks and a thick anti-roll bar. There is a 9-inch rear end with 3.91:1 gears and a Traction-Lok differential. Power front disc brakes and a four-speed manual transmission are standard.

Staggered rear shock absorbers

351 Cleveland V8

THE POWER PACK

Baddest Boss?

The basis for the Boss 351 engine was the 351-cubic inch Cleveland V8. This cast-iron unit has canted-valve cylinder heads and huge ports in the intake manifold. For the Boss, the connecting rods were shot-peened and Magna-fluxed for strength, and forged aluminum pistons were specified, as was an aggressive camshaft with solid lifters. Atop the intake is a 750-cfm four-barrel carburetor. The result is an incredibly robust and powerful engine that cranks out 330 bhp.

Staggered valves

Solid lifters

Cast-iron block and cylinder heads

Magnafluxed forged-steel connecting rods

Final fling

While the Boss 351 isn't as popular as the Boss 302 or 429, it still has strong collectible status. The large Boss 351 was also one of the quickest cars to come out of Detroit in 1971. Only 1,806 Boss 351s were built before it was dropped.

Although collectible, Boss 351s are cheaper than earlier muscle Mustangs.

Ford released its largest ever Mustang in 1971, and the tip of the performance sword was the Boss 351. It was arguably the last of the true muscle Mustangs and today appeals to a generation of car enthusiasts.

Cleveland V8

The Boss 351 came with a 330-bhp 351 Cleveland V8. It has large angled valves and huge ports allowing it to breathe better than the 351 Windsor. It is strengthened to run safely at high rpm and high power.

Four-speed transmission

All 351s were equipped with a Hurst-shifted Borg-Warner T10 four-speed and a 9-inch differential with 3.91:1 final drive. This made it the quickest-accelerating Mustang in 1971.

Live axle

The 1971 Boss 351 has a heavy duty 9-inch rear axle and semi-elliptic leaf springs. Performance models have staggered rear shocks (one behind and one in front of the axle) to help reduce wheelspin off the line. Boss 351s also have a larger-diameter anti-roll bar.

Flat rear window

One of the main styling features of the 1971 model year SportsRoof Mustangs was a near-horizontal rear deck. Unfortunately it hindered rearward vision somewhat.

Wishbone front suspension

The double wish-bone front suspension features stiffer springs and shock absorbers and a massive front anti-roll bar. The suspension had been strengthened for the earlier Boss 302 with reinforcement to the shock housings and larger-diameter wheel spindles to withstand cornering forces.

Front discs

Boss 351s came standard with large, vented front disc brakes and smaller drums at the rear. They could stop the 351 in about 250 feet from 80 mph.

Polyglas tires

Back in 1971, very few cars had radials, and so Boss 351s ran on bias- ply tires. This one has the optional Goodyear Polyglas GTs and Magnum 500 wheels, which give it good at-the-limit handling.

Color-coded graphics

The air-scooped hood includes a color-coded center section. Dark-colored cars have this painted silver, while light-colored cars have it painted semi-gloss black. This reduces glare from the sunlight bouncing off the hood and into the driver's direct line of sight.

Specifications

1971 Ford Mustang Boss 351

ENGINE

Type: V8

Construction: Cast-iron block and heads

Valve gear: Two valves per cylinder operated by a single camshaft via pushrods, solid valve lifters and rockers

Bore and stroke: 4.0 in. x 3.0 in.

Displacement: 351 c.i.

Compression ratio: 11.0:1

Induction system: Autolite four-barrel carburetor

Maximum power: 330 bhp at 5,400 rpm

Maximum torque: 370 lb-ft at 4,000 rpm

Top speed: 116 mph

0-60 mph: 5.8 sec.

TRANSMISSION

Borg-Warner T10 four-speed manual

BODY/CHASSIS

Steel unitary chassis with two-door 2+2 SportsRoof body

SPECIAL FEATURES

Ram Air induction was standard on Boss 351s and optional on Mach 1s.

This car is unusual in that it has a two-spoke steering wheel in place of the deluxe leather-rimmed wheel.

RUNNING GEAR

Steering: Recirculating ball

Front suspension: Double wishbones with coil springs, telescopic shock absorbers and anti-roll bar

Rear suspension: Live axle with semi-elliptic leaf springs, angled telescopic shock absorbers and anti-roll bar

Brakes: Vented discs, 11.3-in. dia. (front), drums, 10-in. dia. (rear)

Wheels: Pressed-steel discs, 7 x 15 in.

Tires: Goodyear Polyglas GT, F60-15

DIMENSIONS

Length: 189.5 in. **Width:** 74.1 in.

Height: 50.1 in. **Wheelbase:** 109.0 in.

Track: 61.5 in. (front), 61.0 in. (rear)

Weight: 3,550 lbs.

Ford MUSTANG MACH 1

1973 was the final year of the big, original-style Mustang. The pick of the range was the Mach 1. It looked sporty, had special interior trim, competition suspension and standard V8 power. It was one of the most popular of Ford's ponycar range.

"...sporty aspirations."

"A standard 1973 Mustang is a long way from the original 1964 model. It became known as the Mustang that was bigger, heavier and plusher but not really as sporty as its forebearer. The Mach I, with its 302-cubic inch V8 changed that myth. It may not have a sense of urgency to it, but the Mach 1 offers adequate acceleration compared to other 1973 muscle missiles. The com-petition suspension virtually eliminates body roll, while ride comfort remains soft for a car with sporty aspirations."

The Mach 1's sporty theme extends to the cabin, with extra gauges and tach as standard.

Milestones

1969 The very first Mach 1 performance SportsRoof model is launched by Ford in response to demand.

A matte-black hood section with an aggressive hood scoop were typical trademarks of the 1969 Mach 1.

1971 The Mustang grows in all dimensions, addressing previous criticisms of cramped passenger space on early ponycars. There is extra space under the hood, too. Among other options, the 429 Cobra Jet V8 is offered, packing all of 375 bhp.

By 1974, in Mustang II guise, the Mach 1 was built for an environmentally conscious market.

1973 In its last year before it was replaced by the slimmer, more economical Mustang II (fitting, given the approaching fuel crisis), the Mustang is offered in a range of five variations topped by the sporty Mach 1.

UNDER THE SKIN

Competition bias

Front and rear anti-roll bars

Stiffened suspension

Leaf-sprung rigid rear axle

V8 varieties

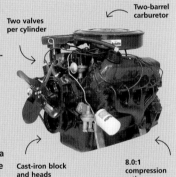

The sporty Mach 1 boasted a number of tweaks under the skin to justify this description, including a competition suspension package, anti-roll bars front and rear and bias-belted E70 x 14 tires. Otherwise, it shares the standard 1973 Mustang specification: independent coil front suspension, leaf-sprung live rear axle and drum brakes. Options included power steering, power front disc brakes, Cruise-O-Matic or Hurst four-speed trans-mission and various rear axle ratios.

THE POWER PACK

Two-barrel terror

In the 1973 Mustang lineup, the Mach 1 was the only model to come with a standard V8. The base V8 was the 302-cubic inch overhead-valve unit, fitted with a Motorcraft two-barrel carburetor. It made 136 bhp. For an extra $128 you could choose the 351-cubic inch Windsor V8 with the two-barrel carb and 156 bhp, or the 351 Cleveland with a two-barrel carb and 154 bhp. Among further options was a four-barrel 351 V8. It made much more power and had large-port cylinder heads and a different intake manifold.

Two valves per cylinder

Two-barrel carburetor

Cast-iron block and heads

8.0:1 compression ratio

Best of breed

Although it was hardly recognizable as a first generation Mustang, the 1973 model, though restyled, was just that. While the Mach 1 isn't the most desirable of the early 1970 Mustangs—the earlier Boss 351 model takes the top honors here—it was still very fast and sporty.

Of all the 1973 Mustangs, the Mach 1 is the most collectable today.

The Mach 1 line, which began in 1969, enhanced the sporty qualities of the Mustang, picking up on some of the themes of Carroll Shelby's modifications. The 1973 Mach 1 boasted a variety of enhancements.

Standard V8 power

All Mustangs for 1973 came with a six-cylinder engine as standard except the Mach 1, with its 302-cubic inch V8. Because it had an emissions-restricted output of 136 bhp, ordering one of the optional V8 engines was an attractive choice.

Competition suspension

Justifying its reputation as the sporty member of the Mustang group, the Mach 1 received a standard competition suspension, with heavy-duty front and rear springs and revalved shock absorbers.

SportsRoof style

The Mach 1 was offered in one body style only, a fastback coupe known as the SportsRoof. This is characterized by a near-horizontal rear roof line, in contrast to the cut-away style of the Mustang hardtop coupe. The rear window is tinted on the Mach 1 and a rear spoiler was optional.

Impact bumpers

In 1973 it was federally mandated that all cars had to have 5-mph impact protection bumpers. To try and retain its sporty appearance, the Mach 1's bumpers were painted the same color as the rest of the car.

Choice of hoods

Two hood styles were offered for the Mach 1—one had functional NACA-type ducts the other had non functional duct work. Two-tone hood paint was an option on all Mach 1s.

Specifications

1973 Ford Mustang Mach 1

ENGINE

Type: V8

Construction: Cast-iron block and heads

Valve gear: Two valves per cylinder operated by a single camshaft with pushrods and rocker arms

Bore and stroke: 4.00 in. x 3.00 in.

Displacement: 302 c.i.

Compression ratio: 8.5:1

Induction system: Single Motorcraft two-barrel carburetor

Maximum power: 136 bhp at 4,200 rpm

Maximum torque: 232 lb-ft at 2,200 rpm

Top speed: 110 mph

0-60 mph: 10.4 sec.

TRANSMISSION

Three-speed automatic

BODY/CHASSIS

Unitary monocoque construction with steel two-door coupe body

SPECIAL FEATURES

Fold-down rear seats allow access to the trunk from inside. It also permits more room to carry unusually long items.

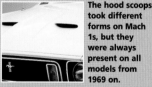

The hood scoops took different forms on Mach 1s, but they were always present on all models from 1969 on.

RUNNING GEAR

Steering: Recirculating ball

Front suspension: Wishbones with lower trailing links, coil springs, shock absorbers and anti-roll bar

Rear suspension: Live axle with semi-elliptic leaf springs, shock absorbers and anti-roll bar

Brakes: Discs (front), drums (rear)

Wheels: Steel, 14-in. dia.

Tires: E70 x 14

DIMENSIONS

Length: 189.0 in.   **Width:** 74.1 in.

Height: 50.7 in.   **Wheelbase:** 109.0 in.

Track: 61.5 in. (front), 59.5 in. (rear)

Weight: 3,090 lbs.

Ford MUSTANG GT

Fox-bodied Mustangs rekindled America's love affair with performance cars. An easy-to-tweak 5.0-liter V8 is just one reason why these cars are so popular. The owner of this particular car went wild bolting on many aftermarket body panels.

"...spaceship-like exterior"

"Similar to many of its rivals, the driver sits fairly low in the Mustang. The gauges are easy to read and an aftermarket monster tachometer keeps the driver totally informed. The reworked 5.0-liter V8 gives a loud roar when the accelerator pedal hits the floor and the tach needle hits 4,000 rpm. Unlike older Mustangs, this one handles like it's on rails. Its spaceship-like exterior has been modified and the only remaining factory panel is the roof, giving it a one-of-a-kind look."

A set of auxiliary gauges replaces the center air vents and everything is color-coded.

Milestones

1979 A new Mustang, with sharp-edged styling, makes its debut.

1982 After several years of pseudo-performance cars, Ford offers the genuine article in the shape of a new Mustang GT. Producing 157 bhp from a 302-cubic inch V8 and with sports suspension, it is fun to drive.

By 1984, the Mustang GT had a four-barrel carburetor and produced 175 bhp.

1987 A heavily-facelifted Mustang goes on sale. The V8 is available in both GT and LX models.

The pinnacle of 'Fox' Mustang development was the 1993 SVT Cobra.

1993 This year sees the end of 'Fox'-platform Mustangs, and a special Cobra is released. It looks similar to the GT, but has larger wheels and tires, slightly different styling and an engine tweaked to 240 bhp.

UNDER THE SKIN

Codename 'Fox'

Rear-wheel drive

MacPherson strut front suspension

In 1979 the Mustang adopted the 'Fox'platform, and for the next 14 years the chassis remained unchanged. It is of a unitary construction, with strut suspension at the front and a live axle at the rear. Common chassis upgrades include fitting lowering springs and replacing the rear drum brakes with discs.

Unitary construction

Fuel-injected V8

THE POWER PACK

The high five

The venerable 5.0-liter V8 has its origins in the 260-cubic inch thin-walled unit introduced in 1962. In 1982, a high-performance version of the engine re-emerged. It initially developed 157 bhp, but a switch to a four-barrel carburetor and then fuel injection resulted in 225 bhp by 1987. Power can be bumped up to 280 bhp by fitting a set of custom exhaust headers and a larger intake; by adding a supercharger 400 bhp is easily obtainable. Some units are stroked and fitted with nitrous to produce 600 bhp.

Tubular exhaust manifolds

Sequential electronic fuel injection

Cast-iron block and cylinder heads

Aluminum pistons

Street or track

'Fox'-platform Mustangs are an ideal base for one-off street machines. Most are turned into drag-style rides, but these cars also make fantastic street freaks as well. There is often no limit to what can be achieved, given the money and imagination.

Thanks to the aftermarket, modifications to 1980s Mustangs are limitless.

More than a million 'Fox' Mustangs were built between 1979 and 1993 and, today, they are perhaps America's favorite late-model street machines. In addition, an entire aftermarket industry is devoted to these cars.

V8 engine
The 5.0-liter V8 has been bored .030 over, fortified with ceramic-coated headers, a K&N filter, an ACUFAB Billet throttle body and a high-lift camshaft. This results in an increase of power from 225 to 370 bhp.

Opening hatch
An opening decklid offers a useful amount of space, but body stiffness suffers as a result.

Road racing suspension
Corner carving and head turning is what this Mustang GT was built to do. To help it zig, it has been lowered with a Saleen Racecraft suspension.

Steeper gearing
The Mustang 5.0-liter came with 2.73 or 3.08 rear gears. For better acceleration, the rear end has been fitted with 3.55 cogs.

Outlandish rear wing
Subtle is not a word used to describe this Mustang. It is modified with full MPH body extensions, including a large IMSA-type rear wing.

Cowl induction hood
A popular aftermarket addition is a fiberglass cowl induction hood. This draws high-pressure air from the base of the windshield, forcing it through the intake and thus increasing power.

Specifications

1987 Ford Mustang GT

ENGINE
Type: V8
Construction: Cast-iron block and heads
Valve gear: Two valves per cylinder operated by pushrods and rockers
Bore and stroke: 4.0 in. x 3.0 in.
Displacement: 306 c.i.
Compression ratio: 10.0:1
Induction system: Sequential electronic fuel injection
Maximum power: 370 bhp at 4,800 rpm
Maximum torque: 300 lb-ft at 3,000 rpm
Top speed: 150 mph
0-60 mph: 5.2 sec.

TRANSMISSION
Borg-Warner 'World Class' T-5 five-speed manual

BODY/CHASSIS
Unitary monocoque with steel and fiberglass three-door hatchback body

SPECIAL FEATURES

A very distinctive feature of this car is its high rear wing.

Ford's 5.0-liter V8 is an easy engine to tune for more power.

RUNNING GEAR
Steering: Recirculating ball
Front suspension: MacPherson struts with coil springs and telescopic shock absorbers
Rear suspension: Live axle with coil springs and quad telescopic shock absorbers
Brakes: Vented discs (front), discs (rear)
Wheels: HRE alloy, 10 x 17 in. (front), 13 x 17 in. (rear)
Tires: 17-in. dia

DIMENSIONS
Length: 178.0 in.　　**Width:** 78.2 in.
Height: 48.3 in.　　**Wheelbase:** 100.4 in.
Track: 63.0 in. (front), 64.0 in. (rear)
Weight: 3,560 lbs.

Ford MUSTANG LX

If any car deserves the credit for bringing back American performance, it is the Ford Mustang 5.0L. Though available in a variety of styles, enthusiasts who wanted unbridled power in an unassuming package ordered the LX notchback model.

"...legendary late model."

"In contrast to most of the late 1980s muscle cars, the 5.0 liter powered Mustangs were actually fast. With 300 lb-ft of torque only a prod of the throttle away, this legendary late model's rear tires will easily be set ablaze through second gear. Oversteer is a fact of life in the 5.0 LX and takes some getting used to. But, there's more to this boulevard brawler than outright power. With Goodyear Eagle ZR tires and large anti roll bars, this premier performer is a fine handler with pleasant road manners."

The LX's interior offers its driver easy-to-read instrumentation and supportive bucket seats.

Milestones

1984 The LX Series replaces the previous GL and GLX models. They are available with 175-bhp, 5.0-liter engines and uprated suspensions.

1985 saw a smoother exterior and beefier wheels and tires on performance models like this GT.

1985 Mustangs are facelifted with smoother front nose styling. The L versions are dropped, 15-inch wheels are available, and the carbureted 302 V8 in its last season is up to 210 bhp and 270 lb-ft of torque.

1986 Electronic fuel injection and 8.8-inch rear axles are standard on V8 models.

For 1987, GTs were dressed with attention-getting body panels and a large rear spoiler.

1987 A major facelift sees aero headlights, smoother glass and a redesigned instrument panel. Power is up to 225 bhp on the 5.0 liter V8.

1994 A new Mustang with swoopier styling is launched.

UNDER THE SKIN

11-inch-diameter front disc brakes

Quadra-Shock rear axle

Unitary construction

Small-block V8

Ubiquitous Fox

A member of the unitary Fox platform of Ford cars, the LX has a modified MacPherson strut front suspension and a live rear axle suspended by coil springs. All 5.0-liter-powered Mustang LXs received an upgraded suspension that included 1.30-inch front and 0.83-inch rear anti-roll bars and gas-pressurized shock absorbers and struts to further improve its roadholding ability.

THE POWER PACK

Fantastic five

The key to the Mustang's outstanding performance is its V8 engine. These cars ran circles around their larger-engined arch rivals: the Firebirds and Camaros. In fact, when it came to 1980s muscle, the 5.0 liter Mustang was at the top. Its powerful power plant is a variation of the 1968-vintage 302-cubic inch Windsor block. Performance made a comeback in 1982 with a special cam and exhaust system. The ultimate evolution of the engine arrived in 1986, with free-breathing heads, tubular exhaust manifolds, electronic fuel injection 19-lb fuel injectors and EEC-IV electronic engine management. Hypereutectic pistons were fitted in 1992. In 1993, the power rating changed from 225 to 205 bhp.

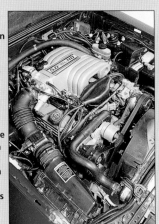

Street stripper

Most Fox-bodied Mustang aficionados will tell you that the LX coupe has the most bang for the buck. It has the same engine and running gear as the flashy GT but weighs less and benefits from a stiffer structure. The LX runs the ¼ mile in 14.3 seconds dead stock.

The LX notchback has the GT's get-up-and-go but without all the garb.

Between 1987 and 1993, the byword in American performance was Mustang. In fact, the V8-powered LX was so quick that law enforcement agencies across the country chose the car for high-speed patrol work.

High Output V8

Producing 225 bhp and 300 lb-ft of torque, the 5.0-liter V8 was the benchmark against which other U.S. performance cars were judged. Another factor in its popularity was the willingness with which the engine responded to modifications.

Embracing safety

Ford added a driver's airbag in 1990 but in the process deleted the tilt steering wheel option. The remote fuel filler release was also dropped that year.

Manual transmission

For the best ETs and acceleration, the Borg-Warner T-5 manual was the transmission of choice. Those into more sedate driving could order the AOD four-speed automatic and a 3.27:1 rear axle ratio This gear set wasn't available with the 5-speed.

Quadra-Shock rear suspension

With more torque than originally intended, wheel hop was a common problem on early 5.0-liter Fox Mustangs. A solution was to fit an extra pair of horizontally-opposed rear shocks.

Improved aerodynamics

Flush-mounted headlights, smoother taillights and slicker side glass fitted for 1987 helped reduce drag. From 1992 the only body styling enhancements to the LX models were body-colored side moldings.

Simple interior

LXs came with a basic interior, which includes standard manual windows and no air conditioning. Buyers could, however, add these as options.

Specifications

1992 Ford Mustang 5.0 LX

ENGINE

Type: V8

Construction: Cast-iron block and heads

Valve gear: Two valves per cylinder operated by pushrods and rockers

Bore and stroke: 4.00 in. x 3.00 in.

Displacement: 5.0 liter

Compression ratio: 9.2:1

Induction system: Sequential multipoint fuel injection

Maximum power: 225 bhp at 4,400 rpm

Maximum torque: 300 lb-ft at 3,000 rpm

Top speed: 138 mph

0-60 mph: 6.2 sec.

TRANSMISSION

Borg-Warner T-5 five-speed manual

BODY/CHASSIS

Steel unitary chassis with two-door coupe body

SPECIAL FEATURES

'Pony logo' wheels appear only on 1991-1993 Mustangs.

The High Output V8 produces a useful 225 bhp in this installation.

RUNNING GEAR

Steering: Rack-and-pinion

Front suspension: MacPherson struts with lower A-arms, telescopic shock absorbers and anti-roll bar

Rear suspension: Live axle with coil springs, trailing arms, telescopic shock absorbers and anti-roll bar

Brakes: Discs (front), drums (rear)

Wheels: Cast-aluminum, 7 x 16 in.

Tires: Goodyear Eagle ZR, P225/55 ZR16

DIMENSIONS

Length: 179.5 in.   **Width:** 68.3 in.

Height: 53.1 in.   **Wheelbase:** 100.5 in.

Track: 57.1 in. (front and rear)

Weight: 3,145 lbs.

Ford MUSTANG COBRA

With its 235 bhp and true muscle car performance, the 1993 Mustang Cobra was a fitting finale for the tremendously successful Fox-platform Mustang, which lasted an incredible 14 seasons with more than 2 million cars sold.

"...civilized performer."

"It takes a second glance to distinguish the Cobra from a regular GT, but once the car is in motion, the differences begin to surface. A lighter clutch makes for faster shifting and the small-block V8 has a useful increase in both power and torque. An SVT altered chassis and suspension mean that the Cobra has better grip than its stock counterpart. When it comes to hard cornering, the Cobra is reminiscent of the Shelby Mustangs of the 1960s."

The bland interior of the Cobra masks the exciting performance that can be unleashed.

Milestones

1987 The Mustang receives a facelift. All models get flush headlights, revised side glass and a new instrument panel. The series is reduced to just the LX and GT with two powerplants—a 2.3-liter four and 5.0-liter V8.

The two-door coupe was the most inexpensive model of the Mustang 5.0-liter lineup in 1993.

1989 Instead of an option package, the LX 5.0L becomes a separate model.

1990 A driver's airbag and door map pockets are standard.

For 1996, the Mustang Cobra got a new 305-bhp, 4.6-liter engine.

1991 LX 5.0Ls and GTs are fitted with bigger 16-inch wheels as standard.

1993 A special Cobra model is released.

UNDER THE SKIN

Subtle changes

Rear disc brakes

Modified MacPherson-strut front suspension

Gas-pressurized shock absorbers

Small-block V8

SVT's engineers took the basic 100.5-inch Fox-platform chassis, with its modified MacPherson-strut front suspension and coil-sprung live axle and added a few subtle improvements. The bushings in the rear upper control arms have been stiffened and the gas-pressurized shock absorbers have been softened. Combined with the bigger rolling stock it is easier to keep the rear in line under power. The rear disc brakes substantially improve braking.

THE POWER PACK

Legendary Powerplant

Possibly one of the most amazing traits of the 5.0L Mustang is its 302-cubic inch, small-block V8. The little Windsor unit cranked out a credible 205 bhp and 275 lb-ft of torque in 1993, but for the Cobra more performance was needed. A bigger throttle body and mass air meter were coupled with Ford Motorsport GT40 free-breathing cylinder heads, 24-lb. fuel injectors, stronger valve springs and a new intake plenum. A revised camshaft was specified with less overlap and roller rockers helped minimize valvetrain friction. The result was 30 more bhp and 10 lb-ft of torque, with 0-60 mph taking just 5.8 seconds.

Collectible

Besides being the best-performing factory Fox Mustang, the 1993 model is also the most collectible. Including the 107 "R" models, only 5,100 Cobras were built. They were sold at only 200 select SVT dealers. A clean, original Cobra can cost more than $20,000.

The limited availability of the Cobra has ensured its desirable status.

In many ways, the Cobra was a more subtle alternative to the GT. It boasts greater levels of performance and, at the same time, was more civilized. From the Dearborn factory, Cobras came with either red, black or teal paint.

Small-block V8 engine
Although power was only increased modestly from 205 to 235 bhp, it translated into a useful amount of mid-range grunt that greatly helped in the acceleration department.

Traction-Lok rear
All Mustangs with automatic transmissions could be ordered with 3.27:1 gears. Cars with 5-speed transmissions could only get gears as steep as 3.07:1.

Subtle styling changes
From the outside, the Cobra differs little from the GT. The front grill houses a running horse emblem, the side scoops have been eliminated and a new rear bumper and decklid spoiler fitted. The taillights are from the SVO.

Revised suspension tuning
Although the modified MacPherson-strut and coil-sprung live axle was retained, SVT engineers fitted stiffer bushings in the upper control arms and actually softened damping rates. The result is a smoother ride and greater cornering stability.

Minimal interior changes
The only difference between the Cobra and the GT is a set of Cobra-embroidered floor-mats. The dashboard, gauges and seats are all unchanged, and, like the GT, all Cobras came with power windows and mirrors.

Specifications

1993 Ford Mustang Cobra

ENGINE
Type: V8
Construction: Cast-iron block and heads
Valve gear: Two valves per cylinder operated by a single V-mounted camshaft
Bore and stroke: 4.0 in. x 3.0 in.
Displacement: 5.0 liter
Compression ratio: 9.0:1
Maximum power: 235 bhp at 5,000 rpm
Maximum torque: 285 lb-ft at 4,000 rpm
Top speed: 151 mph
0-60 mph: 5.8 sec.
Fuel system: Sequential multipoint electronic fuel injection

TRANSMISSION
Borg-Warner T-5 five-speed manual

BODY/CHASSIS
Steel unitary chassis with three-door hatchback body

SPECIAL FEATURES

The factory-fitted flip-open sunroof was available as an option.

The Cobra has a unique decklid spoiler with two center pedestals.

RUNNING GEAR
Steering: Rack-and-pinion
Front suspension: MacPherson struts, lower A-arm, coil springs and anti-roll bar
Rear suspension: Live axle with coil springs, semi-trailing arms, telescopic shock absorbers (two longitudinally, two horizontally) and anti-roll bar
Brakes: Vented discs, 10.8-in. (front), solid disc 10.1-in. (rear)
Wheels: Cast aluminum, 17x7.5 in.
Tires: Goodyear Eagle GT, P245/45 ZR17

DIMENSIONS
Length: 179.3 in. **Width:** 69.1 in.
Height: 52.1 in. **Wheelbase:** 100.5 in.
Track: 56.6 in. (front), 57.0 in. (rear)
Weight: 3,225 lbs.

Ford MUSTANG COBRA R

The name Cobra is synonymous with high-performance Ford automobiles. In 1995, Ford's Special Vehicle Team (SVT) unveiled a very special Mustang, which was built to compete on the track. It was known as the Cobra R.

"...well-balanced."

"Massive torque at low rpm is a good recipe and that's what the Cobra R has. All the power you're going to get has come by 4,800 rpm, and so there is no point revving the big motor beyond that; however the torque comes along with instant throttle response. It is a hard ride on anything but a smooth surface, but it's worth it as it turns a fine-handling Mustang into an excellent one—well-balanced and responsive with superb braking ability."

The Cobra is only equipped with the absolute necessities, which does not include a radio.

Milestones

1993 Ford builds a limited edition homologation special known as the Cobra R (R for race). All 107 cars were painted Vibrant Red and had a Cobra intake, strut tower brace, 13-inch front brakes and no rear seat.

Among the last of the Fox generation Mustangs was the limited production Cobra R.

1995 In the never-ending war with the Camaro Z28, Ford SVT fit a heavily-modified all-iron, pushrod, overhead-valve, 351-cubic inch V8 into the Mustang, which produces 300 bhp. Only 250 of the limited edition Cobra Rs are built.

For 1998 the Mustang Cobra received R-type alloy wheels.

1996 Both the GT and Cobra receive a new 4.6-liter V8 engine.

1998 The spirit of the Cobra R lives on in the standard 300-bhp, 4.6-liter Cobra, which is fitted with new R model type five-spoke alloy wheels.

UNDER THE SKIN

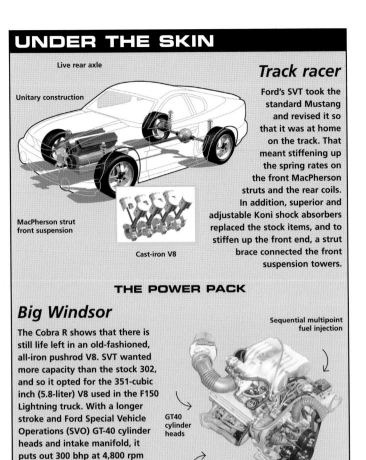

Live rear axle

Unitary construction

MacPherson strut front suspension

Cast-iron V8

Track racer

Ford's SVT took the standard Mustang and revised it so that it was at home on the track. That meant stiffening up the spring rates on the front MacPherson struts and the rear coils. In addition, superior and adjustable Koni shock absorbers replaced the stock items, and to stiffen up the front end, a strut brace connected the front suspension towers.

THE POWER PACK

Big Windsor

The Cobra R shows that there is still life left in an old-fashioned, all-iron pushrod V8. SVT wanted more capacity than the stock 302, and so it opted for the 351-cubic inch (5.8-liter) V8 used in the F150 Lightning truck. With a longer stroke and Ford Special Vehicle Operations (SVO) GT-40 cylinder heads and intake manifold, it puts out 300 bhp at 4,800 rpm and an incredible 365 lb-ft of torque at 3,750 rpm. On the street, few factory-stock cars can outdrag the muscular Cobra R.

Sequential multipoint fuel injection

GT40 cylinder heads

Tubular exhaust manifolds

Cast-iron block and cylinder heads

Less is more

Ford commissioned SVT to build only 250 1995 Cobra Rs. All are Crystal White and have minimal sound-deadening and no air-conditioning or radio. Although they were built for racing, the Rs are fully street legal and command premium prices.

Despite being built as a racer, the Cobra is surprisingly usable.

Produced by Ford's Special Vehicle Team as a limited production special and designed to compete in SCCA showroom stock racing, the Cobra R is the ultimate factory-stock SN95 Mustang.

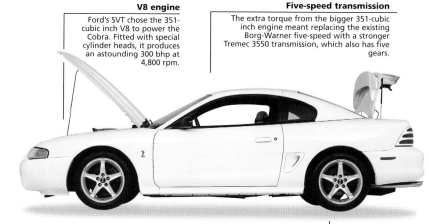

V8 engine

Ford's SVT chose the 351-cubic inch V8 to power the Cobra. Fitted with special cylinder heads, it produces an astounding 300 bhp at 4,800 rpm.

Five-speed transmission

The extra torque from the bigger 351-cubic inch engine meant replacing the existing Borg-Warner five-speed with a stronger Tremec 3550 transmission, which also has five gears.

Low-profile tires

The extra stiff suspension springs ensure the low-profile, unidirectional 245/45 ZR17 BF Goodrich Comp T/As remain 'square' to the track, so that the maximum amount of rubber is in contact with the road.

Huge fuel load

The thirsty, high-powered V8 engine required a change to the fuel tank for racing. The standard tank was swapped for a custom fabricated fuel cell. It has more resistance to rupturing on impact and a larger capacity of 20 gallons.

Adjustable brake balance

Braking in the Cobra R is excellent due to the combination of twin-piston calipers. What really sets it apart from a standard road car is the adjustable brake balance front to rear.

Composite hood

The flat factory hood has been replaced with this lightweight high rise cowl induction piece. The extra clearance is needed to fit the taller intake manifold.

Specifications

1995 Ford Mustang Cobra R

ENGINE

Type: V8

Construction: Cast-iron block and heads

Valve gear: Two valves per cylinder operated by pushrods and rockers

Bore and stroke: 4.00 in. x 3.50 in.

Displacement: 351 c.i.

Compression ratio: 9.2:1

Induction system: Electronic fuel injection

Maximum power: 300 bhp at 4,800 rpm

Maximum torque: 365 lb-ft at 3,750 rpm

Top speed: 150 mph

0-60 mph: 5.5 sec.

TRANSMISSION

Tremec 3550 five-speed manual

BODY/CHASSIS

Steel monocoque two-door coupe body

SPECIAL FEATURES

On all R models the foglights were removed to save weight, but the holes were left open. They feed air to a power steering and oil cooler.

A Cobra emblem on the injection plenum signifies that this is no run-of-the-mill Mustang.

RUNNING GEAR

Steering: Rack-and-pinion

Front suspension: Modified MacPherson struts with adjustable Koni inserts and anti-roll bar

Rear suspension: Live axle with upper and lower trailing links, coil springs, telescopic adjustable Koni shock absorbers and anti-roll bar

Brakes: Vented discs, 13.0-in. dia. (front), 11.65-in. dia. (rear)

Wheels: Alloy, 8 x 17 in.

Tires: BF Goodrich Comp T/A, 245/45 ZR17

DIMENSIONS

Length: 182.5 in. **Width:** 71.8 in.

Height: 53.2 in. **Wheelbase:** 101.3 in.

Track: 60.0 in. (front), 58.7 in. (rear)

Weight: 3,325 lbs.

Ford MUSTANG GT/SC

Although the Mustang enjoyed a performance renaissance during the 1980s, it did not have the same romance as the original. For 1994, an all-new retro-styled car arrived, which has become progressively more sophisticated.

"...truly refined performance."

"Compared to third-generation Mustangs, the current GT has much better ergonomics and feels tighter with no rattling or squeaking. The 4.6 liter modular V8, however, does not have as much torque and doesn't feel as fast as the 5.0-liter engine it replaced. Handling is noticeably better than the previous model and with much less understeer. Braking is excellent and safe, with standard ABS and four-wheel discs. The current 4.6 liter Mustang GT offers truly refined performance."

A twin-cowl dashboard layout is a retro touch which harks back to the original Mustang.

Milestones

1993 In the last month of the year the fourth-generation Mustang is launched in 3.8-liter V6 or 5.0-liter V8 forms, and in coupe or convertible body styles. The hatchback version is no longer offered.

Third-generation 5.0-liters were very powerful and had the same performance as 1960s muscle cars.

1994 The Mustang celebrates its 30th birthday and a 240-bhp Cobra version joins the range.

1995 A new modular 4.6-liter V8 engine arrives for 1996. All Mustangs receive new taillights and the GT gets revised 17-inch wheels.

The Mustang is heavily facelifted for 1999.

1998 Responding to criticisms of lack of power, the GT gets an additional 10 bhp. A standard value performance package is also offered to help boost flagging sales.

UNDER THE SKIN

Old hat

Although substantially revised for 1994, the current Mustang still shares characteristics of the 1979-1993 'Fox' platform, with a conventional front engined, rear-drive format. The front suspension uses modified MacPherson struts on lower 'A'-arms, with a standard front anti-roll bar. The rear is an 8.8-inch live axle which features both horizontal and vertical shocks to reduce axle tramp.

Live rear axle

Unitary construction

MacPherson strut front suspension

Modular V8

THE POWER PACK

Modular-mania

Known as the SN95, the current Mustang's base engine is a 3.8-liter V6. Early fourth-generation GTs were powered by the venerable 5.0 liter V8, although for 1996 this was replaced by a version of Ford's overhead-cam 'Modular V8.' Displacing 4.6 liters, this engine has an alloy block and cylinder heads, with a single overhead cam layout and a composite intake manifold. In current trim it puts out the same power as the old 5.0-liter unit—225 bhp—but with slightly less torque.

Single chain-driven camshaft per bank

Lightweight valvetrain

Teflon-coated pistons

Alloy block and heads

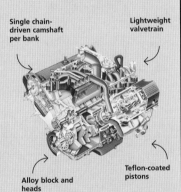

Five liter

Although the 4.6 is undeniably sophisticated, many prefer the 1994-1995 5.0-liter cars. The old pushrod V8 is still satisfying and simpler to maintain. Best of all, there is an abundance of speed equipment to make these cars go even faster.

Many enthusiasts prefer the older 5.0-liter Mustangs.

The GT was essentially a sport appearance package on the original Mustang and, since 1982, has been the mainstream performance variant. Current GTs are often loaded with options, although they still offer plenty of power.

Choice of body styles
Current Mustangs come in either two-door coupe or convertible forms. In the interests of torsional rigidity, the hatchback style, as seen on the 1979-1993 model, was discontinued.

Modern V8 engine
The Mustang underwent something of a revolution in 1996 when the old pushrod V8 was replaced by a modern overhead-cam unit. The engine, although smaller in displacement (4.6 liters versus 5.0 liters), comes close to duplicating the power of the 5.0 liter engine it replaces.

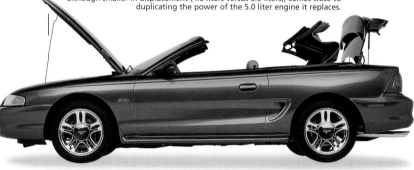

Four-wheel disc brakes
Braking was always a problem on late third-generation cars. However, the current Mustang is fitted with four-wheel ABS-assisted disc brakes which are a tremendous improvement.

Luxury equipment
Cruise control, twin airbags, air-conditioning, tilt steering and foglights are popular optional equipment. Power windows, door locks, mirrors and lumbar support are all standard on the Mustang GT.

Quadrashock rear suspension
Since 1985, all factory V8-powered Mustangs have had an extra pair of rear shocks, mounted horizontally, to reduce axle wind-up under hard, standing-start acceleration.

Retro-styling
When Ford consulted enthusiasts on how the fourth-generation Mustang should look, many wanted a return to the original 1965. Thus, the current car features retro touches such as side scoops and triple taillights and the pony emblem in the grill. However, it remains contemporary and aerodynamically efficient.

Five-speed transmission
All Mustangs can be ordered with the Borg-Warner T-45 five-speed manual transmission, with two sets of final-drive ratios: 2.73 or 3.08:1. Many buyers specify the optional 4R70W four-speed automatic, which is remarkably refined.

Specifications
1998 Ford Mustang GT

ENGINE
Type: V8
Construction: Alloy block and heads
Valve gear: Two valves per cylinder operated by a single overhead camshaft per bank
Bore and stroke: 3.60 in. x 3.60 in.
Displacement: 4.6 liter
Compression ratio: 9.0:1
Induction system: Sequential electronic fuel injection
Maximum power: 225 bhp at 4,400 rpm
Maximum torque: 285 lb-ft at 3,500 rpm
Top speed: 141 mph
0-60 mph: 6.3 sec.

TRANSMISSION
Borg-Warner T-45 five-speed manual

BODY/CHASSIS
Integral chassis with two-door steel convertible body

SPECIAL FEATURES

A strut tower brace helps to improve body stiffness.

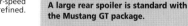

A large rear spoiler is standard with the Mustang GT package.

RUNNING GEAR
Steering: Rack-and-pinion
Front suspension: MacPherson struts with coil springs and shock absorbers
Rear suspension: Live axle with coil springs and quad shock absorbers
Brakes: Discs (front and rear)
Wheels: Alloy, 17-in. dia.
Tires: Goodyear Eagle 245/45 ZR17

DIMENSIONS
Length: 181.5 in.   **Width:** 71.5 in.
Height: 53.0 in.   **Wheelbase:** 101.2 in.
Track: 60.0 in. (front), 58.6 in. (rear)
Weight: 3,462 lbs.

275

Ford **GT40**

The GT40 showed that when a company the size of Ford decides to go into racing, their vast resources will ensure success. After some initial teething trouble, the mighty V8 Ford humiliated the Ferraris with a sweep at Le Mans in 1966.

"...V8 thumps you in the back."

"Even in the road car, with its milder engine and rubber-bushed suspension it's easy to get a realistic impression of what it was like to drive the GT40s through the June heat at Le Mans. The open road and wide, sweeping corners soon beckon; somewhere you can floor the throttle and feel the gutsy V8 thump you in the back as it tears to 100 mph in just 12 seconds. If it's this good on the road, it must have been fantastic on the Mulsanne Straight."

The cabin is small and claustrophobic. Tall drivers cannot even fit in and miss out on one of the greatest driving experiences available.

Milestones

1963 After failing to buy Ferrari, Ford joins forces with Lola to turn the Lola GT into the prototype Ford GT.

1964 Now known as the GT40, the Ford makes its racing debut at the Nurburgring 1000 km. It is forced to retire, as it does in every race this year.

GT40 was so named because its overall height was 40 inches.

1965 Production starts for homologation and a GT40 wins its first race: the 2000-km Daytona Continental.

1966 The big-block cars finish 1-2-3 at Le Mans and win the International Sports Car Championship for GTs.

GT40 won Le Mans in 1968 and '69 after Ford had withdrawn from sports car racing in '67.

1967 Once again the car wins both the International Sports Car Championship and the 24 Hours of Le Mans. Although Ford withdraws from racing at the end of '67, the GT40 races on in the hands of the Gulf team, winning Le Mans again in '68 and '69.

UNDER THE SKIN

Fuel tanks in deep sills

Sheet steel semi-monocoque structure

Suspension mounted in subframes

Mid-mounted engine

Sedan-derived V8

Stiff and strong

As a race car, the GT40 needed to be light as well as stiff and strong. To achieve this, it uses a sheet steel semi-monocoque structure with very deep sills (which hold the fuel cells). At either end of the center monocoque are subframes to hold the engine, transmission and suspension. The later MkIV racers use a more advanced alloy honeycomb construction.

THE POWER PACK

Tuning potential

Most GT40s used the 289-cubic inch V8 also found in the Sunbeam Tiger, Ford Mustang and early AC Cobra. With a cast-iron block and cylinder heads, a single camshaft operating two valves per cylinder via pushrods and rockers, it is not a sophisticated engine. Its design dates back to the 1950s, but it has huge tuning potential. In full racing tune, it can produce around 400 bhp which was more than enough to blow past the more sophisticated, but often less reliable, Ferraris.

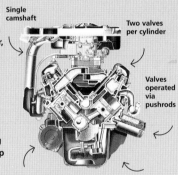

Single camshaft

Two valves per cylinder

Valves operated via pushrods

Eight cylinders in vee-configuration

Iron block and cylinder heads

Big blocks

Ford's first Le Mans-winning GT40 used the big-block 427-cubic inch engine; a unit that proved in the tough world of NASCAR racing it had the strength required for 24-hour racing. Only a few big-block cars were built.

Big-block cars had extra power and strength to compete in endurance racing.

Fast and immensely strong, the GT40 showed what a production car company could do when it wanted to go racing, particularly with Carroll Shelby, father of the AC Cobra, running the racing program.

Final specification
Although this car first raced in 1965, it was later brought up to the final racing specs, those of the Le Mans-winning cars of 1968 and '69.

Mid-engined design
By the 1960s, it was obvious that a successful racing car had to be mid-engined and Ford followed suit. The engine is behind the driver, mounted lengthwise, and by 1968, the displacement of the small-block engine had risen to 302 cubic inches. With Gurney-Weslake-developed cylinder heads, as on this car, power output was up to 435 bhp.

Front-mounted radiator
Ford decided to keep the radiator in its conventional position rather than mounting it alongside or behind the engine as on some modern mid-engined designs.

Four-speed transmission
The first racers are equipped with a four-speed Colotti transmission with right-hand change. Road cars have a ZF five-speed box with conventional central shifter.

Fiberglass body
The GT40's body played no structural role, so it was made from fiberglass and consisted basically of two large hinged sections, which gave the best access during pit stops.

Opening side windows
GT40s get incredibly hot inside and although the main side windows do not open, there are small hinged windows to allow air to pass through the cockpit.

Radiator outlet
By 1968, the air passing through the radiator was exhausted through this one large vent. It has a small upturned lip on the leading edge to accelerate air flow through the radiator.

Competition record
This car was one of the first driven at Le Mans, in 1965 by Bob Bondurant, but it failed to finish after cylinder head gasket failure. Three years later, it came fourth in the 1000 km at Spa Francorchamps.

Halibrand wheels
The wide Halibrand wheels are made from magnesium, so they are very light. The design also provides good cooling for the disc brakes. They are a knock-off design for quick changes at pit stops.

Magnesium suspension components
The GT40 is a heavyweight racing car, but some effort was still made to save weight—the magnesium suspension uprights, for example.

Specifications
1967 Ford GT40 MkIII (road spec)

ENGINE
Type: V8
Construction: Cast-iron block and heads
Valve gear: Two valves per cylinder operated by single camshaft via pushrods and rockers
Bore and stroke: 4 in. x 2.87 in.
Displacement: 289 c.i.
Compression ratio: 10.5:1
Induction system: Single four-barrel Holley carburetor
Maximum power: 306 bhp at 6,000 rpm
Maximum torque: 328 lb-ft at 4,200 rpm
Top speed: 165 mph
0-60 mph: 5.5 sec.

TRANSMISSION
Five-speed ZF manual transaxle

BODY/CHASSIS
Sheet steel central semi-monocoque with front and rear subframes and fiberglass two-door, two-seat GT body

SPECIAL FEATURES

The GT40 was made as low as possible to help its aerodynamics. On this car, to help fit a driver with helmet into the cockpit, this bump was added onto the roof.

To help achieve a low overall height, the exhaust pipes run over the top of the transmission.

RUNNING GEAR
Steering: Rack-and-pinion
Front suspension: Double wishbones with coil springs, telescopic shocks and anti-roll bar
Rear suspension: Trailing arms and wishbones with coil springs, telescopic shocks and anti-roll bar
Brakes: Discs, 11.5 in. dia. (front), 11.2 in. dia. (rear)
Wheels: Halibrand magnesium 6.5 in. x 15 in. (front), 8.5 in. x 15 in. (rear)
Tires: 5.5 in. x 15 in. (front), 7 in. x 15 in. (rear)

DIMENSIONS
Length: 169 in.   **Width:** 70 in.
Height: 40 in.   **Wheelbase:** 95.3 in.
Track: 55 in. (front), 53.5 in. (rear)
Weight: 2,200 lbs.

Ford **TORINO TALLADEGA**

In the late 1960s Ford and Chrysler were waging war in NASCAR. In 1969 Ford revealed its aero-styled Torinos, which cleaned up in the year's stock car racing by collecting 30 victories. To satisfy homologation rules at least 500 road-going versions had to be built. The result was the Ford Talladega.

"...the car was lethal."

"Though sedate looking, the Torino Talladega was the answer to watching the taillights of quicker Mopars and Chevrolets. Its nose was tapered and stretched five inches, and a flush mounted grill replaced the stock Torino piece. In street trim, the Talladega, named after NASCAR's fastest super-speedway, used a 335 bhp 428 Cobra Jet engine with a Drag Pack oil cooler. On the street the car was lethal, but in NASCAR trim it was deadly."

Talladegas have basic interiors, but they are equipped with full instrumentation.

Milestones

1968 Ford restyles
its Fairlane model with swoopier styling. A new top-of-the-line Torino, including a GT fastback and convertible, joins the line up. The latter can be ordered with a 390-or 428-cubic inch V8 big-block engine.

The Torino made its debut as a top-of-the-range Fairlane in 1968.

1969 In response to
the Dodge Charger 500 built for NASCAR racing, Ford releases the Talladega for NASCAR using the 427 engine at first, but switched to the semi-hemi Boss 429 engines after enough were homologated into the Mustang. Ford's aero-aces trounced the Charger 500 and the even more slippery winged Daytonas by winning 30 races that season.

Restyled 1970 Torinos had smoother styling.

1970 A redesigned
Talladega was disappointing in testing, so Ford retained the 1969 cars for NASCAR. Though successful the previous year, the Fords were no match to Plymouth's winged Superbirds.

UNDER THE SKIN

Fairlane chassis

Based on the Fairlane, the Talladega has the same monocoque chassis as its sibling. The suspension is typical Detroit practice for the time, with unequal length wishbones and coil springs up front. At the rear there is a solid axle and multi-leaf springs, plus staggered rear shocks to reduce axle tramp.

Rear leaf springs

Independent front suspension

Unitary construction

Big-block V8

THE POWER PACK

Motown muscle

All production Talladegas are powered by Ford's stout 428-cubic inch Cobra Jet big-block V8s. Underrated at 335 bhp, this engine was Ford's ace in the late 1960s horsepower race. The engines all had 10.6:1 compression, steel cranks, stronger con rods and received fuel from a Holley four-barrel 735-cfm carburetor. While this was the street engine, the NASCAR competition version used the sinister Boss 429 semi-hemi engine that was homologated the same year in the Boss 429 Mustang.

Two valves per cylinder

Single four-barrel carburetor

Forged steel crankshaft

Cast-iron block and cylinder heads

Two of a Kind

While Ford built only 745 Talladegas, its crosstown brother, Mercury, made similar modifications to 353 of its 1969 Cyclones and called it the Spoiler II. Its body was slightly longer and lower to the ground and included a rear spoiler and unique badging.

Cyclone IIs were offered with a 351 cubic inch V8 but a 428 was optional.

Through the use of aerodynamics and the Boss 429 engine, the purpose-built Talladegas accomplished its mission—to take the 1969 NASCAR championship. Once again, Ford's 'Total Performance' campaign shines through.

Cobra Jet power

The standard engine is the monster 428-cubic inch Cobra Jet unit. It was factory rated at 335 bhp for insurance reasons, but the true output is probably somewhere in the region of 450 bhp. In race trim the engine of choice was the Boss 429 that was homologated for racing in the Mustang Boss 429.

Rocker Panel Modifications

The rocker panels were raised over an inch so the NASCAR prepared cars could be lowered while being in full compliance with the ride height requirements.

Handling suspension

All Talladegas are equipped with a 'handling' suspension, which basically consists of stiffer springs and shocks plus a thick front anti-roll bar.

Lack of ornamentation

The exterior of the Talladega is very plain and does not have any nameplates. Instead, it carries 'T' motifs on the fuel cap and above the door handles.

Nose modifications

The Talladega was based on the Fairlane SportsRoof but with some aerodynamic advantages. The nose was stretched more than five inches and brought closer to the ground. It also features a flush mounted grill and a narrowed Fairlane bumper.

Traction-Lok rear

Ford's Traction-Lok differential, with a 3.25:1 final-drive ratio, was the only rear gearing available. It makes the Talladega surprisingly capable at high-speed cruising, although all-out acceleration suffers as a result.

Staggered rear shocks

Like many Detroit cars of the era, the Talladega has a solid axle and rear leaf springs. Staggered shocks are used to prevent severe axle tramp during hard acceleration.

Lightweight interior

To keep weight to a minimum, the Talladega uses a base interior, with a standard vinyl front bench seat and column shifter for the C6 automatic transmission.

Specifications

1969 Ford Torino Talladega

ENGINE

Type: V8

Construction: Cast-iron block and heads

Valve gear: Two valves per cylinder operated by a single camshaft via pushrods and rockers

Bore and stroke: 4.13 in. x 3.98 in.

Displacement: 428 c.i.

Compression ratio: 10.6:1

Induction system: Single Holley four-barrel carburetor

Maximum power: 335 bhp at 5,200 rpm

Maximum torque: 440 lb-ft at 3,400 rpm

Top speed: 130 mph

0-60 mph: 5.8 sec.

TRANSMISSION

Ford C-6 Cruise-O-Matic

BODY/CHASSIS

Steel monocoque with two-door fastback body design

SPECIAL FEATURES

'T' (for Talladega) emblems are carried in the coach stripe on each side.

All Talladegas left the factory with 428 Cobra Jet V8 engines. In NASCAR-prepped cars they ran the notorious Boss 429.

RUNNING GEAR

Steering: Recirculating ball

Front suspension: Unequal length wishbones with coil springs, telescopic shocks and anti-roll bar

Rear suspension: Live axle with semi-elliptical multi-leaf springs and staggered telescopic shocks

Brakes: Discs (front), drums (rear)

Wheels: Ford slotted chrome steel, 14-in. dia.

Tires: Goodyear Polyglas F70-14

DIMENSIONS

Length: 209.8 in.   **Width:** 84.4 in.

Height: 59.1 in.   **Wheelbase:** 116 in.

Track: 64.7 in. (front), 62 in. (rear)

Weight: 3,536 lbs.

Ford **TORINO**

Ford fielded a larger, more curvaceous Torino for 1970. The Cobra was a bare bones performance version of the sporty Torino GT. With a standard 429 Cobra Jet engine and a Hurst-shifted four-speed, it was a serious racer and owning one was certain to gain you instant respect on the drag strip.

"...traction is excellent."

"The first thing that you notice is the room inside—this is one of the larger muscle intermediates and there are acres of space. Traction off the line is excellent, the Hurst-shifted four-speed is precise and in just 5.9 seconds you're hitting 60 mph. What strikes you even more is the level of refinement—the seats are comfortable and the ride soft and composed. Despite all the weight over the front wheels, the Cobra handles well too, thanks to the wide track."

With a four-speed transmission and a full set of gauges this Torino Cobra means business.

Milestones

1970 Ford releases a new crop of intermediate-sized cars, which are longer, lower and wider with new streamlined styling. They are now split into two series: the Fairlane 500 and the Torino. The standard sporty machine is the Torino GT. A serious performance version, the Cobra, has exposed headlights and standard 429-cubic inch V8 power.

The Torino GT was the standard sporty Ford intermediate.

1971 Returning with a facelift, the mid-size line is back for its second and last outing in this form. The Torino Cobra is still offered, although the standard engine is now a 285-bhp, 351-cubic inch small-block.

The Torino was popularized in the TV series Starsky and Hutch.

1972 An all-new Torino with unitized construction is built this year. A token performance model, the Sports GT fastback, is also offered.

UNDER THE SKIN

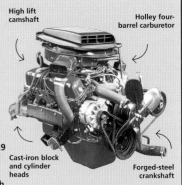

Leaf-sprung live rear axle

Unitary construction

Power front disc brakes

429-powered V8

Reworked

Mid-size Fords were completely revised for 1970, becoming longer and wider. The Torino still had a unitary body, with unequal length wishbones at the front and a live rear axle. The Cobra added heavy-duty front coil springs and rear leaf springs along with staggered rear shock absorbers. The track was also widened, resulting in fairly composed handling for a muscle car.

THE POWER PACK

Sign of the times

In 1970, all Torino Cobras, even the base model, were powered by the 429 (not to be confused with the Boss 429 engine). The base engine had 10.5:1 compression and made 360 bhp, while the intermediate engine came with 11.3:1 compression, different heads, high lift cam, and a 700 cfm Holley carburetor for 370 bhp. If the Drag Pack was ordered with the Cobra 429 the engine received a solid cam, oil cooler forged pistons, a four-bolt main block and a 780 cfm carb which made 375 bhp. Ram air was also available on any of the 429s.

High lift camshaft

Holley four-barrel carburetor

Cast-iron block and cylinder heads

Forged-steel crankshaft

Fully optioned

The 1970 Torino Cobra is, without doubt, the most desirable of these cars. Find one equipped with the 370-bhp 429, Drag Pack and Ram Air and you have one of the muscle era's finest specimens. A good Cobra will set you back $20,000-$30,000 today.

Fast and refined, the Torino Cobra is a cut above many muscle cars.

From any angle, the Torino Cobra has presence. It also has unrivaled handling, comfort and 0-60 mph acceleration. Other muscle cars may be quicker, but few offered so much in a single, tailor-made package.

Wicked 429

In standard form the 429 engine is rated at 360 bhp, although the Cobra Jet version produces 370 bhp thanks to a hotter camshaft, free-flowing cylinder heads and a high-riser intake manifold. The baddest engine option was the 375 bhp version with four-bolt mains, forged pistons, solid cam and larger carburetor. This model happens to be the intermediate model with 370 bhp.

Four-speed transmission

Backing the 429 engine is a standard four-speed transmission, including a Hurst T-shaped shifter. This combination made the Cobra a threat to any car on the street, even with the most average driver behind the wheel.

Beefed-up suspension

Like most muscle machines of its period, the Cobra has standard suspension which has been uprated with a thicker front anti-roll bar and stiffer springs and shocks. The 2-inch wider track results in one of the best-handling muscle cars.

Swoopy styling

The 1970-1971 Torinos are arguably the best-looking, with their fluid styling and fastback roof. Although they look aerodynamic, tests in stock car racing proved that the older 1969 styling was more efficient and therefore Ford continued using 1969 Talladegas on the big NASCAR ovals.

Low rear axle gearing

If equipped with the Drag Pack, Torino Cobras came with either Traction-Lok 3.91:1 rear axle ratio or with the deadly Detroit locker 4.30:1 gears.

Ram Air induction

With the addition of the shaker scoop, the engine became known as the 429 Cobra Jet Ram Air. The scoop attaches directly to the engine's air cleaner.

Specifications
1970 Ford Torino Cobra

ENGINE

Type: V8

Construction: Cast-iron block and heads

Valve gear: Two valves per cylinder operated by pushrods and rockers

Bore and stroke: 4.36 in. x 3.59 in.

Displacement: 429 c.i.

Compression ratio: 11.3:1

Induction system: Single Holley four-barrel carburetor

Maximum power: 370 bhp at 5,400 rpm

Maximum torque: 450 lb-ft at 3,400 rpm

Top speed: 118 mph

0-60 mph: 5.9 sec.

TRANSMISSION

Borg-Warner T10 four-speed with Hurst shifter

BODY/CHASSIS

Unitary steel monocoque with two-door fastback body

SPECIAL FEATURES

The Ram Air induction quickly forced cool air into the carburetor.

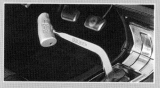

A four-speed manual is standard, as is this Hurst T-handle shifter.

RUNNING GEAR

Steering: Recirculating ball

Front suspension: Unequal length wishbones with coil springs, telescopic shock absorbers and anti-roll bar

Rear suspension: Live 9-in. axle with multi-leaf springs and staggered telescopic shock absorbers

Brakes: Discs, 10-in. dia. (front), finned drums, 9-in. dia. (rear)

Wheels: Steel, 15-in. dia.

Tires: ZBF Goodrich Radial T/A, F60-15

DIMENSIONS

Length: 203.6 in.   **Width:** 80.0 in.

Height: 49.3 in.   **Wheelbase:** 117.0 in.

Track: 60.3 in. (front), 58.4 in. (rear)

Weight: 4,000 lbs.

Ford **F350 LIGHTNING**

Ford's Super Duty series of light- and medium-weight trucks are intimidating enough in stock form, but for some, too much is never enough. Witness this high-riding F-350, which, with its substantial lift, is worthy of being called a junior monster truck.

"...moves along effortlessly."

"As imposing as it looks, this truck rides relatively smoothly even with an 8-inch lift and monster tires, due in part to the custom multistage leaf packs on the front and rear. Four-wheel drive is activated simply by the touch of a button in the cockpit. This lets the monster rig move effortlessly over the most challenging terrain, while protecting its occupants from the extremities of the great outdoors."

SVO leather-trimmed seats give the cabin a luxurious feel, and a CB radio enables contact with the outside world.

Milestones

1996 Ford introduces a brand-new
F-150, which adopts the aero look. It is sold as a 1997 model and production is allocated to three of the five plants used to build F-series trucks. The square-rigged 1996 model continues to be produced until the end of the year.

First of the new wave of F-series trucks was the F-150, the world's best-selling vehicle.

1998 The bigger F-series trucks are
supplanted by an all-new Super Duty series, starting with the F-250 and F-350 formats. The standard engine is the 5.4-liter V8, but a 6.8-liter V10 and Power Stroke diesel are optional.

With the 1999 Super Duty rigs, Ford has redefined the concept of big, workhorse pickups.

1999 The biggest members of the F-series—
the Super Duty F-600 and F-700—go on sale, replacing the previous 1980-vintage models.

Made tough

Ford's Super Duty rigs have a separate box-section steel chassis, with the fuel tank mounted inside the frame rails for maximum protection. Suspension hardware consists of Ford's Twin Traction beams (on 4x4 models), live axles front and rear with a central viscous coupling, and leaf springs all around. This monster features an 8-inch suspension lift and five-way adjustable twin Rancho shocks on each corner. Traction bars and 4.30:1 gears are among its modifications.

Separate box-section steel chassis

Twin Rancho shocks at each corner

Eight-inch suspension lift

Triton V10

THE POWER PACK

The Power of Ten

Realizing that Dodge had cornered a considerable part of the heavy-duty market with its V10-powered 2500 and 3500 rigs, Ford needed a rival engine. The result is the 412-cubic inch (6.8-liter) Triton V10. It has a cast-iron block and cylinder heads and two valves for each cylinder, but these are actuated by a single overhead camshaft on each bank rather than by a single block camshaft. This means that although the engine still produces masses of torque (410 lb-ft), it does not run out of breath at higher rpm like its rival's engines. For extra smoothness, the V10 employs a counter-rotating balancer shaft.

Single overhead camshaft design

Electronic fuel injection

Cast iron block

Counter-rotating balancer shaft

Aiming high

Since they rolled onto the dealers' lots, the new Super Dutys have proved to be popular and are competitively priced. Some owners cannot resist modifying their trucks, and dual exhaust, larger tires, lift kits and extra lights may be fitted.

Oversize tires, bars and winches are popular with the four-wheel drive crowd.

Super Dutys have already found their way into the hands of four-wheeling enthusiasts. This one probably has everything you could possibly need for a long trek into the unforgiving wilds of the Yukon.

Triton V10 engine

In the full-size pickup world, the old adage 'bigger and better' still holds true, especially when it comes to engines. The 6.8-liter V10 is Ford's torquiest production engine of 1999, packing a walloping 410 lb-ft of pulling power.

Twin winches

Off-roading can be hazardous and vehicles can sometimes become stranded. The twin winches on this F-350 (one at the front and one at the rear) can haul loads of up to 12,000 and 9,000 lbs., respectively—far greater weights than the average truck or SUV.

Monster tires

Off-roaders require big, low-pressure tires, which are both durable and grippy. The Dick Cepek F/C radials, measuring a huge 38 x 14.5 x 16.5 inches, are more than adequate for scrambling through rough terrain and suspending the 6,710-lbs. curb weight of the truck. A full-size spare is carried in the pickup bed.

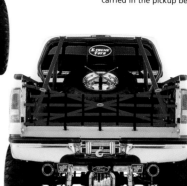

Limiting straps

Although off-roaders require considerable suspension travel in order to clear obstacles, too much can cause problems. For this reason, limiter straps are fitted at the front and rear to prevent the axles from damaging the underside of the vehicle.

Dual shocks

Good damping is essential for four-wheelers, especially when the terrain gets rugged. Dual Rancho shocks at each corner ensure that the driver and passengers are as comfortable as possible when traveling over bumpy ground and that the vehicle remains as stable and as level as possible.

Eight-inch lift

The off-road phenomenon really took off in the 1980s, and there are still a number of people who want to build the ultimate off-road vehicle. This rig has an 8-inch lift kit, which means it can clear all but the biggest rocks when out in the wilderness.

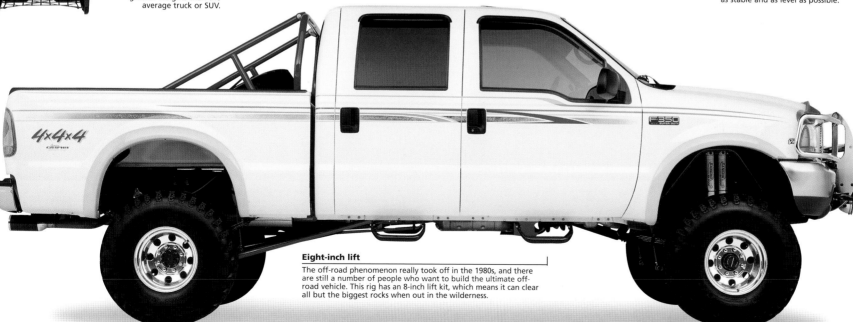

Specifications

1999 Ford F-350 Super Duty

ENGINE
Type: V10

Construction: Cast-iron block and heads

Valve gear: Two valves per cylinder operated by a single overhead camshaft for each cylinder bank

Bore and stroke: 3.55 in. x 4.16 in.

Displacement: 412 c.i.

Compression ratio: 9.0:1

Induction system: Sequential multipoint fuel injection

Maximum power: 275 bhp at 4,250 rpm

Maximum torque: 410 lb-ft at 2,650 rpm

Top speed: 96 mph

0-60 mph: 10.2 sec.

TRANSMISSION
Four-speed automatic

BODY/CHASSIS
Separate steel chassis with four-door pickup body

SPECIAL FEATURES

Due to this truck's substantial step-in height, step plates are essential.

A bed liner helps protect cargo.

RUNNING GEAR
Steering: Recirculating-ball

Front suspension: Twin traction beams with coil springs, quad telescopic shock absorbers and anti-roll bar

Rear suspension: Live axle with coil springs and quad telescopic shock absorbers

Brakes: Discs (front and rear)

Wheels: American Eagle, 16.5 x 12 in.

Tires: Dick Cepek, 38 x 14.5 x 16.5

DIMENSIONS
Length: 265.6 in.   **Width:** 104.7 in.

Height: 97.6 in.   **Wheelbase:** 156 in.

Track: 86.2 in. (front), 87.6 in. (rear)

Weight: 6,710 lbs.

GMC **STEPSIDE**

Affectionately nicknamed the 'Bullnose,' the FC series appeared halfway through 1947 and ushered in a new era in styling and comfort for light-duty trucks. Today, these vehicles are coveted collectibles.

"...workman-like vehicle."

"Utilitarian is the best way to describe the Stepside. Compared to modern pickups, the interior is spartan, but in its time it was regarded as luxurious. With a straight six under the bulbous hood, this truck is no hot rod but pulls well at low revs, and the floor-mounted gear shifter is quite smooth for such a workman-like vehicle. The ride is quite harsh and bumpy, especially unloaded. Its cornering can be interesting, but all this is part of the Bullnose charm."

The dashboard is dominated by the large speedometer and clock.

Milestones

1947 GMC reveals a new line of light-duty trucks, with smoother styling and a revamped cab and front suspension. The sole engine is a 228-cubic inch, in-line six, carried over from the old CC/EC series. A total of 49,187 of the new trucks are registered this year.

Chevrolet's version of the GMC FC series is the popular 3100, a straight-six powered pickup.

1950 Power from the six-cylinder engine increases from 93 to 96 bhp. New shock absorbers help smooth the ride, and improved electricals also arrive.

Chevrolet® (and GMC) trucks were restyled for 1955. This is a 1957 model.

1954 A restyle results in flashier appearance, and chrome hubcaps and trim return. The six is bored out to 249 inches and a one-piece windshield is fitted.

UNDER THE SKIN

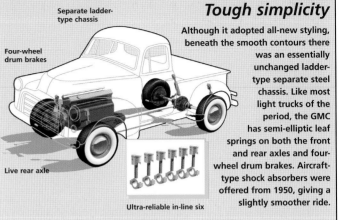

Separate ladder-type chassis

Four-wheel drum brakes

Live rear axle

Ultra-reliable in-line six

Tough simplicity

Although it adopted all-new styling, beneath the smooth contours there was an essentially unchanged ladder-type separate steel chassis. Like most light trucks of the period, the GMC has semi-elliptic leaf springs on both the front and rear axles and four-wheel drum brakes. Aircraft-type shock absorbers were offered from 1950, giving a slightly smoother ride.

THE POWER PACK

Faithful 'Stovebolt'

Until 1955, GMCs came exclusively with straight-six engines. The 228-cubic inch unit that powers this 1951 FC is of Chevrolet origin and dates back to 1927. It is an all-iron, L-head unit with a four-main-bearing crankshaft. Engineered by Ormond E. Hunt, it was affectionately known as the 'Stovebolt Six,' so named because of the engine's cast-iron pistons and slotted head bolts. Outfitted with hydraulic valve lifters and a Carter one-barrel carburetor, it produces 100 bhp at just 3,400 rpm.

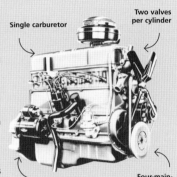

Two valves per cylinder

Single carburetor

Four-main-bearing crankshaft

Cast-iron block and cylinder heads

Big brother

Essentially, the FC series is an upmarket Chevrolet 3100 with virtually identical sheet metal and cab. But the GMC version has a larger, more powerful engine (100-bhp, 228-cubic inch versus 92-bhp, 217-cubic inch). The GMC attracts less collector interest than the Chevrolet, but buyers get more for their money.

Better refined and more powerful post-1950 models are the best buy.

Smooth styling and improved ergonomics marked GMC's first 'new' post-war pickups. More powerful, better trimmed and more exclusive than rival Chevrolets, they signaled a move toward the leisure market.

Improved cab
One of the most noticeable differences of the 1947-1955 GMCs was a more spacious cab than earlier CC/EC-series trucks. The headroom was increased by one inch and legroom by seven inches. A larger glass area improved visibility.

Stepside bed
Traditional pickup beds were called 'stepsides' because running boards enabled people to step up into the bed.

Dual shocks
Buyers could order a set of auxiliary shock absorbers at the rear. These were especially welcomed by those who purchased the FC to carry heavy loads.

Leaf-sprung suspension
Traditionally, trucks had leaf-sprung suspensions. This setup is simple and rugged and can cope admirably with rough roads, but does not sacrifice too much in the way of ride comfort.

Optional lights
Back in 1951, twin tail and stop lights were optional. Today, due to the density of traffic, many owners have chosen to fit these items.

Optional gas tank
Buyers could choose a number of options on their new GMC in 1951. Among them was the position of the gas tank. This is mounted under the pickup bed as standard, although a cab-mounted tank could be ordered instead.

Stovebolt Six
One of the most reliable engines ever built, the veteran Chevy six was a mainstay in GMCs until 1955. GMCs had a larger unit as standard than the rival Chevrolet 3100.

Specifications

1951 GMC FC-101 Stepside

ENGINE
Type: In-line six
Construction: Cast-iron block and heads
Valve gear: Two valves per cylinder operated by pushrods and rockers
Bore and stroke: 3.56 in. x 3.81 in.
Displacement: 228 c.i.
Compression ratio: 6.6:1
Induction system: Carter single-barrel carburetor
Maximum power: 100 bhp at 3,400 rpm
Maximum torque: 187 lb-ft at 1,700 rpm
Top speed: 83 mph
0-60 mph: 22.0 sec

TRANSMISSION
Four-speed manual

BODY/CHASSIS
Steel ladder frame with steel cab and bed

SPECIAL FEATURES

A 100 badge on the side of the hood signifies a 100-bhp 'Stovebolt Six.'

Single circular headlights were fitted to all GMCs up until 1957.

RUNNING GEAR
Steering: Recirculating ball
Front suspension: Solid axle with leaf springs and telescopic shock absorbers
Rear suspension: Live axle with leaf springs and telescopic shock absorbers
Brakes: Drums (front and rear)
Wheels: Pressed steel, 15-in. dia.
Tires: Bias-ply, 6.00 x 16

DIMENSIONS
Length: 196.6 in.   **Width:** 68.0 in.
Height: 67.0 in.   **Wheelbase:** 116.0 in.
Track: 57.6 in. (front), 60.0 in. (rear)
Weight: 3,275 lbs.

GMC **SYCLONE**

Sports cars are for speed, pickup trucks are for hauling around cargo, right? But what if you could combine the two and build a pickup as fast as a Vette™? No, it's not impossible and GM proved it with 280 bhp of turbocharged V6.

"...pure attitude."

"You've seen custom trucks cruising Saturday nights for years. But you've got one of only 3,000 Syclones ever made and there's nothing like it. With big wheels, spoilers, skirts and an intercooled turbo, this hot-rod truck is pure attitude. Finally, a factory show-and-go truck! Hit the gas and you've got instant acceleration—a thump in the back that sends you rocketing off the line to 30 mph in less than two seconds. OK, it's not a sports car, but for a small pickup, there's surprising handling and comfort."

Sport seats and a leather steering wheel give the Syclone's interior a sports car feel.

Milestones

1970s Japanese manufacturers start to make a real impact in the pickup truck market in the U.S. with smaller, nimbler trucks that are more fun than anything from Ford or GM. Some American manufacturers go so far as to offer Japanese trucks with American badges.

The success of the Japanese mini-trucks pushed U.S. manufacturers to produce faster trucks.

1982 America hits back with small trucks of its own: GMC brings out the S15 sports pickup with a new V6 engine, while Ford, reacting in the same way, improves the Ranger pickup.

1991 Adding a liquid-cooled intercooler to the 4.3-liter V6, GMC produces the limited-edition 280-bhp Syclone. It's General Motors' showcase to prove just what performance you can get from a truck. Only 800 were built during this Syclone's short production run.

Once the Syclone was dropped in 1992, the S10 series lost its performance variant.

UNDER THE SKIN

Sports car in disguise

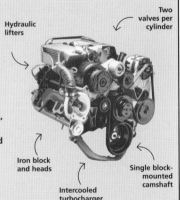

Center viscous coupling

Turbocharged engine

Four-wheel drive

Four-speed automatic gearbox

Turbocharged V6

Traction and handling are what GMC needed with the Syclone, so the springs are shortened and the truck lowered, while the drivetrain incorporates four-wheel drive with a center viscous coupling to divide the torque between the front and rear wheels. The solid rear axle has its own limited slip differential. The V6 is joined to a four-speed automatic, but that doesn't harm the performance.

THE POWER PACK

Blowing hot

Just like American engines were always meant to be, this V6 has an iron block and heads. There's just one camshaft deep in the vee of the block to work the two valves per cylinder through its pushrods and hydraulic lifters. Compared to the larger V8s of some of its competitors, the Syclone's 4.3-liter engine is not that big, so it relies on an intercooled turbocharger to produce its impressive 280 bhp. Even more impressive is its 350 lb-ft of torque, the equal of much larger V8s.

Hydraulic lifters

Two valves per cylinder

Iron block and heads

Single block-mounted camshaft

Intercooled turbocharger

Show and go

GMC gussied up the Syclone so much—with alloy wheels, pointless front spoiler and deep side skirts—you might not take it seriously the first time you come across one. That would be your mistake; from a standstill, this truck can reach 100 mph in less than 18 seconds.

The Syclone is a truck on the outside, sports car on the inside.

When Porsche builds something with an intercooled turbocharger and four-wheel drive, it can cost as much as a house. When GMC did it with the Syclone, you could afford one and have just as much fun while moving the family furniture.

Liquid intercooler
Turbocharged engines work more efficiently if the air that's being forced in can stay dense and cool. To do that, GM uses an intercooler, essentially a radiator for the intake air, which is liquid cooled rather than the more normal air cooling.

Turbocharged V6
With no room for a big V8 under the hood, GMC opted to turbocharge the existing 4.3-liter V6. That instantly gave more than an extra 120 bhp and in excess of another 100 lb-ft of torque, the ingredient you need for serious acceleration.

Low-profile tires
Wide, low-profile tires are installed in the Syclone to help traction and road holding. They work well enough to generate 0.8g around the skid pad. Not many pickups can manage that.

Side skirts
To make the Syclone look even lower, add-on skirts bring the body line lower between the wheels. They're cosmetic only—there's no real need to manage the airflow under the truck.

Rear drum brakes
Because its front brakes do all the work, the Syclone can get by with drum brakes at the rear working in conjunction with the ABS. Brakes are just as impressive as the acceleration.

Borla Exhaust
To further exploit power, this Syclone has been modified with a free-flowing Borla cat-back exhaust system.

Automatic transmission
The combination of four-speed auto with a torque converter suits the power characteristics of the turbocharged V6 perfectly.

Specifications
1992 GMC Syclone

ENGINE
Type: V6
Construction: Cast-iron block and head
Valve gear: Two valves per cylinder operated by single block-mounted camshaft via pushrods, rockers and hydraulic lifters
Bore and stroke: 4 in. x 3.48 in.
Displacement: 4,293 cc
Compression ratio: 8.35:1
Induction system: Electronic multi-point fuel injection with intercooled turbocharger
Maximum power: 280 bhp at 4,400 rpm
Maximum torque: 350 lb-ft at 3,600 rpm
Top speed: 126 mph
0-60 mph: 4.9 sec

TRANSMISSION
Four-speed automatic with four-wheel drive and center viscous coupling

BODY/CHASSIS
Steel frame with two-door pickup body

SPECIAL FEATURES

The sporting theme carries on inside the Syclone. Body-hugging bucket seats hold driver and passenger firmly in position under hard cornering.

An intercooled turbocharger helps the V6 give the power of a much larger V8.

RUNNING GEAR
Steering: Recirculating ball
Front suspension: Unequal-length control arms, torsion bars, anti-roll bar and telescopic shock absorbers
Rear suspension: Live axle with semi-elliptic leaf springs and telescopic shocks
Brakes: Discs (front), drums (rear) with ABS
Wheels: Alloy, 8 in. x 16 in.
Tires: Yokohama AVS 245/50 VR16

DIMENSIONS
Length: 180.5 in.   **Width:** 68.2 in.
Height: 60 in.   **Wheelbase:** 108.3 in.
Track: 55.7 in. (front), 54.1 in. (rear)
Weight: 3,599 lbs.

GMC **TYPHOON**

It's quicker than a Ferrari 348, and has greater luggage capacity. It also boasts all-wheel drive and is powered with a turbocharged engine. However, this vehicle is not an ultra-expensive supercar, but a high performance sport utility from GMC.

"...heart-stopping acceleration."

"With the ride height lowered and the springs and shocks stiffened, you soon realize that you can use as much of the Typhoon's 280 bhp as you like. The all-wheel drive system puts down maximum traction, which results in heart-stopping acceleration with 0-100 mph taking just 16.3 seconds. Cornering ability comes close to matching straight-line performance, while the steering has more than enough feel to inspire confidence."

The Typhoon is like a luxury SUV inside, with leather seats and power everything.

Milestones

1990 GMC turns a Sonoma pickup truck into the extraordinary Syclone in time for the 1991 model year. It cannot carry a great deal, but it can accelerate to 60 mph faster than a Ferrari 348 or even a Corvette® ZR-1®. It is part of GMC's plan to improve its image.

GM'S other muscle truck at the time was the Chevrolet 454 SS®.

1992 A year after the Syclone, GMC introduces the Typhoon, which uses the same all-wheel-drive chassis and turbocharged V6 engine combined with a two-door GMC Jimmy® body. Like the Syclone®, the Typhoon is well received by the press and achieves status as the world's fastest SUV.

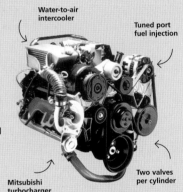

The Typhoon is based on the popular GMC Jimmy.

1992 The Syclone is dropped, but the Typhoon continues. Only 2,200 are built and production ends this year.

UNDER THE SKIN

Old and new

All-wheel drive

HD 8.5-inch front and rear axles with 3.42:1 gears

Four-wheel anti-lock brakes

It is hard to imagine that an SUV that goes this fast started life as an ordinary GMC Jimmy. The Typhoon has a number of traditional features, including a separate chassis frame, live rear axle and recirculating ball steering. However, it also has big vented ABS-assisted disc brakes, stiffer springs and shocks, plus all-wheel drive with a center viscous coupling and rear limited-slip differential.

Turbocharged V6

THE POWER PACK

Vortech turbo

The Typhoon's outrageous performance is provided by GM's 262-cubic inch Vortech V6—an all-iron pushrod two-valve-per-cylinder unit with hydraulic lifters. The key to its 280-bhp capability is turbocharging. This is achieved by using a water-cooled Mitsubishi 12 psi. blower and intercooler coupled with a tuned port fuel injection system. To make the engine more adaptable to turbocharging, the compression ratio is lowered to 8.4:1 by flat-top pistons.

Water-to-air intercooler

Tuned port fuel injection

Two valves per cylinder

Mitsubishi turbocharger

Whirlwind

Sharing the same running gear as the Typhoon but with a Sonoma pickup truck body, the Syclone has an even more savage character. When it appeared in 1991 its 0-60 mph time of 4.9 seconds made it one of the quickest production vehicles on sale in the U.S.

A unique drivetrain and low production ensures future collectability.

Many Sports Utility Vehicles (SUVs) are misnamed. Most of them do not have nearly enough power to provide real sport performance. The Typhoon is different; it combines sport and utility like no other vehicle.

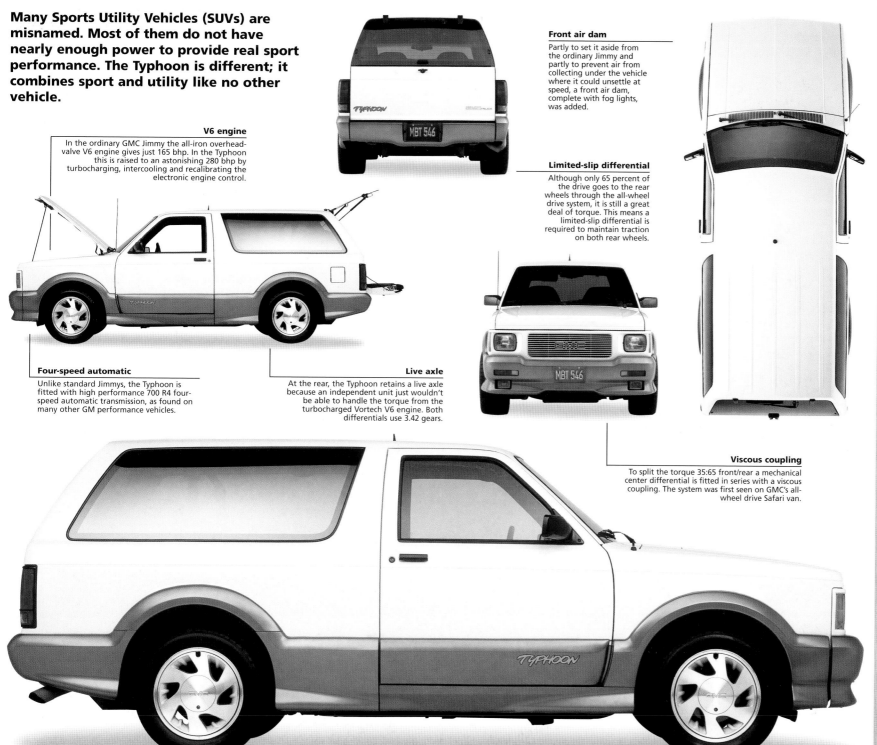

V6 engine

In the ordinary GMC Jimmy the all-iron overhead-valve V6 engine gives just 165 bhp. In the Typhoon this is raised to an astonishing 280 bhp by turbocharging, intercooling and recalibrating the electronic engine control.

Front air dam

Partly to set it aside from the ordinary Jimmy and partly to prevent air from collecting under the vehicle where it could unsettle at speed, a front air dam, complete with fog lights, was added.

Limited-slip differential

Although only 65 percent of the drive goes to the rear wheels through the all-wheel drive system, it is still a great deal of torque. This means a limited-slip differential is required to maintain traction on both rear wheels.

Four-speed automatic

Unlike standard Jimmys, the Typhoon is fitted with high performance 700 R4 four-speed automatic transmission, as found on many other GM performance vehicles.

Live axle

At the rear, the Typhoon retains a live axle because an independent unit just wouldn't be able to handle the torque from the turbocharged Vortech V6 engine. Both differentials use 3.42 gears.

Viscous coupling

To split the torque 35:65 front/rear a mechanical center differential is fitted in series with a viscous coupling. The system was first seen on GMC's all-wheel drive Safari van.

Specifications

1992 GMC Typhoon

ENGINE

Type: V6

Construction: Cast-iron block and heads

Valve gear: Two valves per cylinder operated by pushrods and rockers

Bore and stroke: 4.0 in x 3.5 in

Displacement: 262 c.i.

Compression ratio: 8.4:1

Induction system: Electronic fuel injection with intercooled Mitsubishi RH06 turbocharger

Maximum power: 280 bhp at 4,400 rpm

Maximum torque: 350 lb-ft at 3,600 rpm

Top speed: 124 mph

0-60 mph: 5.4 sec.

TRANSMISSION

GM 700 R4 four-speed automatic

BODY/CHASSIS

Separate steel frame with steel two-door SUV body

SPECIAL FEATURES

Typhoons have these special Turbine-style wheels as standard equipment.

> **NOTICE**
> DO NOT TOW A TRAILER WITH THIS VEHICLE.
> TOWING CAN CAUSE SEVERE DAMAGE TO ENGINE AND TRANSMISSION. THE POWERTRAIN IS NOT DESIGNED FOR TRAILER TOWING.
> PRINTED IN USA   PAS 15897

GMC warns owners not to use the Typhoon for towing.

RUNNING GEAR

Steering: Recirculating ball

Front suspension: Double wishbones with torsion bars, telescopic shock absorbers and anti-roll bar

Rear suspension: Live axle with semi-elliptic leaf springs, telescopic shock absorbers and automatic self-levelling

Brakes: Vented discs, 11.9-in. dia. (front), drums, 11.2-in. dia. (rear)

Wheels: Alloy, 8 x 16 in.

Tires: Firestone Firehawk SVX 245/50 VR16

DIMENSIONS

Length: 170.3 in.   **Width:** 68.2 in.

Height: 60.0 in.   **Wheelbase:** 100.5 in.

Track: 57.8 in. (front), 58.0 in. (rear)

Weight: 3,822 lbs.

Graham HOLLYWOOD

When Auburn-Cord-Duesenberg went out of business, two companies tried to save the incredible Cord. One was Graham-Paige, which transformed the front-wheel drive 810/812 into the rear-drive Hollywood.

"...in a class all its own."

"It may be based on the Cord 810, but the Hollywood behaves differently due to its rear-wheel drive chassis. Narrow tires and vague steering can be somewhat disconcerting at first, especially with so much power on command from the supercharged engine. The three-speed transmission is surprisingly smooth, and for cruising at high speed, the Graham is in a class all its own. A short wheelbase results in fair handling, though stopping needs care."

A stainless steel dashboard and split windshield give a typical 1940s look.

Milestones

1935 The Auburn Motor Co. introduces the Cord 810 at the New York Show. It has completely new styling and front-wheel drive.

Brothers Joe, Robert and Ray Graham started building cars in 1928 as Graham-Paige.

1936 Production gets underway with four bodystyles.

1937 The more powerful supercharged 812 is launched.

Graham production jumped in 1935, to 18,500 cars.

1939 Joe Graham approaches Norm de Vaux to build a version of the Cord 810 using a rear-drive chassis. De Vaux, owner of Cord tooling, agrees and the Hollywood goes into production in 1940. It is expensive to produce and is a slow seller. Graham ends production in late 1940.

UNDER THE SKIN

A simpler way

Graham had to make significant changes to the original Cord 810 to suit a simpler, rear-drive format. This required a new front suspension with a proven but somewhat archaic beam axle suspended on leaf springs. At the rear is a solid axle mating the driveshaft to the differential. It is also located and suspended by semi-elliptic leaf springs. Like most cars of the period, braking is by four-wheel, non-adjusting drums.

Separate steel chassis
Four-wheel drum brakes
Beam-axle front suspension
Supercharged six

THE POWER PACK

Continental engine

The original Cord 810/812 series relied on a Lycoming V8 engine, but the Graham brothers chose a different, less expensive route. In this case, it was Continental that supplied the 218-cubic inch, inline six-cylinder engine. This sidevalve design, with an iron block and alloy head, was available in normally aspirated form, producing 93 bhp (95 for 1941). Fitting Graham's own supercharger gave an extra 26 bhp (29 in 1941). Like most sidevalve engines, it had a long stroke (in this case 4.38 inches) and was designed for low-rpm torque. All the valves are on one side, operated by a single camshaft.

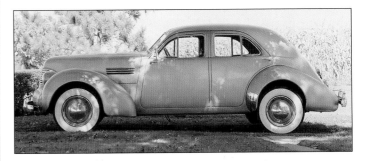

Hip Hup

Even rarer than the Graham Hollywood, with just 354 built, is the Hupmobile Skylark. Like the Hollywood, it was a way of keeping the look of the Cord 812 alive. It has a different engine and rear-wheel drive layout, as well as a restyled nose.

Hupmobile's Skylark looks almost identical to the Graham.

Graham-Paige chose the four-door Beverly Sedan shape rather than the two-door convertible from the various Cord bodystyles because it was intended to make the car a popular, mass-market contender.

Split windshield
Technology to produce compound curved glass had not been perfected in 1940. Even Cadillacs had split windshields, and the Cord and Graham Hollywood followed suit. The design is mirrored in the back window, which is also a two-piece split unit.

Pod headlights
The idea behind the Graham Hollywood was to produce a simpler, and less expensive car than the Cord. One of the complicated items to be dispensed with was the pop-up headlights. The lights were replaced by free-standing units mounted in pods on top of the fenders.

Side-valve engine
The Graham-Paige company had used six-cylinder, side-valve engines supplied by Continental since the late 1920s when the three Graham brothers took over Paige-Detroit to form Graham-Paige. The 218-cubic inch six used for the Graham Hollywood was by no means the largest. Previous models featured a 287-cubic inch six.

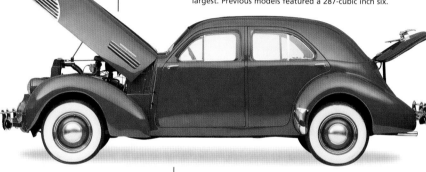

Three-speed transmission
While the Cord has a complicated remote electromagnetic-vacuum gear shifter with its own miniature gate (a system that could also be used as a pre-selector transmission), the Graham Hollywood uses a much simpler conventional manual unit. Like many Detroit cars of the time, the transmission has a column shift.

Live rear axle
With a switch from front to rear drive, the Cord beam rear axle was replaced by a live unit and differential, located and sprung on semi-elliptic leaf springs like most contemporary automobiles.

1941 Graham Hollywood

ENGINE

Type: Inline six-cylinder

Construction: Cast-iron block and alloy head

Valve gear: Two inline sidevalves per cylinder operated by a single block-mounted camshaft and solid valve lifters

Bore and stroke: 3.25 in. x 4.38 in.

Displacement: 218 c.i.

Compression ratio: 7.1:1

Induction system: Single Carter carburetor with Graham supercharger

Maximum power: 124 bhp at 4,000 rpm

Maximum torque: 182 lb-ft at 2,400 rpm

Top speed: 89 mph

0-60 mph: 14.6 sec.

TRANSMISSION
Three-speed manual

BODY/CHASSIS
Separate box-section steel frame with four-door sedan body

SPECIAL FEATURES

A split rear window is standard on all Graham Hollywoods.

In addition to fixed headlights, the Graham also has a different grill.

RUNNING GEAR

Steering: Worm-and-roller

Front suspension: Beam axle with semi-elliptic leaf springs and telescopic shock absorbers

Rear suspension: Live axle with semi-elliptic leaf springs and telescopic shock absorbers

Brakes: Drums (front and rear)

Wheels: Pressed steel discs, 5 x 16 in. dia.

Tires: Bias-ply, 6.00 x 16

DIMENSIONS

Length: 190.5 in. **Width:** 71.0 in.

Height: 60.5 in. **Wheelbase:** 115.0 in.

Track: 57.5 in. (front), 61.0 in. (rear)

Weight: 3,240 lbs.

Hudson **TERRAPLANE**

By the mid 1930s, Terraplanes were considered to be inexpensive, rugged and reliable automobiles. But that was to ignore the fact that these cars had a number of ingenious design features that set them aside from their more mainstream rivals from Ford and Chevrolet.

"...its appeal is obvious."

"You don't drive a Terraplane to go fast. Revel instead in the comfort of the softly sprung chassis and the refinement from such an apparently crude, simple engine. The side-valve six is surprisingly quiet. Its long stroke gives a large torque output at low rpm so it will pull from incredibly slow speeds in top gear. Add light steering once the car is underway, and very effective brakes and its appeal is obvious."

The spartan cabin includes a speedometer and a unique steering column-mounted semi-automatic gear shift selector.

Milestones

1924 Hudson develops a flathead, side-valve, six-cylinder engine for the new Essex Six.

1932 The first Terraplane appears. It is designed to undercut rivals from Ford and Chevrolet.

The most famous Hudson is the Hornet, made from 1949-1952.

1934 The Terraplane range is improved. The biggest news this year is the introduction of 'Axleflex'— a design that combines a beam front axle and an independent front suspension. The bodies are also restyled.

Dating from 1954, the compact Jet was the last true Hudson.

1947 The last link with the Terraplane comes to an end. The 212-cubic inch, side-valve six engine that began life in the stylish coupe was replaced with a larger 262-cubic inch engine.

UNDER THE SKIN

Semi-automatic gear shift

Channel section frame

Spirit of the age

Like most cars of the time, the Hudson is built on a massive channel-section frame. It is a large central 'X' member that is used to give it extra reinforcement. A beam axle at the front and a live axle at the rear are mounted to the chassis. Both are sprung by semi-elliptic leaf springs and damped by telescopic shock absorbers. Naturally, brakes are drums all around, but there are advanced features like the 'Electric Hand' semi-automatic gear shifter.

Live rear axle

Flathead six

THE POWER PACK

Old faithful

Hudson's flathead, six engine was already an old design by 1936 but had been steadily improved since it first appeared in 1924. It is a cast-iron unit with a three-bearing crank-shaft and sidevalves operated upward by block-mounted camshafts. One oddity, even for the time, is the lack of full-pressure lubrication to the bearings, although oiling improvements were made in 1934 when the veteran engine was stretched to 212 cubic inches. This, along with a low 6.3:1 compression ratio, was enough to give the Terraplane 88 bhp and surprising performance—0-60 mph in 23.2 seconds.

Short-lived

Although they started life under the Essex brand, the Terraplanes soon became a make in their own right. From 1936, they adopted a tasteful wraparound style grill. They were fast too, able to reach 60 mph in under 27 seconds and top 80 mph. Most desirable of all are perhaps the coupes and convertibles. A short production run means rarity today.

The Terraplane lasted only through 1937.

Even though Terraplanes were not intended to be the most flamboyant and stylish cars on the road, features like the attractive grill helped make these cars stand out in a crowd.

Side-valve engine

In an L-head sidevalve engine like the 3.5-liter Hudson six, both the intake and exhaust valves are on one side of the engine. Effectively, they work upsidedown, compared with an overhead-valve engine, with the combustion chambers in the head but to one side of the engine over the valves.

Low-pressure tires

To make its cars as comfortable as possible, Hudson had a tendency to fit larger, wider tires than its rival companies. These also ran at a relatively low pressure to improve the ride.

Solid front axle

Hudson's normal front- suspension system was more complicated than most. It fitted a radius arm on each side that was bolted to a solid axle. These ran back from the axle to pivots on the frame and provided better location than the semi-elliptic leaf springs could manage by them-selves. They also provide a measure of antidive under severe braking.

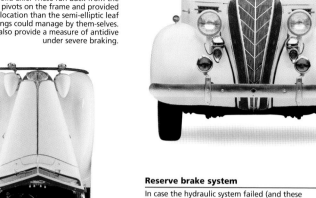

Reserve brake system

In case the hydraulic system failed (and these were the days before dual circuits), Hudson developed Duo-Automatic as a safety feature. Should the pedal get near the floor, it operates a cable to activate the rear brakes.

Welded-on body

Although the Terraplane had an unusual and immensely strong steel chassis for its time, Hudson made the whole car stiffer by welding on the all-steel bodywork at more than 30 points rather than simply bolting it in place like other manufacturers were doing.

Specifications

1936 Hudson Terraplane

ENGINE
Type: Inline six cylinder
Construction: Cast-iron block and head
Valve gear: Two valves operated by single camshaft mounted on side of block
Bore and stroke: 3.0 in. x 5.0 in.
Displacement: 212 c.i.
Compression ratio: 6.0:1
Induction system: Single downdraft Carter carburetor
Maximum power: 88 bhp at 3,800 rpm
Maximum torque: Not quoted
Top speed: 80 mph
0-60 mph: 23.2 sec.

TRANSMISSION
Three-speed manual

BODY/CHASSIS
Separate channel-section frame with X-brace and welded-on steel body

SPECIAL FEATURES

The Hudson Terraplane was know for its ornate details such as this interesting grill ornament.

A fold-out rear rumble seat can easily accommodate two people in total comfort.

RUNNING GEAR
Steering: Worm-and-sector
Front suspension: Solid axle with radius rods, semi-elliptic leaf springs and telescopic shock absorbers
Rear suspension: Live axle with semi-elliptic leaf springs and telescopic shock absorbers
Brakes: Drums (front and rear)
Wheels: Pressed steel, 16-in. dia.
Tires: 6.00 x 16

DIMENSIONS
Length: 195.0 in.   **Width:** 70.0 in.
Height: 70.8 in.   **Wheelbase:** 115.0 in.
Track: 56.0 in. (front), 57.5 in. (rear)
Weight: 2,740 lbs.

Hudson SUPER SIX

In 1948, Hudson introduced its 'step-down' range. Smooth and sleek, the Super Six has a low center of gravity and makes an excellent, though unusual, starting point for a lead sled. Custom body work and a modern fuel injected engine makes a very radically modified Hudson hot rod.

"...attention wherever it goes."

"Classic style meets 1990s technology—that's the best description of the interior of this Hudson. The custom upholstery contrasts with the small windows and the classic steering wheel. With a late-model LT1® V8 engine and automatic transmission, performance is good. But this car feels most at home cruising the strip and attracting attention wherever it goes."

No expense has been spared on this incredible customized Hudson, including radical changes to the interior.

Milestones

1948 After fielding warmed-over 1942 models for the past two years, Hudson introduces its radical 'step-down'. An all-new straight-six engine makes these Hudsons some of the fastest cars on sale in America.

1951 Hudson introduces the powerful Hornet with an enlarged straight-six engine.

From any angle the Hudson 'step-down' looks sleek.

1952 Although the Hornet proves to be an outstanding success in NASCAR, sales begin to slump due to lack of change. Hudson cannot afford tooling for a new body.

Hudson's Hornet was a successful NASCAR competitor.

1954 The 'step-down' returns for its last year. Styling is very dated, despite an attractive facelift.

UNDER THE SKIN

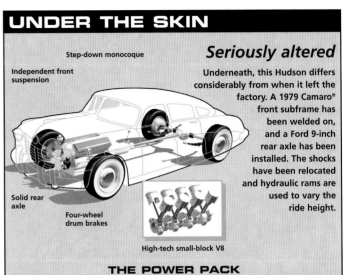

Step-down monocoque

Independent front suspension

Solid rear axle

Four-wheel drum brakes

High-tech small-block V8

Seriously altered

Underneath, this Hudson differs considerably from when it left the factory. A 1979 Camaro® front subframe has been welded on, and a Ford 9-inch rear axle has been installed. The shocks have been relocated and hydraulic rams are used to vary the ride height.

THE POWER PACK

Late-model motor

A late-model LT1 small-block Chevy™ powers this super-cool Hudson. Unlike many other customizers, the owner of this car has chosen to leave the powerplant fairly stock, only replacing the exhaust manifolds with Hooker headers. In this form the LT1 produces 310 bhp and 340 lb-ft of torque, more than enough to propel this heavy-weight lead sled. Although fitted with aluminum heads, the block is cast-iron and its design dates back to 1955.

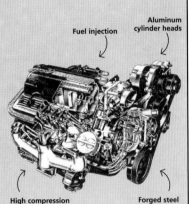

Fuel injection

Aluminum cylinder heads

High compression ratio

Forged steel connecting rods

Sleek shape

Although radical when it first appeared in 1948, the Hudson 'step-down' was a monocoque which made it difficult to alter. This meant that sales soon began to fall, despite the advent of the sporty Hornet. True Hudsons were history after 1954.

Even stock Hudson Sixes look low and perform well.

No expense was spared during the creation of this one-of-a-kind Hudson Super Six. The list of modifications is almost endless, and the result is a striking and unique car.

Sun visor
Despite the radical contemporary modifications, this Hudson is fitted with a period 1940s sun visor. On this car it is perfectly blended into the roof line.

Unique rear-end styling
The rear has been completely smoothed out and fitted with a single strip LED tail light taken from a 1993 Cadillac®.

Special wheels
Full dish aluminum wheels, like those used on Bonneville flats racers, are fitted and stand out against the dark paintwork.

Shaved doors
The doors have been 'shaved' of their handles and locks. Thanks to modern electronics, this lead sled uses a device that electronically activates latches hidden inside the doors to allow easy entry.

Custom hinges
Even the trunk-lid hinges have been altered, with the deck lid hinging to the right on opening.

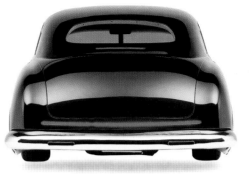

Fastback shape
Fastbacks were in vogue in the late 1940s. At the time of its introduction the 'step-down' Hudson had one of the sleekest shapes around. A low center of gravity ensures good handling.

Mildly modified
Although most of the car has been drastically modified, the LT1 small-block Chevy engine remains nearly stock to maintain reliability.

Specifications

1949 Hudson Super Six

ENGINE
Type: V8

Construction: Cast-iron block with aluminum heads

Valve gear: Two valves per cylinder operated by pushrods and rockers

Bore and stroke: 4 in. x 3.48 in.

Displacement: 350 c.i.

Compression ratio: 10.5:1

Induction system: Multiport electronic fuel injection

Maximum power: 310 bhp at 5,000 rpm

Maximum torque: 340 lb-ft at 2,400 rpm

Top speed: 124 mph

0-60 mph: 9.0 sec.

TRANSMISSION
GM 700R4 four-speed automatic

BODY/CHASSIS
Dropped floorpan monocoque

SPECIAL FEATURES

Flip-out door mirrors are a unique feature on this customized lead sled.

Even the valve covers have been custom-made and include Hudson script.

RUNNING GEAR
Steering: Recirculating ball

Front suspension: Unequal length wishbones with hydraulic rams and telescopic shocks

Rear suspension: Live axle with hydraulic rams, Watt linkage, and telescopic shocks

Brakes: Servo-assisted drums

Wheels: Custom alloy, 15-in. dia.

Tires: Firestone Firehawk F670-15.

DIMENSIONS
Length: 195.6 in. **Width:** 73.4 in.

Height: 54 in. **Wheelbase:** 124 in.

Track: 60.4 in. (front), 57.6 in. (rear)

Weight: 3,554 lbs.

Imperial CROWN

Imperial became a marque in its own right in 1955 in order to compete with Cadillac and Lincoln. Virgil Exner's spectacular 1957 Imperials took American luxury cars to new heights in terms of styling and roadholding.

"...superior road manners."

"Imperials have superior road manners compared with their rivals. Their torsion-bar front suspension ensures a soft ride, combined with much better handling than other Detroit offerings from this era. The larger-capacity V8 is tuned for maximum torque to make the journey as effortless as possible, but you can still hustle the Imperial along at a rapid pace. The steering is responsive but the drum brakes require a gentle touch."

A squarish steering wheel is one of a number of slightly unusual touches.

Milestones

1955 Chrysler nominates Imperial as a marque in its own right.

1957 Flamboyant new Imperials make a big impact in the luxury market.

1958 A mild facelift simplifies the front end and power rises to 345 bhp.

Chrysler's 1958 top-of-the-range staple was the New Yorker.

1959 A 350-bhp, 413-cubic inch 'wedge' engine now powers the car.

Chrysler's 300 letter cars were an alternative to the Imperial.

1960 A new body-shell accentuates the outlandish style of the range.

1962 The rear fins are cut down. Imperials are completely restyled for 1964.

1975 The Imperial is dropped by Chrysler.

UNDER THE SKIN

Live rear axle

Separate-perimeter frame

Torsion bar front suspension

Separate chassis

Chrysler really stole the stage from its rivals in 1957 by producing superbly engineered cars. Longitudinal torsion-bar front suspension made it one of the best-riding luxury cars around. A live axle is retained at the rear, sprung by semi-elliptic leaf springs. The hydraulic four-wheel drum brakes are power-assisted, as is the recirculating ball steering.

Wedge-head V8

THE POWER PACK

From Hemi to Wedge

When the new-series Imperial debuted for 1957, it used an expanded 392-cubic inch version of the classic Chrysler Hemi-head V8 first seen in 1951. This developed an impressive 325 bhp on a 9.25:1 compression ratio. For 1958, it was bumped up to 345 bhp, except on the Crown Imperial limousine. The following year a new 413-cubic inch wedge-head engine replaced the Hemi in all Imperials, except the limousine. Developing a modest amount of extra power (350 bhp), it was chosen because tooling and production costs were much lower than those of the Hemi, plus it was more tractable and flexible and required less frequent tune ups.

Fab fifties

All second-generation Imperials are dramatic-looking cars, but the earlier 1957-1959 models, with more power and arguably better lines, are the ones to go for. Southampton coupes, convertibles and Crown limousines are favorites.

This 1958 Crown Southampton is one of just 1,939 built that year.

The arresting appearance of the 1957 Imperial brought it to the attention of consumers, even though its style quickly became dated. In truth, the Imperial succeeded in challenging the supremacy of rival Cadillac.

Brushed steel inserts

A distinctive feature of these Imperials is their brushed steel roof panel trim. In style, the coupe roof echoes the 'sedanca de ville' look, while the hardtop sedan has a more restrained panel above the windows. From 1959, there was a corresponding brush-finish applique on the rocker panels, too.

Luxury cabin

Imperials were fully equipped to give them an edge in the closely fought luxury market. In the early 1960s, there was a huge range of push buttons, thick padded high-back seating and sumptuous upholstery. Air conditioning, six-way power seats and cruise control were optional.

Separate chassis

Unlike lesser Chryslers, Imperials stayed with a separate frame in 1960. This design is more effective at isolating road noise and vibration, an important element in luxury cars. Imperials finally adopted unitary construction in 1967.

Quad headlights

The Imperial was among the first cars to have four headlights as standard in 1957 (in states that permitted them). Stylist Virgil Exner gave the 1961 models free-standing headlights, set back in small fender coves.

Big tailfins

In size and profile, the tailfins of the 1957 Imperial were on par with those of others in the Chrysler stable that year. They had distinctive rocketship taillights and a trademark 'gunsight' treatment on the top end of the fin that lasted until 1961. The fins were cut right down in 1962 and small gunsights mounted on top of them. These were eliminated for 1963.

TorqueFlite transmission

Chrysler's major engineering accomplishment in 1957 was its brand-new TorqueFlite three-speed automatic transmission. Even by 1963, when this Crown was built, it was still smoother and more responsive than those from rivals Cadillac and Lincoln.

USA 1976-1986

Jeep **CJ-7**

Building on the legendary reputation of the Jeep name, the CJ-7 added flair and creature comforts to the basic durability for which Jeep was so well known. It was a massive sales hit.

"...unrivaled durability."

"When you've got the proven military record of the post-war Jeeps to build on, you already have the makings of a stunning recreational off-roader. The standard 232-cubic inch six-cylinder engine comfortably pulls the CJ-7 up all but the steepest hills—for which the V8 is needed—and the Jeep's durability is unrivaled among its peers. On-road, the CJ's responsive steering gives surprisingly capable handling, and there's a pliant ride, too."

The CJ-7 addresses passenger comfort with improved legroom and supportive seating.

Milestones

1976 After the success of the Jeep CJ-5, AMC responds to the growth of the leisure industry with the CJ-7, which has a longer wheelbase and six-cylinder power. It is also the first Jeep available with both TurboHydramatic and full-time Quadra-Trac 4WD. Hard-top and soft-top versions are available.

The original Jeep shows how little the design has changed in the transition to a leisure vehicle.

1978 The growth in Jeep sales prompts AMC to turn its Brampton, Ontario, plant over to Jeep production exclusively. The special-edition 'Golden Eagle' goes on sale.

The modern Wrangler Sport keeps the Jeep tradition alive.

1984 A new 2.5-liter engine is introduced, while the 'Limited' CJ-7 is discontinued.

1986 After 10 years of production, the last '7' is made.

UNDER THE SKIN

Classic evolution

Ladder-type chassis

Part- or full-time four-wheel drive

At the heart of the Jeep's rugged construction is a standard ladder-type frame— little changed from versions of the Jeep used in World War II. The suspension is by semi-elliptic leaf springs on a live axle with tube shocks. The standard transmission is a three-speed manual, with part-time four-wheel drive with a Dana 20 transfer case. The real change was that 'Quadra-Trac' four-wheel drive was optional on the automatic version.

In-line six

THE POWER PACK

Tough torquing

No-nonsense off-road utility vehicles need strong, reliable engines, and the Jeep is no exception. Although three engines were offered—two in-line sixes and a V8—the standard powerplant was AMC's torquey 232-cubic inch 100 bhp engine. Emissions regulations in California meant that models sold there used the 258-cubic inch single-barrel carburetor version of the engine, which was cleaner but had the same power output. The popular Renegade model has a 304-cubic inch V8 with 110 bhp.

Cast-iron block and cylinder head

Two valves per cylinder

Simple, durable construction

Top of the line

Offered from 1980, the Laredo was a top-line trim package on the CJ-5 and CJ-7. It included 8x15-inch chrome plated wheels with center caps, Goodyear Wrangler 9R tires, chromed front and rear bumpers, hood latch and mirrors, plus an uprated interior with high-back front bucket seats and a leather- rimmed steering wheel.

Laredo models tapped into the growing 4x4 luxury market.

While most of the U.S. car market faced a depression in the mid-1970s, AMC's Jeep witnessed a positive boom, thanks in part to the many available variations.

Soft- or hard-top
A soft-top had been used on Jeeps since the post-war years. The CJ-7 broke new ground when it became the first Jeep to offer a polycarbonate removable hard-top attachment. It included metal doors and roll-down windows.

Consistent identity
Although the Jeep has appeared in many different styles and finishes, the basic body shape and distinctive grill design have remained unchanged since World War II. The CJ-7 marked major under-the-skin changes, but nothing altered the vehicle's essential character.

Engine options
Although a V8 and large-capacity in-line six were also available, the standard, 232-cubic inch AMC in-line six is torquey enough to deal with all but the worst off-road conditions.

Four-wheel drive options
Standard manual CJ-7s use a part-time four-wheel drive system, while automatic models used the 'Quadra-Trac' permanent arrangement.

Renegade models
One of a number of variations on the standard CJ-7, the sporty Renegade model shown here includes a 'swing-away' spare tire attachment as standard equipment as well as other interior creature comforts.

Roll-bar design
By the time the CJ-7 arrived, the central roll-bar structure had become a permanent fixture on the Jeep. Roll bar padding was offered as an accessory from 1981.

ENGINE
Type: In-line six-cylinder
Construction: Cast-iron block and head
Valve gear: Two valves per cylinder operated by a single camshaft with pushrods and rockers
Bore and stroke: 3.75 in. x 3.50 in.
Displacement: 232 c.i.
Compression ratio: 8.0:1
Induction system: Single two-barrel carburetor
Maximum power: 100 bhp at 3,600 rpm
Maximum torque: 185 lb-ft at 1,800 rpm
Top speed: 73 mph
0-60 mph: 11.4 sec.

TRANSMISSION
Three-speed manual

BODY/CHASSIS
Ladder-type frame chassis with steel body

SPECIAL FEATURES

The hood attachment levers are unique and, like everything else, built to last.

A fold-down windshield was optional on later CJ-7s.

RUNNING GEAR
Steering: Recirculating ball
Front suspension: Live axle with semi-elliptic leaf springs and tube shock absorbers
Rear suspension: Live axle with semi-elliptic leaf springs and tube shock absorbers
Brakes: Discs, 12-in. dia. (front), drums, 11 x 2-in. (rear)
Wheels: Steel, 6 x 15 in.
Tires: Tracker A/T, 9 x 15 in.

DIMENSIONS
Length: 147.9 in.   **Width:** 65.3 in.
Height: 67.6 in.   **Wheelbase:** 93.5 in.
Track: 54.0 in. (front), 52.5 in. (rear)
Weight: 3,100 lbs.

Jeep **WRANGLER**

Almost a million Jeeps were built during World War II. They were simple, rugged, reliable and could go almost anywhere. It is these qualities that customers look for in the current Wrangler, introduced in 1997.

"...original off-roader"

"What began as the original purpose-built military off-roader is still built today, but is used more as a trendy transporter than the capable four-wheeler that it is. The Jeep is a fun and very capable off-road vehicle, where its short wheel-base is an asset and the suspension gives more wheel travel and better approach and departure angles. This means the Jeep's abilities are now better than ever. Acceleration and refinement are also notably improved."

The interior of the latest Wrangler is much more comfortable than that of the old model.

Milestones

1987 A new Jeep, called the Wrangler, replaces the long-running CJ series. The latest model features a restyled body with square headlights, an improved interior and smoother ride, but it retains the go-anywhere capability.

Current Wranglers still bear a resemblance to the original Jeep.

1991 Having bought American Motors in 1988, Chrysler introduces a performance Wrangler known as the Renegade, with wider body extensions and a 4.0-liter six-cylinder engine.

The forerunner of the Wrangler was the CJ, which lasted from 1954 to 1986.

1996 Rounded headlights signal the new Wrangler, brought out early for the 1997 model year. It has a stiffer chassis, coil-sprung suspension and an improved interior with air bags.

UNDER THE SKIN

Traditional Jeep

Like its Willys' ancestor, the Wrangler has a sturdy ladder-type frame chassis. Live rear axles are used in the front and rear. Coil springs replace the leaf springs of the earlier Wrangler and give a smoother ride. The Wrangler also features high and low four-wheel-drive ratios. The standard transmission is a five-speed manual, although a three-speed automatic is also available.

Ladder-type frame

Coil-sprung suspension

Live front and rear axles

Robust in-line six

THE POWER PACK

Enduring six

Extremely robust, the 4.0-liter cast-iron straight-six is an AMC design. It features a single block-mounted camshaft driving two valves per cylinder with pushrods, rockers and hydraulic lifters. The engine is torquey and reliable, producing its peak power of 184 bhp at just 4,600 rpm. This makes it ideal for off-roading. A concession to modern times is the sophisticated sequential electronic fuel injection system.

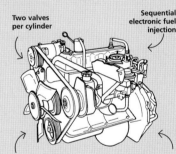

Two valves per cylinder

Sequential electronic fuel injection

Hydraulic valve lifters

Cast-iron block and cylinder head

Super Sahara

The original Jeep has come a long way since 1942. Top of the current range is the Wrangler Sahara, fitted with a 4.0-liter straight-six as standard. It features a deluxe interior and handsome spoked alloy wheels. European Saharas also have full-size doors and come with an optional lift-off hard top.

The latest Wrangler Sahara is refined compared to the previous model.

Still instantly recognizable, the current Jeep Wrangler has been considerably reworked, both inside and out, resulting in the best all around traditional Jeep ever built.

Alloy wheels
Today, many Wranglers are bought as much for image as for their off-road ability. Five-spoke aluminum wheels are standard equipment on the Sahara version.

Disc brakes
The first military Jeeps had four-wheel drum brakes, but the modern vehicles have large discs at the front with drums at the rear.

New bodywork
Although outwardly similar, the current Wrangler shares no body panels with its predecessor, except for the doors. The shape has been softened and round headlights are used again for the first time since 1986. Chrysler has also strengthened the already strong ladder-type frame.

Hard top
A detachable hard top, with glass side and rear windows, plus a rear wiper and a heated rear window, is standard equipment. It is 15 lbs. lighter than the hard top on the old model.

Six-cylinder engine
Wranglers use the same 4.0-liter in-line six-cylinder engine that is also found in the Cherokee. The camshaft profile is conservative and the engine tuned for torque at low rpm for optimal off-road ability.

Part-time four-wheel drive
The Jeep's four-wheel drive system is not permanently engaged like in some 4WD vehicles. It can be selected when required for ice, snow or off-road driving and can be switched in and out of four-wheel and two-wheel drive when the vehicle is moving.

Specifications
1998 Jeep Wrangler Sahara

ENGINE
Type: In-line six
Construction: Cast-iron block and head
Valve gear: Two valves per cylinder operated by one block-mounted camshaft via pushrods, rockers and hydraulic valve lifters
Bore and stroke: 3.88 in. x 3.41 in.
Displacement: 4.0 liter
Compression ratio: 8.75:1
Induction system: Electronic sequential fuel injection
Maximum power: 184 bhp at 4,600 rpm
Maximum torque: 220 lb-ft at 3,600 rpm
Top speed: 112 mph
0-60 mph: 8.8 sec.

TRANSMISSION
Five-speed manual or three-speed automatic with switch-on-the-fly two- or four-wheel drive and high and low ratios

BODY/CHASSIS
Separate ladder-type frame with steel two-door utility body

SPECIAL FEATURES

Factory-fitted tires are, appropriately, Goodyear Wrangler off-roaders.

An automatic transmission is available on the current Wrangler and is ideal for city driving conditions.

RUNNING GEAR
Steering: Recirculating ball
Front suspension: Solid live axle with leading links, coil springs and anti-roll bar
Rear suspension: Solid live axle with four trailing links, coil springs, gas shocks and anti-roll bar
Brakes: Vented discs, 11-in. dia. (front), drums, 9.0-in. dia. (rear)
Wheels: Alloy, 7 x 15 in.
Tires: Goodyear Wrangler 215/75 R15

DIMENSIONS
Length: 152.8 in.   **Width:** 68.1 in.
Height: 70.2 in.   **Wheelbase:** 93.4 in.
Track: 57.9 in. (front and rear)
Weight: 3,349 lbs.

USA 1993-PRESENT

Jeep GRAND CHEROKEE

Capitalizing on the past success of the Jeep name and heritage, Chrysler launched the Grand Cherokee for 1993. It's a large, luxurious, all-purpose machine and is capable of the sort of high performance normally reserved for sports cars.

"...an off-road sports car."

"Equipped with a V8 engine, the Grand Cherokee can take on all comers with the acceleration to rival sports cars. Furthermore, it does not roll through corners like most off-roaders. Ride quality is also good, even in rough conditions, and the sophisticated 4x4 system makes light work of difficult terrain. Inside, the Grand Cherokee Limited is fully equipped, better than many luxury cars on the market."

The Grand Cherokee has full instrumentation and features such luxuries as power seats and climate control.

Milestones

1992 Chrysler boss Bob Lutz reveals the Grand Cherokee by driving the first one from the factory, along the streets of Detroit and through a plate-glass window at the Detroit Auto Show.

The Wrangler is currently the entry-level vehicle and the most traditional in the Jeep range.

1994 European production begins at Chrysler's plant in Graz, Austria.

1996 The 1,000,000 Grand Cherokee rolls off the assembly line.

Since 1984 the Cherokee has remained a consistent winner in terms of sales.

1997 The new Grand Cherokee 5.9 Limited, equipped with a larger, 360-cubic inch V8, makes its debut to American buyers.

UNDER THE SKIN

Car-like construction

Coil springs all-around

Powerful Chrysler V8

All-steel body

5.9-liter V8

The Grand Cherokee boasts Chrysler's Uni-frame structure, a monocoque body/chassis mostly crafted from steel. The Quadra-Coil suspension consists of live front and rear axles suspended by coil springs, with anti-roll bars at both ends. Low-pressure gas-filled shock absorbers are standard all around.

THE POWER PACK

Awesome pulling power

While the Grand Cherokee is available with a six-cylinder engine and smaller V8, the Limited LX has the throaty growl of a 360-cubic inch V8, which dates from the 1960s. This engine also powers the mid-size Dodge Dakota, Durango sport-utility vehicle, and the full-size Ram pick-up. In the Limited, it produces 237 bhp and a huge 345 lb-ft of torque. This large engine enables the Grand Cherokee Limited LX to pull a trailer of up to 5,000 lbs.

Overhead valves

Single camshaft

Heavy cast-iron block and heads

Oversquare design

Limited LX

Launched in September 1997, the 5.9 Limited is the current flagship. The fastest Jeep ever marketed, it is also exceedingly capable off road and has one of the most luxurious and well-equipped interiors of any sport-utility vehicle. It may not be for everyone, but the 5.9 Limited is one of the best 4x4s in the world.

Enduring style is part of the Grand Cherokee's popularity.

Taking up its position at the top of the Chrysler Jeep tree, the 5.9 Limited provides the performance of a sports car, the luxury of a limousine, and the off-road ability of a Jeep.

Big V8 engine

The 360-cubic inch V8 runs smooth and provides ample torque. Sophisticated fuel injection and tough cast-iron construction, make for a reliable and robust powerplant.

Quadra-Trac four-wheel drive

An on-demand 4x4 system uses a viscous coupling center differential to split the torque between front and rear axles depending on ground surface conditions.

Aerodynamic design

Compared to contemporary cars, a drag coefficient figure of 0.45 seems quite high. The Grand Cherokee, however, is one of the most aerodynamic sports-utility vehicles ever built thanks to its raked front windshield and relatively low roof line.

Built-in roof rack

The sleek, contoured built-in roof rack increases the already-large luggage capacity.

Steep approach angle

With its small front overhang, the Grand Cherokee has an approach angle up hills of 37 degrees and a departure angle of 30 degrees.

Specifications
1998 Jeep Grand Cherokee Limited LX

ENGINE

Type: V8

Construction: Cast-iron block and heads

Valve gear: Two overhead valves per cylinder with hydraulic lifters

Bore and stroke: 4.02 in. x 3.58 in.

Displacement: 360 c.i.

Compression ratio: 8.7:1

Induction system: Fuel injection

Maximum power: 245 bhp at 4,050 rpm

Maximum torque: 345 lb-ft at 3,050 rpm

Top speed: 124 mph

0-60 mph: 8.2 sec.

TRANSMISSION

Four-speed automatic

BODY/CHASSIS

Steel monocoque five-door sport-utility

SPECIAL FEATURES

It's a tight squeeze under the hood, but the 360-cubic inch V8 engine gives outstanding performance.

Hood vents distinguish the 5.9 Limited from lesser models.

RUNNING GEAR

Steering: Power-assisted recirculating ball

Front suspension: Live axle suspended by coil springs with leading arms, shocks, and anti-roll bar

Rear suspension: Live axle suspended by coil springs with trailing arms, shocks, and anti-roll bar

Brakes: Vented discs front and rear, anti-lock brake system

Wheels: Alloy, 16-in. dia.

Tires: 225/70 R16

DIMENSIONS

Length: 177.2 in. **Width:** 70.7 in.

Height: 64.9 in. **Wheelbase:** 105.9 in.

Track: 58.5 in. (front), 58.8 in. (rear)

Weight: 4,218 lbs.

Lincoln ZEPHYR

Introduced as a 'junior' Lincoln, the Zephyr was the car that saved the division during the late 1930s. It revitalized the range and brought a combination of style and V12 power at a price rivals could not match.

"...relaxed performance."

"Effortless, relaxed performance sums up the Zephyr. The V12 is silky-smooth and pulls from extremely low revs yet still has enough top-end power to move the car to a relaxed 87 mph. With its synchromesh gears and a light clutch, gear shifts are easy. The steering is light thanks to the low-geared ratio, with 4.5 turns lock to lock. Despite having a fairly dated suspension, the ride is smooth, making long-distance journeys an enjoyable experience."

A distinctive feature of the Zephyr is its large-faced, center-mounted speedometer.

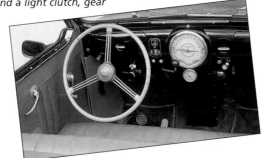

Milestones

1934 Briggs exhibits a concept car designed by John Tjaarda at the Chicago World's Fair. It has a rear-mounted V8 engine, fully independent suspension, unitary construction and radically new streamlined body styling.

The Zephyr was initially offered in two- and four-door sedan forms.

1936 A production Zephyr goes on sale. It is powered by a 267-cubic inch V12 and is styled is by Bob Gregorie.

1938 Zephyrs get a longer wheelbase and styling changes including a mouth organ grill.

A restyle for 1938 set a styling trend for the rest of the decade.

1940 The Zephyr gains an all-new body and a V12 stroked to 292 cubic inches. The convertible sedan is dropped, but production reaches 21,944.

1942 Civilian auto production is suspended.

UNDER THE SKIN

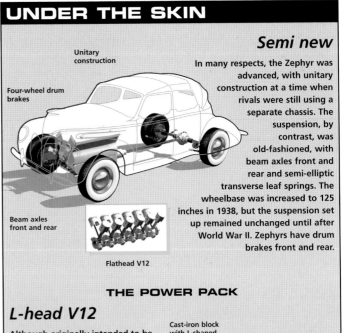

Unitary construction

Four-wheel drum brakes

Beam axles front and rear

Flathead V12

Semi new

In many respects, the Zephyr was advanced, with unitary construction at a time when rivals were still using a separate chassis. The suspension, by contrast, was old-fashioned, with beam axles front and rear and semi-elliptic transverse leaf springs. The wheelbase was increased to 125 inches in 1938, but the suspension set up remained unchanged until after World War II. Zephyrs have drum brakes front and rear.

THE POWER PACK

L-head V12

Although originally intended to be powered by a V8, the Zephyr was actually fitted with a V12 on the orders of Edsel Ford. It is a four-main-bearing L-head unit based on the flathead V8, but with a 75-degree angle. Initially, it produced only 110 bhp, and early versions suffered from overheating, warped bores and oil sludge buildup due to inadequate crankcase ventilation. The addition of hydraulic lifters in 1938 and cast-iron heads in 1941 improved reliability.

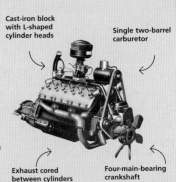

Cast-iron block with L-shaped cylinder heads

Single two-barrel carburetor

Exhaust cored between cylinders

Four-main-bearing crankshaft

Open air

For its day, the Zephyr was revolutionary in many ways, with its unitary construction and trend-setting styling. Perhaps the most desirable of all body styles is the four-door convertible, built only in small numbers and lasting through 1939.

Convertible Zephyr sedans were offered only in 1938 and 1939.

The Zephyr was a curious mixture of new technology—with unitary construction and smooth styling—combined with the old, including mechanical drum brakes and beam axle suspension front and rear.

Vacuum wipers
There is no electric motor for the windshield wipers, so they are powered by the inlet manifold vacuum. The speed of the wipers varies with engine load, resulting in a slower wiper speed up hills.

V12 engine
The Zephyr V12 is a compromise as it is based on the flathead V8. Quiet and refined, it is tuned for torque, not horsepower. The biggest problem is reliability and, consequently, many owners chose to replace the V12 with later Mercury flathead V8s.

Three-speed transmission
Geared more for torque than power, the V12 is perfectly mated to the three-speed manual transmission. Synchromesh is fitted to second and top gear to make shifting easier.

Steel disc wheels
By 1936, most American automobile manufacturers had abandoned wire wheels in favor of discs, and the Zephyr was no exception.

Two-speed axle
From 1936 to 1940 a two-speed Columbia rear axle was offered. This effectively doubles the number of gears, giving six forward speeds.

Beam axles
Due to the stubbornness of Henry Ford, the Zephyr retained beam-axle suspension with transverse leaf springs. To improve the handling, adjustable hydraulic shocks were offered.

Unitary construction
Adopting aircraft techniques, the Zephyr has a light, steel-covered girder-like framework onto which the body is welded. This results in a lighter structure than most rival luxury cars of the time.

Specifications

1939 Lincoln Zephyr

ENGINE
Type: V12

Construction: Cast-iron block and alloy heads

Valve gear: Two sidevalves per cylinder operated by a side-mounted camshaft

Bore and stroke: 2.75 in. x 3.75 in.

Displacement: 267 c.i.

Compression ratio: 7.2:1

Induction system: Single two-barrel downdraft carburetor

Maximum power: 110 bhp at 3,900 rpm

Maximum torque: 180 lb-ft at 3,500 rpm

Top speed: 87 mph

0-60 mph: 16.0 sec.

TRANSMISSION
Three-speed manual

BODY/CHASSIS
Unitary steel construction with four-door convertible sedan body.

SPECIAL FEATURES

A special V12 engine was commissioned for the Zephyr.

The spare tire mount can be hinged outward for easier luggage access.

RUNNING GEAR
Steering: Worm-and-roller

Front suspension: Beam axle with transverse semi-elliptic leaf spring and hydraulic shock absorbers

Rear suspension: Live axle with transverse semi-elliptic leaf spring and hydraulic shock absorbers

Brakes: Drums (front and rear)

Wheels: Steel discs, 16-in. dia.

Tires: 7.00 x 16 in.

DIMENSIONS
Length: 210.0 in.   **Width:** 73.0 in.

Height: 67.0 in.   **Wheelbase:** 122.0 in.

Track: 55.5 in. (front), 58.25 in. (rear)

Weight: 3,790 lbs.

Lincoln CAPRI

A new overhead-valve V8 engine, pioneering suspension and smart styling made the 1954 Lincoln one of the quickest and most roadable luxury cars of its time—so much so that it even won the Carrera Panamericana.

"...speed and agility."

"By 1950s standards, the 1954 Lincoln Capri was an exceptional car to drive, in terms of handling and performance. For three years running, the Capri took first and second place in the Pan Americana Road Race in Mexico—a testament to its excellent handling capabilities and reliability over the roughest terrain. There was even a popular song written about it—Hot Rod Lincoln— praising the car's speed and agility."

Tasteful use of chrome in the cabin helped give the Capri ground-breaking styling impact on the inside as well as out.

Milestones

1952 An all-new restyled Lincoln is launched. The more modern, racy-looking car also boasts a new overhead 317-cubic inch V8. Lincolns take first, second, third and fourth places in the Pan American Mexican Road Race.

The success of the Panamericana cars defined the image of the Capri.

1953 Lincoln takes the top four positions in the Pan American Mexican Road Race for the second year.

The Capri name was passed to Mercury and used for cars like this 1986 model.

1954 A slight change in fortune sees Lincoln take only first and second places in the Pan American Mexican Road Race.

1956 A complete restyle signals the next development of the Capri.

UNDER THE SKIN

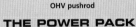

Separate chassis

Ball-joint front suspension with MacPherson struts

Recirculating ball steering

OHV pushrod

Stiff competition

In addition to a powerful engine, a good chassis is equally important to road racing. Fortunately, the 1954 Lincoln Capri had both. This era still used separate body-on-chassis design. The car's all-new chassis had increased torsional stiffness from the frame with its six crossmembers. The Capri was one of the first cars to utilize ball-joint suspension on MacPherson struts at the front.

THE POWER PACK

Smooth operator

The 1952 Lincolns were fitted with a new engine —a 317-cubic inch overhead-valve V8—which succeeded the old 337 flathead that had been used in everything from Ford trucks to Lincolns. The 317 is a wonderfully smooth engine, no doubt due to the crankshaft, which has no fewer than eight counterbalances (rather than the usual six). It is also highly suited to tuning; from an initial output of 160 bhp, Lincoln engineers managed to get 205 bhp out of it by 1954. And aftermarket items such as oversize inlet valves, mechanical cam followers and truck cams meant it was possible to coax up to 300 bhp from it.

All mod cons

Not many cars can claim both luxury and perfor-mance—the 1954 Lincoln Capri can. The option list was extraordinary: power-operated leather seats, power windows, power steering and brakes, and even a Hydramatic automatic transmission.

The 1952-1954 Lincolns could be very lavishly equipped.

Triumphs in the Pan Americana Mexican Road Race moved Lincoln upmarket in consumers' imaginations. The marque was once again perceived as competing with Cadillac, Packard and Imperial.

Powerful OHV V8

Lincoln engineers succeeded in coaxing more power from the overhead valve 317-cubic inch V8. First introduced in 1952, it was the first overhead-valve engine ever to be offered in a Lincoln. Initially output was a mere 160 bhp, but by 1954 it was up to 205 bhp.

Stiff chassis

The chassis is regarded as the Capri's great strength. Featuring additional K-braces with six crossmembers, stiffer rear springs and massive brake drums, it had the control and torsional stiffness needed for success in the Pan Americana Mexican Road Race for three consecutive years.

Revolutionary front suspension

In addition to a stiff chassis, Lincolns of this era also benefited from a revolutionary new front suspension setup. Ball-joint suspension with MacPherson struts proved to be much more flexible and rugged than traditional kingpins—ideal for arduous racing conditions.

Wraparound bumper

Wraparound bumpers give the 1954 Lincoln Capri greater visual impact than its predecessor, as do the torpedo-like protrusions at the front, called 'dagmars.'

Specifications

1954 Lincoln Capri

ENGINE

Type: V8

Construction: Cast-iron block and heads

Valve gear: Two valves per cylinder operated by a single camshaft with pushrods and rockers

Bore and stroke: 3.8 in. x 3.5 in.

Displacement: 317.5 c.i.

Compression ratio: 8.0:1

Induction system: Holley 2,140 four-barrel carburetor

Maximum power: 205 bhp at 4,200 rpm

Maximum torque: 280 lb-ft at 1,800 rpm

Top speed: 108 mph

0-60 mph: 13.4 sec.

TRANSMISSION

Hydramatic automatic

BODY/CHASSIS

Separate six crossmembered chassis with steel four-door or two-door body

SPECIAL FEATURES

The striking hood ornament was first seen on a 1949 Cosmopolitan.

The Capri is distinguished from the lesser Cosmopolitan series by its liberal use of chrome.

RUNNING GEAR

Steering: Recirculating-ball

Front suspension: Ball-joint suspension with MacPherson struts and coil springs

Rear suspension: Live axle with semi-elliptic leaf springs and telescopic shock absorbers

Brakes: Drums (front and rear)

Wheels: Stamped steel, 15-in. dia.

Tires: 8.00 x 15

DIMENSIONS

Length: 215.0 in.   **Width:** 77.6 in.

Height: 62.6 in.   **Wheelbase:** 123.0 in.

Track: 58.5 in. (front and rear)

Weight: 4,250 lbs.

Lincoln **CONTINENTAL MK IV**

Ford's luxury division revealed one of its largest cars ever for 1958. The following year, the Continental returned as a separate Lincoln sub series offered in coupe, convertible, town car and limousine forms. Priced at just over $7,000, it was not, surprisingly, rare and exclusive.

"...unparalleled level of opulence."

"It's apt to describe this car as huge! The Mark IV is longer and wider than just about any of its contemporaries. Although it has 350 bhp on tap, this Continental is more of a cruiser than muscle car, but it still remains effortless to drive and extremely smooth on the open road. The power steering is very light and taking corners at speed can produce some interesting results. The cabin has an unparalleled level of opulence."

Dominating the interior are the jumbo-sized steering wheel and unique instruments.

Milestones

1958 Lincoln issues its largest car yet for
public consumption. It is offered in Capri and Premiere series and both are powered by a 375-bhp, 430-cubic inch V8. In a recession year, sales are a modest 17,134. A similar, separate machine, the Continental Mk III, priced much economically than its predecessor is also offered; 12,500 are sold.

The first Continental arrived for 1940 as an upmarket Zephyr.

1959 Continental
Mk IV becomes part of the Lincoln line with its own range of models. It is priced above the Capri and Premiere. Power on the 430-cubic inch V8 drops to 350 bhp. Production reaches 15,780.

A much smaller and neater Continental debuts for 1961.

1960 The 131-inch wheelbase Lincolns make
their final appearance this year. Production falls yet again to below 15,000. A new, smaller Continental bows for 1961.

UNDER THE SKIN

On a huge scale

Unitary construction

Independent front suspension

Four-wheel drum brakes

Big-block V8

Built on a 131-inch wheelbase unitary chassis, the new-for-1958 Lincoln was one of the biggest cars of its time. Despite its size and unique slab-sided bodywork, it is conventional. Suspension is by unequal length wishbones suspended by coil springs at the front, while a live axle and semi-elliptic leaf springs are used at the rear. The Lincoln uses four-wheel, power-assisted, drum brakes.

THE POWER PACK

Biggest yet

Powering Lincoln's biggest car was, naturally, its biggest engine yet. The enormous 430-cubic inch V8, which debuted for 1958, was the largest passenger car engine up to that time. An outgrowth of the 1956 vintage 368, it is a heavy cast-iron unit, which in initial tune thumped out 375 bhp with a dual-plane intake manifold and four-barrel Holley carburetor. For 1959, power actually dropped to 350 bhp, but its stout 490 lb-ft of torque made it ideal for big, luxury cruisers.

Two valves per cylinder

Holley 4150 four-barrel carburetor

Cast-iron block and cylinder heads

Seven main bearings

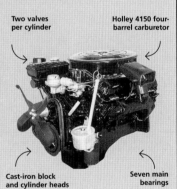

Slow seller

Making its debut on the eve of a recession, these big Lincolns were never built in large numbers. Among Continental Mk IVs, the convertible is the most valuable—only 2,195 were built. Good examples are highly sought after by collectors today.

Despite its huge size, the Mk IV has surprisingly clean lines.

At 227 inches long and weighing 5,192 lbs., the Continental Mk IV was no lightweight. In fact, it was so big that owners in certain parts of the country were required to place clearance lights on their cars for use on the road.

Monster big-block V8

Weighing more than 5,000 lbs., the Mk IV needed a massive engine to move it around. Nestling between the fenders is a monster 430-cubic inch V8, producing 350 bhp and an earth-moving 490 lb-ft of torque.

Power top

The Lincoln's power-operated soft top retracts behind the rear seats and is hidden under a metal tonneau cover, giving it a neat top-down appearence. An unusual option was available in 1958. If the car was parked outside with its top down and it started to rain, the top would automatically raise. Ford had many problems with this option which resulted in its ultimate demise in 1959.

Independent front suspension

The Mk IV uses typical 1950s Detroit suspension at the front, with unequal length wishbones, coil springs and telescopic shocks. Air suspension was offered for 1958, but few buyers chose it.

Automatic transmission

By 1959, most buyers expected automatic transmissions. Thus, the Mk IV came with a Ford Turbo-drive three-speed automatic operated with the column-shifter.

Unitary construction

A surprising feature for 1958-1960 Continentals and Lincolns was the adoption of unitary construction, making them stiffer and stronger than rival luxury cars.

Breezway rear window

With the top up, the 'Breezway' rear window gives a distinctive inverted profile. This style feature allows a smaller window, plus it reduces glare from sunlight and helps to keep the interior cool.

Panoramic windshield

First seen on the 1953 Cadillac Eldorado, the panoramic windshield was a feature of most U.S.-built cars by 1959. These provide excellent forward vision due to moving the A-pillars further back.

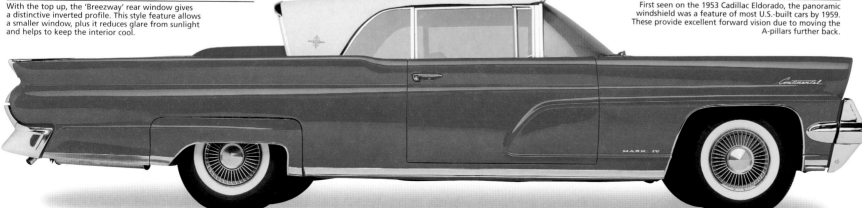

Specifications

1959 Lincoln Continental Mk IV

ENGINE

Type: V8

Construction: Cast-iron block and heads

Valve gear: Two valves per cylinder operated by a single camshaft with pushrods and rockers

Bore and stroke: 4.30 in. x 3.70 in.

Displacement: 430 c.i.

Compression ratio: 10.0:1

Induction system: Holley 4150 four-barrel carburetor

Maximum power: 350 bhp at 4,400 rpm

Maximum torque: 490 lb-ft at 2,800 rpm

Top speed: 118 mph

0-60 mph: 10.4 sec.

TRANSMISSION

Turbo-drive three-speed automatic

BODY/CHASSIS

Unitary monocoque construction steel coupe body

SPECIAL FEATURES

A 'Breezway' power window allowed open air driving for the rear passengers.

Compared to rival 1959 luxury cars, the fins on the Mk IV are quite modest.

RUNNING GEAR

Steering: Recirculating ball

Front suspension: Unequal length wishbones with coil springs and telescopic shock absorbers

Rear suspension: Live axle with semi-elliptic leaf springs and telescopic shock absorbers

Brakes: Drums (front and rear)

Wheels: Steel disc, 14-in. dia.

Tires: 9.50 x 15 in.

DIMENSIONS

Length: 227.1 in. **Width:** 80.1 in.

Height: 56.7 in. **Wheelbase:** 131.0 in

Track: 61.0 in. (front and rear)

Weight: 5,192 lbs.

Lincoln CONTINENTAL COUPE

In the mid-1970s, if a Rolls-Royce or Mercedes was not big, quiet, or luxurious enough, American buyers could get those qualities by buying a Lincoln Continental, one of the biggest and luxurious cars of its time.

"...smoothest ride possible."

"The Continental insulates you from the outside world. The big V8 is unstressed, producing power without a murmur, and the sound-deadening works superbly. Suspension is set up to give the smoothest ride possible. Despite its luxury role, this land yacht can be driven hard, partly thanks to surprisingly direct steering. Soft damping, though, means it's tricky keeping the body's movement under control."

Put the cruise control on, relax on the massive bench seat and enjoy the Continental.

Milestones

1970 The annual restyling of the Continental goes further this year, as it includes a longer wheelbase. Power comes from the 460-c.i. V8, pushing out 365-bhp at 4,600 rpm.

Most elegant and collectible of all Continentals is the 1956–1957 MKII.

1974 Lincoln gives the Continental a facelift. The most obvious difference is the radiator grill which loses its chrome top in place of painted metal with 'Lincoln' written across it. By this stage, power output from the V8 has dropped down to 220 bhp, an effect of emissions controls.

Lincoln's personal luxury offering in the late 1970s was the MKV.

1975 This year's variation on the Continental theme sees a new look to the roof and taillights. Underneath are improved brakes, steering and the option of four-wheel discs.

UNDER THE SKIN

Separate chassis

Live rear axle

Coil-sprung front suspension

Front disc brakes

V8 engine

Whereas other manufacturers moved from separate chassis to unitary construction, Lincoln went the other way with the Continental for the 1970s. It discovered that this was the best way to give the quietest and most refined feel. It has a well-located live rear axle with coil springs and an independent front suspension, along with recirculating-ball steering and a front disc/rear drum setup with optional anti-lock for the rear brakes.

THE POWER PACK

More Power!

A big car needs a big engine, and the Lincoln's V8 had grown from 430 to 460 cubic inches. Both bore and stroke are larger to give an oversquare (4.36 inches x 3.85 inches) layout in the conventional 90-degree V8 format, with cast-iron block and heads and a single camshaft mounted in the V driving two valves per cylinder with pushrods and rockers. Back in 1966, compression ratio was a high 10.25:1, helping account for its excellent 340 bhp at 4,600, an output that would rise over the years before plummeting to 215 by the time of the 1975 model and the onset of emissions regulations.

Early versions

More stylish than the sedan version, the Continental coupe is the model to go for. Pre-emissions cars are the best bets, as with over 300 bhp on tap, they have more than enough power to allow comfortable cruising in a majestic luxo-liner.

The Continental coupe has a massive road presence.

With the Continental, Lincoln was after an image of refinement. It was huge, but the slow, steady evolving styling was intended to be subdued rather than brash, radiating good taste and high quality.

V8 engine

Part of the explanation for the huge difference in power output between the first 460-c.i. V8's output and the far lower figures from the mid-1970s, is that the early outputs were gross figures and the later ones net. Increasingly strict emissions regulations played an influential part.

Auxiliary fuel tank

To increase the thirsty Lincoln's range, an auxiliary fuel tank was part of the options list. This holds around eight gallons, which is about enough to stretch the range by another 100 miles. It fills through an overflow from the standard fuel tank.

Perimeter chassis

In a move that seems counter to automotive progress, Lincoln switched from a modern unitary structure for the Continental back to an old-fashioned chassis frame. This was first done in the late 1960s, and a perimeter-style frame was chosen. The explanation was that it allowed a softer, more luxurious and quieter ride to be engineered into the car.

Front disc brakes

Even though these big Continentals weigh in at well over 5,000 lbs., Lincoln felt that disc brakes only on the front would be sufficient. They are large vented discs, 11.8 inches in diameter, and are supplemented by drums on the rear axle.

Lower rear wheel arches

On the 1975 model, Lincoln wanted to emphasize the long, low look, and so almost half of the rear wheel arch opening is enclosed by a removable cover.

9-inch Live rear axle

To prevent the rear axle from swaying around, there are trailing arms, an upper torque arm and a transverse link to stop sideways movement. Coil springs are fitted for support.

Specifications

1975 Lincoln Continental Coupe

ENGINE

Type: V8

Construction: Cast-iron block and heads

Valve gear: Two valves per cylinder operated by a single block-mounted cam shaft with pushrods and rockers

Bore and stroke: 4.36 in. x 3.85 in.

Displacement: 460 c.i.

Compression ratio: 8.0:1

Induction system: Single Motorcraft 9510 four-barrel carburetor

Maximum power: 215 bhp at 4,000 rpm

Maximum torque: 338 lb-ft at 2,800 rpm

Top speed: 118 mph

0-60 mph: 10.4 sec.

TRANSMISSION

C6 Three-speed automatic

BODY/CHASSIS

Separate steel-perimeter frame and steel two-door coupe body

SPECIAL FEATURES

Headlights are hidden behind covers, which are vacuum operated.

 There is a wide array of gadgets in the Continental. Even the front vent windows are power-operated.

RUNNING GEAR

Steering: Recirculating-ball

Front suspension: Unequal-length A-arms with coil springs, telescopic shock absorbers and anti-roll bar

Rear suspension: Live axle with trailing and radius arms, coil springs and telescopic shock absorbers

Brakes: Discs, 11.8-in. dia. (front), drums (rear)

Wheels: Stamped steel discs, 15-in. dia.

Tires: 230 x 15 steel belted radial

DIMENSIONS

Length: 232.9 in.	**Width:** 78.0 in.
Height: 55.3 in.	**Wheelbase:** 127.2 in.

Track: 64.3 in. (front and rear)

Weight: 5,219 lbs.

Lincoln MARK VII

If the MK VI had been somewhat somber, its successor was anything but. It combined both modern aero and classic retro styling touches. It also offered remarkable straight-line grunt with exceptional road manners.

"...matured Mustang GT."

"Settle yourself behind the wheel and take it all in. The plush leather seats are comfortable and supportive, and there are electric devices to cater to your every need. If the Mark VII feels like a matured Mustang GT that's because it shares the same 5.0-liter V8 as its sinister stablemate. The engine has plenty of get up and go once you hit the gas. The transmission does a fine job in harnessing its power. An air suspension ensures a smooth ride, but not at the expense of handling."

Electrically adjustable seats, climate control and power everything adorn the Mk VII.

Milestones

1984 Lincoln unveils its new personal luxury coupe, the Continental Mk VII, which has slippery styling. It is initially offered in base, Bill Blass, Versace and LSC editions. The latter is the performance model with fatter tires and a ridged suspension.

The MK VII is based on the 1983-1988 Ford Thunderbird chassis.

1985 Anti-lock disc brakes are standard on the LSC. This is one of the first cars offered with ABS.

1986 LSCs get the 200-bhp Ford Mustang GT fuel-injected V8, and ABS is standard on lesser VIIs.

Replacing the MK VII for 1993 was the swoopy Mk VIII.

1987 Larger wheels and tires plus a 225-bhp 5.0-liter V8 come in the LSC. 27,119 VIIs are built.

1990 Exclusive BBS wheels and a driver's-side airbag are new items.

UNDER THE SKIN

Floating 'Fox'

Built on a 108.5-inch wheelbase 'Fox' platform (shared with the shorter Ford Thunderbird and Mercury Cougar), the MK VII has a typical front-engined, rear-wheel drive configuration with struts at the front and a live rear axle. In place of conventional coil springs are cylindrical airbags. LSCs have thicker anti-roll bars, wider, high-speed tires and sure-grabbing, four-wheel, ABS disc brakes.

Rear wheel drive
Air suspension
Four-wheel disc brakes
Unitary construction
Small-block V8

THE POWER PACK

Mustang mill

All Mk VIIs came from the factory powered by 5.0-liter, small-block, Windsor V8s, but the LSC version is the most muscular. In 1985, power rose from 140 to 165 bhp. A year later, electronic fuel injection arrived, giving a solid 200 bhp and a ground-rippling 285 lb-ft of torque. In 1987, revised cylinder heads and dished pistons helped the engine produce an even greater 225 bhp and its 300 lb-ft of torque made for hasty acceleration. It was the same engine that powered the street-menacing Mustang GTs. This made the LSC a true gentleman's GT.

Luxury sport

Greatly undervalued today, the Mk VII LSC is a refined luxury grand tourer with noticeable performance and handling to match. Post-1987 cars with their 225-bhp engines and larger wheels and tires are the ones to go for. 1992 models are especially rare.

Of all MK VII variants, LSCs are the most powerful.

LSC stands for Luxury Sport Coupe, and in this form the Mk VII was the hot-rod Lincoln that came to life. It offered similar performance to more exotic and prestigious coupes, but at a fraction of the price.

Aero headlights

Aero-style headlights were not permitted on U.S.-market cars in the early 1980s, but the Mk VII was one of the first to use them, resulting in a very clean frontal appearance. They are flanked by parking and turn signal/running lights.

Ford Mustang V8

Heart of the LSC is its formidable 225-bhp 5-liter small-block V8. This engine gives the MK VII outstanding performance for a heavyweight machine; in bone stock configuration, 16.1-second quarter-miles are possible.

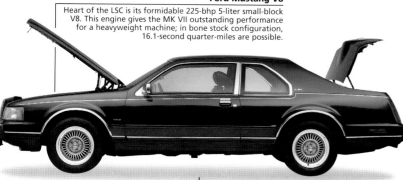

Air suspension

Instead of coil springs, cylindrical airbags are fitted at all four corners. Pressure, ranging from 75 to 100 psi, is controlled automatically by a compressor that optimizes settings for load, ride and handling.

Bigger wheels and tires

LSC models got stouter power steering (2.5 turns lock to lock), stiffer shock valving and air springs stiffened by 70 percent. From 1987, tire size was increased to P225/60R16 and BBS cross-lace wheels were added for the 1990 model year.

Retro styling touches

Although heavily based on the contemporary Thunderbird, Lincoln stylists sought to differentiate the Mark by adding more formal taillights, a traditional simulated spare tire mount on the trunk, thicker C-pillars, and a chromed grill and trim.

Luxurious interior

Inside, the MK VII is well appointed with standard power windows, door locks, mirrors, tilt steering wheel, cruise and climate control, and 12-way power front seats.

Specifications

1990 Lincoln Mk VII LSC

ENGINE

Type: V8

Construction: Cast-iron block and heads

Valve gear: Two valves per cylinder operated by pushrods and rockers

Bore and stroke: 4.00 in x 3.00 in

Displacement: 5.0 liter

Compression ratio: 9.2:1

Induction system: Sequential electronic fuel injection

Maximum power: 225 bhp at 4,200 rpm

Maximum torque: 300 lb-ft at 3,000 rpm

Top speed: 137 mph

0-60 mph: 8.0 sec.

TRANSMISSION

AOD four-speed automatic

BODY/CHASSIS

Unitary monocoque construction with steel two-door coupe body

SPECIAL FEATURES

In mid-1987, LSCs were shod with larger, 16-inch aluminum wheels and Goodyear Eagle GT+4 tires. BBS wheels arrived in 1990.

A humped trunklid maintained a link with Lincoln's past.

RUNNING GEAR

Steering: Recirculating ball

Front suspension: Struts, lower control arms, air springs, telescopic shock absorbers and anti-roll bar

Rear suspension: Live axle, radius arms, airsprings, telescopic shock absorbers and anti-roll bar

Brakes: Discs (front and rear)

Wheels: 7 x 16 in. cast aluminum

Tires: Goodyear Eagle GT+4 P225/60R16

DIMENSIONS

Length: 202.8 in.   **Width:** 70.9 in.

Height: 54.2 in.   **Wheelbase:** 108.5 in.

Track: 58.4 in. (front), 59.0 in. (rear)

Weight: 3,779 lbs.

Lincoln MK VIII

The stylish, quad-cam 32-valve Mk VIII not only carried on the pioneering work of the Mk VII—the car that started Lincoln's assault against luxury exotic imports—it took it onto a totally new level.

"...air-cushioned ride."

"Remarkably, slowing the steering for the final version actually improved the feel of the big Lincoln. With just 2.6 turns lock to lock, it tended to dart around on lock, but by making it more stable, it allows drivers to enjoy a mix of agile handling and a supple, air-cushioned ride. The refined V8 gives enough power to make the Mk VIII really get up and go—moving its large mass to 60 mph in seven seconds takes plenty of horsepower and torque."

The futuristic, wraparound fascia design incorporates driver and passenger airbags.

Milestones

1984 The first of a new generation of streamlined modern-looking Lincolns appears in the form of the Mk VII.

The predecessor to the MK VIII was the more upright MK VII.

1992 Lincoln's response to the dominant European and Japanese luxury sedan imports becomes the sleek Mk VIII.

1996 New and far more effective high-intensity discharge (HID) headlights are fitted to the Mk VIII LSC model.

The 1995 Continental sedan shows styling cues from the Mark VIII.

1997 All Mk VIIIs get the HID lights. The steering is recalibrated for greater stability, and a new, more prominent grill appears.

UNDER THE SKIN

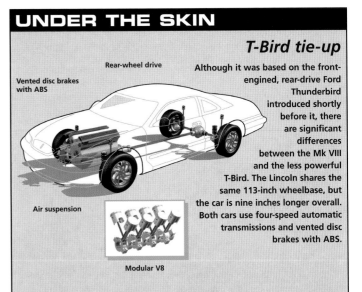

Rear-wheel drive

Vented disc brakes with ABS

Air suspension

Modular V8

T-Bird tie-up

Although it was based on the front-engined, rear-drive Ford Thunderbird introduced shortly before it, there are significant differences between the Mk VIII and the less powerful T-Bird. The Lincoln shares the same 113-inch wheelbase, but the car is nine inches longer overall. Both cars use four-speed automatic transmissions and vented disc brakes with ABS.

THE POWER PACK

Modular motion

Though not as torquey as the 5.0 liter push-rod V8, the 4.6 liter unit is starting to gain a favorable reputation. This engine is part of Ford's modular V8 family, also found in the Mustang, and has both the block and the heads made in alloy. Also, there are four valves per cylinder rather than two. They are opened by four overhead camshafts. With electronic fuel injection and a fairly high (9.8:1) compression ratio, power output is now an impressive 290 bhp, plus an equally impressive 285 lb-ft of torque.

Luxury LSC

The 1998 Mk VIII LSC was the best model ever—thanks to alterations to the steering ratio, which is now more sutiable for this heavyweight. Recalibrated shock absorbers give firm yet comfortable suspension control and a more secure feel.

Suspension modifications transformed the feel of the LSC.

The staid looks of the old Lincolns are long gone, and there are big changes under the skin, too. Modern Lincolns have the high performance and handling to match their advanced and racy styling.

V8 engine
The top-of-the-range LSC model uses the same 4.6-liter alloy quad-cam 32-valve V8 as the rest of the Mk VIIIs, but for the LSC it has an extra 10 bhp. Compared with a traditional iron pushrod V8, the power and the torque are both produced at higher rpm.

Sideview signaling
Small LEDs (light-emitting diodes) are incorporated in the sideview mirrors and light up when the turn signals are used. These lights can be seen by following traffic but not by the driver, to avoid distraction.

Air suspension
The Lincoln dispenses with conventional steel coil springs in favor of pressurized air bags that act as springs.

Vented discs
For 1997, Lincoln made the vented disc brakes thicker and more durable. The heavy Mk VIII takes just 183 feet to stop from 70 mph.

Neon rear light
A single neon light is used to illuminate the rear lights in the band across the back of the car.

Traction control
A sending unit tells the computer if one or both wheels are spinning and then engages the car's traction control system until grip is regained.

Alloy hood
Lincoln needed to save weight wherever possible. One ploy was to make a composite hood, although that policy changed—for 1997 the LSC had an alloy piece.

Specifications

1995 Lincoln Mk VIII LSC

ENGINE
Type: V8

Construction: Alloy block and heads

Valve gear: Four valves per cylinder operated by twin chain-driven overhead camshafts per bank of cylinders

Bore and stroke: 3.54 in. x 3.54 in.

Displacement: 4,601 cc

Compression ratio: 9.8:1

Induction system: Electronic fuel injection

Maximum power: 290 bhp at 5,750 rpm

Maximum torque: 285 lb-ft at 4,500 rpm

Top speed: 123 mph

0-60 mph: 7.0 sec.

TRANSMISSION
Four-speed automatic

BODY/CHASSIS
Unitary monocoque construction with steel two-door sedan body

SPECIAL FEATURES

All Mk VIIIs have these distinctive wraparound front lights.

The security system includes an electronic memory keypad under the door handle to unlock it.

RUNNING GEAR
Steering: Rack-and-pinion

Front suspension: Upper and lower wishbones with air springs, telescopic shock absorbers and anti-roll bar

Rear suspension: Upper and lower wishbones with air springs, telescopic shock absorbers and anti-roll bar

Brakes: Vented discs, 11.5-in. dia., (front), 10.1-in. dia. (rear)

Wheels: Chromed alloy, 7 x 16 in.

Tires: 225/60 R16

DIMENSIONS
Length: 207.2 in.   **Width:** 74.8 in.

Height: 53.6 in.   **Wheelbase:** 113.0 in.

Track: 61.6 in. (front), 60.2 in. (rear)

Weight: 3,765 lbs.

Lincoln **NAVIGATOR**

With the boom in upscale sport-utility vehicles, Ford decided it wanted a slice of the market. Enter the Navigator, an F-series based off-roader with a powerful 5.4-liter 230-bhp V8 engine and luxury interior appointments.

"...does the driving for you."

"Sitting in a Navigator is much like getting behind the wheel of a Lincoln Town Car, though the high driving position offers a better view of the road. Off the highway, the Navigator is surprisingly capable. Select low range four-wheel drive and the vehicle rises an inch higher at speeds under 25 mph, helping it clear difficult obstacles. On the highway, the Navigator is relaxing to drive, being quite comfortable and refined."

A spacious interior offers power everything and standard leather upholstery.

Milestones

1996 The last of the F-150-based two-door Bronco off-roaders goes on sale.

Mercury launched its first sport utility, the Mountaineer, in 1997.

1997 Ford launches its first full-size four-door sport-utility vehicle, the Expedition. Based on the new 1997 F-150, it is designed to compete with the Chevrolet Tahoe and has selectable four-wheel drive.

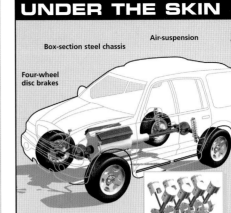

The Navigator is based on the full-size Ford Expedition.

1998 Lincoln introduces an upscaled version of the Ford Expedition. Called the Navigator, it has styling touches to differentiate it from lesser models, a standard 5.4-liter V8 and a luxury interior. It is available in two- or four-wheel drive and can tow up to 8,000 lbs.

UNDER THE SKIN

Box-section steel chassis

Air-suspension

Four-wheel disc brakes

Subtle changes

The body may look a little bit different from the Ford Expedition, but the floorpan and running gear are shared and can be traced back to the F-150 pickup. The Navigator is more sophisticated, however. There is a choice of rear or four-wheel drive models, both with four-speed automatic. The four-wheel drive has air shocks and springs to give a softer ride.

Modular V8

THE POWER PACK

High-tech V8

All Navigators use the 5.4-liter Triton version of Ford's modular V8 engine. Although it is a cast-iron engine with two valves per cylinder, it has a single overhead camshaft per bank and sequential multi-point electronic fuel injection. It produces a stump-pulling 325 lb-ft at a low 3,000 rpm, allowing the Navigator to scramble over rough terrain with ease. The modular V8 also has platinum-tipped spark plugs which will last for 100,000 miles.

Platinum tipped spark plugs

Sequential electronic fuel injection

Cast-iron block and heads

Single overhead camshafts

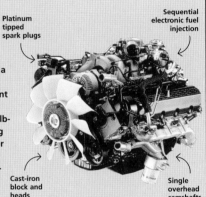

Better buy

Although a two-wheel drive version is available, the four-wheel drive model is the better choice. It costs just over $3,000 more, but it is far more tractable and easier to drive. Off-road, the 4WD version will handle itself in just about any terrain.

Navigators have one of the highest towing capacities of any off-roader.

Equally at home in the most elegant of residential areas, roaming through a national park or towing a power boat, the Navigator is the most versatile vehicle Lincoln has ever built.

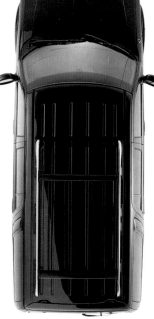

Air suspension
Like the Lincoln Mk VIII coupe, air springs are are used on all four wheels of the 4WD Navigator. They work in conjunction with the automatic load leveling facility which senses the load and adjusts the suspension pressure accordingly.

V8 engine
Ford's most modern V8 engine, in its largest format of 5.4 liters, is used in the Navigator. It boasts features like individual coil ignition for each cylinder and needs no tuning for 100,000 miles.

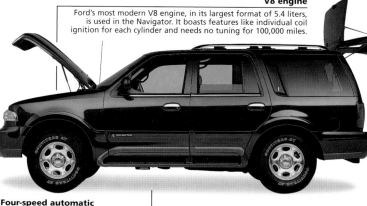

Four-speed automatic
The only transmission available is Ford's four-speed overdrive automatic with a column-mounted shift lever.

Speed sensitive steering
Although old-fashioned, a recirculating ball steering system is used on this Lincoln. It's allied to speed-sensitive power assistance.

Illuminated running boards
To save knocked or bruised shins and the sort of undignified stumbles quite inappropriate to a Lincoln owner, the running boards are illuminated at night when the doors are unlocked.

Skid plates
The Navigator is the only Lincoln ever made to need skid plates. They are fitted under the vehicle to prevent damage to engine or transmission when the Navigator goes off road.

Live rear axle
The one area in which the Navigator shows its Ford F-150 truck chassis origins is the live rear axle. It is well located, however, with upper and lower trailing arms and a Panhard rod to prevent lateral movement.

Rear tailgate
For extra convenience the rear tailgate is split so that either the upper glass section or the whole door can be opened depending on the size of the load.

Perfect accommodation
Not only do the power front seats have a memory function with three settings but there are bucket seats for the second row of passengers and a bench seat for the third row. All seats can be leather trimmed if desired and the third-row bench can be removed for extra luggage space.

Specifications

1998 Lincoln Navigator

ENGINE
Type: V8

Construction: Cast iron block and alloy heads

Valve gear: Two valves per cylinder operated by single overhead cam per bank of cylinders

Bore and stroke: 3.55 in. x 4.16 in.

Displacement: 5.4 liter

Compression ratio: 9.0:1

Induction system: Multi-port sequential fuel injection

Maximum power: 230 bhp at 4,250 rpm

Maximum torque: 325 lb-ft at 3,000 rpm

Top speed: 109 mph

0-60 mph: 11.4 sec.

TRANSMISSION
Four-speed auto with four-wheel drive, high and low ratio

BODY/CHASSIS
Separate box section frame with steel SUV four-door seven- or eight-passenger body

SPECIAL FEATURES

High-intensity headlights give excellent illumination at night.

Directional arrows appear in the mirrors at night when the indicators are in use.

RUNNING GEAR
Steering: Recirculating ball

Front suspension: Double wishbones with air springs and anti-roll bar

Rear suspension: Live axle with air springs, trailing arms, Panhard rod and anti-roll bar

Brakes: Vented discs, (front), solid discs, (rear), ABS standard

Wheels: alloy, 7.5 in. x 17 in.

Tires: P255/75R 17

DIMENSIONS
Length: 204.8 in.   **Width:** 79.9 in.

Height: 76.7 in.   **Wheelbase:** 119 in.

Track: 65.4 in. (front), 65.5 in. (rear)

Weight: 5,557 lbs.

Lincoln TOWN CAR

One of the last of the traditional-style big luxury sedans, the Town Car continues to be a consistent seller, thanks to its long list of standard features, competitive pricing and outstanding attention to detail.

"...allows total comfort."

"Once upon a time, most full-size cars were like this, but today there are few traditional-style, full-size choices. A truly huge interior welcomes you, allowing the driver and passengers to stretch out in total comfort at any speed. At speed the Town Car is whisper-quiet, and for a 4,000-lb. car it handles as well as can be expected. Its anti-lock braking is reassuring and the 220-bhp V8 is creamy smooth, offering plenty of torque for brisk acceleration."

Changes for 1999 include revised wood appliqués and storage space in the armrest.

Milestones

1990 Smoother styling on a carried-over chassis and suspension marks Lincoln's new Town Car. It wins *Motor Trend*'s coveted 'Car of the Year' award.

1991 A 4.6-liter modular V8 replaces the pushrod 5.0-liter unit.

The boxy first-generation Panther platform Town Car lasted until 1989.

1995 A revised grill and taillights, plus a standard anti-theft system, selectable steering and new optional wheels, appear on the new model.

1996 A special Diamond anniversary model briefly goes on sale.

1990-1997 Town Cars are refined and popular luxury cruisers.

1998 A new, more aerodynamic body and interior and bigger brakes are just a few of the many changes.

UNDER THE SKIN

Rock steady

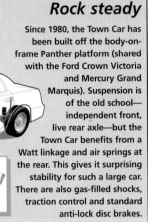

Body-on-frame construction

Dual exhausts

Coil-sprung independent front suspension

Smooth V8

Since 1980, the Town Car has been built off the body-on-frame Panther platform (shared with the Ford Crown Victoria and Mercury Grand Marquis). Suspension is of the old school—independent front, live rear axle—but the Town Car benefits from a Watt linkage and air springs at the rear. This gives it surprising stability for such a large car. There are also gas-filled shocks, traction control and standard anti-lock disc brakes.

THE POWER PACK

Modular power

Since 1991, all Town Cars have been powered by Ford's modular 4.6-liter (281-cubic inch) single overhead-cam V8. This smooth, silky V8 has Ford's EEC-V processor that controls the sequential multipoint electronic fuel injection, electronic voltage regulator, mandatory on-board diagnostics II programming and a distributorless ignition. The engine is offered in two states of tune: 205 bhp or 220 bhp, enabling 0-60-mph sprints in a shade less than eight seconds.

Touring

Offered in Executive, Signature and Cartier editions, the Town Car is a tremendous luxury buy. To get the most for your money, order the top-of-the-line Cartier edition with the Touring package, which adds a stiff suspension and provides an extra 15 bhp.

The Touring package is available only on Signature and Cartier series.

The Town Car is the most traditional and luxurious vehicle in the Lincoln lineup—customers undoubtedly agree because this fabulous four-door is the company's best seller hands down.

Overhead-cam V8

Since its introduction in Town Cars back in 1991, the 4.6-liter single overhead-cam engine has become a mainstay of FoMoCo products. In Touring package-equipped Town Cars, it produces 220 bhp and 290 lb-ft of torque, giving good mid range power.

Touring suspension

Lincoln offers a sport suspension on the Signature and Cartier editions. This adds 60-series Touring tires on cast-aluminum wheels, revised spring rates and revalved shocks along with a 3.55:1 rear axle ratio.

Subtle differences

Touring package-equipped Town Cars also have a small number of external differences. The lower-body cladding and fascias are body-colored and the grill is painted argent silver with chrome trim.

Side airbags

A new feature is the standard side airbags located in the bolsters of the front seats. These are designed to provide incremental head and chest protection. Inflation time upon impact is 30 milliseconds.

Well-located axle

A major criticism of large U.S. cars in the past was their wayward handling. Ford engineers paid considerable attention to handling on the Town Car, with better location of the rear axle with the use of a Watt linkage. This results in reduced oversteer at the limit.

Spacious interior

Classified as a large car by the Environmental Protection Agency, the Town Car boasts one of the biggest interiors of any production car. Rear-seat leg room is 41 inches and head room is 39.2 inches in the front.

Specifications

1999 Lincoln Town Car Cartier

ENGINE

Type: V8

Construction: Cast-iron block and heads

Valve gear: Two valves per cylinder operated by a single overhead camshaft per bank of cylinders

Bore and stroke: 3.60 in. x 3.60 in.

Displacement: 4.6 liter

Compression ratio: 9.0:1

Induction system: Sequential multipoint electronic fuel injection

Maximum power: 220 bhp at 4,500 rpm

Maximum torque: 290 lb-ft at 3,500 rpm

Top speed: 130 mph

0-60 mph: 7.9 sec.

TRANSMISSION

Four-speed automatic

BODY/CHASSIS

Steel-perimeter chassis with separate four-door sedan body

SPECIAL FEATURES

All Lincolns now have a Jaguar-like chromed license plate holder.

Cartier badges signify this car is the top-of-the-line model.

RUNNING GEAR

Steering: Recirculating ball

Front suspension: Unequal-length wishbones with coil springs, telescopic shock absorbers and anti-roll bar

Rear suspension: Live axle, four-bar link, air springs, Watt Linkage, telescopic shock absorbers and anti-roll bar

Brakes: Discs (front and rear)

Wheels: Cast aluminum, 16-in. dia.

Tires: P235/60TR16

DIMENSIONS

Length: 215.3 in. **Width:** 78.2 in.

Height: 58.0 in. **Wheelbase:** 117.7 in.

Track: 63.4 in. (front), 65.3 in. (rear)

Weight: 4,015 lbs.

Mercury **SPORTSMAN**

With the Sportsman, Mercury management created the most collectible car the division would ever build. However, it was based on a pre-WWII design so there weren't many innovative mechanical features and it relied on an old sidevalve V8 engine.

"...quiet and refined."

"The Sportsman was designed for comfort and style. While it may have an ancient suspension, this Mercury can soak up the bumps and potholes without ruffling its occupants. The flathead V8 is quiet and refined offering plenty of torque to compensate for its use of a less-than-desirable three-speed transmission. Hitting 60 mph in just over 21 seconds was fine performance for 1946 and its maximum speed of 82 mph is as fast as you'd want to go back then, too."

The large white plastic steering wheel adds character to the wood-finished dashboard.

Milestones

1939 Spotting a gap in the market, the Ford Motor Company launches the Mercury brand name. It is a success right from its inception. 80,000 cars are sold within a few years.

Chrysler released the wooded Town & Country in 1946, too.

1946 Following the end of World War II, Mercury cars go back into production using updated 1942 models. There isn't time to make fundamental mechanical changes, so the two-door convertible receives some hardwood body paneling. The newly restyled model is know as the Sportsman.

The Ford Sportsman sold very well during the two years it was built.

1947 It is not the end for the Sportsman concept, as the base Ford version carries on the line. Despite strong sales the design is too expensive to build and production ends at the end of the year, although some 1947 cars were sold as 1948 models.

UNDER THE SKIN

Three-speed manual transmission
Hydraulic drum brakes
Solid front axle
Sidevalve V8

Old fashioned

Underneath the Sportsman is an old-fashioned Ford chassis. It has a solid front axle, sprung by transverse leaf springs. The rear axle is also located on another transverse spring. Rival GM cars had automatic transmissions available, but the Sportsman had to make do with a three-speed manual. For stopping power, the Sportsman relies on four-wheel, hydraulically-operated drum brakes.

THE POWER PACK

Proven pre-war V8

The design of Ford's classic flathead V8 dates back to 1932. By the time it found its way into the Mercury Sportsman it had grown to 239 cubic inches. The sidevalve layout was the same, with a cast-iron block and cylinder heads. The valves operate upwards into an overhanging head rather than having the combustion chambers directly over the pistons as in modern engines. By this stage the engine's early reliability problems had been long since remedied. It is a long-stroke design with good low-rpm torque. There was no shortage of tuning parts for what was a race-winning engine in its day.

Rare wood

If you can't find a Mercury Sportsman, there's always the Ford version. Also wood trimmed, it has the same engine and performance and almost as much style. However, because the Ford is more common, the Mercury commands quite a premium with collectors.

Rarity ensures the Mercury Sportsman will always be collectable.

Mercury used the design genius of Bob Gregorie, who had created the look of the famous 1940 Lincoln Continental to make the Sportsman stand apart. He did it with extensive and stylish wood paneling.

Split windshield

Along with all post-war U.S. auto manufacturers, Ford and Mercury had to make do with flat windshield glass. The only way the windshield could be angled backward was by having a central join.

V8 engine

It would not be until the 1954 model year that Mercury cars would receive standard overhead-valve V8 engines. The early post-war models used the existing, modest L-head sidevalve V8. The Sportsman managed just 100 bhp from a 239-cubic inch engine.

Drum brakes

Like every other car on sale in the U.S. at the time, the Sportsman has hydraulically-operated drum brakes. Ford introduced these for the 1939 model year.

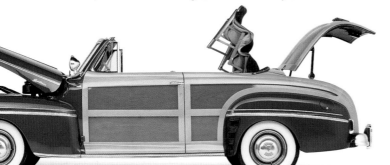

Separate chassis

Like all Mercury cars of the time, the Sportsman is built on a separate steel chassis frame. One feature of the design is a very deep central tunnel, necessary to make room for the movement of the torque tube connected to the rear axle.

Wood trim

The wood trim on the Sportsman is nothing like the trim used on today's cars. The frame is maple or yellow birch, and each part dovetails to the next perfectly. The darker wood paneling is mahogany.

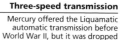

Three-speed transmission

Mercury offered the Liquamatic automatic transmission before World War II, but it was dropped for the 1946 line. The only transmission was a three-speed manual with a column shifter.

Mercury LEAD SLED

In the late 1950s lowered, nosed, decked and shaved cars with chopped tops were known as lead sleds. They were a popular part of American car culture, and still are today. This radical 1949 Mercury is one of the finest around.

"...style is everything."

"When you climb into this rolling juke box the whole car seems to engulf you. It becomes apparent that styling is everything. The windows appear as tiny slits because the roof pillars have been shortened, bringing the roofline closer to the car's body. The interior sings with originality with its custom upholstery, billet knobs and late-model steering column. This heavily modified Merc isn't much of a street racer but it sure is fun to cruise in."

The custom upholstery in this wild Merc is just as outrageous as the exterior.

Milestones

1949 A radically new Mercury, with smoother Lincoln-type styling and a completely re-engineered chassis including independent suspension, helps to make its appearance. Power is still provided by the venerable 'flathead' V8.

Until 1949, Mercury's cars were essentially little more than rehashed pre-war designs.

1950 No changes this year, although a new entry-level model and a special limited edition coupe, the Monterey, join the line up. Nearly 294,000 Mercurys are sold.

The 1949-1951 Mercury was a far more modern design.

1951 The Mercury receives another facelift with more upright rear fenders and larger headlights and tail lights. A three-speed automatic transmission becomes available.

UNDER THE SKIN

Radical chassis

Underneath the body is a 1971 Pontiac frame, complete with coil-sprung independent front suspension and a leaf-sprung live rear end. It also has a 1-inch front and a ⅝-inch rear anti-roll bar, which help handling. Unique features include the braided fuel and brake lines, the special aluminum surge tank, and the alloy radiator.

Separate Pontiac frame
Live rear axle
Independent front suspension
Front disc brakes
Small-block V8

THE POWER PACK

Pontiac power

Unlike the majority of rodders, the owner of this Mercury has chosen to fit a 1968-vintage Pontiac 350 engine (similar to the one shown). Basically a stroked version of the 326 V8, it retains a cast-iron block, cylinder heads and connecting rods, plus a forged-steel crankshaft with five main bearings and two-bolt main bearing caps. Modifications include a radical lift cam, an Edelbrock aluminum intake manifold and a chromed 650-cfm double pumper carburetor, which help to increase power output to 380 bhp.

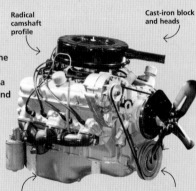

Radical camshaft profile
Cast-iron block and heads
Forged-steel crankshaft
Aluminum intake manifold

Rolling art

In the late 1950s, 1949-1951 Fords and Mercurys were cheap and plentiful. There were dozens of different ways to customize them with varying degrees of difficulty. From GM bumpers and a DeSoto grill to extensive metal work, this one has it all.

The custom paintwork includes 140 hand-painted flames.

This Mercury has it all: the classic appearance of a 1950s custom sled, the reliability and brute power of early 1970s mechanicals and the comfort of 1990s interior fittings.

Pontiac V8
Taken from a 1968 Pontiac Le Mans, the 350-cubic inch V8 has a new intake manifold and an aggressive camshaft. It makes 380 bhp and 380 lb-ft of torque, more than enough to make this car really move.

Chopped top
This Mercury has been 'chopped'—its window pillars have been cut down bringing the roof closer to the body. This modification reduces the car's overall height by a few inches and is also makes the windows look like tiny slits.

Fabricated front metal work
Like many customized Mercury's, this one has been 'nosed and decked,' which simply means that all of the chrome trim has been removed and the holes were filled in with lead. The surfaced was smoothed and painted, leaving no indication that there was ever any trim in the first place. The hood and fenders have also been reworked to make the hood opening more rounded.

Custom fit grill
The stock grill has been removed and replaced with one from a 1954 DeSoto. The factory-installed bumper has also been shelved in favor of a modified 1957 Chevy part.

GM chassis
Although it has a Mercury body, underneath it is almost totally Pontiac, with a full-size Pontiac frame and front and rear suspension.

Shaved doors
The door handles and locks have been removed and the existing holes filled with lead. Like on the hood, the lead work is smoothed and painted. The doors are now opened using an electronic device.

Rear wheel skirts
The large wheel coverings give the Mercury a more streamlined look, but can easily be removed to change a flat tire or any other rear wheel maintenance.

Custom paint
Several coats of purple were applied to the entire car. Following the purple, custom flames were added to the nose then the Mercury received wild pinstriping to accentuate its outrageous body modifications.

Frenched headlights
The headlight bezels were originally chrome but they have since been 'frenched.' This is a very subtle modification where the bezels are welded to the fender, smoothed, sanded and painted for a sleeker look.

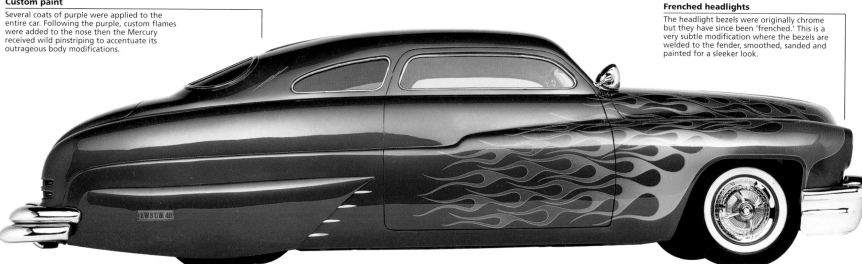

Specifications
1949 Mercury Lead Sled

ENGINE
Type: V8

Construction: Cast-iron block and heads

Valve gear: Two valves per cylinder operated by pushrods and rockers

Bore and stroke: 3.89 in. x 3.75 in.

Displacement: 350 c.i.

Compression ratio: 10.5:1

Induction system: Single Holley four-barrel downdraft carburetor

Maximum power: 380 bhp at 5,100 rpm

Maximum torque: 380 lb-ft at 3,200 rpm

Top speed: 120 mph

0-60 mph: 7.8 sec.

TRANSMISSION
GM TurboHydramatic 350 with 2,500-rpm stall torque converter

BODY/CHASSIS
Steel and aluminum coupe body on separate Pontiac sub-frame

SPECIAL FEATURES

In true 1950s style, this car has twin Appleton spotlights.

Two sets of 1955 Pontiac bumpers give the rear a waterfall effect.

RUNNING GEAR
Steering: Recirculating ball

Front suspension: Unequal length wishbones with coil springs and telescopic shocks

Rear suspension: Live rear axle with leaf springs and telescopic shocks

Brakes: Discs (front), drums (rear)

Wheels: 5 x 14 in., with custom trims

Tires: Marshall whitewalls, 14 in. dia.

DIMENSIONS
Length: 200 in.   **Width:** 73 in.

Height: 51.6 in.   **Wheelbase:** 124 in.

Track: 59.1 in. (front), 62.1 in. (rear)

Weight: 3,374 lbs.

Mercury MONTCLAIR

When most people think of Mercury customs, the 1949-1951 models come to mind. However, this unusual and individual 1955 Montclair illustrates that the later Mercurys have just as much potential for customizing into one-of-a-kind vehicles.

"...a comfortable ride."

"The blue dashboard and white tuck-and-roll upholstery evoke a feeling of spaciousness. Take your place on the comfortable bench seat and start the motor. On the highway the torquey V8 enables the Mercury to do better than just keep up with the traffic and the automatic transmission is perfectly suited to laid-back cruising. The air suspension also results in a more comfortable ride than that felt in many modern cars."

This 1955 Montclair has a number of period touches, like the tuck-and-roll upholstery.

Milestones

1954 Mercury introduces its revolutionary Y-block V8 engine. Created in response to the modern GM V8s, it features overhead valves and produces 161 bhp, making for the fastest accelerating Mercurys yet seen.

Earlier model Mercurys are popular cars to customize.

1955 Retaining the basic 1952 bodyshell, this year's Mercury has more angular styling and greater expanses of chrome. A new Montclair is introduced as the top-of-the-range model.

Mercurys were entirely redesigned for the 1957 model year. This is a top-of-the-line Turnpike Cruiser.

1956 Having proved a success, the 1955 model receives a minor styling update. The Montclair returns and a four-door model is added to the range. An all-new Mercury debuts for 1957.

UNDER THE SKIN

Updated

In Detroit during the 1950s most cars featured a separate chassis and the 1955 Mercury was no exception. This car has been modified with an independent front suspension and a live rear axle taken from a 1981 Camaro. It also has airbags in place of the standard coil springs, and power front disc brakes are an additional safety feature.

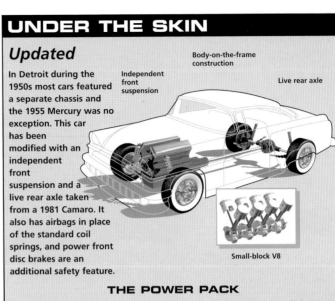

Body-on-the-frame construction

Independent front suspension

Live rear axle

Small-block V8

THE POWER PACK

Venerable V8

Holley four-barrel carburetor

Two valves per cylinder

Five main-bearing cast-iron crankshaft

Cast-iron block and cylinder heads

Like many customized cars, this Mercury has been fitted with a late-model small- block Chevrolet V8. This particular unit, displacing 350 cubic inches, was taken from a 1983 C10 pickup. It is of cast-iron construction, with two valves per cylinder, and features a five main- bearing crankshaft. It has been fitted with an Edelbrock intake manifold and a 750-cfm Holley four-barrel carburetor. With these modifications it has a power output of 210 bhp at 4,000 rpm.

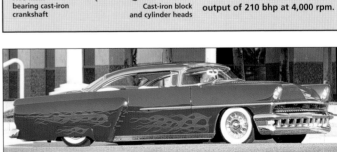

Top model

In 1955 the Montclair Sun Valley hardtop coupe was the top-of-the-range Mercury. Today, most of these cars are restored to stock specifications and, therefore, a custom version makes an interesting alternative to the popular 1949-1951 Mercurys.

The Montclair makes an interesting choice for a modern custom.

The Montclair Sun Valley was eye-catching when it first appeared in the mid-1950s. And with its chopped roof and custom paint, this customized Mercury continues to make a statement wherever it goes.

Chevrolet V8 engine
For practicality and power output this Mercury has a small-block Chevrolet V8 installed in place of the original Y-block engine.

Tuck-and-roll upholstery
Despite the engine and running gear this car has a number of period custom features, including the 1950s-style tuck-and-roll upholstery.

Modified grill
Although not obvious at first, the original bumper/grill has been reworked with additional chromed teeth.

Modern running gear
A Camaro front subframe and suspension have been grafted onto the original chassis. The Salisbury rear axle was also taken from the same Camaro.

Smoothed body
Like most lead sleds the body has been smoothed out, with the headlights and taillights frenched into the body. The door handles and exterior badging have also been removed.

Air suspension
Air bags on the rear suspension give a smooth ride and also allow the car to be raised for driving or lowered for show purposes.

Custom paint
As this car is driven regularly, the body has been coated in tough PPG blue acrylic urethane metallic paint. In true 1950s style, flames have been added below the beltline.

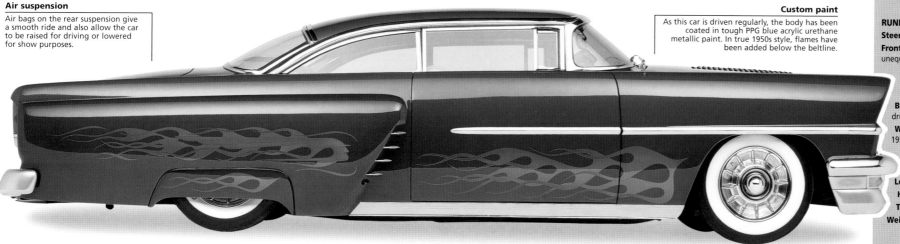

Specifications

1955 Mercury Montclair

ENGINE

Type: V8

Construction: Cast-iron block and heads

Valve gear: Two valves per cylinder operated by pushrods and rockers

Bore and stroke: 4 in. x 3.48 in.

Displacement: 350 c.i.

Compression ratio: 9.5:1

Induction system: Single Holley four-barrel carburetor

Maximum power: 210 bhp at 4,000 rpm

Maximum torque: 285 lb-ft at 2,800 rpm

Top speed: 120 mph

0-60 mph: 9.3 sec.

TRANSMISSION

Three-speed GM TurboHydramatic

BODY/CHASSIS

Separate chassis with two-door steel hardtop body

SPECIAL FEATURES

In popular lead sled style, even the radio antenna has been frenched into the bodywork.

There is even a pair of fuzzy dice hanging from the rear-view mirror—a very period custom accessory.

RUNNING GEAR

Steering: Recirculating ball

Front suspension: Independent with unequal length wishbones, air bags, front stabilizer bar and telescopic shocks

Rear suspension: Live rear axle with airbags and telescopic shocks

Brakes: Power discs, 9.5-in. dia. (front), drums, 9-in. dia. (rear)

Wheels: Steel discs, 15-in. dia. (with 1957 Cadillac hub caps)

Tires: G78 x 15 Whitewalls

DIMENSIONS

Length: 198.6 in.   **Width:** 82.7 in.

Height: 51.8 in.   **Wheelbase:** 119 in.

Track: 62.5 in (front and rear)

Weight: 3,558 lbs.

Mercury **COUGAR GT-E**

Introduced as a 1967 model, the Cougar was more of a refined boulevard cruiser than an all-out muscle car. However, for its sophomore year it turned into a real fire-breather when it was equipped with a 427-cubic inch V8.

"...tremendous torque."

"If you thought that early Cougars were little more than puffed-up Mustangs, the GT-E will undoubtedly change your mind. It does boast upscale appointments, but nail the throttle and be prepared to hold on for dear life. The big 427 packs a tremendous dose of torque and traction is good, thanks to a fairly substantial curbweight and long wheelbase. The Cougar isn't the handling champ of all time, but it won't disappoint."

As the GT-E was based on the XR-7 model, it has a fully loaded interior.

Milestones

1967 Mercury gets its own pony car, the Cougar. It shares many components with the Ford Mustang but rides on a longer 111-inch wheelbase and comes standard with V8 power. Offered in base, GT, or XR-7 form, a total of 150,893 Cougars is built.

The Eliminator supplanted the GT-E as the Hi-Po Cougar in 1969-1970.

1968 Changes are few, but the GT option is dropped. In its place is a special GT-E model, which is essentially an XR-7 with a 427 V8 and heavy-duty suspension. 358 are built before the 428 engine replaces the 427 midyear. In all, 602 GT-Es are built.

The last of the real muscle Cougars was the 1971 429 CJ.

1969 The Cougar is heavily facelifted and the performance model is now called the Eliminator.

UNDER THE SKIN

Mustang Merc

The GT-E shares its underpinnings with the Mustang. The Cougar boasts a unitary chassis with a separate front subframe to carry the engine, transmission and front suspension. Up front are a set of double wishbones with coil springs, while at the rear is a live axle suspended on leaf springs. GT-E models have heavy-duty suspensions to handle the added weight of the 427/428 engine and a thicker front anti-roll bar. Front disc brakes could be specified.

Live rear axle

Unitary body/chassis

Front disc brakes

Large-bore FE V8

THE POWER PACK

Fearsome 427

When the Cougar was launched in 1967, the mainstream performance model—the GT—was available with a 320-bhp, 390-cubic inch engine. But for 1968, things got even wilder. The magical number 427 appeared on the option sheet. This was the side-oiler engine, so named because it has a different block to the original 427 with the oil galley mounted on the left side to reduce engine wear. The cast-iron FE-series engine in the Cougar GT-E has a forged-steel crank, cross-bolted main-bearing caps, a 10.9:1 compression ratio and a dual-plane intake with a single four-barrel carburetor. Dual quad setups could be ordered.

Most power

The Cougar GT-E is among the most underrated 1960s muscle machines, but it also ranks as one of the most powerful Cougars ever built. Fitted with either the 427 or 428 engine, it is a terrific buy today and still has a lot of power.

The sultry though sinister Cougar GT-Es were only built in 1968.

It may have been almost indistinguishable from other Cougars, but the GT-E was in a different league altogether. With 427 cubes and 460 lb-ft of torque, it was arguably one of the quickest factory ponycars in 1968.

427 V8

It was the hallowed 427 that made the Cougar into a real screamer. Its 460 lb-ft of torque put the GT-E firmly in the true muscle car league.

Unitary chassis

Like most Ford Motor Company products of the time, the Cougar features unitary construction almost identical to the popular Mustang.

Heavy-duty suspension

With so much performance on tap, the Cougar needed a heavy-duty suspension. However, with so much weight at the front, it can be a handful through the turns.

Automatic transmission

Unlike the 428 Mustangs, all Cougar GT-Es came with automatic transmissions in the shape of Ford's proven C6 Cruise-O-Matic unit. Even so, the car could run high 14s with a super tuning and an experienced drive behind the wheel.

Improving traction

To get the most from the 427, it was wise to order a Traction-Lok rear end with a set of 3.91:1 gears. This car also has traction bars that help to reduce the car's ability to wheelhop during spells of overly aggressive acceleration.

Hardtop styling

Although its little brother—the Mustang—had a choice of bodystyles, all Cougars in 1967 and 1968 were exclusively two-door coupes. A convertible arrived for 1969.

Specifications

1968 Mercury Cougar GT-E

ENGINE

Type: V8

Construction: Cast-iron block and heads

Valve gear: Two valves per cylinder operated by a single V-mounted camshaft with pushrods and rockers

Bore and stroke: 4.23 in. x 3.78 in.

Displacement: 427 c.i.

Compression ratio: 10.9:1

Induction system: Two Holley 652-cfm four-barrel carburetors

Maximum power: 390 bhp at 5,600 rpm

Maximum torque: 460 lb-ft at 3,200 rpm

Top speed: 128 mph

0-60 mph: 7.0 sec.

TRANSMISSION

C6 Cruise-O-Matic three-speed automatic

BODY/CHASSIS

Steel unitary chassis with two-door coupe body

SPECIAL FEATURES

An overhead console with twin map lights could be ordered.

The hood scoop is a distinguishing feature of the GT-E.

RUNNING GEAR

Steering: Recirculating-ball

Front suspension: Unequal-length wishbones with coil springs, telescopic shock absorbers and anti-roll bar

Rear suspension: Live axle with semi-elliptic leaf springs and telescopic shock absorbers

Brakes: Discs (front), drums (rear)

Wheels: Styled steel, 14x6 in.

Tires: Goodyear Polyglas, G60-14

DIMENSIONS

Length: 190.3 in. **Width:** 73.6 in.

Height: 54.6 in. **Wheelbase:** 111.0 in.

Track: 61.2 in. (front), 60.3 in. (rear)

Weight: 3,174 lbs.

Mercury COUGAR ELIMINATOR

A true performance Cougar emerged in 1969 and continued through 1970. Available with a long list of sports options, it posed a considerable threat to the established muscle cars both on the street and at the drag strip. Despite its potential, the Eliminator is often overlooked by enthusiasts today.

"...a gentleman's muscle car."

"With its wood-rimmed steering wheel and full instrumentation, the Cougar appears to be a gentleman's muscle car. Starting up the monster 428 engine reveals a totally different character. The big engine demands high-octane fuel and concentration on the open road. Its greatest asset is the huge amount of mid-range torque. A drag racer's dream, it is enough to humble any would-be challenger. It's quick enough to run the ¼ mile in 14.1 seconds."

This Eliminator has base model trim and is fitted with vinyl seats instead of leather ones.

Milestones

1967 Two years after Mustang, Mercury launches its own pony car, the Cougar. It features a distinctive front end with a razor-style grill and hidden headlights. Initially it is offered only as a hardtop.

Mercury's other 1969 muscle car was the Cyclone. This one is a Spoiler II.

1969 After minor updates for 1968, the Cougar is restyled the following year and a convertible is now offered. A high performance model, the Eliminator, is launched mid-year and is available with a host of extra performance options, and was painted with 'high impact' exterior colors such as yellow blue, and orange.

The Cougar share the 302 and 428 engines with the Mustang.

1970 The Eliminator returns for its second and final season. Its body restyling is more refined than the 1969 model. Just over 2,000 cars are sold and the model is dropped after only two years of production.

UNDER THE SKIN

Mustang stretch

Unitary construction · Live rear axle · Wishbone front suspension · Front disc brakes · Big-block V8

Essentially a stretched Mustang, the Cougar has independent front suspension with double wishbones, coil springs, telescopic shocks and an anti-roll bar. At the rear are twin semi-elliptical leaf springs, and staggered heavy-duty shocks are fitted to limit wheel hop during a brisk standing start.

THE POWER PACK

Snake bite

The Eliminator was available with either a 302 V8 or a 428 Cobra Jet V8 (identical to the Mustang engine shown here). The 428 came with or without a ram air system. The engine benefits from a modified crankshaft, stronger connecting rods, and, if the Drag Pak was specified, the owner would receive an oil cooler and 4.30:1 gears. At the time, headers, dual quads, and quadruple Weber carbs could be ordered from dealer parts counters to make the Eliminator more of a street terror than what it already was.

Ram-air induction · Four-barrel carburetor · Heavy duty connecting rods · Oil cooler

Street racer

Since the Eliminator is longer and heavier than the Mustang, it is able get more grip and harness the power from the mighty 428 V8. Though the engine had a factory rating of 335 bhp it actually made closer to 410. The lower rating was to fool insurance companies.

The 1970 Eliminator is offers more refined body panels than the 1969 car.

This is Mercury's version of the high-performance Mustang. More refined than its baby brother, it still keeps the Ford heritage with bright paint, side stripes, spoilers, a hood scoop, and big block power.

'High Impact' paintwork
'High Impact' exterior colors was the order of the day in 1970. The Cougar was available in bright blue, yellow and Competition Orange as seen here.

Restyled front
For 1970 the Cougar received a revised front grill with vertical bars and a more pronounced nose. The tail panel was also slightly altered.

Cobra Jet engine
The Eliminator is available with either the 290-bhp Boss 302 or the more stout 428 Cobra Jet with a conservatively rated 335 bhp. This example is powered by the larger 428, often thought of as one of the finest muscle car engines ever produced.

Staggered shocks
Axle tramp can be a serious problem with smaller-sized performance Fords from this era, especially those with big engines. The Cougar Eliminator has staggered rear shock absorbers to help overcome this problem.

Interior trim
Although more luxurious than the Mustang, the Eliminator is a base model Cougar and has vinyl upholstery. Full instrumentation is standard and includes a tachometer.

Sequential turn indicators
The rear indicators, which are also combined with the brake lights, flash in sequence when the driver flicks the lever. These are also found on contemporary Shelby Mustangs.

Drag Pak
This Eliminator is garnished with the legendary 'Drag Pak' option, which includes the 428 Super Cobra Jet engine, an oil cooler, and ultra-low rear-end gearing (3.91:1 or 4.30:1). This makes the Cougar one of the fastest accelerating muscle cars.

Specifications
1970 Mercury Cougar Eliminator

ENGINE

Type: V8

Construction: Cast-iron block and heads

Valve gear: Two valves per cylinder operated by pushrods and rockers

Bore and stroke: 4.0 in. x 3.5 in.

Displacement: 428 c.i.

Compression ratio: 10.6:1

Induction system: Four-barrel carburetor

Maximum power: 335 bhp at 5,200 rpm

Maximum torque: 440 lb-ft at 3,400 rpm

Top speed: 106 mph

0-60 mph: 5.6 sec.

TRANSMISSION

C-6 Cruise-O-Matic

BODY/CHASSIS

Steel monocoque two-door coupe body

SPECIAL FEATURES

The headlights are concealed behind special 'flip-up' panels.

A rear Cougar spoiler is standard Eliminator equipment.

RUNNING GEAR

Steering: Recirculating ball

Front suspension: Unequal length wishbones with coil springs, telescopic shocks and anti-roll bar

Rear suspension: Semi-elliptical multi-leaf springs with staggered rear telescopic shocks

Brakes: Discs (front), drums (rear)

Wheels: Styled steel, 5 x 14 in.

Tires: F60-14 Goodyear Polyglas GT

DIMENSIONS

Length: 191.6 in.   **Width:** 77.6 in.

Height: 52.8 in.   **Wheelbase:** 111 in.

Track: 60 in. (front), 60 in. (rear)

Weight: 3,780 lbs.

USA 1970-1971

Mercury CYCLONE SPOILER

Mercury redesigned its intermediates for 1970, which spelled big changes for the Cyclone. Besides the smoother, more flowing contours, it got a new engine. Packing a massive amount of torque, it could run rings around rival muscle cars.

"...unique and distinctive style."

"A four-speed with a Hurst shifter, high-back bucket seats and acres of black vinyl greet you when you take your place behind the wheel. Being a Mercury, the Cyclone rides extremely well on the highway. The Cyclone also has a unique and distinctive style. The steering may feel light and the Spoiler can feel a little unwieldy around sharp corners, but in a straight line it really goes. Accelerating hard from 20 mph, the force is incredible."

A three-spoke steering wheel and a Hurst shifter complete the businesslike cockpit.

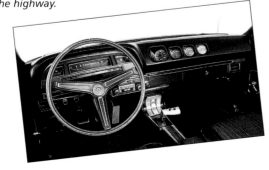

Milestones

1968 The midsize Mercury gets new styling and a new name—the Montego. A semi-sporty Montego– the GT—is offered, but only 334 are built.

A limited-edition spoiler for 1969 was the Dan Gurney Special.

1969 A new Cyclone CJ appears, fitted with a standard 428-cubic inch V8 producing 335 bhp. A Spoiler version also arrives but has a standard 351-cubic-inch small-block V8.

Ford's Torino Cobra is a close relative of the Cyclone Spoiler.

1970 Midsize Mercs are rebodied and get a longer wheelbase. The Cyclone now comes in three different trims: base, GT and Spoiler. The 351 and 390 are offered in lesser Cyclones, but the 370-bhp 429 is standard in the Spoiler. 13,490 Cyclones are built.

1971 The Cyclone returns with few changes. Production plummets to 3,084 in this, its final year.

UNDER THE SKIN

Steady progress

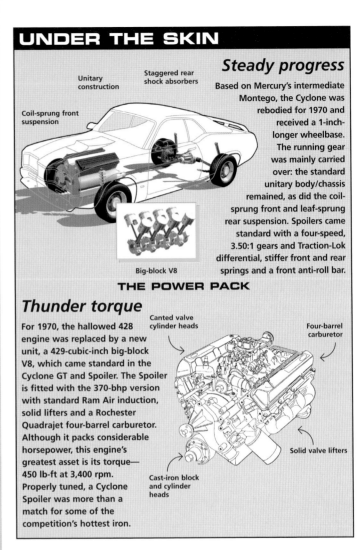

Big-block V8

Based on Mercury's intermediate Montego, the Cyclone was rebodied for 1970 and received a 1-inch-longer wheelbase. The running gear was mainly carried over: the standard unitary body/chassis remained, as did the coil-sprung front and leaf-sprung rear suspension. Spoilers came standard with a four-speed, 3.50:1 gears and Traction-Lok differential, stiffer front and rear springs and a front anti-roll bar.

THE POWER PACK

Thunder torque

For 1970, the hallowed 428 engine was replaced by a new unit, a 429-cubic-inch big-block V8, which came standard in the Cyclone GT and Spoiler. The Spoiler is fitted with the 370-bhp version with standard Ram Air induction, solid lifters and a Rochester Quadrajet four-barrel carburetor. Although it packs considerable horsepower, this engine's greatest asset is its torque—450 lb-ft at 3,400 rpm. Properly tuned, a Cyclone Spoiler was more than a match for some of the competition's hottest iron.

Unspoiled

The most desired car among the second-generation Cyclones is the 1970 Spoiler, with its Ram Air V8. Add a few other options, such as the Drag Pak with lower rear gearing and the Hurst shifted four-speed, and good ones can cost $15,000.

Cyclone Spoilers are still undervalued muscle cars.

In 1970, Mercury really came together, launching its best-ever muscle car. The Cyclone Spoiler had its own distinctive style, packing a wallop, which made it a real threat on the street no matter who was driving it.

Luxury interior
The Cyclone boasts a plusher cabin than the closely related Ford Torino. This includes hounds-tooth vinyl seats and a dash with all auxiliary controls angled toward the driver.

Thunder Jet engine
The canted valve-head 429 came with standard Ram Air in the Spoiler, producing 370 bhp and 450 lb-ft of earth-moving torque. It made the Spoiler a strong runner, especially on the street, which is what counted most of all.

Hidden headlights
By the late 1960s, hideaway headlights were popular in Detroit. The Cyclone's quad circular units are hidden behind flip-up grill panels operated by vacuum tubes. A second set of running lights is mounted astride the grill.

Drag Pak
The Drag Pak option gives the Spoiler even more straight line grunt. This adds an engine oil cooler, stronger bearings and main caps, plus steeper rear axle ratios in the form of 3.91:1 or 4.30:1 cogs.

Safety emphasis
Ford was one of the first U.S. manufacturers to seriously market safety features. The Cyclone boasts such items as dual hydraulic braking systems with warning light, glare-reducing dashboard, energy-absorbing steering wheel and column, standard front and rear lap belts, safety rimmed wheels and corrosion-resistant brake lines.

Swoopy styling
Like its relative the Ford Torino, the Cyclone was rebodied for 1970 with smoother, more flowing lines. A distinctive feature is the projecting snout with gunsight grill treatment. This gave rise to the nickname 'Coffin Nose' and wasn't universally well received. At 209.9 inches overall, the Cyclone is one of the larger 1970 muscle intermediates.

Heavy-duty suspension
In an effort to give the car a more balanced enthusiast flavor, a heavy-duty suspension was standard on the Spoiler. This included stiffer springs, shocks and a front anti-roll bar.

Specifications

1970 Mercury Cyclone Spoiler

ENGINE
Type: V8

Construction: Cast-iron block and heads

Valve gear: Two valves per cylinder operated by a single camshaft with pushrods and rockers.

Bore and stroke: 4.36 in. x 3.59 in.

Displacement: 429 c.i.

Compression ratio: 11.3:1

Induction system: Rochester Quadrajet four-barrel carburetor

Maximum power: 370 bhp at 5,400 rpm

Maximum torque: 450 lb-ft at 3,400 rpm

Top speed: 126 mph

0-60 mph: 6.2 sec.

TRANSMISSION
Borg-Warner T-10 four-speed manual with Hurst shifter

BODY/CHASSIS
Steel unitary chassis with two-door fastback body

SPECIAL FEATURES

A Hurst T-handle was offered with the Borg-Warner T-10 four-speed.

The protruding front end contains a distinctive 'gunsight'-type grill.

RUNNING GEAR
Steering: Recirculating ball

Front suspension: Unequal-length A-arms with coil springs, telescopic shock absorbers and anti-roll bar

Rear suspension: Live axle with semi-elliptic leaf springs and telescopic shock absorbers

Brakes: Discs (front), drums (rear)

Wheels: Steel, 7 x 14 in.

Tires: Goodyear Polyglas, G60-14

DIMENSIONS
Length: 209.9 in.   **Width:** 77.3 in.

Height: 52.2 in.   **Wheelbase:** 117.0 in.

Track: 60.5 in. (front), 60.0 in. (rear)

Weight: 3,773 lbs.

USA 1979-1986

Mercury CAPRI 5.0L

Reborn in 1979 as Mercury's version of the Mustang, the Capri 5.0L offered all the performance attributes of its popular brother but in a more refined package. Offered only as a hatchback, by the time it bowed out it had become one of the quickest GTs in its class.

"...guaranteed to please."

"From behind the wheel, it feels and behaves exactly like a Mustang GT. The steering may feel a little vague, but with this car it's all about throttle control. The T-5 shifter is precise for a mass-market Detroiter, and the endless supply of torque from the 5.0-liter V8 is truly satisfying. Big Gatorback tires give excellent traction and grip, but like rip-roaring muscle cars of the 1960s it is still easy to induce controlled oversteer, something guaranteed to please."

Capris ordered with cruise control have a two-spoke wheel. Sport seats are RS items.

Milestones

1979 Unfavorable exchange rates result in the demise of the German-built Capri. Its replacement is introduced this year, riding a 100.4-inch wheelbase Fox platform.

In 1979, the RS was available with a 2.3-liter turbo four with 140 bhp.

1982 The RS gets a firm suspension and a 157-bhp, 5.0-liter V8 arrives.

1983 A four-barrel carburetor boosts power to 175 bhp. A 'bubble' back window is now standard.

ASC McLaren modified a small number of Capri 5.0Ls

1985 Bigger wheels and tires are standard on the RS. This is the last year for the carbureted V8 which puts out 210 bhp and 270 lb-ft of torque.

1986 With sales of less than 21,000, the Capri is unprofitable and is dropped.

UNDER THE SKIN

Fox-trotting

Like many FoMoCo cars built during the late 1970s and early 1980s the Carpi rides a version of the 'Fox' platform, in this case shared with the Mustang. Capris have modified MacPherson strut suspension at the front, with a live axle on coils and semi-trailing arms at the rear. Late 5.0L cars have gas-filled shocks, front and rear anti-roll bars and ride on 15-inch cast-aluminum wheels with 60 series tires. Brakes are front discs and rear drums.

THE POWER PACK

Five liter havoc wreaker

Capris could be optioned with a 302-cubic inch V8 in 1979, but it was in 1982 that the engine really came into its own. A veteran from 1968, the small-block cast-iron Windsor underwent a power boost to 157 bhp with a special camshaft and low restriction exhaust, and up to 175 bhp the following year with the addition of a four-barrel carburetor. In 1985, a higher-lift camshaft and roller lifters resulted in a formidable 210 bhp (the final year for the Holley carburetor). In 1986, the High Output engine received flat-top pistons and high swirl combustion heads, plus sequential multiport fuel injection giving 200 bhp and 285 lb-ft of torque.

Cheap speed

Having lived its life in the shadow of the Mustang, the Capri is almost forgotten today. It is mechanically identical to its more popular brother and will readily accept the same modifications, but as it is less desirable it is also much more of a bargain.

Late-model Capri 5.0Ls are rare today but less expensive than Mustangs.

By 1986, the Capri 5.0L had matured into a fast and fun-to-drive GT. Poor sales, competition from the Mustang and a dated appearance all conspired to an early demise for Mercury's pony car.

Single body style

Although the Mustang was available as a two-door notchback coupe, convertible or hatchback, the Capri was only produced as a hatchback. This factor, plus the bulging fenders and a bulbous back window contributed to a decline in sales during the 1980s.

High Output V8

Like the Mustang GT, the Capri's 5.0 liter HO V8 received almost annual improvements. By 1986, when this car was built, it boasted roller lifters for reduced friction, an EEC IV processor and sequential multiport fuel injection.

Motorsport suspension

For 1985, RS models received gas-pressurized shocks, with an extra pair mounted horizontally at the rear to reduce axle tramp, and meaty Goodyear Eagle GT tires, with unidirectional rims, mounted on 15-inch wheels. This gave handling ability that could only be dreamed of when the chassis was designed.

Bigger rear end

With the increased torque from the V8, engineers fitted a bigger 8.8-inch rear axle to the Capri 5.0L. Standard final drive was 2.73:1, though 3.27:1 cogs were offered in cars with automatic transmissions.

Option package

Lesser models, like this car, could get all the handling and performance hardware of the top-line RS for a few dollars less. By 1986, however, the V8-engined cars were simply called 5.0L but were still a bargain at $10,223.

Specifications

1986 Mercury Capri 5.0L

ENGINE

Type: V8

Construction: Cast-iron block and heads

Valve gear: Two valves per cylinder operated by a single centrally-mounted camshaft via pushrods and rockers

Bore and stroke: 4.00 in. x 3.00 in.

Displacement: 5.0 liter

Compression ratio: 9.2:1

Induction system: Sequential electronic fuel injection

Maximum power: 200 bhp at 4,000 rpm

Maximum torque: 285 lb-ft at 3,000 rpm

Top speed: 134 mph

0-60 mph: 6.5 sec.

TRANSMISSION

Borg-Warner T-5 five-speed manual

BODY/CHASSIS

Steel unitary chassis with three-door hatchback body

SPECIAL FEATURES

Only ever offered as a hatchback, the Capri boasts exceptional luggage space and easy trunk access.

Like Mustangs, V8-powered Capri 5.0Ls got a revised dual exhaust for 1986.

RUNNING GEAR

Steering: Rack-and-pinion

Front suspension: Modified MacPherson struts with coil springs, telescopic shock absorbers and anti-roll bar

Rear suspension: Live axle with semi-trailing arms, coil springs, telescopic shock absorbers and anti-roll bar

Brakes: Discs (front), drums (rear)

Wheels: Cast-aluminum, 7 x 15 in.

Tires: Goodyear Eagle GT, P225/60 VR15

DIMENSIONS

Length: 179.3 in.　　**Width:** 69.1 in.

Height: 52.1 in.　　**Wheelbase:** 100.5 in.

Track: 56.6 in. (front), 57.0 in. (rear)

Weight: 3,150 lbs.

Mercury **COUGAR**

The restyled Cougar is supposed to be the car to transform Mercury's image from a conservative auto manufacturer to a builder of truly innovative automobiles. It is a front-drive sports coupe with outstanding handling developed overseas.

"...extremely responsive."

"Expectations are high for such a bold shape, and the Cougar doesn't disappoint. Its real strength is in its European-developed handling. To get the best out of Mercury's wild cat, you have to drive the car fast. Biased to give mild understeer, it is extremely responsive and easy to control. The steering, particularly, has great feel. With its advanced chassis, it has exceptional roadholding, which seems to get better the faster the car goes."

The Cougar has some of the best ergonomics and interior room of any car in its class.

Milestones

1994 In the fall, the first computer designs for the new Cougar are made, and by November there is already agreement on how the new car will look.

The previous Cougar was a V8-powered rear-drive luxury coupe.

1997 Mercury shows its MC2 concept car and there is a positive reaction to its bold, aggressive styling from buyers. The decision is made to put the new car into production.

The MC2 concept car was shown at the 1997 Detroit Auto Show.

1998 In a very short time, the MC2 goes from a concept car to the production Cougar. It is sold as a 1999 model. The basic structure makes use of the Ford Contour and Mercury Mystique floorpan. Engine choices consist of a 2.0-liter four-cylinder or a 2.5-liter Duratec V6.

UNDER THE SKIN

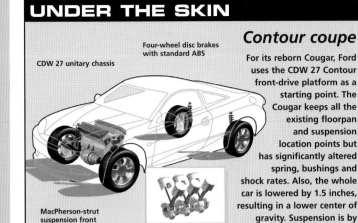

Four-wheel disc brakes with standard ABS

CDW 27 unitary chassis

MacPherson-strut suspension front and rear

Duratec V6

Contour coupe

For its reborn Cougar, Ford uses the CDW 27 Contour front-drive platform as a starting point. The Cougar keeps all the existing floorpan and suspension location points but has significantly altered spring, bushings and shock rates. Also, the whole car is lowered by 1.5 inches, resulting in a lower center of gravity. Suspension is by struts all around but with multilinks at the rear.

THE POWER PACK

New-age V6

Uplevel Cougars are powered by the Ford Duratec, a very lightweight 60-degree, 2.5-liter short-stroke V6 designed to rev beyond 6,250 rpm. The alloy block has dry cast-iron liners and alloy heads, plus a reinforcing 'ladder' between the block and oil pan to stiffen the engine. Its four overhead camshafts are belt-driven and hollow, contributing to the overall lightness. The maximum power output is 170 bhp, although it is rumored that Ford will offer a more powerful V6.

Four-valves per cylinder

Free-flowing cylinder heads

Cast-alloy block and cylinder heads

Engine brace for greater stiffness

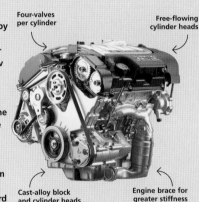

Smooth cat

The new Cougar is one of Ford's global cars and is successfully sold in several markets around the world. Although the four-cylinder is likely to be the undisputed bestseller, the V6 model is more satisfying to drive with its greater torque and smoothness.

V6-powered Cougars are a tremendous value for the money.

'New Edge' styling is all about clean, bold lines intersecting to create shapes that are individually interesting. Crucially, as on the Cougar, it also creates an impression of movement.

Traction control

At low speeds, the front brakes are triggered by ABS sensors, giving just enough power to stop wheelspin. At higher rpm, power is backed off to prevent wheelspin.

V6 engine

The light Duratec, 170-bhp, 24-valve, quad-cam V6 may lack variable valve timing, but it does have a dual-phase, ram-induction system in which the intake tract is varied to allow the engine to breathe much easier.

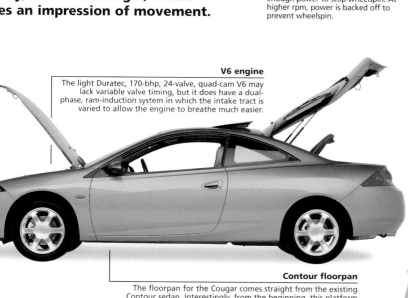

Contour floorpan

The floorpan for the Cougar comes straight from the existing Contour sedan. Interestingly, from the beginning, this platform (code name CDW 27) was designed with a coupe version in mind.

Quadralink rear suspension

Rear suspension location is excellent, thanks to long struts and one trailing link per side. This results in progressive and linear wheel movement.

Rear-wheel steer

Ford has built passive rear-wheel steering into the Cougar. When cornering, one of the transverse links in the rear suspension effectively moves the wheel to give a slight measure of toe-in. The result is that the car is less likely to oversteer or, in more extreme cases, to spin.

Strut front suspension

Although the Cougar has the same strut front suspension as the Contour, spring rates are stiffened to improve handling.

Specifications

1999 Mercury Cougar

ENGINE

Type: V6

Construction: Alloy block and heads

Valve gear: Four valves per cylinder operated by twin belt-driven overhead camshafts per cylinder bank

Bore and stroke: 3.24 in. x 3.13 in.

Displacement: 2,540 cc

Compression ratio: 9.7:1

Induction system: Electronic fuel injection

Maximum power: 170 bhp at 6,250 rpm

Maximum torque: 165 lb-ft at 4,250 rpm

Top speed: 135 mph

0-60 mph: 8.0 sec.

TRANSMISSION

Five-speed manual

BODY/CHASSIS

Unitary monocoque construction with steel two-door coupe body

SPECIAL FEATURES

A sliding steel sunroof is a welcome option for open-air driving.

The 2.5-liter V6 is also offered in the Contour and Mystique sedans.

RUNNING GEAR

Steering: Rack-and-pinion

Front suspension: MacPherson struts with lower control arms, telescopic shock absorbers and anti-roll bar

Rear suspension: MacPherson struts with transverse and trailing arms, telescopic shock absorbers and anti-roll bar

Brakes: Vented discs (front and rear)

Wheels: Alloy, 6.5 x 16 in.

Tires: 215/50 VR16

DIMENSIONS

Length: 185.0 in.   **Width:** 69.6 in.

Height: 52.2 in.   **Wheelbase:** 106.4 in.

Track: 59.3 in. (front), 58.7 in. (rear)

Weight: 3,065 lbs.

Nash **METROPOLITAN**

To answer the demands of a tiny but practical automobile, Nash introduced the Metropolitan. Though it was considered a domestic car, its body was built by Fisher and Ludlow in Birmingham, England, and wrapped around an Austin rolling chassis in Longbridge, England complete with an A40 engine.

"...cute though cramped."

"The glitzy interior of the Metropolitan is pure 1950s American style. The car can seat two adults semi-comfortably; a third can be squeezed in for short journeys. Despite its small engine, it's quite lively, thanks mainly to its torque output and low gearing—top gear can be used right down to 10 mph. It handles exactly like a full-size car. It wallows and rolls on corners, but not too excessively. Even so, this is no sports car just a cute, though cramped, cruiser."

The large speedometer and built-in radio dominate the Nash's dashboard.

Milestones

1950 The Nash Kelvinator corporation displays a prototype at the New York Auto Show. Known as the NXI, it is used to test the public's reaction to the idea of a small car.

The Metropolitan was sold alongside the Nash Ambassador.

1952 Following negotiations, Nash announces that the car will be built in Britain by Austin.

The Metropolitan was available as a hardtop or convertible.

1954 The Nash Metropolitan hits the showroom with a 1.2-liter four-cylinder engine.

1956 The engine is enlarged to 1.5 liters. Power is increased from 42 to 52 bhp.

1961 Production ends after 104,368 coupes and convertibles have been built.

UNDER THE SKIN

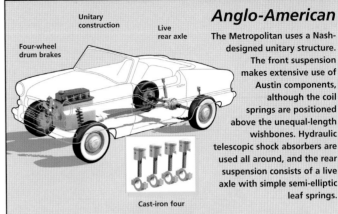

Unitary construction
Live rear axle
Four-wheel drum brakes
Cast-iron four

Anglo-American

The Metropolitan uses a Nash-designed unitary structure. The front suspension makes extensive use of Austin components, although the coil springs are positioned above the unequal-length wishbones. Hydraulic telescopic shock absorbers are used all around, and the rear suspension consists of a live axle with simple semi-elliptic leaf springs.

THE POWER PACK

Little four

The Metropolitan started life with the 1.2-liter four-cylinder unit from the Austin A40. This overhead-valve engine evolved into the B-series engine that later powered the MGB. In 1956, the Metro gained the B-series engine itself, in 1,489-cc form. Like many engines found in low-and medium-priced cars of the time, the B-series is an all-cast-iron unit with two valves per cylinder operated by a single camshaft with pushrods and rockers. Fuel delivery is by a single Zenith downdraft carburetor and a mechanical fuel pump. Producing just 44 bhp (52 from 1956), performance is leisurely rather than swift.

Tiny tearaway

The most sought after of the Metropolitan variants are the later 1.5-liter cars that are fortified with extra power and torque. The convertible bodystyle is the most valuable, and post-1959 models with the opening trunk add practicality. The neat Continental tire kit is standard equipment.

An open top and 1,489-cc engine make the most desirable Metropolitan.

After the Nash-Healey venture, Donald Healey was the conduit for another Anglo-American project between Austin and Nash. The Austin-built Metropolitan provided Nash with a new small car.

B-series engine
The Metropolitan was first fitted with a 42-bhp, 1.2-liter four-cylinder engine. A forerunner of the famous B-series unit that later powered the MGA and MGB, the B-series remained in production until 1980.

Wishbone front suspension
Although it uses many Austin components, the wishbone front suspension follows typical Nash practice in having the coil springs mounted on the upper wishbone. The telescopic shock absorbers are mounted on the lower wishbone.

Large turning circle
The small, square-topped wheel cutouts limited how far the front wheels could turn, giving the Metropolitan a rather large turning circle for a car of its size.

No trunklid
Until 1959, the Metropolitan had no trunklid. Luggage had to be fed into the trunk from behind the seats.

Three-speed transmission
The transmission is derived from the four-speed used in the Austin A40. The bottom gear is removed, so the Nash just uses the upper three ratios. This is possible because of the Nash's good power-to-weight ratio.

Specifications

1957 Nash Metropolitan

ENGINE
Type: Inline four-cylinder
Construction: Cast-iron block and head
Valve gear: Two valves per cylinder operated by a single camshaft with pushrods and rockers
Bore and stroke: 2.87 in. x 3.50 in.
Displacement: 1,489 cc
Compression ratio: 7.2:1
Induction system: Single Zenith downdraft carburetor
Maximum power: 52 bhp at 4,500 rpm
Maximum torque: 69 lb-ft at 2,100 rpm
Top speed: 75 mph
0-60 mph: 24.1 sec.

TRANSMISSION
Three-speed manual

BODY/CHASSIS
Unitary monocoque construction with two-door convertible body

SPECIAL FEATURES

The tiny, 13-inch steel wheels are shod with whitewall tires.

The compact Metropolitan even has a miniaturized Continental kit.

RUNNING GEAR
Steering: Cam-and-peg
Front suspension: Double wishbones with coil springs and telescopic shock absorbers
Rear suspension: Live axle with semi-elliptic leaf springs and telescopic shock absorbers
Brakes: Drums (front and rear)
Wheels: Pressed steel, 13-in. dia.
Tires: 5.20 x 13

DIMENSIONS
Length: 149.5 in. **Width:** 61.5 in.
Height: 54.5 in. **Wheelbase:** 85.0 in.
Track: 45.3 in. (front), 44.8 in. (rear)
Weight: 1,885 lbs.

USA 1954-1956

Oldsmobile 88

Compared to rival designs, the 1954-1956 Oldsmobile 88, with its relatively clean lines and panoramic front and rear windows, is one of the most attractive cars of its period.

"...as fast as a modern sedan."

"When you climb inside a car that is well over 40 years old, the last thing you expect is high performance. But, thanks to its J-2 Rocket powerplant with 312 bhp, the Oldsmobile 88 flies along. Despite its size and weight, the 88 can accelerate as fast as a modern-day performance sedan and has all the torque you'd expect from a classic V8 engine. Lowering the suspension all around has certainly helped to reduce body roll around the bends."

Base model 88s were fairly glitzy inside and two-tone was the order of the day.

Milestones

1954 New 88 series launched on a 122-inch wheelbase in standard and Super 88 forms. A number of body styles are available: two and four-door sedan, Holiday two-door hardtop coupe and convertible.

The convertible body style was available from the start.

1955 A substantial facelift for 1955 introduces a bold oval grill and extra two-tone paintwork options. A new two-door Holiday hardtop sedan joins the range.

By the end of the 1950s, the Oldsmobile range had much crisper styling.

1956 Another styling update adds a 'gaping mouth' front grill and different shaped chrome side accents on the body.

1957 New Golden Rocket models replace the existing line-up.

UNDER THE SKIN

Low technology from Lansing

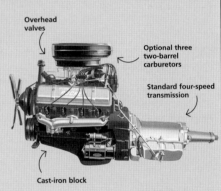

The 88 series is typical for its era, boasting a coil-sprung front and leaf-sprung rear suspension with four-wheel drum brakes. Compared to the 1949-1953 88s, the 1954-1956 88 series has a longer (122-inch) wheelbase and a larger (324-cubic inch) engine. The owner of this car has fitted a 1937 La Salle three-speed transmission, although the car was originally delivered from the factory with a four-speed manual.

371-cubic inch V8 engine · All-steel body · Separate chassis · J-2 Rocket V8

THE POWER PACK

More power for the infamous 'Rocket'

Based on the familiar Olds Rocket V8, the 1954 engine was bored out to 324-cubic inches and could develop between 170 and 185 bhp. This was increased to 185-202 bhp in 1955 and 230-240 bhp in 1956. The owner of this 88 has installed a 1957 371-cubic inch J-2 engine which, with its three two-barrel carburetor induction system, can produce more than 300 bhp in stock form.

Overhead valves · Optional three two-barrel carburetors · Standard four-speed transmission · Cast-iron block

Open air

The most desirable of the 1954-1956 Oldsmobiles is the convertible. It has all the luxury and style of the sedans and hardtops, but gives the added benefit of wind-in-the-hair driving. Between 1954 and 1956, Olds built nearly 50,000 convertibles.

Classic 1950s style and a convertible top combine to make a great cruising car.

Between 1954 and 1957, Oldsmobile set a new production record, manufacturing some 583,000 cars in 1955 alone. Here's an example of a modified 1956.

J2 power

This car has been fitted with a 1957 371-cubic inch engine and features the J-2 option with three two-barrel carburetors. The engine has been tuned to deliver 312 bhp.

Pre-war transmission

The owner has opted to fit a vintage-style transmission from a 1937 La Salle—a prewar 'junior' Cadillac.

Thunderbird paint

Coating the body in 1990 Thunderbird Bright Red enamel paint produces a strikingly different effect and is well suited to the handsome lines on this 1956 88.

Lowered suspension

The suspension on this car has been lowered. At the front end, 1957 coil springs were added and cut, while lowering blocks have been mounted on the rear leaf springs.

Chrome wheels

The full chrome 7 inch x 15 inch wheels are shod with Remington tires front and rear.

Hardtop coupe style

Undoubtedly the most elegant of all the Oldsmobile 88 body variations, the Holiday hardtop coupe was also the most popular.

Wraparound windows

For its time, the 88 was a styling sensation, featuring sleek lines and fully wraparound glass both front and rear. The so-called Panoramic wraparound treatment was pioneered by the 1953 Oldsmobile Ninety-Eight Fiesta.

Specifications
1956 Oldsmobile 88 Holiday hardtop coupe

ENGINE

Type: V8

Construction: Cast-iron cylinder block and cylinder heads

Valve gear: Two valves per cylinder operated by single camshaft via pushrods and rockers

Bore and stroke: 4.0 in. x 3.69 in.

Displacement: 371 c.i.

Compression ratio: 8.4:1

Induction system: Three two-barrel carburetors

Maximum power: 312 bhp at 4,600 rpm

Maximum torque: 410 lb-ft at 2,800 rpm

Top speed: 121 mph

0-60 mph: 8.7 sec.

TRANSMISSION

1937 La Salle three-speed manual

BODY/CHASSIS

Steel chassis with two-door hardtop coupe body

SPECIAL FEATURES

The grill of the 1956 Oldsmobile was unique to that year, with a big divider and horizontal bars.

Outer space was a popular theme among stylists in the 1950s which is evident on this 88's taillights.

RUNNING GEAR

Steering: Recirculating ball

Front suspension: Independent with coil springs

Rear suspension: Live axle with semi-elliptic leaf springs

Brakes: Drums, front and rear

Wheels: Pressed steel, 15-in. dia.

Tires: Remington G-78 (front), L-78 (rear)

DIMENSIONS

Length: 203.4 in.

Width: 77 in.

Height: 60 in.

Wheelbase: 122 in.

Track: 59 in. (front), 58 in. (rear)

Curb weight: 3,771 lbs.

Oldsmobile **TORONADO**

Ultraconservative Oldsmobile produced one of the most innovative cars of the 1960s with its Toronado coupe. The bold styling was just a teaser, for underneath lay Detroit's first front-wheel drive layouts. This endowed the Toronado with first-rate handling finesse.

"...fantastic front wheeler."

"The Toronado was one of the most well balanced drivers that came out of Detroit in the 1960s. The first thing you'll notice about this fantastic front wheeler is the lack of any transmission tunnel. Fire up the engine and the muted Rocket V8 revs happily and is an eager performer on the road. The real revelation comes when you turn your first corner—the car really handles. The payoff is a rather hard ride, but its light steering and easy cruising keep you smiling."

Needles and rocker switches fill the dash-board, but it's all clear and accessible.

Milestones

1966 General Motors turns history on its head with its most radical car of the decade, the front-drive Oldsmobile Toronado.

1967 Optional front disc brakes and radial tires improve the package.

The second generation 1971-1978 Toronado was bigger and heavier.

1968 A semi-notchback rear end is grafted on. Under the hood the engine displacement grows to 455 cubic inches, although standard power output falls by 10 bhp.

E-bodies, including the Toronado, were downsized in 1979.

1970 In its final year before being replaced by an all-new Toronado, fixed headlights replace the pop-up ones.

UNDER THE SKIN

Perimeter frame

All-around drum brakes

Front-wheel drive

Rocket V8

A front-drive first

America had not built a front-wheel-drive car since the Cord 812 of the 1930s, so the Toronado grabbed buyers' attention. The layout set the tone for GM cars for the next two decades. The torque converter sits directly behind the engine, with a remote three-speed Hydramatic transmission linked forward to the differential.

THE POWER PACK

Full-size V8

Originally, chief engineer John Beltz requested an all-alloy transverse V6 engine in the Toronado, but the GM chiefs knew that the market wanted a V8 in a flagship model. So Oldsmobile turned to the familiar full-size Rocket V8. Standard in Olds' big cars, the 425-cubic inch, cast-iron engine was rated at 385 bhp in the Toronado. Engineers mounted it in a rubber-insulated subframe, resulting in less cabin noise and vibration. From 1968, the engine size grew to 455 cubic inches and, though power dropped to 375 bhp, there was an optional W-34 package with twin exhausts and a special cam, capable of 400 bhp.

'66 Toronado

The original is the best when it comes to Toronados, and the first fastback body-style is preferred over the semi-notchback form adopted for 1968. And unless you find a modified 400-bhp version, the original 1966 Toronado has more power than later cars.

Today, the earlier models are the most sought after.

Front-wheel drive was one thing, but an innovative engine/transmission layout freed up a lot of space inside and allowed engineers to deliver class-leading handling.

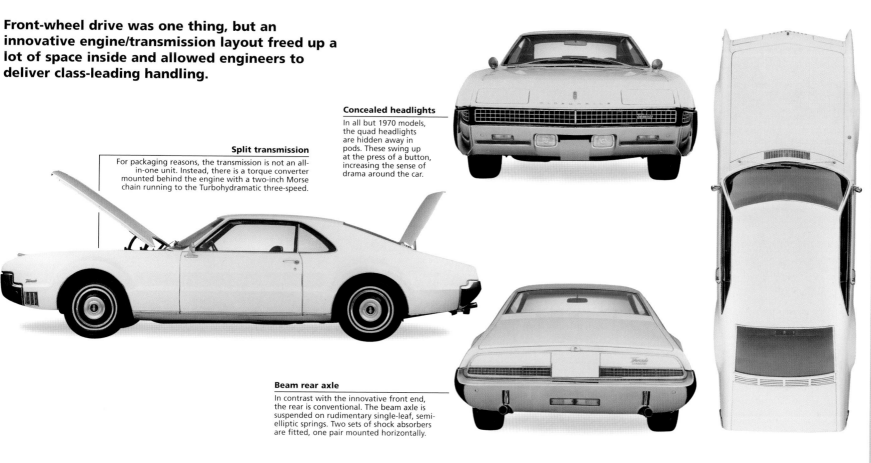

Concealed headlights
In all but 1970 models, the quad headlights are hidden away in pods. These swing up at the press of a button, increasing the sense of drama around the car.

Split transmission
For packaging reasons, the transmission is not an all-in-one unit. Instead, there is a torque converter mounted behind the engine with a two-inch Morse chain running to the Turbohydramatic three-speed.

Beam rear axle
In contrast with the innovative front end, the rear is conventional. The beam axle is suspended on rudimentary single-leaf, semi-elliptic springs. Two sets of shock absorbers are fitted, one pair mounted horizontally.

Bold styling
The Toronado combines European and American styling influences. Its designer, David North, created a clean and dramatic shape dominated by swoopy rear pillars, smooth flanks and heavy chrome bumpers.

Big cabin
Enormous doors open wide to provide access to a very spacious six-passenger interior. A long, 119-inch wheelbase coupled with the compact drivetrain gives ample room for passengers.

Front-wheel drive
In 1966, front-wheel drive cars were unique to the U.S market. The Toronado was easily the world's biggest example.

Specifications
1966 Oldsmobile Toronado

ENGINE
Type: V8

Construction: Cast-iron block and heads

Valve gear: Two valves per cylinder operated by a single camshaft with pushrods and rockers

Bore and stroke: 4.13 in. x 3.98 in.

Displacement: 425 c.i.

Compression ratio: 10.5:1

Induction system: Single four-barrel carburetor

Maximum power: 385 bhp at 4,800 rpm

Maximum torque: 475 lb-ft at 3,200 rpm

Top speed: 124 mph

0-60 mph: 9.9 sec.

TRANSMISSION
Turbohydramatic three-speed automatic

BODY/CHASSIS
Separate chassis with steel two-door coupe body

SPECIAL FEATURES

Cornering lights on the front fenders were an option on 1967 Toronados.

The heavily chromed rear bumper has cutouts for twin exhaust pipes.

RUNNING GEAR
Steering: Recirculating ball

Front suspension: Wishbones with longitudinal torsion bars, shock absorbers and anti-roll bar

Rear suspension: Beam axle with semi-elliptic springs and shock absorbers

Brakes: Drums, front and rear

Wheels: Steel 15-in. dia.

Tires: 8.85 x 15

DIMENSIONS
Length: 211.0 in.   **Width:** 78.5 in.

Height: 52.8 in.   **Wheelbase:** 119.0 in.

Track: 63.5 in. (front), 63.0 in. (rear)

Weight: 4,655 lbs.

Oldsmobile 4-4-2

While the 1968 4-4-2 had plent of power with its 400-cubic inch V8 engine, this stock-looking Oldsmobile street machine has been modified with a massive 455 V8 that makes the kind of power found only in the limited edition Hurst-modified cars.

"...fast and fun street machine."

"The 1968 Oldsmobile 4-4-2 came with a W-30 360-bhp 400-cubic inch engine with the new, forced-air option. This custom example, however, has a full-size 455-cubic inch Rocket motor with added performance parts, similar to the Hurst/Olds introduced that same year. With a 410 bhp under the hood and a convertible top, this 4-4-2 is a fast and fun street machine. It accelerates like a rocket and handles better than most cars of its era."

The interior remains relatively stock, but the engine under the hood is a different story.

Milestones

1964 The 4-4-2 nameplate debuts as a package option on the mid-size F-85™.

1965 The standard 4-4-2 engine is a destroked and debored 425 V8 creating the new 400-cubic inch V8.

Early 4-4-2s have more square bodywork than the later cars.

1967 Tri-power induction is offered for one year and the engine makes 360 bhp.

1968 A restyled body gives the 4-4-2 a more elegant look. 3,000 modified versions known as the Hurst/Olds are offered with 455 engines.

The 1970 W-30 came with a big 455 V8 and fiberglass hood.

1970 A 455-cubic inch engine becomes available with Oldsmobile's "select fit" parts. The W-30 455 makes 370 bhp, but its 14.3 quarter mile time suggests this car made more power. These cars had fiberglass hoods and plastic fender liners.

UNDER THE SKIN

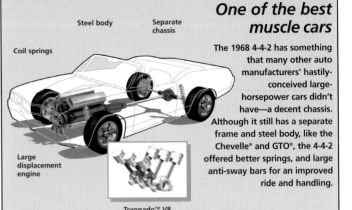

One of the best muscle cars

Steel body | Separate chassis

Coil springs

Large displacement engine

Toronado™ V8

The 1968 4-4-2 has something that many other auto manufacturers' hastily-conceived large-horsepower cars didn't have—a decent chassis. Although it still has a separate frame and steel body, like the Chevelle® and GTO®, the 4-4-2 offered better springs, and large anti-sway bars for an improved ride and handling.

THE POWER PACK

Full-size V8

After 1965 the first '4' in 4-4-2 stood for the size of the standard 400-cubic inch engine. Oldsmobile destroked and debored its full-size 425 V8 engine just for the 4-4-2. For 1966, Olds™ offered a tri-carburetors boosting power to 360 bhp (right). In 1970, its size was increased again to 455. It was the biggest and most powerful engine Olds ever offered. The owner of the model featured here has replaced the factory 400 V8 engine with a 455-cubic inch Rocket motor that makes 410 bhp thanks to special modifications.

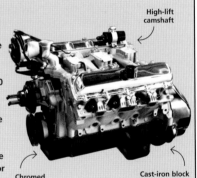

High-lift camshaft

Cast-iron block

Chromed pulleys

Convertible

The new 1968 range of 4-4-2 models updated the earlier cars. At the top of the new range, above the hardtop coupe, was the convertible. It offered incredible value for this type of car, not to mention loads of fun with the top down in the summer.

The convertible top and stock wheels give this 4-4-2 a stealth-like look.

The 4-4-2 was one of the best muscle cars of the 1960s. It has incredible performance and, unlike many of its rivals, it also has the agility and braking to match the speed.

Custom paint
The bodywork has been sprayed with a base coat of Infinity White paint, followed by a clear coat to give a deep, high gloss finish.

4-4-2 badging
By 1968 the 4-4-2 nameplate had become familiar and sought-after property. Badging in the grill announced that you were driving something special.

Uprated wheels and tires
The 1968 4-4-2 had 14-inch diameter wheels, but the owner of this car has chosen to upgrade to 15-inch Super Stock II rims, shod with Goodyear Eagle ST tires.

Sharp steering
To improve handling, the owner installed a quick-ratio steering box. This means the wheel has to be turned less when cornering.

Heavy-duty suspension
The rear end has been beefed up by replacing the stock coil springs with heavy-duty springs from a station wagon. Modern polyurethane bushings and 1 7/8-inch thick front and rear anti-roll bars have also been added to tighten the suspension further.

Improved cabin
As well as 1970 Gold Madrid interior, this particular car features full GM and AutoGauge instruments and a 'Rallye' steering wheel.

Big 455 V8
Although the 455 V8 engine was not offered in the 1968 4-4-2, it was available in a special edition called the Hurst/Olds. It became standard for all 4-4-2 models in 1970.

Oldsmobile 4-4-2 Convertible

ENGINE

Type: V8

Construction: Cast-iron cylinder block and cylinder heads

Valve gear: Two valves per cylinder operated by a single camshaft

Bore and stroke: 4.12 in. x 4.25 in.

Displacement: 455 c.i.

Compression ratio: 10.5:1

Induction system: Four-barrel carburetor

Maximum power: 410 bhp at 5,500 rpm

Maximum torque: 517 lb-ft at 3,500 rpm

Top speed: 134 mph

0-60 mph: 6.2 sec.

TRANSMISSION

Turbo HydraMatic 350 three-speed automatic

BODY/CHASSIS

Separate chassis with two-door convertible steel body

SPECIAL FEATURES

The interior has been taken from a 1970 Oldsmobile and features Gold Madrid vinyl upholstery.

On this modified car, the exhaust tips exit behind the rear tires rather than out of the back as on the standard 4-4-2s.

RUNNING GEAR

Steering: Recirculating ball

Front suspension: Wishbones with coil springs, shocks, and anti-roll bar

Rear suspension: Rigid axle with coil springs, shocks, and anti-roll bar

Brakes: Discs front, drums rear

Wheels: Super Stock II, 15-in. dia.

Tires: Goodyear Eagle ST

DIMENSIONS

Length: 201.6 in.   **Width:** 76.2 in.

Height: 52.8 in.   **Wheelbase:** 112 in.

Track: 59.1 in. (front), 59.1 in. (rear)

Curb weight: 3,890 lbs.

Oldsmobile **CUTLASS RALLYE 350**

Due to rocketing insurance premiums on big-block muscle cars, manufacturers began offering alternatives. One of the best-balanced was the small-block powered Oldsmobile Cutlass Rallye 350, offered only for the 1970 model year.

"...similar to a 4-4-2."

"Sitting behind the wheel, the Rallye 350 seems similar to a 4-4-2. When you drive away, however, the difference really becomes apparent. The small-block Cutlass feels slightly better balanced and more agile—easier to coax through sharp corners at high speeds. It may not have earth-shattering torque, but the willing small-block has a decent amount of power and sounds as deadly as its big-cubed brother. With less weight over the front wheels, the Cutlass also stops better than a 4-4-2."

A four-spoke steering wheel indicates that this was intended to be more than a straightline screamer.

344

Milestones

1970 All GM intermediates get new styling, including the Oldsmobile Cutlass. The 4-4-2 returns, now with standard 455 power, but is joined by a small-block derivative, the Cutlass W31™, packing a 325-bhp 350 engine. A further small-block muscle car, the Rallye 350, arrives. It has Sebring yellow paint with body-colored bumpers and wheels and a standard 310-bhp 350 engine.

Oldsmobile's standard muscle car was the 4-4-2; this is a 1968 model.

1971 Both the W31 and Rallye 350 are dropped. The most powerful 350-cubic inch V8 offered on the Cutlass cranks out just 260 bhp.

The limited-edition Hurst/Olds was based on the Cutlass.

1972 The 4-4-2 reverts to an option package with a standard 350 instead of a 455. The Hurst/Olds makes a welcome return and is selected to pace the Indy 500.

UNDER THE SKIN

Posi-traction limited-slip differential

Body-on-frame construction

Power front disc brakes

Small-block V8

Sophistication

As it was based on the A-body Cutlass, the Rallye 350 is very conventional in engineering terms. It has a separate steel 112-inch wheelbase chassis and a unequal length A-arm front suspension with coils and shocks. The 12-bolt rear axle is also suspended by coil springs and located by upper and lower control arms. Front and rear anti-roll bars, plus heavy-duty springs and shocks result in better-than-average handling. Power front disc brakes are also fitted.

THE POWER PACK

Rowdy Rallye 350

Oldsmobile's 350-cubic inch V8 appeared for 1968 as an enlarged version of the 330 small-block. Used mainly in standard Cutlass sedans, coupes, and wagons, its moment of glory arrived in 1970. The Rallye 350 package Oldsmobile specified the L34 version of its small-block, with a 10.3:1 compression ratio and a Rochester four-barrel Quadrajet carburetor. Rated at 310 bhp and with 390 lb-ft of torque, it could propel the Rallye 350 through the ¼-mile in 15.2 seconds. A second hi-po small-block, the 325-bhp W31, was available for the Cutlass in 1970, but it was not installed in the Rallye 350.

W-45

Undoubtedly the most sought after of all 1970 Oldsmobiles is the 4-4-2 W30, but the small-block cars—the Rallye 350 in particular—deserve a look. All Rallye 350s have Sebring Yellow paint, and with 390 lb-ft of torque they have quite a punch, too.

Just 3,547 Rallye 350s were built for 1970.

Arguably one of the most handsome GM intermediates of 1970, the Cutlass was also one of the most sophisticated and driveable, especially in Rallye 350 form.

V8 engine
The peppy little 350-cubic inch V8, with 310 bhp and 390 lb-ft of torque, made the Rallye 350 more than a match for some other big-block muscle cars. This is because of its lighter weight and lower torque, which enable the bias-ply tires to hook up more effectively.

Dual exhaust
Like any true muscle car, the Rallye 350 has full-length dual exhaust pipes. Smog equipment consists of a PCV valve, which was recommended to be replaced every 12,000 miles.

Sebring Yellow paint
The Rallye 350 was available in only one color—Sebring Yellow. All of the cars have yellow bumpers, sport mirrors, and Rally wheels, and black stripes on the hood and around the back window, outlined in orange and black.

TH350 Automatic
The base transmission on the Cutlass range was a three-speed manual, though in order to get the most from the free-revving L34 small-block, the optional four-speed was perhaps the best choice. A TurboHydramatic three-speed automatic could be specified, with either a column or floor-mounted shifter.

Two body styles
As an option package on the Oldsmobile F-85 Cutlass two-door, the Rallye 350 could be ordered either as a pillared coupe (seen here) or as a hardtop. One small flaw with the pillared coupe is that the vent windows cannot be fully opened because of the twin sport mirrors.

Independent front suspension
Like most Detroit cars of the time, the Cutlass has independent unequal length A-arm front suspension. To improve handling, Rallye 350s have anti-roll bars front and back, plus heavy-duty springs and shocks.

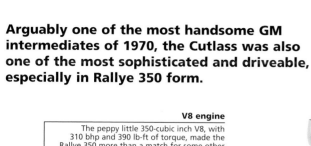

Specifications
1970 Oldsmobile Cutlass Rallye 350

ENGINE

Type: V8

Construction: Cast-iron block and heads

Valve gear: Two valves per cylinder operated by a block-mounted camshaft

Bore and stroke: 4.06 in. x 3.38 in.

Displacement: 350 c.i.

Compression ratio: 10.25:1

Induction system: Single Rochester four-barrel carburetor

Maximum power: 310 bhp at 4,600 rpm

Maximum torque: 390 lb-ft at 3,200 rpm

Top speed: 122 mph

0-60 mph: 7.0 sec.

TRANSMISSION

TH 350 Automatic

BODY/CHASSIS

Body on frame construction; all steel

SPECIAL FEATURES

The body-colored front and rear bumpers are unique to Rallye 350s.

The hood is identical to that on the 4-4-2 W30™ and includes hood locks.

RUNNING GEAR

Steering: Recirculating ball

Front suspension: Unequal length A-arms with coil springs, telescopic shock absorbers and anti-roll bar

Rear suspension: Live axle with upper and lower control arms, coil springs, telescopic shock absorbers and anti-roll bar

Brakes: Discs (front), drums (rear)

Wheels: Stamped-steel, 14 x 6 in.

Tires: Goodyear Polyglas, G-70 14

DIMENSIONS

Length: 203.2 in.   **Width:** 76.2 in.

Height: 52.8 in.   **Wheelbase:** 112.0 in.

Track: 59.0 in. (front and rear)

Weight: 3,574 lbs.

Oldsmobile **VISTA CRUISER**

Most muscle cars were built as two-door hard tops or convertibles, but some people love playing with the options list, resulting in cars with very unusual combinations. This is the case with this Oldsmobile Vista Cruiser wagon, one of three built with full 4-4-2™ W-30™ components.

"...far from sluggish."

"The interior of this car is unusual to say the least. The four-spoke steering wheel seems out of place, but all doubts soon fade once you hit the highway. The sound of the 455-cubic inch V8 resonating through the dual exhaust is music to the ears and even with so much behind you, acceleration is far from sluggish. The heavy-duty suspension helps handling tremendously, and braking is also surprisingly good, with power discs at the front."

A four-spoke wheel is a stock 4-4-2 item and hints at this wagon's performance.

Milestones

1968 GM A-body cars are now built on split wheelbases, 112 inches for two-doors, 116 inches for sedans and 121 inches for wagons. The Vista Cruiser is a separate series in the Cutlass™ range and 36,143 are built.

The sportiest of the Cutlass range is the 4-4-2.

1970 The Cutlass range receives a facelift and a 455-cubic inch V8 is now offered in the Cutlass-based 4-4-2. GM decides to build a performance Vista Cruiser station wagon to test public reaction.

A best-seller in the 1970s, the Cutlass was downsized for 1978.

1972 Despite being favored by the press, the Vista Cruiser W-30 is not officially offered through dealers, but three of these special wagons are built using stock 4-4-2 components.

UNDER THE SKIN

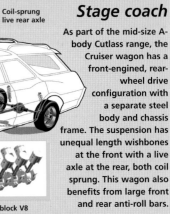

Body-on-frame construction

Coil-sprung live rear axle

Power front disc brakes

Big-block V8

Stage coach

As part of the mid-size A-body Cutlass range, the Cruiser wagon has a front-engined, rear-wheel drive configuration with a separate steel body and chassis frame. The suspension has unequal length wishbones at the front with a live axle at the rear, both coil sprung. This wagon also benefits from large front and rear anti-roll bars.

THE POWER PACK

Big-block wagon

Most Vista Cruisers came from the factory with 350 small-block V8s, but this one is different. Residing between the fenders is a monster 455-cubic inch big-block motor. A bored-out version of the 425-cubic inch engine, it arrived for 1970 and powered Oldsmobiles until 1976. In some eyes, it may seem low-tech, but this particular engine is fully balanced and blueprinted. In the Vista Cruiser it puts out 300 bhp and an earth-shattering 410 lb-ft of torque—more than enough to transport the family.

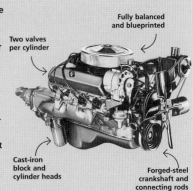

Two valves per cylinder

Fully balanced and blueprinted

Cast-iron block and cylinder heads

Forged-steel crankshaft and connecting rods

Fast hauler

These special wagons combine all the performance attributes of a 4-4-2 with seating for nine. Records indicate that only three cars were built, and if you are after something truly special, yet fast and practical, the Vista Cruiser W-30 is a must.

Only three of these W-30 wagons are known to have been built.

The largest and heaviest of the Cutlass family, the Vista Cruiser may not be a first choice for a performance car, but this example shows how much potential early 1970s GM intermediates have for becoming muscle machines.

Forced air induction
The W-30 package offered on 4-4-2s is also fitted to this Vista Cruiser. It includes a fiberglass hood with twin functional scoops which force air into the carburetor with the assistance of a dual snorkel air cleaner.

Big-block power
Instead of a wheezy small-block, this wagon is powered by an enormous 455-cubic inch V8. It has an aluminum intake, Rochester Quadrajet four-barrel carburetor and is fully balanced and blueprinted. It puts out a respectable 300 bhp at 4,700 rpm.

Power front disc brakes
Although most American cars of this period can go better than they can stop, this Vista Cruiser is fitted with power front discs which help to haul it down from three-figure speeds.

Wood-panel trim
Like most Detroit station wagons of the period, the Vista Cruiser has its lower panels covered in simulated wood veneer.

Single exhaust
Back in the early 1970s, a dual exhaust system was mandatory to extract the power from big-block V8 engines. Unusually, this Oldsmobile has a single full-length pipe.

Limited-slip differential
Housed in the 10-bolt rear end are a set of long-legged 3.73:1 gears and a Positraction limited-slip differential, which prevents both back tires from spinning helplessly under hard acceleration.

Specifications

1972 Oldsmobile Vista Cruiser

ENGINE
Type: V8
Construction: Cast-iron block and heads
Valve gear: Two valves per cylinder operated by pushrods and rockers
Bore and stroke: 4.13 in. x 4.25 in.
Displacement: 455 c.i.
Compression ratio: 8.5:1
Induction system: Rochester Quadrajet four-barrel carburetor
Maximum power: 300 bhp at 4,700 rpm
Maximum torque: 410 lb-ft at 3,200 rpm
Top speed: 120 mph
0-60 mph: 6.5 sec.

TRANSMISSION
GM TurboHydramatic 400

BODY/CHASSIS
Steel perimeter chassis with steel four-door station wagon body

SPECIAL FEATURES

Access to the cargo area can be gained three different ways.

Functional dual hood scoops are part of the W-30 package.

RUNNING GEAR
Steering: Recirculating ball
Front suspension: Unequal length wishbones with coil springs, telescopic shock absorbers and anti-roll bar
Rear suspension: Live axle with coil springs, telescopic shock absorbers and anti-roll bar
Brakes: Discs (front), drums (rear)
Wheels: Oldsmobile Rally, 7 x 15
Tires: Goodyear Polyglas,15-in. dia

DIMENSIONS
Length: 205.0 in.   **Width:** 60.9 in.
Height: 51.4 in.   **Wheelbase:** 121.0 in.
Track: 45.5 in. (front), 47.7 in. (rear)
Weight: 4,150 lbs.

Oldsmobile **HURST/OLDS**

In 1983, 15 years after the appearance of the first Hurst/Olds, a special anniversary version was released. With a tuned 307-cubic inch V8, uprated suspension, bigger tires and limited production run, it was destined to become a future collectible.

"...takes to curves."

"Like previous Hurst/Olds cars, this one lets you shift between first and second manually, for a quick snap off the line. The high-output V8, combined with relatively short gearing, gives adequate 0-60 mph performance. A special suspension means that this H/O takes to curves with much more confidence than previous versions. At highway speeds the car feels comfortable and composed, though the steering may be a little light for some tastes."

The unusual Hurst Lightning Rod shifter came standard in all 1983 Hurst/Olds models.

Milestones

1978 Oldsmobile's intermediate Cutlass™ is downsized to a 108.1-inch wheelbase and sheds over 400 lbs. It still proves a runaway success and 527,606 are sold.

The Hurst/Olds burst onto the scene in 1968, packing a 455 V8.

1979 The Hurst/Olds appears as a limited edition package on the Cutlass Supreme coupe. All 2,499 cars come with two-tone black and gold paint, plus a 350-cubic inch V8.

1983 An eighth incarnation of the Hurst/Olds appears. Only available in two-tone black and silver, it has a tweaked V8 and suspension; 3,000 are sold.

The 307 V8 was standard in 1983 Custom Cruiser™ wagons.

1984 With reversed silver and black paint, the H/O makes its final showing. A reborn 4-4-2 replaces it for 1985.

UNDER THE SKIN

Cutlass based

Body-on-frame construction
Live rear axle
Stiffer coil springs front and rear

All Hurst/Olds models were built from the mid-size Cutlass two-door versions. Though smaller than previous editions, the car still retained a separate steel perimeter chassis and a front-engined, rear-drive format. Improvements over the standard Cutlass include thicker front and rear anti-roll bars, stiffer springs and shocks, quicker steering, shorter gearing and large 15 x 7 inch wheels.

Small-block V8

THE POWER PACK

High output 307

By 1983, engine choices on the Cutlass had been whittled down to a Buick-built 231-cubic inch V6, a 307-cubic inch V8 or a 350-cubic inch diesel V8. In keeping with its sporty tradition, the 15th Anniversary Hurst/Olds had a V8 engine, but the veteran 307 unit underwent some tweaks. It has a performance Delco ignition, an electronically-controlled Rochester Quadrajet carburetor, stiffer valve springs and a low restriction cat-back dual exhaust. This boosted power from 140 to 180 bhp.

Two valves per cylinder
Rochester Quadrajet four-barrel carburetor
Cast-iron block and cylinder heads
Five main-bearing nodular-cast-iron crankshaft

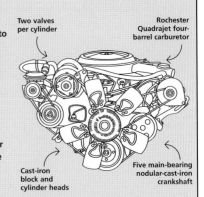

Hurst handler

Although all Hurst/Olds models gain collector interest, the 1983 version stands out as being an anniversary commemorative edition. Although it may not pack the same punch as previous incarnations, it handles better and is more practical to drive every day.

The 1983 Hurst/Olds places more emphasis on balance than acceleration.

As Detroit came to terms with emissions regulations in the early 1980s, performance cars began to make a comeback. The 1983 Hurst/Olds exemplified the breed, being able to handle and go fast in a straight line.

Tuned small-block V8

Back in 1983, the biggest Oldsmobile engine was the 307-cubic inch V8. Not content with the standard 140-bhp mill, engineers fitted a fortified version, with high-energy ignition, a four-barrel carburetor and low restriction exhaust. The result was an extra 40 bhp.

Aero styling

In 1981, Cutlass coupes were fitted with a raked-back nose cap, which improved drag coefficient. The 1983 Hurst/Olds went a stage further and has an air dam integrated into the lower bumper to smooth airflow under the car.

Lightning Rod shifter

To say the least, the three-handled shifter was unique. The lever closest to the driver operated like a traditional automatic transmission with park, reverse neutral, drive and overdrive. If this lever was left in drive the transmission would operate in a normal fashion. The other two shifters were a neat performance option. The shifter furthest from the driver only engaged first and second, while the middle shift lever brought the 2004R automatic from second to third.

Performance rear gearing

A standard set of 3.73:1 rear gears gives the Hurst/Olds considerable snap off the line by early- 1980s standards. A limited-slip differential was offered as an option to further improve traction.

Superlift shocks

Superlift self-levelling air shock absorbers are fitted at the rear, but Oldsmobile recommended that pressure should not exceed 90 psi.

Two-tone paint

All 1983 Hurst/Olds were painted black, with silver on the lower body and bumpers. When the car reappeared in 1984 the color pattern was reversed.

Specifications

1983 Oldsmobile Hurst/Olds

ENGINE

Type: V8

Construction: Cast-iron block and heads

Valve gear: Two valves per cylinder operated by a single camshaft with pushrods and rocker arms.

Bore and stroke: 3.80 in. x 3.89 in.

Displacement: 307 c.i.

Compression ratio: 8.0:1

Induction system: Single GM Rochester Quadrajet four-barrel carburetor

Maximum power: 180 bhp at 4,000 rpm

Maximum torque: 245 lb-ft at 3,200 rpm

Top speed: 120 mph

0-60 mph: 8.4 sec.

TRANSMISSION

GM 2004R four-speed automatic

BODY/CHASSIS

Separate steel chassis with two-door coupe body

SPECIAL FEATURES

The Hurst Lightning Rods shifter permits first and second, and second and third to be engaged manually.

All 1983 Hurst/Olds have a subtle hood bulge, hinting at the car's performance.

RUNNING GEAR

Steering: Recirculating ball

Front suspension: Unequal length A-arms with coil springs, telescopic shock absorbers and anti-roll bar

Rear suspension: Live axle with coil springs, telescopic shock absorbers and anti-roll bar

Brakes: Discs (front), drums (rear)

Wheels: Steel Rallye, 7 x 15 in.

Tires: Goodyear Eagle GT, 225/60 VR15

DIMENSIONS

Length: 200.0 in. **Width:** 71.6 in.

Height: 57.1 in. **Wheelbase:** 108.1 in.

Track: 51.8 in. (front and rear)

Weight: 3,535 lbs.

Packard **6/110**

Packing a 100-bhp six cylinder, the Six (later called the 110) was very much a 'junior' Packard, costing around $150 less than a comparable eight. It turned the company from a purveyor of specialty cars into one of Detroit's top ten.

"...smooth and silent."

"Packard customers expected a smooth, silent and ultra-refined engine, and the 110 met those requirements despite having just six cylinders instead of 8 or 12. It is punchy, but performance can best be described as brisk. With an independent front suspension, ride is impressive and the cabin feels like it is suspended on air. The steering is fantastic, with plenty of feel and accuracy, yet it's so light you would think it was power-assisted."

A comfortable leather bench seat and luxury fittings are very much part of the 110.

Milestones

1937 The success of the small eight-cylinder 120 introduced in 1935 is followed up by an even smaller model, the 115-inch wheelbase six.

Among the most exclusive Packards of 1940 were the Darrin-bodied convertibles.

1938 There are really significant changes to the junior Packards this year, with the wheelbase growing to 122 inches and the longer chassis carrying new and wider all-steel bodywork. Engine size grows to 245 cubic inches, thanks to a larger bore, and it is improved with a new cam.

The 120 was Packard's second-best-selling car before World War II.

1940 The smallest Packard in the range is now called the 110, even though it is built on the 122-inch wheelbase. Styling is revised, with a longer hood, resulting in a more upright look. Production ends in 1942.

UNDER THE SKIN

X-braced separate chassis

Hydraulically operated drum brakes

Independent front suspension

Smooth inline six

Eight parentage

The Packard has a massive chassis frame with two deep-section main rails running lengthwise and braced by an equally deep elongated X-member, drilled to save weight. The Six/110 has a live rear axle on leaf springs, and at the front the same independent setup used by the 120 line, with wishbones and coil springs. The brakes are hydraulically activated drums in the front and rear.

THE POWER PACK

Not much in common

For the 1937 model year, the new small Packard received a new engine. An inline six-cylinder unit, it shared the same bore and stroke dimensions of the existing V12 but surprisingly few of its components. The block is cast-iron and the head in alloy with a row of inline sidevalves operating upwards, in an L-shaped head, worked by a single block-mounted camshaft with adjustable lifters. The original bore and stroke dimensions were 3.44 x 4.25 inches, though the bore was increased in 1938 to bring displacement up to 245 cubic inches. Power output remained unchanged, however.

Fresh air

Today, the most sought after of all the 110 range is the 1940 two-door convertible coupe. This is worth more than twice the value of other variations, like the sedan and two-door sedan, and around $10,000 more than both coupe versions offered.

Rarest of all 1940 110s was the business coupe; only 836 were built.

While other marques adopted more sweeping contours in the 1940s, Packards—including the 110—retained a more traditional upright look. This is befitting a maker that built its fortune on luxury cars.

Sidevalve six

Packard engineering was more than capable of producing an overhead-valve, inline six powerplant, but the com-pany chose to retain the sidevalves for smooth and quiet running. In its L-shaped cylinder head, the valves are inline alongside one side of the head, with both intake and exhaust ports on the same side.

Steel bodywork

In the mid-1930s, Packard bodywork featured metal panels attached to hard-wood sills and roofrails. Although the rear floor was steel, the front was wooden. This changed for 1938, when all-steel bodywork was introduced.

Electric windshield wipers

Throughout the 1930s Packard's windshield wipers operated on the vacuum principle. Although their action was much more regular than some other systems in which the wipers could slow to a crawl depending on engine load, the switch to electric wipers by the 1940s on the junior Packards was a very welcome move.

Overdrive

In the late 1930s, Packard introduced an overdrive to supplement the three-speed manual. This operates very smoothly. Above 20 mph the driver just has to ease off the accelerator and engage an extra epicyclic gear, which is much higher than the normal top gear. Normal top gear can be re-engaged by pressing down on the accelerator.

Optional air conditioning

Packard brought large-car luxury to the small six-cylinder 1940's cars. Air conditioning was a $300 option. This was a huge amount considering that the basic price of the most expensive 110 models was $1,200.

Separate chassis

Weight was never a serious factor for Packard. It was more important to make the cars as high quality as possible and a separate chassis frame reflects that.

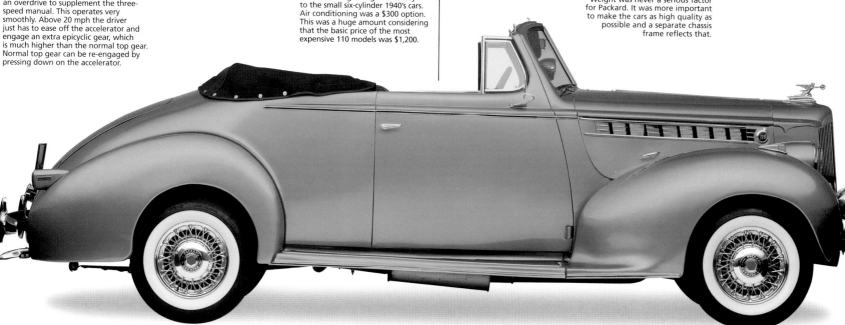

Specifications
1940 Packard 110

ENGINE

Type: Inline sidevalve six-cylinder

Construction: Cast-iron block and alloy cylinder head

Valve gear: Two inline sidevalves per cylinder operated by a single side-mounted camshaft in L-head cylinder head

Bore and stroke: 3.50 in. x 4.25 in.

Displacement: 245.3 c.i.

Compression ratio: 6.4:1

Induction system: Single Stromberg downdraft carburetor

Maximum power: 100 bhp at 3,600 rpm

Maximum torque: 195 lb-ft at 1,500 rpm

Top speed: 75 mph

0-60 mph: 20.1 sec.

TRANSMISSION

Three-speed manual

BODY/CHASSIS

Separate X-braced steel chassis with steel body

SPECIAL FEATURES

The external spotlight can be operated from inside the car.

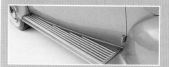

Running boards were still fitted to most cars in 1940.

RUNNING GEAR

Steering: Worm-and-roller

Front suspension: Double wishbones with torque reaction rods, coil springs and lever-arm shock absorbers

Rear suspension: Live axle with semi-elliptic leaf springs and telescopic shock absorbers

Brakes: Drums, 10.7-in. dia. (front and rear)

Wheels: Pressed steel disc, 15-in. dia.

Tires: Biasply, 6.50 x 15

DIMENSIONS

Length: 201.1 in. **Width:** 73.8 in.

Height: 66.8 in. **Wheelbase:** 122.0 in.

Track: 59.2 in. (front) 60.5 in. (rear)

Weight: 3,200 lbs.

Packard CARIBBEAN

In the early 1950s, the Packard company decided its conservative image needed a transformation. One result was an exclusive luxury car, the straight-eight powered, 100 mph Caribbean convertible.

"...a pleasant surprise."

"When mated with the Ultramatic transmission, the big and wonderfully smooth straight eight gives leisurely performance, although it will eventually top 100 mph. Even at low speeds, the car leans through corners, but there is a pleasant surprise in store; as the speed rises the Caribbean steadies itself and can be hustled along quickly and with superb comfort, even over rough roads. The steering is very light, and the brakes need only the slightest touch."

The strawberries-and-cream interior of the Caribbean looks good enough to eat.

Milestones

1951 Packard boosts its image with a show car from the Henney Body Co. The car appears the following year as the Pan American.

The top-of-the-range 1956 Clipper was the last of the true Packards.

1953 Reaction to the Pan American is so strong that Packard decides to go into production with a luxury convertible, the Caribbean.

1954 A facelift adds new headlight rims, a chromed hood scoop, semi-enclosed rear wheels, two-tone paint, new taillights and a color-keyed interior.

Studebaker's financial troubles contributed to Packard's demise.

1955 An all-new Caribbean arrives with innovative new self-leveling suspension. It lasts for a further year. Financial concerns shift the focus to high-volume models.

UNDER THE SKIN

Conservative nature

Power-assisted steering
Live rear axle
Drum brakes front and rear
Inline eight

The 1955 Packard has a really innovative chassis and running gear, and by comparison the 1954 is very conservative. The chassis has channel-section frame rails with a big X-brace carrying A-arms and coil-spring suspension at the front and a live rear axle on semi-elliptic leaf springs at the rear. Transmission is a two-speed Ultramatic automatic with torque converter.

THE POWER PACK

Straight eight

Packard kept faith with inline straight-eight engines while its rivals were making more modern V8s. Engine design was old-fashioned with a long cast-iron block carrying a crankshaft on nine main bearings. On top is an alloy head, but the two inline side valves per cylinder work in an L-head design. The valve lifters are hydraulic, and thus adjustment-free. It is a long-stroke design and output compared well with its V8 rivals. There were very few engines as powerful for the size as the Packard 359 with its 212 bhp.

'53 or '54?

Some aficionados prefer the 1953 Carribean, with its fully open rear wheelarch design, but the 1954 version is rarer (400 were built). The later Caribbean, with 212 bhp, also boasts more power than its predecessor.

1954 was the last year for straight eights in Packards.

With two-tone paintwork, lots of chrome and wire wheels, the Caribbean was an impressive showpiece. It was ideally suited for wealthier Americans to cruise around in on Sunday afternoon drives.

Inline eight cylinder
Prestige and smooth running apart, there were clear disadvantages to the straight-eight design. The design was inherently heavier and larger than a V8. The length of the crankshaft also kept engine speeds down. The 1954 engine was the final flowering of the straight-eight concept and has an alloy head and one of the highest compression ratios of any U.S. engine at the time.

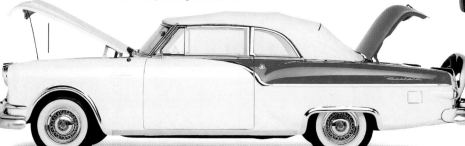

Two-speed Ultramatic
The idea of a two-speed automatic transmission may sound frustrating, but Packard's Ultramatic with torque converter is extremely smooth. It shifts into high gear at speeds ranging from 15 mph to 50 mph depending on how hard the driver accelerates.

Live rear axle
Packard used a live axle that is both located and suspended by semi-elliptic leaf springs. There are telescopic shock absorbers and an anti-roll bar. Packard was working on a sophisticated system of torsion-bar self-leveling suspension but this would not debut until the following year.

Power steering
Although the steering gear on the Caribbean is very low-geared and needs a full 4.4 turns to get from lock to lock, it still has power assistance, although the system chosen is slow to self- center after a turn.

Power top
For the price Packard charged, Caribbean buyers were not expected to have to lower the convertible top manually and there was a hydraulically powered system that could raise or lower the roof completely in around 30 seconds. When lowered, the top disappeared completely.

Specifications

1954 Packard Caribbean

ENGINE
Type: Inline eight cylinder

Construction: Cast-iron block and alloy head

Valve gear: Two inline side valves per cylinder operated upwards by a single block-mounted camshaft

Bore and stroke: 3.56 in. x 4.50 in.

Displacement: 359 c.i.

Compression ratio: 8.7:1

Induction system: Single Carter WCFB four-barrel carburetor

Maximum power: 212 bhp at 4,000 rpm

Maximum torque: 310 lb-ft at 2,000 rpm

Top speed: 101 mph

0-60 mph: 15.8 sec.

TRANSMISSION
Two-speed Ultramatic automatic

BODY/CHASSIS
Separate box-section steel chassis frame with two-door convertible body

SPECIAL FEATURES

Chrome-plated flat-top rear wheel arches are a feature unique to the 1954 Caribbean.

The spare wheel is neatly incorporated into the rear bodywork and was color-coded, too.

RUNNING GEAR
Steering: Spiral-bevel

Front suspension: A-arms with coil springs and telescopic shock absorbers

Rear suspension: Live axle with semi-elliptic leaf springs, telescopic shock absorbers and anti-roll bar

Brakes: Drums front and rear, 12.0-in. dia. (front and rear)

Wheels: Wire spoke, 15-in. dia.

Tires: 8.00 x 15

DIMENSIONS
Length: 211.5 in.   **Width:** 77.8 in.

Height: 64.0 in.   **Wheelbase:** 122.0 in.

Track: 60.0/60/8 front and rear

Weight: 4,400 lbs.

Panoz **ROADSTER**

Despite its youth, the Panoz has made big waves as a superfast, hand-built roadster. Its bare-boned style and advanced aluminum construction make it intriguing and exciting to drive.

"...pure, modern magic."

"To get into the Panoz you have to open a tiny door and step over the sill. The narrow cockpit feels like one of the great sports cars of the 1960s, but when you turn the key and hear the throb of a Mustang V8, you know this has to be a 1990s car. Floor the throttle and you are catapulted off the line at tremendous speed. The pleasure of prowling along twisty roads in the Roadster is pure, modern magic."

The cockpit may be in the spirit of 1960s sports cars, but ergonomically-designed seats and a heater are welcomed modern features.

Milestones

1994 Danny Panoz

sets out to create a car that offers pure driving thrills for the American driver. Having taken over an Irish motorsports company that had an inspired car design, Panoz develops the vehicle to meet U.S. regulations and shows the Roadster this year.

In 1997, Panoz entered the GT endurance series with the sleek new GTR-1.

1995 At the Geneva Motor Show, the Swiss

tuning company Rinspeed presents a mildly-modified version of the Panoz, known as the Rinspeed Roadster.

The latest car from Panoz is the sleek Esperante coupe.

1996 Panoz AIV

Roadster (AIV stands for aluminum-intensive vehicle) debuts in the U.S. to a rapturous reception from the press.

UNDER THE SKIN

Race car technology

The original chassis design was conceived by the legendary British racing car engineer Frank Costin (the 'cos' of the Marcos company). It consists of a frame with large bore aluminum tubes and backbone, to which tubular steel sub-frames are attached. The suspension design is race-bred with wishbones on both the front and the rear.

Aluminum body and frame
Live rear axle
All-aluminum V8 engine
Independent front suspension
Four-cam 32-valve V8

THE POWER PACK

Mustang Cobra V8 power

Taken straight from the current Ford Mustang Cobra, the 4.6-liter modular V8 is state-of-the-art and features four camshafts, 32 valves, fuel injection and sophisticated emissions control. In both the Mustang Cobra and the Panoz Roadster this engine develops 305 bhp, and when combined with the aluminum construction of the Panoz it produces outstanding performance and refinement. The use of a standard Ford engine also means that the Panoz Roadster can be serviced by Ford dealerships.

Distributorless ignition
Sequential electronic fuel injection
Borg-Warner T-45 five-speed transmission
All-aluminum block and cylinder heads

Hand-built

Although it also produces the Esperante Le Mans road-racing car, Panoz offers just one version of its hand-built AIV Roadster. However, there is a range of options to suit an individual's preferences. A sports suspension package is available, as are a trunk-mounted luggage rack and side wind deflectors.

Panoz owners can personalize their cars with factory options.

With Ford Mustang Cobra V8 power, awesome performance and few creature comforts, the American-built Panoz AIV Roadster is the true Shelby Cobra of the 1990s.

Ultra-low profile tires
The wide, 18-inch alloy wheels are fitted with ultra-low profile BF Goodrich Competition T/A tires—245/40 at the front and 295/35 at the rear.

Different suspension settings
Two different suspension settings are available: standard and sport. The latter offers stiffer spring rates and a much firmer, but still comfortable ride.

Classically simple interior
Inside, in classic sports car fashion, form follows function. Interior choices are burr walnut or carbon fiber trim, and dark- or beige-colored leather upholstery. Air-conditioning and a monster stereo are available as options.

Ford sub-systems
Choosing standard Ford parts for the engine, drivetrain, and electrics results in excellent reliability and servicing that can be carried out by Ford dealerships.

Vented disc brakes
The Roadster has one of the world's most effective braking systems, consisting of large diameter vented disc brakes on all four corners. The front discs also boast twin-piston calipers.

Race car chassis
The chassis is descended from an original design by the ex-Marcos and Lotus engineer Frank Costin. The integrity of Costin's original aluminum frame is retained, despite modifications to house the drivetrain.

Elemental styling
The original style of the Panoz was co-created by Danny Panoz and Freeman Thomas, and draws on many influences, particularly the Jaguar E-type and Austin Healey, as well as traditional American hot rods.

Aircraft-technology body
The Roadster's aluminum body panels are built for safety and strength and are similar to those used on aircraft.

Specifications
1997 Panoz AIV Roadster

ENGINE

Type: V8

Construction: Aluminum cylinder block and heads

Valve gear: Four valves per cylinder operated by two chain-driven overhead camshafts per cylinder bank

Bore and stroke: 3.55 in. x 3.54 in.

Displacement: 4.6 liters

Compression ratio: 9.9:1

Induction system: Fuel injection

Maximum power: 305 bhp at 5,800 rpm

Maximum torque: 300 lb-ft at 4,800 rpm

Top speed: 131 mph

0-60 mph: 4.5 sec.

TRANSMISSION

Borg-Warner T-4S five-speed manual

BODY/CHASSIS

Aluminum space frame with two-door roadster body

SPECIAL FEATURES

Small 'cycle-wing' fenders turn with the front wheels to prevent debris from being thrown over the car and driver.

Extensive use of aluminum results in a very light, but strong, frame.

RUNNING GEAR

Steering: Power rack-and-pinion

Front suspension: Unequal length wishbones, with coil spring/shock units, and anti-roll bar

Rear suspension: Unequal length wishbones with coil/spring shock units, and anti-roll bar

Brakes: Vented disc brakes all around

Wheels: Aluminum, 18-in. dia.

Tires: 245/40 ZR18 (front), 295/35 ZR18 (rear)

DIMENSIONS

Length: 155 in.   **Width:** 76.5 in.

Height: 47 in.   **Wheelbase:** 104.5 in.

Track: 65 in. (front), 64.2 in. (rear)

Weight: 2,459 lbs.

Plymouth FURY

Plymouth was once America's number three make, and in the golden years of the late 1950s, the name was carried by cars such as the Fury—a high-performance luxury car with great styling.

"...great pulling power."

"A number of road testers described the Fury as having many of the qualities of a sports car, and they weren't dreaming. For a start, there's the engine. In 1958 Golden Commando guise, it has 305 bhp and is capable of clean and very quick takeoffs. There's great pulling power from just above idle, too. Combined with the superbly smooth-acting, if slightly heavy, TorqueFlite automatic transmission, this was one of the best drives in Detroit."

Classic 1950s style, notably the full-width front bench, defines the Fury's cabin.

Milestones

1956 The Fury name is first used on a Plymouth.

1957 As the range-topping model in the stunning new 1957 lineup, the Fury hardtop coupe gives buyers the luxury of performance and style in equal measure.

1957 was the first year torsion bars were used on the Fury.

1958 A mild facelift includes quad headlights, a revised grill and new taillights. A new Golden Commando V8 is offered with optional fuel injection. The Fury is also offered as a sedan.

Dodge's version of the Fury was the D500.

1959 A controversial restyle extends the tailfins and adds bigger bumpers.

1960 All-new unibody Plymouths replace the old lineup.

UNDER THE SKIN

Separate chassis
Longitudinal torsion-bar front suspension
Live rear axle
Cast-iron V8

Low and lean

Deserving its reputation for being Detroit's best-handling car in 1957, the Plymouth Fury relied on a relatively low center of gravity. All 1957-1959 Plymouths retained the old separate chassis layout. Plymouth switched to a more modern 'Torsion Air Ride' longitudinal torsion-bar front suspension, which was quite adventurous for Detroit in 1957.

THE POWER PACK

One year only 350

The Fury was always fitted with the biggest and most powerful engine in Plymouth's powerplant armory—the name chosen to describe these big V8s was 'wedgehead.' For 1957, there was an all-new range of engines at Plymouth and the Fury got a unique, optional new 318-cubic inch V8 with 290 bhp on tap. The following year, the engine size and output remained the same, but the big news was the optional availability of a larger 350-cubic inch Golden Commando unit with 305 bhp. Even more desirable, but ultra-rare because of the high sticker price, was fuel injection, which added an extra 10 bhp.

Class of '58

While the 1957 Fury is undoubtedly the most cleanly styled of the 1957-1959 models, the most desirable model in collector terms is the rarer 1958 car. It came with the option of a more powerful engine. A few models came with fuel injection.

The 1958 model is the most sought after, but examples are ultra rare.

Living up to its name, the Fury was a full-size coupe that could outperform and outhandle many contemporary sports cars. This was due to fairly advanced engineering by 1957 Detroit standards.

Golden Commando power

While the Fury stopped short of the one-horsepower-per- cubic-inch claim of its DeSoto and Chrysler stablemates, it was not far off. For 1958, the 350-cubic inch motor pumped out 305 bhp or, with fuel injection, 315 bhp.

Torsion-bar front suspension

The Fury was available with a suspension unlike GM's or Ford's. Torsion-bar springing was first applied to the 1957 DeSoto. This 1958 Fury uses the same system.

Long, low and lean

The long, wide stance of the Fury is not just due to style. It significantly lowers the center of gravity, making the Fury one of the best-handling cars of its day.

Tailfins

1957 was the biggest year yet for tailfins, and Virgil Exner's contribution made the Fury one of the year's tailfin stars. Although they were claimed to add directional stability at speed, the real reason for their existence is, of course, cosmetic.

Slimline roofline

The arching shape of the coupe roofline is one of the best styling features. It enhances the sporty feel of the car and, together with the wraparound front and rear windows, contributes toward excellent all-around visibility.

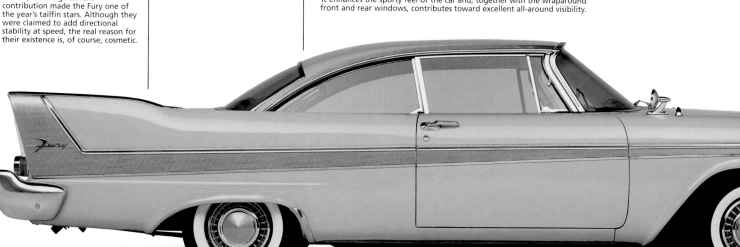

Specifications
1958 Plymouth Fury

ENGINE

Type: V8

Construction: Cast-iron block and heads

Valve gear: Two valves per cylinder operated via pushrods and rockers

Bore and stroke: 4.06 in. x 3.38 in.

Displacement: 350 c.i.

Compression ratio: 10.0:1

Induction system: Dual Carter carburetors

Maximum power: 305 bhp at 5,000 rpm

Maximum torque: 370 lb-ft at 3,600 rpm

Top speed: 122 mph

0-60 mph: 8.0 sec.

TRANSMISSION

Three-speed automatic

BODY/CHASSIS

Separate chassis with two-door coupe body

SPECIAL FEATURES

The 'V' emblem on the grill signifies that a V8 engine is fitted.

The quad-headlight treatment was new for the 1958 model year.

RUNNING GEAR

Steering: Rack-and-pinion

Front suspension: Independent by upper and lower wishbones with longitudinal torsion bars and shock absorbers

Rear suspension: Live axle with semi-elliptic leaf springs and shock absorbers

Brakes: Drums (front and rear)

Wheels: Steel, 14-in. dia.

Tires: 8.00 x 14

DIMENSIONS

Length: 206.0 in.   **Width:** 78.0 in.

Height: 57.0 in.   **Wheelbase:** 118.0 in.

Track: 60.9 in. (front), 59.6 in. (rear)

Weight: 3,510 lbs.

Plymouth **SAVOY 426**

In the early 1960s, Ford, GM and Chrysler were battling to be the victor in NHRA's Super Stock class. Plymouth aptly dubbed its lightweight, race-prepared Savoy the Super Stock. By 1963 they were dominating the drag strips.

"...it borders on insanity."

"With a 13.5:1 compression, 426 cubic-inch, Stage II Max Wedge engine this factory-built race car wasn't really meant for street use. The high strung engine idles rough and loud. The neck-snapping acceleration of this race machine borders on insanity. Take your place behind the steering wheel and you'll notice that the heater, carpeting and radio are removed to reduce weight. Shifting the automatic transmission is done with the push-buttons on the left side of the instrument panel. "

Built only for drag racing, this Savoy has a very plain interior without a radio or heater.

Milestones

1962 Plymouth fields downsized cars with unusual styling. A new 413-cubic inch Wedge engine is offered as an option in its full-size cars.

Arlen Vanke was one of the quickest Max Wedge drivers.

1963 Body styles change and this year's cars have prettier lines. Plymouths still retain a 116-inch wheelbase, but the 413 engine is bored out to 426 cubic inches. The Stage I engine comes with an 11:1 compression ratio, while the Stage II, mainly designed for drag racing, comes with 13.5:1 compression.

The Dodge version of the 426 was called the Ram Charger.

1964 Styling is mildly revised again. The Max Wedge engine is still offered, but in Stage III form with 12.5:1 compression. It takes the back seat to the new 426 Hemi.

UNDER THE SKIN

Perfect racer

In 1962, while the rest of Detroit was upsizing, Plymouth fielded downsized full-size cars on a 116-inch wheelbase. Although not popular with mainstream buyers, they were ideal for drag racers. Less bulk means less weight, and racers were quick to exploit this. This car has unitary construction, torsion bar front suspension and could be ordered with 4.56:1 gearing.

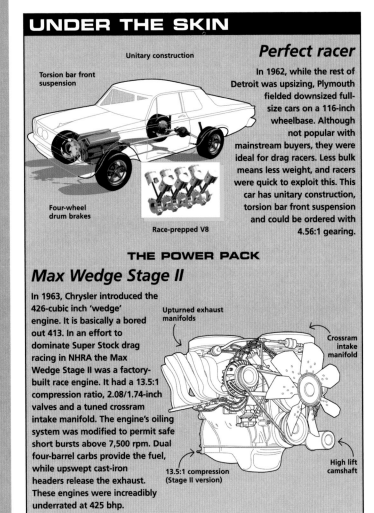

Unitary construction

Torsion bar front suspension

Four-wheel drum brakes

Race-prepped V8

THE POWER PACK

Max Wedge Stage II

In 1963, Chrysler introduced the 426-cubic inch 'wedge' engine. It is basically a bored out 413. In an effort to dominate Super Stock drag racing in NHRA the Max Wedge Stage II was a factory-built race engine. It had a 13.5:1 compression ratio, 2.08/1.74-inch valves and a tuned crossram intake manifold. The engine's oiling system was modified to permit safe short bursts above 7,500 rpm. Dual four-barrel carbs provide the fuel, while upswept cast-iron headers release the exhaust. These engines were incredibly underrated at 425 bhp.

Upturned exhaust manifolds

Crossram intake manifold

13.5:1 compression (Stage II version)

High lift camshaft

Second Stage

Though the Plymouth Super Stock was sold as a production car, it was solely designed for drag racing. Its brochure warned that '... it wasn't a street machine' but was 'built to compete in supervised racing events.' It didn't even come with a factory warranty.

The S/SA 426 Stage II Savoy stands for NHRA's Super Stock Automatic class.

This early 1963 Plymouth Savoy 426 was built at Chrysler's Lynch Road factory in Detroit and was delivered to its first owner in California in May of that year. It was restored in 1989.

Max Wedge engine
A derivative of the previous years 413 engine, the 426 Stage I was rated at 415 bhp with 470 lb-ft of torque. The sinister Max Wedge Stage II made a drastically underrated 425 bhp. These typical race- prepared Savoys would run 12.60 ETs at over 112 mph.

Lightened front
In mid 1963, weight-saving aluminum front fenders, hood and bumpers became available, although this early car retains a steel front end.

Drum brakes
With handling and braking taking a back seat to acceleration, this Savoy is fitted with drum brakes front and rear. They are barely adequate and prone to overheating, especially during repeated drag duty.

Savoy two-door sedan
To maximize the massive engine's power, Plymouth put it between the fenders of its lightest full size—the Savoy.

Torsion bar suspension
There are many advantages to this set up. Torsion bars are extremely tough and inexpensive to replace, plus racers can crank them up a few notches to increase ride height, which aids weight transfer and traction off the line.

Smaller and lighter
In an unusual move, Plymouth fielded shorter full-size cars in 1962 with very unusual styling. Sales were poor, however, and 1963 models adopted more conservative contours.

TorqueFlite transmission
Although a manual transmission was offered with the 426 engine, most buyers specified the 727 TorqueFlite automatic. Chrysler's engineering department was able to design an automatic transmission that was stronger and much more sophisticated than its competitors.

Specifications
1963 Plymouth Savoy 426

ENGINE

Type: V8

Construction: Cast-iron block and heads

Valve gear: Two valves per cylinder operated by a single camshaft via pushrods and solid lifters

Bore and stroke: 4.25 in. x 3.75 in.

Displacement: 426 c.i.

Compression ratio: 13.5:1

Induction system: Twin Carter four-barrel carburetors

Maximum power: 425 bhp at 5,600 rpm

Maximum torque: 470 lb-ft at 4,400 rpm

Top speed: 125 mph

0-60 mph: 5.0 sec.

TRANSMISSION

TorqueFlite 727 three-speed automatic

BODY/CHASSIS

Unitary steel chassis with two-door sedan body

SPECIAL FEATURES

The crossram intake manifold ensures maximum power delivery in short bursts.

For better weight distribution, the battery is mounted in the trunk.

RUNNING GEAR

Steering: Recirculating ball

Front suspension: Longitudinally-mounted torsion bars with coil springs and telescopic shock absorbers

Rear suspension: Live axle with semi-elliptic multi-leaf springs and telescopic shock absorbers

Brakes: Drums, 10-in. dia (front and rear)

Wheels: American Racing Torque Thrust-D, 15-in. dia

Tires: BF Goodrich Silvertown 7-10-15 (front), Hoosier 275/45 R15 (rear)

DIMENSIONS

Length: 197.0 in.   **Width:** 80.5 in.

Height: 58.3 in.   **Wheelbase:** 116.0 in.

Track: 64.8 in. (front), 61.0 in. (rear)

Weight: 3,400 lbs.

Plymouth ROAD RUNNER

By the late 1960s, many muscle cars were beyond the financial reach of their would-be buyers. To corner this segment of the market, Plymouth offered the Road Runner. It was a no-frills coupe with a 383 V8 engine as standard power. The result proved to be an instant sales success and owners were well respected on the street.

"...back to the basics."

"Getting back to the basics is what the Road Runner is all about. It is all business, from the steel wheels to the rubber floormats. The 383 is a strong engine and thrives at low rpm. With the four-speed shifter in your right hand and your foot on the gas, its acceleration is unreal. Because it was a bare-bones muscle car its weight was kept as low as possible for an even better power-to-weight ratio. With 335 bhp, this was a car that really lived up to its name."

The 1968 model is the Road Runner in its purest form with a no-frills interior.

Milestones

1968 With a growing number of enthusiasts wanting a no-frills factory hot rod, Plymouth decides to take the plunge and offer the Road Runner—a two-door coupe with a standard 383-cubic inch V8. Chrysler pays Warner Bros. $50,000 to use the Road Runner name. Projected sales are 2,500, but in the end, 44,589 are sold.

The Super Bee was Dodge Division's equivalent to the Road Runner.

1969 The Road Runner goes upmarket. A convertible model is added to the range. Mid-year, a new 440-cubic inch Six-Barrel joins the 383 and 426 Hemi engine options.

The sporty Road Runner was extensively revamped for 1971.

1970 A new loop-type grill and revised taillights mark the 1970 edition. Fifteen inch Rallye wheels are now a popular option.

UNDER THE SKIN

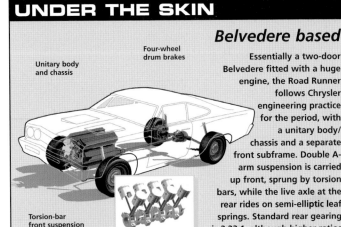

Belvedere based

Four-wheel drum brakes

Unitary body and chassis

Torsion-bar front suspension

Big-block V8

Essentially a two-door Belvedere fitted with a huge engine, the Road Runner follows Chrysler engineering practice for the period, with a unitary body/chassis and a separate front subframe. Double A-arm suspension is carried up front, sprung by torsion bars, while the live axle at the rear rides on semi-elliptic leaf springs. Standard rear gearing is 3.23:1, although higher ratios were available.

THE POWER PACK

Big block brawler

While other muscle cars relied on increasingly complex engines for propulsion, Plymouth decided that simplicity was essential to the Road Runner. For maximum effect and in order to keep costs down, the division decided to install the 383-cubic inch big-block as the standard engine. This cast-iron V8 had been in production since the 1950s, but for the Road Runner it received some upgrades. The heads, exhaust manifolds, camshaft, heavy-duty valve springs, and crankshaft windage tray are all from the 440. With a four-barrel carburetor and a low-restriction air cleaner, it makes 335 bhp at 5,200 rpm.

Hemi first

The first-generation Road Runner is an undisputed muscle car classic, and the first-year (1968) model is its purest form. Collectors prefer the 426 Hemi-engined cars. They can easily run 13-second ¼-mile ETs, but only 1,019 were built.

Steel wheels were standard on 1968 Road Runners.

The Road Runner was so successful that it inspired rival manufacturers to offer budget muscle cars of their own. Anyone who drove a Road Runner was soon mesmerized by its incredible performance.

Torsion-bar front suspension

A typical 1960s Chrysler feature is a torsion-bar front suspension. Twin longitudinal bars provide springing for the front wishbones and give a smoother ride than coil setups. Road Runners have bigger front bars in an attempt to improve handling.

Big-block V8

Inexpensive to build, yet with a few simple tweaks mightily effective, the 383 V8 was the ideal engine for Plymouth's budget muscle-car. Packing 335 bhp and a monster 425 lb-ft of torque, even in stock trim it was a street terror.

Hardtop styling

When introduced, the Road Runner was only available in one body-style—a pillared coupe. A hardtop version appeared mid year and a convertible was introduced in 1969.

Four-speed transmission

An essential performance ingredient on any real street racer is a manual transmission, and the Road Runner has a standard four-on-the-floor. A TorqueFlite automatic was optional.

Drum brakes

Most muscle cars are about going fast in a straight line and little else. Stopping the Road Runner could be quite entertaining, with the standard four-wheel drums, so ordering front discs was a wise option.

Steel wheels

In keeping with its frugal image, the Road Runner came with standard 14-inch steel wheels and center hub caps. However, 14-inch Magnum 500 rims were a popular upgrade.

Specifications

1968 Plymouth Road Runner

ENGINE

Type: V8

Construction: Cast-iron block and heads

Valve gear: Two valves per cylinder operated by a single camshaft

Bore and stroke: 4.25 in. x 3.38 in.

Displacement: 383 c.i.

Compression ratio: 10.0:1

Induction system: Carter AFB four-barrel downdraft carburetor

Maximum power: 335 bhp at 5,200 rpm

Maximum torque: 425 lb-ft at 3,400 rpm

Top speed: 130 mph

0-60 mph: 6.7 sec.

TRANSMISSION

Four-speed manual

BODY/CHASSIS

Unitary steel construction with stamped steel body panels

SPECIAL FEATURES

To extract the most power out of the engine, Road Runners were equipped with standard dual exhaust.

The flat black hood center gave this potent Plymouth a very aggressive look.

RUNNING GEAR

Steering: Recirculating-ball

Front suspension: Unequal-length A-arms with torsion bars, telescopic shock absorbers and anti-roll bar

Rear suspension: Live axle with semi-elliptic leaf springs and telescopic shock absorbers

Brakes: Drums (front and rear)

Wheels: Pressed steel, 14-in. dia.

Tires: F70-14

DIMENSIONS

Length: 202.7 in. **Width:** 81.7 in.

Height: 56.3 in. **Wheelbase:** 116.0 in.

Track: 59.5 in. (front and rear).

Weight: 3,400 lbs.

Plymouth **SUPERBIRD**

Developed from the budget Road Runner coupe, the Superbird was designed to defeat Ford's Talladegas in NASCAR superspeedway races. Shortly after Plymouth's powerful rocket appeared, NASCAR had changed the rules, and Superbirds were only allowed to race the 1970 season.

"...NASCAR racing warrior."

"Plymouth built more than 1,935 Superbirds as a follow up to Dodge's less-than-victorious 1969 Daytonas that were designed to slaughter Ford's Talladegas. The strikingly similar looking Superbird proved to be a NASCAR racing warrior. The aluminum wing, flush mounted rear window, Hemi engine, and 18-inch metal nose cone all added up to victory in 1970. In race trim at speeds in excess of 190 mph, the Superbird's nose cone actually added more weight to the front wheels, while the rear wing had to be properly adjusted or the rear tires would wear prematurely."

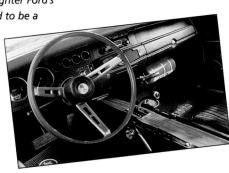

Stock Superbirds had typical Plymouth interiors with only the necessary gauges, console and shifter.

Milestones

1963 Chrysler decides to take on Ford in NASCAR. As owners of Plymouth and Dodge, they had the 426-cubic inch Hemi V8 engine, whose power should have been enough to guarantee supremacy.

1964-68 Power alone is not enough. On stock car ovals, Ford's supremacy continues because their cars have better aerodynamics.

1969 Dodge Charger Daytona appears with a rear wing giving downforce to keep the car on the track at 200 mph speeds. They win 18 NASCAR races this year. Unfortunately, Ford takes home more than 30.

The Superbirds proved their worth on the superspeedways.

1970 Superbird has better aerodynamics than the Dodge Charger and wins 21 races (including the Daytona 500) and beating Ford. Not very many people liked its unusual styling, so many were stripped of their wings and nose cones and turned back into Road Runners just so Plymouth could sell them.

1971 NASCAR rules, designed to keep racing equal, impose a 25 percent engine volume restriction on rear-winged cars, which spells the end of the Superbird in competition.

UNDER THE SKIN

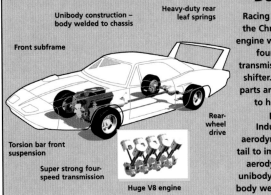

Unibody construction – body welded to chassis

Heavy-duty rear leaf springs

Front subframe

Torsion bar front suspension

Super strong four-speed transmission

Rear-wheel drive

Huge V8 engine

Beefed up

Racing Superbirds use the Chrysler 426 Hemi engine with close-ratio, four-speed manual transmission and Hurst shifter. All mechanical parts are strengthened to handle the extra power. Creative Industries built the aerodynamic nose and tail to improve the car's aerodynamics. It uses unibody construction— body welded to chassis.

THE POWER PACK

More horsepower

The Hemi—so called because the combustion chamber (the area where the fuel is actually burned) is hemispherical—was the first mass-produced engine of its type in America. The Hemi head promoted even burning and more room for bigger valves (to get more fuel and air in). It also produced more horsepower per cubic inch than any other design, and forced Chevy and Ford to think about copies. Finally, it was the victim of NASCAR rule changes.

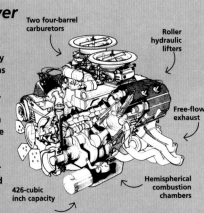

Two four-barrel carburetors

Roller hydraulic lifters

Free-flow exhaust

Hemispherical combustion chambers

426-cubic inch capacity

Vinyl Top

Did you ever notice that all Superbirds had vinyl tops? Plymouth was in a hurry to homologate these cars for NASCAR racing. Instead of properly doing the body work around the flush mounted rear window, it just hid the rough body work with a vinyl top.

The fender scoops cover a cut out giving better tire clearance at high speeds.

The Superbird could achieve over 200 mph on the race track using the vital downforce generated by the huge rear wing. Even the tamer street version could easily reach 140 mph.

Roll cage
The NASCAR version used a tubular roll cage welded to the frame that stiffened it tremendously as well as protected the driver at 200 mph.

Front suspension
Front torsion bars resulted in better front suspension than competitors.

Four-speed transmission
Heavy-duty four-speed Chrysler model 883 was the strongest transmission available at the time.

Standard steel wheels
Steel wheels are still standard in NASCAR—wider 9.5 inch x 15 inch are used now, 15 inch x 7 inch when the Superbird ran. All NASCAR tires then were bias ply with inner tubes.

Live rear axle
Dana-built rear axle was originally intended for a medium-duty truck. Even in drag racing, the mighty Hemi could break it.

Rear suspension
Asymmetric rear leaf springs (the front third was stiffer than the rear two-thirds) helped locate the rear axle.

High-mounted rear wing
The rear wing provided downforce at the rear. Its angle was adjustable—too much and the increased force would shred the tires.

Cowl induction
Carburetor intake air was picked up from the high-pressure area at the base of the windshield—called cowl induction.

Aerodynamic nose
The nose was designed to lower drag and increase top speed while adding downforce—it actually put more weight on the front as speed increased.

Specifications
1970 Plymouth Superbird

ENGINE

Type: Hemi V8

Construction: Cast-iron block and heads; hemispherical combustion chambers

Valve gear: Two valves per cylinder operated by single block-mounted camshaft

Bore and stroke: 4.25 in. x 3.74 in.

Displacement: 426 c.i.

Compression ratio: 12:1

Induction system: Two four-barrel carbs, aluminum manifold

Maximum power: 425 bhp at 5,000 rpm

Maximum torque: 490 lb-ft at 4,000 rpm

Top speed: 140 mph

0-60 mph: 6.1 sec.

TRANSMISSION

Torqueflite three-speed auto plus torque converter or Mopar 883 four-speed manual

BODY/CHASSIS

Steel channel chassis welded to body with bolted front subframe

SPECIAL FEATURES

Front spoiler overcomes front-end lift.

The rear wing's height means it operates in less-disturbed airflow.

RUNNING GEAR

Steering: Recirculating ball steering, power-assisted on road cars

Front suspension: Double wishbones with torsion bars and telescopic shocks

Rear suspension: Live axle with asymmetric leaf springs and telescopic shocks

Brakes: Vented discs 11 in. dia. (front), drums 11 in. dia. (rear)

Wheels: Steel disc, 7 in. x 15 in.

Tires: Goodyear 7.00/15

DIMENSIONS

Length: 218 in.   **Width:** 76.4 in.

Wheelbase: 116 in.

Height: 1159.4 in. (including rear wing)

Track: 59.7 in. (front), 58.7 in. (rear)

Weight: 3,841 lbs.

Plymouth HEMI 'CUDA

As a muscle car legend, there are few cars to rival a 1970 Hemi 'Cuda. It has classic, well-proportioned good looks and an engine that is just as famous as the car itself. Despite its relative rarity, some owners feel the need to build themselves a better Hemi 'Cuda.

"...the definitive Plymouth."

"The Hemi 'Cuda is the definitive Plymouth muscle car. It combines a great looking body style with the fearsome Hemi powerplant. Slip behind the steering wheel of this modified 'Cuda and prepare for an adventure. Off the line it is obvious that this engine has been modified. Next you notice that the huge modern tires grip fantastically. Power-shifting into second causing the rear tires to screach reveals this Hemi 'Cuda's explosive acceleration."

This 'Cuda retains a stock interior including a pistol grip shifter and multiple gauges.

Milestones

1964 The Barracuda is launched as Plymouth's retaliation to Ford's successful Mustang. It is built on the Valiant platform and has fastback coupe styling. Top engine option is the 273-cubic inch V8.

The 1967 GTX was just one of Plymouth's many Hemi powered muscle cars.

1967 A more powerful 383-cubic inch V8 gives the Barracuda more performance.

1968 The Hemi engine is finally fitted to a small number of 'Cudas.

The Duster was Plymouth's entry level muscle car for 1970.

1970 The 'Cuda is restyled with Chrysler's new E-body. The Hemi is now a real production option, and 652 hardtops and 14 convertibles are manufactured.

1971 The Hemi engine is retained for one final year. Power remains at 425 bhp and 490 lb-ft of torque.

UNDER THE SKIN

Solid as a rock

Based on Chrysler's E-body, the 'Cuda uses a steel monocoque. The front suspension uses double wishbones with torsion bar springing. The rear is more conventional with a semi-elliptic leaf-sprung live rear axle. This car has Koni adjustable shock absorbers in place of the standard Chrysler units. Disc brakes are in the front, while drums are in the rear.

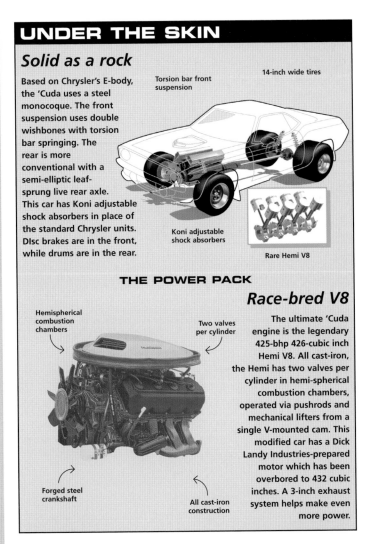

Torsion bar front suspension

14-inch wide tires

Koni adjustable shock absorbers

Rare Hemi V8

THE POWER PACK

Race-bred V8

The ultimate 'Cuda engine is the legendary 425-bhp 426-cubic inch Hemi V8. All cast-iron, the Hemi has two valves per cylinder in hemi-spherical combustion chambers, operated via pushrods and mechanical lifters from a single V-mounted cam. This modified car has a Dick Landy Industries-prepared motor which has been overbored to 432 cubic inches. A 3-inch exhaust system helps make even more power.

Hemispherical combustion chambers

Two valves per cylinder

Forged steel crankshaft

All cast-iron construction

King 'Cuda

Of all the Barracuda range, the 1970 Hemi 'Cuda is the pick of the bunch. Its race-bred engine and rarity make it a real collector's piece, popular with purists and performance freaks alike. Not many are modified as they command higher prices in stock condition.

This car is finished in the original factory color of Lime Light.

Lime Light green was only one of the factory optioned 'High Impact' colors available for the 1970 'Cuda. If you have an engine as powerful as this one, why not have a paint scheme that's equally outrageous?

Hemi V8
The Hemi V8 was so called because of its hemispherical combustion chambers. These promote more efficient combustion of the air/fuel mixture. It was one of the most powerful engines ever put in any muscle car.

Low ratio back axle
The lowest standard axle ratio available was 4.10:1. This car has an even lower 4.56:1 ratio axle for more urgent acceleration.

Hood-retaining pins
These race-style hood-retaining pins were actually factory fitted with the shaker hood which came as standard equipment on the Hemi 'Cuda.

Torsion bar front suspension
The 'Cuda uses double wishbone front suspension sprung by longitudinally-mounted torsion bars. Adjustable Koni shock absorbers are used on this car.

Drag racing tires and wheels
For looks and performance, huge 14-inch wide Weld Racing Pro-Star alloy wheels and super-sticky Mickey Thompson tires have been added to this wild Hemi 'Cuda.

Hardtop body
This, like most Hemi 'Cudas, has a two-door hardtop body. There were only 14 Hemi convertibles made in 1970.

Custom tail pipes
Even with the free-flow system fitted to this car, the owner has managed to retain the neat feature of having the twin tail pipes exiting through the rear valance.

Limited-slip differential
The 'Cuda has a Chrysler 'Sure-Grip' limited-slip differential as standard equipment.

Specifications
1970 Plymouth Hemi 'Cuda

ENGINE
Type: V8

Construction: Cast-iron block and heads

Valve gear: Two valves per cylinder actuated by a single camshaft via mechanical lifters and pushrods

Bore and stroke: 4.25 in. x 3.75 in.

Displacement: 432 c.i.

Compression ratio: 10.25:1

Induction system: Twin Carter AFB four-barrel carburetors

Maximum power: 620 bhp at 6,500 rpm

Maximum torque: 655 lb-ft at 5,100 rpm

Top speed: 137 mph

0-60 mph: 4.3 sec.

TRANSMISSION
Chrysler A-833 four-speed manual

BODY/CHASSIS
Steel monocoque two-door coupe body

SPECIAL FEATURES

This Hemi 'Cuda has the popular shaker hood. The Shaker was often a different color from the bodywork.

The most obvious change from stock on this car is the enormous rear wheels and tires.

RUNNING GEAR
Steering: Recirculating ball

Front suspension: Double wishbones with longitudinal torsion bars, Koni adjustable telescopic shock absorbers and anti-roll bar

Rear suspension: Live axle with semi-elliptic leaf springs, Koni adjustable shock absorbers

Brakes: Discs (front), drums (rear)

Wheels: Weld Racing Pro-Star, 15 x 7 (front), 15 x 14 (rear)

Tires: P225/70R-15 General (front), 18.5-31 Mickey Thompson (rear)

DIMENSIONS
Length: 186.7 in.   **Width:** 74.9 in.

Height: 50.9 in.   **Wheelbase:** 108 in.

Track: 59.7 in. (front), 60.7 in. (rear)

Weight: 3,945 lbs.

Plymouth 'CUDA 383

Few Detroit muscle machines have the same impact as the E-body Plymouth 'Cuda. With a 383-cubic inch V8 under the hood, lightning acceleration and flamboyant paint, its styling is obviously well mated to its performance.

"...retina-scorching hue."

"Chrysler products of the early 1970s—especially E-bodies—have a magic all their own. Slide yourself into the seat, turn the key and grab the Pistol Grip shifter. Floor the throttle and the rear spins violently as the tires fight for traction. To optimize the power band, shift the transmission when the engine reaches 5,000 rpm. The 'Cuda jolts off the line and pulls extremely hard, even in 383 guise. With its meaty-sounding exhaust and retina-scorching hue, it really turns heads."

A three-spoke rim-blow steering wheel and Rally-pack gauges were standard on 'Cudas.

366

Milestones

1968 Plymouth squeezes a 383-cubic inch V8 into the compact A-body 'Cuda, but the results are disappointing. ETs are slower than the 340-equipped cars.

The 1970 'Cuda 440 introduced the new body shape.

1969 Riding a new E-body platform, the Barracuda now has more than enough room for a large displacement V8. The top 'Cuda performance version is offered with a 383, 440, or Hemi V8. It can run 14.4-second ETs. Only 19,515 'Cudas are built for 1970.

Dodge produced the Challenger in 1970—its own version of the Barracuda.

1971 A new grill, with quad headlights, front fender vents and revised side graphic, highlight this year's 'Cuda. The 383 engine is detuned to 300 bhp, and because of falling demand, the 'Cuda 383 is axed for 1972.

UNDER THE SKIN

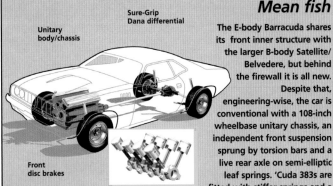

Sure-Grip Dana differential

Unitary body/chassis

Front disc brakes

Big-block V8

Mean fish

The E-body Barracuda shares its front inner structure with the larger B-body Satellite/Belvedere, but behind the firewall it is all new. Despite that, engineering-wise, the car is conventional with a 108-inch wheelbase unitary chassis, an independent front suspension sprung by torsion bars and a live rear axle on semi-elliptic leaf springs. 'Cuda 383s are fitted with stiffer springs and a standard Sure-Grip differential with 3.23:1 gearing.

THE POWER PACK

383 Motorvation

For 1970, Barracuda engines started with the lowly 225-cubic inch Slant Six, but with the performance-oriented 'Cuda, something more was required to satisfy muscle car aficionados. The solution was to make the big-block 383 the standard engine. It is essentially the same as that in the Road Runner, featuring parts from the 440 including the cylinder heads, exhaust manifolds, camshaft and windage tray. Heavy-duty valve springs were also specified. Fuel is delivered with a single Carter four-barrel carburetor and a low-restriction air cleaner. Rated at 300 bhp and 410-lb-ft of torque, the 383 V8 could haul the 'Cuda to 60 mph in less than 8 seconds.

Tough lives

On the street, the E-body 'Cuda was one of the cars to beat. Many cars led hard lives and with poor quality control, many did not last long, either. Today, however, enthusiasts and collectors are buying up 'Cudas and restoring them to their former glory.

1971 was the second and last year for the formidable 'Cuda 383.

Chrysler was at the forefront of building factory street rods in the early 1970s and the 'Cuda was one of the most shining examples. High-impact colors, like Lemon Twist, made a statement on the street.

Big 383 V8

Using parts from the bigger 440 turned the 383 into a street racer's dream. Smooth, streetable and affordable, it enabled E-bodies to turn in mid-14-second ¼-mile elapsed times on street tires.

Plenty of room

The 'Cuda shared its front subframe with the bigger B-body cars, and thus had ample room for big engines. It could be optioned with all the hard-hitters, right up to the fire-breathing Hemi. Only 115 Hemi 'Cudas were built in 1971.

High-impact colors

Chrysler's high-impact color option was unique in the early 1970s. Colors included Tor Red, In-Violet, Vitamin C Orange, Go-Mango, Plum Crazy, Curious Yellow and Lemon Twist, which is painted on this example.

Torsion bar front suspension

Chrysler's proven torsion-bar front suspension was still in widespread use in 1971 and was simple, strong and delivered an excellent ride. In the early 1970s, most serious racers cranked the bars up a few notches to help weight transfer during hard launches.

Dana differential

All 'Cudas came with a Sure-Grip differential with 3.23:1 gears. Shorter 3.55, 3.90 and 4.10 ratios were optional.

Dual-scoop hood

Performance-oriented 'Cudas got a standard steel hood with twin integral scoops. The hood could be equipped with hood pins to keep it from lifting at speed.

Specifications

1971 Plymouth 'Cuda 383

ENGINE

Type: V8

Construction: Cast-iron block and heads

Valve gear: Two valves per cylinder operated by a single V-mounted camshaft with pushrods and rockers

Bore and stroke: 4.25 in. x 3.375 in.

Displacement: 383 c.i.

Compression ratio: 9.5:1

Induction system: Carter AFB four-barrel carburetor

Maximum power: 300 bhp at 4,800 rpm

Maximum torque: 410 lb-ft at 3,400 rpm

Top speed: 120 mph

0-60 mph: 7.8 sec.

TRANSMISSION

Four-speed manual

BODY/CHASSIS

Steel unitary chassis with steel bodywork

SPECIAL FEATURES

Non-functional fender vents are only seen on 1971 model 'Cudas.

The **four-speed transmission** includes this standard and unique **Pistol Grip shifter.**

RUNNING GEAR

Steering: Recirculating-ball

Front suspension: Unequal-length A-arms with longitudinal torsion bars, telescopic shock absorbers and anti-roll bar

Rear suspension: Live axle with semi-elliptic leaf springs, telescopic shock absorbers and anti-roll bar

Brakes: Discs (front), drums (rear)

Wheels: Steel Rallye, 14 x 7 in.

Tires: Goodyear Polyglas, F70-14

DIMENSIONS

Length: 186.6 in.   **Width:** 71.8 in.

Height: 51.4 in.   **Wheelbase:** 108.1 in.

Track: 53.8 in. (front and rear)

Weight: 3,475 lbs.

Plymouth **DUSTER 340**

At the end of the 1960s the Chrysler Corporation attempted to create a new entry-level muscle car. This was achieved by combining the powerful 340-cubic inch V8 with a light, two-door version of the Plymouth Valiant bodyshell to create the high-performance Duster 340.

"...a budget street racer."

"The Duster 340, Plymouth's budget muscle machine, is in essence a down-sized Road Runner. The 340-cubic inch V8 provides smooth power delivery and is capable of embarrassing drivers of other high-performance cars. Combined with a Torqueflite automatic transmission, it makes the Duster a perfect low-cost street racer. Standard front disc brakes provide exceptional stopping power, and the torsion bar suspension is extremely rugged."

Like all Plymouth cars, the Duster's interior is simple but very functional.

Milestones

1970 Plymouth

division introduces its Valiant-based Duster 340, with a swoopy coupe body and a high-power V8. With 275 bhp and a $3,300 list price, it is one of the best muscle car bargains of the year.

In 1971 Dodge introduced a Duster clone, the Demon 340.

1971 Performance

is unchanged, but the appearance is updated with the addition of a vertical bar grill, vivid graphics and an optional hood with huge '340' script.

The Challenger T/A was also powered by a 340-cubic inch V8 but it used three two barrels.

1972 New power and

emissions regulations take their toll and power is at 230 bhp.

1974 The Duster

340 is replaced by the Duster 360 with a larger V8 producing 245 bhp. Performance Dusters are retired after 1976.

UNDER THE SKIN

Classic Chrysler

Standard front disc brakes

Torsion bar front suspension

Live rear axle

Small-block V8

Like other Chrysler cars of the period, the Duster has monocoque construction, with torsion bar suspension at the front mounted on a separate subframe and a live rear axle suspended by leaf springs. Stiffer spring rates, a front anti-roll bar and E70 x 14 tires improve handling. It is the only one of Plymouth's performance cars to have standard front disc brakes.

THE POWER PACK

Hi-po exclusive

Unlike the 318-cubic inch V8, the high-revving 340 is exclusively a high perform-ance engine. For use in the Duster 340, it is fitted with a single Carter AVS four-barrel carburetor, has a high 10.5:1 compression ratio—requiring it to run on premium fuel—and a high-lift camshaft. Optional dual exhausts and more aggressive rear gears help to further enhance perform-ance. Factory rated at 275 bhp, the V8 propels the Duster to 60 mph in just 6.0 seconds and gives elapsed times of 14.7 seconds at 94.3 mph.

Four-barrel carburetor

Wedge-shaped combustion chambers

High-lift camshaft

Cast-iron block and heads

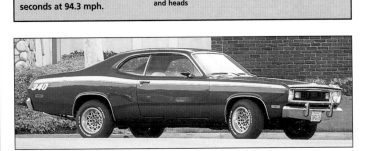

A good buy

The original Duster 340s are the most understated. 1971 editions retain all the performance credentials, but feature louder graphics. After 1971 performance is noticeably reduced, but today, at around $5,000 a good Duster 340 is an excellent buy.

In their day the Duster 340s were a good muscle car buy.

Although sometimes viewed as little more than a coupe version of the Valiant, the Duster 340 combined light weight, Mopar V8 power and heavy-duty suspension at a very attractive price.

V8 engine
The 340-cubic inch V8 is one of Detroit's most tractable small-blocks of the muscle car era. With hydraulic lifters and a single four-barrel carburetor, it is easy to tune and its 275 bhp was more than adequate for street races.

Optional transmissions
The standard transmission is a three-speed manual, but a four-speed or the excellent TorqueFlite automatic were available as options.

Performance tires
The Duster 340 came with standard Goodyear Polyglas E70 x 14 tires and Rallye wheels, although this example has been fitted with period aftermarket wheels and later Jetzon Revenger 15-inch radials.

Rear axle ratios
At the rear, the live axle is suspended by leaf springs. Standard rear gearing is 3.23:1, although shorter gears and a Sure Grip limited-slip differential were also available.

Loud graphics
From 1971 the Duster 340 was given larger side stripes with a 340 script carried on the rear quarter panels. Two different hoods were available—one with fake scoops and the other with a large 340 script.

Power steering
In base form the Duster 340 has manual steering, although the optional power set-up at extra cost was a sensible choice. Very light by today standards, it nevertheless makes the Duster easy to maneuver, especially at lower speeds.

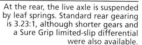

Specifications
1971 Plymouth Duster 340

ENGINE

Type: V8

Construction: Cast-iron block and heads

Valve gear: Two valves per cylinder operated by a single camshaft via pushrods, rockers and hydraulic lifters

Bore and stroke: 4.03 in. x 3.30 in.

Displacement: 340 c.i.

Compression ratio: 10.5:1

Induction system: Single Carter four-barrel carburetor

Maximum power: 275 bhp at 5,000 rpm

Maximum torque: 340 lb-ft at 3,200 rpm

Top speed: 120 mph

0-60 mph: 6.0 sec.

TRANSMISSION

Three-speed TorqueFlite automatic

BODY/CHASSIS

Unitary steel construction with two-door coupe body

SPECIAL FEATURES

An optional matt-black hood introduced in 1971 includes '340' in large script.

The 340-cubic inch V8 was previously used in the Dart and the 'Cuda.

RUNNING GEAR

Steering: Recirculating ball

Front suspension: Double wishbones with longitudinal torsion bars, telescopic shocks and anti-roll bar

Rear suspension: Live axle with semi-elliptic leaf springs and telescopic shocks

Brakes: Ventilated discs, 10.5-in. dia. (front), drums, 9-in. dia. (rear)

Wheels: Cragar, 5.5 x 15 in.

Tires: Jetzon Revenger, 70 x 15

DIMENSIONS

Length: 192 in.   **Width:** 71.6 in.

Height: 52.7 in.   **Wheelbase:** 108 in.

Track: 57.5 in. (front), 55.5 (rear)

Weight: 3,500 lbs.

Plymouth PROWLER

The prototype of the Prowler drew crowds at all the auto shows in 1993. More than 100,000 buyers put down their orders before a single car went on sale.

"...pure bred American Jazz."

"It's hard not to grin when you drive the Prowler for the first time—the engineers at Chrysler must have been 'Rodders' themselves to build such a breakthrough car. This may be the first real factory hot rod ever. The front wishbone suspension actually works as good as it looks. And the big rear rubber gives the back end the right look. Sure there's no V8...yet. But the look, feel and sound are pure bred American Jazz. Be prepared to be the center of attention at every 'Hot Car Nite' from now on!"

Compared to the car's outrageous exterior, the Prowler's interior is a rather strait-laced affair.

Milestones

1990 A brainstorming session of design suggestions produces a throwback to an earlier age. What if hot rods could be built with modern styling and engine technology?

Early styling sketch shows an even wilder proposal.

1993 Prowler appears as a concept car at the Detroit International Auto Show. The crowds love it and the idea of production takes off.

Designers used 1/5 scale models to assess different design proposals.

1995 Five 'Prangler' test cars are made, a combination of Jeep Wrangler bodywork over the Prowler mechanicals.

1996 The Detroit Show sees the Prowler return, this time in production form.

1997 Prowler goes on sale, initially with 5,000 built to minimize owners' chances of seeing an identical car. There are few changes between the original concept car and the production model.

UNDER THE SKIN

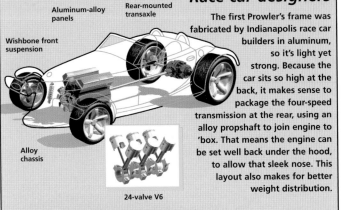

Aluminum-alloy panels

Rear-mounted transaxle

Wishbone front suspension

Alloy chassis

24-valve V6

Race car designers

The first Prowler's frame was fabricated by Indianapolis race car builders in aluminum, so it's light yet strong. Because the car sits so high at the back, it makes sense to package the four-speed transmission at the rear, using an alloy propshaft to join engine to 'box. That means the engine can be set well back under the hood, to allow that sleek nose. This layout also makes for better weight distribution.

THE POWER PACK

What no V8?

With no suitable V8 still in production, Chrysler uses their modern 3.5-liter V6 found in cars like the Dodge Intrepid. Its alloy cylinder heads have four valves per cylinder, operated by a single overhead camshaft per bank of cylinders via hydraulic lifters. The engine is fed by electronic fuel injection, a far cry from the side-valve engines of the first hot rods. Its maximum power of 214 bhp is produced much higher up the rev range (at 5,850 rpm) than those old engines, and its cam profile is designed to give very quick throttle response.

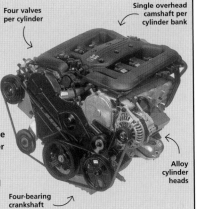

Four valves per cylinder

Single overhead camshaft per cylinder bank

Four-bearing crankshaft

Alloy cylinder heads

It's not unique

Chrysler worried that as hot rods were traditionally unique, each the result of its maker's creativity, a mass-produced hot rod would be a contradiction in terms. Reaction was so positive, though, that they made each one purple, making them all identical.

Classic hot rod looks guarantee head-turning ability.

Nothing combines the old and the new like the Prowler. Alloy wheels and a multi-valve engine are tacked onto a shape that's more 1950s than 1990s. It shouldn't work...but it does, brilliantly.

Minimal top
The Prowler is meant to be enjoyed with the top down, but it looks even more stylish with the top in place. It's low, which emphasizes the larger rear trunk and gives the car a custom look.

Wishbone front suspension
The front suspension is on view for all to see—the Prowler's double-wishbone system looks perfect and has pushrod-style activation for the front springs and shocks.

V6 engine
The engine is an advanced design, a multi-valve V6 with overhead camshafts rather than an old-fashioned all-iron V8.

Retro grill and ellipsoid lights
The radiator grill is the perfect shape and size, exactly the right retro look. Yet it doesn't look out of place alongside those ultra-modern headlights, fared in behind their plastic lenses. They are an ellipsoid design and do not require traditional large reflectors to work effectively.

Run flat tires
There's no room for a spare, so the Prowler uses Goodyear's Extended Mobility tires with a run-flat capability. There's also a tire pressure warning system on the dashboard.

Massive rear tires
The Prowler doesn't actually need those huge 295/40 tires on tall 20-inch rims to cope with its 214 bhp, but the hot-rod look just wouldn't work with anything smaller.

Aluminum construction
Knowing the car would not have a vast amount of power, the Prowler design team went for aluminum construction wherever possible to save weight. That included the chassis frame, suspension arms and most of the body panels. Even the seat frames and rear brake hubs are alloy.

Twin tail pipes
The diameter of those two big tail pipes suggests there's a monster engine under the hood. In fact, they are that size just for show—the 3.5-liter V6 would work just as well with much smaller pipes.

Exposed front bumper
The biggest styling problem designers faced was fitting the compulsory modern energy-absorbing bumper onto such a shape without making it look ridiculous. They managed it, but just barely.

Specifications
1997 Plymouth Prowler

ENGINE
Type: V6
Construction: Cast-iron block and alloy heads
Valve gear: Four valves per cylinder operated by single overhead camshaft per bank of cylinders
Bore and stroke: 3.8 in. x 3.3 in.
Displacement: 3,518 cc
Compression ratio: 9.6:1
Induction system: Electronic fuel injection
Maximum power: 214 bhp at 5,850 rpm
Maximum torque: 225 lb-ft at 3,100 rpm
Top speed: 118 mph
0-60 mph: 7.0 sec.

TRANSMISSION
Rear-mounted four-speed transaxle switchable between semi-automatic and fully automatic selection

BODY/CHASSIS
Alloy chassis frame with alloy hot-rod two-door bodywork

SPECIAL FEATURES

The Prowler is designed to tow a special trailer for extra luggage capacity.

The Prowler's chassis and suspension are made from aluminum.

RUNNING GEAR
Steering: Rack and pinion
Front suspension: Double wishbones with pushrod/pullrod actuated inboard coil springs and shocks
Rear suspension: Multi-link with coil springs, telescopic shocks and anti-roll bar
Brakes: Vented discs 11.1 in. (front), 13 in. (rear)
Wheels: Alloy, 7.5 in. x 17 in. (front), 10 in. x 20 in. (rear)
Tires: Goodyear Eagle GS-D Extended Mobility, 225/45 HR17 (front), 295/40 HR20 (rear)

DIMENSIONS
Length: 165.3 in. **Width:** 76.5 in.
Height: 51 in. **Wheelbase:** 113.3 in.
Track: 62.2 in. (front), 63.5 in. (rear)
Weight: 2,856 lbs.

Pontiac **TORPEDO EIGHT**

Before World War II, Pontiac was fighting to beat Buick in the intermediately-priced car market. In 1940 the company had a new weapon, the Torpedo, and because of its huge success rate, it was built through 1948.

"...beautifully relaxed."

"Don't underestimate the attractions and abilities of a big, sidevalve, 4.1-liter, straight eight. It revs almost silently, producing 190 lb-ft of torque at a very low rpm that wafts along the massive Custom Torpedo in a beautifully relaxed way. Its weight guarantees an incredibly smooth ride, there's hardly any roll through corners, and the handling characteristics are nearly neutral. The interior and dashboard have typical 1940s styling.

Hand-crafted embellishments give the Pontiac's interior real charm.

Milestones

1940 Pontiac introduces a new name into its lineup, the Torpedo or the Series 29. It is only built as a four-door sedan or two-door coupe. Both bodies are new and built on a longer chassis. The L-head, straight-eight engine has its compression ratio increased to 6.5:1.

The 1934 Pontiac 8 was advanced in using coil-spring suspension.

1941 The Torpedo range is extended with a wide range of bodies, including a convertible and a six-window, four-door sedan. There is also a sleek fastback body style for the Streamliner Torpedo.

Pontiacs, such as this Chieftain, used straight eights until 1955.

1946 Post-war production continues with basically the same models as before the war, until more modern styling is introduced in 1949. For 1950, the L-head is stretched and continues until Pontiac's V8 appears for 1955.

UNDER THE SKIN

Long lasting

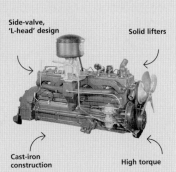

Live rear axle

Independent front suspension

Hydraulic brakes

In-line eight

For 1941, the Torpedo range rode on the longest wheelbase (122 inches) used by Pontiac. As usual, there is a separate chassis frame with few crossmembers but a large central X-brace and two main side rails close together at the rear of the engine and widening out to the rear live axle on semi-elliptic leaf springs. The front suspension is an advanced fully independent system and the brakes are hydraulically-operated, four-wheel drums.

THE POWER PACK

Going straight

Pontiac had yet to enter the V8 age and for the biggest-engined Torpedoes it relied on a straight-eight. It is all cast-iron and uses sidevalves arranged in a line along one side of the engine, making it what's known as an L-head. The valves are opened with solid lifters by a block-mounted camshaft on one side and operate upside down compared to modern overhead-valve engines. By 1941, its dimensions are undersquare with a long stroke for high torque output and 103 bhp at a relaxed 3,500 rpm.

Side-valve, 'L-head' design

Solid lifters

Cast-iron construction

High torque

Super soft top

The most desirable of all the Torpedoes is the two-door convertible. But it's worth considering either of the two coupes in the range, the two-door Business Coupe or two-door Sports Coupe, evenif their performance is slightly less impressive.

The Sports Coupe has conservatively sophisticated styling.

The Custom Torpedo might lack the dramatic flowing lines of the fastback Streamliner Torpedoes but it still showed the way of things to come in body design, marking an end to separate headlights.

Rectangular grill
The switch to an almost rectangular radiator grill for 1941 was a sign of things to come as the old-fashioned upright grills gave way to lower, wider ones through the 1950s and 1960s.

In-line eight-cylinder
Sidevalve engines seem very old-fashioned now, particularly in-line, eight-cylinder units, but they did have their advantages. At moderate engine speeds they run very smoothly and with a long stroke produce large amounts of torque.

Integrated headlights
It was only a few years before the Torpedo that Pontiac had separate headlights mounted on the fenders, so the evolution of faired-in headlights built right into the fenders came very quickly.

Separate chassis
The chassis is of the perimeter type with two main outer box-section sidemembers and a central X-brace. The body is held on to the chassis by rubber mounts.

Live rear axle
Like virtually all contemporary American cars the Torpedo uses a live rear axle. Pontiac gave it a name—'Duflex'—and promoted its telescopic shocks that reduced sway.

Sealed beam headlights
In 1940, General Motors pioneered the sealed beam-type headlight in which the glass, reflector and bulb came as one unit and were replaced together instead of changing a separate bulb. They were regarded as a great advancement giving more light than standard headlights during the 1940s.

Specifications
1941 Pontiac Torpedo Eight

ENGINE

Type: In-line eight-cylinder

Construction: Cast-iron block and head

Valve gear: Two in-line side valves per cylinder operated by a single block-mounted camshaft

Bore and stroke: 3.25 in. x 3.75 in.

Displacement: 249 c.i.

Compression ratio: 6.5:1

Induction system: Single, twin-choke, Carter carburetor

Maximum power: 103 bhp at 3,500 rpm

Maximum torque: 190 lb-ft at 2,000 rpm

Top speed: 88 mph

0-60 mph: 18.9 sec.

TRANSMISSION

Three-speed manual

BODY/CHASSIS

Separate box-section steel chassis frame with central X-brace and steel two-door coupe body

SPECIAL FEATURES

Pontiac's distinctive Indian's head mascot adorns the hood of this Torpedo.

Some critics termed the rectangular radiator grill the 'tombstone' grill.

RUNNING GEAR

Steering: Worm-and-sector

Front suspension: Double wishbones with coil springs and telescopic shocks

Rear suspension: Live axle with semi-elliptic leaf springs and telescopic shock absorbers

Brakes: Hydraulically-operated drums

Wheels: Pressed steel disc, 16-in. dia.

Tires: 6.0 x 16

DIMENSIONS

Length: 201.0 in **Width:** 64.5 in.

Height: 65.0 in. **Wheelbase:** 122.0 in.

Track: 58.0 in. (front), 61.5 in. (rear)

Weight: 3,325 lbs.

Pontiac CHIEFTAIN

In the immediate post-war years, buyers were hungry for new cars. The straight-eight Chieftain helped GM's sole surviving companion marque achieve more than 300,000 sales during the 1949 model year.

"...smooth riding cruiser."

"With only 104 bhp from its straight-eight and weighing over 3,500 lbs., the Chieftain is definitely not a sports car. What it is, though, is a smooth-riding cruiser. Soft spring settings help smooth out the bumps without causing wallowing under normal driving conditions. Attempting high-speed cornering results in extreme body lean and the narrow tires squeal under the weight. For relaxing summer drives, this Poncho is hard to beat."

Column-mounted shifters were almost universal in most cars by 1949.

Milestones

1949 Replacing the Torpedo line is the Chieftain. Beneath the new styling is the venerable straight-six or eight and 'Knee-Action' front suspension. Front fenders are now integrated with the body.

Only a mild facelift was made for its sophomore year in 1950.

1950 The Chieftain line is expanded with the addition of a Super Deluxe Catalina two-door hardtop. The straight-eight's displacement is enlarged to 268.4 cubic inches and power is up to 108 bhp.

The 1953 Pontiac is longer and now has power steering.

1952 The Business Sedan and Coupes are dropped. Korean war restrictions and a steel strike limit Pontiac's output to 271,000 units.

1953 One piece windshields and power steering are fitted.

UNDER THE SKIN

120-inch wheelbase, separate steel chassis

Coil-sprung front suspension

Four-wheel drum brakes

Straight-eight

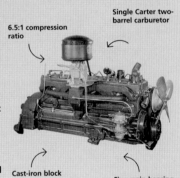

Cautious update

For 1949 Pontiac revised its long-running separate chassis by adding an 'X'-braced box section, enabling a lower body line. GM's Knee Action independent ball joint front suspension with coil springs was standard, while at the rear was a live axle with semi-elliptic leaf springs. Drum brakes were fitted both front and rear. Although a three-speed transmission was standard, a Hydramatic automatic was optional.

THE POWER PACK

Veteran eight

Designed by Benjamin Anibal, Pontiac's straight-eight engine made its debut in 1933. By 1949 it was still powering Pontiacs, though by this stage it had been enlarged to 248.9 cubic inches. An all-cast-iron design, it was typical of L-head engines with side-valve lay-out that resulted in offset combustion chambers. The use of a long-stroke crankshaft produced 188 lb-ft of torque at 2,000 rpm. The basic engine remained in production until 1954, by which time it had 127 bhp.

6.5:1 compression ratio

Single Carter two-barrel carburetor

Cast-iron block and cylinder head

Five main bearing crankshaft

Delux

For 1949 all Pontiacs got a single A-body chassis and were both longer and lower. The most expensive of all was the Deluxe Chieftain Eight convertible The basic design continued through 1954. Today, good examples sell for serious money.

A pristine Deluxe convertible is worth up to $30,000 today.

It took until 1949 before Pontiac offered its first new post-war cars. Longer, lower and wider than pre-war models, with cleaner, more integrated styling, they were also offered with more luxury features.

Side-valve, in-line eight
Although rival Oldsmobile® got a V8 for 1949, Pontiac stuck with its tried and tested L-head six and eight engines. Steady improvement, however, saw the power increase every year during the early 1950s as the horsepower race intensified. In 1949, it put out 104/106 bhp, but by 1954 it was up to 127.

Sealed beam headlights
GM had pioneered sealed beam lights in the late 1930s and these were still standard for 1949. Three years later, the famous Autotronic Eye arrived. This system dimmed the headlights auto-matically at oncoming traffic.

Whitewall tires
Classy whitewall tires became increasingly popular on medium-priced cars during the 1940s. In 1952, due to the conflict in Korea, supplies of whitewalls were restricted along with supplies of copper, used on bumpers and chrome trim.

Power convertible top
Deluxe Chieftain convertibles came with a mohair-lined, power-operated top and a small glass rear window. Plexiglas windows did not become popular until the late 1950s.

Drum brakes
Drum brakes were the industry standard in 1949. The Chieftain's were hydraulically operated and could stop the car in just over over 200 feet from 60 mph—more than adequate by contemporary standards.

1949 Pontiac Chieftain

ENGINE
Type: In-line eight-cylinder
Construction: Cast-iron block and head
Valve gear: Two side-mounted valves per cylinder driven by a single, block-mounted camshaft with solid lifters
Bore and stroke: 3.25 in. x 3.75 in.
Displacement: 248.9 c.i.
Compression ratio: 6.5:1
Induction system: Single Carter WCD two-barrel carburetor
Maximum power: 104 bhp at 3,800 rpm
Maximum torque: 188 lb-ft at 2,000 rpm
Top speed: 86 mph
0-60 mph: 19.0 sec.

TRANSMISSION
Four-speed Hydramatic automatic

BODY/CHASSIS
Separate steel chassis with two-door convertible body

SPECIAL FEATURES

The Pontiac Indian Chief hood ornament illuminates when the headlights come on.

Rear fender skirts were dealer-installed options in 1949.

RUNNING GEAR
Steering: Worm-and-sector
Front suspension: Double wishbones with coil springs and telescopic shock absorbers
Rear suspension: Live axle with semi-elliptic leaf springs and telescopic shock absorbers
Brakes: Drums (front and rear)
Wheels: Stamped steel, 15-in. dia.
Tires: 7.10 x 15

DIMENSIONS
Length: 202.5 in.　**Width:** 75.8 in.
Height: 63.3 in.　**Wheelbase:** 120.0 in.
Track: 58.0 in. (front), 59.0 in. (rear)
Weight: 3,670 lbs.

Pontiac **VENTURA**

Stylish, both then and now, the 1961 Ventura combines both luxury and performance. The owner of this car has chosen to upgrade its performance while retaining the Ventura's classic looks.

"...plenty of power to spare."

"With its big V8 and four-barrel carburetor, the 1961 Ventura has plenty of power to spare, taking less than seven seconds to reach 60 mph. In a straight line, the heavy Ventura can outrun plenty of modern sports cars. Around corners, though, the car shows its age. The steering is vague and there's a lot of body roll, and despite its modern tires, the back end easily breaks loose."

The dash is original, but the seats have been reupholstered for a custom look.

Milestones

1960 Pontiac introduces the Ventura nameplate as a trim level on its Catalina™ line. Two body styles, a hardtop coupe and Vista sedan, are available.

Ed 'Fireball' Roberts was a highly successful stock-car racer in early 1960s full-size Pontiacs.

1961 Slightly shorter and lighter, this year's full-size Pontiacs are established as performance cars. Pontiacs take the first three places in the NASCAR Daytona 500 Stock Car race.

Roberts won the Daytona 500 in 1962 in this Pontiac Catalina.

1962 The Ventura is dropped, although a sporty new Grand Prix™ makes its debut. It features bucket seats and a full instrumentation pack. A 389-cubic inch V8 is the only engine available.

UNDER THE SKIN

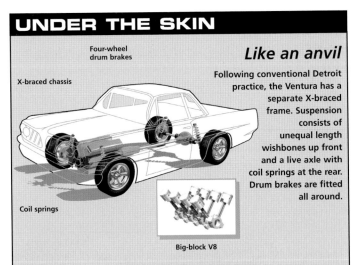

Four-wheel drum brakes

X-braced chassis

Coil springs

Big-block V8

Like an anvil

Following conventional Detroit practice, the Ventura has a separate X-braced frame. Suspension consists of unequal length wishbones up front and a live axle with coil springs at the rear. Drum brakes are fitted all around.

THE POWER PACK

Torque monster

The biggest engine available in the 1961 Ventura was a 389-cubic inch V8 with up to 348 bhp. This car has been fitted with a later Pontiac engine, a 400-cubic inch from a 1969 GTO®. The top engine was the Ram Air IV that gave 370 bhp, but the engine in this car is a tuned Ram Air III that gives more power than the radical Ram Air IV. With free-flow exhaust and ported cylinder heads, this engine makes 380 bhp. Torque has also been increased to 450 lb-ft.

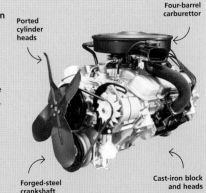

Ported cylinder heads

Four-barrel carburettor

Forged-steel crankshaft

Cast-iron block and heads

Down-sized

The 1961 Pontiacs received shorter, narrower bodies and weighed slightly less. The Ventura was based on the Catalina platform and came in just two body styles. The hardtop coupe proved to be the least popular, though 13,297 were built.

Full size and full power; this Ventura is a stunning customized street machine.

Full-size early-1960s Pontiacs have a special feel about them. This Ventura, with its Tri-Power induction and Torque Thrust wheels, is straight from the muscle-car era.

Wide-track ride
Since 1959, the large Pontiacs adopted a wider track, helping to make them some of the most stable full-size cars of the era.

Custom paint
Many customizers adopt late-model paint finishes. This Ventura has been resprayed in 1993 Ford 'Coronado Red' paint.

Racing wheels
This Pontiac has been fitted with a set of American Racing Torque Thrust wheels, a popular aftermarket item in the 1960s.

Youthful appeal
The Pontiac was emerging as a more sporty, younger person's car in the early 1960s and the Ventura was available with bucket seats and a four-speed manual transmission. This example, however, retains the traditional front bench seat.

Bubble-top fastback
The 'bubble'-type rear window looks stylish and actually improved aerodynamics on the NASCAR Pontiacs.

Chrome accents
The huge chrome side spears running along the beltline are a trademark of General Motors cars from the period.

Stainless-steel exhaust
To extract maximum power, an Edelbrock stainless-steel exhaust with 2½-inch diameter pipes has been fitted.

Ram Air III engine
This particular car has a Ram Air III 400-cubic inch engine from a 1969 Pontiac GTO. Mild tuning means it gives 380 bhp.

Specifications
1961 Pontiac Ventura

ENGINE
Type: V8
Construction: Cast-iron block and heads
Valve gear: Single camshaft operated by pushrods and rockers
Bore and stroke: 4.12 in. x 3.75 in.
Displacement: 400 c.i.
Compression ratio: 10.75:1
Induction system: Single four-barrel carburetor
Maximum power: 380 bhp at 5,500 rpm
Maximum torque: 450 lb-ft at 3,900 rpm
Top speed: 124 mph
0-60 mph: 6.5 sec.

TRANSMISSION
GM TurboHydramatic 400 three-speed automatic with a 2,000-rpm stall converter

BODY/CHASSIS
Steel X-braced frame with separate two-door coupe steel body

SPECIAL FEATURES

Torque Thrust wheels add a period touch to this Ventura.

Although toned down, there is still plenty of chrome.

RUNNING GEAR
Steering: Recirculating ball with power assistance
Front suspension: Unequal length upper and lower wishbones with coil springs and telescopic shocks
Rear suspension: Live rear axle with coil springs and telescopic shocks
Brakes: Drums (front and rear)
Wheels: Cast-magnesium, 15 in.
Tyres: BF Goodrich radial T/A 215/65-15 (front), 235/75-15 (rear)

DIMENSIONS
Length: 207.8 in.   **Width:** 118.9 in.
Height: 66.1 in.   **Wheelbase:** 119 in.
Track: 61 in. (front), 59.5 in. (rear)
Weight: 3,687 lbs.

Pontiac **TEMPEST**

With its alloy V8, rear transaxle, torque tube drive and independent rear suspension, the compact Tempest was one of the boldest and most innovative designs ever to come out of General Motors in the 1960s.

"...rides extremely well."

"Almost-perfect weight distribution is something rarely associated with early-1960s U.S. cars, but the Tempest is not your average Detroiter. It rides extremely well, and in V8 form it has considerable grunt, too. Push the little Poncho on a twisty section of road and you'll be amazed at its poise. The all-independent suspension results in predictable handling and the car remains well planted. That said, it is still possible to provoke oversteer."

Bucket seats and a four-on-the-floor were optional and lent a sporty feel.

Milestones

1960 Of three GM compacts entering production in 1961, the Tempest is the most radical, employing an all-independent suspension and rear mounted transaxle, plus a standard 194-cubic inch inline four engine, with the aluminum 215-cubic inch Buick V8 optional.

Much of the Tempest's chassis and suspension technology came from the rear-engined Chevrolet® Corvair™.

1961 A convertible is introduced. A new three-piece grill and revised lower body contours mark the 1962 models.

Hottest of the midsize 1964 Tempests is the GTO.

1963 Squared up sheet metal and the 215 V8 is replaced by a 326-cubic inch unit. A bigger, more conventional Tempest debuts for 1964.

UNDER THE SKIN

Rear-mounted transaxle

Unitary body/chassis

Independent double-wishbone front suspension

Swinging 60s

Fairly advanced for its day, the Tempest has a unitary body/ chassis. Subframes at the front and rear carry the front unequal length a-arms suspension and the rear swing-axle and coil spring independent setup. A rear-mounted transaxle is fitted to achieve the best possible weight distribution and it's connected to the engine via a rigid torque tube and an innovative flexible driveshaft. Brakes are less high tech, with drums employed at all four corners.

All-aluminum V8

THE POWER PACK

Buick-borrowed V8

Most powerful of all the early Tempest engines is the 215-cubic inch V8 Pontiac, borrowed from Buick. This has a lightweight all-alloy block with the pistons running on dry iron liners pressed into the block. The rest of the design is standard American V8 practice, with a single V-mounted camshaft working two valves per cylinder through pushrods, rockers and hydraulic lifters. To begin with, power output was a conservative 155 bhp, but for 1962 Pontiac wisely decided to up the compression ratio to 10.25:1 and raised output to 190 bhp at a higher 4800 rpm with torque climbing to 240 lb-ft.

Two seasons

Most collectible of the early Tempests is the convertible, offered only for 1962 and 1963. These early cars, despite their innovative engineering, were not the most reliable of Detroit cars and this is a major factor in keeping prices fairly low.

A total of 25,647 open-top Tempests were built.

Despite its radical engineering, the Tempest shares the same basic sheet-metal as the Oldsmobile F-85 and much of the look of the Buick Special, but the front-end treatments are quite different on all three cars.

Alloy V8 engine
Although the standard Tempest engine was a 194-cubic inch Slant Four, its paltry 110 bhp made performance rather lackluster. The optional Buick 215-cubic inch V8 was well worth considering and with 190 bhp and 240 lb-ft, it gave 0-60 mph times of around 9.9 seconds.

Swing-axle rear suspension
It may be fully independent, but the Tempest's rear suspension is very simple. The driveshafts form two swing axles, with one universal joint and a sliding spline next to the final drive. An angled lower A-arm carries the end of the driveshaft and there is a concentric spring/shock unit between the wishbone and the frame.

New front grill
When the Tempest debuted as a 1961 model, it featured Pontiac's trademark split grill though this was altered for 1962 with a small grill replacing the center divider.

A-arm independent front suspension
One of the more conventional parts of the Tempest is the front suspension, which is an unequal length A-arm system with coil springs and telescopic shock absorbers. The top A-arm is one piece but the bottom one is formed with one large pressing and an adjustable drag link which gives adjustment for the caster angle.

Deluxe interior
A convertible was introduced as part of the new Le Mans line for 1962, using better-quality trim than that on the base Tempests. Bucket seats were a popular option and added a dash of sportiness.

Convertible roof
To save weight and complexity, Pontiac decided that the convertible roof on the open Tempest should be manually operated rather than powered, but it was designed in such a way that it is very easy and light to move both up and down, requiring no extra strength or special technique.

Flat floor
One of the advantages to the rear transaxle design, apart from giving an excellent weight distribution, is the elimination of the transmission tunnel, permitting a flat floor.

Pontiac **GTO**

To circumvent a corporate edict which limited GM's intermediate cars to a maximum engine displacement of 330 cubic inches, the GTO option package for the Tempest created a new type of vehicle—the muscle car.

"...unlike any other car."

"With its lightweight body and 348 horses under the hood, the 1964 GTO was unlike any other car at the time. Putting the shifter into first and flooring the gas delivers a neck-straining launch off the line. The GTO will cover the ¼-mile in a surprising 14.8 seconds. The heavy duty floorshifter easily handles the engine's huge power and torque output. Handling and braking aren't as powerful, but it's the high levels of torque that define the GTO."

The GTO has bucket seats, four gauges and a sure-shifting four-speed.

Milestones

1964 For the 1964 model year, Pontiac begins the muscle car era with the GTO. It comes in three body styles and with a standard 325-bhp, 389-cubic inch V8.

The 1966 GTO was longer and curvier than earlier models.

1965 Power grows to 335 bhp, with an optional 360-bhp engine. A restyle adds vertically-stacked headlights.

The colorful GTO Judge was introduced in 1969.

1966 Power is now rated at 335 bhp in base form, and a new 3-inch longer model arrives. The GTO is now a separate Pontiac series.

1967 A new 400-cubic inch V8 debuts with 335 or 360 bhp.

1968 An all-new GTO makes its debut.

UNDER THE SKIN

Sporty bargain

Separate body and chassis

Sintered metallic brake linings

Live axle with limited-slip differential

Powerful V8

Based on the Tempest, the GTO naturally shares its body-on-frame construction, A-arm front suspension and coil-sprung live axle, but has a thicker front anti-roll bar, heavy-duty shocks, stiff springs and high-speed tires. For an extra $75, you could get a 'roadability' group, which added sintered metallic brake linings and a limited-slip differential.

THE POWER PACK

Muscle car genesis

The 389-cubic inch V8 is the centerpiece of the GTO package. Even in standard tune with a 10.75:1 compression ratio and a single four-barrel carburetor it boasted 325 bhp. With Tri-Power carburetion, power rose to 348 bhp. In the sophomore season, its output rose to 335 and 360 bhp, respectively. In such a light body, this was exceptionally potent. For 1967, a 400-cubic inch engine replaced the 389, with a single four-barrel carburetor (the Tri-power option was dropped midway through 1966).

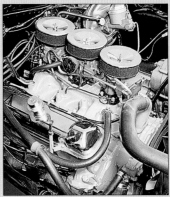

64 flyer

All first-generation GTO models have a special place in collectors' hearts as the first of the muscle car species, especially the original 1964 model. Tri-Power-equipped first-year coupes seem to have a special aura among enthusiasts.

Initial sales were estimated to be around 5,000, but 32,450 GTOs were sold.

It was amazing how much torque the GTO had for an essentially stock six-passenger car. Its specification could be tailored to your individual wishes, and it became a legend in its own time.

Big V8 power

It is the powerful V8 engine that gives the GTO its special character—namely its muscle. With up to 348 bhp available from the 389-cubic inch engine, the GTO could accelerate from 0 to 60 mph in under 7 seconds.

Choice of transmission

A floorshifted three-speed manual transmission was standard for the GTO, although a heavy-duty three-speed, a Muncie close-ratio four-speed with Hurst linkage and a two-speed automatic were optional.

Three body styles

You could buy a GTO in any of three body configurations. The most popular was the hardtop coupe (commonly referred to as the Sport Coupe), but there was also a standard coupe and a convertible. Today, the drop-top models are the most collectable.

Hood scoops

There are twin, non functional air scoops in the hood—1965 models had single hood scoops.

Stiff suspension

The uprated suspension package consisted of stiffer shocks and springs, heavy-duty front anti-roll bar and special tires, that sharpen the GTO's handling.

Specifications

1964 Pontiac GTO

ENGINE

Type: V8

Construction: Cast-iron block and heads

Valve gear: Two valves per cylinder operated by a single camshaft via pushrods and rockers

Bore and stroke: 4.06 in. x 3.75 in.

Displacement: 389 c.i.

Compression ratio: 10.75:1

Induction system: Three carburetors

Maximum power: 348 bhp at 4,900 rpm

Maximum torque: 428 lb-ft at 3,600 rpm

Top speed: 120 mph

0-60 mph: 6.6 sec.

TRANSMISSION

Four-speed manual

BODY/CHASSIS

Separate steel chassis with two-door coupe body

SPECIAL FEATURES

Dual exhaust pipes were a standard feature on the GTO.

A Motorola reverb sound system was state-of-the-art in 1964.

RUNNING GEAR

Steering: Recirculating ball

Front suspension: A-arms with coil springs, shock absorbers and anti-roll bars

Rear suspension: Live axle with coil springs and shock absorbers

Brakes: Drums (front and rear)

Wheels: Steel, 14-in. dia.

Tires: 6.95 x 14

DIMENSIONS

Length: 203.0 in.   **Width:** 73.3 in.

Height: 54.0 in.   **Wheelbase:** 115.0 in.

Track: 58.0 in. (front and rear)

Weight: 3,126 lbs.

Pontiac **GTO**

Taking a huge engine and putting it into a smaller vehicle was the concept behind the GTO. Pontiac's original muscle car grew larger for 1966 but retained the essential performance ingredients that made it a winner from day one.

"...few cars are cooler."

"Even today, there are few cars as cool as the 1966 GTO. The front bucket seats may be lacking support by today's standards, but the dash is a delight and the interior tastefully restrained. Once on the road, acceleration is tremendous, and the four-speed shifter is well mated to the 389 V8. However, on damp surfaces wheelspin is almost unavoidable if you're heavy on the gas pedal. The GTO is no corner-carver and tends to oversteer if you don't take care."

A two-spoke steering wheel is standard, although a three-spoke one was available.

Milestones

1964 A new, larger and more conventional Tempest® line arrives. The biggest news is the debut of the GTO (Gran Turismo Omologato), with a standard 389-cubic inch V8 and sporty touches. 32,450 GTOs are sold in the first year.

The GTO got a crisp restyle for 1965, that included vertical headlights.

1966 The GTO gets a larger, curvier body, but the basic style and performance remain the same. By this stage muscle car competition is getting tougher. However, the GTO sets an all-time muscle car production record with 96,946 cars built.

In 1969 Pontiac releases The Judge™ option to strike more interest in perspective buyers.

1967 Pontiac turns its attention to improving the car. The grill and taillights are altered, and the V8 is bored out to 400 cubic inches.

UNDER THE SKIN

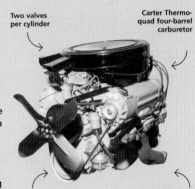

Coil-sprung live rear axle

Wishbone front suspension

Body-on-frame construction

Big-block V8

Classic mid-size

The GTO became a separate model for 1966, although it was still based on the Pontiac Tempest, one of GM's mid-sized 'A'-body cars. The GTO has an all-steel body on a separate perimeter chassis with wishbone front and live axle rear coil-sprung suspension to provide a smooth ride. A front anti-roll bar and four-wheel drum brakes are standard.

THE POWER PACK

Torque monster

From 1964 until 1967, the GTO's standard engine was the 389-cubic inch V8, first seen in 1959 as an option on Pontiac's big cars. A heavy cast-iron unit, the 389 was upgraded for the GTO with a hotter camshaft and 421 High Output free-flowing cylinder heads. In 1966, the base 389 was rated at 335 bhp with a single Carter four-barrel carburetor, but the optional Tri-Power set up with three two-barrel carburetors was rated at 360 bhp. However, mid-year GM outlawed multi-carb set ups.

Two valves per cylinder

Carter Thermo-quad four-barrel carburetor

Seven main-bearing crankshaft

Cast-iron block and cylinder heads

Loaded Goat

Among muscle car aficionados, the 1966 GTO ranks as an all-time great. Desirable options include Rally I wheels, a four-speed transmission and Tri-Power carb set-up. Add these to a convertible body and you've got one fantastic summer cruiser.

The 1966 GTO is one of the most desirable muscle cars of all time.

Pontiac set an all-time production record with the 1966 GTO, thanks to the car's combination of outstanding performance, eye-catching looks and attractive pricing.

Big-block V8
In 1966, the GTO could be ordered with the 389-cubic inch engine in two different states of tune. This car is one of 19,045 ordered with the optional Tri-Power set up, which boosted power output to 360 bhp.

Power convertible top
The GTO, if ordered in convertible form, was available with a power top

Ram Air kit
The standard hood scoop was purely for decoration, but a dealer-installed Ram Air kit was also available. Quoted horsepower remained unchanged, but fresh air induction would probably add a few additional bhp.

Coil-sprung suspension
Like the other General Motors 'A'-body intermediates of the time, the GTO has coil springs front and rear. This results in a much smoother ride than rival Ford and Chrysler muscle cars.

Four-speed transmission
In order to extract maximum performance from the big-block V8, a four-speed manual was the hot ticket, although a TurboHydramatic automatic was offered.

Fluted taillights
Although base model Tempests and Le Mans have simple rear lights, the GTO has a unique tail end treatment with fluted taillight lenses. These are unique to this model year, as the rear end was revised for 1967.

Promotional license plate
GTOs quickly became known on the streets and at the race tracks for their unbelievable performance. One of Pontiac's campaign slogans compared the car's power with that of a tiger, hence the 'growling' license plate.

Restyled body
Still Tempest-based, the GTO grew dimensionally larger for 1966 with a longer body and more flowing lines. It was offered in pillared coupe, hardtop and convertible forms. The hardtop was by far the most popular model.

Optional axle gearing
Since the GTO was after all a muscle car it had to have considerable torque to get it out ahead of the competition. Naturally, Pontiac offered it with a variety of rear axle ratios ranging from econo-wise 3.08:1 gears to the tire-frying 4.33:1s.

Specifications
1966 Pontiac GTO

ENGINE

Type: V8

Construction: Cast-iron block and heads

Valve gear: Two valves per cylinder operated by a single camshaft with pushrods and rockers

Bore and stroke: 4.06 in. x 3.75 in.

Displacement: 389 c.i.

Compression ratio: 10.75:1

Induction system: Three Rochester two-barrel carburetors

Maximum power: 360 bhp at 5,200 rpm

Maximum torque: 424 lb-ft at 3,600 rpm

Top speed: 125 mph

0-60 mph: 6.2 sec.

TRANSMISSION

Muncie M21 four-speed manual

BODY/CHASSIS

Steel perimeter chassis with separate steel convertible two-door body

SPECIAL FEATURES

1966 was the last year for Tri-Power carburetion on all GM mid-size cars.

Its sinister look is attributed to the vertical headlights and split front grill.

RUNNING GEAR

Steering: Recirculating ball

Front suspension: Unequal length wishbones with coil springs, telescopic shock absorbers and anti-roll bar

Rear suspension: Live axle with coil springs and lower control arms

Brakes: Drums (front and rear)

Wheels: Steel Rally I, 14-in. dia.

Tires: Uniroyal 155/F70 14

DIMENSIONS

Length: 199.0 in. **Width:** 79.8 in.

Height: 54.8 in. **Wheelbase:** 116.0 in.

Track: 53.8 in. (front), 50.1 in. (rear)

Weight: 3,555 lbs.

Pontiac GTO JUDGE

Looking to boost sales of its muscle cars, Pontiac created The Judge option package for its 1969 model lineup and made it available on the tire-incinerating GTO. With its attention-getting paint scheme and outrageous graphics, a Ram Air-powered GTO Judge was a street-wise combination of flamboyance and force.

"...All rise for the GTO Judge."

"With its legendary Ram Air engines, the GTO is the quintessential muscle car. In 1969, a new option gave this powerful Poncho a new image—all rise for the GTO Judge. The Judge makes a statement even when it stands still. On the move its true intentions become evident. Push down on the throttle and feel its torque as your body sinks into its bucket seat. Bang second gear and listen to the tires chirp—now that's power. This honorable hot rod gives a very judicious jaunt."

A firm bucket seat, Hurst shifter and a hood mounted tach—what more do you need?

Milestones

1969 Although originally conceived as a single-color, bare-bones GTO at a low price, the Judge debuts as an option package on the Goat. It is equipped with the standard Ram III or optional Ram Air IV engines. The first 2,000 cars are painted Carousel Red, but later variants are available in any factory GTO color.

This 1968 GTO was one of the first cars to use a plastic Endura front bumper.

1970 GM A-bodies undergo a major restyle, and the GTO has more bulging lower sheet metal, plus new front and rear styling. Powertrain choices on the Judge are unchanged, but there are new colors, and spring and suspension settings are altered. Late in the model year, a 455-cubic inch V8 becomes available.

The final, 1971 incarnation of the Judge is noticeably different from its predecessors.

1971 The Judge is retired due to a lack of consumer interest.

UNDER THE SKIN

A-stounding

Body-on-frame construction

Safe-T-Track differential with 3.55:1 gearing

All-coil-sprung suspension

Ram Air V8

From 1968, the GTO was built on the 112-inch-wheelbase A-body platform. Beneath its stylish sheet metal is a separate-perimeter chassis with an independent front and a live rear-axle suspension. Compared to its Tempest parent, the GTO (and Judge) has stiffer coil springs, a thicker front anti-roll bar and revalved shock absorbers. Options included a limited-slip, Safe-T-Track differential. The Safe-T-Track was standard on cars with the Ram Air IV engines

THE POWER PACK

Ramming air—III or IV

With outrageous styling, The Judge had to have the power to match. Its standard engine was a 400-cubic inch, Ram Air III, V8. This engine had D-port cylinder heads, a hydraulic camshaft, free-flowing exhaust manifolds and a Rochester Quadrajet 4-barrel carburetor. It made 366 bhp. Three is keen but with four you definitely get more. Owners who wanted to maximize performance ordered their Judge with the barely streetable Ram Air IV 400. It came with forged pistons, round-port cylinder heads and 1.65:1 rocker arms. According to the factory, this engine only made 4 more bhp than the III, but this figure was grossly underrated.

In session

Offered for sale for only three model years, the Judge has long been coveted by collectors. 1969 models boast cleaner styling, and Carousel Red is the definitive color. Due to high demand, buyers should be aware of GTO Judge imitations.

A Carousel Red Judge with the Ram Air IV is a highly desirable car.

Despite taking its name from the popular *Laugh-In* TV show, the Judge was no joke. Fitted with the Ram Air IV, it was one of the most respected muscle cars on the street.

III or IV for the road
Whereas regular GTOs came with a 350-bhp 400 as the standard V8, Judges got the 366-bhp Ram Air III. The hot setup, however, was the $389.68 Ram Air IV engine option with a 4-speed transmission. It was endowed with an aluminum intake manifold, 4-bolt mains and, of course, oval-port heads with 67cc combustion chambers. Only 34 buyers ordered their GTO Judges with the RA IV/4-speed option.

Standard Ram Air IV equipment
If you ordered your GTO with the Ram Air IV engine, you automatically received a heavy-duty cooling system. The standard gear ratio with this engine was a set of 3.90:1s and a Safe-T-Track limited slip differential. If these gears weren't steep enough, a set of 4.33:1s could be specified.

Heavy-duty suspension
Judges came with heavy-duty suspension, which includes stiff springs and shocks. Drum brakes were standard, but front discs were optional—and at a mere $64.25, highly advisable.

Eye-catching paint scheme
By 1969, image was everything in the muscle car stakes. The Judge was launched with one of the loudest schemes around, Carousel Red, set off by blue stripes outlined in yellow and with Judge logos on the front fenders and decklid spoiler.

Endura nose
One of the first cars to have energy-absorbing bumpers, the GTO's optional Endura nose could withstand parking lot shunts of up to four mph. Hidden headlights were a very popular option, however this GTO retains the fixed headlights.

Well-laid-out interior
The second-generation GTO had one of the best interiors of all its peers. All of the gauges were clearly visible, front bucket seats were very supportive and the floor-mounted Hurst shifter never missed a gear.

Specifications
1969 Pontiac GTO Judge

ENGINE

Type: V8

Construction: Cast-iron block and heads

Valve gear: Two valves per cylinder operated by a single camshaft with pushrods and rockers

Bore and stroke: 4.12 in. x 3.75 in.

Displacement: 400 c.i. (R/A III)

Compression ratio: 10.75:1

Induction system: GM Rochester Quadrajet four-barrel carburetor

Maximum power: 366 bhp at 5,400 rpm

Maximum torque: 445 lb-ft at 3,600 rpm

Top speed: 123 mph

0-60 mph: 6.2 sec.

TRANSMISSION

Muncie M-21 four-speed manual

BODY/CHASSIS

Separate steel chassis with two-door coupe body

SPECIAL FEATURES

'The Judge' decals are prominently displayed all around the car.

The hood-mounted tachometer was not only stylish but very useful, too.

RUNNING GEAR

Steering: Recirculating ball

Front suspension: Unequal-length A-arms with coil springs, telescopic shock absorbers and anti-roll bar

Rear suspension: Live axle with coil springs, trailing arms and telescopic shock absorbers

Brakes: Discs (front), drums (rear)

Wheels: Steel Rally II, 14-in. dia.

Tires: Goodyear Polyglas, G-60 14

DIMENSIONS

Length: 195.0 in.   **Width:** 75.0 in.

Height: 52.0 in.   **Wheelbase:** 112.0 in.

Track: 64.0 in. (front and rear)

Weight: 3,503 lbs.

Pontiac **CATALINA 2+2**

Taking a hint from the "Super Duty" Pontiacs of the early 1960s, the Catalina 2+2 was created in 1964 as a sporty option package. With a 421-cubic inch engine, it was one of the quickest full-size cars to emerge from Detroit at the time.

"...nimble brute."

"This cruiser has a sporty flair missing from rival domestic cars. Turn on the radio, put the car in gear, and feel the back tires motivate you. Pontiacs are known for their monster-torque engines, and the Catalina 2+2 is a perfect example. It will accelerate to 60 mph in less than seven seconds, and the power and torque are all in by 5,000 rpm. The wide track makes this big brute feel nimble and stable, but weighing in at almost two tons, it is by no means agile."

The large steering wheel and bucket seats are designed to give cruise-oriented appeal.

Milestones

1964 A new model joins the ranks of Pontiac's full-size cars. A 2+2 performance package is made available on the Catalina. It includes an uprated suspension and a standard 389 V8; a 421-cubic inch V8 is optional.

The smaller GTO adopted many 2+2 styling cues for 1966.

1965 Pontiac's big cars are redesigned with more aggressive grills. The 2+2 now has a standard 421 V8, rated at 338 bhp, and a three-speed manual transmission. Pontiac builds 11,521 2+2s this year.

More 2+2s were made in 1965 than in any other year.

1966 In the division's 40th year, Pontiac makes the 2+2 a model in its own right. Shorter by three inches, it is the only Poncho with standard 421 power, offered in three different states of tune. Production drops to 6,383 this year, and the 2+2 reverts to an option package for 1967, its final year.

UNDER THE SKIN

Huge chassis

Heavy-duty anti-roll bar

Muncie four-speed manual transmission

Four-wheel drum brakes

Cast-iron V8

Based on the standard Catalina, the 1965-1967 2+2 has a huge steel-perimeter chassis with a 121-inch wheel-base. it has a conventional suspension with upper and lower A-arms suspended by coil springs at the front and a live rear axle held in place by semi-trailing arms and coil springs. The 2+2 package adds stiffer spring rates and shocks, plus a thick front anti-roll bar and Safe-T-Track limited-slip differential.

THE POWER PACK

Strong V8s

Although a 389-cubic inch engine was standard 2+2 equipment for 1964, the following year the car became exclusively powered by the 421. This cast-iron engine first appeared in 1961, and for 1965 it was offered in three states of tune in the 2+2. The first, rated at 338 bhp, has a four-barrel carburetor, but the other two have Tri-Power intake manifolds and three two-barrel carburetors. Four-bolt main bearings and a forged-steel crankshaft make them strong runners on the street, and despite 10.75:1 compression ratios, they are surprisingly tractable. These two engines are rated at 356 and 376 bhp, the latter having special exhaust manifolds.

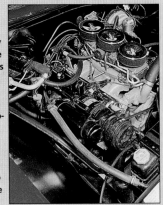

Full-size fun

Though most enthusiasts feel the GTO® is the defin-itive example of mid-1960s muscle, the big 2+2 stands out as one of the few full-size performance cars from that year. The 1965 model, with its bold, aggressive styling, is probably the most desirable.

The 2+2 is regarded by some enthusiasts as the definitive full-size muscle car.

Despite the success midsize cars were starting to enjoy in the 1960s, Pontiac persevered with the full-size Catalina 2+2. Properly tuned and equipped, it was one of the fastest big cars of its day.

Big V8

One of the most respected engines around in 1965, the 421 was a serious force anywhere hot cars gathered. Although a four-barrel version was standard, the two optional Tri-Power engines were the ones most enthusiasts craved. The top 421 Tri-Power makes 376 bhp and 461 lb-ft of torque.

Eight-lug wheels

One of the most desirable options on a 2+2 is a set of the famed eight-lug wheels. These are rims that bolt directly to the brake drums. The effect is both striking and stylish.

Four-speed transmission

To get the best performance from the 421 engine, the four-speed manual transmission with Hurst short-throw shifter is a must. An automatic transmission was available as an option.

Stiffer suspension

The big 1960s Pontiacs are among the most capable full-sizers of their day. Because the 2+2 is sportier than the others, it has stiffer springs and shocks, plus a heavy-duty anti-roll bar.

Stacked headlights

A Pontiac trademark during the mid-1960s was stacked headlights that first appeared in 1963. On 1965 models they have very pronounced brows, giving an aggressive appearance. This was toned down for 1966.

Two bodystyles

The 2+2 was available as a hardtop or convertible. When the big Ponchos were redesigned for 1965, the hardtop gained a much slicker profile with a fastback roofline, similar to that year's Impala.

Sporty interior

Adding to the 2+2's overall sporty character are front bucket seats and a center console with a floor shifter. A horizontal speedometer is standard, and so is a tachometer and a Sports steering wheel.

Specifications
1965 Pontiac 2+2

ENGINE

Type: V8

Construction: Cast-iron block and heads

Valve gear: Two valves per cylinder operated by a single V-mounted camshaft with pushrods and rockers

Bore and stroke: 4.09 in. x 4.00 in.

Displacement: 421 c.i.

Compression ratio: 10.75:1

Induction system: Three Rochester two-barrel downdraft carburetors

Maximum power: 376 bhp at 5,500 rpm

Maximum torque: 461 lb-ft at 3,600 rpm

Top speed: 125 mph

0-60 mph: 7.0 sec.

TRANSMISSION

Muncie M21 four-speed manual with Hurst shifter

BODY/CHASSIS

Separate steel chassis with two-door hardtop body

SPECIAL FEATURES

The stacked quad headlights became a defining feature of 1960s Pontiacs.

2+2s came standard with an under-the-hood light so owners could safely perform unscheduled repairs—even at night.

RUNNING GEAR

Steering: Recirculating ball

Front suspension: Unequal-length A-arms with coil springs, telescopic shock absorbers, and anti-roll bar

Rear suspension: Live axle with semi-trailing arms, coil springs, and telescopic shock absorbers

Brakes: Drums (front and rear)

Wheels: Steel, 7 x 14 in.

Tires: 8.25 x 14

DIMENSIONS

Length: 214.6 in. **Width:** 86.5 in.

Height: 57.0 in. **Wheelbase:** 121.0 in.

Track: 62.5 in. (front) 64.0 in. (rear)

Weight: 3,748 lbs.

Pontiac **FIREBIRD**

The 1968 Firebird was a huge hit among those who wanted performance. It was offered with a 175-bhp six-cylinder all the way up to the 335-bhp Ram Air® 400. Those who wanted the perfect compromise of power and economy chose the 350 H.O.

"...handles extremely well."

"The best kept secret in the 1968 Firebird had to be the 350 H.O. model. As with all first generation Firebirds, this one handled extremely well for a car with multiple rear leaf springs and unitary construction. The interior utilizes bucket seats and center console. With an ample 320 bhp, it nearly rivaled the performance of the base 330-bhp 400 V8, but was made available at much lower price. It offered a 0-60 mph time of 6.9 seconds.

Vinyl bucket seats and deep-set instruments give the cabin a sporty feel.

Milestones

1966 In September, GM introduces the Chevrolet® Camaro®. The Pontiac version is delayed.

First-generation Firebirds were heavily facelifted for 1969.

1967 The Pontiac Firebird is introduced in February. Although mechanically similar to the Camaro, it has a different nose and tail treatment.

In 1988, after 19 years, a Firebird convertible reappeared.

1969 After minor changes in 1968, there is a restyle for both the Camaro and the Firebird. The top Pontiac performance variant is the Firebird Trans Am.

1970 A second-generation Firebird makes its debut in February. It later proves to be a modern classic with the 345-bhp Ram Air IV 400 cubic-inch V8 being the pinnacle performance engine.

UNDER THE SKIN

Leaf-sprung live rear axle

Optional power-assisted front disc brakes

Independent front suspension

High-output V8

Classic recipe

Firebirds follow the classic recipe for high-performance American cars. A big V8 at the front driving the rear wheels through a live axle. Base models are fitted with manual steering and brakes. However, the majority of Firebird 350 buyers requested most of the optional extras which transform the car, such as power disc brakes and power steering.

THE POWER PACK

High output

Pontiac's 350-cubic inch engine is the same mix as most big American V8s—all iron construction with the cylinder banks at a 90-degree angle to each other and with a single camshaft in the center of the engine working two valves per cylinder through pushrods and rockers. In its H.O. (High Output) role the 350 with its short-stroke, 10.25:1 compression ratio, long duration camshaft, D-port cylinder heads with 1.96/1.66-inch intake and exhaust valves was a great alternative to the 400 H.O.

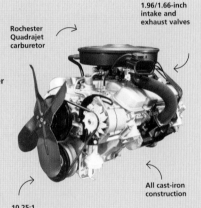

1.96/1.66-inch intake and exhaust valves

Rochester Quadrajet carburetor

All cast-iron construction

10.25:1 compression ratio

350 H.O.

The 1968 Firebird offered the perfect compromise of power, handling and economy all wrapped up in an extremely sporty shell. As the more popular muscle car prices sore, the Firebird 350 remains relatively affordable and easily obtainable.

Many 1968 350 H.O. models are readily available and easily affordable.

Even before the Trans Am® appeared, Pontiac already had a performance version of the Firebird—the 400. However, its intermediate version—the 350 H.O.— nearly rivaled its performance, but at a bargain price.

V8 engine
The biggest and most powerful engine available in early Firebirds is a Pontiac 400-cubic inch V8. It could be ordered with Ram Air to boost the power output. However this model is equipped with the intermediate 350 H.O. engine

Optional disc brakes
The standard brakes on all early Firebirds are four-wheel drums, but with the immense power and torque of the 350 V8, optional front disc brakes are a wise and safe option.

Convertible top
The Firebird was available in both convertible and coupe forms. In 1968, only about 15 percent of production were convertibles.

Revisions from the 1967 model
For 1968, the Firebird now had wraparound front parking lights around the lower valance. In addition, small marker lights in the shape of the Pontiac Arrowhead were installed on the rear quarters. A new Astro ventilation system eliminated the vent windows.

Three-speed manual
A three-speed manual transmission was standard on 1967 Firebirds, although a four-speed manual and TurboHydramatic three-speed automatic were available as options.

Rear suspension
The factory 10-bolt rear end housing with the optional Safe-T-Track limited slip could be ordered with a variety of axle ratios from 2.56:1 to 3.23:1. Any higher ratio would require a 12-bolt unit.

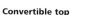

Specifications
1968 Pontiac Firebird 350 H.O.

ENGINE

Type: V8

Construction: Cast-iron block and heads

Valve gear: Two valves per cylinder operated by a single V-mounted camshaft, pushrods and rockers

Bore and stroke: 3.88 in. x 3.75 in.

Displacement: 350 c.i.

Compression ratio: 10.25:1

Induction system: One four-barrel Rochester carburetor

Maximum power: 320 bhp at 5,000 rpm

Maximum torque: 380 lb-ft at 3,400 rpm

Top speed: 114 mph

0-60 mph: 6.9 sec.

TRANSMISSION

Four-speed manual

BODY/CHASSIS

Steel unitary construction with two-door coupe body

SPECIAL FEATURES

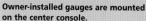

Early Firebirds have dummy scoops on the rear quarter panels.

Owner-installed gauges are mounted on the center console.

RUNNING GEAR

Steering: Recirculating ball

Front suspension: Double wishbones with coil springs, telescopic shock absorbers and anti-roll bar

Rear suspension: Live axle with semi-elliptic leaf springs and telescopic shock absorbers

Brakes: Optional discs (front), drums, 11-in dia (rear)

Wheels: Steel, Rally II, 6 x 14 in.

Tires: F70 x 14

DIMENSIONS

Length: 189.2 in. **Width:** 72.8 in.

Height: 49.3 in. **Wheelbase:** 109.0 in.

Track: 60.0 in. (front and rear)

Weight: 3,740 lbs.

Pontiac **FIREBIRD**

The second-generation Firebird is one of Pontiac's most successful cars ever and it remained in production for 11 years. Perhaps the purest and best-performing cars are the early-1970s Firebird Formulas®.

"...plenty of low-end power."

"While most muscle cars were scrapped by 1972, Pontiac refused to let go. It continued to charge hard with the popular ponycar. Those who wanted attention bought the Trans Am®, but the more sedate looking Formula shared its power. The Formula has a 400-cubic inch V8 under its dual-scooped hood. Although power in the 1973 model is down because of the government's strict emissions regulations, this car is still very quick and has plenty of low-end power."

In 1973, Formulas had plush bucket seats and a sporty center console.

Milestones

1970 The second-generation Firebird makes its debut in February. It is longer, lower and wider, with an Endura flexible nose. Four models are available: Firebird, Esprit®, Formula and Trans Am. The latter two are the performance models.

The first-generation Firebird made its debut in February 1967.

1973 The last of the true muscle Firebirds appear as the 455 Super Duty Formula and the Trans Am.

1974 A facelift for the second-generation Firebird introduces new front and rear styling to satisfy crash requirements.

The 1979 model was the most popular year, with 211,000 Firebirds being sold.

1979 This is the last year for the 400- and 403-cubic inch V8s. The 400-cubic inch V8 was the more powerful engine and was used with a 4-speed transmission, while the lower performance 403 V8 was used with an automatic.

UNDER THE SKIN

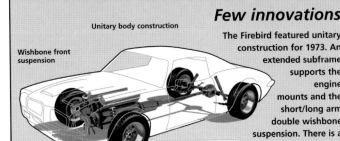

Few innovations

The Firebird featured unitary construction for 1973. An extended subframe supports the engine mounts and the short/long arm double wishbone suspension. There is a live axle with leaf springs at the rear, and a front-mounted anti-roll bar aids handling. Front disc brakes are standard equipment.

Unitary body construction

Wishbone front suspension

Front disc brakes

400-cubic inch V8

THE POWER PACK

Big and torquey

The second-generation Pontiac Firebird was available with a wide range of engines and power outputs, with everything from a lowly 110-bhp 250-cubic inch six to the mighty 455-cubic inch V8 with up to 335 bhp. In between there was the intermediate 230-bhp, 400-cubic inch Pontiac V8. The biggest 455 V8 catered to those who craved real muscle car performance. This brutal engine was only reserved for the outrageous Trans Am models, while a few Formula owners opted for the mighty engine in their cars.

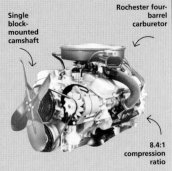

Single block-mounted camshaft

Rochester four-barrel carburetor

8.4:1 compression ratio

Fiery flagship

The flagship of the Firebird line in 1973 was the Trans Am. Apart from spoilers, decals and a shaker hood scoop, it is mechanically identical to the 455 Formula. The toughest engine available in 1973 was the 455-cubic inch Super Duty, with 310 bhp.

1970-1973 Firebirds are the cleanest-looking second-generation models.

For those who did not have the money to buy the Trans Am but still wanted performance, the Formula was a good choice. It had the same mechanicals as its more renowned stablemate.

400-cubic inch engine

This large bore 400-cubic inch engine features 8.4:1 compression cast-iron pistons, large chamber D-port cylinder heads with 2.11-inch intake and 1.77-inch exhaust valves, a low lift hydraulic camshaft and a Rochester Quadrajet.

Steel wheels

Firebirds have steel Pontiac Rally wheels as standard, although special 'honeycomb' wheels were available at extra cost.

Limited-slip differential

Standard equipment with the four-speed manual transmission is the limited-slip differential. It was much easier to offer this as an aid to traction than to re-engineer the Firebird with independent rear suspension.

Separate rear bumper

In contrast to the front color-coded, impact-absorbing Endura nose, there is still a traditional-style chrome bumper at the rear. The last year for this very clean rear-end styling was 1973.

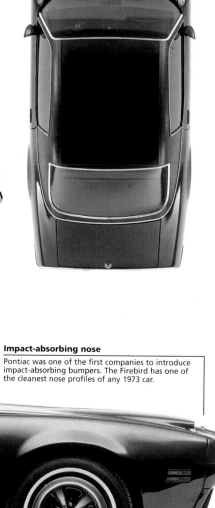

Optional air-conditioning

Unlike its import rivals, even the lowest model of the Firebird could be ordered with air-conditioning as an option.

Impact-absorbing nose

Pontiac was one of the first companies to introduce impact-absorbing bumpers. The Firebird has one of the cleanest nose profiles of any 1973 car.

Specifications
1973 Pontiac Firebird Formula 400

ENGINE

Type: V8

Construction: Cast-iron block and heads

Valve gear: Two valves per cylinder operated by a single block-mounted camshaft, pushrods and rockers

Bore and stroke: 4.13 in. x 3.74 in.

Displacement: 400 c.i.

Compression ratio: 8.4:1

Induction system: Single Rochester 7043263 four-barrel carburetor

Maximum power: 230 bhp at 4,400 rpm

Maximum torque: 177 lb-ft at 3,200 rpm

Top speed: 118 mph

0-60 mph: 9.4 sec.

TRANSMISSION

Four-speed manual

BODY/CHASSIS

Steel monocoque with ladder-type front chassis rails and two-door coupe body

SPECIAL FEATURES

Twin hood scoops are unique to the high-performance Formula model.

Rally II wheels are standard equipment on the Formula and optional on lesser models.

RUNNING GEAR

Steering: Recirculating ball

Front suspension: Double unequal length wishbones, with coil springs, telescopic shocks and anti-roll bar

Rear suspension: Live axle with semi-elliptic leaf springs, telescopic shocks and anti-roll bar

Brakes: Discs, 11-in. dia. (front), drums (rear)

Wheels: Steel disc, 7 in. x 14 in.

Tires: F70-14

DIMENSIONS

Length: 191.5 in.   **Width:** 73.4 in.

Height: 50.4 in.   **Wheelbase:** 108.1 in.

Track: 61.6 in. (front), 61.6 in. (rear)

Weight: 3,766 lbs.

Pontiac TRANS AM

Since Pontiac only made eight Firebird Trans Am convertibles in 1969, over the years many enthusiasts decided to build their own. The owner of this modified Trans Am drop-top decided to give it a modern touch by adding a late-model fuel injected 350-cubic inch engine and automatic transmission with overdrive.

"...an original stoplight warrior."

"This modified classic takes you back to cruising the boulevard in the summer of '69. But there's a twist—the 350 Chevy® engine puts out a serious rumble to ward off pretenders as you prepare for "The Stoplight Grand Prix." You're running fuel injection and a Positraction rear end to get all that power to the ground. Ready? Red...green...blast off! Light up the tires, and listen to the righteous sound of 250 horses slam you back in the seat and leave them all in a cloud of smoke! You're driving an original stoplight warrior."

The interior of this modified gem is perfect for cruisin'. There's lots of room to spread out and listen to old time rock 'n roll on the 8-Track.

Milestones

1967 Firebird is introduced with a range of engines; the most powerful is the 400 c.i. V8, pumping out 325 bhp.

1969 Most sought after of all the Firebirds becomes the Trans Am, named after the racing series.

1970 Shape is changed. All Firebirds now look longer, lower and sleeker. The convertible Firebird is discontinued.

1974 facelift proved popular with buyers.

1974 A facelift gives the Firebird a new lease on life.

1982 Third-generation Firebird appears. It's smaller and lighter than before, but by this stage even the Trans Am produces only 155 bhp.

Camaro IROC Z28 lent its engine to the car featured overleaf.

1989 Power rises steadily—the 350 c.i. V8 is available with 220 bhp in Camaro Z28 IROC trim. A modified version is transplanted into this 1969 Trans Am.

UNDER THE SKIN

BFG Radial T/A tires

All-steel body and chassis

Heavy duty rear axle

Double-wishbone front suspension

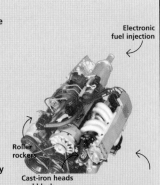

1989 Camaro IROC V8

Heavy duty

The first Trans Am arrived when America was making the transition from body-on-frame construction to unitary build. The car shown overleaf has discarded the original single-leaf spring per side rear end in favor of the heavy-duty Chevy Nova® axle on to which later Trans Am disc brakes have been added. Front suspension is the original double-wishbone system and the whole car is better balanced with the big Pontiac V8 replaced by the lighter Chevy V8.

THE POWER PACK

Small-block power

Chevrolet's 350-cubic inch V8 is one of the all-time greats, fitted in various forms in everything from the Blazer® to the Corvette®. In the 1989 Camaro® IROC trim, it has cast-iron block and heads, roller rockers and fuel injection. Cast-iron headers were installed as standard, but tuners would replace those with freer-flowing steel headers to increase output. There's a vast number of other tuning parts for the 350—higher lift cams with longer overlap, and reworked ports, combustion chambers and valves. It's easy to tune to 300 bhp or beyond; it's just a question of how fast you want to go.

Electronic fuel injection

Roller rockers

Cast-iron heads and block

Five-bearing crankshaft

Plush Pontiac

Pontiac's answer to the Camaro Z28 appeared a year after its in-house rival. It was made a bit plusher in keeping with Pontiac's higher status in the GM hierarchy. In Trans Am form, it uses a bigger, 400-cubic inch V8, rather than the Z28's 302 cubic inch.

First-year Trans Ams were white with blue stripes.

Why take a genuine collector's car and modify it? Why replace an immensely powerful 400-cubic inch V8 with a smaller 350? Look deeper at all the other modifications and improvements, and drive the car. Then it becomes obvious.

350-cubic inch V8

Pontiac's 400-cubic inch V8 was not one of America's greatest V8s, even though it produced plenty of power. Here it's been replaced by the superior, lighter and smaller 350 Chevrolet V8, as found in the Camaro Z28 and close to the specs found in the Corvette.

Taller wheels

The 1969 Trans Am ran on 14-inch wheels. They have been replaced by taller 15-inch wheels that fill the wheel arches to a greater extent and improve the car's overall look.

Positraction limited slip

The Nova axle is complemented by the Positraction limited slip differential with its 3.42:1 final drive ratio, taken from the 1979 Camaro Z28. This combination means the car can put its power down far more effectively than the original 1969 model.

Rear disc brakes

In the late-1960s, even front disc brakes were only an option on Firebirds and the rears were always drums. To help deal with the car's performance in the modern world, it's been fitted with the rear discs taken from a 1979 model Trans Am.

Power top

When the power convertible top was fitted to the Trans Am, all the effort was taken out of raising and lowering the top.

Hood scoops

The two hood scoops look impressive, but their function was to force air to the intake of the appropriately named Ram Air engine.

Rear spoiler

Part of the Trans Am package on the early Firebirds was the rear spoiler. It wasn't huge, but it was big enough to provide some downforce and, just as important, to make the car stand out from other Firebirds.

Chevy Nova rear end

Chevrolet produced Novas for Police Departments across the country. They have a heavy-duty rear suspension designed to cope with lots of power and sustained chases and abuse. This suspension has been incorporated into this Trans Am.

Specifications

1969 Modified Pontiac Trans Am

ENGINE

Type: Chevrolet small-block V8
Construction: Cast-iron block and heads
Valve gear: Two valves per cylinder operated by single block-mounted camshaft via pushrods, rockers and hydraulic tappets
Bore and stroke: 4 in. x 3.48 in.
Displacement: 350 c.i.
Compression ratio: 10:1
Induction system: Throttle body electronic fuel injection
Maximum power: 250 bhp at 5,000 rpm
Maximum torque: 295 lb-ft at 3,650 rpm
Top speed: 140 mph
0-60 mph: 6.8 sec

TRANSMISSION

1989 700R4 automatic transmission with overdrive

BODY/CHASSIS

Semi-unitary body/chassis with two-door convertible body

SPECIAL FEATURES

Rear disc brakes come from a 1979 model Trans Am.

Fuel injection on IROC Z28 engine gives cleaner emissions and smoother pick-up. With a modified engine management chip, as used on this car, it also gives more horsepower.

RUNNING GEAR

Steering: Recirculating ball
Front suspension: Double wishbones with coil springs, telescopic shocks and anti-roll bar
Rear suspension: Live axle from 1979 Chevrolet Nova Police specification with elliptic leaf springs and telescopic shocks
Brakes: Discs (front), with discs from a 1979 model Trans Am (rear)
Wheels: Steel 15 in. x 6 in.
Tires: BF Goodrich 235/60R15

DIMENSIONS

Length: 191.1 in. **Width:** 173.9 in.
Height: 49.6 in. **Wheelbase:** 108.1 in.
Track: 60 in. (front and rear)
Weight: 3,649 lbs.

Pontiac **TRANS AM SD455**

By 1974, only GM could offer anything even vaguely approaching the performance machines of the late 1960s and early 1970s, with the Chevrolet Corvette and the more powerful Pontiac Trans Am SD-455.

"...raucous take-offs."

"The 1974 Trans Am was strictly 'old school' American muscle in the performance and handling departments. Like its predecessors a decade earlier, it was great in a straight line. The massive 455-cubic inch engine plays a part in the car's front-heavy handling, although it gives fantastic midrange acceleration. Standard disc brakes up front and a limited-slip differential for raucous take-offs are major plus points."

There is a comfortable feel to the interior, which is unmistakably 1970s.

Milestones

1967 Pontiac introduces the Firebird, it shares its basic shell with the Chevrolet Camaro, which debuted a few months earlier. Both are aimed at the 'pony market' created by the Mustang.

Chevrolet dropped the Camaro in 1975, leaving the Trans Am as GM's only muscle car.

1969 The Trans Am is offered for the first time in the Firebird lineup as the top-of-the-line performance Firebird. Standard was the Ram Air III, 335 bhp 400 HO engine.

The Trans Am had a bold redesign for 1979.

1974 First major body and engineering restyle for the Firebird/Trans Am series.

1976 Last year of the Pontiac 455-c.i. engine, only available in the Trans Am as a limited edition.

UNDER THE SKIN

Better balance

The second-generation Firebird was introduced in 1970, and the 1974 Trans Am was a continuation of that design. The early 1970s Trans Ams have improved steering linkage and a redesigned front suspension setup. There were new stabilizer bars on the front and rear suspensions. A lower center of gravity was made possible by utilizing bucket seats in the rear and raising the transmission tunnel relative to the floorplan, lowering the car overall.

Live rear axle

Coil-sprung front suspension

Front disc brakes

455-c.i. V8

THE POWER PACK

Super-Duty punch

Pontiac's Super Duty 455 was the last bastion of big-cube power for the performance enthusiast. With a compression ratio of 8.4:1, output was down as the first of the mandatory emissions controls began to sap power. Nonetheless, the engine still sported all the performance features of the soon-to-be-gone muscle car era. This includes a lot of displacement, four-bolt mains, forged-aluminum pistons and an 800-cfm Quadrajet carb. There was even built-in provision for dry-sump lubrication. Earlier 1974 cars make use of the Ram IV camshaft and are capable of 310 bhp; later 1974 cars do not and are rated at 290 bhp.

Last of its kind

If you wanted a muscle car in 1974, there was only one choice: the Trans Am SD-455. Big-block Camaros had been discontinued and MOPAR, the purveyor of some of the hot muscle car property, had pulled the plug on performance.

For 1974, Pontiac gave the Trans Am new front-end treatment.

Pontiac Firebirds were offered in four series for 1974: Firebird, Esprit, Formula and Trans Am. The 455-SD engine could be ordered only in the Formula and the Trans Am. Super-Duty equipped Formulas are the rarest.

Special dash

Trans Ams featured a special steering wheel, a faux metal dash and a rally gauge cluster, which included a clock and dash-mounted tachometer. As a sign of the times, a new 'fuel economy' gauge was introduced later in the year.

LSD

Standard on the Trans Am was a limited-slip differential, ensuring minimal wheelspin and consistent launches.

New tires

For 1974, all General Motors cars had to use steel-belted radials. Hence, the old Firestone Wide-Oval F60-15 bias-belted tires were replaced with new Firestone 500 F60 x 15 steel-belted radials.

'Soft' bumpers

New for 1974 was a soft bumper treatment front and rear, utilizing molded urethane foam. These were faced with black rubber front bars to absorb parking bumps.

Scoops galore

Pontiac made sure that the Trans Am looked aggressive and powerful with flared wheel arches and front fender air extractors. The menacing-looking, rear-facing Shaker hood scoop finishes off the whole effect with SD-455 decals on the side.

Restyled rear end

The rear-end treatment includes a full-width rear spoiler. Taillights are wider, in a horizontal casing, giving a more integrated appearance.

ENGINE

Type: V8

Construction: Cast-iron cylinder block and cylinder head

Valve gear: Two valves per cylinder

Bore and stroke: 4.15 in. x 4.21 in.

Displacement: 455 c.i.

Compression ratio: 8.4:1

Induction system: 800-cfm Quadrajet four-barrel carburetor

Maximum power: 310 bhp at 4,000 rpm

Maximum torque: 390 lb-ft at 3,600 rpm

Top speed: 132 mph

0-60 mph: 5.4 sec.

TRANSMISSION

Three-speed automatic M40 Turbo Hydramatic

BODY/CHASSIS

Steel unibody construction

SPECIAL FEATURES

The SD-455 logos are seen only on Trans Ams and Formulas.

A holographic applique on the dash perfectly reflects mid-1970s style.

RUNNING GEAR

Steering: Variable-ratio, ball-nut

Front suspension: A-arms with coil springs and telescopic shock absorbers

Rear suspension: Live rear axle with leaf springs and telescopic shock absorbers

Brakes: Discs (front), drums (rear)

Wheels: Steel, 15-in. Rally II

Tires: F60 x 15 (raised white letters) Firestone steel belted

DIMENSIONS

Length: 196.0 in.   **Width:** 73.4 in.

Height: 50.4 in.   **Wheelbase:** 108.0 in.

Track: 61.6 in. (front), 60.3 in. (rear)

Weight: 3,655 lbs.

Pontiac **TRANS AM**

Although it almost died in 1972, the Trans Am came back with a vengeance in the late 1970s, becoming the best-selling Firebird® of all. If ordered with the optional 400-cubic inch V8 and 4-speed transmission it was a real muscular late 1970s car.

"...in a class of its own."

"There's one thing you notice when sliding behind the wheel of this Trans Am—everything is silver. You may sit low down and the seat may not recline, but once in motion, who cares? The 400 V8 and four speed are perfectly matched, and the sound resonating from the mufflers lets everyone know you're coming. Handling is in a class of its own compared with other American cars of the period. The Trans Am stops, too, thanks to the four-wheel disc brakes."

All 10th Anniversary Trans Ams had silver interiors, but only a few had four speeds.

Milestones

1970 An all-new Trans Am arrives. It is available in either blue or white. Standard power is 330-bhp, Ram Air III 400-cubic inch V8.

The Trans Am is introduced at the 1969 Chicago Auto Show.

1971 The Trans Am gets a 455 HO engine.

1973 While other muscle cars are dropping in power, Pontiac unleashes the 310-bhp Super Duty 455.

Fourth-generation Firebirds still retain real muscle performance.

1976 This is the last year for 455 engines in Trans Ams. A special black and gold model is built to celebrate Pontiac's 50th anniversary.

1978 After a facelift the previous year, the big news is a new WS6™ handling suspension and a 200-bhp 400 V8.

1979 A special Trans Am is built to celebrate the model's 10th anniversary.

UNDER THE SKIN

Simple approach

Unitary construction

Double-wishbone front suspension

Four-wheel disc brakes

In production for a remarkable 12 years, the second-generation Trans Am has a unitary body/chassis with separate front and rear subframes, plus an independent wishbone front suspension with coil springs and a leaf-sprung live rear axle. In 1978, a special handling suspension added stiffer springs and revised shocks. Four-wheel disc brakes arrived for 1979.

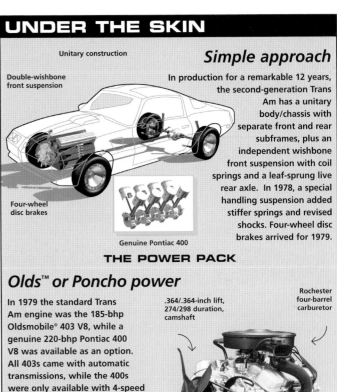

Genuine Pontiac 400

THE POWER PACK

Olds™ or Poncho power

In 1979 the standard Trans Am engine was the 185-bhp Oldsmobile® 403 V8, while a genuine 220-bhp Pontiac 400 V8 was available as an option. All 403s came with automatic transmissions, while the 400s were only available with 4-speed manuals. Without looking inside there is little to differentiate which engine the car has. However if the T/A has an autotrans, the shaker hood scoop will read '6.6 liter.' All 400 V8equipped models will read 'T/A 6.6.' The car featured here has a 400 V8 engine.

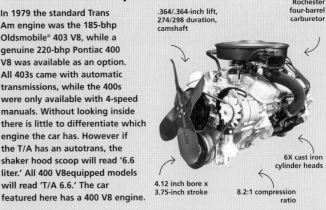

.364/.364-inch lift, 274/298 duration, camshaft

Rochester four-barrel carburetor

4.12 inch bore x 3.75-inch stroke

8.2:1 compression ratio

6X cast iron cylinder heads

Four-speed

Although only 7,500 10th Anniversary Trans Ams were built for 1979, regular Trans Am sales reached an all-time high, with 109,609 built. If you are looking for one of these, a 220-bhp, 400-cubic inch four-speed car with the WS6 handling suspension is a must.

The 220-bhp, 400-cubic-inch-powered Trans Am is the most sought after.

To celebrate 10 years of Trans Ams, Pontiac released a special-edition model in 1979. It had special two-tone gray and silver paint, unique turbine wheels and other touches, and paced the Daytona 500.

400-cubic inch V8
In 1978, the optional W72 high-output 400 was boosted to 220 bhp. In 1979, it was only available in the Formula or Trans Am. Still rated at 220 bhp, it was only ordered by 1,817 astute buyers in the special anniversary edition.

Hood decal
The infamous D53 'Screaming Eagle' hood decal was popular in the late 1970s. The 10th Anniversary Trans Ams had an even larger decal, which extended to the windshield cowl and over the front of the doors.

T-tops
With the absence of convertibles, T-tops became popular in the late 1970s. Trans Ams were offered with two different types: Hurst and Fisher. This car has Fishers, because Hurst T-tops were only available on 1976-1977 models

Distinct wheels
Whereas standard 1979 Trans Ams have snowflake wheels, 10th Anniversary cars are fitted with these unique 15-inch turbine-style aluminum wheels.

Rear disc brakes
A first for Pontiac was the option of four-wheel disc brakes for 1979. These could be specified with or without the WS6 handling suspension package.

Plastic spoilers
Up until 1978, the front air dam, front and rear wheel spats, and rear spoiler were made of semi-hard composite. For 1979, these were replaced by softer, more flexible plastic items. These look great and are functional, increasing downforce at high speed.

Restrictive exhaust
Although the chromed splitters give the impression of twin pipes, stock 1979 Trans Ams have a single exhaust and catalytic convertor, restricting the V8's power.

Front style
1979 was the year of the grill-less front end with the four headlights set in four separate square housings. Halogen headlights were a first-time option.

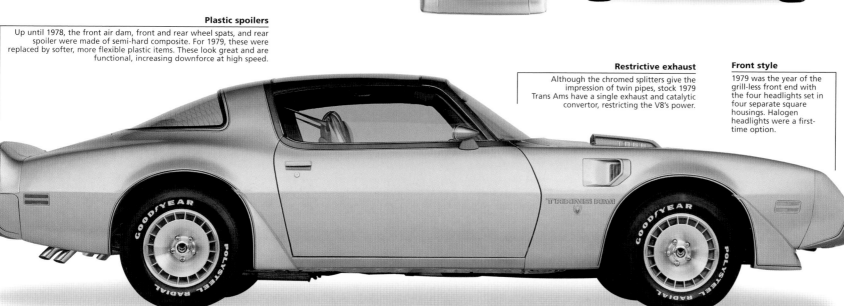

Specifications

1979 Pontiac Trans Am '10th Anniversary'

ENGINE

Type: V8

Construction: Cast-iron block and 6X cylinder heads

Valve gear: Two valves per cylinder

Bore and stroke: 4.12 in. x 3.75 in.

Displacement: 400 c.i.

Compression ratio: 8.2:1

Induction system: Single Rochester four-barrel carburetor

Maximum power: 220 bhp at 4,000 rpm

Maximum torque: 320 lb-ft at 2,800 rpm

Top speed: 125 mph

0-60 mph: 7.0 sec.

TRANSMISSION

Borg-Warner Super T10 four-speed manual

BODY/CHASSIS

Two-door semi-unitary body/chassis with separate front and rear subframes

SPECIAL FEATURES

T/A 6.6 callout on the shaker indicates this car has the W72 400-cubic inch V8.

Brake and taillights glow through the smoke-tinted rear lens panel.

RUNNING GEAR

Steering: Recirculating ball

Front suspension: Double wishbones with coil springs, telescopic shock absorbers and anti-roll bar.

Rear suspension: Live rear axle with semi-elliptic leaf springs, telescopic shock absorbers and anti-roll bar

Brakes: Discs (front and rear)

Wheels: Turbine cast-aluminum, 7 x 15 in.

Tires: Goodyear Polysteel, FR78-15

DIMENSIONS

Length: 196.8 in.   **Width:** 73.0 in.

Height: 49.5 in.   **Wheelbase:** 108.0 in.

Track: 61.3 in. (front), 61.6 in. (rear)

Weight: 3,551 lbs.

Pontiac **TURBO TRANS AM**

Externally it may have looked like the 1979 edition, but with a turbocharged, small-bore engine and an automatic transmission, the 1980 Firebird Trans Am was an entirely different breed. It was, however, still deemed quick enough to pace that year's Indianapolis 500, which it did in style.

"...agile on twisty roads."

"1980 is often considered the dark time for U.S. performance cars, but you would never know it from driving the Firebird Turbo Trans Am. Although an automatic transmission was mandatory, this Bird still has some bite. The turbo 301 V8 delivers power like a big bore engine and pulls hard up to 4,000 rpm, but if you think this car is just a straightline screamer, think again. It is much more agile on twisty roads than can be expected, but oversteer is still easily provoked."

All Pace Car replicas came with charcoal vinyl and oyster cloth interiors.

Milestones

1978 After a facelift the previous year, few changes occur for the Firebird Trans Am. The optional 400-cubic inch engine gets an extra 20 bhp, and a new WS6 suspension, including eight-inch wide wheels, is used. Larger Fisher T-tops supplement the Hurst Hatches. Pontiac stops building 400 engines but stockpiles them for 1979.

Pontiac released the Silver Anniversary model in 1979.

1980 Firebird Trans Am sales reach an all-time high with 117,109 units sold. A special 10th Anniversary model goes on sale; 7,500 of these $10,620 specials are built.

In 1989, a second Firebird Turbo Trans Am paces the Indy 500. It is powered by a turbocharged 3.8 liter V6.

1980 The 400 and 403 V8s are replaced by a turbocharged 301. The Firebird Trans Am is also chosen for Indy 500 pace car duty.

UNDER THE SKIN

Four-wheel disc brakes
Unitary body/chassis
Handling suspension

Turbocharged V8

Old but good

By 1980, the Pontiac Trans Am was an old design. It may have had unitary construction, but the suspension setup of front A-arms and coil springs, plus a live axle on leaf springs out back, is straight from the 1960s. A WS6 suspension package was available, which included stiffer springs, bigger anti-roll bars, and recalibrated shocks for improved handling. Four-wheel disc brakes were optional, while an automatic transmission was standard.

THE POWER PACK

America's first

With the Pontiac 400 V8s and Oldsmobile 403 V8s having fallen victim to tightening emissions and fuel economy standards, Pontiac needed a solution for its premier performance car. PMD's engineers started with the 301-cubic inch V8 (found mostly in station wagons) and bolted a turbocharger onto it. To aid in its reliability, lower 7.5:1 compression pistons, solid-core head gaskets, a reprofiled camshaft and baffled oil pan were specified. Boost on the Garret T3 was limited to 9 psi to enable the engine to run on low-octane gasoline without suffering from detonation.

Indy race car

While collector interests mainly revolve around the older cars, the 1980 model is worth considering. The Pace Car replica (coded X87) came fully loaded and because only 5,700 were built, its value is greater than many other models.

Pace Car replicas are the most collectible 1980 Pontiacs.

Similar to most cars built in 1980, the Pontiac Firebird Turbo Trans Am wasn't very powerful. However, it did point GM in the right direction for highly successful turbocharged supercars that came on the scene by the end of the decade.

Automatic transmission

Reduced emissions was the priority in 1980, therefore all Pace Car replicas used TH350 automatic transmissions. The 301 turbo engine could not clear California's tougher emissions hurdles and was not certified for sale in the Golden State, even though the cars were built there.

ENGINE

Type: V8

Construction: Cast-iron block and heads

Valve gear: Two valves per cylinder operated by a single V-mounted camshaft with pushrods and rockers

Bore and stroke: 4.00 in. x 3.00 in.

Displacement: 301 c.i.

Compression ratio: 7.5:1

Induction system: Rochester Quadrajet four-barrel carburetor and Garrett AiResearch T3 turbocharger

Maximum power: 210 bhp at 4,000 rpm

Maximum torque: 345 lb-ft at 2,000 rpm

Top speed: 116 mph

0-60 mph: 8.2 sec.

TRANSMISSION

TH350 three-speed automatic

BODY/CHASSIS

Unitary steel construction with steel panels

SPECIAL FEATURES

Pace Car door decals came in the trunk and were installed by the dealer at the owner's request.

Appliance Industries Turbine wheels were standard on all Pace Car replicas.

RUNNING GEAR

Steering: Recirculating-ball

Front suspension: Unequal-length A-arms with coil springs, telescopic shock absorbers and anti-roll bar

Rear suspension: Live axle with semi-elliptic multi leaf springs, telescopic shock absorbers and anti-roll bar

Brakes: Discs (front and rear)

Wheels: Turbine aluminum, 15 x 8 in.

Tires: Goodyear Polysteel, P225/70 R15

DIMENSIONS

Length: 192.1 in. **Width:** 73.4 in.

Height: 50.4 in. **Wheelbase:** 108.0 in.

Track: 61.6 in. (front), 60.3 in. (rear)

Weight: 3,673 lbs.

Turbocharged V8

Adding a Garret AiResearch T3 turbocharger to the 301-cubic inch V8 boosted power from 140 to 210 bhp. Some of the changes it required included a sturdier bottom end, stronger rods and pistons, and heavy-duty head gaskets. Amazingly, the turbo motor put out greater torque than the old 400: 345 lb-ft versus 320 lb-ft.

Turbine wheels

These Turbine style wheels first appeared on the 1979 10th Anniversary models and were standard on all 1980 Pace Car replicas. Built by Appliance Industries, they were a Firebird option in 1981.

Pace Car package

In order to get a Pace Car replica, you had to order the X87 package, which included special white and charcoal silver paint, two-tone interior, four-wheel disc brakes, air conditioning, power windows and an AM/FM stereo.

WS6 handling suspension

Introduced in 1978, the WS6 handling package added thicker front and rear anti-roll bars, stiffer springs and shocks, and wider wheels. This setup made the Pace Car replica one of the best cornering cars on sale in the U.S.

Four-wheel disc brakes

In 1980, only Pontiacs were available with four-wheel disc brakes. Its Mustang and Camaro rivals only offered front discs while still retaining rear drums.

Pontiac TURBO TRANS AM

To commemorate the 20th anniversary of the original Trans Am, Pontiac installed a slightly altered turbocharged V6 from the Buick Grand National in its top-of-the-line Firebird GTA. The result was Pontiac's most potent production car of the 1980s.

"...high-tech and tantalizing."

"Sliding behind the wheel of the Turbo Trans Am is like entering the bridge of the Starship Enterprise, with gadgets galore. However, it what's under the hood that really makes your heart skip a beat. Nail the throttle from a stop and you'll be doing 70 mph before you can say "anniversary." Besides being blindingly quick, the Trans Am is also a cornering champion, with its WS6 suspension capable of reaching a 0.89 lateral g on the skid pad."

Most Turbo Trans Ams were ordered with power everything and a remote control radio.

Milestones

1982 Pontiac launches a new Firebird. It is smaller and lighter than the previous model but is no longer available with a true Pontiac V8. The most potent engine is a 165-bhp, 305-cubic inch V8.

The turbo V6 was first used in Buick T-types™ and GNs™.

1985 The Firebird line gets a minor facelift; the Trans Am is still the top model. Power from the V8s now ranges from 170 bhp to 205 bhp.

1987 Pontiac turns up the heat again, with the announcement of the Trans Am GTA. This model comes fully loaded and is equipped with the 210-bhp L98 350 V8.

The regular top-line Firebird from 1987 to 1992 was the V8 GTA.

1989 To celebrate the 20th Anniversary of the Trans Am, Pontiac builds a limited number of special Trans Ams powered by a Buick turbo V6.

UNDER THE SKIN

Updated

When the redesigned Firebird debuted for 1982 it was considerably altered. Rear-wheel drive format was retained, but the car now boasted MacPherson struts up front and a live rear axle located by coil springs, torque arm and a Panhard rod in place of the old leaf springs.

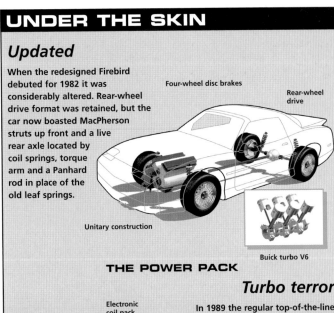

Four-wheel disc brakes

Rear-wheel drive

Unitary construction

Buick turbo V6

THE POWER PACK

Turbo terror

In 1989 the regular top-of-the-line Firebird was the GTA, which boasted a 225-bhp, 350-cubic inch V8. For the 20th Anniversary model, Pontiac decided to adopt the turbo V6 from the recently departed Buick Grand National. Though it only has a maximum displacement of 231 cubic inches, the turbo-charger helps it make the power and torque that can only be compared to a big block V8. The engine included a Garrett AiResearch turbo and intercooler, 3800 Series cylinder heads; an electronic coil pack ignition system replaces the antiquated distributor.

Electronic coil pack

Garrett turbocharger

Steel crankshaft

Air-to-air intercooler

Convertible

In 1989 the American Sunroof Corporation converted a small number of T-top Firebirds into convertibles, some of which were 20th Anniversary Trans Ams. These came with full factory warranties and are highly sought after.

Turbo Trans Am convertibles are as rare and only three or four were built.

You could have any color you wanted, as long as it was white. With a 0-60 time of just 5.1 seconds and a top speed of 157 mph, this all-American muscle machine was capable of embarrassing most performance cars that were on sale in the U.S. in 1989.

Turbo engine

Instead of using a big V8, this Trans Am relies on a sophisticated Buick 3.8-liter V6. For optimum performance it is both turbocharged and intercooled. Recalibrated engine electronics, upgraded turbo, GNX-style intercooler and header style exhaust manifolds help the engine produce 255 bhp—10 bhp more than the equivalent engine in the Buick Grand National.

Pop-up headlights

Like many sporty cars of the era, the Trans Am has pop-up headlights. For greater aerodynamic efficiency these are positioned underneath panels which continue the shape of the hood.

1LE suspension

All 20th Anniversary models came with the WS6 handling suspension including the 1LE package. This consists of revised shock valving, stiffer springs and a 38 mm front and 24 mm rear anti-roll bars.

Live rear axle

The Turbo Trans Am retains a traditional live rear axle with 3.27:1 gears. The differential is well located, with coil springs, gas-adjustable shocks, torque arm and Panhard rod.

T-top roof

About 1,500 of the 1,555 special Trans Ams came with T-tops

Fully electronic interior

Inside, the Turbo Trans Am boasts full luxury garnishings, with power windows, automatic transmission, power steering, tilt wheel, plus cruise control and stereo controls located in the center of the steering wheel.

Specifications

1989 Pontiac Turbo Trans Am

ENGINE

Type: V6

Construction: Cast-iron block and heads

Valve gear: Two valves per cylinder operated by pushrods and rockers

Bore and stroke: 3.80 in. x 3.40 in.

Displacement: 231 c.i.

Compression ratio: 8.0:1

Induction system: Electronic fuel injection with Garrett intercooled turbocharger

Maximum power: 255 bhp at 4,000 rpm

Maximum torque: 340 lb-ft at 2,800 rpm

Top speed: 157 mph

0-60 mph: 5.1 sec.

TRANSMISSION

GM 700R4 four-speed automatic

BODY/CHASSIS

Unitized frame with steel coupe body

SPECIAL FEATURES

The 20th Anniversary Trans Am paced the Indianapolis 500 in 1989.

Most of the limited edition cars came with T-top roof panels.

RUNNING GEAR

Steering: Recirculating ball

Front suspension: MacPherson struts with coil springs, telescopic shock absorbers and anti-roll bar

Rear suspension: Live axle with coil springs, Panhard rod and control arms, telescopic shock absorbers and anti-roll bar

Brakes: Discs, 12-in. dia. front, and 11.65-in. dia. rear

Wheels: Cast-aluminum, 8 x 16 in.

Tires: Goodyear 245//50/16 ZR50

DIMENSIONS

Length: 177.0 in. **Width:** 77.3 in.

Height: 50.4 in. **Wheelbase:** 101.0 in.

Track: 62.5 in. (front and rear)

Weight: 3,406 lbs.

Pontiac HURST SSJ

Redesigned for 1969, the Grand Prix became a perennial best-seller during the 1970s. Among the most exclusive and desirable models was the special Hurst SSJ, which was offered for only three model years. With big-block V8 power, it was also a very fast highway cruiser.

"...peculiar performer."

"A well laid-out interior with an angled dashboard and good seats makes the Grand Prix a joy to drive on longer road trips. It may have light steering and will lean through hard corners, but the Hurst SSJ was conceived as a fast cruiser—in this role it excels. With phenomenal torque, the Hurst shifter enables you to get the most out of the 455-cubic inch V8. It's not the leanest, or quickest Pontiac muscle car, but the Hurst SSJ just might be the most peculiar performer."

A curved dash with all instruments facing the driver is a Grand Prix trait.

Milestones

1969 A new downsized Grand Prix arrives, built off the intermediate A-body Tempest chassis. It comes as a two-door hardtop only and with a standard 350-bhp, 400-cubic inch V8. A 428 with 370 bhp is optional. 112,486 are sold during its first year.

The Monte Carlo was Chevrolet's version of the Grand Prix.

1970 Hurst works its magic on the Grand Prix, resulting in the SSJ model. It has a Cadillac sunroof and can be built to order. Two exterior colors are offered, Cameo White or Starlight Black, both with gold accents and performance wheels.

With a supercharged V6, the current Grand Prix is as fast as a Hurst SSJ.

1972 Making its third and final appearance, the Hurst SSJ is offered with 400- or 455-cubic inch V8 power and a long list of options. Production comes to an end this year.

UNDER THE SKIN

Smaller package

Body-on-frame construction

Safe-T-Track differential

Independent front suspension

From 1969, the Grand Prix shifted to the mid-size A-body platform, but with a unique 118-inch wheel-base. Body-on-frame construction was retained, as was an all-coil-sprung suspension. Hurst SSJs were outfitted with heavy-duty suspension and power front disc brakes. Most came with an automatic transmission and Hurst Auto/Stick shifter.

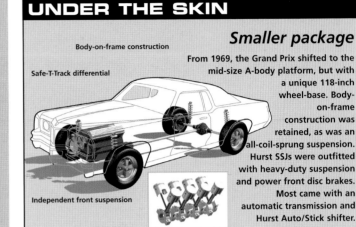

Big-block V8

THE POWER PACK

Big bore exclusive

From 1969 until 1975, all Grand Prixs relied exclusively on big-bore Pontiac V8s for propulsion. Standard equipment in 1972 was the 400-cubic inch D-port unit, rated at 250 bhp, breathing through a cast-iron, dual-plane intake and four-barrel carburetor. For added power, buyers could order the monster 455-cubic inch mill. Hurst Performance Research modified the engines by blueprinting the internals and installing a more aggressive cam-shaft. The reworked cylinder heads included larger combustion chambers and 2.11/1.77-inch valves. Horsepower is underrated at 250 bhp with a mighty 375 lb-ft of torque at a low 2,400 rpm.

Well equipped

Only around 450 Hurst SSJs were built between 1970 and 1972, making them rare. Desirable options include the 455 engine, Hurst Digital Computer and even a telephone. Performance-wise, these cars are capable of 15-second ETs.

Hurst SSJs were marketed as personal luxury cars with a performance bias.

One of the rarest and most exclusive Detroit personal luxury performers of the 1970s, the Hurst SSJ had to be specially ordered, and although an out-of-house conversion, it was sold through Pontiac dealers with a full warranty.

Big-block power
Although emissions standards were beginning to take their toll on high-compression V8s, the Pontiac Grand Prix still packed a considerable punch from its 400- or 455-cubic inch V8. Hurst Performance rebuilt each engine, but output was unchanged from factory specs for insurance reasons.

Unique wheelbase
Although it shared its perimeter chassis with the A-body Tempest/Le Mans, the Grand Prix rode a unique 118-inch wheelbase, freeing up more interior room.

Dual exhaust system
All Grand Prixs up until 1975 came with dual exhaust. With the optional Hurst exhaust system the 455 engines would breathe more freely thanks to larger pipes and low-restriction mufflers.

Vinyl top
Hurst SSJs were offered in two exterior colors: Starlight Black and Cameo White. A half-vinyl roof was standard, although the owner of this one chose to remove it, resulting in a cleaner, more uncluttered appearance.

Stiffer suspension
Hurst SSJs were most often ordered with heavy-duty suspension, which meant stiffer springs and shock absorbers, plus a bigger front anti-roll bar.

Sliding sunroof
A factory-installed item, the sliding steel sunroof was taken from the equally enormous Cadillac Eldorado. It is electrically operated with a switch between the sun visors.

Longest hood
When launched for 1969, the new intermediate-size Grand Prix boasted the longest hood of any Detroit production car, measuring six feet in length. This idea was soon copied (notably by the Chevrolet Monte Carlo) and became prevalent on domestic cars during the 1970s.

Pontiac **GRAND VILLE**

At one time, Pontiac offered six convertibles in its lineup, but by 1973, the Grand Ville was the sole surviving example. It, too, would retire after 1975. This massive car was a victim of buyer preference for coupes and sedans, not to mention the gasoline crisis.

"...effortless to drive."

"The Grand Ville comes from a time when cars peaked in size, and this Pontiac is no exception. With a total of 455 cubes under the long hood, it is effortless to drive, with plenty of torque at the tip of your right foot. It is happy to cruise along the freeway at high speed and the ride remains comfortable. Show it some twisty road and things begin to get interesting. The big Poncho leans through corners, yet the radial tires help it grip better than earlier Pontiacs."

A huge bench seat and sizeable footwells give you plenty of room to spread out.

Milestones

1971 A new crop of big GM full-size cars arrives. The Grand Ville is the new top-of-the-line Pontiac, riding on a 126-inch wheelbase. It comes as a sedan, coupe, wagon and a convertible. Standard power is a 455 V8.

In 1969, the full-size Bonneville was available with a drop top.

1972 Slightly altered trim and a new grill mark the 1972 models. Under the hood, all engines switch to SAE power ratings. The 455 makes 185 bhp.

Chevy's version of the Grand Ville was the Caprice, here a 1975 model.

1974 Styling is altered again with 5 mph bumpers fitted at the front and rear. Just 3,000 droptops are sold.

1975 Modified grill, square headlights and a catalytic converter arrive. Just 4,519 Grand Ville convertibles are built during its final year.

UNDER THE SKIN

Live rear axle

Separate chassis

Front disc brakes

455 c.i. V8

Let it grow

General Motors' big cars were redesigned for 1971 and were larger and heavier. Engineering-wise, the Grand Ville is typical with a separate frame, double-wishbone front suspension and a live rear axle suspended by coil springs and located by upper and lower semi-trailing arms. By 1974, steel-belted radial tires were standard, as were power front disc brakes and a front anti-roll bar.

THE POWER PACK

Big is beautiful

For the Bonneville, the standard engine was Pontiac's venerable 400-cubic inch V8 introduced in 1967. By 1974, all U.S. passenger cars were required to have strict emissions controls. An EGR (Exhaust Gas Recirculation) system, which vents spent exhaust gas back through the combustion chamber, low octane fuel and retarded ignition timing resulted in a mere 200 bhp and 320-lb ft of torque. Its more upmarket sister, the Grand Ville got the big 455 as standard Pontiac's largest engine. Even so, emissions controls took their toll on horsepower, which dropped from 325 bhp in 1971 to just 200 by 1975.

Soft-top

Without any doubt, the model in the Grand Ville range most likely to attract collector interest is the convertible. Only 15,968 were built between 1971 and 1975. Desirable options include dual exhaust and steel-belted radials with rally wheels.

Expect to pay around $6,000 for a good, clean Grand Ville.

With a two-door convertible and V8 engine, the early 1970s Grand Ville droptop represents the finale of the huge V8 gas-guzzlers. Many owners had their cars equipped with every imaginable option, resulting in an auto that was close to a Cadillac Eldorado in terms of luxury.

Radial tuned suspension

In 1974, Grand Villes came with RTS (Radial Tuned Suspension) and steel-belted tires, giving these enormous cars improved roadholding compared with their predecessors. The standard wheels were stamped steel with hub caps, but Rally II rims were listed as an option.

Monster V8 engine

Before 1973, fuel was still inexpensive, so big V8s were still common. Even by 1974, when the fuel crisis hit, the Grand Ville still came with a 455-cubic inch V8 (the largest production Pontiac engine ever built), though emissions controls resulted in a maximum output of 250 bhp.

Five-mph bumpers

Among the many federal requirements in the early 1970s was the adoption of five-mph bumpers on all cars sold in North America. The Grand Ville's are basically composed of huge steel bumpers mounted on twin hydraulic rams that were surrounded by Endura flexible plastic.

Body-on-the-frame construction

Although redesigned for 1971, GM's big cars stuck with a separate body and chassis. A separate chassis design also permitted greater isolation from the road resulting in a smooth ride—something that large-car buyers of the era expected.

Dual exhausts

1974 was the last year that most V8s could run on leaded fuel and high compression. These changes resulted in a modest horsepower gain and were standard with the 250 bhp V8 (available as an option on the Grand Ville).

Power top

Like most convertibles of the era, the Grand Ville came with a power-operated soft-top that would fit behind the rear seat.

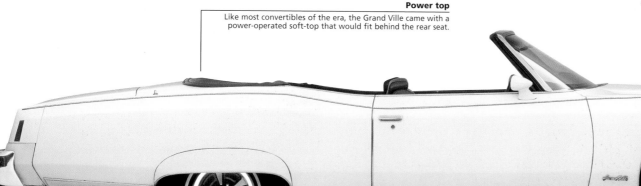

Specifications

1974 Pontiac Grand Ville

ENGINE

Type: V8

Construction: Cast-iron block and heads

Valve gear: Two valves per cylinder operated by a single V-mounted camshaft with pushrods and rockers

Bore and stroke: 4.15 in. x 4.21 in.

Displacement: 455 c.i.

Compression ratio: 8.0:1

Induction system: Rochester Quadrajet four-barrel downdraft carburetor

Maximum power: 250 bhp at 4,000 rpm

Maximum torque: 370 lb-ft at 2,800 rpm

Top speed: 124 mph

0-60 mph: 7.8 sec.

TRANSMISSION

GM TH400 three-speed automatic

BODY/CHASSIS

Separate steel chassis with two-door convertible body

SPECIAL FEATURES

1974 was the first year for five-mph impact bumpers at the rear.

Front cornering lights were a popular option on the Grand Ville.

RUNNING GEAR

Steering: Recirculating-ball

Front suspension: Unequal-length A-arms, coil springs, telescopic shock absorbers and anti-roll bar

Rear suspension: Live axle, upper and lower control arms, coil springs and telescopic shock absorbers

Brakes: Discs (front), drums (rear)

Wheels: 15 x 7 in. stamped steel

Tires: Goodyear Polysteel radials 175/50R 15

DIMENSIONS

Length: 226 in. **Width:** 87.8 in.

Height: 58.9 in. **Wheelbase:** 124.0 in.

Track: 58.9 in. (front and rear)

Weight: 4,476 lbs.

Pontiac CAN AM

Although it is often said that performance died during the 1970s, there were some bright spots. In 1977, Pontiac dropped a 400-cubic inch V8 into the LeMans to create the Can Am, a limited production sports coupe.

"...something different."

"Based on the mid-1970s LeMans, the Can Am has a low-set driving position and feels wide on the road. The interior may be bland, but the floor shifter at the end of your right hand indicates something different is going on. The 400 V8 works best at low rpm, and while not fast on paper, the Can Am still feels quick. A nice surprise is the handling—stiffer springs and anti-roll bars, along with radial tires give assuring grip."

Velour upholstery and every gauge one could imagine come standard in all Can Ams.

Milestones

1973 Pontiac fields a restyled intermediate line, now called LeMans. Convertibles and hardtop coupes are not offered, but pillared sedans, coupes and wagons are. This is also the last year for the A-body GTO™.

Pontiac's popular Trans Am also used 400- or 403-cubic inch V8s.

1975 Pontiac drops its only surviving performance intermediate, the Grand Am™, after sales reach only 10,769.

Pontiac's original muscle car, the GTO was also based on the midsize LeMans.

1977 In an attempt to inject more performance into its lineup, Pontiac offers the Can Am, based on the LeMans Sport. It has big V8 power, handling suspension and white paint with orange and black graphics. A downsized LeMans arrives for 1978 on a 108.1-inch wheelbase. The sporty Can Am does not return.

UNDER THE SKIN

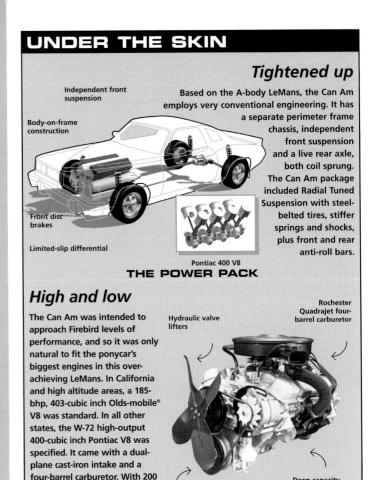

Tightened up

Based on the A-body LeMans, the Can Am employs very conventional engineering. It has a separate perimeter frame chassis, independent front suspension and a live rear axle, both coil sprung. The Can Am package included Radial Tuned Suspension with steel-belted tires, stiffer springs and shocks, plus front and rear anti-roll bars.

Independent front suspension

Body-on-frame construction

Front disc brakes

Limited-slip differential

Pontiac 400 V8
THE POWER PACK

High and low

The Can Am was intended to approach Firebird levels of performance, and so it was only natural to fit the ponycar's biggest engines in this over-achieving LeMans. In California and high altitude areas, a 185-bhp, 403-cubic inch Olds-mobile® V8 was standard. In all other states, the W-72 high-output 400-cubic inch Pontiac V8 was specified. It came with a dual-plane cast-iron intake and a four-barrel carburetor. With 200 bhp at a low 3,600 rpm and 325 lb-ft of torque, it made the Can Am a good performer.

Rochester Quadrajet four-barrel carburetor

Hydraulic valve lifters

Deep-capacity oil pan

Cast-iron block and cylinder heads

White warrior

The Can Am was built only for 1977 and just 3,177 examples left the factory. It may be slower than its 1960s forebears, but thanks to a 400-cubic inch engine packing 200 bhp in top condition, it is undoubtedly a high performance bargain.

Today, good Can Ams can be bought for very a reasonable price.

Fitting a huge engine in a mid-range coupe was the muscle car concept in its purest form. Although not the quickest, one road tester claimed the Can Am was "the strongest thing to come from Motown in years."

Biggest V8

In 1977, the 400 was the biggest engine offered by Pontiac. With a four-barrel carburetor and 200 bhp, it was potent too, and enabled Can Am drivers to flog their machines down the ¼-mile in a shade over 17 seconds.

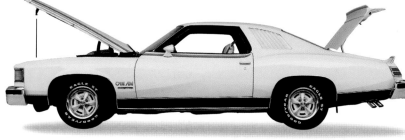

All automatics

Though two different engines were available in the Can Am, only one transmission was available—a TH350 three speed automatic. The transmission included a 2.52 first gear for spirited standing starts.

Driver-oriented interior

Although it is essentially a LeMans, the Can Am has a driver-oriented Grand Prix instrument panel, with large circular gauges that are angled toward the driver.

Live axle

Most American production cars of the 1970s had front-mounted engines, with a live rear axle. Can Ams came with a 10-bolt rear end with a Safe-T-Track limited-slip differential. For economy, 3.23:1 was the shortest ratio offered.

Five-mph bumpers

Beginning in 1973, all manufacturers who sold cars in the U.S. had to comply with federal regulations which required heftier bumpers to withstand low-speed shunts. After a low-speed impact they bounce back to their original position.

Chassis enhancements

Stiffer coil springs, shocks with improved damping and front and rear anti-roll bars were offered as part of the RTS (Radial Tuned Suspension) package, along with 15-inch wheels.

Cosmetic enhancements

Because performance was a scarce commodity in the 1970s, Detroit dressed up its 'hot' offerings. This included a trunk spoiler, shaker hood scoop, plus a white body and wheels.

Specifications

1977 Pontiac Can Am

ENGINE

Type: V8

Construction: Cast-iron block and heads

Valve gear: Two valves per cylinder operated by a single camshaft with pushrods and hydraulic lifters

Bore and stroke: 4.12 in. x 3.75 in.

Displacement: 400 c.i.

Compression ratio: 8.0:1

Induction system: Rochester Quadrajet four-barrel carburetor

Maximum power: 200 bhp at 3,600 rpm

Maximum torque: 325 lb-ft at 2,400 rpm

Top speed: 120 mph

0-60 mph: 8.6 sec.

TRANSMISSION

TurboHydramatic three speed automatic

BODY/CHASSIS

Steel perimeter chassis with separate two-door coupe body

SPECIAL FEATURES

Vents over the quarter windows add a sporty look to this 1970s hot rod.

Chrome-plated exhaust tips, as seen here, were a popular dealer option.

RUNNING GEAR

Steering: Recirculating ball

Front suspension: Unequal length A-arms with coil springs, telescopic shock absorbers and anti-roll bar

Rear suspension: Live axle with lower control arms, coil springs, telescopic shock absorbers and anti-roll bar

Brakes: Discs (front), drums (rear)

Wheels: Cast-steel, 7 x 15 in.

Tires: Goodyear Polysteel, GR70-15

DIMENSIONS

Length: 208.0 in. **Width:** 77.0 in.

Height: 52.7 in. **Wheelbase:** 112.0 in.

Track: 61.6 in. (front), 61.1 in. (rear)

Weight: 4,140 lbs.

Pontiac **FIERO**

No one expected General Motors to have the courage to create a small, mid-engined sports car, particularly one using such a revolutionary form of construction. Surprisingly, and against the odds, it did.

"...doesn't get unbalanced."

"To begin with the Fiero equals the engine's crispness and instant steering response of the car that was its main rival, the Toyota MR2. The faster it is driven the better it feels. It flows through any combination of twisty bends and curves, and because of its mid-engine layout it doesn't get unbalanced. The V6 provides sufficient power to offer exhilarating get up and go for those looking for a reasonably priced performance car."

Like most U.S. cars of the period, Fieros are often loaded with options, including cruise control and power windows and mirrors.

Milestones

1983 Production of the Fiero begins, appropriately in Pontiac, Michigan, for the 1984 model year. Both 2.5-liter four and 2.8-liter V6 engines are offered and come in base or S/E trim levels.

The Fiero went on sale in September 1983 as a 1984 model.

1985 A Fiero paces the Indianapolis 500 in 1984. The following year the GT, with a low-drag nose inspired from the pace car, is launched. It has a standard V6 engine and a larger exhaust.

The 2.8-liter V6 was also used in Pontiac's Euro sedan, the 6000.

1986 The GT is restyled with fastback styled roof panels. A five-speed manual transaxle is also introduced.

1988 Production ends after GM decides that the Fiero is no longer cost effective.

UNDER THE SKIN

Plastic and metal

Steel spaceframe with plastic panels

Transverse-mounted V6 engine

Like most cars, the Fiero is basically a steel monocoque. The difference is that it has composite plastic body panels which are easily detachable. For the suspension, Pontiac raided the parts bin. The front set-up is taken from the humble T-body Chevrolet® Chevette™, while the rear subframe, including the transaxle and engine mountings, are borrowed from the front-drive GM X-body cars—the Chevrolet Citation™ and Pontiac Ventura™.

Four-wheel disc brakes

Cast-iron V6

THE POWER PACK

Two valves per cylinder

Electronic fuel injection

Cast-iron wet cylinder liners

Cast-iron block and heads

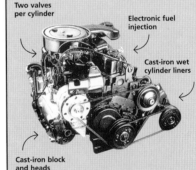

Potent performance

Throughout its life the Fiero was only offered with two engines. One is Pontiac's 2.5-liter 'Iron Duke' four cylinders (as shown), so-named because of its proven reliability and all-iron block and head. The other is a 2.8-liter, 60-degree GM corporate V6. This basic powerplant first saw duty in the front-engined, front-drive X-body cars. In late Fieros, such as the 1988 Formula and GT, it produces a respectable 135 bhp.

Less is more

Although the GT is the most talked about, the V6 was also available in the mid-level S/E and Formula models. Formulas were only built for 1988 and retain the same engine chassis tuning and suspension as GTs but are slightly faster and cheaper.

Formulas are cheaper than Fiero GTs but have better performance.

The Fiero was a bold concept that deserved to succeed. Although initially developed as a commuter car, the Fiero became a sporty, mid-engined two-seater.

SMC body

The roof, hood, deck lid and upper quarter panels are made from a composite material known as SMC (Sheet Molding Compound).

Central fuel tank

What appears to be a conventional transmission tunnel in the center of the cabin actually contains the fuel tank.

Five-speed transmission

Enthusiasts had been crying out for a five-speed transmission since the Fiero was launched. Their prayers were answered when it became an option mid-way through 1986.

V6 engine

The Fiero's 135 bhp and 170 lb-ft of torque is enough to give proper sports car performance. The weight of the all-iron engine does not matter as it is mounted in the middle of the car.

Strut rear suspension

Like the front suspension, the rear is taken from another GM car. It is effectively the front suspension used in the compact X-body cars but mounted at the back.

Steel structure

Despite its composite body construction, under the skin the Fiero is conventional with a pressed-steel structure. This is formed from no fewer than 280 pieces of stamped steel welded together. The spaceframe can also be driven without the body.

Specifications

1988 Pontiac Fiero Formula

ENGINE

Type: V6

Construction: Cast-iron block and heads

Valve gear: Two valves per cylinder operated by a single V-mounted camshaft via pushrods and rockers

Bore and stroke: 3.5 in. x 3.0 in.

Displacement: 173 c.i.

Compression ratio: 8.9:1

Induction system: Bosch multipoint fuel injection

Maximum power: 135 bhp at 5,200 rpm

Maximum torque: 170 lb-ft at 3,600 rpm

Top speed: 120 mph

0-60 mph: 7.4 sec.

TRANSMISSION

Four or five-speed manual or three-speed automatic

BODY/CHASSIS

Steel monocoque underbody with two-door plastic mid-engine coupe body

SPECIAL FEATURES

Pop-up headlights are a feature of both the Fiero and the larger Firebird.

This rear spoiler is exclusive to Formula and GT models.

RUNNING GEAR

Steering: Rack-and-pinion

Front suspension: Double wishbones with coil springs, telescopic shock absorbers and anti-roll bar

Rear suspension: Struts with lower control arms and anti-roll bar

Brakes: Discs (front and rear)

Wheels: Alloy, 6 x 15 in.

Tires: 205/60 HR15 (front), 215/60 HR15 (rear)

DIMENSIONS

Length: 163.1 in. **Width:** 68.9 in.

Height: 46.9 in. **Wheelbase:** 93.4 in.

Track: 59.7 in. (front), 60.4 in. (rear)

Weight: 2,778 lbs.

Pontiac GRAND PRIX

In 1995, a show car made its debut at the New York Auto Show. A year later, a production version, the Pontiac Grand Prix, hit the streets. It provides tremendous performance for a reasonable price.

"...the 3.8 V6 is a revelation."

"Vastly improved over its predecessor, the current GP has a decidedly sporty interior, like a Firebird with extra space. It feels tight, too; the doors shut with a reassuring clunk and on the highway there are no squeaks or rattles. The ride is firm, but still soft enough to keep you comfortable, and the powerful 3.8-liter supercharged V6 is a revelation. That, together with a capable chassis and efficient brakes, makes this car very fun to drive."

A supercharged V6, good chassis and direct power steering make this Pontiac's best ever.

Milestones

1988 The Grand Prix gets an added dose of excitement with front-wheel drive and sporty new styling.

1989 A limited-edition 200-bhp turbo Grand Prix is offered to the public. Exclusivity is guaranteed as only around 2,000 are built.

The Grand Prix became front-wheel drive for the 1988 model year.

1991 The GTP replaces the Turbo as the performance model, with a 200-bhp, 3.1-liter V6.

1994 The Grand Prix is facelifted and has smoother, lower body styling.

The Grand Prix shares its drivetrain with the Bonneville.

1995 Pontiac's GPX show car makes its debut at the New York Auto Show.

1996 A new Grand Prix goes on sale. The GTP has a 240-bhp supercharged engine.

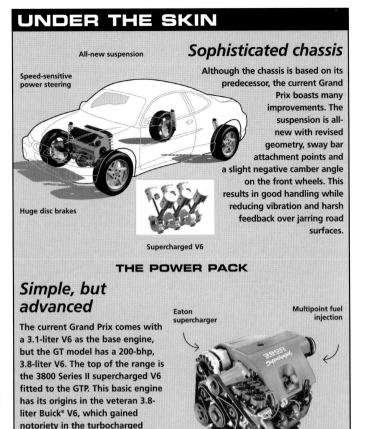

Sophisticated chassis

Although the chassis is based on its predecessor, the current Grand Prix boasts many improvements. The suspension is all-new with revised geometry, sway bar attachment points and a slight negative camber angle on the front wheels. This results in good handling while reducing vibration and harsh feedback over jarring road surfaces.

All-new suspension

Speed-sensitive power steering

Huge disc brakes

Supercharged V6

THE POWER PACK

Simple, but advanced

The current Grand Prix comes with a 3.1-liter V6 as the base engine, but the GT model has a 200-bhp, 3.8-liter V6. The top of the range is the 3800 Series II supercharged V6 fitted to the GTP. This basic engine has its origins in the veteran 3.8-liter Buick® V6, which gained notoriety in the turbocharged Grand National™ and T-Type™ cars of the 1980s. It is a fairly conventional affair, with cast-iron block and heads but gives robust power and torque thanks to the supercharger.

Eaton supercharger

Multipoint fuel injection

Cast-iron block and heads

25 mpg in normal driving conditions

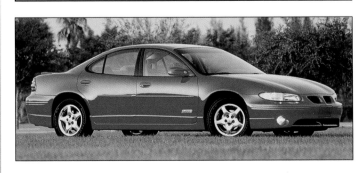

Wide choice

Offered in two- and four-door versions and with three trim levels, the Grand Prix has broad appeal. Enthusiasts are drawn to the GTP with its potent supercharged V6 and enhanced suspension. The GTP is offered as a sedan as well as a coupe.

The four-door version combines advanced performance with practicality.

GM's 'excitement division' has virtually reinvented the American mid-size car with the dramatic-looking and top-performing GTP. Few cars can match its performance and feature content for the price.

Heads-up display

A first for GM and Pontiac is an optional heads-up display unit that projects speed and other functions onto the windshield. It enables the driver to read vital information without having to take his or her eyes off the road.

Automatic transmission

The normally aspirated Grand Prix has GM's 4T60-E four-speed automatic transmission. But with the supercharged V6 imposing greater load on the transmission, GTPs have a beefed-up 4T65-E with a performance shift mode for sportier driving.

Wide-track suspension

Like classic Pontiacs, the Grand Prix has an extra-wide front track and a new suspension with 'low-friction' anti-roll bar points for optimum grip.

Four-wheel disc brakes

GTPs have large four-wheel discs, with the greater swept area being at the front where it is needed most.

Alternative body styles

Throughout most of its history, the Grand Prix was exclusively a two-door, but the current car is offered in both sedan and coupe forms with the same roof panel. Although its design is all new, the Grand Prix is built on the GM corporate W-body, which it shares with the Buick Century™/Regal™ and Oldsmobile™ Intrigue™.

V6 engine

The supercharged 3800 Series II V6 first saw duty in this form in the full-size Bonneville SSEi sport sedan. A durable, torquey engine, it can push the GTP to 60 mph in a brisk 6.6 seconds.

Specifications

1999 Pontiac Grand Prix GTP

ENGINE
Type: V6
Construction: Cast-iron block and heads
Valve gear: Two valves per cylinder operated by a single camshaft via pushrods and rockers
Bore and stroke: 3.80. x 3.40 in.
Displacement: 231 c.i.
Compression ratio: 8.5:1
Induction system: Multipoint fuel injection
Maximum power: 240 bhp at 5,200 rpm
Maximum torque: 280 lb-ft at 3,200 rpm
Top speed: 142 mph
0-60 mph: 6.6 sec.

TRANSMISSION
4T65-E four-speed automatic

BODY/CHASSIS
Steel unitary chassis with two-door body

SPECIAL FEATURES

Both the GT and GTP are fitted with the 3800 Series II V6 as standard.

Five-spoke front wheels are set at a negative camber to enhance grip.

RUNNING GEAR
Steering: Rack-and-pinion
Front suspension: MacPherson struts with coil springs, telescopic shock absorbers and anti-roll bar
Rear suspension: MacPherson struts with trailing arms, coil springs, telescopic shock absorbers and anti-roll bar
Brakes: Discs, 10.9-in. dia. (vented front), 10.9-in. dia. (rear)
Wheels: Cast-aluminum, 7 x 16 in.
Tires: Goodyear Eagle, RS-A 225/60HR-16

DIMENSIONS
Length: 196.5 in.   **Width:** 72.7 in.
Height: 54.7 in.   **Wheelbase:** 110.5 in.
Track: 61.7 in. (front), 61.1 in. (rear)
Weight: 3,396 lbs.

Pontiac FIREHAWK

SLP Engineering offered its first Firehawk street car in 1992. The current car, now available in both Formula and Trans Am format, is the best yet. The uprated suspension gives handling and grip that is matched only by the unequivocal LS1 engine making the Firehawk a contemporary muscle car.

"...supertuned street machine."

"SLP shows what clever modifications can do to the handling and power of a typical Trans Am. The Firehawk's variable rate springs give an excellent ride quality despite its low-profile Firestones while its thicker anti-roll bars allow more aggressive cornering. Under the SLP-installed, forced-air induction hood, the engine generates 327 bhp thanks to a cat-back exhaust system. This supertuned street machine accelerates to 60 mph in 5.1 seconds and has a top speed of 157 mph."

The Firehawk's instruments are easy to read and the high bolstered seats give great support.

Milestones

1987 Ex-drag racer Ed Hamburger forms SLP (Street Legal Performance) Engineering. He negotiates a deal with General Motors to design and make a performance package for the Pontiac Firebird.

The Trans Am is the top-of-the-line factory Firebird with a 305-bhp V8.

1992 SLP offers its first Firehawk street car. It is inspired by the SCCA showroom stock racers.

SLP also offers a package for the Grand Prix® GTP™ called the GTX.

1995 Still using the Formula, SLP offers the Firehawk in both coupe and convertible styles. Power comes from a 315-bhp LT1 engine with a Ram Air induction system.

1998 A new Firehawk, with 327 bhp is previewed but production does not begin until late in the year.

UNDER THE SKIN

Super suspension

In addition to boosting the engine's power, SLP also improves upon the highly street tuned Trans Am suspension. A thicker front anti-roll bar is fitted on the basic package, along with new 17-inch wheels and Firestone Firehawk tires. Optional packages include variable rate springs with Bilstein telescopic shock absorbers, stiffer rear springs and a thicker rear anti-roll bar.

Four-wheel disc brakes

Unitary construction

Bilstein gas-pressurized shock absorbers

Gutsy V8

THE POWER PACK

Forced-air flyer

Because of the new LS1 engine with its all-alloy construction, cutting edge cylinder heads, a single coil for each cylinder, 10.5:1 compression ratio and composite intake manifold, the Formula and Trans Am have never been faster. As if 305 bhp wasn't enough, SLP adds a twin nostrilled, forced-air induction hood and a free flowing cat-back exhaust system. With these hard-core modifications, the Firehawk is able to generate a massive 327 bhp.

Sequential multiport fuel injection

Ignition coil for each cylinder

10.5:1 compression ratio

Cast-aluminum block and heads

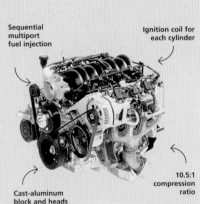

Basic fun

Despite some high-tech features, the Firehawk is a throwback to the old muscle cars of the 1960s. Packing 327 bhp and able to run 13-second ¼-miles right out of the box, it is an affordable driving enthusiast's dream, considering its $30,499 sticker price.

As of 1998, the Firehawks can now be based on the Trans Am.

Exclusivity isn't normally associated with the 1999 Pontiac Trans Am, but if you ordered the top shelf, SLP-modified Firehawk, you would be one of only 500 people with the best-handling Pontiac ever offered.

Heat extractors
In addition to the new forced air hood, SLP designed these heat extractors to draw out hot air from the engine bay.

V8 engine
GM's small-block 5.7-liter V8 is still a classic two-valve pushrod design but shares little with the old LT1. It has a cast-aluminum block and features redesigned cylinder heads, a composite intake manifold and 6-bolt, main-bearing caps.

Functional hood scoop
Firebirds got a restyled twin nostrilled hood for 1998. The SLP forced air induction system is different from the standard Pontiac WS-6 Ram Air hood but works just as effectively.

Six-speed transmission
Because of the extra power they make, Firehawks are only available with Borg-Warner six-speed transmissions. If you want an automatic transmission, you'll have to stay with the standard Firebird or Trans Am models.

Bilstein suspension
On the SLP option list, you can specially order the Bilstein Ultra Performance Suspension System. These revalved shocks will keep the Firehawk composed up to .91gs on the skidpad. This option is only available on coupe models.

Optional differential
The standard factory differential can be upgraded with a severe duty Auburn Gear unit. It is available with an AAM cast aluminum cooling cover.

Performance exhaust
The less restrictive exhaust fitted by SLP helps the engine produce seven extra bhp, but there is very little penalty in extra noise generated.

Specifications
1999 Pontiac Firebird Firehawk

ENGINE

Type: V8

Construction: Aluminum block and heads

Valve gear: Two valves per cylinder operated by a single block-mounted camshaft with pushrods and rocker arms

Bore and stroke: 3.90 in. x 3.62 in.

Displacement: 5.7 liter

Compression ratio: 10.5:1

Induction system: Electronic fuel injection

Maximum power: 327 bhp at 5,200 rpm

Maximum torque: 345 lb-ft at 4,400 rpm

Top speed: 157 mph

0-60 mph: 5.1 sec.

TRANSMISSION

Borg-Warner T56 six-speed manual

BODY/CHASSIS

Steel unitary chassis with composite two-door coupe body

SPECIAL FEATURES

The 1999 Firehawk was intended to have exposed headlights but cost prohibited them.

These chrome plated, five-spoke aluminum wheels are a popular option.

RUNNING GEAR

Steering: Rack-and-pinion

Front suspension: Double wishbones with coil springs, Bilstein telescopic shock absorbers and anti-roll bar

Rear suspension: Live axle with trailing links, control arm, Panhard rod, coil springs, Bilstein telescopic shock absorbers and anti-roll bar

Brakes: Vented discs, 11.8-in. dia. (front), 11.9-in. dia. (rear)

Wheels: Chrome plated alloy, 9 x 17 in.

Tires: Firestone Firehawk, 275/40 ZR17

DIMENSIONS

Length: 193.8 in.   **Width:** 74.5 in.

Height: 52.0 in.   **Wheelbase:** 101.1 in.

Track: 60.7 in. (front), 60.6 in. (rear)

Weight: 3,520 lbs.

Shelby COOPER KING COBRA

The logic behind the immortal Shelby Cobra also gave birth to the King Cobra —Carroll Shelby's front-line racer during 1963 and 1964. It was essentially a Cooper Monaco two-seater sports racer incorporating a fearsomely powerful, mid-mounted, Ford V8 engine tuned by Shelby American.

"...vintage racer."

"Many people consider the King Cobra to be the spiritual forerunner of the Can-Am cars. They should, too, because this vintage racer drives like one. You sit low to the ground, pinned in place by the narrow cockpit and the intrusive engine. The most striking thing about driving the King Cobra is how tractable it is. You can pull away strongly in a high gear and it just keeps going right up to top speed. It's not an easy car to set up, but when it's right, the handling balance is highly rewarding."

In favor of a highly aerodynamic body shell, the rear visibility is virtually non existent.

Milestones

1958 John Cooper introduces the Monaco, a highly competitive mid-engined sports racer.

The Cooper Monaco is the basis on which Shelby created the exhilarating King Cobra.

1963 In his search for the quintessential sports race design, Carroll Shelby mated the Cooper Monaco with a Ford 289 V8 engine to create the first King Cobra.

The AC Cobra uses the same 289-cubic inch Ford V8 powerplant.

1964 The 12th and last King Cobra is made by Shelby, although cars continue to race successfully after this date; the car pictured won the Riverside GP this year.

UNDER THE SKIN

Brilliant chassis

The base Cooper Monaco was dominant on the track thanks to its brilliant chassis. But this had to be adjusted so that it could handle V8 power. The process of turning the Cooper into a King Cobra was a gradual one, with different chassis incorporating changes as they were made. This included modified A-arms and pick up points to increase suspension travel, Armstrong shocks and uprated brakes. This car is fitted with a modified transaxle.

Modified Cooper A-arms
All-around independent suspension
Uprated disc brakes
Ford V8 engine

THE POWER PACK

Ford 289 V8

The idea behind the King Cobra was to replace the Cooper's 2.7-liter Coventry Climax engine with an American V8. Just as he had done with the AC Ace to turn it into the Cobra, Shelby put a Ford V8 into the Monaco chassis. This was the latest 289-cubic inch, Ford, small-block V8 motor. Indeed, space is so tight that the V8 intrudes substantially into the passenger compartment. As in the Monaco, the engine/transaxle forms part of the chassis structure. Racing cars had about 400 bhp, compared with 240 bhp for the Cooper Monaco.

Rare snake

Of the chassis that were supplied to Shelby by Cooper during 1963 and 1964, only four King Cobras are known to survive. That makes them very hot properties and very valuable. However, most of the cars have been modified along the way.

The powerful V8 engine mated to the excellent chassis made for a great racer.

The Shelby Cobra was one of the first cars to successfully mate a British chassis with an American V8 engine. The King Cobra was the first mid-engined two-seater sports racer to do the same. It was a technical triumph.

Mid-mounted V8

Sports racers with centrally mounted engines were pioneered by John Cooper in the late 1950s. Carroll Shelby recognized the potential of a mid-engined chassis with a V8 engine. His team shoehorned a Ford 289 V8 into a very tight space to create the Shelby King Cobra.

Aluminum body

The main front and rear body sections are hand-formed in aluminum. It is also more sculptural and aerodynamic than the Monacos. Like the original cars, this example features a divided undertray and separate side pods.

Challenging brakes

The front brakes are the original Airhart discs, as designed for drag racing in 1962. The rear brakes are Girling BR. A modern Tilton brake balance bar has replaced the Cooper original, and there are Brake Man carbon-Kevlar pads and brake fluid.

Racing transmission

King Cobras used a variety of transmissions including Huffaker and Colotti. The transmission in this particular car is a Shelby/McKee four-speed transaxle with ZF limited slip differential.

Cooper alloy wheels

The original Cooper alloy wheels are still fitted, shod with Dunlop L and M Vintage Racing tires, or in certain cases, Goodyear Vintage Bluestreaks. For road use, vintage-lookalike Panasport wheels are used.

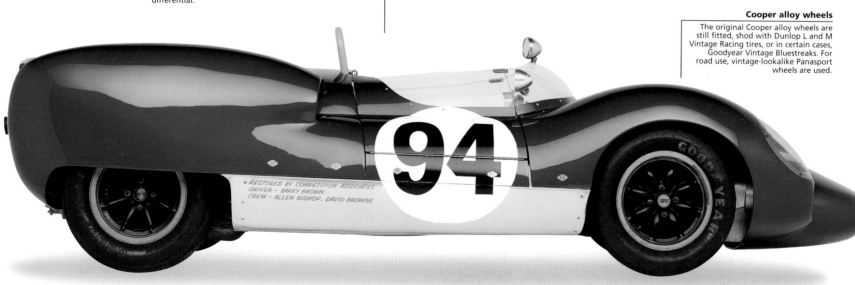

RESTORED BY COMPETITION ASSOCIATES
DRIVER - BARRY BROWN
CREW - ALLEN BISHOP, DAVID BROWNE

Specifications

1964 Cooper King Cobra

ENGINE

Type: V8

Construction: Cast-iron cylinder block and cylinder heads

Valve gear: Two valves per cylinder operated by single camshaft with pushrods and rockers

Bore and stroke: 4.00 in. x 2.90 in.

Displacement: 289 c.i.

Compression ratio: 10.5:1

Induction system: Four Weber 48 IDA carburetors

Maximum power: 400 bhp at 6,800 rpm

Maximum torque: 345 lb-ft at 4,000 rpm

Top speed: 176 mph

0-60 mph: 3.5 sec.

TRANSMISSION

Four-speed manual

BODY/CHASSIS

Separate tubular-steel chassis with two-door sports body in aluminum

SPECIAL FEATURES

The Shelby/McKee transmission is designed to get the most from the V8.

Like the Can Am cars that followed it, the King Cobra has dry-sump lubrication.

RUNNING GEAR

Steering: Rack-and-pinion

Front suspension: Double A-arm with coil springs, anti-roll bar and shock absorbers, and anti-roll bar

Rear suspension: Double A-arm with coil springs, shock absorbers, and anti-roll bar

Brakes: Discs (front and rear)

Wheels: Alloy, 15-in. dia.

Tires: 5.00 (front), 6.50 (rear)

DIMENSIONS

Length: 145.0 in. **Width:** 57.5 in.

Height: 31.5 in. **Wheelbase:** 91.0 in.

Track: 55.0 in. (front and rear)

Weight: 1,400 lbs.

Shelby MUSTANG GT350

When dynamic Texan, Carroll Shelby worked his magic on the best-selling Ford Mustang, he created a classic. The rare top-of-the-line 350-bhp Shelby Mustang GT350 was a great champion—and you could rent the street-legal 306-bhp version from Hertz for $35 a day!

"...tons of upper end power."

"'Rough...nasty...noisy...hard steering...I love it!' were the comments most testers made back in 1965, and it hasn't changed since. The special Detroit Locker limited slip differential makes loud ratcheting noises on slow corners, then locks with a bang when you hit the accelerator. The engine is smaller than most other American muscle cars of the time, but the GT350 is a winner at the track or on the street. Suspension is stiffer than the stock Mustang and really helps the car negotiate sharp turns. The high-performance 289 offers lots of torque and tons of upper end power."

With full instrumentation and a stripped-out interior, it is obvious that the GT350 means business.

Milestones

1964 Mustang introduced in April

and showrooms are mobbed. The first V8 comes slightly later, followed by a bigger V8, then a 271-bhp version (code name 'K'), which is the basis for the GT350.

The Mustang was launched in 1964 as a 'pony' car.

1965 Shelby

American takes time out from building Cobras to produce 100 GT350s and qualifying them to run as SCCA sports cars. They win four out of five of the B-Production regional wins in 1965, and take the overall championship that year and in 1966 and 1967.

1966 Hertz Rent-a-Car

buys about 1,000 GT350Hs (for Hertz), painted with gold stripes—most have automatic transmissions. There are stories about people renting them, racing them, then returning the Rent-a-Racers with brakes smoking and tires worn out.

Hertz gained publicity from renting Shelby Mustangs.

UNDER THE SKIN

New suspension

Engine is mounted in the front, driving through a special Borg Warner T-10 four-speed transmission to a heavy-duty rear axle, taken from a Ford Galaxie station wagon. The Mustang monocoque is steel with Shelby adding a rear seat replacement panel and fiberglass hood (with air scoop). Shelby added a wooden steering wheel—a sports car must-have at the time.

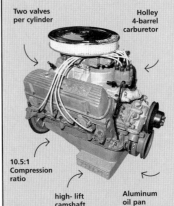

Spare tire on fiberglass rear seat panel

Koni adjustable shocks

Braces from cowl to suspension towers

Optional alloy wheels

Front-mounted V8

THE POWER PACK

Ford 'Hi-Po' 289

Basically a Mustang GT unit, the high-performance 289-cubic inch Ford small block started at 271 bhp before Shelby began working on it, a substantial improvement on the 101 bhp of the first six-cylinder Mustangs. The engine of the GT350 street car with a Holley four-barrel carburetor developed 306 bhp, and the mighty GT350R had another 44 bhp. The main modifications were a higher compression ratio, high-lift cam, larger valves, and improved breathing with the performance carburetor.

Two valves per cylinder

Holley 4-barrel carburetor

10.5:1 Compression ratio

high-lift camshaft

Aluminum oil pan

The GT350R

Only 37 examples of the 'R' (for race) version were built. With a stout 350-bhp engine and stripped interior, it won championships in the Sports Car Club of America's (SCCA) hot B-Production class against Corvettes, Ferraris, Cobras, Lotuses and E-type Jaguars.

GT350R has a fiberglass apron which increased airflow to the radiator.

Ford's Mustang was selling well, but it lacked the high-performance image of the Corvette. So Ford asked Carroll Shelby to develop the GT350, which beat the Corvette on the race track and outperformed it on the road.

High performance 289 V8
Shelby modified Ford's 'Hi-Po' version of the small-block V8 with 10.5:1 compression ratio, improved valve timing and better breathing. This gave 306 bhp at 6,000 rpm.

Rear-exiting exhaust system
The original GT350s had side-exiting exhausts which were noisy and not permitted in some states. 1966 models were given a conventional rear-exiting exhaust system.

Improved front suspension
The standard Mustang front suspension was improved for the GT350 with stiffer springs, revalved Koni shocks and relocated control arms.

Optional Cragar alloy wheels
Conventional steel wheels were standard wear on the GT350, but many owners opted for the lighter Cragar alloys approved by Shelby.

Functional side scoops
The 1966 GT350 had side scoops which fed air to the rear brakes, distinguishing it from the standard fastback Mustang.

Rear drum brakes
The GT350's extra performance dictated the use of Kelsey-Hayes front discs, but drums were retained at the rear.

Custom fuel cap
The 1966-model GT350s were given their very own fuel cap in the middle of the rear of the car, carrying the Cobra logo.

Limited slip differential
Early Shelbys were fitted with the Detroit Locker limited slip differential to improve cornering traction and eliminate wheelspin.

Acrylic rear quarter windows
On the 1966 models the standard Mustang fastback louvers were replaced by acrylic windows to make the car lighter.

Specifications
1966 Shelby Mustang GT350

ENGINE
Type: V8

Construction: Cast-iron block and heads, aluminum intake manifold, tubular steel exhaust manifolds

Valve gear: Two valves per cylinder operated by single block-mounted camshaft via pushrods and rockers

Bore and stroke: 4.02 in. x 2.87 in.

Displacement: 289 c.i.

Compression ratio: 10.5:1

Induction system: Holley four-barrel carburetor

Maximum power: 306 bhp at 6,000 rpm

Maximum torque: 329 lb-ft at 4,200 rpm

Top speed: 135 mph

0-60 mph: 5.7 sec.

TRANSMISSION
Borg Warner T-10 four-speed with close-ratio gears and aluminum case

BODY/CHASSIS
Standard steel Mustang fastback body with Shelby grill; fiberglass hood, removed rear seat, Mustang monocoque with subframes

SPECIAL FEATURES

Goodyear tires were the performance rubber to have on your 1960s muscle car.

Shelby Mustang ID plate is mounted on left fenderwell.

RUNNING GEAR
Front suspension: Wishbones, coil springs, Koni shocks and anti-roll bar

Rear suspension: Live axle with semi-elliptic leaf springs, Koni shocks and traction control arms

Brakes: Kelsey-Hayes disc brakes 11.3 in. dia. (front), drums (rear)

Wheels: Steel 6 in. x 14 in. or magnesium alloy 7 in. x 14 in.

Tires: Goodyear crossply Blue Dot 775-14

DIMENSIONS
Length: 181.6 in.   **Width:** 68.2 in.

Height: 55 in.   **Wheelbase:** 108 in.

Track: 56.5 in. (front), 57 in. (rear)

Weight: 2,792 lbs.

Shelby **MUSTANG GT500**

Softer, roomier and more practical than the original stark GT350, the GT500 still boasted masses of brute strength with over 350 bhp and a gigantic 420 lb-ft of torque from its 428-cubic inch V8.

"...so much power and torque."

"With so much power and torque available, anyone can get stunning performance from the GT500, particularly with the automatic. There are two surprises in store: You expect it to be faster than a 15.6-second quarter mile suggests, but you don't expect it to handle as well as it does. Despite the huge engine making it front heavy, the power steering makes sure the GT500 goes where you want it to. The ride isn't bad for a late-'60s muscle car and the engine isn't very temperamental, although it does throw out an awful lot of heat, making the air conditioning option a must."

The dashboard has a special 140-mph speedometer and 8,000-rpm tachometer as well as plenty of extra gauges.

Milestones

1965 First Shelby GT350s appear as 1966 models, but sell slowly.

1966 Efforts to make it more of a street car lead to the specifications being toned down: The exhaust is quieter, the limited slip differential is an option and Koni shocks are left off.

1968 was the first year you could get a GT500 convertible.

1967 The last year before Ford takes over building the Shelby Mustang. The GT350 is restyled and the bigger engined GT500 is introduced.

1968 GT500 is joined by the GT500KR (King of the Road). It has a 428-cubic inch engine—the Cobra Jet rather than the Police unit.

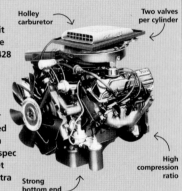

Ford's own Mach 1 Mustang killed off the GT500.

1969 Whole Mustang range is restyled, including the GT500 to the big, flatter looking Mach 1 style.

UNDER THE SKIN

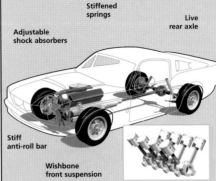

Stiffened springs

Live rear axle

Adjustable shock absorbers

Stiff anti-roll bar

Wishbone front suspension

Police-spec V8

Suspension improvements

Like all performance Mustangs, the GT500 had a straightforward front V8 engine driving a live rear axle. Shelby's improvements saw the springs stiffened and Gabriel adjustable shock absorbers added, and a stiff anti-roll bar at the front. The modification which lowered the pivot for the front upper wishbone was so good Ford adopted it on the stock Mustang.

THE POWER PACK

Simply big

Don't confuse the 428-cubic inch unit installed in the GT500 with the fierce 427 engine in Shelby's Cobras. The 428 has a different bore and stroke and, although it shares the same all-iron pushrod V8 layout, it is a less sophisticated design, and less powerful. It was designed for lower engine speeds and for long sustained use, often in the police chase cars in which it was used. Later the police-spec unit was replaced with the Cobra Jet version which was rated with an extra five bhp but no increase in torque.

Holley carburetor

Two valves per cylinder

High compression ratio

Strong bottom end

Early or open?

Although the GT500 continued until the 1970 model year, by that stage there was very little to set it apart from the rest of the Mustang range. So if you're after one of the big-engined Shelby Mustangs, it's best to go for an earlier, more subtle car or one of the rare convertibles, which are highly collectible and often faked.

The rarest of the GT500s is the factory convertible.

If bigger was better, the GT500 was the best of the Shelby Mustang line. There was no way you could have added a bigger engine to the car, and that made sure it was the most powerful of all.

Fiberglass hood
A new fiberglass hood with functional air scoops helps to accommodate the big engine and also reduces the car's weight.

Power steering
With so much weight over the nose and with wide tires, power steering was a very good idea. In fact you had no choice—it was a standard feature, as were the power brakes and shoulder harnesses.

Front heavy
That huge cast-iron V8 naturally made the GT500 front heavy, with a weight distribution of 58 percent front and 42 percent rear. It was just as well that the hood was fiberglass.

V8 engine
With the GT500, Shelby went for the biggest engine he could fit in the bay, the Police Interceptor type 428-cubic inch V8. It filled the engine compartment so fully you couldn't even see the spark plugs.

Alloy wheels
Steel wheels were a standard feature, but these Shelby alloys were available as an option. They are very desirable today.

Wide tires
The GT500 needed to put as much rubber on the road as possible to cope with its power. Shelby opted for Goodyear Speedway E70-15s, a popular choice for muscle cars of the era that were rated at 140 mph.

Adjustable shocks
The standard shocks were thrown out and replaced by Gabriel adjustables. However, the car left the Shelby works with what was considered the optimum settings.

Unique tail lights
The back of the car was distinguished from the standard Mustang fastback by different tail lights, two very wide ones replacing the two sets of triple lights. Above the lights, the trunk lid was another Shelby fiberglass part.

Specifications
1967 Shelby Mustang GT500

ENGINE
Type: V8
Construction: Cast-iron block and heads
Valve gear: Two valves per cylinder operated by single block-mounted camshaft via pushrods, rockers and hydraulic lifters
Bore and stroke: 4.13 in. x 3.98 in.
Displacement: 428 c.i.
Compression ratio: 10.5:1
Induction system: Two Holley four-barrel carburetors
Maximum power: 355 bhp at 5,400 rpm
Maximum torque: 420 lb-ft at 3,200 rpm
Top speed: 132 mph
0-60 mph: 7.0 sec.

TRANSMISSION
Ford Cruise-O-Matic three-speed automatic or four-speed manual

BODY/FRAME
Unitary steel with two-door coupe body

SPECIAL FEATURES

The hood scoops added by Shelby were changed with each model year. They became more prominent after these rather subtle scoops on this 1967 car.

1967 Shelby GT500s were equipped with two extra driving lights but were spread farther apart toward the end of the 1967 model year.

RUNNING GEAR
Steering: Recirculating ball
Front suspension: Double wishbones with adjustable Gabriel shock absorbers and 1-inch dia. anti-roll bar
Rear suspension: Live axle with semi-elliptic leaf springs and adjustable Gabriel shock absorbers
Brakes: Discs, 11.3 in. dia. (front), drums, 10 in. dia. (rear)
Wheels: Shelby alloy, 7 in. x 15 in. (front and rear)
Tires: E70-15 (front and rear)

DIMENSIONS
Length: 186.6 in.   **Width:** 70.9 in.
Height: 49 in.   **Wheelbase:** 108 in.
Track: 58 in. (front and rear)
Weight: 3,520 lbs.

Shelby **OMNI GLH-S**

Conceived as an economy hatchback, few people could have even conceived that the Dodge Omni could be a performer, too. In 1986, Shelby Automobiles proved that it could be, with the 175-bhp GLH-S.

"...truly astonishing."

"You are not likely to find a car that is more of a 'sleeper' than this. Even inside, it is very subdued, but at least you've got a five-speed stickshifter and a tachometer. This little car is quite happy performing the trip to the grocery store, but put pedal to metal and the little Omni comes alive. It leaps forward with a raspy note, and although the handling requires maximum driving input, the acceleration is truly astonishing."

Much is shared with the sportier Charger, including the dash, seats and steering wheel.

420

Milestones

1978 Dodge introduces perhaps its most significant car of the decade, the front-drive, subcompact Omni. It is powered by a 1.7-liter Volkswagen-based four-cylinder engine.

A Europeanized version of the Omni, badged Talbot Horizon, was Car of the Year in 1977.

1984 Things begin to heat up with the arrival of the Omni GLH created with input from Carroll Shelby. It has blackout exterior trim, body extensions, special aluminum wheels and a 110 bhp, 2.2-liter four-cylinder engine.

Following on from the Omni was the Shelby Charger GLH-S.

1985 A turbocharged 146-bhp four becomes available.

1986 Shelby announces the even hotter GLH-S, of which 500 are built at the new Whittier plant.

UNDER THE SKIN

Unitary body/chassis Stiffened suspension

Five-speed transaxle

Turbocharged four

Omni-potent

Known as the O-body, the front-drive Omni and its Plymouth twin, the Horizon, were conceived in the VW Rabbit idom. A two-box hatchback unibody is featured with Iso-strut-type suspension at the front and a standard anti-roll bar. Out back there is a set of semi-trailing arms and coil springs. GLH-S models got a beefier front anti-roll bar, a rear bar and stiffer suspension settings.

THE POWER PACK

Hot yet cold

For 1981, a 2.2-liter (135-cubic inch) Chrysler-built four became optional in the Omni and it was this engine that formed the basis for the Omni GLH motor. This cast-iron-block, aluminum-head unit features a single overhead camshaft, two valves per cylinder, and a five-main-bearing crank. A beefier camshaft, recalibrated electronics and a higher compression ratio resulted in 110 bhp for 1984. Adding a turbocharger pushed power output up to 146 horses the following year. The ultimate Shelby-built Omnis got equal-length intake runners, an air-to-air intercooler, and other changes, all resulting in a formidable 175 bhp.

Fast Little Rocket

Weighing in at just 2,300 lbs. and with 175 bhp on tap, the little GLH-S is an absolute rocket. It may have ferocious torquesteer and suffer from indifferent workmanship, but considering that only 500 were built and that it will dash from 0-60 mph in 6.4 seconds, collectible status is guaranteed.

Most of the 500 GLH-S cars built were finished in red or black.

Some GLH-S customers removed the graphics from their cars, making the peppy little Omni's just about invisible on the street. Many ponycar drivers fell victim to the little front-drive Shelby.

Five-speeds

All GLH-S Omnis came with Chrysler's five-speed manual transaxle—an automatic was not offered. A competent driver could hustle the little car to 60 mph in just 6.4 seconds.

Turbo four

Bringing out 175 bhp from 2.2 liters was quite a feat in 1980s America. It was achieved by the miracle of electronic fuel injection, turbocharging and intercooling.

Hatchback body

Taking its inspiration from the Volkswagen Rabbit, the Omni was only available as a five-door hatchback. A folding rear seat more than doubled cargo carrying capacity.

Strut suspension

For reasons of packaging, the Omni employs Iso-type struts for the front suspension. This means there is adequate clearance for the engine and transaxle assembly. The GLH-S has stiffer front springs and dampers than lesser Omnis.

Beefy tires

In place of the 14-inch rims found on lesser Omnis, the GLH-S got special aluminum and composite 15-inch wheels shod in Goodyear Eagle GT 50-series tires with uni-directional Gatorback tread.

Specifications
1986 Shelby Omni GLH-S

ENGINE

Type: Inline four

Construction: Cast-iron block with alloy head

Valve gear: Two valves per cylinder operated by a single overhead camshaft

Bore and stroke: 3.44 in. x 3.62 in.

Displacement: 135 c.i.

Compression ratio: 8.5:1

Induction system: Electronic fuel injection

Maximum power: 175 bhp at 5,200 rpm

Maximum torque: 168 lb-ft at 3,600 rpm

Top speed: 130 mph

0-60 mph: 6.4 sec.

TRANSMISSION

Five-speed manual

BODY/CHASSIS

Unitary steel construction with steel four-door hatchback body

SPECIAL FEATURES

Although the speedometer only reaches 85 mph, the GLH-S could rocket all the way up to 130.

Black bumpers and driving lights hint at the GLH-S's performance potential.

RUNNING GEAR

Steering: Rack-and-pinion

Front suspension: Iso struts, coil springs, lower control arms and anti-roll bar

Rear suspension: Beam axle, semi-trailing arms, coil springs and anti-roll bar

Brakes: Discs (front), drums (rear)

Wheels: Aluminum/composite 15-in. dia.

Tires: Goodyear Eagle GT P205/50VR15

DIMENSIONS

Length: 164.8 in. **Width:** 67.2 in.

Height: 52.6 in. **Wheelbase:** 99.1 in.

Track: 56.1 in. (front) 55.7 in. (rear)

Weight: 2,300 lbs.

Shelby **CSX**

With the CSX, Carroll Shelby showed that you could take an ordinary four-cylinder front-drive car such as the Dodge Shadow and turn it into a high-performance, 130-mph-plus sports coupe.

"...impressive power."

"When using all the 175 bhp from a standstill you better hang on because the torque-steer will nearly wrench the steering wheel out of your hands. Slightly ease off the throttle and control will return. With the optional bigger tires, the car fidgets and darts. The ride is very firm, and the payoff is a decent level of grip and handling that lets you use all the engine's power. Because the turbo lag is minimal, there is always plenty of passing power."

The interior of the CSX has a bland, functional appearance.

Milestones

1987 Carroll Shelby turns his attention to the Dodge Shadow compact. He modifies the suspension and adds a Garrett turbocharger.

Carroll Shelby tuned many Chrysler Corp. products during the 1980s.

1989 A limited edition (just 500 cars), with improved interior, lowered and stiffened suspension, rear wing and front air dam, optional larger tires and a new variable intake turbocharger, is launched. It marks the debut of composite fiberglass road wheels.

The Dodge Neon R/T is the spiritual successor to the CSX.

1990 Chrysler builds its own turbocharged version of the Shadow after Shelby stops making the CSX.

1991 The final year of the Shadow sees a reduction in power, even from the 2.2-liter turbo, which pumps out a mere 150 bhp.

UNDER THE SKIN

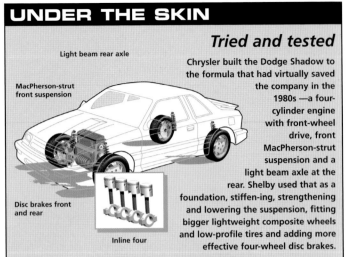

Tried and tested

Chrysler built the Dodge Shadow to the formula that had virtually saved the company in the 1980s —a four-cylinder engine with front-wheel drive, front MacPherson-strut suspension and a light beam axle at the rear. Shelby used that as a foundation, stiffen-ing, strengthening and lowering the suspension, fitting bigger lightweight composite wheels and low-profile tires and adding more effective four-wheel disc brakes.

Light beam rear axle

MacPherson-strut front suspension

Disc brakes front and rear

Inline four

THE POWER PACK

VNT power

Chrysler's familiar overhead-cam, four-cylinder dates back to the early 1980s. It has a cast-iron block with a crankshaft running on five main bearings and topped by an alloy head with a single beltdriven overhead camshaft and two valves per cylinder operated by hydraulic valve lifters. It is undersquare, with a stroke longer than the bore is wide (3.44 inches x 3.62 inches), giving just over 2.2 liters. At first, power output was very low, but the addition of Chrysler's new Variable Nozzle Turbocharger (VNT) not only raised power to 175 bhp, but also considerably reduced turbolag.

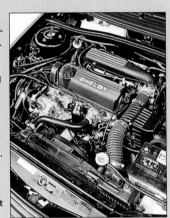

My generation

A second-generation CSX model has to be the one to go for because there were so many improvements over the original. This is especially the case in terms of power delivery, if not outright power, as well as suspension improvements and superior handling.

The understated looks of the CSX belie its performance potential.

The standard Dodge Shadow was not an outstanding-looking car, and Shelby had to dress it up to look the part. This involved lowering it, fitting low-profile tires and adding a full bodykit with front spoiler and rear wing.

Power-assisted steering
A nose-heavy car with front-drive and wide low-profile tires is always going to need power assistance for the rack-and-pinion steering. The steering is also very high-geared, with just 2.1 turns lock to lock, making the car very responsive to driver input.

Overhead-cam engine
Chrysler's overhead-cam four-cylinder engine had been designed with turbocharging in mind and, with the compression ratio dropped to 8.1:1, it was strong enough to take the 12-psi of turbo boost from the VNT turbo.

High front weight bias
Having the iron-block engine mounted transversely at the front with its transmission and turbo makes the CSX front-heavy. The weight distribution is 62:38 front/rear, which would normally create excessive understeer, yet Shelby was able to minimize this.

Discs brakes
Since the front brakes do most of the work, they are vented and fairly large at 10.1 inches in diameter. The solid rear discs are even larger, at 10.6 inches in diameter, but are unvented and have less force exerted on them.

Specifications
1989 Shelby CSX

ENGINE

Type: Inline four-cylinder

Construction: Cast-iron block and alloy cylinder head

Valve gear: Two valves per cylinder operated by a single beltdriven overhead camshaft

Bore and stroke: 3.5 in. x 3.68 in.

Displacement: 2,213 cc

Compression ratio: 8.1:1

Induction system: Electronic fuel injection with Garrett AiResearch VNT-25 turbo

Maximum power: 175 bhp at 5,200 rpm

Maximum torque: 205 lb-ft at 2,400 rpm

Top speed: 133 mph

0-60 mph: 7.1 sec.

TRANSMISSION

Five-speed manual

BODY/CHASSIS

Unitary steel construction

SPECIAL FEATURER

With a top speed of over 130 mph, the CSX needed its rear wing to keep it stable at high speeds.

The turbo boost gauge is the only real indication of what lurks under the hood.

RUNNING GEAR

Steering: Rack-and-pinion

Front suspension: MacPherson struts with lower control arms and anti-roll bar

Rear suspension: Beam axle with trailing arms, Panhard rod, coil springs, telescopic shock absorbers and anti-roll bar

Brakes: Vented discs, 10.1-in. dia. (front), solid discs, 10.6-in. dia. (rear)

Wheels: Plastic fiberglass-reinforced composite, 15 x 6.5 in.

Tires: 225/50 VR15

DIMENSIONS

Length: 171.7 in.   **Width:** 67.3 in.

Height: 52.0 in.   **Wheelbase:** 97.0 in.

Track: 57.6 in. (front and rear)

Weight: 2,790 lbs.

Shelby DAKOTA

Introduced in 1987, the Dakota was one of the first mid-size pickups to uncover a substantial market. With the boom in hot trucks in the late 1980s, Carroll Shelby decided to build a limited-production Dakota.

"...first-rate performance."

"It may feel somewhat dated today, but the Shelby-modified Dakota has plenty of interior space. However, space efficiency is the last reason you would want to own one of these sporty trucks. With a torquey 318 V8 and short gearing, this truck sprints off the line to 60 mph in less than 9.0 seconds. With Shelby's track experience, this truck offers first-rate performance and commendable handling. Furthermore, its precise steering is in a league of its own."

Full instrumentation, including a 6,000-rpm tachometer, tells you this is no average truck.

Milestones

1986 Replacing the Mitsubishi-derived
Ram 50 is the new home-grown Dakota. Bigger than rival compact trucks, it comes with a standard 3.9-liter V6 and is available in two- or four-wheel drive.

Shelby's entry-level vehicle in 1989 was the Dodge Shadow-based CSX subcompact.

1989 A sport model is added
to the range, with blackout trim, cast-aluminum wheels and a 125-bhp, 3.9-liter V6. Carroll Shelby decides to build a hotter version and squeezes a 5.2-liter V8 into the engine bay. Handling suspension, performance tires and graphics highlight the Shelby Dakota. Projected output is 1,500 units per year.

Second-generation Dakotas have either 5.2- or 5.9-liter V8s.

1991 A V8 becomes available on
the regular Dakota, which also receives a new nose.

UNDER THE SKIN

Limited-slip differential

Separate steel chassis

Vented front disc brakes

Small-block V8

Subtle changes

Classified as a mid-size pickup, the Dakota is a very conventional design with a steel box-section chassis with a coil- sprung independent front suspension and a live rear axle. All Shelby Dakotas are rear-wheel drive and feature stiffer springs and revalved shocks to improve handling. A rack-and-pinion steering setup is fitted and vented disc brakes are standard at the front.

THE POWER PACK

Veteran V8

Early first generation Dakotas came stock with rather anemic 3.9-liter V6s, but Shelby decided that his new truck needed a V8 engine. The 318-cubic inch, small-block V8 available in the full-size Ram seemed ideal for the job. This cast-iron V8 was veteran technology by the 1980s, but could still meet emissions requirements and was incredibly easy to tune. The only modification required for installation in the Dakota was replacing the stock fan with twin electric units, primarily for clearance reasons. With 175 bhp and 270 lb-ft of torque, Shelby Dakotas could run 16.5-second ¼-mile elapsed times.

Balancing act

Among hot trucks from the late 1980s and early 1990s, the Shelby Dakota is one of the best balanced. It may not be as quick as current sport trucks, but it is still fun to drive and limited production ensures it will be a future collectable.

Shelby Dakotas were sold through 100 select dealers.

With the growing popularity of customized trucks for leisure use, Carroll Shelby saw an opportunity to market a hot version of the mid-size Dakota, complete with full warranty and dealer backup.

Small-block V8
Dropping the 318-cubic inch V8 into the Dakota Sport transformed the truck into a serious performer. The only modification required was substituting the engine-driven fan for two electric ones. A bonus was an extra 5 bhp and improved cooling efficiency.

Long-lived design
When it first went on sale in 1987, the Dakota was in a class by itself. Bigger than a compact truck yet more manageable than a full-size rig, it attracted an ardent band of followers and the original design remained in production until 1995.

Performance rubber
A set of Goodyear Eagle GT+4 tires helps improve handling and traction. These were some of the best tires available at the time and were also used on Chrysler's police vehicles.

Heavy-duty suspension
Even though it is quick in a straight line, the Shelby is also designed for excellent handling, too. Stiffer springs and revalved shocks help improve cornering. The Shelby is capable of 0.81 lateral g, which is quite remarkable for a truck.

Two-wheel drive
Although stock Dakotas came in two- or four-wheel drive, all Shelby versions were two-wheel drive. A set of 3.90:1 gears and a limited-slip differential give the truck better performance figures than many sporty cars of the era.

Specifications
1989 Shelby Dakota

ENGINE
Type: V8
Construction: Cast-iron block and heads
Valve gear: Two valves per cylinder operated by a single centrally mounted camshaft with pushrods and rockers
Bore and stroke: 3.91 in. x 3.31 in.
Displacement: 318 c.i.
Compression ratio: Not quoted
Induction system: Carter Thermoquad four-barrel downdraft carburetor
Maximum power: 175 bhp at 4,000 rpm
Maximum torque: 270 lb-ft at 2,000 rpm
Top speed: 119 mph
0-60 mph: 8.5 sec.

TRANSMISSION
Four-speed automatic

BODY/CHASSIS
Steel chassis with steel cab and pickup box

SPECIAL FEATURES

To further exploit the Shelby Dakota's handling, Goodyear Eagle GT+4 tires were fitted.

A sports bar behind the cab enhances the appearance but adds no strength to the body's structure.

RUNNING GEAR
Steering: Rack-and-pinion
Front suspension: Upper and lower wishbones with coil springs, telescopic shock absorbers and anti-roll bar
Rear suspension: Live axle with semi-elliptic leaf springs and telescopic shock absorbers
Brakes: Discs (front), drums (rear)
Wheels: Cast aluminum, 6 x 15
Tires: Goodyear Eagle GT+4, P255/75 HR15

DIMENSIONS
Length: 189.9 in. **Width:** 73.9 in.
Height: 66.9 in. **Wheelbase:** 112.0 in.
Track: 59.3 in. (front and rear)
Weight: 3,610 lbs.

Shelby **S.P. 360**

In stock form, the Durango is a class-leading SUV, with a powerful V8 engine and unbeatable towing capacity. Turning it into the awesome S.P. 360 results in a truck that has few peers.

"...sheer opulence."

"The first thing that strikes you when you climb into the S.P. 360 is the sheer opulence of the cabin—this is a rig conceived to transport its occupants in absolute luxury. The sound of the supercharger after you have turned the key is a hint of the performance on command. Planting your right foot to the floor brings a rush of acceleration. A completely reworked suspension also enables the driver to tackle corners with confidence."

Bucket seats, CD changer and plenty of wood elevate the S.P. to ultra-luxury status.

Milestones

1995 A new Dakota makes its debut as a 1996 model. It adopts the styling cues of its big brother, the Dodge Ram, and proves instantly popular. Powertrain choices are expanded to include a 3.9-liter V6, 5.2- and 5.9-liter Magnum V8 engines. The Dakota is the only domestic mid-size pickup.

Shelby's first 'muscle truck' was the 1989 Shelby Dakota.

1997 The new Durango Sport

Utility is based on the Dakota. It shares powertrains, chassis and suspension with its pickup sibling and likewise proves a success.

Launched in 1997, the Durango is a consistent sales champion.

1998 On October 4th, the first Shelby S.P. 360 is revealed as a hot-rod version of the Durango. Only 3,000 copies are slated for the 1999 model year.

UNDER THE SKIN

Live rear axle

Coil-sprung front suspension

V8 engine

Super SUV

Despite an increase in the number of car-derived SUVs on the market, the Durango remains true to the Sport Utility's truck origins. It has a separate boxed-section steel chassis and an independent front suspension, sprung by torsion bars, with a live axle at the rear suspended by leaf springs. For the S.P. the suspension is modified and dropped three inches. Edelbrock shocks are also fitted at all four corners.

THE POWER PACK

Extra power

Standard in the regular Durango is a 3.9-liter V6, though most buyers specify the bigger 5.2- and 5.9-liter V8s. The latter, with 245 bhp, gives this fairly heavy SUV excellent sprinting ability, but there are those who seek still more.

For them, Shelby and Performance West deliver. The S.P. 360 gets a Kenne Bell 2,200 Blowzilla with up to 13 psi of boost, an Optimizer CPU, a Ram Air induction kit, and a pair of Kenne Bell Extractor equal-length exhaust headers. These upgrades are enough to bump power from 250 to a whopping 360 bhp and also take torque from 335 to 414 lb-ft.

Limited build

With an allocated production run of just 3,000 units for 1999, the Shelby Durango is destined to be a collectible vehicle. At the moment, however, it is an immensely fun-to-drive and fairly practical SUV with head-turning looks.

All 1999 S.P. 360s are painted in Viper Blue with white stripes.

As SUVs have risen in popularity, so has the aftermarket dedicated to upgrading them. The 1999 Shelby S.P. 360 is perhaps the most shining example of a new breed of ultra-fast, ultra-luxurious sport utilities.

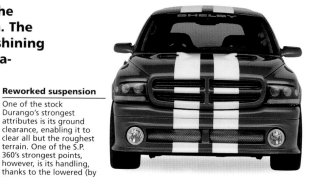

Supercharged V8

Bolting a supercharger, Ram Air system and headers on the 5.9-liter Magnum results in a truly formidable powerplant, with 360 bhp and 414 lb-ft of torque.

GPS system

Most S.P. 360s are loaded to the gills and feature a TV, video and stereo system, plus a Global Positioning System, which pinpoints the Durango's exact location by satellite.

Reworked suspension

One of the stock Durango's strongest attributes is its ground clearance, enabling it to clear all but the roughest terrain. One of the S.P. 360's strongest points, however, is its handling, thanks to the lowered (by three inches) and reengineered suspension, with modified camber, caster and recalibrated springs and steering.

Single paint choice

In keeping with recent Dodge-based performance vehicles, such as the Viper GTS and Ram VTS pickup, the 1999 S.P. 360 is sprayed in Viper Blue, with twin white stripes covering the hood, roof and rear. No other colors are available on the 1999 model.

Four-wheel disc brakes

One major improvement over the stock Durango is in the braking department. Big cross-drilled discs and four-piston calipers at the front translate into a sizeable decrease in stopping distance.

Performance exhaust

No hot-rod vehicle is complete without a performance exhaust, and this applies to the S.P., which has a Kenne Bell stainless steel cat-back dual system.

Specifications

1999 Shelby S.P. 360

ENGINE

Type: V8

Construction: Cast-iron block and heads

Valve gear: Two valves per cylinder operated by a single V-mounted camshaft with pushrods and rockers

Bore and stroke: 4.0 in. x 3.58 in.

Displacement: 360 c.i.

Compression ratio: 8.9:1

Induction system: Sequential multipoint fuel injection

Maximum power: 360 bhp at 4,000 rpm

Maximum torque: 414 lb-ft at 3,200 rpm

Top speed: 132 mph

0-60 mph: 6.4 sec.

TRANSMISSION

Four-speed overdrive automatic

BODY/CHASSIS

Separate steel chassis with four-door station wagon body

SPECIAL FEATURES

Kenne-Bell supplied the dual chromed exhaust tips, which protrude through the rear valance.

A variety of different seating layouts are available, including this six-bucket seat arrangement.

RUNNING GEAR

Steering: Recirculating-ball

Front suspension: Upper and lower A-arms, longitudinal torsion bars, telescopic shock absorbers and anti-roll bar

Rear suspension: Live axle, semi-elliptic leaf springs and telescopic shock absorbers

Brakes: Discs (front and rear)

Wheels: Daytona alloy 18 x 8 in.

Tires: Goodyear F1 GS 295/45 ZR18

DIMENSIONS

Length: 193.3 in. **Width:** 72.4 in.

Height: 69.9 in. **Wheelbase:** 115.9 in.

Track: 63.0 in.

Weight: 4,515 lbs.

Studebaker GOLDEN HAWK

The supercharged, 275-bhp Golden Hawk was an unusually fast car. However, it was so much more expensive than the normally aspirated version that sales were low despite its outstanding performance.

"...extremely stable."

"With the supercharger boosting power and torque, performance is strong. The driving position is excellent and the steering very direct, although without power assistance, it's heavy. At high speeds, the Hawk is extremely stable, and with revised front anti-roll bar and spring rates compensating for the extra weight of the V8 and supercharger, handling is good. Add effective brakes and a smooth ride and the package is near perfect—aside from the price."

The comfortable and functional interior belies the Golden Hawk's performance.

Milestones

1956 Studebaker introduces the Hawk in coupe and hardtop forms. Engines range from a sidevalve inline six, used in the Flight Hawk, to a Packard 275-bhp, 352-cubic inch V8, used in the flagship Golden Hawk.

Packard offered a Hawk for 1958, also with supercharged power.

1957 Studebaker reverts to its own 289-cubic inch engine, adding a belt-driven supercharger to bring power up to 275 bhp.

The Lark compact introduced for 1959 could also get a 289-c.i. V8.

1959 After poor sales, the Hawk range is simplified. Only the 180-bhp Silver Hawk is offered.

1963 The Avanti is launched with the supercharged 289-cubic inch unit.

1964 The final Hawk is built—the Gran Turismo.

UNDER THE SKIN

Big brakes

Four-wheel finned drum brakes

Steel ladder-type frame

Front anti-roll bar

Supercharged V8

Studebaker used the normal body-on-frame approach for the Hawk range, which has two substantial chassis rails running fore and aft with crossmembers. In 1958, asymmetrical rear semi-elliptic leaf springs, with the longer part of the leaves behind the axle line, were fitted. At the front, there are angled double wishbones with coil springs, with an anti-roll bar to improve handling. Brakes are big-finned drums.

THE POWER PACK

Supercharged flyer

Studebaker introduced its first V8 engine in 1951, which helped boost the company's sales by 50 percent. For 1955, the V8 (standard on the Commander) got a power increase to 140 bhp despite being destroked to 224 cubic inches. A bigger 259 arrived as standard on the President. Debuting as the flagship in 1956, it was only natural that the Golden Hawk packed the largest engine—a 352-cubic inch V8 with 275 bhp, sourced from Packard. This was short-lived; for the following year, the Golden Hawk got Studebaker's own 289 V8 with a belt-driven Paxton supercharger producing 275 bhp.

Hard charger

Silver Hawks proved to be far more popular than Golden ones in 1958—4,485 coupes were built against just 878 blown Golden Hawks. But the passage of time changes things, and the latter is more collectible today simply because it is the rarer of the two.

Supercharged Golden Hawks were built for only three model years.

After the Ford Thunderbird had been restyled, the Golden Hawk emerged as just about the best-looking two-door coupe on the market in 1958. And it had the performance to match its styling.

Auto anti-creep

Another option offered by Studebaker was an anti-creep device for the optional automatic transmission. As its name suggests, this stops the car from creeping forward without the driver needing to keep his foot on the brake at the lights or stop signs.

V8 engine

Studebaker developed a V8 engine before Packard (which took over the company in 1954) and so continued to use its own V8. The biggest version, the 289-cubic inch unit, was supercharged for the 1957 Golden Hawk.

Power windows

For the first time with the 1958 models, Studebaker made power front windows available. It was a $102 option and, curiously, power seats cost less than half that price.

Wishbone suspension

Studebaker used independent double-wishbone front suspension but, unusually, angled both wishbones back in the chassis. Most other manufacturers had the inboard ends of the wishbones parallel to the wheels.

Power brakes

Disc brakes were still a rarity in the late 1950s, and so Studebaker used large drums all around. They were given finned casings to help dissipate heat and maintain braking efficiency. At this time, Studebaker charged $38 for power-assisted brakes.

Wraparound rear window

One of the keys to the Golden Hawk's good looks is the wraparound rear window, which permitted the front and rear roof pillars to be set at almost the same angle.

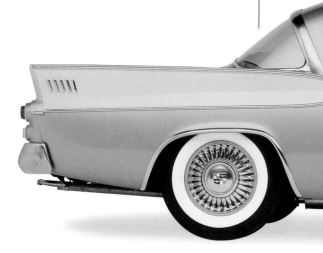

1958 Studebaker Golden Hawk

ENGINE

Type: V8

Construction: Cast-iron block and heads

Valve gear: Two overhead valves per cylinder operated by a single centrally-mounted camshaft with pushrods, rockers and solid valve lifters

Bore and stroke: 3.56 in. x 3.63 in.

Displacement: 289 c.i.

Compression ratio: 7.8:1

Induction system: Single Stromberg two-barrel WW carburetor with supercharger

Maximum power: 275 bhp at 4,800 rpm

Maximum torque: Not quoted

Top speed: 118 mph

0-60 mph: 9.2 sec.

TRANSMISSION

Three-speed Flightomatic

BODY/CHASSIS

Separate steel ladder frame with steel two-door coupe bodywork

SPECIAL FEATURES

The distinctive fins on the Hawks were originally made in fiberglass and later in steel.

A machined aluminum dash was quite a novelty on a 1958 Detroit car.

RUNNING GEAR

Steering: Recirculating ball

Front suspension: Double wishbones with coil springs, telescopic shock absorbers and anti-roll bar

Rear suspension: Live axle with semi-elliptic leaf springs and telescopic shock absorbers

Brakes: Finned drums (front and rear)

Wheels: Pressed steel disc, 14-in. dia.

Tires: 8.00 x 14

DIMENSIONS

Length: 204.0 in.   **Width:** 71.3 in.

Height: 55.5 in.   **Wheelbase:** 120.5 in.

Track: 57.1 in. (front), 56.1 in. (rear)

Weight: 3,470 lbs.

Studebaker **AVANTI**

Looking quite unlike any other American car, the Avanti was an attempt to bolster Studebaker's flagging fortunes. Raymond Loewy's swoopy styling and sports-car feel won many friends.

"...potent road car of its day."

"All Avantis are powerful, and the top versions are among the most potent road cars of their day, with a gutsy V8 engine, suspension tuned for sports-car driving, a low roof line and a long hood stretching out ahead. The ride is hard and the car doesn't roll much because of its anti-roll bars. It's also heavy to drive despite its power-assisted steering. Its overall sensation tells you the Avanti is a special car. After all, it survived for more than three decades with very few changes."

Styling of the Avanti's smart and very functional interior is surprisingly European in design.

Milestones

1962 Studebaker stuns America with its bold new sports coupe, but production is delayed.

1964 The Avanti is dropped after disappointing sales.

Loewy's original Avanti is an all-time design classic.

1965 Two dealers acquire the rights to produce Loewy's design. The Avanti II now uses a Chevrolet engine.

Avanti IIs were hand-built in very small numbers.

1982 The company changes hands, and there are further changes of ownership in 1986 and 1988.

1988 A four-door sedan Avanti is presented, following Raymond Loewy's desire for such a car.

1992 The Avanti finally goes out of production.

UNDER THE SKIN

Old-fashioned chassis

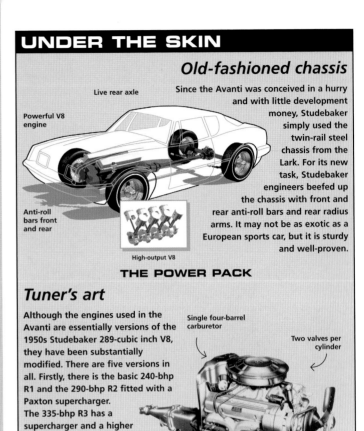

Live rear axle

Powerful V8 engine

Anti-roll bars front and rear

High-output V8

Since the Avanti was conceived in a hurry and with little development money, Studebaker simply used the twin-rail steel chassis from the Lark. For its new task, Studebaker engineers beefed up the chassis with front and rear anti-roll bars and rear radius arms. It may not be as exotic as a European sports car, but it is sturdy and well-proven.

THE POWER PACK

Tuner's art

Although the engines used in the Avanti are essentially versions of the 1950s Studebaker 289-cubic inch V8, they have been substantially modified. There are five versions in all. Firstly, there is the basic 240-bhp R1 and the 290-bhp R2 fitted with a Paxton supercharger. The 335-bhp R3 has a supercharger and a higher compression ratio, the 280-bhp R4 is a twin-carb, four-barrel version and the experimental R5 has twin blowers and fuel injection to produce 575 bhp. The post-Studebaker Avanti IIs use Chevrolet engines like the unit shown here.

Single four-barrel carburetor

Two valves per cylinder

Oversquare cylinder dimensions

Cast-iron block and heads

Going strong

Despite its 1960s design and its fluctuating economic fortunes, the Avanti survived well past its sell-by date. Later, post-Studebaker models lacked the crispness of the original design and attempts to modernize its appearance never looked right.

Late Avantis had color-coded bumpers and alloy wheels.

The Avanti has all the credentials of a hand-built European sports coupe, yet it's 100 percent American made. Nothing else looks like it and, in 1962, very few cars went as fast.

Four-seat interior
Opening up the fiberglass doors reveals an interior which is spacious by the standards of contemporary sports coupes. The rear seats can easily accommodate two adults.

Supercharged V8 engine
Some versions of the Avanti's V8 engine have Paxton superchargers. One experimental version, the R5, has two superchargers and fuel injection, and is claimed to develop 575 bhp and an amazing 196 mph.

Front disc brakes
The Avanti was the first American road car to have standard front disc brakes. They are a Dunlop design with servo assistance.

Sturdy chassis
The simple, twin-rail, box-section ladder chassis is a development of Studebaker's standard sedan car chassis, which dates back to 1953.

Antiquated suspension
Although beefed up with anti-roll bars, the suspension belonged to a previous era. The semi-elliptic leaf springs at the rear are typical of conservative American engineering at the time.

Fiberglass bodywork
To minimize time and tooling costs, Studebaker opted for fiberglass bodywork. The Molded Fiberglass Company had quality problems, however, so Studebaker decided to manufacture its own bodyshells after a critical delay.

Loewy styling
The fantastic and unusual styling of the Avanti was the responsibility of famous designer Raymond Loewy, who also created another design icon—the Coke bottle.

ENGINE

Type: V8

Construction: Cast-iron cylinder block and heads

Valve gear: Two overhead valves per cylinder operated by a single camshaft via pushrods and rockers

Bore and stroke: 3.56 in. x 3.62 in.

Displacement: 289 c.i.

Compression ratio: 10.3:1

Induction system: Single four-barrel carb

Maximum power: 290 bhp at 5,200 rpm

Maximum torque: 330 lb-ft at 3,500 rpm

Top speed: 118 mph

0-60 mph: 8.0 sec.

TRANSMISSION

Four-speed manual or automatic

BODY/CHASSIS

Steel twin-rail box-section ladder chassis with two-door fiberglass coupe body

SPECIAL FEATURES

Highly unusual for an American car of its day, the Avanti has no grill on its nose. The air intake is underneath the front bumper.

To aid cabin ventilation, the Avanti's unusually-shaped rear side windows are hinged at the front edge.

RUNNING GEAR

Steering: Recirculating ball

Front suspension: Wishbones with coil springs, shocks and anti-roll bar

Rear suspension: Live axle with semi-elliptic leaf springs, shocks, upper torque arms and anti-roll bar

Brakes: Discs (front), drums (rear)

Wheels: Steel, 15-in. dia.

Tires: F78 x 15 in.

DIMENSIONS

Length: 192.5 in.   **Width:** 70.4 in.

Height: 53.9 in.   **Wheelbase:** 109 in.

Track: 57.4 in. (front), 56.6 in. (rear)

Weight: 3,405 lbs.

USA 1912-1932

Stutz **BEARCAT**

Developed from an Indianapolis 500 racing car, the Stutz Bearcat has style and charisma but most of all, a huge engine that could take it far beyond the performance of most cars on the roads in the U.S.

"...antique supercar of its time."

"A maximum of 60 bhp doesn't sound like much to get excited about, but the Stutz's big 390-cubic inch four has an enormous amount of torque. Like its maximum power, it seems to be produced right off-idle. The hefty bellowing Bearcat, with its barn-like aerodynamics, could turn a top speed of 80 mph, making it an antique supercar of its time. It'll cruise effortlessly at 60 mph and the sensation of speed is something even a Ferrari driver would be impressed by. It's surprisingly easy to drive, too: the controls are light and the gearshift simple."

It doesn't come more basic than this. Stutz drivers have a bare minimum of instruments and controls.

Milestones

1911 Harry Clayton Stutz builds a car for the first Indianapolis 500. It finishes 11th out of a field of 44 and inspires Stutz to start production.

In 1915 the Stutz White Squadron team dominated racing in the U.S.

1912 Stutz begins to build six- and four-cylinder cars.

1914 A Stutz car finishes fifth in the Indy 500.

1915 Erwin 'Cannonball' Baker breaks the U.S. coast-to-coast record driving a Bearcat over 3,700 miles at an average speed of 13.7 mph. It sounds slow, but there were no proper roads across the country at this time.

Later Stutz cars were more civilized than the Bearcat, but still offered good performance.

1916 Stutz introduces its own 360-cubic inch 'T' head engine giving a top speed of 71 mph. Production continues into the 1930s progressing into a more civilized car.

UNDER THE SKIN

Beefy Bearcat

There is one novelty to the Bearcat's large, robust, ladder-type chassis. In a foretaste of modern racing car design, the engine acts as part of the chassis. Another unusual feature of the overall design is having the three-speed transmission in unit with the final drive and mounted at the rear, where it helps weight distribution, off-setting the bulk of the huge Wisconsin four-cylinder engine at the front. The standard wheels are wooden spoke; wire wheels were only an option.

Monocle windshield — Rear transaxle — Engine is load bearing — Ladder-type chassis — Huge straight-four

THE POWER PACK

'T' head

Stutz bought its engine from the Wisconsin company. It is a large four-cylinder 'T' head side-valve design, so called because the valves are below the cylinder head working up into the combustion chambers, with the intake manifold on one side, and the exhaust manifold on the other. The engine itself is made up of two cast-iron blocks of two cylinders each, mounted on an alloy crankcase. Two plugs per cylinder are used and it produces its maximum power at a very low 1,500 rpm.

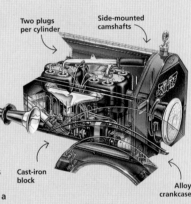

Two plugs per cylinder — Side-mounted camshafts — Cast-iron block — Alloy crankcase

Stutz racer

The Bearcat was a direct development of the Stutz racing car that finished in 11th position in the first Indy 500 in 1911. The production car's minimal bodywork reflects its racing origins. Bearcats used the same 'T' head engines as the original racer.

Stutz racer developed into the Bearcat.

432

Before World War I, both Stutz and Mercer defined their American sports cars—the Bearcat and the Raceabout—as big, brash and fast.

'T' head Wisconsin engine
All Bearcats were built with a Wisconsin 'T' head in-line four. It's much bigger than the side-valve four used in the Mercer Raceabout but only fractionally more powerful.

Bucket seats
Bucket seats were developed to keep the occupants from falling out of the car since it didn't have any doors.

Twin spark ignition
With large cylinders there's an advantage in two spark plugs per cylinder, but they are there for reliability and not to improve the efficiency of the engine.

Advance/retard mechanism
The driver adjusted the engine timing with a control on the steeringwheel. The ignition could be advanced as the engine speed rose.

Rear drum brakes
As usual with pre-World War I cars, there are brakes on the rear wheels only, although there is a manual handbrake also acting on the rear wheels.

Rear transaxle
Harry Clayton Stutz saw the advantage of mounting the transmission to the rear along with the transaxle to improve weight distribution.

Optional wire wheels
Standard equipment for the Bearcat was wooden wheels with detachable rims. Lightweight wire-spoke wheels, such as these, were optional.

Shift and handbrake levers
In the early days of motoring there was no place for the gearshifter inside the cockpit. It stayed outside, in this case mounted alongside the handbrake lever.

High ground clearance
With tall wheels and the semi-elliptic leaf springs mounted on top of the axles, the Bearcat has a lot of ground clearance, keeping the transaxle far above the road.

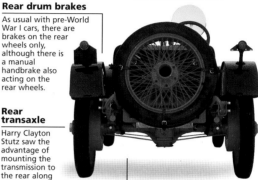

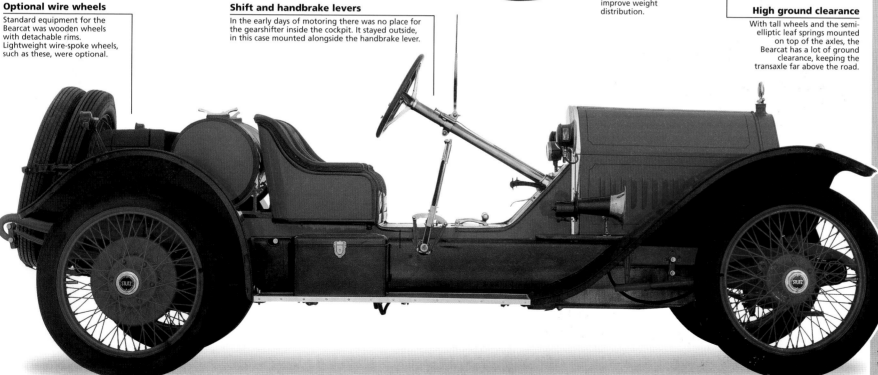

Specifications

1914 Stutz Bearcat

ENGINE
Type: Wisconsin four-cylinder side valve
Construction: Alloy crankcase with two cast-iron blocks and alloy pistons
Valve gear: Two side valves per cylinder operated by side-mounted camshafts on either side of the block
Bore and stroke: 4.76 in. x 5.51 in.
Displacement: 390 c.i.
Compression ratio: 4.0:1
Induction system: Single updraft Stromberg HA carburetor
Maximum power: 60 bhp at 1,500 rpm
Maximum torque: Not quoted
Top speed: 80 mph
0-60 mph: Not quoted

TRANSMISSION
Rear-mounted three-speed manual

BODY/CHASSIS
Steel ladder frame chassis with the engine acting as stressed chassis member. Open speedster-type bodywork

SPECIAL FEATURES

The monocle windshield gave the driver protection from the slipstream.

A radiator-mounted 'Boyce Motometer' is used to monitor water temperature.

RUNNING GEAR
Steering: Worm-and-nut
Front suspension: Beam axle with semi-elliptic leafs and friction shocks
Rear suspension: Live axle with semi-elliptic leafs and friction shocks
Brakes: Rear drums only, 16 in. dia.
Wheels: Wire spoke, 4.5 in. x 34 in.
Tires: 4.5 in. x 34 in.

DIMENSIONS
Length: 160 in. **Width:** 65.9 in.
Height: 63.4 in. **Wheelbase:** 120 in.
Track: 55.9 in. (front and rear)
Weight: 2,500 lbs.

Stutz **BLACKHAWK**

America has its fair share of 'revival marques,' and among the better known is Stutz. Once famous for incredibly powerful roadsters of the early teens, the name reappeared in 1969 on a retro-styled, hand built luxury car which still offered a tremendous amount of torque.

"...early 1970s luxury."

"As can be expected from a car that's virtually all hand built, the Stutz offers early 1970s luxury, but fire up the big-block Pontiac V8 and the sound resonating from under the hood and through the twin tailpipes is awe inspiring. Once on the move, the Stutz glides along the highway, effortlessly soaking up all manner of bumps and potholes. The brakes are on the sensitive side, but the steering is very light and the Hydramatic transmission does a fine job."

Rich leather seats, thick carpeting and acres of polished wood result in a luxurious interior.

Milestones

1969 Reviving a great name, a new retro-styled Stutz is produced. It is derived from the Pontiac Grand Prix. The cars are built in Italy, imported to New York and distributed by Jules Meyers in Los Angeles.

1973 Pontiac's Grand Prix is rebodied.

Blackhawks were styled by Virgil Exner, but the 1950s Chryslers were his more noted designs.

1976 The big 455 V8, by now rated at 200 bhp, is offered for the last time on the Stutz.

The Stutz Blackhawk is based on the Pontiac Grand Prix coupe.

1978 A down-sized Grand Prix arrives. The Stutz returns with smaller dimensions and taller styling. Engine choices are a 130-bhp Pontiac V8, a 175-bhp Chevy or a 425-cubic inch Cadillac V8. A huge Royale limousine arrives for the 1979 model year.

UNDER THE SKIN

Derivative chassis

Rear live axle

Pontiac Grand Prix chassis

Coil-sprung suspension

Cast-iron V8

Beneath the Stutz's Virgil Exner-styled sheet metal lies a Pontiac Grand Prix chassis and running gear. The 1969-1972 Blackhawks were built off the same vintage GP, sharing the 116-inch wheelbase and coil-sprung suspension. At the front, mounted above and below the coils, is a long-arm wishbone setup, while at the rear there is a live GM 10-bolt axle with a Safe-T-Track limited-slip differential and 3.55:1 gears.

THE POWER PACK

Heavy-duty muscle

Conceived during the height of the muscle car craze, early Stutzes are powered by Pontiac V8 400s, 428s and 455s. All these engines were essentially cast from the same block and feature cast-iron construction with heavy-duty main bearing caps and reinforced crank journals. Early 455-cubic inch V8s put out 320 bhp thanks to their high performance cylinder heads, larger camshafts and Rochester Quadrajet carburetors. A fairly low 8.4:1 compression ratio allows low-lead fuel.

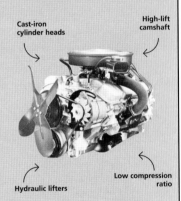

Cast-iron cylinder heads

High-lift camshaft

Low compression ratio

Hydraulic lifters

Cool coupe

The rarest and most expensive cars of this line are the stretched Royale limousines, but if there is a practical choice, it is the two-door Blackhawk coupe. Early examples are worth from $4,000 to $15,000 if equipped with a powerful V8.

The Blackhawk coupe offers the best performance and is the pick of the range.

With its outrageous styling, the Blackhawk may look as though it is all show and no substance, but underneath its flamboyant skin lies a well-engineered, luxury performance machine with considerable merit.

Freestanding headlights

Another retro touch are the free-standing parking and headlights. Exner was fond of such features and also used them on the 1961-1963 Chrysler Imperials.

Big-block V8

Back in the early 1970s, gas was cheap and many cars still had massive V8s. The Stutz is no exception, relying on a monster 455-cubic inch Pontiac V8 for power. With 320 bhp and 420 lb-ft of torque, it offers substantial get-up-and-go.

Safe-T-Track rear

Pontiac's version of the GM limited-slip differential was known as the Safe-T-Track, which considerably reduces wheelspin under hard acceleration.

Pontiac Grand Prix chassis

It may look unique, but the Blackhawk uses a Pontiac Grand Prix chassis. Early cars such as this one have a 116-inch wheelbase. GM parts helped keep production costs down, partly to offset the expense of the coachbuilt bodies.

Side exhausts

One distinctive Stutz feature is the side-mounted exhaust, which is reminiscent of 1930s styling. The ribbed aluminum finish resembles that used on Mercedes SSKs, but here they are strictly for decoration. The real exhaust—twin pipes and mufflers—exits under the rear bumper.

Built in Italy

Capitalizing on the prestige of Italian supercars, the Stutz body was hand built by Carrozzeria Padama coachworks in Turin, Italy. The bodies were then shipped to a foundry in Modena (home of Ferrari), where they were mated to the chassis and running gear. The final touches and quality control were carried out in Italy before the cars were shipped to the U.S.

Flamboyant styling

Stylist Virgil Exner was best known for designing Chryslers in the 1950s and early 1960s. His Stutz design embodies many Exner trademarks, such as the sweeping beltline and creases behind the wheels.

Specifications

1972 Stutz Blackhawk

ENGINE

Type: V8

Construction: Cast-iron block and heads

Valve gear: Two valves per cylinder

Bore and stroke: 4.15 in. x 4.21 in.

Displacement: 455 c.i.

Compression ratio: 8.4:1

Induction system: Rochester Quadrajet four-barrel downdraft carburetor

Maximum power: 320 bhp at 4,400 rpm

Maximum torque: 420 lb-ft at 3,200 rpm

Top speed: 130 mph

0-60 mph: 8.4 sec.

TRANSMISSION

GM TurboHydramatic 400 three-speed automatic

BODY/CHASSIS

Separate steel chassis with hand-built coupe body

SPECIAL FEATURES

This particular car was ordered by entertainer Sammy Davis Junior.

The trunk lid features a cut out to clear the spare tire.

RUNNING GEAR

Steering: Recirculating ball

Front suspension: Unequal length wishbones with coil springs, telescopic shock absorbers and anti-roll bar

Rear suspension: Live axle with coil springs, radius arms and telescopic shock absorbers

Brakes: Discs (front), drums (rear)

Wheels: Kelsey Hayes wires, 7 x 15 in.

Tires: 175/70 R15

DIMENSIONS

Length: 203.8 in. **Width:** 78.7 in.

Height: 51.6 in. **Wheelbase:** 116.0 in.

Track: 62.1 in. (front), 61.2 in. (rear)

Weight: 4,021 lbs.

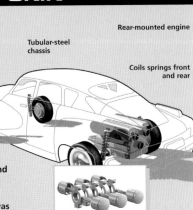

USA 1948

Tucker **TORPEDO**

Preston Tucker had a dream to make the most advanced, the safest and one of the fastest cars ever seen in the U.S. But along the way, he made enough enemies in the business to doom the project.

"...ahead of its time."

"It would have taken drivers of the 1940s a while to get used to the rear-engined Torpedo. This is a fast car and its torquey flat-six gives acceleration to match. It is quiet, due in part to the rear engine. The assisted steering is far more direct than most cars of the time, so if the back end does break traction and step out, it can be easily controlled. The advanced suspension is firm and high-speed stability is good. This car was way ahead of its time"

For safety reasons, all the controls are deeply recessed behind a padded dash.

Milestones

1946 Preston Tucker assembles a team to help him design and build a car. He also sponsors a car in the Indianapolis 500—a Miller-engined Gulf Oil Special—and renames it the Tucker Torpedo Special to gain exposure for his new road car. Tucker acquires the immense Dodge plant in Chicago.

MGM released a movie about Tucker 40 years after his Torpedo.

1947 Built in an amazingly short time, the prototype Tucker is ready in June.

The next U.S. production car with a rear-mounted engine was the Chevrolet Corvair.

1949 Development problems delay the car and Tucker is investigated for fraud. It is thought that vested interests among Detroit car companies are behind the allegations.

1950 Tucker is cleared, but the damage is done. The company folds after just 51 cars have been made.

UNDER THE SKIN

Unique features

A massive chassis of box-section steel tubes makes the Tucker extremely strong. A separate chassis is about the only ordinary part of this car, with its rear-mounted engine and novel rubber-sprung wish-bone suspension. In addition, the center headlight turns with the steering wheel and automatically lights up when darkness falls. The proposed torque-converter transmission was discarded in favor of the complex preselector from a pre-war Cord.

Rear-mounted engine

Tubular-steel chassis

Coils springs front and rear

Flat six

THE POWER PACK

Helicopter engine

Tuckers went into production with a 334-cubic inch, flat-six, helicopter engine. To suit air duty, it was light and designed to run for long periods of time at a relatively low rpm for reliability. Although the engine was converted from air cooled to water cooled, it is still a low-revving engine with a low compression ratio. It produces its 166 bhp maximum power output at only 3,600 rpm. Designed for torque, rather than outright power or fast running, it has side valves in L-head cylinder heads, yet is also advanced in having an alloy block when virtually all car engines were cast iron.

Refined looks

Even if thousands of Tuckers had been built as planned, it would still be much more collectible than the majority of 1948 U.S. production cars. Nothing else built at the time could match its looks and refinement, handling and performance.

From any angle, the Torpedo is a stunning machine.

Preston Tucker hired Alex Tremulis, one of the best car designers, to style the Torpedo. He had worked on the great pre-war Cords and produced an elegant and aerodynamic design years ahead of its rivals.

Flat-six engine

When his own engine proved impossible to develop, Tucker turned to a converted 5.5-liter, flat-six, water cooled, helicopter engine produced by Air Cooled Motors of Syracuse.

Rear radiator

The prototype Tucker was intended to have a front-mounted radiator connected to the rear engine by copper tubes. When the converted helicopter engine was fitted, the radiator moved behind the engine.

Wishbone suspension

Tucker wanted to use a double-wishbone suspension up front with rubber in torsion for springing. The rear was intended to have trailing links, again with rubber springs. This proved troublesome in the prototype because the alloy suspension arms were too fragile and had to be reengineered. Later cars had coil springs fitted both front and rear.

Safety features

Tucker was obsessed with safety so the Torpedo was years ahead of its time in making the interior safe. The dashboard rail is padded, the steering column is collapsible, and the passenger side footwell is large enough to act as a survival cell.

24-volt electrics

The prototype engine had hydraulic valve gear. The valves remained closed until the engine finally turned over during start ups. Therefore, a 24-volt starter was required.

Specifications

1948 Tucker Torpedo

ENGINE

Type: Air cooled flat six

Construction: Alloy block and heads

Valve gear: Two sidevalves per cylinder in an L-head operated by single block-mounted camshaft per bank of cylinders

Bore and stroke: 4.57 in. x 3.56 in.

Displacement: 334 c.i.

Compression ratio: 7.0:1

Induction system: Single Autolite carburetor

Maximum power: 166 bhp at 3,200 rpm

Maximum torque: Not quoted

Top speed: 130 mph

0-60 mph: 10.0 sec

TRANSMISSION

Four-speed manual preselector

BODY/CHASSIS

Separate steel-perimeter chassis with steel four-door sedan bodywork

SPECIAL FEATURES

The column-mounted gearshift is an unusual design, in keeping with the rest of the interior.

No fewer than six exhaust pipes stick out from the rear of the car, three for each bank of the flat-six engine.

RUNNING GEAR

Steering: Recirculating-ball

Front suspension: Double wishbones with coil springs and telescopic shock absorbers

Rear suspension: Twin wishbones with rubber springs and telescopic shock absorbers

Brakes: Drums (front and rear)

Wheels: Pressed steel disc, 15-in. dia.

Tires: 7.00 x 15

DIMENSIONS

Length: 219.0 in. **Width:** 79.0 in.

Height: 60.0 in. **Wheelbase:** 130.0 in.

Track: 64.0 in. (front), 65.0 in. (rear)

Weight: 4,235 lbs.

Vector **W8-M12**

The best way of describing the exotic Vector is that it's America's answer to Lamborghini. It boasts phenomenal power output and has the performance to make it a contender for the title of the fastest car on earth.

"...American exotica."

"If you have ever wondered what a fighter pilot must feel like, slide into the Vector and you'll have a good idea. Everything is designed for ultra-high speeds. Its controls resemble those of a jet fighter and the overall ride is the same. As for the acceleration, it's American exotica that can compete with Italian supercars. The Vector offers unearthly performance and is a pleasure to drive—especially in the three digit mph range."

The Vector is by no means your everyday car. Inside it is more like a Space Shuttle than a conventional car.

Milestones

1977 Gerald A. Wiegert's Vector W2 is presented in Los Angeles as "the fastest car in the world."

1990 After years of preparation, the W8 is launched using a Donovan small-block Chevy®-designed engine.

Originally, Vectors were built with domestic drivelines.

1992 A WX3 model has a new aerodynamic body, twin turbos and makes up to 1100 bhp.

1993 After a power struggle, Megatech eventually emerges as the new owner and the company moves to Florida. Since they also own Lamborghini, future plans include building the car with the Diablo's V12. By using the underpowered Italian engine, the Vector will no longer be a full-blooded and extremely powerful U.S. supercar.

On looks, the Vector is a match for any Lamborghini or Ferrari.

1995 With a Diablo 492 bhp V12 engine and a much cheaper price tag, the new M12 model is marketed.

UNDER THE SKIN

Like an aircraft

Based in a part of California well known for its advanced aerospace industry, Vector took full advantage of its location. Under the super-lightweight composite bodywork there is an aircraft-inspired aluminum chassis which is both light and very strong. The Vector's running gear may be state of the art, but it is also practical. The front end boasts independent double-wishbone suspension, while the rear end consists of a well-located de Dion tube and coil/shock units.

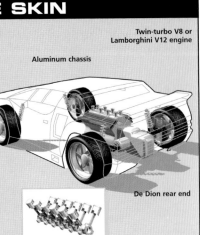

Twin-turbo V8 or Lamborghini V12 engine

Aluminum chassis

De Dion rear end

Lamborghini V12

THE POWER PACK

Four valves per cylinder

Two overhead camshafts per bank

Lamborghini V12 engine

Manual transmission

More means less

The Vector was originally powered by a Donovan aluminum engine based on Corvette's® 350 V8. It featured electronic fuel injection and twin turbochargers, with power ranging from 500 bhp to 1100 bhp. After a short production run using this engine, Vector Aeromotive was bought out and started using Lamborghini's Diablo 5.7-liter V12. Who would have thought that four extra cylinders from an Italian supercar company, would have cut the Vector's power output in half to 492 bhp?

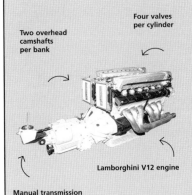

Vector M12

When Megatech acquired Vector Aeromotive, it restyled its body and gave it an Italian supercar engine. While the new body panels bring the car into the 1990s, it should have kept the 1,100-bhp Chevy-designed V8. In comparison, the new V12 only makes 492 bhp.

The M12 uses Lamborghini's bigger but less powerful V-12 engine.

Originally marketed as an all-American supercar using a Chevy-designed engine and a Toronado® transmission, the Vector W8 pulled the rug out from under both Lamborghini and Ferrari.

Advanced bodywork
Years before other manufacturers began using sophisticated composites in cars, the Vector's bodywork contained Kevlar, fiberglass and carbon fiber.

Aircraft-influenced design
As well as using aerospace materials and construction methods, the Vector's styling also recalls aircraft practice.

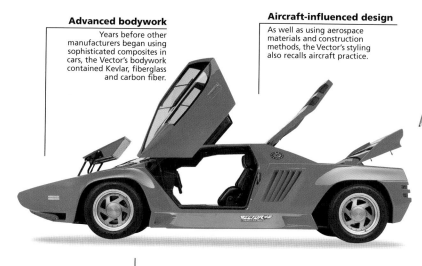

Honeycomb chassis
The advanced chassis is a semi-monocoque structure. Like an aircraft frame, it is constructed from tubular steel and bonded aluminum honeycomb, and is extremely light and incredibly strong.

Turbocharged Chevy V8
In a bid to make this an all-American supercar, the engine was derived from a Corvette V8 unit. To produce enough power to make this the fastest car in the world, Vector used twin intercooled Garrett H3 turbochargers.

Oldsmobile® transmission
To transfer the immense power of the mid-mounted engine, Vector selected a suitably modified Toronado automatic transmission.

Exotic 'scissor' doors
The large gull-wing doors open up in scissor fashion, similar to the Lamborghini Countach and Diablo.

Powerful braking
With performance as breathtaking as the Vector's, brakes that can deal with speeds of up to 218 mph are required. The Vector has vented four-wheel discs measuring a massive 13 inches in diameter. Naturally, there is a sophisticated ABS system.

Specifications
1992 Vector W8

ENGINE
Type: V8
Construction: Cast-iron cylinder block and head
Valve gear: Two valves per cylinder operated by a single camshaft
Bore and stroke: 4.08 in. x 3.48 in.
Displacement: 5,973 cc
Compression ratio: 8.0:1
Induction system: Tuned port electronic fuel injection
Maximum power: 625 bhp at 5,700 rpm
Maximum torque: 630 lb-ft at 4,900 rpm
Top speed: 195 mph
0-60 mph: 4.1 sec.

TRANSMISSION
Three-speed automatic

BODY/CHASSIS
Semi-monocoque honeycomb chassis with two-door coupe body in composite materials

SPECIAL FEATURES

Twin Garrett turbochargers can boost power up to 1100 bhp, a figure the Diablo engine could never match.

The radiator is mounted horizontally in the nose of the car, leaving little space for luggage up front.

RUNNING GEAR
Steering: Rack-and-pinion
Front suspension: Double wishbones with coil springs and shocks
Rear suspension: De Dion axle with longitudinal and transverse arms and coil spring/shock units
Brakes: Four-wheel discs
Wheels: Alloy, 16-in. dia.
Tires: 255/45 ZR16 front, 315/40 ZR16 rear

DIMENSIONS
Length: 172 in.
Width: 76 in.
Height: 42.5 in.
Wheelbase: 103 in.
Track: 63 in. (front), 65 in. (rear)
Weight: 3,572 lbs.

Willys **KNIGHT**

The combination of excellent workmanship and quality, coupled with the refined sleeve-valve engine and the pricing made the four-cylinder Willys 65-Knight a very popular choice in the 1920s.

"...wonderfully quiet engine."

"The four-cylinder sleeve-valve Willys engine is wonderfully quiet: because of its internal balancer system, few four-cylinder motors come close. It is also torquey for its 3-liter size, so you can get away with the minimum of gearchanging. These cars are solidly built, ride comfortably, and handle well, helped by light and low-geared steering. Braking is adequate though, as front brakes had yet to appear on the four-cylinder."

The plain and simple fascia of the Willys 65-Knight is reflective of the period.

Milestones

1914 Willys-Overland begins to produce a four-cylinder in a new plant at Elyria in Ohio. To begin with, the car is too expensive and sales are slow.

The 6/90 continued Willys' low-priced tradition into the 1930s.

1915 The Willys Knight is moved down market and sold in the $1,000 range. Sales rapidly climb.

Willys is most famous for its World War II Jeep.

1919 John North Willys loses financial control after overextending himself with moves such as buying the Duesenberg plant in New Jersey.

1922 Willys buys himself back into control.

1926 A new six-cylinder model means that the company stops production of the four. By 1932, all sleeve-valve production comes to an end.

UNDER THE SKIN

Usual design

Leaf-sprung suspension front and rear

Three-speed 'crash' transmission

Rear brakes only

Inline four

Like virtually every other car made at the time, the 65-Knight uses a separate steel chassis frame that also carries the same basic form of suspension used everywhere else. This means a live rear axle that is both located and sprung by semi-elliptic leaf springs. The same system is used for the front, which has a solid steel beam connecting the hubs. There are brakes only on the rear wheels because performance is modest.

THE POWER PACK

Complex design

The Willys sleeve-valve engine is a complex design in which two sleeves around the pistons move up and down. Each has a connecting rod joined to a shaft, which acts in the same way as the camshaft in an ordinary engine. Ports are cut in the sleeves, and the movement of the sleeves cover and uncover them, acting like the valves in a conventional engine. This design allows an excellent combustion chamber shape with the spark plug centrally mounted. Another advantage is that it is extremely quiet-running. The design was reasonably powerful for the time, producing 40 bhp at a very low 2,600 rpm.

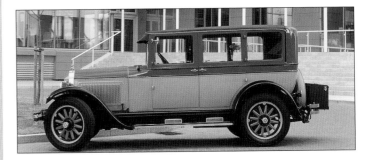

Tourer

For 1925, there was a choice of five different models in the four-cylinder range, but the most sought after now is the five-passenger tourer. Next is the two-door coupe while the ordinary sedan (built in the greatest numbers) is the least valuable.

Back in the 1920s, the Sedan was the most popular model in the range.

Some 1925 Willys cars, such as the coupe and roadster, were extremely attractive and stylish. The sedan, however, was built on upright lines designed to maximize interior space rather than look elegant.

Thermo-siphon cooling

There is no water pump for the engine. It relies on the thermo-siphon effect of the water moving around the engine and radiator as it heats and cools.

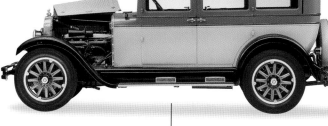

Sleeve-valve engine

One of the advantages of the sleeve-valve engine was that it improved with use. Carbon built up between the sliding sleeves after some miles, improving the sealing. As a result, the power output rose, as genuine independent tests proved.

Engine vibration damper

To make the four-cylinder engine smoother, a Lanchester balancer was added. This uses two rotating cylinders geared together to rotate in different directions. As they rotate, they counteract the movement of the pistons, thereby giving the effect of a smoother engine with more cylinders.

Wooden-spoke wheels

Standard equipment for the four-cylinder Willys were wooden spoke wheels. The smooth disc-type wheel could be ordered as an option and was more suited to the formal-looking sedan.

Live rear axle

The standard form of rear suspension was used on the Willys 65-Knight, namely a live rear axle, which like the front beam axle, uses long, semi-elliptic leaf springs to locate and suspend it. The leaves are 2.25 inches wide and more than four feet long.

Rear brakes

Four-cylinder Knights were not designed with high performance in mind, so they rely on mechanically operated brakes on the rear wheels only. These are the external-contracting type.

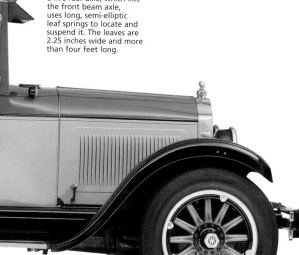

Specifications

1925 Willys 65-Knight

ENGINE

Type: Inline four sleeve valve

Construction: Cast-iron block, cylinders and sleeves

Valve gear: Inlet and exhaust ports cut in sliding sleeves

Bore and stroke: 3.63 in. x 4.50 in.

Displacement: 186 c.i.

Compression ratio: N/A

Induction system: Single MS2B carburetor

Maximum power: 40 bhp at 2,600 rpm

Top speed: 60 mph

0-60 mph: 31.0 sec.

Maximum torque: N/A

TRANSMISSION

Three-speed manual

BODY/CHASSIS

Separate steel chassis frame with sedan bodywork

SPECIAL FEATURES

Brakes lights were a novel feature for the 1920s.

Rear opposite opening doors give access for the driver and passengers.

RUNNING GEAR

Steering: Worm-and-gear

Front suspension: Beam axle with semi-elliptic leaf springs

Rear suspension: Live axle with semi-elliptic leaf springs

Brakes: External contracting drums on rear

Wheels: Wooden spoke

Tires: 5.77 x 30

DIMENSIONS

Length: 183.8 in.   **Width:** 75.6 in.

Height: 77.0 in.   **Wheelbase:** 124.0 in.

Track: 55.5 in. (front), 56.5 in. (rear)

Weight: 3,060 lbs.

USA 1941-1945

Willys JEEP

There are few motoring institutions so essentially American as the Jeep. Despite the fashionable status of the current Wrangler, the Jeep started out as a U.S. army vehicle during World War II.

"...can tackle any terrain."

"When the world's largest army needed an all-purpose vehicle during World War II, it had to be able to withstand virtually any kind of terrain. There are no frills in the Willys Jeep and it's designed for utility alone. The Jeep feels very solid, with rock-hard suspension and a choppy ride. The steering may be vague, but the torquey engine pulls strong in any gear. This gutsy little four-wheeler really proved its worth for the U.S. Armed Forces."

No creature comforts here. Only the bare essentials are found inside the Jeep.

Milestones

1940 The U.S. Quartermaster Corps publishes a requirement for a compact 4x4 ¼-ton truck. A design from Bantam is chosen.

1941 Production begins at the Bantam, Ford, and Willys factories.

Total wartime Jeep production totalled nearly 650,000.

1945 Willys plugs on with the Jeep in civilian CJ-2A form, while the new Jeep Station Wagon becomes America's first steel-bodied station wagon.

A post-war variation was the 1950 Jeep four-wheel drive pick-up.

1948 A civilian Jeepster model, with whitewall tires, bright colors, and luxury fittings, is introduced.

1955 The long-running CJ-5 appears. In 1970 Willys is absorbed by AMC.

UNDER THE SKIN

Simple and effective

Short front and rear overhangs

Four-wheel drive

Four-wheel leaf springs

Side-valve four-cylinder

The Jeep's simple steel frame is composed of box-section side rails connected by five cross-members. Everything bolts into place, including the body. The fully floating Spicer axles at both ends are suspended by aluminum springs (eight leaves at the front, nine at the rear), plus Bendix shocks.

THE POWER PACK

Torquey side-valve

The idea behind the Jeep was to keep things simple, reliable and effective. The low-output, high-torque, four-cylinder side valve Willys Go-Devil L-head engine was therefore entirely appropriate. Conceived as early as 1926, the block and cylinder head are made from cast-iron, but the connecting rods are forged steel and the three-ring pistons aluminum. Maximum torque is attained at a low 2,000 rpm.

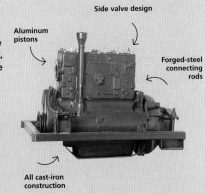

Side valve design

Aluminum pistons

Forged-steel connecting rods

All cast-iron construction

Many makers

The Willys model is best-known, but this vintage four-wheeler was also built by Bantam (which originally designed the vehicle) and Ford (which badged it as the GPW—hence the name, 'Jeep'). All three are almost identical, although Ford stamped its logo on every component.

The Jeep proved highly adaptable for a variety of roles.

Although conceived for wartime use, the Jeep continues to impress today. It is still versatile, effective off-road, simple to work on, and great fun to drive.

Basic seating

There is basic seating for four passengers. Seats are filled with cattle hair and rubber (later, springs and felt) and covered with water-resistant cotton.

Dependable engine

Power comes from a 134 cubic inch, four-cylinder engine producing 60 bhp. A low state of tune ensures excellent reliability.

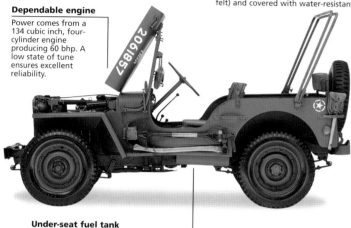

Under-seat fuel tank

A 15-gallon fuel tank is located under the driver's seat. For the sake of practicality, a gasoline can with an extra 5 gallons' capacity is also attached to the rear.

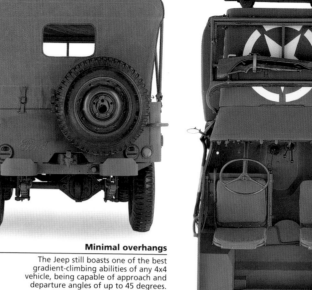

Minimal overhangs

The Jeep still boasts one of the best gradient-climbing abilities of any 4x4 vehicle, being capable of approach and departure angles of up to 45 degrees.

Storage bins

Just behind each front seat is a locker for tools. A small compartment at the far right of the instrument panel was designed to hold gas masks and goggles.

Simple body

The ultra-simple bodywork of the Jeep is designed for ease of manufacture and repair, and is made of low-carbon steel. A variety of Jeeps have been produced, including ambulances, rocket-launchers, and even amphibians (dubbed 'Seeps').

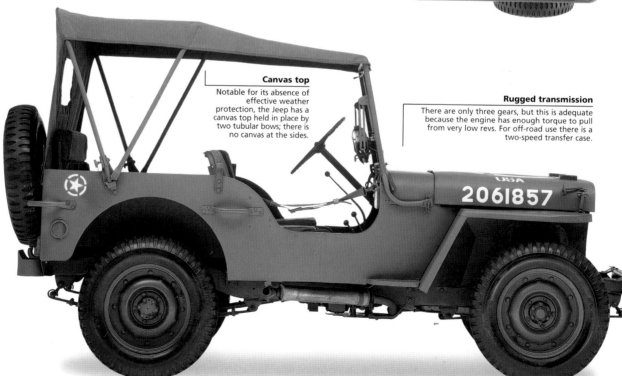

Canvas top

Notable for its absence of effective weather protection, the Jeep has a canvas top held in place by two tubular bows; there is no canvas at the sides.

Rugged transmission

There are only three gears, but this is adequate because the engine has enough torque to pull from very low revs. For off-road use there is a two-speed transfer case.

USA
2061857

Specifications

1942 Ford GPW Jeep

ENGINE

Type: In-line four-cylinder

Construction: Cast-iron cylinder block and cylinder head

Valve gear: Pushrod-operated side-valves with single chain-driven camshaft

Bore and stroke: 3.13 in. x 4.37 in.

Displacement: 134 c.i.

Compression ratio: 6.48:1

Induction system: Single Carter downdraft carburetor

Maximum power: 60 bhp at 3,600 rpm

Maximum torque: 105 lb-ft at 2,000 rpm

Top speed: 62 mph

0-60 mph: 30 sec.

TRANSMISSION

Three-speed manual

BODY/CHASSIS

Steel frame with doorless open steel body

SPECIAL FEATURES

Useful items such as spades and axes can be strapped to the bodywork for excursions deep into the country.

Simple in the extreme, early Jeeps lacked a glove compartment but did include a rifle mount.

RUNNING GEAR

Steering: Variable-ratio cam and twin-lever

Front suspension: Spicer floating axle with alloy leaf springs and Bendix hydraulic shock absorbers

Rear suspension: Spicer floating axle with alloy leaf springs and Bendix hydraulic shock absorbers

Brakes: Drums, front and rear

Wheels: Steel split-rim, 16-in. dia.

Tires: 6.00 x 16 in.

DIMENSIONS

Length: 132.3 in. **Width:** 62 in.

Height: 69 in. **Wheelbase:** 80 in.

Track: 48.3 in. (front), 43.8 in. (rear)

Weight: 2,453 lbs.

Zimmer **QUICKSILVER**

The neo-classic style became an American automotive icon in the 1980s and Zimmer cashed in on its popularity. Then it diversified with the extraordinary Quicksilver, an unusual sports car with Pontiac Fiero mechanicals.

"...well-balanced handling."

"Any Pontiac Fiero owner would feel at home in the Quicksilver. Because the suspension and steering remain untouched, the Zimmer drives much like the Fiero. The mid-mounted engine brings advantages to the handling since the car has very sensitive steering. It is well balanced, though, and has plenty of grip from the wide tires. However, the V6 isn't powerful enough for true sports-car performance considering the Quicksilver's weight."

The Quicksilver's instrument layout is taken directly from the Pontiac Fiero.

Milestones

1980 Zimmer, a well-known conversion van company, forms a car division to produce a 'nostalgia' coupe called the Golden Spirit. Using Ford running gear, it is powered by a 4.2-liter V8. Over the next 10 years some 1,500 examples are built.

The mid-engined V6 Pontiac Fiero formed the basis for the Zimmer Quicksilver.

1986 GM designer Don Johnson pens the strikingly styled Quicksilver. It uses the Pontiac Fiero chassis and engine. It is first seen during the summer of 1986.

Zimmer's neo-classic Golden Spirit is based on a Mustang.

1987 Production of the Quicksilver begins.

1988 Zimmer is burdened with financial problems and Pontiac decision to discontinue the Fiero results in the total suspension of Quicksilver production.

UNDER THE SKIN

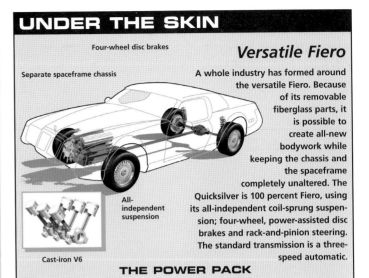

Four-wheel disc brakes

Separate spaceframe chassis

All-independent suspension

Cast-iron V6

Versatile Fiero

A whole industry has formed around the versatile Fiero. Because of its removable fiberglass parts, it is possible to create all-new bodywork while keeping the chassis and the spaceframe completely unaltered. The Quicksilver is 100 percent Fiero, using its all-independent coil-sprung suspension; four-wheel, power-assisted disc brakes and rack-and-pinion steering. The standard transmission is a three-speed automatic.

THE POWER PACK

General Motors V6

Just as the Fiero's spaceframe was left untouched, so was the Pontiac engine. That meant that, deceptively, it was still mid-mounted. While a four-cylinder engine was offered in the Fiero, Zimmer stuck with the larger L44 V6 option, which has a displace-ment of 2.8 liters and is a much more suitable powerplant for a sports car than the 2.5-liter four. The V6 features cast-iron construction, a central chain-driven camshaft, 60-degree V, and Bosch electronic fuel injection. It produces a credible 140 bhp at 5,200 rpm, enough for a top speed of over 120 mph.

Stylish quality

The Quicksilver was one of the first of many specialist coachwork conversions of the popular Pontiac Fiero. The Quicksilver was produced by a recognized high quality coachbuilder, Zimmer, and even used the Fiero's engine and suspension for reliability.

Unlike a lot of other kit cars, the Quicksilver uses only new parts.

Glitz, chrome and neo-classic grills were alive and well at Zimmer during the 1980s. But as well as the usual gigantic V8-powered leviathans, Zimmer produced the unique, mid-engined Quicksilver.

Long hood

The lengthy hood of the Quicksilver is deceptive, because the engine is not under it. Instead, it is located in a central position behind the driver. The long nose contributes to a 28-inch long increase over a stock Fiero.

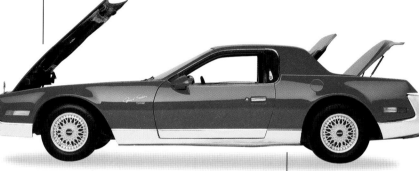

Extensive chrome trim

The Quicksilver is liberally adorned with chrome, from the grill to the bumpers along the entire lower bodywork.

Mid-mounted V6

Basing the Quicksilver on the Pontiac Fiero meant that it kept the Fiero's mid-mounted engine. Zimmer stuck with the 2.8-liter V6, which develops 140 bhp.

Pop-up headlights

A low front end was necessary to keep the proportions looking right, so in addition to thin parking lights, the main headlights are concealed behind pop-up panels.

Fiero spaceframe

Pontiac pioneered a spaceframe construction method to which body panels were bolted on.

Glitzy styling

The Quicksilver's extroverted styling was the responsibility of former GM stylist Don Johnson. The car's low roof contributes to a long and low look.

1988 Zimmer Quicksilver

ENGINE

Type: V6

Construction: Cast-iron block and heads

Valve gear: Two valves per cylinder operated by a single camshaft with pushrods and rocker arms

Bore and stroke: 3.50 in. x 2.99 in.

Displacement: 173 c.i.

Compression ratio: 8.5:1

Induction system: Bosch fuel injection

Maximum power: 140 bhp at 5,200 rpm

Maximum torque: 170 lb-ft at 3,600 rpm

Top speed: 121 mph

0-60 mph: 9.7 sec.

TRANSMISSION

Three-speed automatic

BODY/CHASSIS

Separate spaceframe chassis with fiberglass two-door coupe body

SPECIAL FEATURES

The Zimmer's unmistakable nose is adorned in chrome.

The long hood of the Quicksilver provides excellent luggage space.

RUNNING GEAR

Steering: Rack-and-pinion

Front suspension: Wishbones with coil springs, shock absorbers, and anti-roll bar

Rear suspension: MacPherson struts with lower A-arm, coil springs and shock absorbers

Brakes: Discs (front and rear)

Wheels: Wire, 14-in. dia.

Tires: 205/70 R14

DIMENSIONS

Length: 188.8 in. **Width:** 70.8 in.

Height: 47.6 in. **Wheelbase:** 93.4 in.

Track: 58.3 in. (front), 59.3 in. (rear)

Weight: 2,920 lbs.

Index